STUDENT'S SOLUTIONS MANUAL

NANCY S. BOUDREAU
Bowling Green State University

STATISTICS FOR BUSINESS AND ECONOMICS

ELEVENTH EDITION

James T. McClave
Info Tech, Inc.
University of Florida

P. George Benson
College of Charleston

Terry Sincich
University of South Florida

Prentice Hall
is an imprint of

PEARSON

The author and publisher of this book have used their best efforts in preparing this book. These efforts include the development, research, and testing of the theories and programs to determine their effectiveness. The author and publisher make no warranty of any kind, expressed or implied, with regard to these programs or the documentation contained in this book. The author and publisher shall not be liable in any event for incidental or consequential damages in connection with, or arising out of, the furnishing, performance, or use of these programs.

Reproduced by Pearson Prentice Hall from electronic files supplied by the author.

ISBN-13: 978-0-321-64175-5
ISBN-10: 0-321-64175-2

2 3 4 5 6 BRR 13 12 11

Prentice Hall
is an imprint of

www.pearsonhighered.com

Contents

Chapter 1
Statistics, Data, and Statistical Thinking

1.1   Statistics is a science that deals with the collection, classification, analysis, and interpretation of information or data. It is a meaningful, useful science with a broad, almost limitless scope of applications to business, government, and the physical and social sciences.

1.3   The four elements of a descriptive statistics problem are:

1. The population or sample of interest. This is the collection of all the units upon which the variable is measured.
2. One or more variables that are to be investigated. These are the types of data that are to be collected.
3. Tables, graphs, or numerical summary tools. These are tools used to display the characteristic of the sample or population.
4. Conclusions about the data based on the patterns revealed. These are summaries of what the summary tools revealed about the population or sample.

1.5   The first major method of collecting data is from a published source. These data have already been collected by someone else and is available in a published source. The second method of collecting data is from a designed experiment. These data are collected by a researcher who exerts strict control over the experimental units in a study. These data are measured directly from the experimental units. The third method of collecting data is from a survey. These data are collected by a researcher asking a group of people one or more questions. Again, these data are collected directly from the experimental units or people. The final method of collecting data is observationally. These data are collected directly from experimental units by simply observing the experimental units in their natural environment and recording the values of the desired characteristics.

1.7   A population is a set of existing units such as people, objects, transactions, or events. A variable is a characteristic or property of an individual population unit such as height of a person, time of a reflex, amount of a transaction, etc.

1.9   A representative sample is a sample that exhibits characteristics similar to those possessed by the target population. A representative sample is essential if inferential statistics is to be applied. If a sample does not possess the same characteristics as the target population, then any inferences made using the sample will be unreliable.

1.11   A population is a set of existing units such as people, objects, transactions, or events. A process is a series of actions or operations that transform inputs to outputs. A process produces or generates output over time. Examples of processes are assembly lines, oil refineries, and stock prices.

1.13   The data consisting of the classifications A, B, C, and D are qualitative. These data are nominal and thus are qualitative. After the data are input as 1, 2, 3, and 4, they are still nominal and thus qualitative. The only differences between the two data sets are the names of the categories. The numbers associated with the four groups are meaningless.

1

1.15   a.   The population of interest is all citizens of the United States.

        b.   The variable of interest is the view of each citizen as to whether the president is doing a good or bad job. It is qualitative.

        c.   The sample is the 2000 individuals selected for the poll.

        d.   The inference of interest is to estimate the proportion of all U.S. citizens who believe the president is doing a good job.

        e.   The method of data collection is a survey.

        f.   It is not very likely that the sample will be representative of the population of all citizens of the United States. By selecting phone numbers at random, the sample will be limited to only those people who have telephones. Also, many people share the same phone number, so each person would not have an equal chance of being contacted. Another possible problem is the time of day the calls are made. If the calls are made in the evening, those people who work in the evening would not be represented.

1.17   I.   Qualitative; the possible responses are "yes" or "no," which are nonnumerical.

        II.   Quantitative; age is measured on a numerical scale, such as 15, 32, etc.

        III.   Qualitative; the possible responses are "yes" or "no," which are nonnmerical.

        IV.   Qualitative; the possible responses are "laser printer" or "another type of printer," which are nonnumerical.

        V.   Qualitative; the speeds can be classified as "slower," "unchanged," or "faster," which are nonnumerical.

        VI.   Quantitative; the number of people in a household who have used Windows 95 at least once is measured on a numerical scale, such as 0, 1, 2, etc.

1.19   a.   Whether the data collected on the chief executive officers at the 500 largest U. S. companies is a population or a sample depends on what one is interested in. If one is only interested in the information from the CEO's of the 500 largest U.S. companies, then this data form a population. If one is interested in the information on CEO's from all U.S. firms, then this data would form a sample.

        b.   1.   The industry type of the CEO's company is a qualitative variable. The industry type is a name.

                2.   The CEO's total compensation is a meaningful number. Thus, it is a quantitative variable.

                3.   The CEO's total compensation over the previous five years is quantitative.

                4.   The number of company stock shares (millions) held is a meaningful number. Thus, it is a quantitative variable.

                5.   The CEO's age is a meaningful number. Thus, it is a quantitative variable.

                6.   The CEO's efficiency rating is a meaningful number. Thus, it is a quantitative variable.

1.21   a.   The population of interest is the set of all satellite radio subscribers.

      b.   The variable of interest is whether or not a satellite radio subscriber has a satellite receiver in his/her car.

      c.   The variable would produce qualitative data. The possible responses would be "yes" or "no".

      d.   The sample of interest is the set of 501 satellite radio subscribers. The problem states that the 501 satellite radio subscribers were a random sample. If the sample is a random sample, then it should be representative of the population.

      e.   The proportion of the 501 satellite radio subscribers surveyed that responded that they have a satellite radio receiver in their car would be a good estimate of the proportion of all satellite radio subscribers that have a satellite radio receiver in their car. In this case, the proportion is 396/501 = .79.

1.23   a.   Length of maximum span can take on values such as 15 feet, 50 feet, 75 feet, etc. Therefore, it is quantitative.

      b.   The number of vehicle lanes can take on values such as 2, 4, etc. Therefore, it is quantitative.

      c.   The answer to this item is "yes" or "no," which are not numeric. Therefore, it is qualitative.

      d.   Average daily traffic could take on values such as 150 vehicles, 3,579 vehicles, 53,295 vehicles, etc. Therefore, it is quantitative.

      e.   Condition can take on values "good," "fair," or "poor," which are not numeric. Therefore, it is qualitative.

      f.   The length of the bypass or detour could take on values such as 1 mile, 4 miles, etc. Therefore, it is quantitative.

      g.   Route type can take on values "interstate," U.S.," "state," "county," or "city," which are not numeric. Therefore, it is qualitative.

1.25   a.   The process being studied is the distribution of pipes, valves, and fittings to the refining, chemical, and petrochemical industries by Wallace Company of Houston.

      b.   The variables of interest are the speed of the deliveries, the accuracy of the invoices, and the quality of the packaging of the products.

      c.   The sampling plan was to monitor a subset of current customers by sending out a questionnaire twice a year and asking the customers to rate the speed of the deliveries, the accuracy of the invoices, and the quality of the packaging minutes. The sample is the total numbers of questionnaires received.

      d.   The Wallace Company's immediate interest is learning about the delivery process of its distribution of pipes, valves, and fittings. To do this, it is measuring the speed of deliveries, the accuracy of the invoices, and the quality of its packaging from the sample of its customers to make an inference about the delivery process to all customers. In particular, it might use the mean speed of its deliveries to the sampled customers to estimate the mean speed of its deliveries to all its customers. It might use the mean accuracy of its invoices to the sampled customers to estimate the mean accuracy of its deliveries to all its customers. It might use the mean rating of the quality of its packaging to the sampled customers to estimate the mean rating of the quality of its packaging to all its customers.

e.   Several factors might affect the reliability of the inferences. One factor is the set of customers selected to receive the survey. If this set is not representative of all the customers, the wrong inferences could be made. Also, the set of customers returning the surveys may not be representative of all its customers. Again, this could influence the reliability of the inferences made.

1.27   a.   The population of interest would be all accounting alumni of a large southwestern university.

b.   Age would produce quantitative data – the responses would be numbers.

Gender would produce qualitative data – the responses would be 'male' or 'female'.

Level of education would produce qualitative data – the responses could be categories such college degree, masters degree, or PhD degree.

Income would produce quantitative data – the responses would be numbers.

Job satisfaction score would produce quantitative data. We would assume that a satisfaction score would be a number, where the higher the number, the higher the job satisfaction.

Machiavellian rating score would produce quantitative data. We would assume that a rating score would be a number, where the higher the score, the higher the Machiavellian traits.

c.   The sample is the 198 people who returned the useable questionnaires.

d.   The data collection method used was a survey.

e.   The inference made by the researcher is that Machiavellian behavior is not required to achieve success in the accounting profession.

f.   Generally, those who respond to surveys are those with strong feelings (in either direction) toward the subject matter. Those who do not have strong feelings for the subject matter tend not to answer surveys. Those who did not respond might be those who are not real happy with their jobs or those who are not real unhappy with their jobs. Thus, we might have no idea what type of scores these people would have on the Machiavellian rating score.

1.29   a.   Some possible questions are:

1.   In your opinion, why has the banking industry consolidated in the past few years? Check all that apply.

a.   Too many small banks with not enough capital.
b.   A result of the Savings and Loan scandals.
c.   To eliminate duplicated resources in the upper management positions.
d.   To provide more efficient service to the customers.
e.   To provide a more complete list of financial opportunities for the customers.
f.   Other. Please list.

2.   Using a scale from 1 to 5, where 1 means strongly disagree and 5 means strongly agree, indicate your agreement to the following statement: "The trend of consolidation in the banking industry will continue in the next five years."

1 strongly disagree   2 disagree   3 no opinion   4 agree   5 strongly agree

b.   The population of interest is the set of all bank presidents in the United States.

     c.   It would be extremely difficult and costly to obtain information from all 10,000 bank presidents. Thus, it would be more efficient to sample just 200 bank presidents. However, by sending the questionnaires to only 200 bank presidents, one risks getting the results from a sample which is not representative of the population. The sample must be chosen in such a way that the results will be representative of the entire population of bank presidents in order to be of any use.

1.30   a.   The process being studied is the process of filling beverage cans with softdrink at CCSB's Wakefield plant.

     b.   The variable of interest is the amount of carbon dioxide added to each can of beverage.

     c.   The sampling plan was to monitor five filled cans every 15 minutes. The sample is the total number of cans selected.

     d.   The company's immediate interest is learning about the process of filling beverage cans with softdrink at CCSB's Wakefield plant. To do this, they are measuring the amount of carbon dioxide added to a can of beverage to make an inference about the process of filling beverage cans. In particular, they might use the mean amount of carbon dioxide added to the sampled cans of beverage to estimate the mean amount of carbon dioxide added to all the cans on the process line.

     e.   The technician would then be dealing with a population. The cans of beverage have already been processed. He/she is now interested in the outputs.

1.31   a.   The population of interest is the set of all people in the United States over 14 years of age.

     b.   The variable being measured is the employment status of each person. This variable is qualitative. Each person is either employed or not.

     c.   The problem of interest to the Census Bureau is inferential. Based on the information contained in the sample, the Census Bureau wants to estimate the percentage of all people in the labor force who are unemployed.

Chapter 2
Methods for Describing Sets of Data

2.1   First, we find the frequency of the grade A. The sum of the frequencies for all five grades must be 200. Therefore, subtract the sum of the frequencies of the other four grades from 200. The frequency for grade A is:

$$200 - (36 + 90 + 30 + 28) = 200 - 184 = 16$$

To find the relative frequency for each grade, divide the frequency by the total sample size, 200. The relative frequency for the grade B is $36/200 = .18$. The rest of the relative frequencies are found in a similar manner and appear in the table:

Grade on Statistics Exam	Frequency	Relative Frequency
A: 90 – 100	16	.08
B: 80 – 89	36	.18
C: 65 – 79	90	.45
D: 50 – 64	30	.15
F: Below 50	28	.14
Total	200	1.00

2.3   a.   The type of graph is a pie chart.

b.   The variable measured on each of the industrial robots is task category.

c.   From the graph, the task that uses the highest percentage of industrial robots is Material Handling with 34.0%.

d.   Thirty-two percent or .32 * 184,000 = 58,880. Thus, 58,880 industrial robots were used for spot welding.

e.   The percentage of industrial robots used for either spot welding or arc welding is 32.0% + 20.0% = 52.0%.

2.5   a.   Since the variable measured is manufacturer, the data type is qualitative.

        b.   Using MINITAB, a frequency bar chart for the data is:

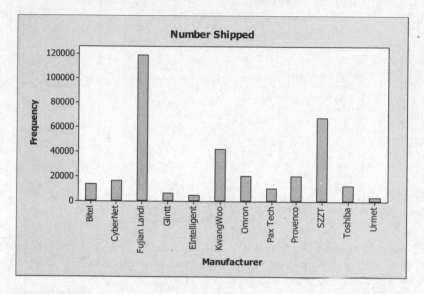

        c.   Using MINITAB, the Pareto diagram is:

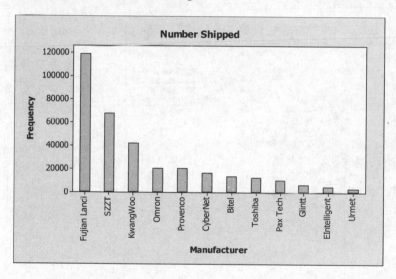

               Most PIN pads shipped in 2007 were manufactured by either Fujian Landi or SZZT Electronics.
               These two categories make up (119,000 + 67,300)/334,039= 186,300/334,039 = .558 of all PIN pads
               shipped in 2007. Urmet shipped the fewest number of PIN pads among these 12 manufacturers.

2.7   a.   The population of interest in this study is all non-cash payments in the U.S.

        b.   The number of non-cash payments in 2007 that were made with credit cards is about
               .23 *93,300,000,000 = 21,459,000,000.

        c.   The percentage of non-cash payments in 2007 that were made with either credit or debit cards is
               27% + 23% = 50%.

d.   Using MINITAB, a Pareto diagram for non-cash payments in the U.S. is:

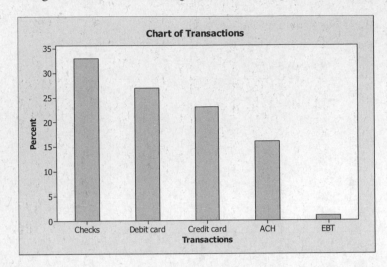

Checks were the most common method of non-cash payment in the U.S. in 2007. However, credit and debit card combined accounted for 50% of the non-cash payments in 2007. EBT was the least common method of non-cash payment in the U.S. in 2007.

2.9   Using MINITAB, the pie chart is:

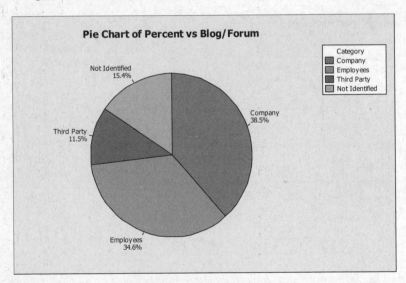

Companies and Employees represent (38.5 + 34.6 = 73.1) slightly more than 73% of the entities creating blogs/forums. Third parties are the least common entity.

2.11   Using MINITAB, the pie charts are:

Color

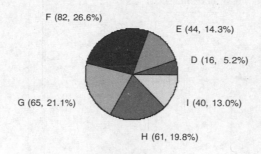

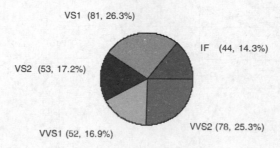

Clarity

The F color occurs the most often with 26.6%. The clarity that occurs the most is VS1 with 26.3%. The D color occurs the least often with 5.2%. The clarity that occurs the least is IF with 14.3%.

2.13   a.   The variable measured by Performark is the length of time it took for each advertiser to respond back.

         b.   The pie chart is:

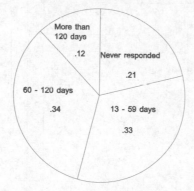

         c.   Twenty-one percent of .21 × 17,000 = 3,570 of the advertisers never respond to the sales lead.

         d.   The information from the pie chart does not indicate how effective the "bingo cards" are. It just indicates how long it takes advertisers to respond, if at all.

2.15   a.   Using MINITAB, bar charts for the 3 variables are:

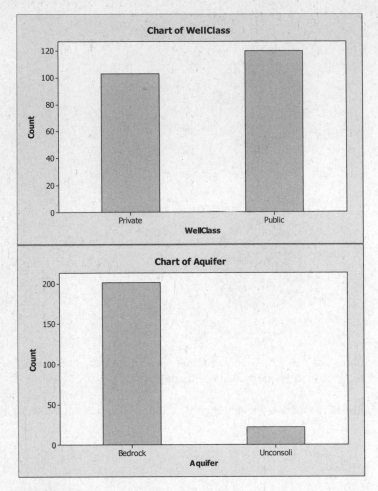

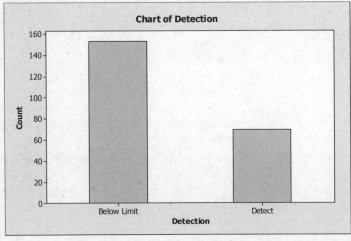

b.   Using MINITAB, the side-by-side bar chart is:

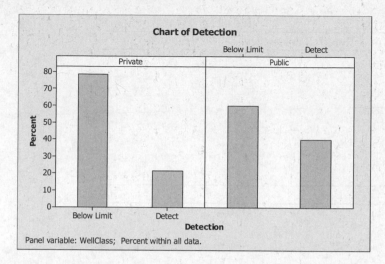

c.   Using MINITAB, the side-by-side bar chart is:

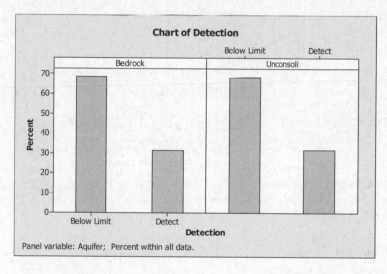

d.   From the bar charts in parts a-c, one can infer that most aquifers are bedrock and most levels of MTBE were below the limit ($\approx 2/3$). Also the percentages of public wells verses private wells are relatively close. Approximately 80% of private wells are not contaminated, while only about 60% of public wells are not contaminated. The percentage of contaminated wells is about the same for both types of aquifers ($\approx 30\%$).

2.17   To find the number of measurements for each measurement class, multiply the relative frequency by the total number of observations, $n = 500$. The frequency table is:

Measurement Class	Relative Frequency	Frequency
.5 – 2.5	.10	$500(.10) = 50$
2.5 – 4.5	.15	$500(.15) = 75$
4.5 – 6.5	.25	$500(.25) = 125$
6.5 – 8.5	.20	$500(.20) = 100$
8.5 – 10.5	.05	$500(.05) = 25$
10.5 – 12.5	.10	$500(.10) = 50$
12.5 – 14.5	.10	$500(.10) = 50$
14.5 – 16.5	.05	$500(.05) = 25$
		500

The frequency histogram is:

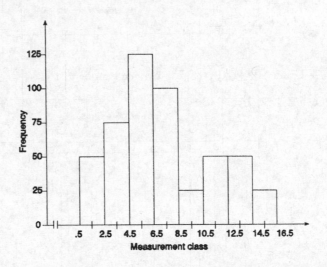

2.19   a.   This is a frequency histogram because the number of observations is graphed for each interval rather than the relative frequency.

b.   There are 14 measurement classes.

c.   There are 49 measurements in the data set.

2.21   a.   For male USGA golfers, there are about ≈30% with handicaps greater than 20.

b.   For female USGA golfers, there are about ≈80% with handicaps greater than 20.

2.23　a.　Using MINITAB, a dot plot of the data is:

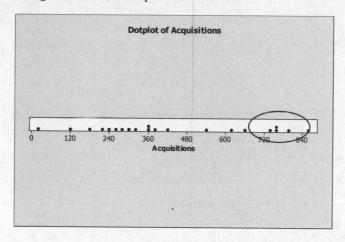

b.　By looking at the dot plot, one can conclude that the years 1996-2000 had the highest number of firms with at least one acquisition. The lowest number of acquisitions in that time frame (748) is almost 100 higher than the highest value from the remaining years.

2.25　a.　Using MINITAB, the relative frequency (percent) histogram is:

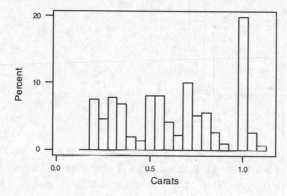

b.　Using MINITAB, the relative frequency (percent) histogram for the GIA group is:

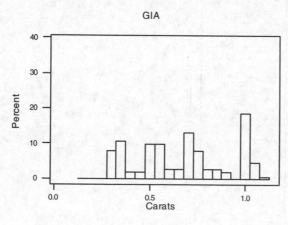

c.   Using MINITAB, the relative frequency (percent) histograms for the HRD and IGI groups are:

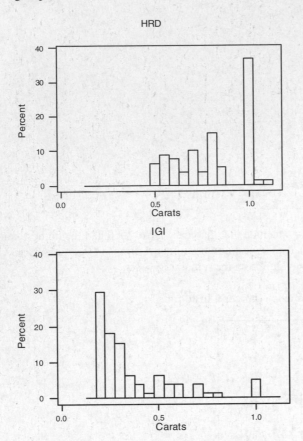

d.   The HRD group does not assess any diamonds less than .5 carats and almost 40% of the diamonds they assess are 1.0 carats or higher. The IGI group does not assess very many diamonds over .5 carats and more than half are .3 carats or less. More than half of the diamonds assessed by the GIA group are more than .5 carats, but the sizes are less than those of the HRD group.

2.27   a.   Using MINITAB, the stem-and-leaf display is:

```
Stem-and-Leaf of PENALTY           N = 38
Leaf Unit = 10000

(28)     0  0  0 ① ① 111 ② ② 222222 ③ ③ 33334444899
  10     1 ⓪ 0239
   5     2
   5     3 0
   4     4 0
   3     5
   3     6
   3     7
   3     8 5
   2     9 3
   1    10 0
```

b.   See the circled leaves in part **a**.

c.   Most of the penalties imposed for Clean Air Act violations are relatively small compared to the penalties imposed for other violations. All but one of the penalties for Clean Air Act violations are below the median penalty imposed.

2.29   a.   Using MINITAB, the frequency histograms for the 2 years of SAT scores are:

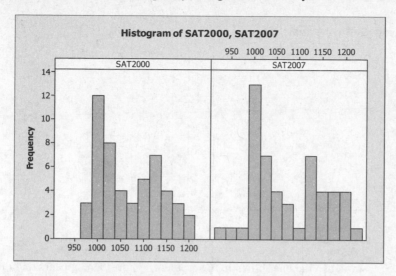

The data from 2007 appear to be somewhat shifted to the right of those for 2000.

   b.   Using MINITAB, the frequency histogram of the differences is:

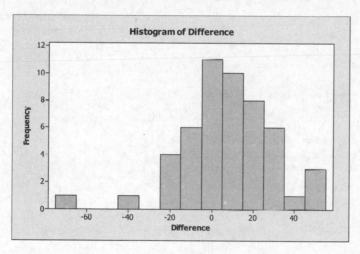

   c.   There appear to be 12 differences that were less than -5. Thus, for these states, the 2007 SAT scores were worse than the SAT scores for 2000. There were also 11 differences that were between -5 and 5. There was very little change in the SAT scores for those states. The rest of the states (28) had differences of more than 5. This would indicate a moderate shift to the right of the SAT scores.

   d.   Based on the graph, the greatest improvement was around 50, with 3 states having values around 50. These states are Colorado, Illinois, and Wyoming. Colorado has the highest improvement.

2.31   Using MINITAB, the histogram of the data is:

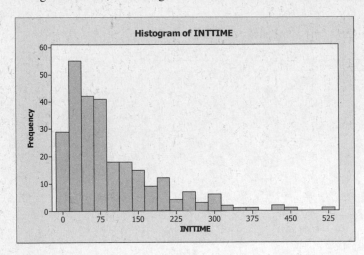

Histogram of INTTIME

This histogram looks very similar to the one shown in the problem. Thus, there appears that there was minimal or no collaboration or collusion from within the company. We could conclude that the phishing attack against the organization was not an inside job.

2.33   a. $\sum x = 5 + 1 + 3 + 2 + 1 = 12$

b. $\sum x^2 = 5^2 + 1^2 + 3^2 + 2^2 + 1^2 = 40$

c. $\sum (x-1) = (5-1) + (1-1) + (3-1) + (2-1) + (1-1) = 7$

d. $\sum (x-1)^2 = (5-1)^2 + (1-1)^2 + (3-1)^2 + (2-1)^2 + (1-1)^2 = 21$

e. $\left(\sum x\right)^2 = (5 + 1 + 3 + 2 + 1)^2 = 12^2 = 144$

2.35   Using the results from Exercise 2.33:

a. $\sum x^2 - \dfrac{\left(\sum x\right)^2}{5} = 40 - \dfrac{144}{5} = 40 - 28.8 = 11.2$

b. $\sum (x-2)^2 = (5-2)^2 + (1-2)^2 + (3-2)^2 + (2-2)^2 + (1-2)^2 = 12$

c. $\sum x^2 - 10 = 40 - 10 = 30$

2.37   Assume the data are a sample. The sample mean is:

$$\bar{x} = \frac{\sum x}{n} = \frac{3.2+2.5+2.1+3.7+2.8+2.0}{6} = \frac{16.3}{6} = 2.717$$

The median is the average of the middle two numbers when the data are arranged in order (since $n = 6$ is even). The data arranged in order are: 2.0, 2.1, 2.5, 2.8, 3.2, 3.7. The middle two numbers are 2.5 and 2.8. The median is:

$$\frac{2.5+2.8}{2} = \frac{5.3}{2} = 2.65$$

2.39   The mean and median of a symmetric data set are equal to each other. The mean is larger than the median when the data set is skewed to the right. The mean is less than the median when the data set is skewed to the left. Thus, by comparing the mean and median, one can determine whether the data set is symmetric, skewed right, or skewed left.

2.41   Assume the data are a sample. The mode is the observation that occurs most frequently. For this sample, the mode is 15, which occurs three times.

The sample mean is:

$$\bar{x} = \frac{\sum x}{n} = \frac{18+10+15+13+17+15+12+15+18+16+11}{11} = \frac{160}{11} = 14.545$$

The median is the middle number when the data are arranged in order. The data arranged in order are: 10, 11, 12, 13, 15, 15, 15, 16, 17, 18, 18. The middle number is the 6th number, which is 15.

2.43   a.   For a distribution that is skewed to the left, the mean is less than the median.

b.   For a distribution that is skewed to the right, the mean is greater than the median.

c.   For a symmetric distribution, the mean and median are equal.

2.45   a.   The mean amount exported on the printout is 653. This means that in 2007, the average amount of money per market from exporting sparkling wine was $653,000.

b.   The median amount exported on the printout is 231. Since the median is the middle value, this means that in 2007, half of the 30 sparkling wine export values were above $231,000 and half of the sparkling wine export values were below $231,000.

c.   The mean 3-year percentage change on the printout is 481. This means that in the last three years, the average change is 481%, which indicates a large increase.

d.   The median 3-year percentage change on the printout is 156. Since the median is the middle value, this means that in 2007, half, or 15 of the 30 countries' 3-year percentage change values were above 156% and half, or 15 of the 30 countries' 3-year percentage change values were below 156%.

2.47   a.   The median is the middle number (18th) once the data have been arranged in order because n = 35 is odd. The honey dosage data arranged in order are:

           4,5,6,8,8,8,9,9,9,9,10,10,10,10,10,10,<u>11</u>,11,11,11,12,12,12,12,12,12,13,13,14,15,15,15,15,16

           The 18th number is the median = 11.

     b.   The median is the middle number (17th) once the data have been arranged in order because n = 33 is odd. The DM dosage data arranged in order are:

           3,4,4,4,4,4,4,6,6,6,7,7,7,7,7,8,<u>9</u>,9,9,9,9,10,10,10,11,12,12,12,12,12,13,13,15

           The 17th number is the median = 9.

     c.   The median is the middle number (19th) once the data have been arranged in order because n = 37 is odd. The No dosage data arranged in order are:

           0,1,1,1,3,3,4,4,5,5,5,6,6,6,6,7,7,7,<u>7</u>,7,7,7,7,8,8,8,8,8,9,9,9,9,10,11,12,12

           The 19th number is the median = 7.

     d.   Since the median for the Honey dosage is larger than the other two, it appears that the honey dosage leads to more improvement than the other two treatments.

2.49   a.   The sample mean is:

$$\bar{x} = \frac{\sum_{i=1}^{n} x_i}{n} = \frac{.30+.30+.30+...+1.09}{308} = \frac{194.32}{308} = .63$$

           The average number of carats for the 308 diamonds is .63

     b.   The median is the average of the middle two observations once they have been ordered. The 154th and 155th observations are .62 and .62. The average of these two observations is .62.

           Half of the diamonds weigh less than .62 carats and half weigh more.

     c.   The mode is 1.0. This observation occurred 32 times.

     d.   Since the mean and median are close in value, either could be a good descriptor of central tendency.

2.51   The mean is 141.31 hours. This means that the average number of semester hours per candidate for the CPA exam is 141.31 hours. The median is 140 hours. This means that 50% of the candidates had more than 140 semester hours of credit and 50% had less than 140 semester hours of credit. Since the mean and median are so close in value, the data are probably not skewed, but close to symmetric.

2.53 For the "Joint exchange offer with prepack" firms, the mean time is 2.6545 months, and the median is 1.5 months. Thus, the average time spent in bankruptcy for "Joint" firms is 2.6545 months, while half of the firms spend 1.5 months or less in bankruptcy.

For the "No prefiling vote held" firms, the mean time is 4.2364 months, and the median is 3.2 months. Thus, the average time spent in bankruptcy for "No prefiling vote held" firms is 4.2364 months, while half of the firms spend 3.2 months or less in bankruptcy.

For the "Prepack solicitation only" firms, the mean time is 1.8185 months, and the median is 1.4 months. Thus, the average time spent in bankruptcy for "Prepack solicitation only" firms is 1.8185 months, while half of the firms spend 1.4 months or less in bankruptcy.

Since the means and medians for the three groups of firms differ quite a bit, it would be unreasonable to use a single number to locate the center of the time in bankruptcy. Three different "centers" should be used.

2.55 a. Due to the "elite" superstars, the salary distribution is skewed to the right. Since this implies that the median is less than the mean, the players' association would want to use the median.

b. The owners, by the logic of part **a**, would want to use the mean.

2.57 a. Range $= 4 - 0 = 4$

$$s^2 = \frac{\sum x^2 - \frac{\left(\sum x\right)^2}{n}}{n-1} = \frac{22 - \frac{8^2}{5}}{4-1} = 2.3 \qquad s = \sqrt{2.3} = 1.52$$

b. Range $= 6 - 0 = 6$

$$s^2 = \frac{\sum x^2 - \frac{\left(\sum x\right)^2}{n}}{n-1} = \frac{63 - \frac{17^2}{7}}{7-1} = 3.619 \qquad s = \sqrt{3.619} = 1.90$$

c. Range $= 8 - (-2) = 10$

$$s^2 = \frac{\sum x^2 - \frac{\left(\sum x\right)^2}{n}}{n-1} = \frac{154 - \frac{30^2}{10}}{10-1} = 7.111 \qquad s = \sqrt{7.111} = 2.67$$

d. Range $= 1 - (-3) = 4$

$$s^2 = \frac{\sum x^2 - \frac{\left(\sum x\right)^2}{n}}{n-1} = \frac{25.04 - \frac{(-6.8)^2}{17}}{17-1} = 1.395 \qquad s = \sqrt{1.395} = 1.18$$

2.59 a. $\sum x = 3 + 1 + 10 + 10 + 4 = 28$

$\sum x^2 = 3^2 + 1^2 + 10^2 + 10^2 + 4^2 = 226$

$\bar{x} = \dfrac{\sum x}{n} = \dfrac{28}{5} = 5.6$

$s^2 = \dfrac{\sum x^2 - \dfrac{\left(\sum x\right)^2}{n}}{n-1} = \dfrac{226 - \dfrac{28^2}{5}}{5-1} = \dfrac{69.2}{4} = 17.3$ $\qquad s = \sqrt{17.3} = 4.1593$

b. $\sum x = 8 + 10 + 32 + 5 = 55$

$\sum x^2 = 8^2 + 10^2 + 32^2 + 5^2 = 1213$

$\bar{x} = \dfrac{\sum x}{n} = \dfrac{55}{4} = 13.75 \text{ feet}$

$s^2 = \dfrac{\sum x^2 - \dfrac{\left(\sum x\right)^2}{n}}{n-1} = \dfrac{1213 - \dfrac{55^2}{4}}{4-1} = \dfrac{456.75}{3} = 152.25 \text{ square feet}$

$s = \sqrt{152.25} = 12.339 \text{ feet}$

c. $\sum x = -1 + (-4) + (-3) + 1 + (-4) + (-4) = -15$

$\sum x^2 = (-1)^2 + (-4)^2 + (-3)^2 + 1^2 + (-4)^2 + (-4)^2 = 59$

$\bar{x} = \dfrac{\sum x}{n} = \dfrac{-15}{6} = -2.5$

$s^2 = \dfrac{\sum x^2 - \dfrac{\left(\sum x\right)^2}{n}}{n-1} = \dfrac{59 - \dfrac{(-15)^2}{6}}{6-1} = \dfrac{21.5}{5} = 4.3$ $\qquad s = \sqrt{4.3} = 2.0736$

d. $\sum x = \dfrac{1}{5} + \dfrac{1}{5} + \dfrac{1}{5} + \dfrac{2}{5} + \dfrac{1}{5} + \dfrac{4}{5} = \dfrac{10}{5} = 2$

$\sum x^2 = \left(\dfrac{1}{5}\right)^2 + \left(\dfrac{1}{5}\right)^2 + \left(\dfrac{1}{5}\right)^2 + \left(\dfrac{2}{5}\right)^2 + \left(\dfrac{1}{5}\right)^2 + \left(\dfrac{4}{5}\right)^2 = \dfrac{24}{25} = .96$

$\bar{x} = \dfrac{\sum x}{n} = \dfrac{2}{6} = \dfrac{1}{3} = .33 \text{ ounce}$

$s^2 = \dfrac{\sum x^2 - \dfrac{\left(\sum x\right)^2}{n}}{n-1} = \dfrac{\dfrac{24}{25} - \dfrac{2^2}{6}}{6-1} = \dfrac{.2933}{5} = .0587 \text{ square ounce}$

$s = \sqrt{.0587} = .2422 \text{ ounce}$

2.61 This is one possibility for the two data sets.

Data Set 1: 0, 1, 2, 3, 4, 5, 6, 7, 8, 9
Data Set 2: 0, 0, 1, 1, 2, 2, 3, 3, 9, 9

The two sets of data above have the same range = largest measurement − smallest measurement = 9 − 0 = 9.

The means for the two data sets are:

$$\bar{x}_1 = \frac{\sum x}{n} = \frac{0+1+2+3+4+5+6+7+8+9}{10} = \frac{45}{10} = 4.5$$

$$\bar{x}_2 = \frac{\sum x}{n} = \frac{0+0+1+1+2+2+3+3+9+9}{10} = \frac{30}{10} = 3$$

The dot diagrams for the two data sets are shown below.

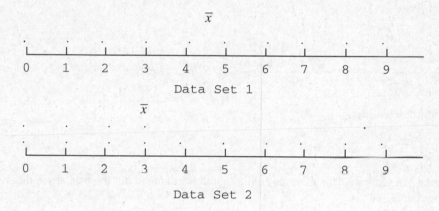

2.63 a. Range = 3 − 0 = 3

$$s^2 = \frac{\sum x^2 - \dfrac{\left(\sum x\right)^2}{n}}{n-1} = \frac{15 - \dfrac{7^2}{5}}{5-1} = 1.3 \qquad s = \sqrt{1.3} = 1.14$$

b. After adding 3 to each of the data points,

Range = 6 − 3 = 3

$$s^2 = \frac{\sum x^2 - \dfrac{\left(\sum x\right)^2}{n}}{n-1} = \frac{102 - \dfrac{22^2}{5}}{5-1} = 1.3 \qquad s = \sqrt{1.3} = 1.14$$

c. After subtracting 4 from each of the data points,

Range = −1 − (−4) = 3

$$s^2 = \frac{\sum x^2 - \dfrac{\left(\sum x\right)^2}{n}}{n-1} = \frac{39 - \dfrac{(-13)^2}{5}}{5-1} = 1.3 \qquad s = \sqrt{1.3} = 1.14$$

d. The range, variance, and standard deviation remain the same when any number is added to or subtracted from each measurement in the data set.

2.65   a.   The range is the difference between the largest observation and the smallest observation. From the printout, the largest observation is $4,852 thousand and the smallest observation is $70 thousand. The range is:

R = $4,852 - $70 = $4,882 thousand

      b.   From the printout, the standard deviation is s = $1,113 thousand.

      c.   The variance is the standard deviation squared. The variance is:

$s^2 = 1,113^2 = 1,238,769$ million dollars squared

2.67   a.   The maximum weight is 1.1 carats. The minimum weight is .18 carats. The range is $1.1 - .18 = .92$ carats.

      b.   The variance is:

$$s^2 = \frac{\sum_i x_i^2 - \dfrac{\left(\sum_i x_i\right)^2}{n}}{n-1} = \frac{146.19 - \dfrac{194.32^2}{308}}{308-1} = .0768 \text{ square carats}$$

      c.   The standard deviation is:

$$s = \sqrt{s^2} = \sqrt{.0768} = .2772 \text{ carats}$$

      d.   The standard deviation. This gives us an idea about how spread out the data are in the same units as the original data.

2.69   a.   The range is the largest observation minus the smallest observation or $11 - 1 = 10$

The variance is:

$$s^2 = \frac{\sum_i x_i^2 - \dfrac{\left(\sum_i x_i\right)^2}{n}}{n-1} = \frac{463 - \dfrac{81^2}{20}}{20-1} = 7.10$$

The standard deviation is:

$$s = \sqrt{s^2} = \sqrt{7.1026} = 2.67$$

b.   The largest observation is 11. It is deleted from the data set. The new range is: $9 - 1 = 8$.

The variance is:

$$s^2 = \frac{\sum_i x_i^2 - \frac{\left(\sum_i x_i\right)^2}{n}}{n-1} = \frac{342 - \frac{70^2}{19}}{19-1} = 4.67$$

The standard deviation is:

$$s = \sqrt{s^2} = \sqrt{4.6725} = 2.16$$

When the largest observation is deleted, the range, variance and standard deviation decrease.

c.   The largest observation is 11 and the smallest is 1. When these two observations are deleted from the data set, the new range is: $9 - 1 = 8$.

The variance is:

$$s^2 = \frac{\sum_i x_i^2 - \frac{\left(\sum_i x_i\right)^2}{n}}{n-1} = \frac{341 - \frac{69^2}{18}}{18-1} = 4.50$$

The standard deviation is:

$$s = \sqrt{s^2} = \sqrt{4.5} = 2.12$$

When the largest and smallest observations are deleted, the range, variance and standard deviation decrease.

2.71   a.   The unit of measurement of the variable of interest is dollars (the same as the mean and standard deviation). Based on this, the data are quantitative.

b.   Since no information is given about the shape of the data set, we can only use Chebyshev's Rule.

$900 is 2 standard deviations below the mean, and $2100 is 2 standard deviations above the mean. Using Chebyshev's Rule, at least 3/4 of the measurements (or $3/4 \times 200 = 150$ measurements) will fall between $900 and $2100.

$600 is 3 standard deviations below the mean and $2400 is 3 standard deviations above the mean. Using Chebyshev's Rule, at least 8/9 of the measurements (or $8/9 \times 200 \approx 178$ measurements) will fall between $600 and $2400.

$1200 is 1 standard deviation below the mean and $1800 is 1 standard deviation above the mean. Using Chebyshev's Rule, nothing can be said about the number of measurements that will fall between $1200 and $1800.

$1500 is equal to the mean and $2100 is 2 standard deviations above the mean. Using Chebyshev's Rule, at least 3/4 of the measurements (or $3/4 \times 200 = 150$ measurements) will fall between $900 and $2100. It is possible that all of the 150 measurements will be between $900 and $1500. Thus, nothing can be said about the number of measurements between $1500 and $2100.

2.73   According to the Empirical Rule:

a.   Approximately 68% of the measurements will be contained in the interval $\bar{x} - s$ to $\bar{x} + s$.

b.   Approximately 95% of the measurements will be contained in the interval $\bar{x} - 2s$ to $\bar{x} + 2s$.

c.   Essentially all the measurements will be contained in the interval $\bar{x} - 3s$ to $\bar{x} + 3s$.

2.75   Using Chebyshev's Rule, at least 8/9 of the measurements will fall within 3 standard deviations of the mean. Thus, the range of the data would be around 6 standard deviations. Using the Empirical Rule, approximately 95% of the observations are within 2 standard deviations of the mean. Thus, the range of the data would be around 4 standard deviations. We would expect the standard deviation to be somewhere between Range/6 and Range/4.

For our data, the range = 760 − 135 = 625.

The Range/6 = 625/6 = 104.17 and Range/4 = 625/4 = 156.25.

Therefore, I would estimate that the standard deviation of the data set is between 104.17 and 156.25.

It would not be feasible to have a standard deviation of 25. If the standard deviation were 25, the data would span 625/25 = 25 standard deviations. This would be extremely unlikely.

2.77   a.   The 2 standard deviation interval around the mean is:

$\bar{x} \pm 2s \Rightarrow 141.31 \pm 2(17.77) \Rightarrow 141.31 \pm 35.54 \Rightarrow (105.77, \quad 176.85)$

b.   Using Chebyshev's Theorem, at least ¾ of the observations will fall within 2 standard deviations of the mean. Thus, at least ¾ of first-time candidates for the CPA exam have total credit hours between 105.77 and 176.85.

c.   In order for the above statement to be true, nothing needs to be known about the shape of the distribution of total semester hours.

2.79   a.   From the information given, we have $\bar{x} = 375$ and $s = 25$. From Chebyshev's Rule, we know that at least three-fourths of the measurements are within the interval:

$\bar{x} \pm 2s$, or (325, 425)

Thus, at most one-fourth of the measurements exceed 425. In other words, more than 425 vehicles used the intersection on at most 25% of the days.

b.   According to the Empirical Rule, approximately 95% of the measurements are within the interval:

$\bar{x} \pm 2s$, or (325, 425)

This leaves approximately 5% of the measurements to lie outside the interval. Because of the symmetry of a mound-shaped distribution, approximately 2.5% of these will lie below 325, and the remaining 2.5% will lie above 425. Thus, on approximately 2.5% of the days, more than 425 vehicles used the intersection.

2.81   The sample mean is:

$$\bar{x} = \frac{\sum_{i=1}^{n} x_i}{n} = \frac{240.9 + 248.8 + 215.7 + \cdots + 238.0}{10} = \frac{2347.4}{10} = 234.74$$

The sample variance deviation is:

$$s^2 = \frac{\sum_{i=1}^{n} x_i^2 - \frac{\left(\sum_{i=1}^{n} x_i\right)^2}{n}}{n-1} = \frac{551,912.1 - \frac{2347.4^2}{10}}{9} = \frac{883.424}{9} = 98.1582$$

The sample standard deviation is:

$$\sqrt{s^2} = \sqrt{98.1582} = 9.91$$

The data are fairly symmetric, so we can use the Empirical Rule. We know from the Empirical Rule that almost all of the observations will fall within 3 standard deviations of the mean. This interval would be:

$$\bar{x} \pm 3s \Rightarrow 234.74 \pm 3(9.91) \Rightarrow 234.74 \pm 29.73 \Rightarrow (205.01, \ 264.47) \text{ or } (205.0, 264.5) \text{ or } (205.0, 264.5)$$

2.83   a.   Since no information is given about the distribution of the velocities of the Winchester bullets, we can only use Chebyshev's Rule to describe the data. We know that at least 3/4 of the velocities will fall within the interval:

$$\bar{x} \pm 2s \Rightarrow 936 \pm 2(10) \Rightarrow 936 \pm 20 \Rightarrow (916, 956)$$

Also, at least 8/9 of the velocities will fall within the interval:

$$\bar{x} \pm 3s \Rightarrow 936 \pm 3(10) \Rightarrow 936 \pm 30 \Rightarrow (906, 966)$$

b.   Since a velocity of 1,000 is much larger than the largest value in the second interval in part **a**, it is very unlikely that the bullet was manufactured by Winchester.

2.85   Since we do not know if the distribution of the heights of the trees is mound-shaped, we need to apply Chebyshev's Rule. We know $\mu = 30$ and $\sigma = 3$. Therefore,

$$\mu \pm 3\sigma \Rightarrow 30 \pm 3(3) \Rightarrow 30 \pm 9 \Rightarrow (21, 39)$$

According to Chebyshev's Rule, at least 8/9 or .89 of the tree heights on this piece of land fall within this interval and at most $\frac{1}{9}$ or .11 of the tree heights will fall above the interval. However, the buyer will only purchase the land if at least $\frac{1000}{5000}$ or .20 of the tree heights are at least 40 feet tall. Therefore, the buyer should not buy the piece of land.

2.87   We know $\mu = 25$ and $\sigma = .1$. Therefore,

$$\mu \pm 2\sigma \Rightarrow 25 \pm 2(.1) \Rightarrow 25 \pm .2 \Rightarrow (24.8, 25.2)$$

The machine is shut down for adjustment if the contents of two consecutive bags fall more than 2 standard deviations from the mean (i.e., outside the interval (24.8, 25.2)). Therefore, the machine was shut down yesterday at 11:30 (25.23 and 25.25 are outside the interval) and again at 4:00 (24.71 and 25.31 are outside the interval).

2.89   Using the definition of a percentile:

	Percentile	Percentage Above	Percentage Below
a.	75th	25%	75%
b.	50th	50%	50%
c.	20th	80%	20%
d.	84th	16%	84%

2.91   We first compute z-scores for each x value.

a. $z = \dfrac{x - \mu}{\sigma} = \dfrac{100 - 50}{25} = 2$

b. $z = \dfrac{x - \mu}{\sigma} = \dfrac{1 - 4}{1} = -3$

c. $z = \dfrac{x - \mu}{\sigma} = \dfrac{0 - 200}{100} = -2$

d. $z = \dfrac{x - \mu}{\sigma} = \dfrac{10 - 5}{3} = 1.67$

The above z-scores indicate that the x value in part **a** lies the greatest distance above the mean and the x value of part **b** lies the greatest distance below the mean.

2.93   The mean score of U.S. eighth-graders on a mathematics assessment test is 279. This is the average score. The 10th percentile score is 231. This means that 10% of the U.S. eighth-graders score below 231 on the test and 90% score higher. The 25th percentile is 255. This means that 25% of the U.S. eighth-graders score below 255 on the test and 75% score higher. The 75th percentile is 304. This means that 75% of the U.S. eighth-graders score below 304 on the test and 25% score higher. The 90th percentile is 324. This means that 90% of the U.S. eighth-graders score below 324 on the test and 10% score higher.

2.95   A median starting salary of \$41,100 indicates that half of the University of South Florida graduates had starting salaries less than \$41,100 and half had starting salaries greater than \$41,100. At mid-career, half of the University of South Florida graduates had a salary less than \$71,100 and half had salaries greater than \$71,100. At mid-career, 90% of the University of South Florida graduates had salaries under \$131,000 and 10% had salaries greater than \$131,000.

2.97   Since the 90th percentile of the study sample in the subdivision was .00372 mg/L, which is less than the USEPA level of .015 mg/L, the water customers in the subdivision are not at risk of drinking water with unhealthy lead levels.

2.99 a. The 10th percentile is the score that has at least 10% of the observations less than it. If we arrange the data in order from the smallest to the largest, the 10th percentile score will be the $.10(75) = 7.5$ or 8th observation. When the data are arranged in order, the 8th observation is 0. Thus, the 10th percentile is 0.

   b. The 95th percentile is the score that has at least 95% of the observations less than it. If we arrange the data in order from the smallest to the largest, the 95th percentile score will be the $.95(75) = 71.25$ or 72nd observation. When the data are arranged in order, the 72nd observation is 21. Thus, the 95th percentile is 21.

   c. The sample mean is:

$$\bar{x} = \frac{\sum_{i=1}^{n} x_i}{n} = \frac{393}{75} = 5.24$$

The sample variance is:

$$s^2 = \frac{\sum_i x_i^2 - \frac{\left(\sum_i x_i\right)^2}{n}}{n-1} = \frac{5943 - \frac{393^2}{75}}{75-1} = 52.482$$

The standard deviation is:

$$s = \sqrt{s^2} = \sqrt{52.482} = 7.24$$

The z-score for a county with 48 Superfund sites is:

$$z = \frac{x - \bar{x}}{s} = \frac{48 - 5.24}{7.24} = 5.90$$

   d. Yes. A score of 48 is almost 6 standard deviations from the mean. We know that for any data set almost all (at least 8/9 using Chebyshev's Theorem) of the observations are within 3 standard deviations of the mean. To be almost 6 standard deviations from the mean is very unusual.

2.101   Not necessarily. Because the distribution is highly skewed to the right, the standard deviation is very large.
         Remember that the z-score represents the number of standard deviations a score is from the mean. If the
         standard deviation is very large, then the z-scores for observations somewhat near the mean will appear to
         be fairly small. If we deleted the schools with the very high productivity scores and recomputed the mean
         and standard deviation, the standard deviation would be much smaller. Thus, most of the z-scores would
         be larger because we would be dividing by a much smaller standard deviation. This would imply a bigger
         spread among the rest of the schools than the original distribution with the few outliers.

2.103   To determine if the measurements are outliers, compute the z-score.

   a. $z = \dfrac{x - \bar{x}}{s} = \dfrac{65 - 57}{11} = .727$ Since this z-score is less than 3 in magnitude, 65 is
                                                                                  not an outlier.

   b. $z = \dfrac{x - \bar{x}}{s} = \dfrac{21 - 57}{11} = -3.273$ Since this z-score is more than 3 in magnitude, 21 is
                                                                                  an outlier.

   c. $z = \dfrac{x - \bar{x}}{s} = \dfrac{72 - 57}{11} = 1.364$ Since this z-score is less than 3 in magnitude, 72 is
                                                                                  not an outlier.

   d. $z = \dfrac{x - \bar{x}}{s} = \dfrac{98 - 57}{11} = 3.727$ Since this z-score is more than 3 in magnitude, 98 is
                                                                                  an outlier.

2.105   The interquartile range is IQR = $Q_U - Q_L$ = 85 − 60 = 25.

         The lower inner fence = Q_L − 1.5(IQR) = 60 − 1.5(25) = 22.5.

         The upper inner fence = Q_U + 1.5(IQR) = 85 + 1.5(25) = 122.5.

         The lower outer fence = Q_L − 3(IQR) = 60 − 3(25) = −15.

         The upper outer fence = Q_U + 3(IQR) = 85 + 3(25) = 160.

         With only this information, the box plot would look something like the following:

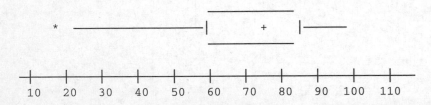

         The whiskers extend to the inner fences unless no data points are that small or that large. The upper inner
         fence is 122.5. However, the largest data point is 100, so the whisker stops at 100. The lower inner fence
         is 22.5. The smallest data point is 18, so the whisker extends to 22.5. Since 18 is between the inner and
         outer fences, it is designated with a *. We do not know if there is any more than one data point below
         22.5, so we cannot be sure that the box plot is entirely correct.

2.107 a.   The average expenditure per full-time employee is $6,563. The median expenditure per employee is $6,232. Half of all expenditures per employee were less than $6,232 and half were greater than $6,232. The lower quartile is $5,309. Twenty-five percent of all expenditures per employee were below $5,309. The upper quartile is $7,216. Seventy-five percent of all expenditures per employee were below $7,216.

      b.   IQR = $Q_U - Q_L$ = $7,216 − $5,309 = $1,907.

      c.   The interquartile range goes from the 25th percentile to the 75th percentile. Thus, .5(.75 − .25) of the 1,751 army hospitals have expenses between $5,309 and $7,216.

2.109 a.   The z-score is:

$$z = \frac{x - \bar{x}}{s} = \frac{160 - 141.31}{17.77} = 1.05$$

Since the z-score is not large, it is not considered an outlier.

      b.   Z-scores with values greater than 3 in absolute value are considered outliers. An observation with a z-score of 3 would have the value:

$$z = \frac{x - \bar{x}}{s} \Rightarrow 3 = \frac{x - 141.31}{17.77} \Rightarrow 3(17.77) = x - 141.31 \Rightarrow 53.31 = x - 141.31 \Rightarrow x = 194.62$$

An observation with a z-score of −3 would have the value:

$$z = \frac{x - \bar{x}}{s} \Rightarrow -3 = \frac{x - 141.31}{17.77} \Rightarrow -3(17.77) = x - 141.31 \Rightarrow -53.31 = x - 141.31 \Rightarrow x = 88.00$$

Thus any observation of semester hours that is greater than or equal to 194.62 or less than or equal to 88 would be considered an outlier.

2.111 a.   Using MINITAB, the boxplots for each type of firm are:

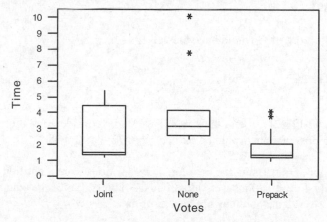

      b.   The median bankruptcy time for Joint firms is about 1.5. The median bankruptcy time for None firms is about 3.2. The median bankruptcy time for Prepack firms is about 1.4.

      c.   The range of the "Prepack" firms is less than the other two, while the range of the "None" firms is the largest. The interquartile range of the "Prepack" firms is less than the other two, while the interquartile range of the "Joint" firms is larger than the other two.

d.   No. The interquartile range for the "Prepack" firms is the smallest which corresponds to the smallest standard deviation. However, the second smallest interquartile range corresponds to the "none" firms. The second smallest standard deviation corresponds to the "Joint" firms.

e.   Yes. There is evidence of two outliers in the "Prepack" firms. These are indicated by the two *'s. There is also evidence of two outliers in the "None" firms. These are indicated by the two *'s.

2.113   a.   Using MINITAB, the boxplot is:

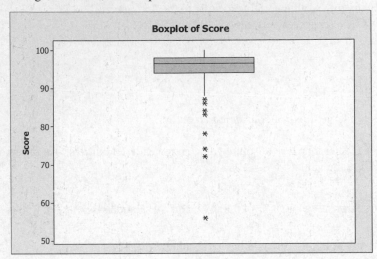

From the boxplot, there appears to be 8 outliers: 56, 72, 74, 78, 83, 83, 84, and 84.

b.   From Exercise 2.80, $\bar{x} = 95.044$ and $s = 5.391$. Since the data are skewed to the left, we will consider observations more than 3 standard deviations from the mean to be outliers. An observation with a z-score of 3 would have the value:

$$z = \frac{x - \bar{x}}{s} \Rightarrow 3 = \frac{x - 95.044}{5.391} \Rightarrow 3(5.391) = x - 95.044 \Rightarrow 16.173 = x - 95.044 \Rightarrow x = 111.217$$

An observation with a z-score of -3 would have the value:

$$z = \frac{x - \bar{x}}{s} \Rightarrow -3 = \frac{x - 95.044}{5.391} \Rightarrow -3(5.391) = x - 95.044 \Rightarrow -16.173 = x - 95.044 \Rightarrow x = 78.871$$

Observations greater than 111.217 or less than 78.871 would be considered outliers. Using this criterion, the following observations would be outliers: 56, 72, 74, and 78.

c.   No, these methods do not agree. Using the boxplot, 8 observations were identified as outliers. Using the z-score method, only 4 observations were identified as outliers. Since the data are very highly skewed to the left, the z-score method may not be appropriate.

2.115   a.   Using MINITAB, the box plot is:

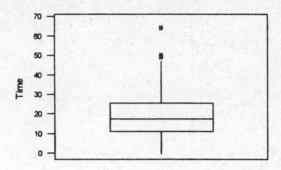

The median is about 18. The data appear to be skewed to the right since there are 3 suspect outliers to the right and none to the left. The variability of the data is fairly small because the IQR is fairly small, approximately $26 - 10 = 16$.

b.   The customers associated with the suspected outliers are customers 268, 269, and 264.

c.   In order to find the z-scores, we must first find the mean and standard deviation.

$$\bar{x} = \frac{\sum x}{n} = \frac{815}{40} = 20.375$$

$$s^2 = \frac{\sum x^2 - \frac{\left(\sum x\right)^2}{n}}{n-1} = \frac{24129 - \frac{815^2}{40}}{40-1} = 192.90705$$

$$s = \sqrt{192.90705} = 13.89$$

The z-scores associated with the suspected outliers are:

Customer 268 $z = \dfrac{49 - 20.375}{13.89} = 2.06$

Customer 269 $z = \dfrac{50 - 20.375}{13.89} = 2.13$

Customer 264 $z = \dfrac{64 - 20.375}{13.89} = 3.14$

All the z-scores are greater than 2. These are very unusual values.

2.117   Using MINITAB, the scatterplot is:

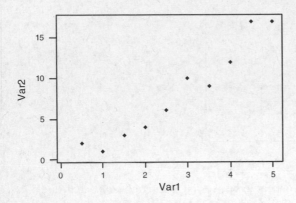

2.119   Using MINITAB, a scattergram of the data is:

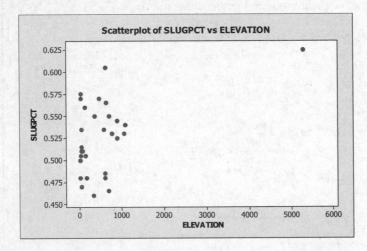

If we include the observation from Denver, then we would say there was a linear relationship between slugging percentage and elevation. If we eliminated the observation from Denver, it appears that there might not be a relationship between slugging percentage and elevation.

2.121   Using MINITAB, the scatterplot is:

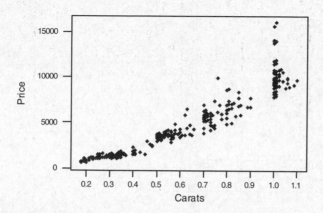

As the number of carats increases the price of the diamond tends to increase.

2.123   a.   Using MINITAB, a scatterplot of the data is:

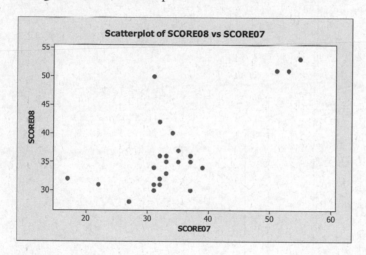

There is a moderate positive trend to the data. As the scores for 2007 increase, the scores for 2008 also tend to increase.

b.   From the graph, two agencies that had greater than expected PARS evaluation scores for 2008 were USAID and State.

2.125   Using MINITAB, the scattergram of the data is:

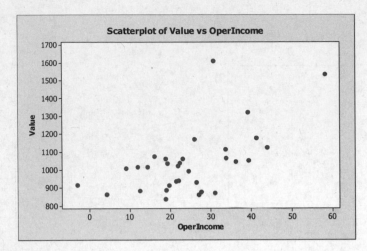

There is a moderate positive trend to the data. As operating income increases, the 2008 value also tends to increase. Since the trend is moderate, we would recommend that an NFL executive use operating income to predict a team's current value.

2.127   The relative frequency histogram is:

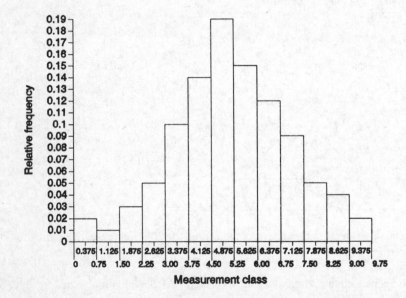

2.129 a. $z = \dfrac{x-\mu}{\sigma} = \dfrac{50-60}{10} = -1$

            $z = \dfrac{70-60}{10} = 1$

            $z = \dfrac{80-60}{10} = 2$

    b. $z = \dfrac{x-\mu}{\sigma} = \dfrac{50-50}{5} = 0$

            $z = \dfrac{70-50}{5} = 4$

            $z = \dfrac{80-50}{5} = 6$

    c $z = \dfrac{x-\mu}{\sigma} = \dfrac{50-40}{10} = 1$

            $z = \dfrac{70-40}{10} = 3$

            $z = \dfrac{80-40}{10} = 4$

    d. $z = \dfrac{x-\mu}{\sigma} = \dfrac{50-40}{100} = .1$

            $z = \dfrac{70-40}{100} = .3$

            $z = \dfrac{80-40}{100} = .4$

2.131 a. $\sum x = 13 + 1 + 10 + 3 + 3 = 30$

          $\sum x^2 = 13^2 + 1^2 + 10^2 + 3^2 + 3^2 = 288$

          $\bar{x} = \sum x = \dfrac{30}{5} = 6$

$$s^2 = \dfrac{\sum x^2 - \dfrac{\left(\sum x\right)^2}{n}}{n-1} = \dfrac{288 - \dfrac{30^2}{5}}{5-1} = \dfrac{108}{4} = 27 \qquad s = \sqrt{27} = 5.20$$

    b. $\sum x = 13 + 6 + 6 + 0 = 25$

          $\sum x^2 = 13^2 + 6^2 + 6^2 + 0^2 = 241$

          $\bar{x} = \sum x = \dfrac{25}{4} = 6.25$

$$s^2 = \dfrac{\sum x^2 - \dfrac{\left(\sum x\right)^2}{n}}{n-1} = \dfrac{241 - \dfrac{25^2}{4}}{4-1} = \dfrac{84.75}{3} = 28.25 \qquad s = \sqrt{28.25} = 5.32$$

c. $\sum x = 1 + 0 + 1 + 10 + 11 + 11 + 15 = 49$

$\sum x^2 = 1^2 + 0^2 + 1^2 + 10^2 + 11^2 + 11^2 + 15^2 = 569$

$\bar{x} = \sum x = \dfrac{49}{7} = 7$

$s^2 = \dfrac{\sum x^2 - \dfrac{\left(\sum x\right)^2}{n}}{n-1} = \dfrac{569 - \dfrac{49^2}{7}}{7-1} = \dfrac{226}{6} = 37.67$ $s = \sqrt{37.67} = 6.14$

d. $\sum x = 3 + 3 + 3 + 3 = 12$

$\sum x^2 = 3^2 + 3^2 + 3^2 + 3^2 = 36$

$\bar{x} = \sum x = \dfrac{12}{4} = 3$

$s^2 = \dfrac{\sum x^2 - \dfrac{\left(\sum x\right)^2}{n}}{n-1} = \dfrac{36 - \dfrac{12^2}{4}}{4-1} = \dfrac{0}{3} = 0$ $s = \sqrt{0} = 0$

2.133   The range is found by taking the largest measurement in the data set and subtracting the smallest measurement. Therefore, it only uses two measurements from the whole data set. The standard deviation uses every measurement in the data set. Therefore, it takes every measurement into account—not just two. The range is affected by extreme values more than the standard deviation.

2.135   Using MINITAB, the scatterplot is:

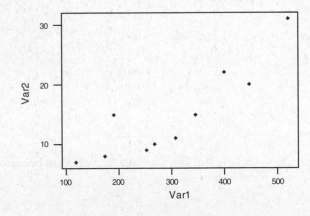

2.137   a.   The relative frequency for each response category is found by dividing the frequency by the total sample size. The relative frequency for the category "Global Marketing" is 235/2863 = .082. The rest of the relative frequencies are found in a similar manner and are reported in the table.

Area	Number	Relative Frequencies
Global Marketing	235	235/2863 = .082
Sales Management	494	494/2863 = .173
Buyer Behavior	478	478/2863 = .167
Relationships	498	498/2863 = .174
Innovation	398	398/2863 = .139
Marketing Strategy	280	280/2863 = .098
Channels/Distribution	213	213/2863 = .074
Marketing Research	131	131/2863 = .046
Services	136	136/2863 = .048
TOTAL	2,863	1.00

Relationships and sales management had the most articles published with 17.4% and 17.3%, respectively. Not far behind was Buyer Behavior with 16.7%. Of the rest of the areas, only innovation had more than 10%.

b.   Using MINITAB, the pie chart of the data is:

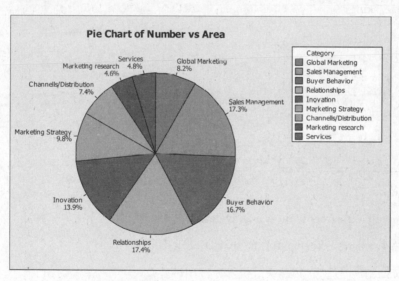

The slice for Marketing Research is smaller than the slice for Sales Management because there were fewer articles on Marketing Research than for Sales Management.

2.139   Using MINITAB, the pie chart is:

Pie Chart of DrivStar

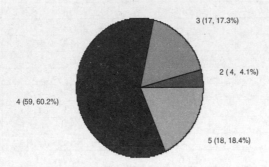

60% of cars have 4-star rating.

2.141   a.   Using MINITAB, a Pareto diagram for the data is:

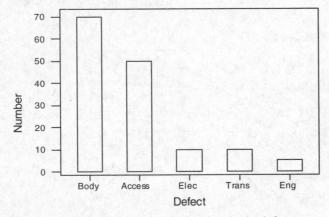

The most frequently observed defect is a body defect.

b.   Using MINITAB, a Pareto diagram for the Body Defect data is:

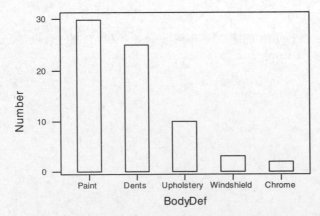

Most body defects are either paint or dents. These two categories account for (30 + 25) / 70 = 55 / 70 = .786 of all body defects. Since these two categories account for so much of the body defects, it would seem appropriate to target these two types of body defects for special attention.

2.143   The sample mean is:

$$\bar{x} = \frac{\sum\limits_{i=1}^{n} x_i}{n} = \frac{185.00 + 56.70 + 56.70 + \cdots + 63.00}{14} = \frac{728.59}{14} = 52.04$$

The median is found as the average of the 7th and 8th observations, once the data have been ordered. The ordered data are:

9.00 11.95 20.95 21.95 29.99 35.00 56.70 56.70 56.70 56.70 61.95 63.00 63.00 185.00

The 7th and 8th observations are 56.70 and 56.70. The median is:

$$\frac{56.70 + 56.70}{2} = \frac{113.40}{2} = 56.70$$

The mode is the number which occurs the most. In this case, the mode is 56.70, which occurs 4 times.

Since the data are somewhat skewed to the right, the mode and median are better measures of central tendency than the mean.

2.145   a.   The sample mean is:

$$\bar{x} = \frac{\sum\limits_{i=1}^{n} x_i}{n} = \frac{529 + 355 + 301 + ... + 63}{26} = \frac{3757}{26} = 144.5$$

The sample median is found by finding the average of the 13th and 14th observations once the data are arranged in order. The 13th and 14th observations are 100 and 105. The average of these two numbers (median) is:

$$\text{median} = \frac{100 + 105}{2} = \frac{205}{2} = 102.5$$

The mode is the observation appearing the most. For this data set, the mode is 70, which appears 3 times.

Since the mean is larger than the median, the data are skewed to the right.

b. The sample mean is:

$$\bar{x} = \frac{\sum_{i=1}^{n} x_i}{n} = \frac{11+9+6+\ldots+4}{26} = \frac{136}{26} = 5.23$$

The sample median is found by finding the average of the 13th and 14th observations once the data are arranged in order. The 13th and 14th observations are 5 and 5. The average of these two numbers (median) is:

$$\text{median} = \frac{5+5}{2} = \frac{10}{2} = 5$$

The mode is the observation appearing the most. For this data set, the mode is 6, which appears 6 times.

Since the mean and median are about the same, the data are somewhat symmetric.

c. Using MINITAB, the histogram of the number of lawyers is:

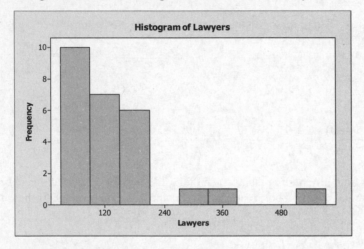

Since this data are skewed to the right, the median is a better measure of central tendency than the mean.

d. Using MINITAB, the stem-and-leaf display of the number of offices is:

Stem-and-Leaf Display: Offices

```
Stem-and-leaf of Offices   N  = 26
Leaf Unit = 0.10

     3    1    000
     4    2    0
     7    3    000
    11    4    0000
   (3)    5    000
    12    6    000000
     6    7    00
     4    8
     4    9    00
     2   10
     2   11    0
     1   12    0
```

Since the mean and the median are almost the same, both are good measures of central tendency.

e.   Using MINITAB, the histogram of the data is:

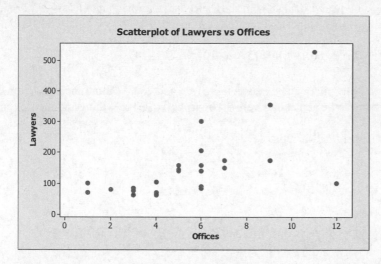

As the number of offices increase, the number of lawyers also tends to increase.

2.147   a.   Using MINITAB, a bar graph of the data is:

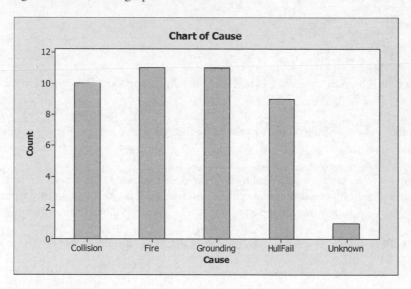

Fire and grounding are the two most likely causes of puncture.

b.   Using MINITAB, the descriptive statistics are:

Descriptive Statistics: Spillage

```
Variable   N   Mean   StDev   Minimum     Q1   Median     Q3   Maximum
Spillage   42  66.19  56.05     25.00  32.00    43.00  77.50    257.00
```

The mean spillage amount is 66.19 thousand metric tons, while the median is 43.00. Since the median is so much smaller than the mean, it indicates that the data are skewed to the right. The standard deviation is 56.05. Again, since this value is so close to the value of the mean, it indicates that the data are skewed to the right.

Since the data are skewed to the right, we cannot use the Empirical Rule to describe the data. Chebyshev's Rule can be used. Using Chebyshev's Rule, we know that at least 8/9 of the observations will fall within 3 standard deviations of the mean.

$$\bar{x} \pm 3s \Rightarrow 66.19 \pm 3(56.05) \Rightarrow 66.19 \pm 168.15 \Rightarrow (-101.96, \ 234.34)$$

Thus, at least 8/9 of all oil spills will be between -101.96 and 234.34 thousand metric tons. Since a spill cannot be less than 0, the actual interval will be from 0 to 234.34 thousand metric tons.

2.149   a.   Using MINITAB, the stem-and-leaf display is:

```
Stem-and-leaf of C1
Leaf Unit = 0.10      N = 46

    4      0    34 4 4
  (25)     0    5 5 5 5 5 5 5 556666 6 6 6 7 7 7 7 7 8 8 8 8 9
   16      1    000011222 3 34
    4      1    7 7
    2      2
    2      2
    2      3
    2      3    9
    1      4
    1      4    7
```

   b.   The leaves that represent those brands that carry the American Dental Association seal are circled above.

   c.   It appears that the cost of the brands approved by the ADA tend to have the lower costs. Thirteen of the twenty brands approved by the ADA, or $(13/20) \times 100\% = 65\%$ are less than the median cost.

2.151   a.   One reason the plot may be interpreted differently is that no scale is given on the vertical axis. Also, since the plot almost reaches the horizontal axis at 3 years, it is obvious that the bottom of the plot has been cut off. Another important factor omitted is who responded to the survey.

   b.   A scale should be added to the vertical axis. Also, that scale should start at 0.

2.153   a.   Since the mean is greater than the median, the distribution of the radiation levels is skewed to the right.

   b. $\bar{x} \pm s \Rightarrow 10 \pm 3 \Rightarrow (7, 13)$; $\bar{x} \pm 2s \Rightarrow 10 \pm 2(3) \Rightarrow (4, 16)$; $\bar{x} \pm 3s \Rightarrow 10 \pm 3(3) \Rightarrow (1, 19)$

Interval	Chebyshev's	Empirical
(7, 13)	At least 0	≈68%
(4, 16)	At least 75%	≈95%
(1, 19)	At least 88.9%	≈100%

Since the data are skewed to the right, Chebyshev's Rule is probably more appropriate in this case.

   c.   The background level is 4. Using Chebyshev's Rule, at least 75% or .75(50) ≈ 38 homes are above the background level. Using the Empirical Rule, ≈ 97.5% or .975(50) ≈ 49 homes are above the background level.

   d. $z = \dfrac{x - \bar{x}}{s} = \dfrac{20 - 10}{3} = 3.333$

It is unlikely that this new measurement came from the same distribution as the other 50. Using either Chebyshev's Rule or the Empirical Rule, it is very unlikely to see any observations more than 3 standard deviations from the mean.

2.155   a.   Both the height and width of the bars (peanuts) change. Thus, some readers may tend to equate the area of the peanuts with the frequency for each year.

   b.   The frequency bar chart is:

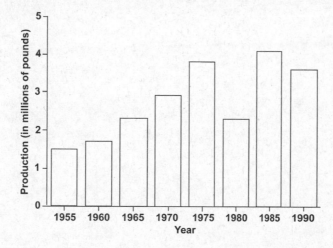

2.157   First we make some preliminary calculations.

Of the 20 engineers at the time of the layoffs, 14 are 40 or older. Thus, the probability that a randomly selected engineer will be 40 or older is $14/20 = .70$. A very high proportion of the engineers is 40 or over.

In order to determine if the company is vulnerable to a disparate impact claim, we will first find the median age of all the engineers. Ordering all the ages, we get:

29, 32, 34, 35, 38, 39, 40, 40, 40, 40, 40, 41, 42, 42, 44, 46, 47, 52, 55, 64

The median of all 20 engineers is $\dfrac{40+40}{2} = \dfrac{80}{2} = 40$

Now, we will compute the median age of those engineers who were not laid off. The ages underlined above correspond to the engineers who were not laid off. The median of these is $\dfrac{40+40}{2} = \dfrac{80}{2} = 40$.

The median age of all engineers is the same as the median age of those who were not laid off. The median age of those laid off is $\dfrac{40+41}{2} = \dfrac{81}{2} = 40.5$, which is not that much different from the median age of those not laid off. In addition, 70% of all the engineers are 40 or older. Thus, it appears that the company would not be vulnerable to a disparate impact claim.

2.159   There is evidence to support this claim. The graph peaks at the interval above 1.002. The heights of the bars decrease in order as the intervals get further and further from the peak interval. This is true for all bars except the one above 1.000. This bar is greater than the bar to its right. This would indicate that there are more observations in this interval than one would expect, suggesting that some inspectors might be passing rods with diameters that were barely below the lower specification limit.

Chapter 3
Probability

3.1   a.   Since the probabilities must sum to 1,

$$P(E_3) = 1 - P(E_1) - P(E_2) - P(E_4) - P(E_5) = 1 - .1 - .2 - .1 - .1 = .5$$

        b. $P(E_3) = 1 - P(E_3) - P(E_2) - P(E_4) - P(E_5)$
$$\Rightarrow 2P(E_3) = 1 - .1 - .2 - .1 \Rightarrow 2P(E_3) = .6 \Rightarrow P(E_3) = .3$$

        c. $P(E_3) = 1 - P(E_1) - P(E_2) - P(E_4) - P(E_5) = 1 - .1 - .1 - .1 - .1 = .6$

3.3 $P(A) = P(1) + P(2) + P(3) = .05 + .20 + .30 = .55$
$P(B) = P(1) + P(3) + P(5) = .05 + .30 + .15 = .50$
$P(C) = P(1) + P(2) + P(3) + P(5) = .05 + .20 + .30 + .15 = .70$

3.5   a. $\dbinom{N}{n} = \dbinom{5}{2} = \dfrac{5!}{2!(5-2)!} = \dfrac{5 \cdot 4 \cdot 3 \cdot 2 \cdot 1}{2 \cdot 1 \cdot 3 \cdot 2 \cdot 1} = \dfrac{120}{12} = 10$

        b. $\dbinom{N}{n} = \dbinom{6}{3} = \dfrac{6!}{3!(6-3)!} = \dfrac{6 \cdot 5 \cdot 4 \cdot 3 \cdot 2 \cdot 1}{3 \cdot 2 \cdot 1 \cdot 3 \cdot 2 \cdot 1} = \dfrac{720}{36} = 20$

        c. $\dbinom{N}{n} = \dbinom{20}{5} = \dfrac{20!}{5!(20-5)!} = \dfrac{20 \cdot 19 \cdot 18 \cdots 3 \cdot 2 \cdot 1}{5 \cdot 4 \cdot 3 \cdot 2 \cdot 1 \cdot 15 \cdot 14 \cdot 13 \cdots 3 \cdot 2 \cdot 1}$

$$= \dfrac{2.432902008 \times 10^{18}}{1.569209242 \times 10^{14}} = 15{,}504$$

3.7   a.   If we denote the marbles as B_1, B_2, R_1, R_2, and R_3, then the ten sample points are:

(B_1, B_2) (B_1, R_1) (B_1, R_2) (B_1, R_3) (B_2, R_1) (B_2, R_2) (B_2, R_3) (R_1, R_2) (R_1, R_3) (R_2, R_3)

        b.   Each of the sample points would be equally likely. Thus, each would have a probability of 1/10 of occurring.

        c.   There is one sample point in A: (B_1, B_2). Thus, $P(A) = \dfrac{1}{10}$.

There are 6 sample points in B: (B_1, R_1) (B_1, R_2) (B_1, R_3) (B_2, R_1) (B_2, R_2) (B_2, R_3).

Thus, $P(B) = 6\left(\dfrac{1}{10}\right) = \dfrac{6}{10} = \dfrac{3}{5}$.

There are 3 sample points in C: (R_1, R_2) (R_1, R_3) (R_2, R_3). Thus, $P(C) = 3\left(\dfrac{1}{10}\right) = \dfrac{3}{10}$.

3.9   a.   The sample points of this experiment correspond to each of the 6 possible colors of the M&M's. Let
             Br=brown, *Y*=yellow, *R*=red, *Bl*=blue, *O*=orange, *G*=green. The six sample points are: *Br, Y, R,*
             Bl, O, and *G*

       b.   From the problem, the probabilities of selecting each color are:

             $P(Br) = 0.13,   P(Y) = 0.14,   P(R) = 0.13,   P(Bl) = 0.24, P(O) = 0.2,   P(G) = 0.16$
       c.   The probability that the selected M&M is brown is P(Br) = 0.13

       d.   The probability that the selected M&M is red, green or yellow is:

             $P(R \text{ or } G \text{ or } Y) = P(R) + P(G) + P(Y) = 0.13 + 0.16 + 0.14 = 0.43$

       e. $P(\text{not } Bl) = P(R) + P(G) + P(Y) + P(Br) + P(O) = 0.13 + 0.16 + 0.14 + 0.13 + 0.20 = 0.76$

3.11   Define the following events:
       M: {Nanny who was placed in a job last year is a male}
       $$P(M) = \frac{24}{4,176} = .0057$$

3.13   a.   The 5 sample points are the possible responses of a randomly selected person who participated in
             Harris Poll:

             None, 1-2, 3-5, 6-9, 10 or more
       b.   The probabilities are:

             $P(\text{none}) = 0.25,   P(1\text{-}2) = 0.31, P(3\text{-}5) = 0.25,   P(6\text{-}9) = 0.05,   P(10 \text{ or more}) = 0.14$

       c.   Define the following event:

             A: {Respondent looks for healthcare information online more than two times per month}

             $P(A) = P(3\text{-}5) + P(6\text{-}9) + P(10 \text{ or more}) = 0.25 + 0.05 + 0.14 = 0.44$

3.15   a.   Define the following event:

             C: {Slaughtered chicken passes inspection with fecal contamination}

             $$P(C) = \frac{1}{100} = .01$$

       b.   Based on the data, $P(C) = \frac{306}{32,075} = .0095 \approx .01$

             Yes. The probability of a slaughtered chicken passing inspection with fecal contamination rounded
             off to 2 decimal places is .01.

3.17   Define the following events:

   E: {Industrial accident caused by faulty Engineering & Design}

   P: {Industrial accident caused by faulty Procedures & Practices}

   M = {Industrial accident caused by faulty Management & Oversight }

   T = {Industrial accident caused by faulty Training & Communication}

   a. $P(E) = 27 / 83 = .325$. Approximately 32.5% of all industrial accidents are caused by faulty Engineering and Design.

   b. P(Industrial accident caused by something other than procedures & practices) $= (27 + 22 + 10) / 83 = 59 / 83 = .711$. Approximately 71.1% of all industrial accidents are caused by something other than faulty procedures & practices.

3.19   Since one would be selecting 3 stocks from 15 without replacement, the total number of ways to select the 3 stocks would be a combination of 15 things taken 3 at a time.

   The number of ways would be

$$\binom{15}{3} = \frac{15!}{3!(15-3)!} = \frac{15 \cdot 14 \cdot 13 \cdots 3 \cdot 2 \cdot 1}{3 \cdot 2 \cdot 1 \cdot 12 \cdot 11 \cdot 10 \cdots 3 \cdot 2 \cdot 1} = \frac{1.307674368 \times 10^{12}}{2874009600} = 455$$

3.21   a.   Since we want to maximize the purchase of grill #2, grill #2 must be one of the 3 grills in the display. Thus, we have to pick 2 more grills from the 4 remaining grills. Since order does not matter, the number of different ways to select 2 grill displays from 4 would be a combination of 4 things taken 2 at a time. The number of ways is:

$$\binom{4}{2} = \frac{4!}{2!(4-2)!} = \frac{4 \cdot 3 \cdot 2 \cdot 1}{2 \cdot 1 \cdot 2 \cdot 1} = \frac{24}{4} = 6$$

   Let *Gi* represent Grill *i*. The possibilities are:

   $G_1 G_2 G_3$, $G_1 G_2 G_4$, $G_1 G_2 G_5$, $G_2 G_3 G_4$, $G_2 G_3 G_5$, $G_2 G_4 G_5$

   b.   To find reasonable probabilities for the 6 possibilities, we divide the frequencies by the total sample size of 124. The probabilities would be:

   $P(G_1 G_2 G_3) = 35 / 124 = .282$

   $P(G_1 G_2 G_4) = 8 / 124 = .065$

   $P(G_1 G_2 G_5) = 42 / 124 = .339$

   $P(G_2 G_3 G_4) = 4 / 124 = .032$

   $P(G_2 G_3 G_5) = 1 / 124 = .008$

   $P(G_2 G_4 G_5) = 34 / 124 = .274$

   c. P(display contained Grill #1) $= P(G_1 G_2 G_3) + P(G_1 G_2 G_4) + P(G_1 G_2 G_5)$
$$= .282 + .065 + .339 = .686$$

3.23 a. The odds in favor of an Oxford Shoes win are $\frac{1}{3}$ to $1 - \frac{1}{3} = \frac{2}{3}$ or 1 to 2.

b. If the odds in favor of Oxford Shoes are 1 to 1, then the probability that Oxford Shoes wins is
$\frac{1}{1+1} = \frac{1}{2}$.

c. If the odds against Oxford Shoes are 3 to 2, then the odds in favor of Oxford Shoes are
2 to 3. Therefore, the probability that Oxford Shoes wins is $\frac{2}{2+3} = \frac{2}{5}$.

3.25 a. The number of ways the 5 commissioners can vote is $2(2)(2)(2)(2) = 2^5 = 32$ (Each of the 5 commissioners has 2 choices for his/her vote – For or Against.)

b. Let F denote a vote 'For' and A denote a vote 'Against'. The 32 sample points would be:

FFFFF FFFFA FFFAF FFAFF FAFFF AFFFF FFFAA FFAFA FAFFA AFFFA
FFAAF FAFAF AFFAF FAAFF AFAFF AAFFF FFAAA FAFAA FAAFA FAAAF
AFFAA AFAFA AFAAF AAFFA AAFAF AAAFF FAAAA AFAAA AAFAA AAAFA
AAAAF AAAAA

Each of the sample points should be equally likely. Thus, each would have a probability of 1/32.

c. The sample points that result in a 2-2 split for the other 4 commissioners are:

FFAAF FAFAF AFFAF FAAFF AFAFF AAFFF FFAAA FAFAA FAAFA
AFFAA AFAFA AAFFA

There are 12 sample points.

d. Let V = event that your vote counts. $P(V) = 12/32 = .375$.

e. If there are now only 3 commissioners in the bloc, then the total number of ways the bloc can vote is $2(2)(2) = 2^3 = 8$. The sample points would be:

FFF   FFA   FAF   AFF   FAA   AFA   AAF   AAA

The number of sample points where your vote would count is 4: *FAF, AFF, FAA, AFA*

Let W = event that your vote counts in the bloc. $P(W) = 4/8 = .5$.

3.27 a. A: {*HHH, HHT, HTH, THH, TTH, THT, HTT*}
B: {*HHH, TTH, THT, HTT*}
$A \cup B$: {*HHH, HHT, HTH, THH, TTH, THT, HTT*}
A^c: {*TTT*}
$A \cap B$: {*HHH, TTH, THT, HTT*}

b. $P(A) = \frac{7}{8}$ $\qquad$ $P(B) = \frac{4}{8} = \frac{1}{2}$ $\qquad$ $P(A \cup B) = \frac{7}{8}$

$P(A^c) = \frac{1}{8}$ $\qquad$ $P(A \cap B) = \frac{4}{8} = \frac{1}{2}$

c. $P(A \cup B) = P(A) + P(B) - P(A \cap B) = \dfrac{7}{8} + \dfrac{1}{2} - \dfrac{1}{2} = \dfrac{7}{8}$

d. No. $P(A \cap B) = \dfrac{1}{2}$ which is not 0.

3.29   a. $P(A) = P(E_1) + P(E_2) + P(E_3) + P(E_5) + P(E_6) = \dfrac{1}{5} + \dfrac{1}{5} + \dfrac{1}{5} + \dfrac{1}{20} + \dfrac{1}{10} = \dfrac{15}{20} = \dfrac{3}{4}$

b. $P(B) = P(E_2) + P(E_3) + P(E_4) + P(E_7) = \dfrac{1}{5} + \dfrac{1}{5} + \dfrac{1}{20} + \dfrac{1}{5} = \dfrac{13}{20}$

c. $P(A \cup B) = P(E_1) + P(E_2) + P(E_3) + P(E_4) + P(E_5) + P(E_6) + P(E_7)$
$$= \dfrac{1}{5} + \dfrac{1}{5} + \dfrac{1}{5} + \dfrac{1}{20} + \dfrac{1}{20} + \dfrac{1}{10} + \dfrac{1}{5} = 1$$

d. $P(A \cap B) = P(E_2) + P(E_3) = \dfrac{1}{5} + \dfrac{1}{5} = \dfrac{2}{5}$

e. $P(A^c) = 1 - P(A) = 1 - \dfrac{3}{4} = \dfrac{1}{4}$

f. $P(B^c) = 1 - P(B) = 1 - \dfrac{13}{20} = \dfrac{7}{20}$

g. $P(A \cup A^c) = P(E_1) + P(E_2) + P(E_3) + P(E_4) + P(E_5) + P(E_6) + P(E_7)$
$$= \dfrac{1}{5} + \dfrac{1}{5} + \dfrac{1}{5} + \dfrac{1}{20} + \dfrac{1}{20} + \dfrac{1}{10} + \dfrac{1}{5} = 1$$

h. $P(A^c \cap B) = P(E_4) + P(E_7) = \dfrac{1}{20} + \dfrac{1}{5} = \dfrac{5}{20} = \dfrac{1}{4}$

3.31   a. $P(A) = .50 + .10 + .05 = .65$

b. $P(B) = .10 + .07 + .50 + .05 = .72$

c. $P(C) = .25$

d. $P(D) = .05 + .03 = .08$

e. $P(A^c) = .25 + .07 + .03 = .35$ (Note: $P(A^c) = 1 - P(A) = 1 - .65 = .35$)

f. $P(A \cup B) = P(B) = .10 + .07 + .50 + .05 = .72$

g. $P(A \cap C) = 0$

h. Two events are mutually exclusive if they have no sample points in common or if the probability of their intersection is 0.

$P(A \cap B) = P(A) = .50 + .10 + .05 = .65$. Since this is not 0, A and B are not mutually exclusive.

$P(A \cap C) = 0$. Since this is 0, A and C are mutually exclusive.

$P(A \cap D) = .05$. Since this is not 0, A and D are not mutually exclusive.

$P(B \cap C) = 0$. Since this is 0, B and C are mutually exclusive.

$P(B \cap D) = .05$. Since this is not 0, B and D are not mutually exclusive.

$P(C \cap D) = 0$. Since this is 0, C and D are mutually exclusive.

3.33 a. The analyst makes an early forecast and is only concerned with accuracy is the event $A \cap B$.

b. The analyst is not only concerned with accuracy is the event A^c.

c. The analyst is from a small brokerage firm or makes an early forecast is the event $C \cup B$.

d. The analyst makes a late forecast and is not only concerned with accuracy is the event $B^c \cap A^c$.

3.35 Define the following events:

IM: {18-to-34 year-old cell phone user uses instant messaging}

NA: {18-to-34 year-old cell phone user uses none of the featurees}

a. $P(IM) = .43$

b. P(18-to-34 year-old cell phone user uses at least one of the features)
$= 1 - P(NA) = 1 - .16 = .84$

3.37 Define the following events:

A: {oil structure is active}

I: {oil structure is inactive}

C: {oil structure is caisson}

W: {oil structure is well protector}

F: {oil structure is fixed platform}

a. The simple events are all combinations of structure type and activity type. The simple events are:

$AC, \ AW, \ AF, IC, IW, \ IF$

b. Reasonable probabilities would be the frequency divided by the sample size of 3,400. The probabilities are:

$P(AC) = 503 / 3,400 = .148$ $P(AW) = 225 / 3,400 = .066$

$P(AF) = 1,447 / 3,400 = .426$ $P(IC) = 598 / 3,400 = .176$

$P(IW) = 177 / 3,400 = .052$ $P(IF) = 450 / 3,400 = .132$

c. $P(A) = P(AC) + P(AW) + P(AF) = .148 + .066 + .426 = .640$
d. $P(W) = P(AW) + P(IW) = .066 + .052 = .118$

e. $P(IC) = .176$

f. $P(I \cup F) = P(IC) + P(IW) + P(IF) + P(AF) = .176 + .052 + .132 + .426 = .786$

g. $P(C)^c = 1 - P(C) = 1 - \{P(AC) + P(IC)\} = 1 - \{.148 + .176\} = 1 - .324 = .676$

3.39   a. $P \cap S \cap A$

Products 6 and 7 are contained in this intersection.

b. $P(\text{possess all the desired characteristics}) = P(P \cap S \cap A)$
$$= P(6) + P(7) = \frac{1}{10} + \frac{1}{10} = \frac{1}{5}$$

c. $A \cup S$

$P(A \cup S) = P(2) + P(3) + P(5) + P(6) + P(7) + P(8) + P(9) + P(10)$
$$= \frac{1}{10} + \frac{1}{10} + \frac{1}{10} + \frac{1}{10} + \frac{1}{10} + \frac{1}{10} + \frac{1}{10} + \frac{1}{10} = \frac{8}{10} = \frac{4}{5}$$

d. $P \cap S$

$P(P \cap S) = P(2) + P(6) + P(7) = \frac{1}{10} + \frac{1}{10} + \frac{1}{10} = \frac{3}{10}$

3.41   a. $P(A) = \dfrac{1,465}{2,143} = .684$

b. $P(B) = \dfrac{265}{2,143} = .124$

c.   No. There is one sample point that they have in common: Plaintiff trial win – reversed, Jury

d. $P(A^c) = 1 - P(A) = 1 - .684 = .316$

e. $P(A \cup B) = \dfrac{194 + 71 + 429 + 111 + 731}{2,143} = \dfrac{1,536}{2,143} = .717$

f. $P(A \cap B) = \dfrac{194}{2,143} = .091$

3.43   a. $P(A) = 8/28.44 = .281$

        $P(B) = 7.84/28.44 = .276$

        $P(C) = 1.24/28.44 = .044$

        $P(D) = (1.0 + 1.24)/28.44 = 2.24/28.44 = .079$

        $P(E) = 1.24/28.44 = .044$

   b. $P(A \cap B) = 0/28.44 = 0$

   c. $P(A \cup B) = (7.84 + 8)/28.44 = 15.84/28.44 = .557$

   d. $P(B^c \cap E) = 0$

   e. $P(A \cup E) = 9.24/28.44 = .325$

   f.   Two events are mutually exclusive if they have no sample points in common or if the probability of their intersection is 0.

        $P(A \cap B) = 0$. Since this is 0, A and B are mutually exclusive.

        $P(A \cap C) = 0$. Since this is 0, A and C are mutually exclusive.

        $P(A \cap D) = 0$. Since this is 0, A and D are mutually exclusive.

        $P(A \cap E) = 0$. Since this is 0, A and E are mutually exclusive.

        $P(B \cap C) = 1.24/28.44 = .044$. Since this is not 0, B and C are not mutually exclusive.

        $P(B \cap D) = 2.24/28.44 = .079$. Since this is not 0, B and D are not mutually exclusive.

        $P(B \cap E) = 1.24/28.44 = .044$. Since this is not 0, B and E are not mutually exclusive.

        $P(C \cap D) = 1.24/28.44 = .044$. Since this is not 0, C and D are not mutually exclusive.

        $P(C \cap E) = 1.24/28.44 = .044$. Since this is not 0, C and E are not mutually exclusive.

        $P(D \cap E) = 1.24/28.44 = .044$. Since this is not 0, D and E are not mutually exclusive.

3.45   Define the following events:

   A: {Air pressure is over-reported by 4 psi or more}
   B: {Air pressure is over-reported by 6 psi or more}
   C: {Air pressure is over-reported by 8 psi or more

   a.   For gas station air pressure gauges that read 35 psi, $P(B) = .09$.

   b.   For gas station air pressure gauges that read 55 psi, $P(C) = .09$.

   c.   For gas station air pressure gauges that read 25 psi, $P(A^c)$ $1 - P(A) = 1 - .16 = .84$.

d.   No. If air pressure is over-reported by 6 psi or more, then it is also over-reported by 4 psi or more. Thus, these 2 events are not mutually exclusive.

e.   The columns in the table are not mutually exclusive. All events in the last column (% Over-reported by 8 psi or more) are also part of the events in the first and second columns. All events in the second column are also part of the events in the first column. In addition, there is no column for the event 'Over-reported by less than 4 psi or not over-reported'.

3.47   a. $P(A\,|\,B) = \dfrac{P(A\cap B)}{P(B)} = \dfrac{.1}{.2} = .5$

b. $P(B\,|\,A) = \dfrac{P(A\cap B)}{P(A)} = \dfrac{.1}{.4} = .25$

c.   Events A and B are said to be independent if $P(A|B) = P(A)$. In this case, $P(A|B) = .5$ and $P(A) = .4$. Thus, A and B are not independent.

3.49   a.   If two events are independent, then $P(A\cap B) = P(A)P(B) = .4(.2) = .08$.

b.   If two events are independent, then $P(A\,|\,B) = P(A) = .4$.

c. $P(A\cup B) = P(A) + P(B) - P(A\cap B) = .4 + .2 - .08 = .52$

3.51   a. $P(A) = P(E_1) + P(E_2) + P(E_3)$
$$= .2 + .3 + .3$$
$$= .8$$

$P(B) = P(E_2) + P(E_3) + P(E_5)$
$$= .3 + .3 + .1$$
$$= .7$$

$P(A\cap B) = P(E_2) + P(E_3)$
$$= .3 + .3$$
$$= .6$$

b. $P(E_1\,|\,A) = \dfrac{P(E_1\cap A)}{P(A)} = \dfrac{P(E_1)}{P(A)} = \dfrac{.2}{.8} = .25$

$P(E_2\,|\,A) = \dfrac{P(E_2\cap A)}{P(A)} = \dfrac{P(E_2)}{P(A)} = \dfrac{.3}{.8} = .375$

$P(E_3\,|\,A) = \dfrac{P(E_3\cap A)}{P(A)} = \dfrac{P(E_3)}{P(A)} = \dfrac{.3}{.8} = .375$

The original sample point probabilities are in the proportion .2 to .3 to .3 or 2 to 3 to 3.

The conditional probabilities for these sample points are in the proportion .25 to .375 to .375 or 2 to 3 to 3.

c.   (1) $P(B|A) = P(E_2|A) + P(E_3|A)$
                 $= .375 \quad + \quad .375 \quad \text{(from part \textbf{b})}$
                 $= .75$

    (2) $P(B|A) = \dfrac{P(A \cap B)}{P(A)} = \dfrac{.6}{.8} = .75 \quad \text{(from part \textbf{a})}$

The two methods do yield the same result.

d.   If A and B are independent events, $P(B|A) = P(B)$.

From part **c**, $P(B|A) = .75$. From part **a**, $P(B) = .7$.

Since $.75 \ne .7$, A and B are not independent events.

3.53   a. $P(A) = P(E_1) + P(E_3) = .22 + .15 = .37$

b. $P(B) = P(E_2) + P(E_3) + P(E_4) = .31 + .15 + .22 = .68$

c. $P(A \cap B) = P(E_3) = .15$

d. $P(A|B) = \dfrac{P(A \cap B)}{P(B)} = \dfrac{.15}{.68} = .2206$

e. $P(B \cap C) = 0$

f. $P(C|B) = \dfrac{P(C \cap B)}{P(B)} = \dfrac{0}{.68} = 0$

g.   For pair A and B: A and B are not independent because $P(A|B) \ne P(A)$ or $.2206 \ne .37$.

For pair A and C:

$$P(A \cap C) = P(E_1) = .22$$
$$P(C) = P(E_1) + P(E_5) = .22 + .1 = .32$$
$$P(A|C) = \dfrac{P(A \cap C)}{P(C)} = \dfrac{.22}{.32} = .6875$$

A and C are not independent because $P(A|C) \ne P(A)$ or $.6875 \ne .37$.

For pair B and C: B and C are not independent because $P(C|B) \ne P(C)$ or $0 \ne .32$.

3.55 a. $P(A \cap C) = 0 \Rightarrow A$ and C are mutually exclusive.
$P(B \cap C) = 0 \Rightarrow B$ and C are mutually exclusive.

b. $P(A) = P(1) + P(2) + P(3) = .20 + .05 + .30 = .55$
$P(B) = P(3) + P(4) = .30 + .10 = .40$
$P(C) = P(5) + P(6) = .10 + .25 = .35$
$P(A \cap B) = P(3) = .30$

$$P(A \mid B) = \frac{P(A \cap B)}{P(B)} = \frac{.30}{.40} = .75$$

A and B are independent if $P(A \mid B) = P(A)$. Since $P(A \mid B) = .75$ and $P(A) = .55$, A and B are not independent.

Since A and C are mutually exclusive, they are not independent. Similarly, since B and C are mutually exclusive, they are not independent.

c. Using the probabilities of sample points,
$P(A \cup B) = P(1) + P(2) + P(3) + P(4) = .20 + .05 + .30 + .10 = .65$

Using the additive rule,
$P(A \cup B) = P(A) + P(B) - P(A \cap B) = .55 + .40 - .30 = .65$

Using the probabilities of sample points,
$P(A \cup C) = P(1) + P(2) + P(3) + P(5) + P(6)$
$\quad\quad\quad\quad = .20 + .05 + .30 + .10 + .25 = .90$

Using the additive rule,
$P(A \cup C) = P(A) + P(C) - P(A \cap C) = .55 + .35 - 0 = .90$

3.57 Define the following events:

A: {Company is a banking company}
B: {Company is based in United Kingdom}

From the problem, we know that $P(A \cap B) = \dfrac{3}{20} = .15$ and $P(B) = \dfrac{5}{20} = .25$

$$P(A \mid B) = \frac{P(A \cap B)}{P(B)} = \frac{.15}{.25} = .60$$

3.59 Define the following events:
G: {Adult owns at least one gun}
H: {Adult owns a hand gun}

a. $P(G) = .26$
b. From the exercise, $P(H|G) = .05$.
$P(G \cap H) = P(H|G)P(G) = .05(.26) = .013$

3.61   Define the following events:

A: {Internet user owns at least one computer}
B: {Internet user logs on to the internet for more than 30 hours per week}

From the exercise, $P(A) = .80$, $P(B) = .25$ and $P(A \cap B) = .15$.

a. $P(B \mid A) = \dfrac{P(A \cap B)}{P(A)} = \dfrac{.15}{.80} = .1875$

b. $P(A \mid B) = \dfrac{P(A \cap B)}{P(B)} = \dfrac{.15}{.25} = .60$

3.63   Define the following events:

P: {Capital punishment case had serious, reversible error}
R: {Acquittal for defendant on retrial}

a. $P(P) = .68$
        $P(R|P) = .07$

b. $P(R \cap P) = P(R \mid P)P(P) = .07(.68) = .048$

3.65   Define the following events as in Exercise 3.44:

A: {Wheelchair user had an injurious fall}
B: {Wheelchair user had all five features installed in the home}
C: {Wheelchair user had no falls}
D: {Wheelchair user had none of the features installed in the home}

a. $P(A \mid B) = \dfrac{P(A \cap B)}{P(B)} = \dfrac{\frac{2}{306}}{\frac{9}{306}} = \dfrac{2}{9} = .222$

b. $P(A \mid D) = \dfrac{P(A \cap D)}{P(D)} = \dfrac{\frac{20}{306}}{\frac{109}{306}} = \dfrac{20}{109} = .183$

3.67   Define the following events:

A: {Alarm A sounds alarm}

B: {Alarm B sounds alarm}

I: {Intruder}

a.   From the problem:

        $P(A \mid I) = .9$
        $P(B \mid I) = .95$
        $P(A \mid I^c) = .2$
        $P(B \mid I^c) = .1$

b.   Since the two systems are operating independently of each other,

$$P(A \cap B \mid I) = P(A \mid I)\, P(B \mid I) = .9(.95) = .855$$

c. $P(A \cap B \mid I^c) = P(A \mid I^c)\, P(B \mid I^c) = .2(.1) = .02$

d. $P(A \cup B \mid I) = P(A \mid I) + P(B \mid I) - P(A \cap B \mid I) = .9 + .95 - .855 = .995$

3.69   Define the following event:
        A: {The specimen labeled "red snapper" was really red snapper}

a.   The probability that you are actually served red snapper the next time you order it at a restaurant is
        $P(A) = 1 - .77 = .23$

b.   P(at least one customer is actually served red snapper)
        $= 1 - P$(no customer is actually served red snapper)
        $= 1 - P(A^c \cap A^c \cap A^c \cap A^c \cap A^c)$

        $= 1 - P(A^c)\, P(A^c)\, P(A^c)\, P(A^c)\, P(A^c)$
        $= 1 - .77^5$
        $= 1 - .271$
        $= .729$

        Note: In order to compute the above probability, we had to assume that the trials or events are independent. This assumption is likely to not be valid. If a restaurant served one customer a look-a-like variety, then it probably served the next one a look-a-like variety.

3.71   Define the following events:

        A: {Patient receives PMI sheet}
        B: {Patient was hospitalized}

        $P(A) = .20,\ P(A \cap B) = .12$
        $$P(B \mid A) = \frac{P(A \cap B)}{P(A)} = \frac{.12}{.20} = .60$$

3.73   a.   If the coin is balanced, then $P(H) = .5$ and $P(T) = .5$ on any trial. Also, we can assume that the results of any coin toss is independent of any other. Thus,

        $$P(H \cap H \cap H \cap H \cap H \cap H \cap H \cap H \cap H \cap H)$$
        $$= P(H)P(H)P(H)P(H)P(H)P(H)P(H)P(H)P(H)P(H)$$
        $$= .5(.5)(.5)(.5)(.5)(.5)(.5)(.5)(.5) = .5^{10} = .0009766$$

        $$P(H \cap H \cap T \cap T \cap H \cap T \cap T \cap H \cap H \cap H)$$
        $$= P(H)P(H)P(T)P(T)P(H)P(T)P(T)P(H)P(H)P(H)$$
        $$= .5(.5)(.5)(.5)(.5)(.5)(.5)(.5)(.5) = .5^{10} = .0009766$$

        $$P(T \cap T \cap T \cap T \cap T \cap T \cap T \cap T \cap T \cap T)$$
        $$= P(T)P(T)P(T)P(T)P(T)P(T)P(T)P(T)P(T)P(T)$$
        $$= .5(.5)(.5)(.5)(.5)(.5)(.5)(.5)(.5) = .5^{10} = .0009766$$

b.   Define the following events:

A: {10 coin tosses result in all heads or all tails}
B: {10 coin tosses result in mix of heads and tails}

$$P(A) = P(H \cap H \cap H \cap H \cap H \cap H \cap H \cap H \cap H \cap H)$$
$$+ P(T \cap T \cap T \cap T \cap T \cap T \cap T \cap T \cap T \cap T)$$
$$= .0009766 + .0009766 = .0019532$$

c. $P(B) = 1 - P(A) = 1 - .0019532 = .9980468$

d.   From the above probabilities, the chances that either all heads or all tails occurred is extremely rare. Thus, if one of these sequences really occurred, it is most likely sequence   #2.

3.75   Random samples are chosen in such a way that every set of n elements in the population has an equal chance or probability of being selected. The random samples are related to representative samples in such a way that these random samples are likely to be representative of the population that they are selected from.

3.77   a.   The number of samples of size $n = 3$ elements that can be selected from a population of $N = 600$ is:

$$\binom{N}{n} = \binom{600}{3} = \frac{600!}{3!597!} = \frac{600(599)(598)}{3(2)(1)} = 35,820,200$$

b.   If random sampling is employed, then each sample is equally likely. The probability that any sample is selected is 1/35,820,200.

c.   To draw a random sample of three elements from 600, we will number the elements from 1 to 600. Then, starting in an arbitrary position in Table I, Appendix B, we will select three numbers by going either down a column or across a row. Suppose that we start in the first three positions of column 8 and row 17. We will proceed down the column until we select three different numbers, skipping 000 and any numbers between 601 and 999. The first sample drawn will be 448, 298, and 136 (skip 987). The second sample drawn will be 47, 263, and 287. The 20 samples selected are:

Sample Number	Items Selected	Sample Number	Items Selected
1	448, 298, 136	11	345, 420, 152
2	47, 263, 287	12	144, 68, 485
3	153, 147, 222	13	490, 54, 178
4	360, 86, 357	14	428, 297, 549
5	205, 587, 254	15	186, 256, 261
6	563, 408, 258	16	90, 383, 232
7	428, 356, 543	17	438, 430, 352
8	248, 410, 197	18	129, 493, 496
9	542, 355, 208	19	440, 253, 81
10	399, 313, 563	20	521, 300, 15

None of the samples contain the same three elements. Because the probability in part **b** was so small, it would be very unlikely to have any two samples with the same elements.

3.79   a.   First, we need to define the area from which the telephone numbers are to be selected. If the area is the entire country, we will need to include area codes in our random numbers. Suppose we restrict ourselves to a single area code. Within a single area code, assuming that all "first three digits" are possible, we would select 7-digit numbers at random. We would start at a particular point in Table I, Appendix B, say row 7 and the beginning of column 3. We would use the five digits of column 3 plus the first two digits of column 4. We would proceed down the column until we selected the needed sample of different numbers.

       a.   Starting in row 7 and the beginning of column 3, the ten 7-digit numbers selected would be:

              5642069
              0546307
              6366110
              5334253
              8823133
              4823503
              5263692
              8752985
              7104808
              5182151

       c.   If the first three digits are to be 373, then we only need to use 4-digit numbers. Suppose we start in row 32, column 11, using the last four digits in the column, and proceeding down the column. The five numbers would be:

              3736038
              3739841
              3733611
              3734952
              3739080

3.81   a.   If we randomly select one account from the 5,382 accounts, the probability of selecting account 3,241 is 1/5,382 = .000186.

       b.   To draw a random sample of 10 accounts from 5,382, we will number the accounts from 1 to 5,382. Then, starting in an arbitrary position in Table I, Appendix B, we will select 10 numbers by going either down a column or across a row. Suppose that we start in the first four positions of column 10 and row 5. We will proceed down the column until we select 10 different numbers, skipping 0000 and any numbers between 5,382 and 9,999. The sample drawn will be:

            1505, 4884, 1256, 1798, 3159, 2084, 0827, 2635, 4610, 2217

       c.   No. If the samples are randomly selected, any sample of size 10 is equally likely. The total number of ways to select 10 accounts from 5,382 is:

$$\binom{N}{n} = \binom{5,382}{10} = \frac{5,382!}{10!5,372!} = \frac{5,382(5381)(5380)\ldots(5373)}{10(9)(8)\ldots(1)}$$
$$= 5.572377607 \times 10^{30}$$

       The probability that any one sample is selected is $1/5.572377607 \times 10^{30}$. Each of the two samples shown have the same probability of occurring.

3.83   Suppose we want to select 900 intersections by numbering the intersections from 1 to 500,000. We would then use a random number table or a random number generator from a software program to select 900 distinct intersection points. These would then be the sampled markets.

Now, suppose we want to select the 900 intersections by selecting a row from the 500 and a column from the 1,000. We would first number the rows from 1 to 500 and number the columns from 1 to 1,000. Using a random number generator, we would generate a sample of 900 from the 500 rows. Obviously, many rows will be selected more than once. At the same time, we use a random number generator to select 900 columns from the 1,000 columns. Again, some of the columns could be selected more than once. Placing these two sets of random numbers side-by-side, we would use the row-column combinations to select the intersections. For example, suppose the first row selected was 453 and the first column selected was 731. The first intersection selected would be row 453, column 731. This process would be continued until 900 unique intersections were selected.

3.85   First, we find the following probabilities:

$$P(A \cap B_1) = P(A \mid B_1)P(B_1) = .4(.2) = .08$$
$$P(A \cap B_2) = P(A \mid B_2)P(B_2) = .25(.15) = .0375$$
$$P(A \cap B_3) = P(A \mid B_3)P(B_3) = .6(.65) = .5075$$
$$P(A) = P(A \cap B_1) + P(A \cap B_2) + P(A \cap B_3) = .08 + .0375 + .39 = .5075$$

a. $$P(B_1 \mid A) = \frac{P(A \cap B_1)}{P(A)} = \frac{.08}{.5075} = .158$$

b. $$P(B_2 \mid A) = \frac{P(A \cap B_2)}{P(A)} = \frac{.0375}{.5075} = .074$$

c. $$P(B_3 \mid A) = \frac{P(A \cap B_3)}{P(A)} = \frac{.39}{.5075} = .768$$

3.87   From the information given, $P(D) = 1/80$, $P(D^c) = 79/80$, $P(N|D) = 1/2$, $P(N^c|D) = 1/2$, $P(N|D^c) = 1$, and $P(N^c|D^c) = 0$. Using Bayes' Rule

$$P(D \mid N) = \frac{P(D \cap N)}{P(N)} = \frac{P(N \mid D)P(D)}{P(N \mid D)P(D) + P(N \mid D^c)P(D^c)}$$

$$= \frac{\frac{1}{2} \cdot \frac{1}{80}}{\frac{1}{2} \cdot \frac{1}{80} + 1 \cdot \frac{79}{80}} = \frac{\frac{1}{160}}{\frac{1}{160} + \frac{79}{80}} = \frac{\frac{1}{160}}{\frac{1}{160} + \frac{158}{160}} = \frac{1}{159} = .0063$$

3.89   a.   Converting the percentages to probabilities,

$$P(275-300) = .52, \ P(305-325) = .39, \text{ and } P(330-350) = .09.$$

     b.   Using Bayes Theorem,

$$P(275-300 \mid CC) = \frac{P(275-300 \cap CC)}{P(CC)}$$

$$= \frac{P(CC \mid 275-300)P(275-300)}{P(CC \mid 275-300)P(275-300) + P(CC \mid 305-325)P(305-325) + P(CC \mid 330-350)P(330-350)}$$

$$= \frac{.775(.52)}{.775(.52) + .77(.39) + .86(.09)} = \frac{.403}{.403 + .3003 + .0774} = \frac{.403}{.7807} = .516$$

3.91   Define the following events:

A_1: {Fuse made by line 1}
A_2: {Fuse made by line 2}
D: {Fuse is defective}

From the Exercise, we know $P(D|A_1) = .06$ and $P(D|A_2) = .025$. Also, $P(A_1) = P(A_2) = .5$.

Two fuses are going to be selected and we need to find the probability that one of the two is defective. We can get one defective fuse out of two by getting a defective on the first and non-defective on the second ($D \cap D^c$) or non-defective on the first and defective on the second ($D^c \cap D$). The probability of getting one defective out of two fuses given line 1 is:

$$P(D \cap D^c \mid A_1) + P(D^c \cap D \mid A_1) = P(D \mid A_1)P(D^c \mid A_1) + P(D^c \mid A_1)P(D \mid A_1)$$
$$= .06(1-.06) + (1-.06)(.06) = .06(.94) + .94(.06) = .1128 = P(1\ D \mid A_1)$$

The probability of getting one defective out of two fuses given line 2 is:

$$P(D \cap D^c \mid A_2) + P(D^c \cap D \mid A_2) = P(D \mid A_2)P(D^c \mid A_2) + P(D^c \mid A_2)P(D \mid A_2)$$
$$= .025(1-.025) + (1-.025)(.025) = .025(.975) + .975(.025) = .04875 = P(1\ D \mid A_2)$$

The probability of getting one defective out of two fuses is:

$$P(1\ D) = P(1\ D \cap A_1) + P(1\ D \cap A_2) = P(1\ D \mid A_1)P(A_1) + P(1\ D \mid A_2)P(A_2)$$
$$= .1128(.5) + .04875(.5) = .0564 + .024375 = .080775$$

Finally, we want to find:

$$P(A_1 \mid 1\ D) = \frac{P(1\ D \cap A_1)}{P(1\ D)} = \frac{.0564}{.080775} = .6982$$

3.93   Define the following event:

D: {Chip is defective}

From the Exercise, $P(S_1) = .15$, $P(S_2) = .05$, $P(S_3) = .10$, $P(S_4) = .20$, $P(S_5) = .12$, $P(S_6) = .20$, and $P(S_7) = .18$. Also, $P(D|S_1) = .001$, $P(D|S_2) = .0003$, $P(D|S_3) = .0007$, $P(D|S_4) = .006$, $P(D|S_5) = .0002$, $P(D|S_6) = .0002$, and $P(D|S_7) = .001$.

a.   We must find the probability of each supplier given a defective chip.

$$P(S_1 \mid D) = \frac{P(S_1 \cap D)}{P(D)} =$$

$$\frac{P(D \mid S_1)P(S_1)}{P(D \mid S_1)P(S_1) + P(D \mid S_2)P(S_2) + P(D \mid S_3)P(S_3) + P(D \mid S_4)P(S_4) + P(D \mid S_5)P(S_5) + P(D \mid S_6)P(S_6) + P(D \mid S_7)P(S_7)}$$

$$= \frac{.001(.15)}{.001(.15) + .0003(.05) + .0007(.10) + .006(.20) + .0002(.12) + .0002(.02) + .001(.18)}$$

$$= \frac{.00015}{.00015 + .000015 + .00007 + .0012 + .000024 + .00004 + .00018} \quad \frac{.00015}{.001679} = .0893$$

$$P(S_2 \mid D) = \frac{P(S_2 \cap D)}{P(D)} = \frac{P(D \mid S_2)P(S_2)}{P(D)} = \frac{.0003(.05)}{.001679} = \frac{.000015}{.001679} = .0089$$

$$P(S_3 \mid D) = \frac{P(S_3 \cap D)}{P(D)} = \frac{P(D \mid S_3)P(S_3)}{P(D)} = \frac{.0007(.10)}{.001679} = \frac{.00007}{.001679} = .0417$$

$$P(S_4 \mid D) = \frac{P(S_4 \cap D)}{P(D)} = \frac{P(D \mid S_4)P(S_4)}{P(D)} = \frac{.006(.20)}{.001679} = \frac{.0012}{.001679} = .7147$$

$$P(S_5 \mid D) = \frac{P(S_5 \cap D)}{P(D)} = \frac{P(D \mid S_5)P(S_5)}{P(D)} = \frac{.0002(.12)}{.001679} = \frac{.000024}{.001679} = .0143$$

$$P(S_6 \mid D) = \frac{P(S_6 \cap D)}{P(D)} = \frac{P(D \mid S_6)P(S_6)}{P(D)} = \frac{.0002(.20)}{.001679} = \frac{.00004}{.001679} = .0238$$

$$P(S_7 \mid D) = \frac{P(S_7 \cap D)}{P(D)} = \frac{P(D \mid S_7)P(S_7)}{P(D)} = \frac{.001(.18)}{.001679} = \frac{.00018}{.001679} = .1072$$

Of these probabilities, .7147 is the largest. This implies that if a failure is observed, supplier number 4 was most likely responsible.

b. If the seven suppliers all produce defective chips at the same rate of .0005, then $P(D|S_i) = .0005$ for all $i = 1, 2, 3, \ldots 7$ and $P(D) = .0005$.

For any supplier i, $P(S_i \cap D) = P(D \mid S_i)P(S_i) = .0005P(S_i)$ and

$$P(S_i \mid D) = \frac{P(S_i \cap D)}{P(D)} = \frac{P(D \mid S_i)P(S_i)}{.0005} = \frac{.0005P(S_i)}{.0005} = P(S_i)$$

Thus, if a defective is observed, then it most likely came from the supplier with the largest proportion of sales (probability). In this case, the most likely supplier would be either supplier 4 or supplier 6. Both of these have probabilities of .20.

3.95 a. The two probability rules for a sample space are that the probability for any sample point is between 0 and 1 and that the sum of the probabilities of all the sample points is 1.

For this Exercise, all the probabilities of the sample points are between 0 and 1 and

$$\sum_{i=1}^{4} P(S_i) = P(S_1) + P(S_2) + P(S_3) + P(S_4) = .2 + .1 + .3 + .4 = 1.0$$

b. $P(A) = P(S_1) + P(S_4) = .2 + .4 = .6$

3.97 a. If events A and B are mutually exclusive, then $P(A \cap B) = 0$.

$$P(A \mid B) = \frac{P(A \cap B)}{P(B)} = \frac{0}{.3} = 0$$

b. No. If events A and B are independent, then $P(A \mid B) = P(A)$. However, from the Exercise we know $P(A) = .2$ and from part a, we know $P(A \mid B) = 0$. Thus, events A and B are not independent.

3.99 $P(A \cap B) = .4$, $P(A \mid B) = .8$

Since the $P(A \mid B) = \dfrac{P(A \cap B)}{P(B)}$, substitute the given probabilities into the formula and solve for $P(B)$.

$$.8 = \frac{.4}{P(B)} \Rightarrow P(B) = \frac{.4}{.8} = .5$$

3.101   a. $P(A \cap B) = 0$

$P(B \cap C) = P(2) = .2$

$P(A \cup C) = P(1) + P(2) + P(3) + P(5) + P(6) = .3 + .2 + .1 + .1 + .2 = .9$

$P(A \cup B \cup C) = P(1) + P(2) + P(3) + P(4) + P(5) + P(6) = .3 + .2 + .1 + .1 + .1 + .2 = 1$

$P(B^c) = P(1) + P(3) + P(5) + P(6) = .3 + .1 + .1 + .2 = .7$

$P(A^c \cap B) = P(2) + P(4) = .2 + .1 = .3$

$$P(B \mid C) = \frac{P(B \cap C)}{P(C)} = \frac{P(2)}{P(2) + P(5) + P(6)} = \frac{.2}{.2 + .1 + .2} = \frac{.2}{.5} = .4$$

$$P(B \mid A) = \frac{P(B \cap A)}{P(A)} = \frac{0}{P(A)} = 0$$

     b.   Since $P(A \cap B) = 0$, and $P(A) \cdot P(B) > 0$, these two would not be equal, implying A and B are not independent. However, A and B are mutually exclusive, since $P(A \cap B) = 0$.

     c. $P(B) = P(2) + P(4) = .2 + .1 = .3$. But $P(B \mid C)$, calculated above, is .4. Since these are not equal, B and C are not independent. Since $P(B \cap C) = .2$, B and C are not mutually exclusive.

3.103   a.   The number of ways to select 5 graduate students from 50 is a combination of 50 things taken 5 at a time or

$$\binom{50}{5} = \frac{50!}{5!(50-5)!} = \frac{50!}{5!45!} = \frac{50 \cdot 49 \cdot 48 \cdot 47 \cdot 46 \cdot 45!}{5 \cdot 4 \cdot 3 \cdot 2 \cdot 1 \cdot 45!} = 2,118,760$$

     b.   We would number the students from 1 to 50. Start anywhere in the table with 2 digit numbers. Go down the column and select the first 2 digit number between 01 and 50. Continue selecting 2 digit numbers between 01 and 50 until 5 different numbers are selected.

3.105   Define the event:

B: {Small business owned by non-Hispanic white female}

From the problem, $P(B) = .27$

The probability that a small business owned by a non-Hispanic white is male-owned is $P(B^c) = 1 - P(B) = 1 - .27 = .73$.

3.107   a.   This statement is false. All probabilities are between 0 and 1 inclusive. One cannot have a probability of 4.

     b.   If we assume that the probabilities are the same as the percents (changed to proportions), then this is a true statement.

$$P(4 \, or \, 5) = P(4) + P(5) = .6020 + .1837 = .7857$$

     c.   This statement is true. There were no observations with one star. Thus, $P(1) = 0$.

     d.   This statement is false. $P(2) = .0408$ and $P(5) = .1837$. $P(5) > P(2)$.

3.109   a. $B \cap C$

b. A^c

c. $C \cup B$

d. $A \cap C^c$

3.111   Define the following events:

G: {regularly use the golf course}
T: {regularly use the tennis courts}

Given: $P(G) = .7$ and $P(T) = .5$

The event "uses neither facility" can be written as $G^c \cap T^c$ or $(G \cup T)^c$. We are given
$P(G^c \cap T^c) = P[(G \cup T)^c] = .05$. The complement of the event "uses neither facility" is the event "uses at least one of the two facilities" which can be written as $G \cup T$.

$$P(G \cup T) = 1 - P[(G \cup T)^c] = 1 - .05 = .95$$

From the additive rule, $P(G \cup T) = P(G) + P(T) - P(G \cap T)$

$$\Rightarrow .95 = .7 + .5 - P(G \cap T)$$
$$\Rightarrow P(G \cap T) = .25$$

a.   The Venn Diagram is:

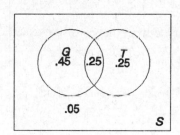

b. $P(G \cup T) = .95$ from above.

c. $P(G \cap T) = .25$ from above.

d. $P(G \mid T) = \dfrac{P(G \cap T)}{P(T)} = \dfrac{.25}{.5} = .5$

3.113   Define the following events:

A: {U.S. household does not own stock}
B: {U.S. household does own stock}
C: {U.S. household spends more and saves less}
D: {U.S. household spends less and saves more}
E: {No effect}

We are given that $P(B) = .50$. Since the figures in the table are only for stockholders, they are all conditional probabilities. $P(E|B) = .85$, $P(C|B) = .034$, and $P(D|B) = .116$

a. $P(A) = 1 - P(B) = 1 - .50 = .50$.

b. $P(C|B) = .034$

c. $P(B \cap D) = P(D|B)P(B) = .116(.50) = .058$

3.115   Define the following events:

A: {The watch is accurate}
N: {The watch is not accurate}

Assuming the manufacturer's claim is correct,

$P(N) = .05$ and $P(A) = 1 - P(N) = 1 - .05 = .95$

The sample space for the purchase of four of the manufacturer's watches is listed below.

(A, A, A, A)   (N, A, A, A)   (A, N, N, A)   (N, A, N, N)
(A, A, A, N)   (A, A, N, N)   (N, A, N, A)   (N, N, A, N)
(A, A, N, A)   (A, N, A, N)   (N, N, A, A)   (N, N, N, A)
(A, N, A, A)   (N, A, A, N)   (A, N, N, N)   (N, N, N, N)

a. All four watches not being accurate as claimed is the sample point *(N, N, N, N)*.

Assuming the watches purchased operate independently and the manufacturer's claim is correct,

$P(N, N, N, N) = P(N)P(N)P(N)P(N) = .05^4 = .00000625$

b. The sample points in the sample space that consist of exactly two watches failing to meet the claim are listed below.

(A, A, N, N)   (N, A, A, N)
(A, N, A, N)   (N, A, N, A)
(A, N, N, A)   (N, N, A, A)

The probability that exactly two of the four watches fail to meet the claim is the sum of the probabilities of these six sample points.

Assuming the watches purchased operate independently and the manufacturer's claim is correct,

$P(A, A, N, N) = P(A)P(A)P(N)P(N) = (.95)(.95)(.05)(.05) = .00225625$

All six of the sample points will have the same probability. Therefore, the probability that exactly two of the four watches fail to meet the claim when the manufacturer's claim is correct is

$6(0.00225625) = .0135$

c. The sample points in the sample space that consist of three of the four watches failing to meet the claim are listed below.

(A, N, N, N) (N, N, A, N)
(N, A, N, N) (N, N, N, A)

The probability that three of the four watches fail to meet the claim is the sum of the probabilities of the four sample points.

Assuming the watches purchased operate independently and the manufacturer's claim is correct,

$$P(A, N, N, N) = P(A)P(N)P(N)P(N) = (.95)(.05)(.05)(.05) = .00011875$$

All four of the sample points will have the same probability. Therefore, the probability that three of the four watches fail to meet the claim when the manufacturer's claim is correct is

$$4(.00011875) = .000475$$

If this event occurred, we would tend to doubt the validity of the manufacturer's claim since its probability of occurring is so small.

d. All four watches tested failing to meet the claim is the sample point (N, N, N, N).

Assuming the watches purchased operate independently and the manufacturer's claim is correct,

$$P(N, N, N, N) = P(N)P(N)P(N)P(N) = (.05)^4 = .00000625$$

Since the probability of observing this event is so small if the claim is true, we have strong evidence against the validity of the claim. However, we do not have conclusive proof that the claim is false. There is still a chance the event can occur (with probability .00000625) although it is extremely small.

3.117 Define the following events:

A: {Never smoked cigars}
B: {Former cigar smoker}
C: {Current cigar smoker}
D: {Died from cancer}
E: {Did not die from cancer}

a. $P(D \mid A) = \dfrac{P(D \cap A)}{P(A)} = \dfrac{782/137,243}{121,529/137,243} = \dfrac{782}{121,529} = .006$

b. $(D \mid B) = \dfrac{P(D \cap B)}{P(B)} = \dfrac{91/137,243}{7,848/137,243} = \dfrac{91}{7,848} = .012$

c. $P(D \mid C) = \dfrac{P(D \cap C)}{P(C)} = \dfrac{141/137,243}{7,866/137,243} = \dfrac{141}{7,866} = .018$

3.119   a. $P(B) = \dfrac{5,021}{833,303} = .0060$

b. $P(A \cap B) = \dfrac{1,808}{833,303} = .0022$

c. $P(A \cup B) = P(A) + P(B) - P(A \cap B)$
$$= \dfrac{341,180}{833,303} + \dfrac{5,021}{833,303} - \dfrac{1,808}{833,303} = \dfrac{344,393}{833,303} = .4133$$

d. $P(A \mid B) = \dfrac{(A \cap B)}{P(B)} = \dfrac{1,808/833,303}{5,021/833,303} = \dfrac{1,808}{5,021} = .3601$

e.   No. If A and B are independent, then $P(A \mid B) = P(A)$. Here, $P(A \mid B) \neq P(A)$ or $.3601 \neq .4094$. Thus, A and B are not independent.

3.121   Define the following events:

S_1:   {Salesman makes sale on the first visit}
S_2:   {Salesman makes a sale on the second visit}

$P(S_1) = .4 \quad P(S_2 \mid S_1^c) = .65$

The sample points of the experiment are:

$S_1 \cap S_2^c$
$S_1^c \cap S_2$
$S_1^c \cap S_2^c$

The probability the salesman will make a sale is:

$P(S_1 \cap S_2^c) + P(S_1^c \cap S_2) = P(S_1) + P(S_2 \mid S_1^c)P(S_1^c) = .4 + .65(1 - .4) = .4 + .39 = .79$

3.123   a.   Suppose we let the four positions in a sample point represent in order (1) Raise a broad mix of crops, (2) Raise livestock, (3) Use chemicals sparingly, and (4) Use techniques for regenerating the soil, such as crop rotation. A farmer is either likely (L) to engage in an activity or unlikely (U). The possible classifications are:

LLLL   LLLU   LLUL   LULL   ULLL   LLUU   LULU   LUUL   ULLU   ULUL   UULL   LUUU
ULUU   UULU   UUUL   UUUU

b.   Since there are 16 classifications or sample points and all are equally likely, then each has a probability of 1/16.

$P(UUUU) = \dfrac{1}{16}$

c.   The probability that a farmer will be classified as likely on at least three criteria is

$$P(LLLL) + P(LLLU) + P(LLUL) + P(LULL) + P(ULLL) = 5\left(\dfrac{1}{16}\right) = \dfrac{5}{16}.$$

3.125   Define the following events:

O_1:   {Component #1 in System A operates properly}
O_2:   {Component #2 in System A operates properly}
O_3:   {Component #3 in System A operates properly}
A: {System A works properly}

$$P(O_1) = 1 - P\left(O_1^c\right) = 1 - .12 = .88$$

$$P(O_2) = 1 - P\left(O_2^c\right) = 1 - .09 = .91$$

$$P(O_3) = 1 - P\left(O_3^c\right) = 1 - .11 = .89$$

a. $P(A) = P(O_1 \cap O_2 \cap O_3)$
     $= P(O_1)P(O_2)P(O_3)$ (since the three components operate independently)
     $= (.88)(.91)(.89) = .7127$

b. $P(A^c) = 1 - P(A)$
     $= 1 - .7127$ (see part **a**)
     $= .2873$

c.   Define the following events:

C_1:   {Component 1 in System B works properly}
C_2:   {Component 2 in System B works properly}
D_3:   {Component 3 in System B works properly}
D_4:   {Component 4 in System B works properly}
C: {Subsystem C works properly}
D: {Subsystem D works properly}

The probability a component fails is .1, so the probability a component works properly is $1 - .1 = .9$.

Subsystem C works properly if both components 1 and 2 work properly.

$$P(C) = P(C_1 \cap C_2) = P(C_1)P(C_2) = .9(.9) = .81$$
$$\text{(since the components operate independently)}$$

Similarly, $P(D) = P(D_1 \cap D_2) = P(D_1)P(D_2) = .9(.9) = .81$

The system operates properly if either subsystem C or D operates properly.

The probability that System B operates properly is:

$$P(C \cup D) = P(C) + P(D) - P(C \cap D) = P(C) + P(D) - P(C)P(D)$$
$$= .81 + .81 - .81(.81) = .9639$$

d.   The probability exactly one subsystem fails in System B is:

$$P(C \cap D^c) + P(C^c \cap D) = P(C)P(D^c) + P(C^c)P(D)$$
$$= .81(1 - .81) + (1 - .81).81 = .1539 + .1539 = .3078$$

e.   The probability that System B fails is the probability that both subsystems fail:

$$P(C^c \cap D^c) = P(C^c)P(D^c) = (1 - .81)(1 - .81) = .0361$$

f.   The system operates correctly 99% of the time means it fails 1% of the time. The probability one subsystem fails is .19. The probability n subsystems fail is $.19^n$. Thus, we must find n such that

$$.19^n \le .01$$

Thus, $n = 3$.

3.127   Define the following events:

A: {Press is correctly adjusted}
B: {Press is incorrectly adjusted}
D: {part is defective}

From the exercise, $P(A) = .90$, $P(D|A) = .05$, and $P(D|B) = .50$. We also know that event B is the complement of event A. Thus, $P(B) = 1 - P(A) = 1 - .90 = .10$.

$$P(B \mid D) = \frac{P(B \cap D)}{P(D)} = \frac{P(D \mid B)P(B)}{P(D \mid B)P(B) + P(D \mid A)P(A)}$$
$$= \frac{.50(.10)}{.50(.10) + .05(.90)} = \frac{.05}{.05 + .045} = \frac{.05}{.095} = .526$$

3.129   Define the flowing events:

A: {Dealer draws a blackjack}
B: {Player draws a blackjack}

a.   For the dealer to draw a blackjack, he needs to draw an ace and a face card. There are

$$\binom{4}{1} = \frac{4!}{1!(4-1)!} = \frac{4 \cdot 3 \cdot 2 \cdot 1}{1 \cdot 3 \cdot 2 \cdot 1} = 4 \text{ ways to draw an ace and}$$

$$\binom{12}{1} = \frac{12!}{1!(12-1)!} = \frac{12 \cdot 11 \cdot 10 \cdots 1}{1 \cdot 11 \cdot 10 \cdot 9 \cdots 1} = 12 \text{ ways to draw a face card (there are 12 face}$$

cards in the deck).

The total number of ways a dealer can draw a blackjack is $4 \cdot 12 = 48$.

The total number of ways a dealer can draw 2 cards is

$$\binom{52}{2} = \frac{52!}{2!(52-2)!} = \frac{52 \cdot 51 \cdot 50 \cdots 1}{2 \cdot 1 \cdot 50 \cdot 49 \cdot 48 \cdots 1} = 1326$$

Thus, the probability that the dealer draws a blackjack is $P(A) = \frac{48}{1326} = .0362$

b. In order for the player to win with a blackjack, the player must draw a blackjack and the dealer does not. Using our notation, this is the event $B \cap A^C$. We need to find the probability that the player draws a blackjack ($P(B)$) and the probability that the dealer does not draw a blackjack given the player does ($P(A^C \mid B)$). Then, the probability that the player wins with a blackjack is $P(A^C \mid B)P(B)$.

The probability that the player draws a blackjack is the same as the probability that the dealer draws a blackjack, which is $P(B) = .0362$.

There are 5 scenarios where the dealer will not draw a blackjack given the player does. First, the dealer could draw an ace and not a face card. Next, the dealer could draw a face card and not an ace. Third, the dealer could draw two cards that are not aces or face cards. Fourth, the dealer could draw two aces, and finally, the dealer could draw two face cards.

The number of ways the dealer could draw an ace and not a face card given the player draws a blackjack is

$$\binom{3}{1}\binom{36}{1} = \frac{3!}{1!(3-1)!} \cdot \frac{36!}{1!(36-1)!} = \frac{3 \cdot 2 \cdot 1}{1 \cdot 2 \cdot 1} \cdot \frac{36 \cdot 35 \cdot 34 \cdots 1}{1 \cdot 35 \cdot 34 \cdot 33 \cdots 1} = 3(36) = 108$$

(Note: Given the player has drawn blackjack, there are only 3 aces left and 36 non-face cards.)

The number of ways the dealer could draw a face card and not an ace given the player draws a blackjack is

$$\binom{11}{1}\binom{36}{1} = \frac{11!}{1!(11-1)!} \cdot \frac{36!}{1!(36-1)!} = \frac{11 \cdot 10 \cdot 9 \cdots 1}{1 \cdot 10 \cdot 9 \cdot 8 \cdots 1} \cdot \frac{36 \cdot 35 \cdot 34 \cdots 1}{1 \cdot 35 \cdot 34 \cdot 33 \cdots 1} = 11(36) = 396$$

The number of ways the dealer could draw neither a face card nor an ace given the player draws a blackjack is

$$\binom{36}{2} = \frac{36!}{2!(36-2)!} = \frac{36 \cdot 35 \cdot 34 \cdots 1}{2 \cdot 1 \cdot 34 \cdot 33 \cdot 32 \cdots 1} = 630$$

The number of ways the dealer could draw two aces given the player draws a blackjack is

$$\binom{3}{2} = \frac{3!}{2!(3-2)!} = \frac{3 \cdot 2 \cdot 1}{2 \cdot 1 \cdot 1} = 3$$

The number of ways the dealer could draw two face cards given the player draws a blackjack is

$$\binom{11}{2} = \frac{11!}{2!(11-2)!} = \frac{11 \cdot 10 \cdot 9 \cdots 1}{2 \cdot 9 \cdot 8 \cdot 7 \cdots 1} = 55$$

The total number of ways the dealer can draw two cards given the player draws a blackjack is

$$\binom{50}{2} = \frac{50!}{2!(50-2)!} = \frac{50 \cdot 49 \cdot 48 \cdots 1}{2 \cdot 1 \cdot 48 \cdot 47 \cdot 46 \cdots 1} = 1225$$

The probability that the dealer does not draw a blackjack given the player draws a blackjack is

$$P(A^c \mid B) = \frac{108 + 396 + 630 + 3 + 55}{1225} = \frac{1192}{1225} = .9731$$

Finally, the probability that the player wins with a blackjack is

$$P(B \cap A^c) = P(A^c \mid B)P(B) = .9731(.0362) = .0352$$

3.131   First, we will list all possible sample points for placing a car (C) and 2 goats (G) behind doors #1, #2, and #3. If the first position corresponds to door #1, the second position corresponds to door #2, and the third position corresponds to door #3, the sample space is:

(*C G G*) (*G C G*) (*G G C*)

Now, suppose you pick door #1. Initially, the probability that you will win the car is 1/3 – only one of the sample points has a car behind door #1.

The host will now open a door behind which is a goat. If you pick door #1 in the first sample point (*C G G*), the host will open either door #2 or door #3. Suppose he opens door #3 (it really does not matter). If you pick door #1 in the second sample point (*G C G*), the host will open door #3. If you pick door #1 in the third sample point (*G G C*), the host will open door #2. Now, the new sample space will be:

(*C G*) (*G C*) (*G C*)

where the first position corresponds to door #1 (the one you chose) and the second position corresponds to the door that was not opened by the host.

Now, if you keep door #1, the probability that you win the car is 1/3. However, if you switch to the remaining door, the probability that you win the car is now 2/3. Based on these probabilities, it is to your advantage to switch doors.

The above could be repeated by selecting door #2 initially or door #3 initially. In either of these cases, again, the probability of winning the car is 1/3 if you do not switch and 2/3 if you switch. Thus, Marilyn was correct.

Chapter 4
Random Variables
and Probability Distributions

4.1   a.   The number of newspapers sold by New York Times each month can take on a countable number of values. Thus, this is a discrete random variable.

        b.   The amount of ink used in printing the Sunday edition of the New York Times can take on an infinite number of different values. Thus, this is a continuous random variable.

        c.   The actual number of ounces in a one gallon bottle of laundry detergent can take on an infinite number of different values. Thus, this is a continuous random variable.

        d.   The number of defective parts in a shipment of nuts and bolts can take on a countable number of values. Thus, this is a discrete random variable.

        e.   The number of people collecting unemployment insurance each month can take on a countable number of values. Thus, this is a discrete random variable.

4.3   Since there are only a fixed number of outcomes to the experiment, the random variable, x, the number of stars in the rating, is discrete.

4.5   The variable x, total compensation in 2008 (in $ millions), is reported in whole number dollars. Since there are a countable number of possible outcomes, this variable is discrete.

4.7   An economist might be interested in the percentage of the work force that is unemployed, or the current inflation rate, both of which are continuous random variables.

4.9   The manager of a clothing store might be concerned with the number of employees on duty at a specific time of day, or the number of articles of a particular type of clothing that are on hand.

4.11   a.   When a die is tossed, the number of spots observed on the upturned face can be 1, 2, 3, 4, 5, or 6. Since the six sample points are equally likely, each one has a probability of 1/6.

        The probability distribution of x may be summarized in tabular form:

x	1	2	3	4	5	6
$p(x)$	$\frac{1}{6}$	$\frac{1}{6}$	$\frac{1}{6}$	$\frac{1}{6}$	$\frac{1}{6}$	$\frac{1}{6}$

b.   The probability distribution of x may
     also be presented in graphical form:

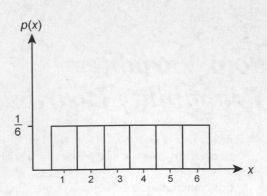

4.13   a.   We know $\sum p(x) = 1$. Thus, $p(2) + p(3) + p(5) + p(8) + p(10) = 1$

$\Rightarrow p(5) = 1 - p(2) - p(3) - p(8) - p(10) = 1 - .15 - .10 - .25 - .25 = .25$

b. $P(x = 2 \text{ or } x = 10) = P(x = 2) + P(x = 10) = .15 + .25 = .40$

c. $P(x \leq 8) = P(x = 2) + P(x = 3) + P(x = 5) + P(x = 8) = .15 + .10 + .25 + .25 = .75$

4.15   a.   The sample points are (where H = head, T = tail):

	HHH	HHT	HTH	THH	HTT	THT	TTH	TTT
x = # heads	3	2	2	2	1	1	1	0

b.   If each event is equally likely, then $P(\text{sample point}) = \dfrac{1}{n} = \dfrac{1}{8}$

$p(3) = \dfrac{1}{8}$, $p(2) = \dfrac{1}{8} + \dfrac{1}{8} + \dfrac{1}{8} = \dfrac{3}{8}$, $p(1) = \dfrac{1}{8} + \dfrac{1}{8} + \dfrac{1}{8} = \dfrac{3}{8}$, and $p(0) = \dfrac{1}{8}$

c.   Using Minitab, the graph of $p(x)$ is:

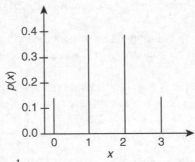

d. $P(x = 2 \text{ or } x = 3) = p(2) + p(3) = \dfrac{3}{8} + \dfrac{1}{8} = \dfrac{4}{8} = \dfrac{1}{2}$

4.17   a. $\mu = E(x) = \sum x p(x) = -4(.02) + (-3)(.07) + (-2)(.10) + (-1)(.15) + 0(.3)$

$+ 1(.18) + 2(.10) + 3(.06) + 4(.02)$

$= -.08 - .21 - .2 - .15 + 0 + .18 + .2 + .18 + .08 = 0$

$\sigma^2 = E[(x - \mu)^2] = \sum (x - \mu)^2 p(x)$

$= (-4 - 0)^2(.02) + (-3 - 0)^2(.07) + (-2 - 0)^2(.10)$

$+ (-1 - 0)^2(.15) + (0 - 0)^2(.30) + (1 - 0)^2(.18)$

$+ (2 - 0)^2(.10) + (3 - 0)^2(.06) + (4 - 0)^2(.02)$

$= .32 + .63 + .4 + .15 + 0 + .18 + .4 + .54 + .32 = 2.94$

$\sigma = \sqrt{2.94} = 1.715$

b.

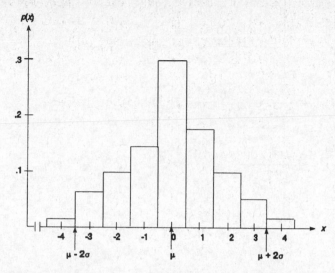

$$\mu \pm 2\sigma \Rightarrow 0 \pm 2(1.715) \Rightarrow 0 \pm 3.430 \Rightarrow (-3.430, 3.430)$$

c. $P(-3.430 < x < 3.430) = p(-3) + p(-2) + p(-1) + p(0) + p(1) + p(2) + p(3)$
$$= .07 + .10 + .15 + .30 + .18 + .10 + .06 = .96$$

4.19 a. The probability distribution for x is found by converting the Percent column to a probability column by dividing the percents by 100. The probability distribution of x is:

x	$p(x)$
2	.0408
3	.1735
4	.6020
5	.1837

b. $P(x = 5) = p(5) = .1837.$

c. $P(x \le 2) = p(2) = .0408.$

d. $\mu = E(x) = \sum_{i=1}^{4} x_i \, p(x_i) = 2(.0408) + 3(.1735) + 4(.6020) + 5(.1837)$
$$= .0816 + .5205 + 2.4080 + .9185 = 3.9286 \approx 3.93$$

The average star rating for a car's drivers-side star rating is 3.9286.

4.21 a. Yes. For all values of x, $0 \le p(x) \le 1$ and $\sum p(x) = .01 + .02 + .03 + .05 + .08 + .09 + .11 + .13 +$
$.12 + .10 + .08 + .06 + .05 + .03 + .02 + .01 + .01 = 1.00.$

b. $P(x = 16) = .06$

c. $P(x \le 10) = p(5) + p(6) + p(7) + p(8) + p(9) + p(10)$
$$= .01 + .02 + .03 + .05 + .08 + .09 = .28$$

d. $P(5 \le x \le 15) = p(5) + p(6) + p(7) + p(8) + p(9) + p(10) + p(11) + p(12) + p(13) + p(14) + p(15)$
$$= .01 + .02 + .03 + .05 + .08 + .09 + .11 + .13 + .12 + .10 + .08$$
$$= .82$$

4.23   a.   X is a discrete random variable because it can take on only values 0, 1, 2, 3, 4, or 5 in this example.

     b. $p(0) = \dfrac{5!(.35)^0(.65)^{5-0}}{0!(5-0)!} = \dfrac{5 \cdot 4 \cdot 3 \cdot 2 \cdot 1(1)(.65)^5}{1 \cdot 5 \cdot 4 \cdot 3 \cdot 2 \cdot 1} = .65^5 = .1160$

$p(1) = \dfrac{5!(.35)^1(.65)^{5-1}}{1!(5-1)!} = \dfrac{5 \cdot 4 \cdot 3 \cdot 2 \cdot 1(.35)^1(.65)^4}{1 \cdot 4 \cdot 3 \cdot 2 \cdot 1} = 5(.35)(.65)^4 = .3124$

$p(2) = \dfrac{5!(.35)^2(.65)^{5-2}}{2!(5-2)!} = \dfrac{5 \cdot 4 \cdot 3 \cdot 2 \cdot 1(.35)^2(.65)^3}{2 \cdot 1 \cdot 3 \cdot 2 \cdot 1} = 10(.35)^2(.65)^3 = .3364$

$p(3) = \dfrac{5!(.35)^3(.65)^{5-3}}{3!(5-3)!} = \dfrac{5 \cdot 4 \cdot 3 \cdot 2 \cdot 1(.35)^3(.65)^2}{3 \cdot 2 \cdot 1 \cdot 2 \cdot 1} = 10(.35)^3(.65)^2 = .1811$

$p(4) = \dfrac{5!(.35)^4(.65)^{5-4}}{4!(5-4)!} = \dfrac{5 \cdot 4 \cdot 3 \cdot 2 \cdot 1(.35)^4(.65)^1}{4 \cdot 3 \cdot 2 \cdot 1 \cdot 1} = 5(.35)^4(.65)^1 = .0488$

$p(5) = \dfrac{5!(.35)^5(.65)^{5-5}}{5!(5-5)!} = \dfrac{5 \cdot 4 \cdot 3 \cdot 2 \cdot 1(.35)^5(.65)^0}{5 \cdot 4 \cdot 3 \cdot 2 \cdot 1 \cdot 1} = (.35)^5 = .0053$

     c.   The two properties of discrete random variables are that $p(x) \geq 0$ for all x and $\Sigma p(x) = 1$. From above, all probabilities are greater than 0 and

$\Sigma p(x) = .1160 + .3124 + .3364 + .1811 + .0488 + .0053 = 1$

     d. $P(x \geq 4) = p(4) + p(5) = .0488 + .0053 = .0541$

4.25   a. $p(1) = (.23)(.77)^{1-1} = (.23)(.77)^0 = .23$. The probability that one would encounter a contaminated cartridge on the first trial is .23.

     b. $p(5) = (.23)(.77)^{5-1} = (.23)(.77)^4 = .0809$. The probability that one would encounter a the first contaminated cartridge on the fifth trial is .0809.

     c. $P(x \geq 2) = 1 - P(x \leq 1) = 1 - P(x = 1) = 1 - .23 = .77$. The probability that the first contaminated cartridge is found on the second trial or later is .77.

4.27   a. $p(0) = \dfrac{\binom{20}{0}\binom{100-20}{3-0}}{\binom{100}{3}} = \dfrac{\dfrac{20!}{0!(20-0)!} \cdot \dfrac{80!}{3!(80-3)!}}{\dfrac{100!}{3!(100-3)!}} = \dfrac{\dfrac{20!}{0!20!} \cdot \dfrac{80!}{3!77!}}{\dfrac{100!}{3!97!}} = \dfrac{1 \cdot \dfrac{80 \cdot 79 \cdot 78}{3 \cdot 2}}{\dfrac{100 \cdot 99 \cdot 98}{3 \cdot 2}}$

$= \dfrac{82,160}{161,700} = .508$

b. $p(1) = \dfrac{\dbinom{20}{1}\dbinom{100-20}{3-1}}{\dbinom{100}{3}} = \dfrac{\dfrac{20!}{1!(20-1)!}\dfrac{80!}{2!(80-2)!}}{\dfrac{100!}{3!(100-3)!}} = \dfrac{\dfrac{20!}{1!19!}\dfrac{80!}{2!78!}}{\dfrac{100!}{3!97!}} = \dfrac{20\cdot\dfrac{80\cdot79}{2}}{\dfrac{100\cdot99\cdot98}{3\cdot2}}$

$= \dfrac{63,200}{161,700} = .391$

c. $p(2) = \dfrac{\dbinom{20}{2}\dbinom{100-20}{3-2}}{\dbinom{100}{3}} = \dfrac{\dfrac{20!}{2!(20-2)!}\dfrac{80!}{1!(80-1)!}}{\dfrac{100!}{3!(100-3)!}} = \dfrac{\dfrac{20!}{2!18!}\dfrac{80!}{1!79!}}{\dfrac{100!}{3!97!}} = \dfrac{\dfrac{20\cdot19}{2}\cdot80}{\dfrac{100\cdot99\cdot98}{3\cdot2}}$

$= \dfrac{15,200}{161,700} = .094$

d. $p(3) = \dfrac{\dbinom{20}{3}\dbinom{100-20}{3-0}}{\dbinom{100}{3}} = \dfrac{\dfrac{20!}{3!(20-3)!}\dfrac{80!}{0!(80-0)!}}{\dfrac{100!}{3!(100-3)!}} = \dfrac{\dfrac{20!}{3!17!}\cdot1}{\dfrac{100!}{3!97!}} = \dfrac{\dfrac{20\cdot19\cdot18}{3\cdot2}\cdot1}{\dfrac{100\cdot99\cdot98}{3\cdot2}}$

$= \dfrac{1,140}{161,700} = .007$

4.29 a. The properties of valid probability distributions are:

$$\sum p(x) = 1 \text{ and } 0 \le p(x) \le 1 \text{ for all } x.$$

For ARC a_1: $0 \le p(x) \le 1$ for all x and $\sum p(x) = .6 + .25 + .1 + .05 = 1.00$
Thus, this is a valid probability distribution.

For ARC a_2: $0 \le p(x) \le 1$ for all x and $\sum p(x) = .6 + .3 + .1 = 1.00$
Thus, this is a valid probability distribution.

For ARC a_3: $0 \le p(x) \le 1$ for all x and $\sum p(x) = .9 + .1 = 1.00$
Thus, this is a valid probability distribution.

For ARC a_4: $0 \le p(x) \le 1$ for all x and $\sum p(x) = .9 + .1 = 1.00$
Thus, this is a valid probability distribution.

For ARC a_5: $0 \le p(x) \le 1$ for all x and $\sum p(x) = .9 + .1 = 1.00$
Thus, this is a valid probability distribution.

For ARC a_6: $0 \le p(x) \le 1$ for all x and $\sum p(x) = .7 + .25 + .05 = 1.00$
Thus, this is a valid probability distribution.

b. For Arc a_1, $P(x > 1) = P(x = 2) + P(x = 3) = .25 + .6 = .85$

c.   For Arc a_2, $P(x > 1) = P(x = 2) = .6$
      For Arc a_3, $P(x > 1) = 0$
      For Arc a_4, $P(x > 1) = 0$
      For Arc a_5, $P(x > 1) = 0$
      For Arc a_6, $P(x > 1) = P(x = 2) = .7$

d.   For Arc a_1,

$$E(x) = \sum xp(x) = 3(.60) + 2(.25) + 1(.10) + 0(.05) = 1.80 + .50 + .1 + 0 = 2.40$$

       The average capacity of Arc a_1 is 2.40.

       For Arc a_2,

$$E(x) = \sum xp(x) = 2(.60) + 1(.30) + 0(.10) = 1.20 + .30 + 0 = 1.50$$

       The average capacity of Arc a_2 is 1.50.

       For Arcs a_3, a_4, and a_5,

$$E(x) = \sum xp(x) = 1(.90) + 0(.10) = .90 + 0 = .90$$

       The average capacity of Arc a_3 is 0.90. The average capacity of Arc a_4 is 0.90.
       The average capacity of Arc a_5 is 0.90.

       For Arc a_6,

$$E(x) = \sum xp(x) = 2(.70) + 1(.25) + 0(.10) = 1.40 + .25 + 0 = 1.65$$

       The average capacity of Arc a_6 is 1.65.

e.   For Arc a_1,

$$\sigma^2 = E\left[(x - \mu)\right]^2 = \sum (x - \mu)^2 p(x)$$

$$= (3 - 2.4)^2(.60) + (2 - 2.4)^2(.25) + (1 - 2.4)^2(.10) + (0 - 2.4)^2(.05)$$

$$= (.6)^2(.60) + (-.4)^2(.25) + (-1.4)^2(.10) + (-2.4)^2(.05)$$

$$= .216 + .04 + .196 + .288 = .74$$

$$\sigma = \sqrt{.74} = .86$$

       We would expect most observations to fall within 2 standard deviations of the mean or
       $2.40 \pm 2(.86) \Rightarrow 2.40 \pm 1.72 \Rightarrow (.68, 4.12)$

       For Arc a_2,

$$\sigma^2 = E\left[(x - \mu)\right]^2 = \sum (x - \mu)^2 p(x)$$

$$= (2 - 1.5)^2(.60) + (1 - 1.5)^2(.30) + (0 - 1.5)^2(.10)$$

$$= (.5)^2(.60) + (-.5)^2(.30) + (-1.5)^2(.10)$$

$$= .15 + .075 + .225 = .45$$

$$\sigma = \sqrt{.45} = .67$$

       We would expect most observations to fall within 2 standard deviations of the mean or
       $1.50 \pm 2(.67) \Rightarrow 1.50 \pm 1.34 \Rightarrow (.16, 2.84)$

For Arcs a_3, a_4, and a_5,

$$\sigma^2 = E\left[(x-\mu)\right]^2 = \sum(x-\mu)^2 p(x)$$

$$= (1-.9)^2(.90) + (0-.9)^2(.10)$$

$$= (.1)^2(.90) + (-.9)^2(.10)$$

$$= .009 + .081 = .090$$

$$\sigma = \sqrt{.09} = .30$$

We would expect most observations to fall within 2 standard deviations of the mean or
$.90 \pm 2(.30) \Rightarrow .90 \pm .60 \Rightarrow (.30, 1.50)$

For Arc a_6,

$$\sigma^2 = E\left[(x-\mu)\right]^2 = \sum(x-\mu)^2 p(x)$$

$$= (2-1.65)^2(.70) + (1-1.65)^2(.25) + (0-1.65)^2(.05)$$

$$= (.35)^2(.70) + (-.65)^2(.25) + (-1.65)^2(.05)$$

$$= .08575 + .105625 + .136125 = .3275$$

$$\sigma = \sqrt{.3275} = .57$$

We would expect most observations to fall within 2 standard deviations of the mean or
$1.65 \pm 2(.57) \Rightarrow 1.65 \pm 1.14 \Rightarrow (.51, 2.79)$

4.31   a.   Let x = the potential flood damages. Since we are assuming if it rains the business will incur damages and if it does not rain the business will not incur any damages, the probability distribution of x is:

x	0	300,000
$p(x)$	.7	.3

   b.   The expected loss due to flood damage is

$$E(x) = \sum_{\text{All } x} xp(x) = 0(.7) + 300{,}000(.3) = 0 + 90{,}000 = \$90{,}000$$

4.33   a.   Since there are 20 possible outcomes that are all equally likely, the probability of any of the 20 numbers is 1/20. The probability distribution of x is:

$P(x = 5) = 1/20 = .05;\quad P(x = 10) = 1/20 = .05;$ etc.

x	5	10	15	20	25	30	35	40	45	50	55	60	65	70	75	80	85	90	95	100
$p(x)$	.05	.05	.05	.05	.05	.05	.05	.05	.05	.05	.05	.05	.05	.05	.05	.05	.05	.05	.05	.05

   b. $E(x) = \sum xp(x) = 5(.05) + 10(.05) + 15(.05) + 20(.05) + 25(.05) + 30(.05) + 35(.05)$
   $+ 40(.05) + 45(.05) + 50(.05) + 55(.05) + 60(.05) + 65(.05) + 70(.05) + 75(.05)$
   $+ 80(.05) + 85(.05) + 90(.05) + 95(.05) + 100(.05) = 52.5$

   c. $\sigma^2 = E(x-\mu)^2 = \sum(x-\mu)^2 p(x) = (5-52.5)^2(.05) + (10-52.5)^2(.05)$
   $+ (15-52.5)^2(.05) + (20-52.5)^2(.05) + (25-52.5)^2(.05) + (30-52.5)^2(.05)$
   $+ (35-52.5)^2(.05) + (40-52.5)^2(.05) + (45-52.5)^2(.05) + (50-52.5)^2(.05)$
   $+ (55-52.5)^2(.05) + (60-52.5)^2(.05) + (65-52.5)^2(.05) + (70-52.5)^2(.05)$
   $+ (75-52.5)^2(.05) + (80-52.5)^2(.05) + (85-52.5)^2(.05) + (90-52.5)^2(.05)$
   $+ (95-52.5)^2(.05) + (100-52.5)^2(.05)$
   $= 831.25$

$\sigma = \sqrt{\sigma^2} = \sqrt{831.25} = 28.83$

Since the uniform distribution is not mound-shaped, we will use Chebyshev's theorem to describe the data. We know that at least 8/9 of the observations will fall with 3 standard deviations of the mean and at least 3/4 of the observations will fall within 2 standard deviations of the mean. For this problem,

$\mu \pm 2\sigma \Rightarrow 52.5 \pm 2(28.83) \Rightarrow 52.5 \pm 57.66 \Rightarrow (-5.16, 110.16)$. Thus, at least 3/4 of the data will fall between -5.16 and 110.16. For our problem, all of the observations will fall within 2 standard deviations of the mean. Thus, x is just as likely to fall within any interval of equal length.

d. If a player spins the wheel twice, the total number of outcomes will be $20(20) = 400$. The sample space is:

5, 5	10, 5	15, 5	20, 5	25, 5...	100, 5
5,10	10,10	15,10	20,10	25,10...	100,10
5,15	10,15	15,15	20,15	25,15...	100,15
.	.	.	.	.	.
.	.	.	.	.	.
.	.	.	.	.	.
5,100	10,100	15,100	20,100	25,100...	100,100

Each of these outcomes are equally likely, so each has a probability of $1/400 = .0025$.

Now, let x equal the sum of the two numbers in each sample. There is one sample with a sum of 10, two samples with a sum of 15, three samples with a sum of 20, etc. If the sum of the two numbers exceeds 100, then x is zero. The probability distribution of x is:

x	$p(x)$
0	.5250
10	.0025
15	.0050
20	.0075
25	.0100
30	.0125
35	.0150
40	.0175
45	.0200
50	.0225
55	.0250
60	.0275
65	.0300
70	.0325
75	.0350
80	.0375
85	.0400
90	.0425
95	.0450
100	.0475

e. We assumed that the wheel is fair, or that all outcomes are equally likely.

f. $\mu = E(x) = \sum xp(x) = 0(.5250) + 10(.0025) + 15(.0050) + 20(.0075) + ... + 100(.0475)$

$\quad\quad = 33.25$

$\sigma^2 = E(x - \mu)^2 = \sum (x - \mu)^2 p(x) = (0 - 33.25)^2(.525) + (10 - 33.25)^2(.0025)$

$\quad\quad + (15 - 33.25)^2(.0050) + (20 - 33.25)^2(.0075) + ... + (100 - 33.25)^2(.0475)$

$\quad\quad = 1471.3125$

$\sigma = \sqrt{\sigma^2} = \sqrt{1471.3125} = 38.3577$

g. $P(x = 0) = .525$

h.   Given that the player obtains a 20 on the first spin, the possible values for x (sum of the two spins) are 0 (player spins 85, 90, 95, or 100 on the second spin), 25, 30, ..., 100. In order to get an x of 25, the player would spin a 5 on the second spin. Similarly, the player would have to spin a 10 on the second spin order to get an x of 30, etc. Since all of the outcomes are equally likely on the second spin, the distribution of x is:

x	$p(x)$
0	.20
25	.05
30	.05
35	.05
40	.05
45	.05
50	.05
55	.05
60	.05
65	.05
70	.05
75	.05
80	.05
85	.05
90	.05
95	.05
100	.05

i.   The probability that the players total score will exceed one dollar is the probability that x is zero.
$P(x = 0) = .20$

j. Given that the player obtains a 65 on the first spin, the possible values for x (sum of the two spins) are 0 (player spins 40, 45, 50, up to 100 on second spin), 70, 75, 80,..., 100. In order to get an x of 70, the player would spin a 5 on the second spin. Similarly, the player would have to spin a 10 on the second spin in order to get an x of 75, etc. Since all of the outcomes are equally likely on the second spin, the distribution of x is:

x	$p(x)$
0	.65
70	.05
75	.05
80	.05
85	.05
90	.05
95	.05
100	.05

The probability that the players total score will exceed one dollar is the probability that x is zero. $P(x = 0) = .65$.

4.35 Let x = bookie's earnings per dollar wagered. Then x can take on values \$1 (you lose) and \$-5 (you win). The only way you win is if you pick 3 winners in 3 games. If the probability of picking 1 winner in 1 game is .5, then $P(www) = p(w)p(w)p(w) = .5(.5)(.5) = .125$ (assuming games are independent).

Thus, the probability distribution for x is:

x	$p(x)$
\$1	.875
\$-5	.125

$$E(x) = \sum xp(x) = 1(.875) - 5(.125) = .875 - .625 = \$.25$$

4.37 a. x is discrete. It can take on only six values.

b. This is a binomial distribution.

c. $p(0) = \binom{5}{0} (.7)^0(.3)^{5-0} = \frac{5!}{0!5!} (.7)^0(.3)^5 = \frac{5 \cdot 4 \cdot 3 \cdot 2 \cdot 1}{1 \cdot 5 \cdot 4 \cdot 3 \cdot 2 \cdot 1} (1)(.00243) = .00243$

$p(1) = \binom{5}{1} (.7)^1(.3)^{5-1} = \frac{5!}{1!4!} (.7)^1(.3)^4 = .02835$

$p(2) = \binom{5}{2} (.7)^2(.3)^{5-2} = \frac{5!}{2!3!} (.7)^2(.3)^3 = .1323$

$p(3) = \binom{5}{3} (.7)^3(.3)^{5-3} = \frac{5!}{3!2!} (.7)^3(.3)^2 = .3087$

$p(4) = \binom{5}{4} (.7)^4(.3)^{5-4} = \frac{5!}{4!1!} (.7)^4(.3)^1 = .36015$

$p(5) = \binom{5}{5} (.7)^5(.3)^{5-5} = \frac{5!}{5!0!} (.7)^5(.3)^0 = .16807$

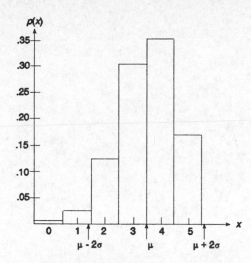

d. $\mu = np = 5(.7) = 3.5$
    $\sigma = \sqrt{npq} = \sqrt{5(.7)(.3)} = 1.0247$

e. $\mu \pm 2\sigma = 3.5 \pm 2(1.0247) \Rightarrow (1.4506, 5.5494)$

4.39 a. $P(x = 1) = \dfrac{5!}{1!4!}(.2)^1(.8)^4 = \dfrac{5 \cdot 4 \cdot 3 \cdot 2 \cdot 1}{(1)(4 \cdot 3 \cdot 2 \cdot 1)}(.2)^1(.8)^4 = 5(.2)^1(.8)^4 = .4096$

     b. $P(x = 2) = \dfrac{4!}{2!2!}(.6)^2(.4)^2 = \dfrac{4 \cdot 3 \cdot 2 \cdot 1}{(2 \cdot 1)(2 \cdot 1)}(.6)^2(.4)^2 = 6(.6)^2(.4)^2 = .3456$

     c. $P(x = 0) = \dfrac{3!}{0!3!}(.7)^0(.3)^3 = \dfrac{3 \cdot 2 \cdot 1}{(1)(3 \cdot 2 \cdot 1)}(.7)^0(.3)^3 = 1(.7)^0(.3)^3 = .027$

     d. $P(x = 3) = \dfrac{5!}{3!2!}(.1)^3(.9)^2 = \dfrac{5 \cdot 4 \cdot 3 \cdot 2 \cdot 1}{(3 \cdot 2 \cdot 1)(2 \cdot 1)}(.1)^3(.9)^2 = 10(.1)^3(.9)^2 = .0081$

     e. $P(x = 2) = \dfrac{4!}{2!2!}(.4)^2(.6)^2 = \dfrac{4 \cdot 3 \cdot 2 \cdot 1}{(2 \cdot 1)(2 \cdot 1)}(.4)^2(.6)^2 = 6(.4)^2(.6)^2 = .3456$

     f. $P(x = 1) = \dfrac{3!}{1!2!}(.9)^1(.1)^2 = \dfrac{3 \cdot 2 \cdot 1}{(1)(2 \cdot 1)}(.9)^1(.1)^2 = 3(.9)^1(.1)^2 = .027$

4.41 a. $\mu = np = 25(.5) = 12.5$

         $\sigma^2 = np(1 - p) = 25(.5)(.5) = 6.25$
         $\sigma = \sqrt{\sigma^2} = \sqrt{6.25} = 2.5$

     b. $\mu = np = 80(.2) = 16$

         $\sigma^2 = np(1 - p) = 80(.2)(.8) = 12.8$
         $\sigma = \sqrt{\sigma^2} = \sqrt{12.8} = 3.578$

c. $\mu = np = 100(.6) = 60$

$\sigma^2 = np(1 - p) = 100(.6)(.4) = 24$
$\sigma = \sqrt{\sigma^2} = \sqrt{24} = 4.899$

d. $\mu = np = 70(.9) = 63$

$\sigma^2 = np(1 - p) = 70(.9)(.1) = 6.3$
$\sigma = \sqrt{\sigma^2} = \sqrt{6.3} = 2.510$

e. $\mu = np = 60(.8) = 48$
$\sigma^2 = np(1 - p) = 60(.8)(.2) = 9.6$
$\sigma = \sqrt{\sigma^2} = \sqrt{9.6} = 3.098$

f. $\mu = np = 1,000(.04) = 40$

$\sigma^2 = np(1 - p) = 1,000(.04)(.96) = 38.4$
$\sigma = \sqrt{\sigma^2} = \sqrt{38.4} = 6.197$

4.43 a. We will check the 5 characteristics of a binomial random variable.

1. The experiment consists of 100 identical trials.
2. There are only 2 possible outcomes for each trial. Let S = internet user goes online at home using a wireless network and F = internet user goes online at home without using a wireless network.
3. The probability of success (S) is the same from trial to trial. For each trial, $p = P(S) = .20$ and $q = 1 - p = 1 - .20 = .80$.
4. The trials are independent.
5. The binomial random variable x is the number of internet users in 100 trials who go online at home using a wireless connection.

Thus, x is a binomial random variable.

b. From the exercise, $p = .20$. For any internet user who goes online at home, the probability of using a wireless connection is .20.

c. $\mu = E(x) = np = 100(.20) = 20$. On average, for every 100 internet users who go online at home, 20 will use a wireless connection.

4.45 a. Let x = number of small businesses owned by non-Hispanic whites that are female owned in 200 trials. Then x is a binomial random variable with $n = 200$ and $p = .27$.

$\mu = E(x) = np = 200(.27) = 54$

b. Let x = number of small businesses owned by non-Hispanic whites that are female owned in 8 trials. Then x is a binomial random variable with n = 8 and p = .27.

$$P(x = 0) = \binom{n}{x} p^x (1 - p)^{n-x} = \binom{8}{0} .27^0 (.73)^{8-0} = .73^8 = .0806$$

$$P(x = 4) = \binom{n}{x} p^x (1 - p)^{n-x} = \binom{8}{4} .27^4 (.73)^{8-4} = \frac{8!}{4!(8-4)!} .27^4 .73^4 = .1056$$

4.47   a.   We will check the 5 characteristics of a binomial random variable.

1.   The experiment consists of $n = 20$ identical trials.
2.   There are only 2 possible outcomes for each trial. Let S = intruding object is detected and F = intruding object is not detected.
3.   The probability of success (S) is the same from trial to trial. For each trial, $p =$ $P(S) =$ .8 and $q = 1 - p = 1 - .8 = .2$.
4.   The trials are independent.
5.   The binomial random variable x is the number of intruding objects in the 20 trials that are detected.

Thus, x is a binomial random variable.

b.   For this experiment, $n = 20$ and $p = .8$.

c.   Using Table II, Appendix B, with $n = 20$ and $p = .8$,

$$P(x = 15) = P(x \le 15) - P(x \le 14) = .370 - .196 = .174$$

d.   Using Table II, Appendix B, with n = 20 and p = .8,

$$P(x \ge 15) = 1 - P(x \le 14) = 1 - .196 = .804$$

e. $E(x) = np = 20(.8) = 16$. For every 20 intruding objects, SBIRS will detect an average of 16.

4.49   Let x = number of major bridges in Denver that will have a rating of 4 or below in 2020 in 10 trials. Then x has an approximate binomial distribution with $n = 10$ and $p = .09$.

a. $P(x \ge 3) = 1 - P(x \le 2) = 1 - P(x = 0) - P(x = 1) - P(x = 2)$

$$= 1 - \binom{10}{0}.09^0(.91)^{10-0} - \binom{10}{1}.09^1(.91)^{10-1} - \binom{10}{2}.09^2(.91)^{10-2}$$

$$= 1 - \frac{10!}{0!10!}.09^0.91^{10} - \frac{10!}{1!9!}.09^1.91^9 - \frac{10!}{2!8!}.09^2.91^8 = 1 - .389 - .385 - .171 = .055$$

b.   Since the probability of seeing at least 3 bridges out of 10 with ratings of 4 or less is so small, we can conclude that the forecast of 9% of all major Denver bridges will have ratings of 4 or less in 2020 is too small. There would probably be more than 9%.

4.51   Define the following events:

A: {Taxpayer is audited}
B: {Taxpayer has income less than $1 million)
C: {Taxpayer has income of $1 million or higher}

a.   From the information given in the problem,

$P(A \mid B) = 1/100 = .01$
$P(A \mid C) = 9/100 = .09$

b. Let x = number of taxpayers with incomes under \$1 million who are audited. Then x is a binomial random variable with $n = 5$ and $p = .01$.

$$P(x = 1) = \binom{5}{1}.01^1.99^{(5-1)} = \frac{5!}{1!4!}.01^1.99^{(4)} = .0480$$

$$P(x > 1) = 1 - [P(x = 0) + P(x = 1)]$$

$$= 1 - \left[\binom{5}{0}.01^0.99^{(5-0)} + .0480 \right]$$

$$= 1 - \left[\frac{5!}{0!5!}.01^0.99^5 + .0480 \right]$$

$$= 1 - [.9510 + .0480] = 1 - .9990 = .0010$$

c. Let x = number of taxpayers with incomes of \$1 million or more who are audited. Then x is a binomial random variable with $n = 5$ and $p = .09$.

$$P(x = 1) = \binom{5}{1}.09^1.91^{(5-1)} = \frac{5!}{1!4!}.09^1.91^4 = .3086$$

$$P(x > 1) = 1 - [P(x = 0) + P(x = 1)]$$

$$= 1 - \left[\binom{5}{0}.09^0.91^{(5-0)} + .3086 \right]$$

$$= 1 - \left[\frac{5!}{0!5!}.09^0.91^5 + .3086 \right]$$

$$= 1 - [.6240 + .3086] = 1 - .9326 = .0674$$

d. Let x = number of taxpayers with incomes under \$1 million who are audited. Then x is a binomial random variable with $n = 2$ and $p = .01$.

Let y = number of taxpayers with incomes \$1 million or more who are audited. Then y is a binomial random variable with $n = 2$ and $p = .09$.

$$P(x = 0) = \binom{2}{0}.01^0.99^{(2-0)} = \frac{2!}{0!2!}.01^0.99^2 = .9801$$

$$P(y = 0) = \binom{2}{0}.09^0.91^{(2-0)} = \frac{2!}{0!2!}.09^0.91^2 = .8281$$

$$P(x = 0)P(y = 0) = .9801(.8281) = .8116$$

e. We must assume that the variables defined as x and y are binomial random variables. We must assume that the trials are identical, the probability of success is the same from trial to trial, and that the trials are independent.

4.53 a. $\mu = E(x) = np = 800(.70) = 560$

$$\sigma = \sqrt{npq} = \sqrt{800(.70)(.30)} = \sqrt{168} = 12.96$$

b.   Half of the 800 food items would be 400. A value of $x = 400$ would have a z-score of:

$$z = \frac{x - \mu}{\sigma} = \frac{400 - 560}{12.96} = -12.35$$

Since the z-score associated with 400 items is so small (-12.35), it would be virtually impossible to observe less than half with any pesticides if the 70% value was correct.

4.55   a.   We must assume that the probability that a specific type of ball meets the requirements is always the same from trial to trial and the trials are independent. To use the binomial probability distribution, we need to know the probability that a specific type of golf ball meets the requirements.

b.   For a binomial distribution,

$$\mu = np$$
$$\sigma = \sqrt{npq}$$

In this example, n = two dozen = $2 \cdot 12 = 24$.

$p = .10$ (Success here means the golf ball *does not* meet standards.)
$q = .90$
$\mu = np = 24(.10) = 2.4$
$\sigma = \sqrt{npq} = \sqrt{24(.10)(.90)} = 1.47$

c.   In this situation,

p = Probability of success
  = Probability golf ball *does* meet standards
  = .90
$q = 1 - .90 = .10$
$n = 24$
$E(x) = \mu = np = 24(.90) = 21.60$
$\sigma = \sqrt{npq} = \sqrt{24(.10)(.90)} = 1.47$ (Note that this is the same as in part **b.**)

4.57   a.   The random variable x is discrete since it can assume a countable number of values (0, 1, 2, ...).

b.   This is a Poisson probability distribution with $\lambda = 3$.

c.   In order to graph the probability distribution, we need to know the probabilities for the possible values of x. Using Table III of Appendix B with $\lambda = 3$:

$p(0) = .050$
$p(1) = P(x \le 1) - P(x = 0) = .199 - .050 = .149$
$p(2) = P(x \le 2) - P(x \le 1) = .423 - .199 = .224$
$p(3) = P(x \le 3) - P(x \le 2) = .647 - .423 = .224$
$p(4) = P(x \le 4) - P(x \le 3) = .815 - .647 = .168$
$p(5) = P(x \le 5) - P(x \le 4) = .916 - .815 = .101$
$p(6) = P(x \le 6) - P(x \le 5) = .966 - .916 = .050$
$p(7) = P(x \le 7) - P(x \le 6) = .988 - .966 = .022$
$p(8) = P(x \le 8) - P(x \le 7) = .996 - .988 = .008$
$p(9) = P(x \le 9) - P(x \le 8) = .999 - .996 = .003$
$p(10) \approx .001$

The probability distribution of x in graphical form is:

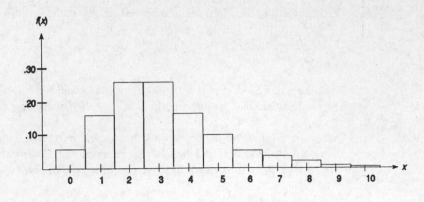

d. $\mu = \lambda = 3$
    $\sigma^2 = \lambda = 3$
    $\sigma = \sqrt{3} = 1.73$

e. The mean of x is the same as the mean of the probability distribution, $\mu = \lambda = 3$.

The standard deviation of x is the same as the standard deviation of the probability distribution, $\sigma = 1.7321$.

4.59   a. $P(x = 1) = \dfrac{\binom{r}{x}\binom{N-r}{n-x}}{\binom{N}{n}} = \dfrac{\binom{3}{1}\binom{5-3}{3-1}}{\binom{5}{3}} = \dfrac{\frac{3!}{1!2!}\frac{2!}{2!0!}}{\frac{5!}{3!2!}} = \dfrac{3(1)}{10} = .3$

b. $P(x = 3) = \dfrac{\binom{r}{x}\binom{N-r}{n-x}}{\binom{N}{n}} = \dfrac{\binom{3}{3}\binom{9-3}{5-3}}{\binom{9}{5}} = \dfrac{\frac{3!}{3!0!}\frac{6!}{2!4!}}{\frac{9!}{5!4!}} = \dfrac{1(15)}{126} = .119$

c. $P(x = 2) = \dfrac{\binom{r}{x}\binom{N-r}{n-x}}{\binom{N}{n}} = \dfrac{\binom{2}{2}\binom{4-2}{2-2}}{\binom{4}{2}} = \dfrac{\frac{2!}{2!0!}\frac{2!}{0!2!}}{\frac{4!}{2!2!}} = \dfrac{1(1)}{6} = .167$

d. $P(x = 0) = \dfrac{\binom{r}{x}\binom{N-r}{n-x}}{\binom{N}{n}} = \dfrac{\binom{2}{0}\binom{4-2}{2-0}}{\binom{4}{2}} = \dfrac{\frac{2!}{0!2!}\frac{2!}{2!0!}}{\frac{4!}{2!2!}} = \dfrac{1(1)}{6} = .167$

4.61   a. For $\lambda = 1$, $P(x \le 2) = .920$ (from Table III, Appendix B)

b. For $\lambda = 2$, $P(x \le 2) = .677$

c. For $\lambda = 3$, $P(x \le 2) = .423$

d. The probability decreases as λ increases. This is reasonable because λ is equal to the mean. As the mean increases, the probability that x is less than a particular value will decrease.

4.63   For this problem, $N = 100$, $n = 10$, and $x = 4$.

     a.   If the sample is drawn without replacement, the hypergeometric distribution should be used. The hypergeometric distribution requires that sampling be done without replacement.

     b.   If the sample is drawn with replacement, the binomial distribution should be used. The binomial distribution requires that sampling be done with replacement.

4.65   a.   For $N = 209$, $r = 10$, and $n = 8$, $E(x) = \dfrac{nr}{N} = \dfrac{10(8)}{209} = .383$

     b. $P(x = 4) = \dfrac{\binom{8}{4}\binom{209-8}{10-4}}{\binom{209}{10}} = \dfrac{\dfrac{8!}{4!(8-4)!} \cdot \dfrac{201!}{6!(201-6)!}}{\dfrac{209!}{10!(209-10)!}} = .0002$

4.67   a.   With $\lambda = 4.5$, $P(x = 0) = \dfrac{4.5^0 e^{-4.5}}{0!} = 0.0111$

     b. $P(x = 1) = \dfrac{4.5^1 e^{-4.5}}{1!} = 0.0500$

     c. $\mu = E(x) = \lambda = 4.5$

        $\sigma = \sqrt{\lambda} = \sqrt{4.5} = 2.12$

4.69   Let x = number of "clean" cartridges selected in 5 trials. For this problem, $N = 158$, $r = 122$, and $n = 5$.

$$P(x = 5) = \dfrac{\binom{r}{x}\binom{N-r}{n-x}}{\binom{N}{n}} = \dfrac{\binom{122}{5}\binom{36}{0}}{\binom{158}{5}} = \dfrac{\dfrac{122!}{5!117!}\dfrac{36!}{0!36!}}{\dfrac{158!}{5!153!}} = .2693$$

4.71   a.   Using Table III, Appendix B, with $\lambda = 5$,

        $P(x < 3) = P(x \le 2) = .125$

     b. $E(x) = \lambda = 5$. The average number of calls blocked during the peak hour of video conferencing call time is 5.

4.73   Let x = number of spoiled bottles in the sample of 3. Since the sampling will be done without replacement, x is a hypergeometric random variable with $N = 12$, $n = 3$, and $r = 1$.

$$P(x = 1) = \dfrac{\binom{r}{x}\binom{N-r}{n-x}}{\binom{N}{n}} = \dfrac{\binom{1}{1}\binom{12-1}{3-1}}{\binom{12}{3}} = \dfrac{\dfrac{1!}{1!0!}\dfrac{11!}{2!9!}}{\dfrac{12!}{3!9!}} = \dfrac{55}{220} = .25$$

4.75   a.   Using Table III, Appendix B, with $\lambda = 10$, $P(x = 24) = P(x \le 24) - P(x \le 23) = 1.000 - 1.000 = .000$

     b.   Using Table III, Appendix B, with $\lambda = 10$, $P(x = 23) = P(x \le 23) - P(x \le 22) = 1.000 - 1.000 = .000$

c. Yes, these probabilities are good approximations for the probability of "fire" and "theft". The researchers estimated these probabilities to be .0001, indicating that these would be extremely rare events. Our probabilities of .000 are very close to .0001.

4.77   Let x = number of females promoted in the 72 employees awarded promotion, where x is a hypergeometric random variable. From the problem, $N = 302$, $r = 73$, and $n = 72$. We need to find if observing 5 females who were promoted was fair.

$$E(x) = \mu = \frac{nr}{N} = \frac{72(73)}{302} = 17.40$$

If 72 employees are promoted, we would expect that about 17 would be females.

$$V(x) = \sigma^2 = \frac{r(N-r)n(N-n)}{N^2(N-1)} = \frac{73(302-73)72(302-72)}{302^2(302-1)} = 10.084$$

$$\sigma = \sqrt{10.084} = 3.176$$

Using Chebyshev's Theorem, we know that at least 8/9 of all observations will fall within 3 standard deviations of the mean. The interval from 3 standard deviations below the mean to 3 standard deviations above the mean is:

$$\mu \pm 3\sigma \Rightarrow 17.40 \pm 3(3.176) \Rightarrow 17.40 \pm 9.528 \Rightarrow (7.872, 26.928)$$

If there is no discrimination in promoting females, then we would expect between 8 and 26 females to be promoted within the group of 72 employees promoted. Since we observed only 5 females promoted, we would infer that females were not promoted fairly.

4.79   Using Table IV, Appendix B:

a. $P(z > 1.46) = .5 - P(0 < z \le 1.46)$
            $= .5 - .4279 = .0721$

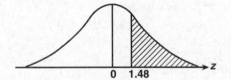

b. $P(x < -1.56) = .5 - P(-1.56 \le z < 0)$
            $= .5 - .4406 = .0594$

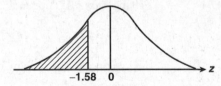

c. $P(.67 \le z \le 2.41)$
            $= P(0 < z \le 2.41) - P(0 < z < .67)$
            $= .4920 - .2486 = .2434$

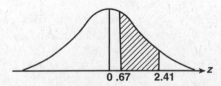

d. $P(-1.96 \le z < -.33)$
            $= P(-1.96 \le z < 0) - P(-.33 \le z < 0)$
            $= .4750 - .1293 = .3457$

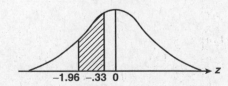

e. $P(z \geq 0) = .5$

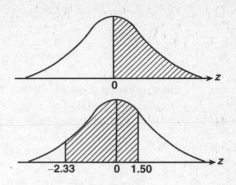

f. $P(-2.33 < z < 1.50)$
$= P(-2.33 < z < 0) + P(0 < z < 1.50)$
$= .4901 + .4332 = .9233$

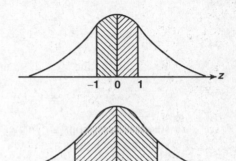

4.81 Using Table IV, Appendix B:

a. $P(-1 \leq z \leq 1)$
$= P(-1 \leq z \leq 0) + P(0 < z \leq 1)$
$= .3413 + .3413 = .6826$

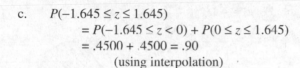

b. $P(-1.96 \leq z \leq 1.96)$
$= P(-1.96 \leq z < 0) + P(0 \leq z \leq 1.96)$
$= .4750 + .4750 = .9500$

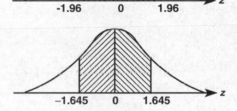

c. $P(-1.645 \leq z \leq 1.645)$
$= P(-1.645 < z < 0) + P(0 \leq z \leq 1.645)$
$= .4500 + .4500 = .90$
(using interpolation)

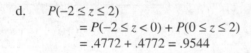

d. $P(-2 \leq z \leq 2)$
$= P(-2 \leq z < 0) + P(0 \leq z \leq 2)$
$= .4772 + .4772 = .9544$

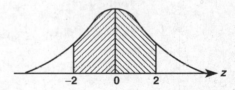

4.83 a. $P(z = 1) = 0$, since a single point does not have an area.

b. $P(z \leq 1) = P(z \leq 0) + P(0 \leq z \leq 1)$
$= .5 + .3413$
$= .8413$
(Table IV, Appendix B)

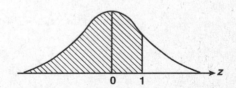

c. $P(z < 1) = P(z \leq 1) = .8413$ (Refer to part **b**.)

d. $P(z > 1) = 1 - P(z \leq 1) = 1 - .8413 = .1587$ (Refer to part **b**.)

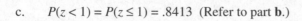

4.85   Using Table IV of Appendix B:

a. $P(z \leq z_0) = .2090$
      $A = .5000 - .2090 = .2910$

      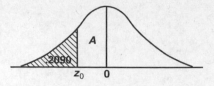

      Look up the area .2910 in the body of Table IV; $z_0 = -.81$.

      (z_0 is negative since the graph shows z_0 is on the left side of 0.)

b. $P(z \leq z_0) = .7090$

      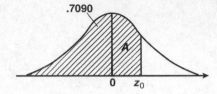

      $P(z \leq z_0) = P(z \leq 0) + P(0 \leq z \leq z_0)$
      $\qquad\qquad = .5 + P(0 \leq z \leq z) = .7090$

      Therefore, $P(0 \leq z \leq z_0) = .7090 - .5 = .2090$

      Look up the area .2090 in the body of Table IV; $z_0 \approx .55$.

c. $P(-z_0 \leq z < z_0) = .8472$

      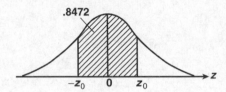

      $P(-z_0 \leq z < z_0) = 2P(0 \leq z \leq z_0)$
      $2P(0 \leq z \leq z_0) = .8472$

      Therefore, $P(0 \leq z \leq z_0) = .4236$.

      Look up the area .4236 in the body of Table IV; $z_0 = 1.43$.

d. $P(-z_0 \leq z < z_0) = .1664$

      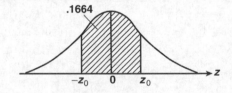

      $P(-z_0 \leq z \leq z_0) = 2P(0 \leq z \leq z_0)$
      $2P(0 \leq z \leq z_0) = .1664$

      Therefore, $P(0 \leq z \leq z_0) = .0832$.

      Look up the area .0832 in the body of Table IV; $z_0 = .21$.

e. $P(z_0 \leq z \leq 0) = .4798$

      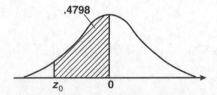

      $P(z_0 \leq z \leq 0) = P(0 \leq z \leq -z_0)$

      Look up the area .4798 in the body of Table IV;
      $z_0 = -2.05$.

f. $P(-1 < z < z_0) = .5328$

      $P(-1 < z < z_0)$
      $\qquad = P(-1 < z < 0) + P(0 < z < z_0)$
      $\qquad = .5328$

      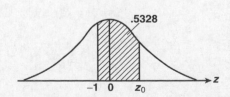

      $P(0 < z < 1) + P(0 < z < z_0) = .5328$

      Thus, $P(0 < z < z_0) = .5328 - .3413 = .1915$

      Look up the area .1915 in the body of Table IV; $z_0 = .50$.

4.87   Using Table IV, Appendix B:

a. $z = \dfrac{x-\mu}{\sigma} = \dfrac{20-30}{4} = -2.50$

b. $z = \dfrac{x-\mu}{\sigma} = \dfrac{30-30}{4} = 0$

c. $z = \dfrac{x-\mu}{\sigma} = \dfrac{27.5-30}{4} = -0.61$

d. $z = \dfrac{x-\mu}{\sigma} = \dfrac{15-30}{4} = -3.75$

e. $z = \dfrac{x-\mu}{\sigma} = \dfrac{35-30}{4} = 1.25$

f. $z = \dfrac{x-\mu}{\sigma} = \dfrac{25-30}{4} = -1.25$

4.89   a. $P(10 \leq x \leq 12) = P\left(\dfrac{10-11}{2} \leq z \leq \dfrac{12-11}{2}\right)$

$= P(-0.50 \leq z \leq 0.50)$
$= A_1 + A_2$
$= .1915 + .1915 = .3830$

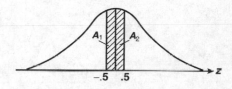

b. $P(6 \leq x \leq 10) = P\left(\dfrac{6-11}{2} \leq z \leq \dfrac{10-11}{2}\right)$

$= P(-2.50 \leq z \leq -0.50)$
$= P(-2.50 \leq z \leq 0) - P(-0.50 \leq z \leq 0)$
$= .4938 - .1915 = .3023$

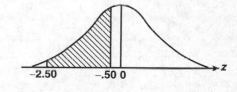

c. $P(13 \leq x \leq 16) = P\left(\dfrac{13-11}{2} \leq z \leq \dfrac{16-11}{2}\right)$

$= P(1.00 \leq z \leq 2.50)$
$= P(0 \leq z \leq 2.50) - P(0 \leq x \leq 1.00)$
$= .4938 - .3413 = .1525$

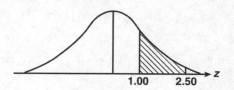

d. $P(7.8 \leq x \leq 12.6)$

$= P\left(\dfrac{7.8-11}{2} \leq z \leq \dfrac{12.6-11}{2}\right)$

$= P(-1.60 \leq z \leq 0.80)$
$= A_1 + A_2$
$= .4452 + .2881 = .7333$

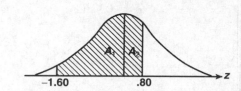

e. $P(x \geq 13.24) = P\left(z \geq \dfrac{13.24-11}{2}\right)$

$= P(z \geq 1.12)$
$= A_2 = .5 - A_1$
$= .5000 - .3686 = .1314$

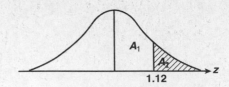

f. $P(x \geq 7.62) = P\left(z \geq \dfrac{7.62-11}{2}\right)$

$= P(z \geq -1.69)$
$= A_1 + A_2$
$= .4545 + .5000 = .9545$

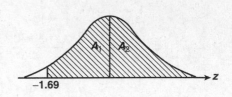

4.91 Let x = age of a powerful woman. The random variable x has a normal distribution with $\mu = 50$ and $\sigma = 5.3$. Using Table IV, Appendix B,

a. $P(55 < x < 60) = P\left(\dfrac{55-50}{6} < z < \dfrac{60-50}{6}\right) = P(.83 < z < 1.67)$

$= P(0 < z < 1.67) - P(0 < z < .83) = .4525 - .2967 = .1558$

b. $P(48 < x < 52) = P\left(\dfrac{48-50}{6} < z < \dfrac{52-50}{6}\right) = P(-.33 < z < .33)$

$= P(-.33 < z < 0) + P(0 < z < .33) = .1293 + .1293 = .2586$

c. $P(x < 35) = P\left(z < \dfrac{35-50}{6}\right) = P(z < -2.5)$

$= .5 - P(-2.5 < z < 0) = .5 - .4933 = .0062$

d. $P(x > 40) = P\left(z > \dfrac{40-50}{6}\right) = P(z > -1.67)$

$= .5 + P(-1.67 < z < 0) = .5 + .4525 = .9525$

4.93 a. Let x = buy-side analyst's forecast error. Then x has an approximate normal distribution with $\mu = .85$ and $\sigma = 1.93$. Using Table IV, Appendix B,

$P(x > 2.00) = P\left(z > \dfrac{2.00-.85}{1.93}\right) = P(z > .60) = .5 - .2257 = .2743$

b. Let y = sell-side analyst's forecast error. Then y has an approximate normal distribution with $\mu = -.05$ and $\sigma = 85$. Using Table IV, Appendix B,

$P(y > 2.00) = P\left(z > \dfrac{2.00-(-.05)}{.85}\right) = P(z > 2.41) = .5 - .4920 = .0080$

4.95   Let x = transmission delay. The random variable x has a normal distribution with $\mu = 48.5$ and $\sigma = 8.5$. Using Table IV, Appendix B,

a. $P(x < 57) = P\left(z < \dfrac{57 - 48.5}{8.5}\right) = P(z < 1.00)$

$$= .5 + P(0 < z < 1) = .5 + .3413 = .8413$$

b. $P(40 < x < 60) = P\left(\dfrac{40 - 48.5}{8.5} < z < \dfrac{60 - 48.5}{8.5}\right) = P(-1 < z < 1.35)$

$$= P(-1 < z < 0) + P(0 < z < 1.35) = .3413 + .4115 = .7528$$

4.97   a.   Let x = rating. Then x has a normal distribution with $\mu = 50$ and $\sigma = 15$. Using Table IV, Appendix B,

$P(x > x_o) = .10$. Find x_o.

$$P(x > x_o) = P\left(z > \dfrac{x_o - 50}{15}\right) = P(z > z_o) = .10$$

$A_1 = .5 - .10 = .4000$
Looking up area .4000 in Table IV, $z_o = 1.28$

$$z_o = \dfrac{x_o - 50}{15} \Rightarrow 1.28 = \dfrac{x_o - 50}{15} \Rightarrow x_o = 50 + 1.28(15) = 69.2$$

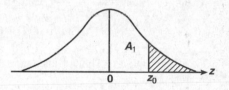

b. $P(x > x_o) = .10 + .20 + .40 = .70$. Find x_o.

$$P(x > x_o) = P\left(z > \dfrac{x_o - 50}{15}\right) = P(z > z_o) = .70$$

$A_1 = .70 - .5 = .2000$
Looking up area .2000 in Table IV, $z_o = -.52$

$$z_o = \dfrac{x_o - 50}{15} \Rightarrow -.52 = \dfrac{x_o - 50}{15} \Rightarrow x_o = 50 - .52(15) = 42.2$$

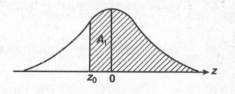

4.99   a.   Using Table IV, Appendix B, and $\mu = 75$ and $\sigma = 7.5$,

$$P(x > 80) = P\left(z > \dfrac{80 - 75}{7.5}\right) = P(z > .67) = .5 - .2486 = .2514$$

Thus, 25.14% of the scores exceeded 80.

b. $P(x \le x_0) = .98$. Find x_0.

$$P(x \le x_0) = P\left(z \le \dfrac{x_0 - 75}{7.5}\right) = P(z \le z_0) = .98$$

$A_1 = .98 - .5 = .4800$
Looking up area .4800 in Table IV, $z_0 = 2.05$.

$$z_0 = \dfrac{x_0 - 75}{7.5} \Rightarrow 2.05 = \dfrac{x_0 - 75}{7.5} \Rightarrow x_0 = 90.375$$

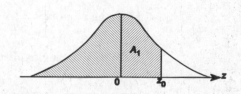

4.101   a.   The contract will be profitable if total cost, x, is less than $1,000,000.

$$P(x < 1,000,000) = P\left(z < \frac{1,000,000 - 850,000}{170,000}\right) = P(z < .88) = .5 + .3106 = .8106$$

b.   The contract will result in a loss if total cost, x, exceeds 1,000,000.

$$P(x > 1,000,000) = 1 - P(x < 1,000,000) = 1 - .8106 = .1894$$

c. $P(x < R) = .99$. Find R.

$$P(x < R) = P\left(z < \frac{R - 850,000}{170,000}\right) = P(z < z_0) = .99$$

$A_1 = .99 - .5 = .4900$

Looking up the area .4900 in Table IV, $z_0 = 2.33$

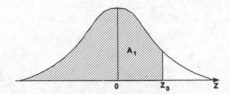

$$z_0 = \frac{R - 850,000}{170,000} \Rightarrow 2.33 = \frac{R - 850,000}{170,000}$$
$$\Rightarrow R = 2.33(170,000) + 850,000 = \$1,246,100$$

4.103   Let x = load. Then x has a normal distribution with $\mu = 20$. We are given $P(10 < x < 30) = .95$. We want to find σ.

$$P(10 < x < 30) = .95 \Rightarrow P(z_1 < z < z_2) = .95 \Rightarrow P(z_1 < z < 0) = P(0 < z < z_2) = .95/2 = .4750$$

Looking up area .4750 in Table IV, Appendix B, $z_2 = 1.96$ and $z_1 = -1.96$.

$$z_2 = \frac{x - 30}{\sigma} = \frac{30 - 20}{\sigma} = 1.96 \Rightarrow \sigma = \frac{10}{1.96} = 5.1$$

4.105   a.   The proportion of measurements that one would expect to fall in the interval $\mu \pm \sigma$ is about .68.

b.   The proportion of measurements that one would expect to fall in the interval $\mu \pm 2\sigma$ is about .95.

c.   The proportion of measurements that one would expect to fall in the interval $\mu \pm 3\sigma$ is about 1.00.

4.107   If the data are normally distributed, then the normal probability plot should be an approximate straight line. Of the three plots, only plot c implies that the data are normally distributed. The data points in plot c form an approximately straight line. In both plots **a** and **b**, the plots of the data points do not form a straight line.

4.109   a.   IQR $= Q_U - Q_L = 54 - 47 = 7$
This agrees with IQR from the printout.

b.   From the printout, $s = 6.444$

c.   If the data are approximately normal, then $\dfrac{\text{IQR}}{s} \approx 1.3$. For this problem,

$\dfrac{\text{IQR}}{s} = \dfrac{7}{6.444} = 1.086 \approx 1.3$. Thus, the distribution is approximately normal.

d.   From Exercise 2.48 d, the histogram is:

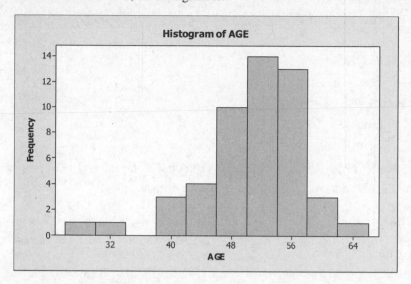

From the histogram, the data appear to be approximately mound-shaped. Thus, the data are approximately normal.

4.111   The information given in the problem states that $\bar{x} = 4.71$, $s = 6.09$, $Q_L = 1$, and $Q_U = 6$. To be normal, the data have to be symmetric. If the data are symmetric, then the mean would equal the median and would be half way between the lower and upper quartile. Half way between the upper and lower quartiles is 3.5. The sample mean is 4.71, which is much larger than 3.5. This implies that the data may not be normal. In addition, the interquartile range divided by the standard deviation will be approximately 1.3 if the data are normal. For this data,

$$\frac{\text{IQR}}{s} = \frac{Q_U - Q_L}{s} = \frac{6-1}{6.09} = .82$$

The value of .82 is much smaller than the necessary 1.3 to be normal. Again, this is an indication that the data are not normal. Finally, the standard deviation is larger than the mean. Since one cannot have values of the variable in this case less than 0, a standard deviation larger than the mean indicates that the data are skewed to the right. This implies that the data are not normal.

4.113   We will look at the 4 methods for determining if the data are normal. First, we will look at a histogram of the data. Using MINITAB, the histogram of the driver's head injury rating is:

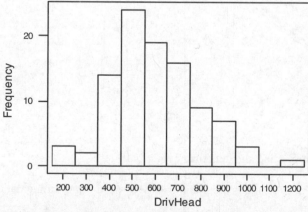

From the histogram, the data appear to be somewhat skewed to the right, but is fairly mound-shaped. This indicates that the data are normal.

Next, we look at the intervals $\bar{x} \pm s$, $\bar{x} \pm 2s$, $\bar{x} \pm 3s$. If the proportions of observations falling in each interval are approximately .68, .95, and 1.00, then the data are approximately normal. Using MINITAB, the summary statistics are:

Descriptive Statistics: DrivHead

Variable	N	Mean	Median	TrMean	StDev	SE Mean
DrivHead	98	603.7	605.0	600.3	185.4	18.7

Variable	Minimum	Maximum	Q1	Q3
DrivHead	216.0	1240.0	475.0	724.3

$\bar{x} \pm s \Rightarrow 603.7 \pm 185.4 \Rightarrow (418.3,\ 789.1)$ 68 of the 98 values fall in this interval. The proportion is .69. This is very close to the .68 we would expect if the data were normal.

$\bar{x} \pm 2s \Rightarrow 603.7 \pm 2(185.4) \Rightarrow 603.7 \pm 370.8 \Rightarrow (232.9,\ 974.5)$ 96 of the 98 values fall in this interval. The proportion is .98. This is a fair amount larger than the .95 we would expect if the data were normal.

$\bar{x} \pm 3s \Rightarrow 603.7 \pm 3(185.4) \Rightarrow 603.7 \pm 556.2 \Rightarrow (47.5,\ 1{,}159.9)$ 97 of the 98 values fall in this interval. The proportion is .99. This is fairly close to the 1.00 we would expect if the data were normal.

From this method, it appears that the data may be normal.

Next, we look at the ratio of the IQR to s. IQR = $Q_U - Q_L$ = 724.3 – 475 = 249.3.

$\dfrac{\text{IQR}}{s} = \dfrac{249.3}{185.4} = 1.3$ This is equal to the 1.3 we would expect if the data were normal. This method indicates the data may be normal.

Finally, using MINITAB, the normal probability plot is:

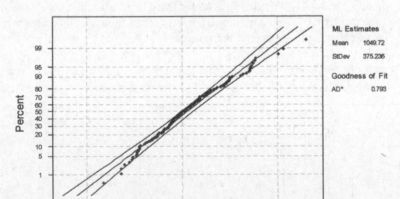

Since the data form a fairly straight line, the data may be normal.

From the 4 different methods, all indications are that the driver's head injury rating data are normal.

4.115   We will look at the 4 methods or determining if the 3 variables are normal.

Distance:
First, we will look at A histogram of the data. Using MINITAB, the histogram of the distance data is:

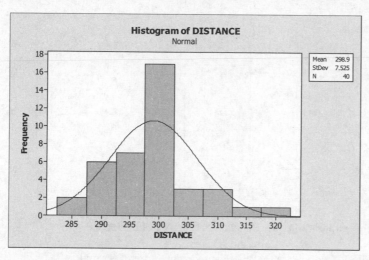

From the histogram, the distance data do not appear to have a normal distribution.

Next, we look at the intervals $\bar{x} \pm s$, $\bar{x} \pm 2s$, $\bar{x} \pm 3s$. If the proportions of observations falling in each interval are approximately .68, .95, and 1.00, then the data are approximately normal. Using MINITAB, the summary statistics are:

Descriptive Statistics: DISTANCE, ACCURACY, INDEX

Variable	N	Mean	StDev	Minimum	Q1	Median	Q3	Maximum
DISTANCE	40	298.95	7.53	283.20	294.60	299.05	302.00	318.90

$\bar{x} \pm s \Rightarrow 298.95 \pm 7.53 \Rightarrow (291.42, \quad 306.48)$ 28 of the 40 values fall in this interval. The proportion is 28/40 = .70. This is fairly close to the .68 we would expect if the data were normal.

$\bar{x} \pm 2s \Rightarrow 298.95 \pm 2(7.53) \Rightarrow 298.95 \pm 15.06 \Rightarrow (283.89, \quad 314.01)$ 37 of the 40 values fall in this interval. The proportion is 37/40 = .925. This is a fair amount below the .95 we would expect if the data were normal.

$\bar{x} \pm 3s \Rightarrow 298.95 \pm 3(7.53) \Rightarrow 298.95 \pm 22.59 \Rightarrow (276.36, \quad 321.54)$ 40 of the 40 values fall in this interval. The proportion is 40/40 =1.00. This is equal to the 1.00 we would expect if the data were normal.

From this method, it appears that the distance data may not be normal.

Next, we look at the ratio of the IQR to s.

IQR = $Q_U - Q_L$ = 302 − 294.6 = 7.4.

$\dfrac{\text{IQR}}{s} = \dfrac{7.4}{7.53} = .983$. This is much smaller than the 1.3 we would expect if the data were normal. This method indicates the distance data may not be normal.

Finally, using MINTAB, the normal probability plot is:

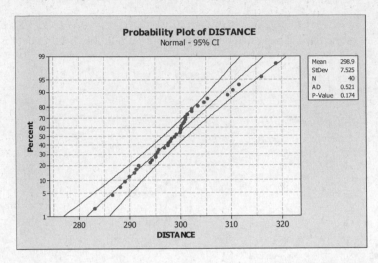

Since the data do not form a fairly straight line, the distance data may not be normal.

From the 4 different methods, all indications are that the distance data are not normal.

Accuracy:

First, we will look at a histogram of the data. Using MINITAB, the histogram of the accuracy data is:

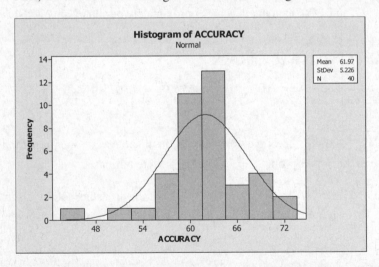

From the histogram, the accuracy data do not appear to have a normal distribution.

Descriptive Statistics: DISTANCE, ACCURACY, INDEX

```
Variable    N    Mean   StDev  Minimum     Q1   Median      Q3  Maximum
ACCURACY   40  61.970   5.226   45.400  59.400  61.950  64.075   73.000
```

$\bar{x} \pm s \Rightarrow 61.97 \pm 5.226 \Rightarrow (56.744, \quad 67.196)$ 30 of the 40 values fall in this interval. The proportion is 30/40 = .75. This is much greater than the .68 we would expect if the data were normal.

$\bar{x} \pm 2s \Rightarrow 61.97 \pm 2(5.226) \Rightarrow 61.97 \pm 10.452 \Rightarrow (51.518, \quad 72.422)$ 37 of the 40 values fall in this interval. The proportion is 37/40 = .925. This is a fair amount below the .95 we would expect if the data were normal.

$\bar{x} \pm 3s \Rightarrow 61.97 \pm 3(5.226) \Rightarrow 61.97 \pm 15.678 \Rightarrow (46.292, \quad 77.648)$ 39 of the 40 values fall in this interval. The proportion is 39/40 = .975. This is a fair amount lower than the 1.00 we would expect if the data were normal.

From this method, it appears that the accuracy data may not be normal.

Next, we look at the ratio of the IQR to s.

IQR = $Q_U - Q_L$ = 64.075 − 59.4 = 4.675.

$\dfrac{IQR}{s} = \dfrac{4.675}{5.226} = .895$. This is much smaller than the 1.3 we would expect if the data were normal. This method indicates the accuracy data may not be normal.

Finally, using MINTAB, the normal probability plot is:

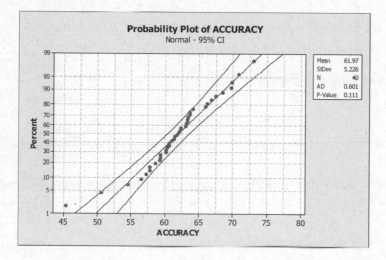

Since the data do not form a fairly straight line, the accuracy data may not be normal.

From the 4 different methods, all indications are that the accuracy data are not normal.

Index:
First, we will look at a histogram of the data. Using MINITAB, the histogram of the index data is:

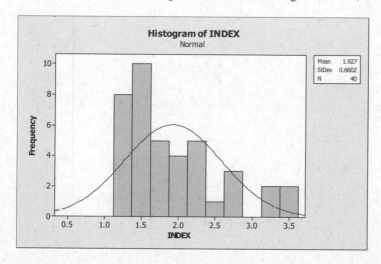

From the histogram, the index data do not appear to have a normal distribution.

Next, we look at the intervals $\bar{x} \pm s$, $\bar{x} \pm 2s$, $\bar{x} \pm 3s$. If the proportions of observations falling in each interval are approximately .68, .95, and 1.00, then the data are approximately normal. Using MINITAB, the summary statistics are:

Descriptive Statistics: DISTANCE, ACCURACY, INDEX

```
Variable    N    Mean  StDev  Minimum      Q1  Median      Q3  Maximum
INDEX      40   1.927  0.660    1.170   1.400   1.755   2.218    3.580
```

$\bar{x} \pm s \Rightarrow 1.927 \pm .660 \Rightarrow (1.267, \quad 2.587)$ 30 of the 40 values fall in this interval. The proportion is 30/40 = .75. This is much greater than the .68 we would expect if the data were normal.

$\bar{x} \pm 2s \Rightarrow 1.927 \pm 2(.660) \Rightarrow 1.927 \pm 1.320 \Rightarrow (.607, \quad 3.247)$ 37 of the 40 values fall in this interval. The proportion is 37/40 = .925. This is a fair amount below the .95 we would expect if the data were normal.

$\bar{x} \pm 3s \Rightarrow 1.927 \pm 3(.660) \Rightarrow 1.927 \pm 1.980 \Rightarrow (-.053, \quad 3.907)$ 40 of the 40 values fall in this interval. The proportion is 40/40 = 1.000. This is equal to the 1.00 we would expect if the data were normal.

From this method, it appears that the index data may not be normal.

Next, we look at the ratio of the IQR to s.

IQR = $Q_U - Q_L$ = 2.218 − 1.4 = .818.

$\dfrac{IQR}{s} = \dfrac{.818}{.66} = 1.23$. This is fairly close to the 1.3 we would expect if the data were normal. This method indicates the index data may normal.

Finally, using MINTAB, the normal probability plot is:

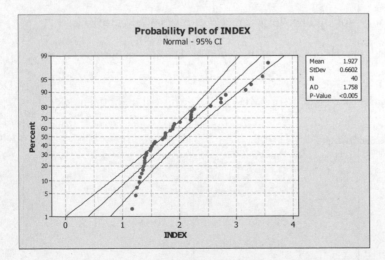

Since the data do not form a fairly straight line, the index data may not be normal.

From 3 of the 4 different methods, the indications are that the index data are not normal.

4.117   From Exercise 2.51, it states that the mean number of semester hours for those taking the CPA exam is 141.31 and the median is 140. It also states that most colleges only require 128 semester hours for an undergraduate degree. Thus, the minimum value for the total semester hours is around 128. The z-score associated with 128 is:

$$z = \frac{x - \mu}{\sigma} = \frac{128 - 141.31}{17.77} = -.75$$

If the data are normal, we know that about .34 of the observations are between the mean and 1 standard deviation below the mean. Thus, .16 of the observations are more than 1 standard deviation below the mean. With this distribution, that is impossible. Thus, the data are not normal. The mean is greater than the median, so we know that the data are skewed to the right.

4.119   a. $\mu = np = 100(.01) = 1.0$, $\sigma = \sqrt{npq} = \sqrt{100(.01)(.99)} = .995$

$\mu \pm 3\sigma \Rightarrow 1 \pm 3(.995) \Rightarrow 1 \pm 2.985 \Rightarrow (-1.985, 3.985)$

Since this interval does not fall in the interval $(0, n = 100)$, the normal approximation is not appropriate.

b. $\mu = np = 20(.6) = 12$, $\sigma = \sqrt{npq} = \sqrt{20(.6)(.4)} = 2.191$

$\mu \pm 3\sigma \Rightarrow 12 \pm 3(2.191) \Rightarrow 12 \pm 6.573 \Rightarrow (5.427, 18.573)$

Since this interval falls in the interval $(0, n = 20)$, the normal approximation is appropriate.

c. $\mu = np = 10(.4) = 4$, $\sigma = \sqrt{npq} = \sqrt{10(.4)(.6)} = 1.549$

$\mu \pm 3\sigma \Rightarrow 4 \pm 3(1.549) \Rightarrow 4 \pm 4.647 \Rightarrow (-.647, 8.647)$

Since this interval does not fall within the interval $(0, n = 10)$, the normal approximation is not appropriate.

d. $\mu = np = 1000(.05) = 50$, $\sigma = \sqrt{npq} = \sqrt{1000(.05)(.95)} = 6.892$

$\mu \pm 3\sigma \Rightarrow 50 \pm 3(6.892) \Rightarrow 50 \pm 20.676 \Rightarrow (29.324, 70.676)$

Since this interval falls within the interval $(0, n = 1000)$, the normal approximation is appropriate.

e. $\mu = np = 100(.8) = 80$, $\sigma = \sqrt{npq} = \sqrt{100(.8)(.2)} = 4$

$\mu \pm 3\sigma \Rightarrow 80 \pm 3(4) \Rightarrow 80 \pm 12 \Rightarrow (68, 92)$

Since this interval falls within the interval $(0, n = 100)$, the normal approximation is appropriate.

f. $\mu = np = 35(.7) = 24.5$, $\sigma = \sqrt{npq} = \sqrt{35(.7)(.3)} = 2.711$

$\mu \pm 3\sigma \Rightarrow 24.5 \pm 3(2.711) \rightarrow 24.5 \pm 8.133 \Rightarrow (16.367, 32.633)$

Since this interval falls within the interval $(0, n = 35)$, the normal approximation is appropriate.

4.121 x is a binomial random variable with $n = 100$ and $p = .4$.

$$\mu \pm 3\sigma \Rightarrow np \pm 3\sqrt{npq} \;\Rightarrow\; 100(.4) \pm 3\sqrt{100(.4)(1-.4)}$$

$$\Rightarrow 40 \pm 3(4.8990) \Rightarrow (25.303, 54.697)$$

Since the interval lies in the range 0 to 100, we can use the normal approximation to approximate the probabilities.

a. $P(x \le 35) \approx P\left(z \le \dfrac{(35+.5)-40}{4.899}\right)$

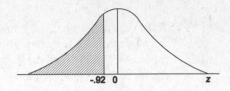

$= P(z \le -.92)$

$= .5000 - .3212 = .1788$

(Using Table IV in Appendix B.)

b. $P(40 \le x \le 50)$

$\approx P\left(\dfrac{(40-.5)-40}{4.899} \le z \le \dfrac{(50+.5)-40}{4.899}\right)$

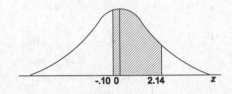

$= P(-.10 \le z \le 2.14)$

$= P(-.10 \le z \le 0) + P(0 \le z \le 2.14)$

$= .0398 + .4838 = .5236$

(Using Table IV in Appendix B.)

c. $P(x \ge 38) \approx P\left(z \ge \dfrac{(38-.5)-40}{4.899}\right)$

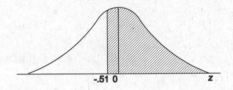

$= P(z \ge -.51)$

$= .5000 + .1950 = .6950$

(Using Table IV in Appendix B.)

4.123   Let x = number of patients who undergo laser surgery who have serious post-laser vision problems in 100,000 trials. Then x is a binomial random variable with n = 100,000 and $p = .01$.

$E(x) = \mu = np = 100,000(.01) = 1,000$.

$\sigma = \sqrt{\sigma^2} = \sqrt{npq} = \sqrt{100,000(.01)(.99)} = \sqrt{990} = 31.464$

To see if the normal approximation is appropriate, we use:

$$\mu \pm 3\sigma \Rightarrow 1,000 \pm 3(31.464) \Rightarrow 1,000 \pm 94.392 \Rightarrow (905.608, \; 1,094.392)$$

Since the interval lies in the range of 0 to 100,000, the normal approximation is appropriate.

$$P(x < 950) \approx P\left(z < \dfrac{949.5 - 1000}{31.464}\right) = P(z < -1.61) = .5 - .4463 = .0537$$

(Using Table IV, Appendix B)

4.125   a. x is a binomial random variable with $n = 1,000$ and $p = .28$.

$$\mu = E(x) = np = 1000(.28) = 280$$

b. $\sigma = \sqrt{npq} = \sqrt{1000(.28)(.72)} = \sqrt{201.6} = 14.2$

$\mu \pm 3\sigma \Rightarrow 280 \pm 3(14.2) \Rightarrow 280 \pm 42.6 \Rightarrow (237.4, \ 322.6)$

Since the interval lies in the range 0 to 1000, we can use the normal approximation to approximate the probability.

$$P(x > 750) \approx P\left(z > \frac{750 + .5 - 280}{14.2} \right) = P(z > 33.1) \approx .5 - .5 = 0$$

4.127   Let x = number of bottles (brands) selected in 65 trials that contain tap water. Then x is binomial random variable with $n = 65$ and $p = .25$.

$$E(x) = \mu = np = 65(.25) = 16.25$$

$$\sigma = \sqrt{\sigma^2} = \sqrt{npq} = \sqrt{65(.25)(.75)} = \sqrt{12.1875} = 3.49$$

To see if the normal approximation is appropriate, we use:

$\mu \pm 3\sigma => 16.25 \pm 3(3.49) => 16.25 \pm 10.47 => (5.78, \ 26.72)$

Since this interval lies in the range from 0 to 65, the normal approximation is appropriate.

$$P(x \geq 20) = P\left(z \geq \frac{(20 - .5) - 16.25}{3.49} \right) = P(z \geq .93) = .5 - P(0 \leq z \leq .93) = .5 - .3238 = .1762$$

(Using Table IV, Appendix B)

4.129   Let x = number of defective CDs in $n = 1,600$ trials. Then x is a binomial random variable with $n = 1,600$ and $p = .006$.

$$E(x) = \mu = np = 1,600(.006) = 9.6.$$

$$\sigma = \sqrt{\sigma^2} = \sqrt{npq} = \sqrt{1,600(.006)(.994)} = \sqrt{9.5424} = 3.089$$

To see if the normal approximation is appropriate, we use:

$\mu \pm 3\sigma \Rightarrow 9.6 \pm 3(3.089) \Rightarrow 9.6 \pm 9.267 \Rightarrow (0.333, \ 18.867)$

Since the interval lies in the range of 0 to 1,600, the normal approximation is appropriate.

$$P(x \geq 12) \approx P\left(z \geq \frac{11.5 - 9.6}{3.089} \right) = P(z \geq 0.62) = .5 - .2324 = .2676$$

(Using Table IV, Appendix B)

Since this probability is fairly large, it would not be unusual to see 12 or more defectives in a sample of 1,600 if 99.4% were defect-free. Thus, there would be no evidence to cast doubt on the manufacturer's claim.

4.131   Let x = number patients out of 150 who wait more than 30 minutes to see a doctor in a typical U.S. emergency room. Then x is a binomial random variable with $n = 150$ and $p = .5$.

$$\mu = np = 150(.5) = 75 \qquad \sigma = \sqrt{npq} = \sqrt{150(.5)(.5)} = \sqrt{37.5} = 6.124$$

To see if the normal approximation is valid, we use:

$$\mu \pm 3\sigma \Rightarrow 75 \pm 3(6.124) \Rightarrow 75 \pm 18.372 \Rightarrow (56.628, \quad 93.372)$$

Since the interval lies in the range 0 to 150, we can use the normal approximation to approximate the probability.

a. $P(x > 75) \approx P\left(z > \dfrac{75 + .5 - 75}{6.124} \right) = P(z > .08) = .5 - .0319 = .4681$

   (Using Table IV, Appendix B)

b. $P(x > 85) \approx P\left(z > \dfrac{85 + .5 - 75}{6.124} \right) = P(z > 1.71) = .5 - .4564 = .0436$

   (Using Table IV, Appendix B)

c. $P(60 < x < 90) = P\left(\dfrac{60 + .5 - 75}{6.124} < z < \dfrac{90 - .5 - 75}{6.124} \right) = P(-2.37 < z < 2.37)$

$$= P(-2.37 < z < 0) + P(0 < z < 2.37) = .4911 + .4911 = .9822$$

   (Using Table IV, Appendix B)

4.133   a. $f(x) = \dfrac{1}{d - c} \quad (c \le x \le d)$

$$\frac{1}{d - c} = \frac{1}{45 - 20} = \frac{1}{25} = .04$$

   So, $f(x) = \begin{cases} .04 & (20 \le x \le 45) \\ 0 & \text{otherwise} \end{cases}$

b. $\mu = \dfrac{c + d}{2} = \dfrac{20 + 45}{2} = \dfrac{65}{2} = 32.5$

$$\sigma = \frac{d - c}{\sqrt{12}} = \frac{45 - 20}{\sqrt{12}} = 7.22$$

c.

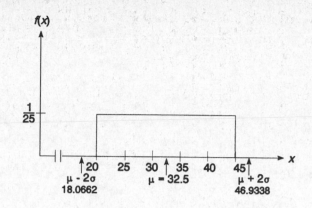

$\mu \pm 2\sigma \Rightarrow 32.5 \pm 2(7.22) \Rightarrow (18.06,\ 46.94)$

$P(18.06 < x < 46.94) = P(20 < x < 45) = (45 - 20).04 = 1$

4.135   a. $f(x) = \dfrac{1}{d - c} \qquad (c \le x \le d)$

$\dfrac{1}{d - c} = \dfrac{1}{7 - 3} = \dfrac{1}{4}$

$f(x) = \begin{cases} \dfrac{1}{4} & (3 \le x \le 7) \\ 0 & \text{otherwise} \end{cases}$

b. $\mu = \dfrac{c + d}{2} = \dfrac{3 + 7}{2} = \dfrac{10}{2} - 5$

$\sigma = \dfrac{d - c}{\sqrt{12}} = \dfrac{7 - 3}{\sqrt{12}} = \dfrac{4}{\sqrt{12}} = 1.155$

c. $\mu \pm \sigma \Rightarrow 5 \pm 1.155 \Rightarrow (3.845,\ 6.155)$

$P(\mu - \sigma \le x \le \mu + \sigma) = P(3.845 \le x \le 6.155) = \dfrac{b - a}{d - c} = \dfrac{6.155 - 3.845}{7 - 3} = \dfrac{2.31}{4}$
$= .5775$

4.137 $P(x \ge a) = e^{-a/\theta} = e^{-a/1}$. Using Table V, Appendix B:

a. $P(x > 1) = e^{-1/1} = e^{-1} = .367879$

b. $P(x \le 3) = 1 - P(x > 3) = 1 - e^{-3/1} = 1 - e^{-3} = 1 - .049787 = .950213$

c. $P(x > 1.5) = e^{-1.5/1} = e^{-1.5} = .223130$

d. $P(x \le 5) = 1 - P(x > 5) = 1 - e^{-5/1} = 1 - e^{-5} = 1 - .006738 = .993262$

4.139 $f(x) = \dfrac{1}{d-c} = \dfrac{1}{200-100} = \dfrac{1}{100} = .01$

$f(x) = \begin{cases} .01 & (100 \le x \le 200) \\ 0 & otherwise \end{cases}$

$\mu = \dfrac{c+d}{2} = \dfrac{100+200}{2} = \dfrac{300}{2} = 150$

$\sigma = \dfrac{d-c}{\sqrt{12}} = \dfrac{200-100}{\sqrt{12}} = \dfrac{100}{\sqrt{12}} = 28.8675$

a. $\mu \pm 2\sigma \Rightarrow 150 \pm 2(28.8675) \Rightarrow 150 \pm 57.735 \Rightarrow (92.265, 207.735)$

$P(x < 92.265) + P(x > 207.735) = P(x < 100) + P(x > 200)$
$$= \quad 0 \quad + \quad 0$$
$$= 0$$

b. $\mu \pm 3\sigma \Rightarrow 150 \pm 3(28.8675) \Rightarrow 150 \pm 86.6025 \Rightarrow (63.3975, 236.6025)$

$P(63.3975 < x < 236.6025) = P(100 < x < 200) = (200 - 100)(.01) = 1$

c.   From **a**, $\mu \pm 2\sigma \Rightarrow (92.265, 207.735)$.

$P(92.265 < x < 207.735) = P(100 < x < 200) = (200 - 100)(.01) = 1$

4.141   a.   Let x = temperature with no bolt-on trace elements. Then x has a uniform distribution.

$f(x) = \dfrac{1}{d-c} \quad (c \le x \le d)$

$\dfrac{1}{d-c} = \dfrac{1}{290-260} = \dfrac{1}{30}$

Therefore, $f(x) = \begin{cases} \dfrac{1}{30} & (260 \le x \le 290) \\ 0 & otherwise \end{cases}$

$P(280 < x < 284) = (284 - 280)\dfrac{1}{30} = 4\left(\dfrac{1}{30}\right) = .133$

Let y = temperature with bolt-on trace elements. Then y has a uniform distribution.

$f(y) = \dfrac{1}{d-c} \quad (c \le y \le d)$

$\dfrac{1}{d-c} = \dfrac{1}{285-278} = \dfrac{1}{7}$

Therefore, $f(y) = \begin{cases} \dfrac{1}{7} & (278 \le y \le 285) \\ 0 & otherwise \end{cases}$

$P(280 < y < 284) = (284 - 280)\dfrac{1}{7} = 4\left(\dfrac{1}{7}\right) = .571$

b. $P(x \le 268) = (268 - 260)\dfrac{1}{30} = 8\left(\dfrac{1}{30}\right) = .267$

$P(y \le 268) = (268 - 260)(0) = 0$

4.143   a. $P(x > 2) = e^{-2/2.5} = e^{-.8} = .449329$ (using Table V, Appendix B)

b. $P(x < 5) = 1 - P(x \ge 5) = 1 - e^{-5/2.5} = 1 - e^{-2} = 1 - .135335 = .864665$
                       (using Table V, Appendix B)

4.145   To construct a relative frequency histogram for the data, we can use 7 measurement classes.

$$\text{Interval width} = \frac{\text{Largest number - smallest number}}{\text{Number of classes}} = \frac{98.0716 - .7434}{7} = 13.9$$

We will use an interval width of 14 and a starting value of .74335.

The measurement classes, frequencies, and relative frequencies are given in the table below.

Class	Measurement Class	Class Frequency	Class Relative Frequency
1	.74335 – 14.74335	6	6/40 = .15
2	14.74335 – 28.74335	4	.10
3	28.74335 – 42.74335	6	.15
4	42.74335 – 56.74335	6	.15
5	56.74335 – 70.74335	5	.125
6	70.74335 – 84.74335	4	.10
7	84.74335 – 98.74335	9	.225
		40	1.000

The histogram looks like the data could be from a uniform distribution. The last class (84.74335 – 98.74335) has a few more observations in it than we would expect. However, we cannot expect a perfect graph from a sample of only 40 observations.

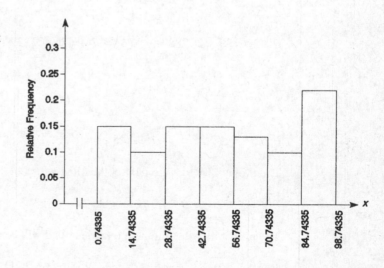

4.147   a.   The amount dispensed by the beverage machine is a continuous random variable since it can take on any value between 6.5 and 7.5 ounces.

   b.   Since the amount dispensed is random between 6.5 and 7.5 ounces, x is a uniform random variable.

$$f(x) = \frac{1}{d-c} \quad (c \le x \le d)$$

$$\frac{1}{d-c} = \frac{1}{7.5-6.5} = \frac{1}{1} = 1$$

Therefore, $f(x) = \begin{cases} 1 & (6.5 \le x \le 7.5) \\ 0 & \text{otherwise} \end{cases}$

The graph is as follows:

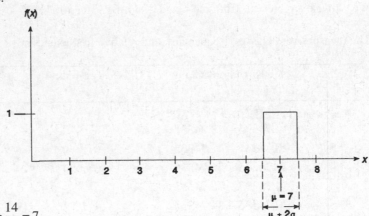

   c. $\mu = \dfrac{c+d}{2} = \dfrac{6.5+7.5}{2} = \dfrac{14}{2} = 7$

$\sigma = \dfrac{d-c}{\sqrt{12}} = \dfrac{7.5-6.5}{\sqrt{12}} = .2887$

$\mu \pm 2\sigma \Rightarrow 7 \pm 2(.2887) \Rightarrow 7 \pm .5774 \Rightarrow (6.422, 7.577)$

   d. $P(x \ge 7) = (7.5 - 7)(1) = .5$

   e. $P(x < 6) = 0$

   f. $P(6.5 \le x \le 7.25) = (7.25 - 6.5)(1) = .75$

   g.   The probability that the next bottle filled will contain more than 7.25 ounces is:

$P(x > 7.25) = (7.5 - 7.25)(1) = .25$

The probability that the next 6 bottles filled will contain more than 7.25 ounces is:

$P[(x > 7.25) \cap (x > 7.25) \cap (x > 7.25) \cap (x > 7.25) \cap (x > 7.25) \cap (x > 7.25)]$
$= [P(x > 7.25)]^6 = .25^6 = .0002$

4.149   a.   For $\mu = 17 = \theta$. To graph the distribution, we will pick several values of x and find the value of $f(x)$, where x = time between arrivals of the smaller craft at the pier.

$$f(x) = \frac{1}{\theta}e^{-x/\theta} = \frac{1}{17}e^{-x/17}$$

$$f(1) = \frac{1}{17}e^{-1/17} = .0555$$

$$f(3) = \frac{1}{17}e^{-3/17} = .0493$$

$$f(5) = \frac{1}{17}e^{-5/17} = .0438$$

$$f(7) = \frac{1}{17}e^{-7/17} = .0390$$

$$f(10) = \frac{1}{17}e^{-10/17} = .0327$$

$$f(15) = \frac{1}{17}e^{-15/17} = .0243$$

$$f(20) = \frac{1}{17}e^{-20/17} = .0181$$

$$f(25) = \frac{1}{17}e^{-25/17} = .0135$$

The graph is:

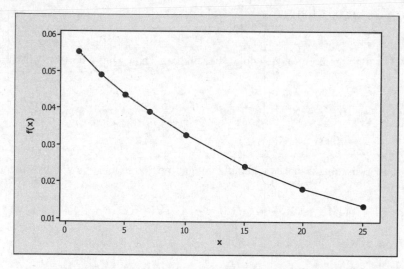

b.   We want to find the probability that the time between arrivals is less than 15 minutes.

$$P(x < 15) = 1 - P(x \geq 15) = 1 - e^{-15/17} = 1 - .4138 = .5862$$

4.151   a.   Let x = product's lifetime at the end of its lifetime. Then x has an exponential distribution with $\mu = 500,000$.

$$P(x < 700,000) = 1 - P(x \geq 700,000) = 1 - e^{-700000/5000000} = 1 - e^{-1.4} = 1 - .246597 = .753403$$

(Using Table V, Appendix B)

     b.   Let y = product's lifetime during its normal life. Then y has a uniform distribution.

$$f(y) = \frac{1}{d-c} \quad (c \leq y \leq d)$$

$$\frac{1}{d-c} = \frac{1}{1,000,000 - 100,000} = \frac{1}{900,000}$$

Therefore, $f(y) = \begin{cases} \dfrac{1}{900,000} & (100,000 \leq y \leq 1,000,000) \\ 0 & otherwise \end{cases}$

$$P(y < 700,000) = (700,000 - 100,000)\left(\frac{1}{900,000}\right) = .667$$

     c. $P(x < 830,000) = 1 - P(x \geq 830,000) = 1 - e^{-830000/5000000} = 1 - e^{-1.66} = 1 - .190139 = .809861$
(Using a calculator)

$$P(y < 830,000) = (830,000 - 100,000)\left(\frac{1}{900,000}\right) = .811$$

4.153   Let x = number of inches a gouge is from one end of the spindle. Then x has a uniform distribution with $f(x)$ as follows:

$$f(x) = \begin{cases} \dfrac{1}{d-c} = \dfrac{1}{18-0} = \dfrac{1}{18} & 0 \leq x \leq 18 \\ 0 & otherwise \end{cases}$$

In order to get at least 14 consecutive inches without a gouge, the gouge must be within 4 inches of either end. Thus, we must find:

$$P(x < 4) + P(x > 14) = (4 - 0)(1/18) + (18 - 14)(1/18) = 4/18 + 4/18 = 8/18 = .4444$$

4.155   a.   For $\theta = 250$, $P(x > a) = e^{-a/250}$

For $a = 300$ and $b = 200$, show $P(x > a + b) \geq P(x > a)P(x > b)$

$$P(x > 300 + 200) = P(x > 500) = e^{-500/250} = e^{-2} = .1353$$

$$P(x > 300)\, P(x > 200) = e^{-300/250}\, e^{-200/250} = e^{-1.2}\, e^{-.8} = .3012(.4493) = .1353$$

Since $P(x > 300 + 200) = P(x > 300)\, P(x > 200)$, then
$P(x > 300 + 200) \geq P(x > 300)\, P(x > 200)$

Also, show $P(x > 300 + 200) \leq P(x > 300)\, P(x > 200)$. Since we already showed that
$P(x > 300 + 200) = P(x > 300)\, P(x > 200)$,
then $P(x > 300 + 200) \leq P(x > 300)\, P(x > 200)$.

b.   Let $a = 50$ and $b = 100$. Show $P(x > a + b) \geq P(x > a) P(x > b)$

$P(x > 50 + 100) = P(x > 150) = e^{-150/250} = e^{-.6} = .5488$

$P(x > 50) P(x > 100) = e^{-50/250} e^{-100/250} = e^{-.2} e^{-.4} = .8187(.6703) = .5488$

Since $P(x > 50 + 100) = P(x > 50) P(x > 100)$, then
$P(x > 50 + 100) \geq P(x > 50) P(x > 100)$

Also, show $P(x > 50 + 100) \leq P(x > 50) P(x > 100)$. Since we already showed that
$P(x > 50 + 100) = P(x > 50) P(x > 100)$,
then $P(x > 50 + 100) \leq P(x > 50) P(x > 100)$.

c.   Show $P(x > a + b) \geq P(x > a) P(x > b)$
$P(x > a + b) = e^{-(a+b)/250} = e^{-a/250} e^{-b/250} = P(x > a) P(x > b)$

4.157   Solution will vary. See page 488 for Guided Solutions.

4.159 $E(x) = \mu = \sum xp(x) = 1(.2) + 2(.3) + 3(.2) + 4(.2) + 5(.1)$
$$= .2 + .6 + .6 + .8 + .5 = 2.7$$

$E(\bar{x}) = \sum \bar{x}p(\bar{x}) = 1.0(.04) + 1.5(.12) + 2.0(.17) + 2.5(.20) + 3.0(.20) + 3.5(.14) + 4.0(.08)$
$$+ 4.5(.04) + 5.0(.01)$$
$$= .04 + .18 + .34 + .50 + .60 + .49 + .32 + .18 + .05 = 2.7$$

4.161   Solution will vary. See page 488 for Guided Solutions.

4.163   The sampling distribution is approximately normal only if the sample size is sufficiently large or if the population being sampled from is normal.

4.165   a. $\mu_{\bar{x}} = \mu = 100, \sigma_{\bar{x}} = \dfrac{\sigma}{\sqrt{n}} = \dfrac{\sqrt{100}}{\sqrt{4}} = 5$

b. $\mu_{\bar{x}} = \mu = 100, \sigma_{\bar{x}} = \dfrac{\sigma}{\sqrt{n}} = \dfrac{\sqrt{100}}{\sqrt{25}} = 2$

c. $\mu_{\bar{x}} = \mu = 100, \sigma_{\bar{x}} = \dfrac{\sigma}{\sqrt{n}} = \dfrac{\sqrt{100}}{\sqrt{100}} = 1$

d. $\mu_{\bar{x}} = \mu = 100, \sigma_{\bar{x}} = \dfrac{\sigma}{\sqrt{n}} = \dfrac{\sqrt{100}}{\sqrt{50}} = 1.414$

e. $\mu_{\bar{x}} = \mu = 100, \sigma_{\bar{x}} = \dfrac{\sigma}{\sqrt{n}} = \dfrac{\sqrt{100}}{\sqrt{500}} = .447$

f. $\mu_{\bar{x}} = \mu = 100, \sigma_{\bar{x}} = \dfrac{\sigma}{\sqrt{n}} = \dfrac{\sqrt{100}}{\sqrt{1000}} = .316$

4.167   In Exercise 4.166, it was determined that the mean and standard deviation of the sampling distribution of the sample mean are 20 and 2 respectively. Using Table IV, Appendix B:

a. $P(\bar{x} < 16) = P\left(z < \dfrac{16-20}{2}\right) = P(z < -2) = .5 - .4772 = .0228$

b. $P(\bar{x} > 23) = P\left(z > \dfrac{23-20}{2}\right) = P(z > 1.50) = .5 - .4332 = .0668$

c. $P(\bar{x} > 25) = P\left(z > \dfrac{25-20}{2}\right) = P(z > 2.5) = .5 - .4938 = .0062$

d. $P(16 < \bar{x} < 22) = P\left(\dfrac{16-20}{2} < z < \dfrac{22-20}{2}\right) = P(-2 < z < 1)$

$$= .4772 + .3413 = .8185$$

e. $P(\bar{x} < 14) = P\left(z < \dfrac{14-20}{2}\right) = P(z < -3) = .5 - .4987 = .0013$

4.169   By the Central Limit Theorem, the sampling distribution of is approximately normal with $\mu_{\bar{x}} = \mu = 30$ and $\sigma_{\bar{x}} = \sigma / \sqrt{n} = 16 / \sqrt{100} = 1.6$. Using Table IV, Appendix B:

a. $P(\geq 28) = P\left(z \geq \dfrac{28-30}{1.6}\right) = P(z \geq -1.25) = .5 + .3944 = .8944$

b. $P(22.1 \leq \bar{x} \leq 26.8) = P\left(\dfrac{22.1-30}{1.6} \leq z \leq \dfrac{26.8-30}{1.6}\right) = P(-4.94 \leq z \leq -2) = .5 - .4772 = .0228$

c. $P(\bar{x} \leq 28.2) = P\left(z \leq \dfrac{28.2-30}{1.6}\right) = P(z \leq -1.13) = .5 - .3708 = .1292$

d. $P(\bar{x} \geq 27.0) = P\left(z \geq \dfrac{27.0-30}{1.6}\right) = P(z \geq -1.88) = .5 + .4699 = .9699$

4.171   a. $\mu_{\bar{x}} = \mu = 141$

b. $\sigma_{\bar{x}} = \dfrac{\sigma}{\sqrt{n}} = \dfrac{18}{\sqrt{100}} = 1.8$

c.   By the Central Limit Theorem, the sampling distribution of $\bar{x}$ is approximately normal.

d. $z = \dfrac{\bar{x} - \mu_{\bar{x}}}{\sigma_{\bar{x}}} = \dfrac{142-141}{1.8} = 0.56$

e. $P(\bar{x} > 142) = P(z > 0.56) = .5 - .2123 = .2877$ (Using Table IV, Appendix B)

4.173   By the Central Limit Theorem, the sampling distribution of $\bar{x}$ is approximately normal with $\mu_{\bar{x}} = \mu = 19$

and $\sigma_{\bar{x}} = \dfrac{\sigma}{\sqrt{n}} = \dfrac{65}{\sqrt{100}} = 6.5$.

Using Table IV, Appendix B,

$$P(\bar{x} < 10) = P\left(z < \frac{10 - 19}{6.5}\right) = P(z < -1.38) = .5 - .4162 = .0838$$

4.175   a.   By the Central Limit Theorem, the sampling distribution of $\bar{x}$ is approximately normal with a mean

$\mu_{\bar{x}} = \mu = .53$ and standard deviation $\sigma_{\bar{x}} = \dfrac{\sigma}{\sqrt{n}} = \dfrac{.193}{\sqrt{50}} = .0273$.

   b. $P(\bar{x} > .58) = P\left(z > \dfrac{.58 - .53}{.0273}\right) = P(z > 1.83) = .5 - .4664 = .0336$

   c.   If Before Tensioning: $\mu_{\bar{x}} = \mu = .53$

$$P(\bar{x} \geq .59) = P\left(z \geq \frac{.59 - .53}{.0273}\right) = P(z \geq 2.20) = .5 - .4861 = .0139$$

If After Tensioning: $\mu_{\bar{x}} = \mu = .58$

$$P(\bar{x} \geq .59) = P\left(z \geq \frac{.59 - .58}{.0273}\right) = P(z \geq 0.37) = .5 - .1443 = .3557$$

Since the probability of getting a maximum differential of .59 or more Before Tensioning is so small, it would be very unlikely that the measurements were obtained before tensioning. However, since the probability of getting a maximum differential of .59 or more After Tensioning is not small, it would not be unusual that the measurements were obtained after tensioning. Thus, most likely, the measurements were obtained After Tensioning.

4.177   a.   By the Central Limit Theorem, the sampling distribution of $\bar{x}$ is approximately normal with a mean

$\mu_{\bar{x}} = \mu = 6$ and standard deviation $\sigma_{\bar{x}} = \dfrac{\sigma}{\sqrt{n}} = \dfrac{10}{\sqrt{326}} = .5538$.

$$P(\bar{x} > 7.5) = P\left(z > \frac{7.5 - 6}{.5538}\right) = P(z > 2.71) = .5 - .4966 = .0034$$

(Using Table IV, Appendix B)

   b.   We first need to find the probability of observing the current data or anything more unusual if the true mean is 6.

$$P(\bar{x} \geq 300) = P\left(z \geq \frac{300 - 6}{.5538}\right) = P(z \geq 530.88) \approx .5 - .5 = 0$$

Since the probability of observing a sample mean of 300 ppb or higher is essentially 0 if the true mean is 6 ppb, we would infer that the true mean PFOA concentration for the population of people who live near DuPont's Teflon facility is not 6 ppb but higher than 6 ppb.

4.179   a.   By the Central Limit Theorem, the sampling distribution of is approximately normal
with $\mu_{\bar{x}} = \mu$ and $\sigma_{\bar{x}} = \sigma / \sqrt{n} = \sigma / \sqrt{50}$.

b. $\mu_{\bar{x}} = \mu = 40$ and $\sigma_{\bar{x}} = \sigma / \sqrt{50} = 12 / \sqrt{50} = 1.6971$.

$$P(\bar{x} \geq 44) = P\left(z \geq \frac{44 - 40}{1.6971} \right) = P(z \geq 2.36) = .5 - .4909 = .0091$$

(using Table IV, Appendix B)

c. $\mu \pm 2\sigma / \sqrt{n} \Rightarrow 40 \pm 2(1.6971) \Rightarrow 40 \pm 3.3942 \Rightarrow (36.6058, 43.3942)$

$$P(36.6058 \leq \bar{x} \leq 43.3942) = P\left(\frac{36.6058 - 40}{1.6971} \leq z \leq \frac{43.3942 - 40}{1.6971} \right)$$
$$= P(-2 \leq z \leq 2) = 2(.4772) = .9544$$
(using Table IV, Appendix B)

4.181   For $n = 50$, we can use the Central Limit Theorem to decide the shape of the distribution of the sample
mean bacterial counts. For the handrubbing sample, the sampling distribution of $\bar{x}$ is approximately
normal with a mean of $\mu = 35$ and standard deviation $\dfrac{\sigma}{\sqrt{n}} = \dfrac{59}{\sqrt{50}} = 8.344$. For the handwashing sample,
the sampling distribution of $\bar{x}$ is approximately normal with a mean of $\mu = 69$ and standard deviation
$\dfrac{\sigma}{\sqrt{n}} = \dfrac{106}{\sqrt{50}} = 14.991$.

For Handrubbing:

$$P(\bar{x} < 30 \mid \mu = 35) = P\left(z < \frac{30 - 35}{8.344} \right) = P(z < -.60) = .5 - .2257 = .2743$$

(using Table IV, Appendix B)

For Handwashing:

$$P(\bar{x} < 30 \mid \mu = 69) = P\left(z < \frac{30 - 69}{14.991} \right) = P(z < -2.60) = .5 - .4953 = .0047$$

(using Table IV, Appendix B)

Since the probability of getting a sample mean of less than 30 for the handrubbing is not small compared
with that for the handwashing, the sample of workers probably came from the handrubbing group.

4.183 $p(x) = \dbinom{n}{x} p^x q^{n-x} \quad x = 0, 1, 2, \ldots , n$

a. $P(x = 3) = p(3) = \dbinom{7}{3} .5^3 .5^4 = \dfrac{7!}{3!4!} .5^3 .5^4 = 35(.125)(.0625) = .2734$

b. $P(x = 3) = p(3) = \dbinom{4}{3} .8^3 .2^1 = \dfrac{4!}{3!1!} .8^3 .2^1 = 4(.512)(.2) = .4096$

c. $P(x = 1) = p(1) = \dbinom{15}{1} .1^1 .9^{14} = \dfrac{15!}{1!14!} .1^1 .9^{14} = 15(.1)(.228768) = .3432$

4.185   From Table II, Appendix B:

a. $P(x = 14) = P(x \le 14) - P(x \le 13) = .584 - .392 = .192$

b. $P(x \le 12) = .228$

c. $P(x > 12) = 1 - P(x \le 12) = 1 - .228 = .772$

d. $P(9 \le x \le 18) = P(x \le 18) - P(x \le 8) = .992 - .005 = .987$

e. $P(8 < x < 18) = P(x \le 17) - P(x \le 8) = .965 - .005 = .960$

f. $\mu = np = 20(.7) = 14$

$\sigma^2 = npq = 20(.7)(.3) = 4.2, \ \sigma = \sqrt{4.2} = 2.049$

g. $\mu \pm 2\sigma \Rightarrow 14 \pm 2(2.049) \Rightarrow 14 \pm 4.098 \Rightarrow (9.902, 18.098)$

$P(9.902 < x < 18.098) = P(10 \le x \le 18) = P(x \le 18) - P(x \le 9) = .992 - .017 = .975$

4.187   a.   Poisson

b.   Binomial

c.   Binomial

4.189   a.   Discrete - The number of damaged inventory items is countable.

b.   Continuous - The average monthly sales can take on any value within an acceptable limit.

c.   Continuous - The number of square feet can take on any positive value.

d.   Continuous - The length of time we must wait can take on any positive value.

4.191   a. $P(z \le 2.1) = A_1 + A_2$
$= .5 + .4821$
$= .9821$

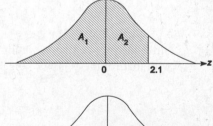

b. $P(z \ge 2.1) = A_2 = .5 - A_1$
$= .5 - .4821$
$= .0179$

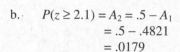

c. $P(z \ge -1.65) = A_1 + A_2$
$= .4505 + .5000$
$= .9505$

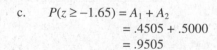

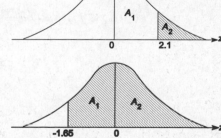

d. $P(-2.13 \le z \le -.41)$

$\qquad = P(-2.13 \le z \le 0) - P(-.41 \le z \le 0)$

$\qquad = .4834 - .1591$

$\qquad = .3243$

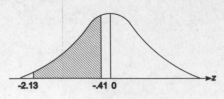

e. $P(-1.45 \le z \le 2.15) = A_1 + A_2$

$\qquad\qquad\qquad\qquad\quad = .4265 + .4842$

$\qquad\qquad\qquad\qquad\quad = .9107$

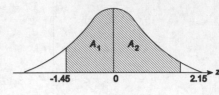

f. $P(z \le -1.43) = A_1 = .5 - A_2$

$\qquad\qquad\qquad\quad = .5000 - .4236$

$\qquad\qquad\qquad\quad = .0764$

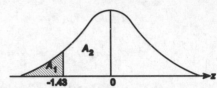

4.193   a.   For the probability density function, $f(x) = \dfrac{e^{-x/7}}{7}$, $x > 0$, x is an exponential random variable.

        b.   For the probability density function, $f(x) = \dfrac{1}{20}$, $5 < x < 25$, x is a uniform random variable.

        c.   For the probability function, $f(x) = \dfrac{e^{-.5[(x-10)/5]^2}}{5\sqrt{2\pi}}$, x is a normal random variable.

4.195   a. $P(x \le 80) = P\left(z \le \dfrac{80 - 75}{10}\right) = P(z \le .5)$

$\qquad\qquad\qquad = .5000 + .1915 = .6915$

$\qquad\qquad\qquad$ (Table IV, Appendix B)

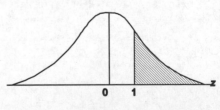

        b. $P(x \ge 85) = P\left(z \ge \dfrac{85 - 75}{10}\right) = P(z \ge 1)$

$\qquad\qquad\qquad = .5000 - .3413 = .1587$

$\qquad\qquad\qquad$ (Table IV, Appendix B)

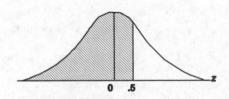

        c. $P(70 \le x \le 75) = P\left(\dfrac{70 - 75}{10} \le z \le \dfrac{75 - 75}{10}\right)$

$\qquad\qquad\qquad\qquad = P(-.5 \le z \le 0)$

$\qquad\qquad\qquad\qquad = P(0 \le z \le .5) = .1915$

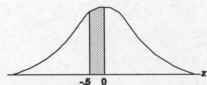

        d. $P(x > 80) = 1 - P(x \le 80) = 1 - .6915 = .3085$ (Refer to part **a**.)

        e. $P(x = 78) = 0$, since a single point does not have an area.

f. $P(x \le 110) = P\left(z \le \dfrac{110-75}{10}\right) = P(z \le 3.5)$

   $\approx .5000 + .5000 = 1.0$
   (Table IV, Appendix B)

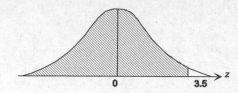

4.197 x is normal random variable with $\mu = 40$, $\sigma^2 = 36$, and $\sigma = 6$.

a. $P(x \ge x_0) = .10$

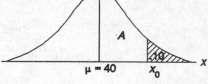

   So, $A = .5000 - .1000 = .4000$.
   $z_0 = 1.28$ (See part **a**.)
   To find x_0, substitute the values into the z-score formula:

   $$z_0 = \frac{x_0 - \mu}{\sigma} \Rightarrow 1.28 = \frac{x_0 - 40}{6} \Rightarrow x_0 = 1.28(6) + 40 = 47.68$$

b. $P(\mu \le x \le x_0) = .40$

   Look up the area .4000 in the body of Table IV,
   Appendix B; (take the closest value) $z_0 = 1.28$.

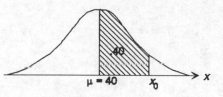

   To find x_0, substitute the values into the z-score formula:

   $$z_0 = \frac{x_0 - \mu}{\sigma} \Rightarrow 1.28 = \frac{x_0 - 40}{6} \Rightarrow x_0 = 40 + 6(1.28) = 47.68$$

c. $P(x < x_0) = .05$

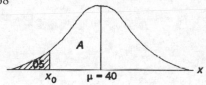

   So, $A = .5000 - .0500 = .4500$.

   Look up the area .4500 in the body of Table IV, Appendix B; $z_0 = -1.645$.   (.45 is halfway between
   .4495 and .4505; therefore, we average the z-scores

   $$\frac{1.64 + 1.65}{2} = 1.645$$

   z_0 is negative since the graph shows z_0 is on the left side of 0.

   To find x_0, substitute the values into the z-score formula:

   $$z_0 = \frac{x_0 - \mu}{\sigma} \Rightarrow -1.645 = \frac{x_0 - 40}{6} \Rightarrow x_0 = -1.645(6) + 40 = 30.13$$

d. $P(x > x_0) = .40$
   So, $A = .5000 - .4000 = .1000$.

   Look up the area .1000 in the body of Table IV, Appendix
   B; (take the closest value) $z_0 = .25$.

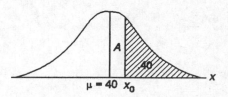

   To find x_0, substitute the values into the z-score formula:

   $$z_0 = \frac{x_0 - \mu}{\sigma} \Rightarrow .25 = \frac{x_0 - 40}{6} \Rightarrow x_0 = 40 + 6(.25) = 41.5$$

e. $P(x_0 \le x < \mu) = .45$

Look up the area .4500 in the body of Table IV, Appendix B; $z_0 = -1.645$. (.45 is halfway between .4495 and .4505; therefore, we average the z-scores

$$\frac{1.64 + 1.65}{2} = 1.645$$

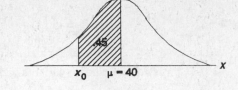

z_0 is negative since the graph shows z_0 is on the left side of 0.

To find x_0, substitute the values into the z-score formula:

$$z_0 = \frac{x_0 - \mu}{\sigma} \Rightarrow -1.645 = \frac{x_0 - 40}{6} \Rightarrow x_0 = 40 - 6(1.645) = 30.13$$

4.199   By the Central Limit Theorem, the sampling distribution of is approximately normal.

$$\mu_{\bar{x}} = \mu = 19.6, \ \sigma_{\bar{x}} = \frac{3.2}{\sqrt{68}} = .388$$

a. $P(\bar{x} \le 19.6) = P\left(z \le \dfrac{19.6 - 19.6}{.388} \right) = P(z \le 0) = .5$ (using Table IV, Appendix B)

b. $P(\bar{x} \le 19) = P\left(z \le \dfrac{19 - 19.6}{.388} \right) = P(z \le -1.55) = .5 - .4394 = .0606$

(using Table IV, Appendix B)

c. $P(\bar{x} \ge 20.1) = P\left(z \ge \dfrac{20.1 - 19.6}{.388} \right) = P(z \ge 1.29) = .5 - .4015 = .0985$

(using Table IV, Appendix B)

d. $P(19.2 \le \bar{x} \le 20.6) = P\left(\dfrac{19.2 - 19.6}{.388} \le z \le \dfrac{20.6 - 19.6}{.388} \right)$

$$= P(-1.03 \le z \le 2.58) = .3485 + .4951 = .8436$$

(using Table IV, Appendix B)

4.201   Given: $\mu = 100$ and $\sigma = 10$

n	1	5	10	20	30	40	50
$\dfrac{\sigma}{\sqrt{n}}$	10	4.472	3.162	2.236	1.826	1.581	1.414

The graph of $\sigma / \sqrt{n}$ against n is given here:

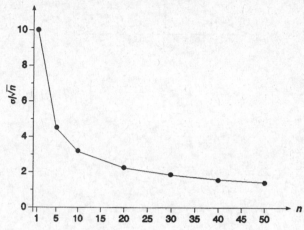

4.203   a. $\displaystyle\sum_{i=1}^{6} p(x_i) = p(0) + p(1) + p(2) + p(3) + p(4) + p(5)$

$= .0102 + .0768 + .2304 + .3456 + .2592 + .0778 = 1.0000$

b. $P(x = 4) = .2592$

c. $P(x < 2) = P(x = 0) + P(x = 1) = .0102 + .0768 = .0870$

d. $P(x \geq 3) = P(x = 3) + P(x = 4) + P(x = 5) = .3456 + .2592 + .0778 = .6826$

e. $\mu = E(x) = \displaystyle\sum_{i=1}^{6} x_i p(x_i) = 0(.0102) + 1(.0768) + 2(.2304) + 3(.3456) + 4(.2592) + 5(.0778)$

$= 0 + .0768 + .4608 + 1.0368 + 1.0368 + .3890 = 3.0002$

On the average, 3 out of every 5 dentists will use nitrous oxide.

4.205   a.   For this problem, $c = 0$ and $d = 1$.

$$f(x) = \begin{cases} \dfrac{1}{d-c} = \dfrac{1}{1-0} & (0 \leq x \leq 1) \\ 0 & \text{otherwise} \end{cases}$$

$\mu = \dfrac{c+d}{2} = \dfrac{0+1}{2} = .5$

$\sigma^2 = \dfrac{(d-c)^2}{12} = \dfrac{(1-0)^2}{12} = \dfrac{1}{12} = .0833$

$\sigma = \sqrt{.0833} = .289$

b. $P(.2 < x < .4) = (.4 - .2)(1) = .2$

c. $P(x > .995) = (1 - .995)(1) = .005$. Since the probability of observing a trajectory greater than .995 is so small, we would not expect to see a trajectory exceeding .995.

4.207   a. $\mu_{\bar{x}} = \mu = 89.34;\ \sigma_{\bar{x}} = \dfrac{\sigma}{\sqrt{n}} = \dfrac{7.74}{\sqrt{35}} = 1.31$

b.

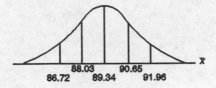

c. $P(\bar{x} > 88) = P\left(z > \dfrac{88 - 89.34}{1.31}\right) = P(z > -1.02) = .5 + .3461 = .8461$

(using Table IV, Appendix B)

d. $P(\bar{x} < 87) = P\left(z < \dfrac{87 - 89.34}{1.31}\right) = P(z < -1.79) = .5 - .4633 = .0367$

(using Table IV, Appendix B)

4.209   Let x = interarrival time between patients.   Then x is an exponential random variable with a mean of 4 minutes.

a. $P(x < 1) = 1 - P(x \geq 1)$
$= 1 - e^{-1/4}$
$= 1 - e^{-.25}$
$= 1 - .778801$
$= .221199$

b.   Assuming that the interarrival times are independent,
P(next 4 interarrival times are all less than 1 minute)
$= \{P(x < 1)\}^{4}$
$= .221199^{4}$
$= .002394$

c. $P(x > 10) = e^{-10/4}$
$= e^{-2.5}$
$= .082085$

4.211   a.   Let x_1 = repair time for machine 1. Then x_1 has an exponential distribution with $\mu_1 = 1$ hour.

$P(x_1 > 1) = e^{-1/1} = e^{-1} = .367879$ (using Table V, Appendix B)

b.   Let x_2 = repair time for machine 2. Then x_2 has an exponential distribution with $\mu_2 = 2$ hours.

$P(x_2 > 1) = e^{-1/2} = e^{-.5} = .606531$ (using Table V, Appendix B)

c.   Let x_3 = repair time for machine 3. Then x_3 has an exponential distribution with $\mu_3 = .5$ hours.

$P(x_3 > 1) = e^{-1/.5} = e^{-2} = .135335$ (using Table V, Appendix B)

Since the mean repair time for machine 4 is the same as for machine 3, $P(x_4 > 1) = P(x_3 > 1) = .135335$.

d.   The only way that the repair time for the entire system will not exceed 1 hour is if all four machines are repaired in less than 1 hour. Thus, the probability that the repair time for the entire system exceeds 1 hour is:

P(Repair time entire system exceeds 1 hour)
$$= 1 - P((x_1 \le 1) \cap (x_2 \le 1) \cap (x_3 \le 1) \cap (x_4 \le 1))$$
$$= 1 - P(x_1 \le 1)P(x_2 \le 1)P(x_3 \le 1)P(x_4 \le 1)$$
$$= 1 - (1 - .367879)(1 - .606531)(1 - .135335)(1 - .135335)$$
$$= 1 - (.632121)(.393469)(.864665)(.864665) = 1 - .185954 = .814046$$

4.213   a.   In order for the number of deaths to follow a Poisson distribution, we must assume that the probability of a death is the same for any week. We must also assume that the number of deaths in any week is independent of any other week.

The first assumption may not be valid. The probability of a death may not be the same for every week. The number of passengers varies from week to week, so the probability of a death may change. Also, things such as weather, which varies from week to week may increase or decrease the chance of derailment.

b. $E(x) = \lambda = 20$
$\sigma = \sqrt{\lambda} = \sqrt{20} = 4.47$

c.   The z-score corresponding to $x = 4$ is:
$$z = \frac{4 - 20}{4.47} = -3.58$$

Since this z-score is more than 3 standard deviations from the mean, it would be very unlikely that only 4 or fewer deaths occur next week.

d.   Using Table III, Appendix B with $\lambda = 20$,

$$P(x \le 4) = 0.000$$

This probability is consistent with the answer in part **c**. The probability of 4 or fewer deaths is essentially zero, which is very unlikely.

4.215   Using MINITAB, the stem-and-leaf display is:

```
Stem-and-leaf of Time      N  = 49
Leaf Unit = 0.10

    (26)    1 00001122222344444445555679
     23     2 11446799
     15     3 002899
      9     4 11125
      4     5 24
      2     6
      2     7 8
      1     8
      1     9
      1    10 1
```

The data are skewed to the right, and do not appear to be normally distributed.

Using MINITAB, the descriptive statistics are:

Variable	N	Mean	Median	TrMean	StDev	SE Mean
Time	49	2.549	1.700	2.333	1.828	0.261

Variable	Minimum	Maximum	Q1	Q3
Time	1.000	10.100	1.350	3.500

$\bar{x} \pm s \Rightarrow 2.549 \pm 1.828 \Rightarrow (0.721, 4.377)$

$\bar{x} \pm 2s \Rightarrow 2.549 \pm 2(1.828) \Rightarrow 2.549 \pm 3.656 \Rightarrow (\pm 1.107, 6.205)$

$\bar{x} \pm 3s \Rightarrow 2.549 \pm 3(1.828) \Rightarrow 2.549 \pm 5.484 \Rightarrow (-2.935, 8.033)$

Of the 49 measurements, 44 are in the interval (0.721, 4.377). The proportion is 44/49 = .898. This is much larger than the proportion (.68) stated by the Empirical Rule.

Of the 49 measurements, 47 are in the interval (−1.107, 6.205). The proportion is 47/49 = .959. This is close to the proportion (.95) stated by the Empirical Rule.

Of the 49 measurements, 48 are in the interval (−2.935, 8.033). The proportion is 48/49 = .980. This is smaller than the proportion (1.00) stated by the Empirical Rule.
This would imply that the data are not normal.
IQR = $Q_U - Q_L$ = 3.500 − 1.350 = 2.15.   IQR/s = 2.15/1.828 = 1.176. If the data are normally distributed, this ratio should be close to 1.3. Since 1.176 is smaller than 1.3, this indicates that the data may not be normal.

Using MINITAB, the normal probability plot is:

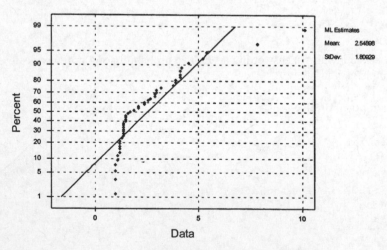

Normal Probability Plot for Time

Since this plot is not a straight line, the data are not normal.

All four checks indicate that the data are not normal.

4.217   Let x equal the difference between the actual weight and recorded weight (the error of measurement). The random variable x is normally distributed with $\mu = 592$ and $\sigma = 628$.

  a.   We want to find the probability that the weigh-in-motion equipment understates the actual weight of the truck. This would be true if the error of measurement is positive.

$$P(x > 0) = P\left(z > \frac{0 - 592}{628}\right)$$
$$= P(z > -.94)$$
$$= .5000 + .3264$$
$$= .8264$$

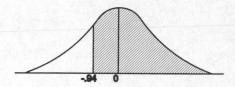

  b. $P(\text{overstate the weight}) = 1 - P(\text{understate the weight})$
$$= 1 - .8264$$
$$= .1736 \quad (\text{Refer to part } \mathbf{a}.)$$

For 100 measurements, approximately $100(.1736) = 17.36$ or 17 times the weight would be overstated.

  c. $$P(x > 400) = P\left(z > \frac{400 - 592}{628}\right)$$
$$= P(z > -.31)$$
$$= .5000 + .1217$$
$$= .6217$$

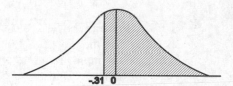

  d.   We want $P(\text{understate the weight}) = .5$
To understate the weight, $x > 0$. Thus, we want to find μ so that $P(x > 0) = .5$

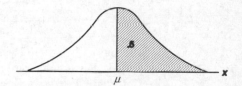

$$P(x > 0) = P\left(z > \frac{0 - \mu}{628}\right) = .5$$

From Table IV, Appendix B, $z_0 = 0$. To find μ, substitute into the z-score formula:
$$z_0 = \frac{x_0 - \mu}{\sigma} \Rightarrow 0 = \frac{0 - \mu}{628} \Rightarrow \mu = 0$$

Thus, the mean error should be set at 0.
We want $P(\text{understate the weight}) = .4$

To understate the weight, $x > 0$. Thus, we want to find μ so that $P(x > 0) = .4$

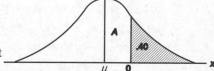

$A = .5 - .40 = .1$. Look up the area .1000 in the body of Table IV, Appendix B, $z_0 = .25$.

To find μ, substitute into the z-score formula:

$$z_0 = \frac{x_0 - \mu}{\sigma} \Rightarrow .25 = \frac{0 - \mu}{628} \Rightarrow \mu = 0 - (.25)628 = -157$$

Thus, the mean error should be set at -157.

4.219   a. $\mu = n \cdot p = 25(.05) = 1.25$

$$\sigma = \sqrt{npq} = \sqrt{25(.05)(.95)} = 1.09$$

Since μ is not an integer, x could not equal its mean.

b.   The event is $(x \geq 5)$. From Table II with $n = 25$ and $p = .05$:

$$P(x \geq 5) = 1 - P(x \leq 4) = 1 - .993 = .007$$

c.   Since the probability obtained in part **b** is so small, it is unlikely that 5% applies to this agency. The percentage is probably greater than 5%.

4.221   Let x = number of grants awarded to the north side in 140 trials. The random variable x has a hypergeometric distribution with $N = 743$, $n = 140$, and $r = 601$.

a. $\mu = E(x) = \dfrac{nr}{N} = \dfrac{140(601)}{743} = 113.24$

$$\sigma^2 = \frac{r(N-r)n(N-n)}{N^2(N-1)} = \frac{601(743-601)140(743-140)}{743^2(743-1)} = 17.5884$$

$$\sigma = \sqrt{17.5884} = 4.194$$

b.   If the grants were awarded at random, we would expect approximately 113 to be awarded to the north side. We observed 140. The z-score associated with 140 is:

$$z = \frac{x - \mu}{\sigma} = \frac{140 - 113.24}{4.194} = 6.38$$

Because this z-score is so large, it would be extremely unlikely to observe all 140 grants to the north side if they are randomly selected. Thus, we would conclude that the grants were not randomly selected.

4.223   We know from the Empirical Rule that almost all the observations are larger than $\mu - 2\sigma$. ($\approx 95\%$ are between $\mu - 2\sigma$ and $\mu + 2\sigma$). Thus $\mu - 2\sigma > 100$.

For the binomial, $\mu = np = n(.4)$ and $\sigma = \sqrt{npq} = \sqrt{n(.4)(.6)} = \sqrt{.24n}$

$$\mu - 2\sigma > 100 \Rightarrow .4n - 2\sqrt{.24n} > 100 \Rightarrow .4n - .98\sqrt{n} - 100 > 0$$

Solving for $\sqrt{n}$, we get:

$$\sqrt{n} = \frac{.98 \pm \sqrt{.98^2 - 4(.4)(-100)}}{2(.4)} = \frac{.98 \pm 12.687}{.8}$$

$$\Rightarrow \sqrt{n} = 17.084 \Rightarrow n = 17.084^2 = 291.9 \approx 292$$

4.225 Even though the number of flaws per piece of siding has a Poisson distribution, the Central Limit Theorem implies that the distribution of the sample mean will be approximately normal with $\mu_{\bar{x}} = \mu = 2.5$ and

$$\sigma_{\bar{x}} = \frac{\sigma}{\sqrt{n}} = \frac{\sqrt{2.5}}{\sqrt{35}} = .2673 \ . \ \text{Therefore,}$$

$$P(\bar{x} > 2.1) + P\left(z > \frac{2.1 - 2.5}{\sqrt{2.5}/\sqrt{35}}\right) = P(z > -1.50) = .5 + .4332 = .9332 \text{ (using Table IV, Appendix B)}$$

4.227 Using MINITAB, the descriptive statistics are:

Descriptive Statistics: INSOMNIA

```
Variable    N    Mean   StDev  Minimum    Q1  Median     Q3  Maximum
INSOMNIA   40   5.935   5.392    1.300  2.250   3.650  7.675   22.800
```

To see if the mean time to fall asleep for those taking melatonin is different from those taking a placebo, we will see how unusual it is to observe a sample mean of 5.935 if the true mean is 15.

$$P(\bar{x} \le 5.935) = P\left(z \le \frac{5.935 - 15}{5.392 / \sqrt{40}}\right) = P(z \le -10.63) \approx .5 - .5 = 0 \quad \text{(Using Table IV, Appendix B.)}$$

Since this probability is so small, we would infer that the mean time to fall asleep for those taking melatonin is not 15 minutes, but something less than 15 minutes.

Chapter 5
Inferences Based on a Single Sample:
Estimation with Confidence Intervals

5.1   a.   For $\alpha = .10$, $\alpha/2 = .10/2 = .05$. $z_{\alpha/2} = z_{.05}$ is the z-score with .05 of the area to the right of it. The area between 0 and $z_{.05}$ is $.5 - .05 = .4500$. Using Table IV, Appendix B, $z_{.05} = 1.645$.

   b.   For $\alpha = .01$, $\alpha/2 = .01/2 = .005$. $z_{\alpha/2} = z_{.005}$ is the z-score with .005 of the area to the right of it. The area between 0 and $z_{.005}$ is $.5 - .005 = .4950$. Using Table IV, Appendix B, $z_{.005} = 2.575$.

   c.   For $\alpha = .05$, $\alpha/2 = .05/2 = .025$. $z_{\alpha/2} = z_{.025}$ is the z-score with .025 of the area to the right of it. The area between 0 and $z_{.025}$ is $.5 - .025 = .4750$. Using Table IV, Appendix B, $z_{.025} = 1.96$.

   d.   For $\alpha = .20$, $\alpha/2 = .20/2 = .10$. $z_{\alpha/2} = z_{.10}$ is the z-score with .10 of the area to the right of it. The area between 0 and $z_{.10}$ is $.5 - .10 = .4000$. Using Table IV, Appendix B, $z_{.10} = 1.28$.

5.3   a.   For confidence coefficient .95, $\alpha = .05$ and $\alpha/2 = .05/2 = .025$. From Table IV, Appendix B, $z_{.025} = 1.96$. The confidence interval is:

$$\bar{x} \pm z_{.025} \frac{\sigma}{\sqrt{n}} \Rightarrow 28 \pm 1.96 \frac{\sqrt{12}}{\sqrt{75}} \Rightarrow 28 \pm .784 \Rightarrow (27.216, 28.784)$$

   b. $$\bar{x} \pm z_{.025} \frac{\sigma}{\sqrt{n}} \Rightarrow 102 \pm 1.96 \frac{\sqrt{22}}{\sqrt{200}} \Rightarrow 102 \pm .65 \Rightarrow (101.35, 102.65)$$

   c. $$\bar{x} \pm z_{.025} \frac{\sigma}{\sqrt{n}} \Rightarrow 15 \pm 1.96 \frac{.3}{\sqrt{100}} \Rightarrow 15 \pm .0588 \Rightarrow (14.9412, 15.0588)$$

   d. $$\bar{x} \pm z_{.025} \frac{\sigma}{\sqrt{n}} \Rightarrow 4.05 \pm 1.96 \frac{.83}{\sqrt{100}} \Rightarrow 4.05 \pm .163 \Rightarrow (3.887, 4.213)$$

   e.   No. Since the sample size in each part was large (n ranged from 75 to 200), the Central Limit Theorem indicates that the sampling distribution of is approximately normal.

5.5   a.   For confidence coefficient .95, $\alpha = .05$ and $\alpha/2 = .05/2 = .025$. From Table IV, Appendix B, $z_{.025} = 1.96$. The confidence interval is:

$$\bar{x} \pm z_{\alpha/2} \frac{s}{\sqrt{n}} \Rightarrow 26.2 \pm 1.96 \frac{4.1}{\sqrt{70}} \Rightarrow 26.2 \pm .96 \Rightarrow (25.24, 27.16)$$

   b.   The confidence coefficient of .95 means that in repeated sampling, 95% of all confidence intervals constructed will include μ.

   c.   For confidence coefficient .99, $\alpha = .01$ and $\alpha/2 = .01/2 = .005$. From Table IV, Appendix B, $z_{.005} = 2.58$. The confidence interval is:

$$\bar{x} \pm z_{\alpha/2} \frac{s}{\sqrt{n}} \Rightarrow 26.2 \pm 2.58 \frac{4.1}{\sqrt{70}} \Rightarrow 26.2 \pm 1.26 \Rightarrow (24.94, 27.46)$$

   d.   As the confidence coefficient increases, the width of the confidence interval also increases.

e.   Yes. Since the sample size is 70, the Central Limit Theorem applies. This ensures the distribution of is normal, regardless of the original distribution.

5.7   A point estimator is a single value used to estimate the parameter, μ. An interval estimator is two values, an upper and lower bound, which define an interval with which we attempt to enclose the parameter, ▯. An interval estimate also has a measure of confidence associated with it.

5.9   Yes. As long as the sample size is sufficiently large, the Central Limit Theorem says the distribution of is approximately normal regardless of the original distribution.

5.11   For confidence coefficient .90, $\alpha = 1 - .90 = .10$ and $\alpha/2 = .10/2 = .05$. From Table IV, Appendix B, $z_{.05} = 1.645$. The 90% confidence interval is:

$$\bar{x} \pm z_{\alpha/2} \frac{s}{\sqrt{n}} \Rightarrow 6,563 \pm 1.645 \frac{2,484}{\sqrt{1,751}} \Rightarrow 6,563 \pm 97.65 \Rightarrow (6,465.35, \ 6,660.65)$$

We are 90% confident that the true mean expenses per full-time equivalent employees of all U.S. Army hospitals is between $6,465.35 and $6,660.65.

5.13   a.   For confidence coefficient .99, $\alpha = 1 - .99 = .01$ and $\alpha/2 = .01/2 = .005$. From Table IV, Appendix B, $z_{.005} = 2.58$. The 99% confidence interval is:

$$\bar{x} \pm z_{\alpha/2} \frac{s}{\sqrt{n}} \Rightarrow 4.25 \pm 2.58 \frac{12.02}{\sqrt{56}} \Rightarrow 4.25 \pm 4.14 \Rightarrow (0.11, \ 8.39)$$

b.   We are 99% confident that the true mean number of blogs/forums per site of all Fortune 500 firms that provide blogs and forums for marketing tools is between 0.11 and 8.39.

c.   No. Since our sample size is 56, the sampling distribution of $\bar{x}$ is approximately normal by the Central Limit Theorem.

5.15   a.   The target parameter is the population mean 2008 salary of these 500 CEOs who participated in the *Forbes'* survey.

b.   Using MINITAB, a sample of 50 CEOs was selected. The ranks of the 50 selected are: 9, 10, 14, 18, 19, 22, 25, 32, 38, 39, 45, 49, 50, 55, 60, 66, 69, 77, 96, 104, 106, 115, 147, 152, 192, 197, 209, 213, 229, 241, 245, 261, 268, 278, 283, 292, 305, 309, 325, 337, 342, 358, 364, 370, 376, 384, 405, 417, 433, 470.

c.   Using MINITAB, the descriptive statistics are:

Descriptive Statistics: PAY2005 ($mil)

Variable	N	Mean	StDev	Minimum	Q1	Median	Q3	Maximum
PAY ($mil)	50	19.56	19.95	1.23	4.70	8.99	32.78	73.17

The sample mean is $\bar{x} = 19.56$ and the sample standard deviation is $s = 19.95$.

d. Using MINITAB, the descriptive statistics for the entire data set is:

Descriptive Statistics: Pay ($mil)

```
Variable       N     Mean    StDev     Minimum      Q1  Median      Q3  Maximum
Pay ($mil)   497   12.874   18.502   0.000000000   3.395   6.470   14.250  192.920
```

From the above, the standard deviation of the population is $18.5 million.

e. For confidence coefficient .99, $\alpha = .01$ and $\alpha/2 = .01/2 = .005$. From Table IV, Appendix B, $z_{.005} = 2.58$. The confidence interval is:

$$\bar{x} \pm z_{\alpha/2} \frac{s}{\sqrt{n}} \Rightarrow 19.56 \pm 2.58 \frac{19.95}{\sqrt{50}} \Rightarrow 19.56 \pm 7.28 \Rightarrow (12.28, \ 26.84)$$

f. We are 99% confident that the true mean salary of all 500 CEOs in the *Forbes'* survey is between $12.28 million and $26.84 million.

g. From part d, the true mean salary of all 500 CEOs is $12.87 million. This value does fall within the 99% confidence interval that we found in part e.

5.17 a. An estimate of the true mean Mach rating score of all purchasing managers is $\bar{x} = 99.6$.

b. For confidence coefficient .95, $\alpha = 1 - .95 = .05$ and $\alpha/2 = .05/2 = .025$. From Table IV, Appendix B, $z_{.025} = 1.96$. The 95% confidence interval is:

$$\bar{x} \pm z_{\alpha/2} \frac{s}{\sqrt{n}} \Rightarrow 99.6 \pm 1.96 \frac{12.6}{\sqrt{122}} \Rightarrow 99.6 \pm 2.24 \Rightarrow (97.36, \ 101.84)$$

c. We are 95% confident that the true Mach rating score of all purchasing managers is between 97.36 and 101.84.

d. Yes, there is evidence to dispute this claim. We are 95% confident that the true mean Mach rating score is between 97.36 and 101.84. It would be very unlikely that the true means Mach scores is as low as 85.

5.19 To answer the question, we will first form 90% confidence intervals for each of the 2 SAT scores.

For confidence coefficient .90, $\alpha = .10$ and $\alpha/2 = .10/2 = .05$. From Table IV, Appendix B, $z_{.05} = 1.645$. The confidence interval is:

$$\bar{x} \pm z_{\alpha/2} \frac{s}{\sqrt{n}} \Rightarrow 19 \pm 1.645 \frac{65}{\sqrt{265}} \Rightarrow 19 \pm 6.57 \Rightarrow (12.43, \ 25.57)$$

We are 90% confident that the mean change in SAT-Mathematics score is between 12.43 and 25.57 points.

For confidence coefficient .90, $\alpha = .10$ and $\alpha/2 = .10/2 = .05$. From Table IV, Appendix B, $z_{.05} = 1.645$. The confidence interval is:

$$\bar{x} \pm z_{\alpha/2} \frac{s}{\sqrt{n}} \Rightarrow 7 \pm 1.645 \frac{49}{\sqrt{265}} \Rightarrow 7 \pm 4.95 \Rightarrow (2.05, \ 11.95)$$

We are 90% confident that the mean change in SAT-Verbal score is between 2.05 and 11.95 points.

The SAT-Mathematics test would be the most likely of the two to have 15 as the mean change in score. This value of 15 is in the 90% confidence interval for the mean change in SAT-Mathematics score. However, 15 does not fall in the 90% confidence interval for the mean SAT-Verbal test.

5.21   a.   For confidence coefficient .80, $\alpha = 1 - .80 = .20$ and $\alpha/2 = .20/2 = .10$. From Table IV, Appendix B, $z_{.10} = 1.28$. From Table V, with df $= n - 1 = 5 - 1 = 4$, $t_{.10} = 1.533$.

         b.   For confidence coefficient .90, $\alpha = 1 - .90 = .05$ and $\alpha/2 = .10/2 = .05$. From Table IV, Appendix B, $z_{.05} = 1.645$. From Table V, with df $= n - 1 = 5 - 1 = 4$, $t_{.05} = 2.132$.

         c.   For confidence coefficient .95, $\alpha = 1 - .95 = .05$ and $\alpha/2 = .05/2 = .025$. From Table IV, Appendix B, $z_{.025} = 1.96$. From Table V, with df $= n - 1 = 5 - 1 = 4$, $t_{.025} = 2.776$.

         d.   For confidence coefficient .98, $\alpha = 1 - .98 = .02$ and $\alpha/2 = .02/2 = .01$. From Table IV, Appendix B, $z_{.01} = 2.33$. From Table V, with df $= n - 1 = 5 - 1 = 4$, $t_{.01} = 3.747$.

         e.   For confidence coefficient .99, $\alpha = 1 - .99 = .02$ and $\alpha/2 = .02/2 = .005$. From Table IV, Appendix B, $z_{.005} = 2.575$. From Table V, with df $= n - 1 = 5 - 1 = 4$, $t_{.005} = 4.604$.

         f.   Both the t- and z-distributions are symmetric around 0 and mound-shaped. The t-distribution is more spread out than the z-distribution.

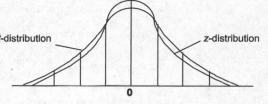

5.23   a. $P(-t_0 < t < t_0) = .95$ where df $= 10$
              Because of symmetry, the statement can be written
              $$P(0 < t < t_0) = .475 \text{ where df} = 10$$
              $$\Rightarrow P(t \geq t_0) = .025$$
              $$t_0 = 2.228$$
         b. $P(t \leq (-t_0 \text{ or } t \geq t_0) = .05$ where df $= 10$
              $$\Rightarrow 2P(t \geq t_0) = .05$$
              $$\Rightarrow P(t \geq t_0) = .025 \text{ where df} = 10$$
              $$t_0 = 2.228$$

         c. $P(t \leq t_0) = .05$ where df $= 10$
              Because of symmetry, the statement can be written
              $$\Rightarrow P(t \geq -t_0) = .05 \text{ where df} = 10$$
              $$t_0 = -1.812$$

         d. $P(t < -t_0 \text{ or } t > t_0) = .10$ where df $= 20$
              $$\Rightarrow 2P(t > t_0) = .10$$
              $$\Rightarrow P(t > t_0) = .05 \text{ where df} = 20$$
              $$t_0 = 1.725$$

         e. $P(t \leq -t_0 \text{ or } t \geq t_0) = .01$ where df $= 5$
              $$\Rightarrow 2P(t \geq t_0) = .01$$
              $$\Rightarrow P(t \geq t_0) = .005 \text{ where df} = 5$$
              $$t_0 = 4.032$$

5.25   First, we must compute $\bar{x}$ and s.

$$\bar{x} = \frac{\sum x}{n} = \frac{30}{6} = 5$$

$$s^2 = \frac{\sum x^2 - \frac{\left(\sum x\right)^2}{n}}{n-1} = \frac{176 - \frac{(30)^2}{6}}{6-1} = \frac{26}{5} = 5.2$$

$$s = \sqrt{5.2} = 2.2804$$

a.   For confidence coefficient .90, $\alpha = 1 - .90 = .10$ and $\alpha/2 = .10/2 = .05$. From Table V, Appendix B, with df $= n - 1 = 6 - 1 = 5$, $t_{.05} = 2.015$. The 90% confidence interval is:

$$\bar{x} \pm t_{0.5} \frac{s}{\sqrt{n}} \Rightarrow 5 \pm 2.015 \frac{2.2804}{\sqrt{6}} \Rightarrow 5 \pm 1.88 \Rightarrow (3.12, 6.88)$$

b.   For confidence coefficient .95, $\alpha = 1 - .95 = .05$ and $\alpha/2 = .05/2 = .025$. From Table V, Appendix B, with df $= n - 1 = 6 - 1 = 5$, $t_{.025} = 2.571$. The 95% confidence interval is:

$$\bar{x} \pm t_{.025} \frac{s}{\sqrt{n}} \Rightarrow 5 \pm 2.571 \frac{2.2804}{\sqrt{6}} \Rightarrow 5 \pm 2.39 \Rightarrow (2.61, 7.39)$$

c.   For confidence coefficient .99, $\alpha = 1 - .99 = .01$ and $\alpha/2 = .01/2 = .005$. From Table V, Appendix B, with df $= n - 1 = 6 - 1 = 5$, $t_{.005} = 4.032$. The 99% confidence interval is:

$$\bar{x} \pm t_{.005} \frac{s}{\sqrt{n}} \Rightarrow 5 \pm 4.032 \frac{2.2804}{\sqrt{6}} \Rightarrow 5 \pm 3.75 \Rightarrow (1.25, 8.75)$$

d.   a)   For confidence coefficient .90, $\alpha = 1 - .90 = .10$ and $\alpha/2 = .10/2 = .05$. From Table V, Appendix B, with df $= n - 1 = 25 - 1 = 24$, $t_{.05} = 1.711$. The 90% confidence interval is:

$$\bar{x} \pm t_{.05} \frac{s}{\sqrt{n}} \Rightarrow 5 \pm 1.711 \frac{2.2804}{\sqrt{25}} \Rightarrow 5 \pm .78 \Rightarrow (4.22, 5.78)$$

b)   For confidence coefficient .95, $\alpha = 1 - .95 = .05$ and $\alpha/2 = .05/2 = .025$. From Table V, Appendix B, with df $= n - 1 = 25 - 1 = 24$, $t_{.025} = 2.064$. The 95% confidence interval is:

$$\bar{x} \pm t_{.025} \frac{s}{\sqrt{n}} \Rightarrow 5 \pm 2.064 \frac{2.2804}{\sqrt{25}} \Rightarrow 5 \pm .94 \Rightarrow (4.06, 5.94)$$

c)   For confidence coefficient .99, $\alpha = 1 - .99 = .01$ and $\alpha/2 = .01/2 = .005$. From Table V, Appendix B, with df $= n - 1 = 25 - 1 = 24$, $t_{.005} = 2.797$. The 99% confidence interval is:

$$\bar{x} \pm t_{.005} \frac{s}{\sqrt{n}} \Rightarrow 5 \pm 2.797 \frac{2.2804}{\sqrt{25}} \Rightarrow 5 \pm 1.28 \Rightarrow (3.72, 6.28)$$

Increasing the sample size decreases the width of the confidence interval.

5.27   For confidence coefficient .90, $\alpha = .10$ and $\alpha/2 = .10/2 = .05$. From Table V, Appendix   B, with df $= n - 1 = 25 - 1 = 24$, $t_{.05} = 1.711$. The 90% confidence interval is:

$$\bar{x} \pm t_{.05}\frac{s}{\sqrt{n}} \Rightarrow 75.4 \pm 1.711\frac{10.9}{\sqrt{25}} \Rightarrow 75.4 \pm 3.73 \Rightarrow (71.67, \ 79.13)$$

We are 90% confident that the mean breaking strength of the white wood is between 71.67 and 79.13.

5.29   a.   From the printout, the 95% confidence interval is $(-320\%, 5,922\%)$. We are 95% confident that the true mean 5-year revenue growth rate for the 2008 12 companies is between -320% and $5,922\%$.

   b.   The population being sampled from must be normally distributed.

   c.   From the stem-and-leaf display in the printout, the data appear to be skewed to the right. The data do not appear to have come from a normal distribution. Therefore, the 95% confidence interval in part **a** may not be valid.

5.31   a.   Using MINITAB, the descriptive statistics are:

Descriptive Statistics: Skid

```
Variable    N   N*    Mean  SE Mean   StDev  Minimum      Q1  Median     Q3  Maximum
Skid       20    0   358.5     26.3   117.8    141.0   276.0   367.5  438.0    574.0
```

For confidence coefficient .95, $\alpha = .05$ and $\alpha/2 = .05/2 = .025$. From Table V, Appendix B, with df $= n - 1 = 20 - 1 = 19$, $t_{.025} = 2.093$. The 95% confidence interval is:

$$\bar{x} \pm t_{.05}\frac{s}{\sqrt{n}} \Rightarrow 358.5 \pm 2.093\frac{117.8}{\sqrt{20}} \Rightarrow 358.5 \pm 55.13 \Rightarrow (303.37, \ 413.63)$$

   b.   We are 95% confident that the mean skidding distance is between 303.37 and 413.63 meters.

c.   In order for the inference to be valid, the skidding distances must be from a normal distribution. We will use the four methods to check for normality. First, we will look at a histogram of the data. Using MINITAB, the histogram of the data is:

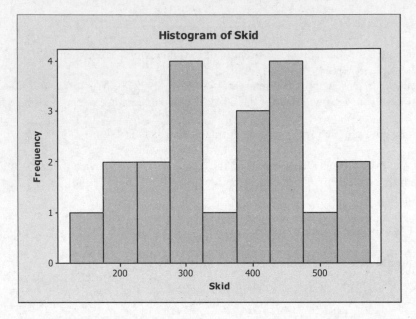

From the histogram, the data appear to be fairly mound-shaped. This indicates that the data may be normal.

Next, we look at the intervals $\bar{x} \pm s$, $\bar{x} \pm 2s$, $\bar{x} \pm 3s$. If the proportions of observations falling in each interval are approximately .68, .95, and 1.00, then the data are approximately normal. Using MINITAB, the summary statistics are:

$\bar{x} \pm s \Rightarrow 358.5 \pm 117.8 \Rightarrow (240.7, \quad 476.3)$ 14 of the 20 values fall in this interval. The proportion is .70. This is very close to the .68 we would expect if the data were normal.

$\bar{x} \pm 2s \Rightarrow 358.5 \pm 2(117.8) \Rightarrow 358.5 \pm 235.6 \Rightarrow (122.9, \quad 594.1)$ 20 of the 20 values fall in this interval. The proportion is 1.00. This is a larger than the .95 we would expect if the data were normal.

$\bar{x} \pm 3s \Rightarrow 358.5 \pm 3(117.8) \Rightarrow 358.5 \pm 353.4 \Rightarrow (5.1, \quad 711.9)$ 20 of the 20 values fall in this interval. The proportion is 1.00. This is exactly the 1.00 we would expect if the data were normal.

From this method, it appears that the data may be normal.

Next, we look at the ratio of the IQR to s. IQR = $Q_U - Q_L = 438 - 276 = 162$.

$\dfrac{\text{IQR}}{s} = \dfrac{162}{117.8} = 1.37$ This is fairly close to the 1.3 we would expect if the data were normal. This method indicates the data may be normal.

Finally, using MINITAB, the normal probability plot is:

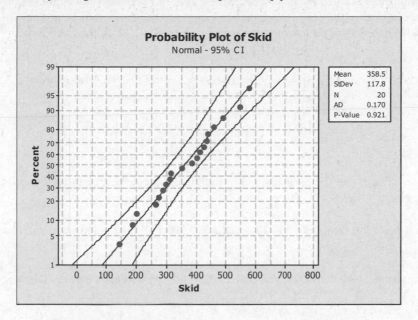

Since the data form a fairly straight line, the data may be normal.

From above, all the methods indicate the data may be normal. It appears that the assumption that the data come from a normal distribution is probably valid.

d. No. A distance of 425 meters falls above the 95% confidence interval that was computed in part **a**. It would be very unlikely to observe a mean skidding distance of at least 425 meters.

5.33 a. Using MINITAB, the descriptive statistics are:

Descriptive Statistics: Alqaeda

Variable	N	Mean	StDev	Minimum	Q1	Median	Q3	Maximum
Alqaeda	21	1.857	1.195	1.000	1.000	1.000	2.000	5.000

The sample mean is $\bar{x} = 1.857$ and the sample standard deviation is $s = 1.195$.

b. Using MINITAB, a histogram of the data is:

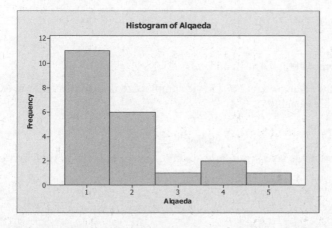

The data are skewed to the right.

c. Since the sample size is small (n = 21), the Central Limit Theorem does not apply. In order to use a small sample confidence interval, the population being sampled from must be normal. In this case, it does not look like the population being sampled from is normal. Thus, the confidence interval may not be valid.

For confidence coefficient .90, $\alpha = 1 - .90 = .10$ and $\alpha/2 = .10/2 = .05$. From Table V, Appendix B, with df = n – 1 = 21 – 1 = 20, $t_{.05} = 1.725$. The 90% confidence interval is:

$$\bar{x} \pm t_{\alpha/2} \frac{s}{\sqrt{n}} \Rightarrow 1.857 \pm 1.725 \frac{1.195}{\sqrt{21}} \Rightarrow 1.857 \pm .450 \Rightarrow (1.407, \quad 2.307)$$

d. We are 90% confident that the mean number of individual suicide bombings and/or attacks per incident is between 1.407 and 2.307.

e. If the distribution being sampled from is normal, then .90 of all intervals formed will contain the true mean.

5.35   a. The population from which the sample was drawn is the Forbes 441 Biggest Private companies.

b. Using MINITAB, the descriptive statistics are:

Descriptive Statistics: Revenue

```
Variable    N  Mean  StDev  Minimum   Q1  Median   Q3  Maximum
Revenue    15  4.61   4.51     1.10  1.75   2.20  5.05   14.32
```

For confidence coefficient .98, $\alpha = .02$ and $\alpha/2 = .02/2 = .01$. From Table V, Appendix B, with df = n – 1 = 15 – 1 = 14, $t_{.01} = 2.624$. The 98% confidence interval is:

$$\bar{x} \pm t_{.025} \frac{s}{\sqrt{n}} \Rightarrow 4.61 \pm 2.624 \frac{4.51}{\sqrt{15}} \Rightarrow 4.61 \pm 3.06 \Rightarrow (1.55, \quad 7.67)$$

c. We are 98% confident that the mean revenue is between $1.554 and $7.666 billion .

d. The population must be normally distributed in order for the procedure used in part **b** to be valid.

e. Yes. The value of $5.0 billion dollars falls in the 98% confidence interval computed in part **b**. Therefore, we should believe the claim.

5.37   The sample size is large enough if both $n\hat{p} \geq 15$ and $n\hat{q} \geq 15$.

a. When n = 400, $\hat{p} = .10$: $n\hat{p} = 400(.10) = 40$ and $n\hat{q} = 400(.90) = 360$

Since both numbers are greater than or equal to 15, the sample size is sufficiently large to conclude the normal approximation is reasonable.

b. When n = 50, $\hat{p} = .10$: $n\hat{p} = 50(.10) = 5$ and $n\hat{q} = 50(.90) = 45$

Since $n\hat{p}$ is less than 15, the sample size is not large enough to conclude the normal approximation is reasonable.

    c.   When n = 20, $\hat{p}$ = .5: $n\hat{p}$ = 20(.5) = 10 and $n\hat{q}$ = 20(.5) = 10

    Since both numbers are less than 15, the sample size is not large enough to conclude the normal approximation is reasonable.

    d.   When n = 20, $\hat{p}$ = .3: $n\hat{p}$ = 20(.3) = 6 and $n\hat{q}$ = 20(.7) = 14

    Since both numbers are less than 15, the sample size is not large enough to conclude the normal approximation is reasonable.

5.39   a.   The sample size is large enough if both $n\hat{p} \geq 15$ and $n\hat{q} \geq 15$.

    $n\hat{p}$ = 225(.46) = 103.5 and $n\hat{q}$ = 225(.54) = 121.5

    Since both numbers are greater than or equal to 15, the sample size is sufficiently large to conclude the normal approximation is reasonable.

    b.   For confidence coefficient .95, α = .05 and $\alpha/2$ = .025. From Table IV, Appendix B, $z_{.025}$ = 1.96. The 95% confidence interval is:

$$\hat{p} \pm z_{.025}\sqrt{\frac{pq}{n}} \Rightarrow \hat{p} \pm 1.96\sqrt{\frac{\hat{p}\hat{q}}{n}} \Rightarrow .46 \pm 1.96\sqrt{\frac{.46(1-.46)}{225}} \Rightarrow .46 \pm .065 \Rightarrow (.395, .525)$$

    c.   We are 95% confident the true value of p will fall between .395 and .525.

    d.   "95% confidence interval" means that if repeated samples of size 225 were selected from the population and 95% confidence intervals formed, 95% of all confidence intervals will contain the true value of *p*.

5.41   a.   The population of interest is all American adults.

    b.   The sample is the 1,000 adults surveyed.

    c.   The parameter of interest is the proportion of all American adults who think Starbucks coffee is overpriced.

    d.   The sample size is large enough if both $n\hat{p} \geq 15$ and $n\hat{q} \geq 15$.

    $n\hat{p}$ = 1,000(.73) = 730 and $n\hat{q}$ = 1,000(.27) = 270

    Since both numbers are greater than or equal to 15, the sample size is sufficiently large to conclude the normal approximation is reasonable.

    For confidence coefficient .95, α = 1 - .95 = .05 and $\alpha/2$ = .05/2 = .025. From Table IV, Appendix B, $z_{.025}$ = 1.96. The 95% confidence interval is:

$$\hat{p} \pm z_{\alpha/2}\sqrt{\frac{pq}{n}} \Rightarrow \hat{p} \pm z_{\alpha/2}\sqrt{\frac{\hat{p}\hat{q}}{n}} \Rightarrow .73 \pm 1.96\sqrt{\frac{.73(.27)}{1000}} \Rightarrow .73 \pm .028 \Rightarrow (.702, .758)$$

    We are 95% confident that the true proportion of all American adults who say Starbucks coffee is overpriced is between .702 and .758.

5.43   a.   The point estimate of p is $\hat{p} = \dfrac{x}{n} = \dfrac{414}{900} = .46$.

        b.   The sample size is large enough if both $n\hat{p} \geq 15$ and $n\hat{q} \geq 15$.

              $n\hat{p} = 900(.46) = 414$ and $n\hat{q} = 900(.54) = 486$

              Since both numbers are greater than or equal to 15, the sample size is sufficiently large to conclude the normal approximation is reasonable.

              For confidence coefficient .90, $\alpha = .10$ and $\alpha/2 = .10/2 = .05$. From Table IV, Appendix B, $z_{.05} = 1.645$. The confidence interval is:

              $$\hat{p} \pm z_{.05}\sqrt{\dfrac{\hat{p}\hat{q}}{n}} \Rightarrow .46 \pm 1.645\sqrt{\dfrac{.46(.54)}{900}} \Rightarrow .46 \pm .027 \Rightarrow (.433, \ .487)$$

        c.   We are 90% confident that the true proportion of contractors in the U.S. who have a company website or will have one by the end of the year is between .433 and .487.

        d.   The meaning of "90% confident" is that in repeated sampling, 90% of all confidence intervals constructed will contain the true proportion and 10% will not.

5.45   a.   The point estimate of p is $\hat{p} = \dfrac{x}{n} = \dfrac{35}{1,165} = .03$.

        b.   The sample size is large enough if both $n\hat{p} \geq 15$ and $n\hat{q} \geq 15$.

              $n\hat{p} = 1,165(.03) = 34.95$ and $n\hat{q} = 1,165(.97) = 1130.05$

              Since both numbers are greater than or equal to 15, the sample size is sufficiently large to conclude the normal approximation is reasonable.

              For confidence coefficient .95, $\alpha = .05$ and $\alpha/2 = .05/2 = .025$. From Table IV, Appendix B, $z_{.025} = 1.96$. The confidence interval is:

              $$\hat{p} \pm z_{.025}\sqrt{\dfrac{\hat{p}\hat{q}}{n}} \Rightarrow .03 \pm 1.96\sqrt{\dfrac{.03(.97)}{1,165}} \Rightarrow .03 \pm .01 \Rightarrow (.02, \ .04)$$

        c.   We are 95% confident that the true proportion of drivers that use their cell phone while driving is between .02 and .04.

5.47   a.   A point estimate for the true percentage of all American adults who have access to a high-speed internet connection is 42%. Changing this to a proportion, the point estimate is $\hat{p} = .42$.

        b.   The sample size is large enough if both $n\hat{p} \geq 15$ and $n\hat{q} \geq 15$.

              $n\hat{p} = 4,000(.42) = 1,680$ and $n\hat{q} = 4,000(.58) = 2,320$

              Since both numbers are greater than or equal to 15, the sample size is sufficiently large to conclude the normal approximation is reasonable.

For confidence coefficient .95, $\alpha = 1 - .95 = .05$ and $\alpha/2 = .05/2 = .025$. From Table IV, Appendix B, $z_{.025} = 1.96$. The 95% confidence interval is:

$$\hat{p} \pm z_{\alpha/2}\sqrt{\frac{pq}{n}} \Rightarrow \hat{p} \pm z_{\alpha/2}\sqrt{\frac{\hat{p}\hat{q}}{n}} \Rightarrow .42 \pm 1.96\sqrt{\frac{.42(.58)}{4,000}} \Rightarrow .42 \pm .015 \Rightarrow (.405, \ .435)$$

We are 95% confident that the true proportion of all American adults who have access to a high-speed internet connection at home is between .405 and .435.

c.   Yes, since the interval constructed in part b contains values greater than .30, we could conclude that the percentage has increased since 2005.

5.49   Of the 2,778 sampled firms, 748 announced one or more acquisitions during the year 2000. Thus,

$$\hat{p} = \frac{x}{n} = \frac{748}{2,778} = .269$$

The sample size is large enough if both $n\hat{p} \geq 15$ and $n\hat{q} \geq 15$.

$n\hat{p} = 2,778(.269) = 747$ and $n\hat{q} = 2,778(.731) = 2031$

Since both numbers are greater than or equal to 15, the sample size is sufficiently large to conclude the normal approximation is reasonable.

For confidence coefficient .90, $\alpha = 1 - .90 = .10$ and $\alpha/2 = .10/2 = .05$. From Table IV, Appendix B, $z_{.05} = 1.645$. The 90% confidence interval is:

$$\hat{p} \pm z_{\alpha/2}\sqrt{\frac{pq}{n}} \Rightarrow \hat{p} \pm z_{\alpha/2}\sqrt{\frac{\hat{p}\hat{q}}{n}} \Rightarrow .269 \pm 1.645\sqrt{\frac{.269(.731)}{2,778}} \Rightarrow .269 \pm .014 \Rightarrow (.255, \ .283)$$

We are 90% confident that the true proportion of all firms that announced one or more acquisitions during the year 2000 is between .255 and .283. Changing these to percentages, the results would be 25.5% and 28.3%.

5.51   a.   The point estimate of p is $\hat{p} = \dfrac{x}{n} = \dfrac{52}{60} = .867$.

b.   For confidence coefficient .95, $\alpha = .05$ and $\alpha/2 = .05/2 = .025$. From Table IV, Appendix B, $z_{.025} = 1.96$. The confidence interval is:

$$\hat{p} \pm z_{.025}\sqrt{\frac{\hat{p}\hat{q}}{n}} \Rightarrow .867 \pm 1.96\sqrt{\frac{.867(.133)}{60}} \Rightarrow .867 \pm .085 \Rightarrow (.781, \ .953)$$

c.   We are 95% confident that the true proportion of Wal-Mart stores in California that have more than 2 inaccurately priced items per 100 scanned is between .781 and .953.

d.   If 99% of the California Wal-Mart stores are in compliance, then only 1% or .01 would not be. However, we found the 95% confidence interval for the proportion that are not in compliance is between .781 and .953. The value of .01 is not in this interval. Thus, it is not a likely value. This claim is not believable.

e. The sample size is large enough if both $n\hat{p} \geq 15$ and $n\hat{q} \geq 15$.

$$n\hat{p} = 60(.867) = 52 \text{ and } n\hat{q} = 60(.133) = 8$$

Since $n\hat{q}$ is less than 15, the sample size is not large enough to conclude the normal approximation is reasonable. Thus, the confidence interval constructed in part b may not be valid. Any inference based on this interval is questionable.

5.53   a. The parameter of interest is p, the proportion of all fillets that are red snapper.

b. The estimate of p is $\hat{p} = \dfrac{x}{n} = \dfrac{22-17}{22} = .23$

The sample size is large enough if both $n\hat{p} \geq 15$ and $n\hat{q} \geq 15$.

$$n\hat{p} = 22(.23) = 5 \text{ and } n\hat{q} = 22(.77) = 17$$

Since $n\hat{p}$ is less than 15, the sample size is not large enough to conclude the normal approximation is reasonable.

c. We will use Wilson's adjustment to form the confidence interval.

Using Wilson's adjustment, the point estimate of the true proportion of all fillets that are not red snapper is

$$\tilde{p} = \frac{x+2}{n+4} = \frac{5+2}{22+4} = \frac{7}{26} = .27$$

For confidence coefficient .95, $\alpha = 1 - .95 = .05$ and $\alpha/2 = .05/2 = .025$. From Table IV, Appendix B, $z_{.025} = 1.96$. Wilson's adjusted 95% confidence interval is:

$$\tilde{p} \pm z_{\alpha/2}\sqrt{\frac{\tilde{p}\tilde{q}}{n}} \Rightarrow .27 \pm 1.96\sqrt{\frac{.27(.73)}{22+4}} \Rightarrow .27 \pm .170 \Rightarrow (.10, \ .44)$$

d. We are 95% confident that the true proportion of all fillets that are red snapper is between .10 and .44.

5.55   We will use a 99% confidence interval to estimate the true proportion of mailed items that are delivered on time.

First, we must compute $\hat{p}$: $\hat{p} = \dfrac{x}{n} = \dfrac{282,200}{332,000} = .85$

The sample size is large enough if both $n\hat{p} \geq 15$ and $n\hat{q} \geq 15$.

$$n\hat{p} = 332,000(.85) = 282,200 \text{ and } n\hat{q} = 332,000(.15) = 49,800$$

Since both numbers are greater than or equal to 15, the sample size is sufficiently large to conclude the normal approximation is reasonable.

For confidence coefficient .99, $\alpha = .01$ and $\alpha/2 = .01/2 = .005$. From Table IV, Appendix B, $z_{.005} = 2.58$. The confidence interval is:

$$\hat{p} \pm z_{.005}\sqrt{\frac{pq}{n}} \approx \hat{p} \pm 2.58\sqrt{\frac{\hat{p}\hat{q}}{n}} \Rightarrow .85 \pm 2.58\sqrt{\frac{.85(.15)}{332{,}000}} \Rightarrow .85 \pm .002 \Rightarrow (.848, .852)$$

We are 99% confident that the true percentage of items delivered on time by the U.S. Postal Service is between 84.8% and 85.2%.

5.57   a.   An estimate of σ is obtained from:

range $\approx 4s$

$$s \approx \frac{\text{range}}{4} = \frac{34-30}{4} = 1$$

To compute the necessary sample size, use

$$n = \frac{\left(z_{\alpha/2}\right)^2\sigma^2}{(SE)^2} \quad \text{where } \alpha = 1 - .90 = .10 \text{ and } \alpha/2 = .05.$$

From Table IV, Appendix B, $z_{.05} = 1.645$. Thus,

$$n = \frac{(1.645)^2(1)^2}{.2^2} = 67.65 \approx 68$$

b.   A less conservative estimate of σ is obtained from:

range $\approx 6s$

$$s \approx \frac{\text{range}}{6} = \frac{34-30}{6} = .6667$$

Thus, $n = \dfrac{\left(z_{\alpha/2}\right)^2\sigma^2}{(SE)^2} = \dfrac{(1.645)^2(.6667)^2}{.2^2} = 30.07 \approx 31$

5.59   For confidence coefficient .90, $\alpha = .10$ and $\alpha/2 = .05$. From Table IV, Appendix B, $z_{.05} = 1.645$.

We know $\hat{p}$ is in the middle of the interval, so $\hat{p} = \dfrac{.54 + .26}{2} = .4$

The confidence interval is $\hat{p} \pm z_{.05}\sqrt{\dfrac{\hat{p}\hat{q}}{n}} \Rightarrow .4 \pm 1.645\sqrt{\dfrac{.4(.6)}{n}}$

We know $.4 - 1.645\sqrt{\dfrac{.4(.6)}{n}} = .26$

$$\Rightarrow .4 - \frac{.8059}{\sqrt{n}} = .26$$

$$\rightarrow .4 - .26 = \frac{.8059}{\sqrt{n}} \Rightarrow \sqrt{n} = \frac{.8059}{.14} = 5.756$$

$$\Rightarrow n = 5.756^2 = 33.1 \approx 34$$

5.61   a.   The width of a confidence interval is $2(SE) = 2z_{\alpha/2}\dfrac{\sigma}{\sqrt{n}}$

For confidence coefficient .95, $\alpha = 1 - .95 = .05$ and $\alpha/2 = .05/2 = .025$. From Table IV, Appendix B, $z_{.025} = 1.96$.

For $n = 16$,
$$W = 2z_{\alpha/2}\frac{\sigma}{\sqrt{n}} = 2(1.96)\frac{1}{\sqrt{16}} = 0.98$$

For $n = 25$,
$$W = 2z_{\alpha/2}\frac{\sigma}{\sqrt{n}} = 2(1.96)\frac{1}{\sqrt{25}} = 0.784$$

For $n = 49$,
$$W = 2z_{\alpha/2}\frac{\sigma}{\sqrt{n}} = 2(1.96)\frac{1}{\sqrt{49}} = 0.56$$

For $n = 100$,
$$W = 2z_{\alpha/2}\frac{\sigma}{\sqrt{n}} = 2(1.96)\frac{1}{\sqrt{100}} = 0.392$$

For $n = 400$,
$$W = 2z_{\alpha/2}\frac{\sigma}{\sqrt{n}} = 2(1.96)\frac{1}{\sqrt{400}} = 0.196$$

b.

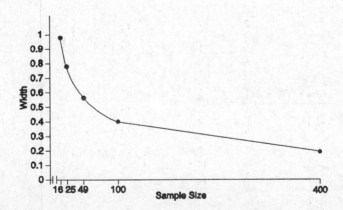

5.63   For confidence coefficient .90, $\alpha = .10$ and $\alpha/2 = .10/2 = .05$. From Table IV, Appendix B, $z_{.05} = 1.645$. Thus,

$$n = \frac{(z_{\alpha/2})^2\sigma^2}{(SE)^2} = \frac{1.645^2(10.9)^2}{4^2} = 20.09 \approx 21$$

Thus, we would need a sample of size 21.

5.65   For confidence coefficient .90, $\alpha = .10$ and $\alpha/2 = .10/2 = .05$. From Table IV, Appendix B, $z_{.05} = 1.645$. Since we have no estimate given for the value of p, we will use .5. The sample size is:

$$n = \frac{z_{\alpha/2}^2 pq}{(SE)^2} = \frac{1.645^2(.5)(.5)}{.02^2} = 1{,}691.3 \approx 1{,}692$$

5.67   For confidence coefficient .99, $\alpha = .01$ and $\alpha/2 = .01/2 = .005$. From Table IV, Appendix B, $z_{.005} = 2.575$. From the previous estimate, we will use $\hat{p} = 1/3$ to estimate p.

$$n = \frac{z_{\alpha/2}^2 pq}{(SE)^2} = \frac{2.575^2(1/3)(2/3)}{.01^2} = 14{,}734.7 \approx 14{,}735$$

5.69   To compute the needed sample size, use

$$n = \frac{\left(z_{\alpha/2}\right)^2 \sigma^2}{(SE)^2} \quad \text{where } \alpha = 1 - .95 = .05 \text{ and } \alpha/2 = .05/2 = .025.$$

From Table IV, Appendix B, $z_{.025} = 1.96$.

Thus, for $s = 10$, $n = \dfrac{(1.96)^2(10)^2}{3^2} = 42.68 \approx 43$

For $s = 20$, $n = \dfrac{(1.96)^2(20)^2}{3^2} = 170.74 \approx 171$

For $s = 30$, $n = \dfrac{(1.96)^2(30)^2}{3^2} = 384.16 \approx 385$

5.71   The bound is $SE = .05$. For confidence coefficient .99, $\alpha = 1 - .99 = .01$ and $\alpha/2 = .01/2 = .005$. From Table IV, Appendix B, $z_{.005} = 2.575$.

We estimate p with $= 11/27 = .407$. Thus,

$$n = \frac{\left(z_{\alpha/2}\right)^2 pq}{(SE)^2} = \frac{2.575^2(.407)(.593)}{.05^2} \approx 640.1 \Rightarrow 641$$

The necessary sample size would be 641. The sample was not large enough.

5.73   a.   Percentage sampled $= \dfrac{n}{N}(100\%) = \dfrac{1000}{2500}(100\%) = 40\%$

Finite population correction factor:
$$\sqrt{\frac{N-n}{N}} = \sqrt{\frac{2500-1000}{2500}} = \sqrt{.6} = .7746$$

b.   Percentage sampled = $\dfrac{n}{N}(100\%) = \dfrac{1000}{5000}(100\%) = 20\%$

Finite population correction factor:

$$\sqrt{\dfrac{N-n}{N}} = \sqrt{\dfrac{5000-1000}{5000}} = \sqrt{.8} = .8944$$

c.   Percentage sampled = $\dfrac{n}{N}(100\%) = \dfrac{1000}{10,000}(100\%) = 10\%$

Finite population correction factor:

$$\sqrt{\dfrac{N-n}{N}} = \sqrt{\dfrac{10,000-1000}{10,000}} = \sqrt{.9} = .9487$$

d.   Percentage sampled = $\dfrac{n}{N}(100\%) = \dfrac{1000}{100,000}(100\%) = 1\%$

Finite population correction factor:

$$\sqrt{\dfrac{N-n}{N}} = \sqrt{\dfrac{100,000-1000}{100,000}} = \sqrt{.99} = .995$$

5.75   a. $\hat{\sigma}_{\bar{x}} = \dfrac{s}{\sqrt{n}}\sqrt{\dfrac{N-n}{N}} = \dfrac{50}{\sqrt{2000}}\sqrt{\dfrac{10,000-2000}{10,000}} = 1.00$

b. $\hat{\sigma}_{\bar{x}} = \dfrac{50}{\sqrt{4000}}\sqrt{\dfrac{10,000-4000}{10,000}} = .6124$

c. $\hat{\sigma}_{\bar{x}} = \dfrac{50}{\sqrt{10,000}}\sqrt{\dfrac{10,000-10,000}{10,000}} = 0$

d.   As n increases, $\sigma_{\bar{x}}$ decreases.

e.   We are computing the standard error of $\bar{x}$. If the entire population is sampled, then $\bar{x} = \mu$. There is no sampling error, so $\sigma_{\bar{x}} = 0$.

5.77   The approximate 95% confidence interval for p is

$$\hat{p} \pm 2\hat{\sigma}_{\hat{p}} \Rightarrow \hat{p} \pm 2\sqrt{\dfrac{\hat{p}(1-\hat{p})}{n}}\sqrt{\dfrac{N-n}{N}}$$

$$\Rightarrow .42 \pm 2\sqrt{\dfrac{.42(.58)}{1600}}\sqrt{\dfrac{6000-1600}{6000}} \Rightarrow .42 \pm .011 \Rightarrow (.409, .431)$$

5.79   a. $\bar{x} = \dfrac{\sum x}{n} = \dfrac{1081}{30} = 36.03$

$$s^2 = \dfrac{\sum x^2 - \dfrac{(\sum x)^2}{n}}{n-1} = 41,747 - \dfrac{1081^2}{30} = 96.3782$$

$\hat{\mu} = \bar{x} = 36.03$

$$\bar{x} \pm 2\hat{\sigma}_{\bar{x}} \Rightarrow \bar{x} \pm 2\dfrac{s}{\sqrt{n}}\sqrt{\dfrac{N-n}{N}}$$

$$\Rightarrow 36.03 \pm 2\dfrac{\sqrt{96.3782}}{\sqrt{30}}\sqrt{\dfrac{300-30}{300}} \Rightarrow 36.03 \pm 3.40$$

$$\Rightarrow (32.63, 39.43)$$

      b. $\hat{p} = \dfrac{x}{n} = \dfrac{21}{30} = .7$

$$\bar{x} \pm 2\hat{\sigma}_{\hat{p}} \Rightarrow \hat{p} \pm 2\sqrt{\dfrac{\hat{p}(1-\hat{p})}{n}}\sqrt{\dfrac{N-n}{N}}$$

$$\Rightarrow .7 \pm 2\sqrt{\dfrac{.7(.3)}{30}}\sqrt{\dfrac{300-30}{300}} \Rightarrow .7 \pm .159 \Rightarrow (.541, .859)$$

5.81   a.   First, we must estimate p: $\hat{p} = \dfrac{x}{n} = \dfrac{759}{1,355} = .560$

For confidence coefficient .95, $\alpha = 1 - .95 = .05$ and $\alpha/2 = .05/2 = .025$. From Table IV, Appendix B, $z_{.025} = 1.96$. Since $n/N = 1,355/1,696 = .799 > .05$, we must use the finite population correction factor. The 95% confidence interval is:

$$\hat{p} \pm z_{\alpha/2}\sqrt{\dfrac{\hat{p}\hat{q}}{n}\left(\dfrac{N-n}{N}\right)} \Rightarrow .560 \pm 1.96\sqrt{\dfrac{.560(.440)}{1,355}\left(\dfrac{1,696-1,355}{1,696}\right)}$$

$$\Rightarrow .560 \pm .012 \Rightarrow (.548, \quad .572)$$

      b.   We used the finite correction factor because the sample size was very large compared to the population size.

      c.   We are 95% confident that the true proportion of active NFL players who select a professional coach as the most influential in their career is between .548 and .572.

5.83   a.   First, we must calculate the sample mean:

$$\bar{x} = \dfrac{\sum_{i=1}^{15} f_i x_i}{n} = \dfrac{3(108) + 2(55) + 1(500) + \cdots + 19(100)}{100} = \dfrac{15,646}{100} = 156.46$$

The point estimate of the mean value of the parts inventory is $\bar{x} = 156.46$.

b.   The sample variance and standard deviation are:

$$s^2 = \frac{\sum_{i=1}^{15} f_i x_i^2 - \frac{\left(\sum f_i x_i\right)^2}{n}}{n-1} = \frac{3(108)^2 + 2(55)^2 + \cdots + 19(100)^2 - \frac{15,646^2}{100}}{100-1}$$

$$= \frac{6,776,336 - \frac{15,646^2}{100}}{99} = 43,720.83677$$

$$s = \sqrt{s^2} = \sqrt{43,720.83677} = 209.10$$

The estimated standard error is:

$$\hat{\sigma}_{\bar{x}} = \frac{s}{\sqrt{n}}\sqrt{\frac{N-n}{N}} = \frac{209.10}{\sqrt{100}}\sqrt{\frac{500-100}{500}} = 18.7025$$

c.   The approximate 95% confidence interval is:

$$\bar{x} \pm 2\hat{\sigma}_{\bar{x}} \Rightarrow \bar{x} \pm 2\left(\frac{s}{\sqrt{n}}\right)\sqrt{\frac{N-n}{N}} \Rightarrow 156.46 \pm 2(18.7025) \Rightarrow 156.46 \pm 37.405$$

$$\Rightarrow (119.055, 193.865)$$

We are 95% confident that the mean value of the parts inventory is between \$119.06 and \$193.87.

d.   Since the interval in part **c** does not include \$300, the value of \$300 is not a reasonable value for the mean value of the parts inventory.

5.85 $\hat{p} = \frac{x}{n} = \frac{15}{175} = .086$

The standard error of $\hat{p}$ is:

$$\hat{\sigma}_{\hat{p}} = \sqrt{\frac{\hat{p}(1-\hat{p})}{n}\left(\frac{N-n}{N}\right)} = \sqrt{\frac{.086(1-.086)}{175}\left(\frac{3000-175}{3000}\right)} = .0206$$

An approximate 95% confidence interval for p is:

$$\hat{p} \pm 2\hat{\sigma}_{\hat{p}} \Rightarrow .086 \pm 2(.0206) \Rightarrow .086 \pm .041 \Rightarrow (.045, .127)$$

Since .07 falls in the 95% confidence interval, it is not an uncommon value. Thus, there is no evidence that more than 7% of the corn-related products in this state have to be removed from shelves and warehouses.

5.87   a. $P(t \leq t_0) = .05$ where df = 20
                   $t_0 = -1.725$

b. $P(t \geq t_0) = .005$ where df = 9
                   $t_0 = 3.250$

c. $P(t \le -t_0 \text{ or } t \ge t_0) = .10$ where df = 8 is equivalent to
$$P(t \ge t_0) = .10/2 = .05 \text{ where df} = 8$$
$$t_0 = 1.860$$

d. $P(t \le -t_0 \text{ or } t \ge t_0) = .01$ where df = 17 is equivalent to
$$P(t \ge t_0) = .01/2 = .005 \text{ where df} = 17$$
$$t_0 = 2.898$$

5.89   a.   For confidence coefficient .99, $\alpha = .01$ and $\alpha/2 = .005$. From Table IV, Appendix B, $z_{.005} = 2.575$.
The confidence interval is:

$$\bar{x} \pm z_{\alpha/2}\frac{s}{\sqrt{n}} \Rightarrow 32.5 \pm 2.575\frac{30}{\sqrt{225}} \Rightarrow 32.5 \pm 5.15 \Rightarrow (27.35, 37.65)$$

b.   The sample size is $n = \dfrac{\left(z_{\alpha/2}\right)\sigma^2}{(SE)^2} = \dfrac{2.575^2(30)^2}{.5^2} = 27{,}870.25 \approx 23{,}871$.

c.   "99% confidence" means that if repeated samples of size 225 were selected from the population and 99% confidence intervals constructed for the population mean, then 99% of all the intervals constructed will contain the population mean.

5.91   The parameters of interest for the problems are:

(1)   The question requires a categorical response. One parameter of interest might be the proportion, p, of all Americans over 18 years of age who think their health is generally very good or excellent.

(2)   A parameter of interest might be the mean number of days, μ, in the previous 30 days that all Americans over 18 years of age felt that their physical health was not good because of injury or illness.

(3)   A parameter of interest might be the mean number of days, μ, in the previous 30 days that all Americans over 18 years of age felt that their mental health was not good because of stress, depression, or problems with emotions.

(4)   A parameter of interest might be the mean number of days, μ, in the previous 30 days that all Americans over 18 years of age felt that their physical or mental health prevented them from performing their usual activities.

5.93   a.   Of the 1000 observations, 29% said they would never give personal information to a company $\Rightarrow \hat{p} = .29$

The sample size is large enough if both $n\hat{p} \ge 15$ and $n\hat{q} \ge 15$.

$n\hat{p} = 1000(.29) = 290$ and $n\hat{q} = 1000(.71) = 710$

Since both numbers are greater than or equal to 15, the sample size is sufficiently large to conclude the normal approximation is reasonable.

b.   For confidence coefficient .95, $\alpha = 1 - .95 = .05$ and $\alpha/2 = .05/2 = .025$. From Table IV, Appendix B, $z_{.025} = 1.96$. The 95% confidence interval is:

$$\hat{p} \pm z_{.025}\sqrt{\frac{\hat{p}\hat{q}}{n}} \Rightarrow .29 \pm 1.96\sqrt{\frac{.29(.71)}{1000}} \Rightarrow .29 \pm .028 \Rightarrow (.262, .318)$$

We are 95% confident that the proportion of Internet users who would never give personal information to a company is between .262 and .318.

5.95   For confidence coefficient .95, $\alpha = .05$ and $\alpha/2 = .05/2 = .025$. From Table IV, Appendix B, $z_{.025} = 1.96$. For this study,

$$n = \frac{(z_{\alpha/2})^2 \sigma^2}{SE^2} \approx \frac{1.96^2 (5)^2}{1^2} = 96.04 \approx 97$$

The sample size needed is 97.

5.97   First, we must estimate p: $\hat{p} = \dfrac{x}{n} = \dfrac{50}{72} = .694$. The 95% confidence interval is:

$$\hat{p} \pm 2\sqrt{\frac{\hat{p}\hat{q}}{n}\left(\frac{N-n}{N}\right)} \Rightarrow .694 \pm 2\sqrt{\frac{.694(.306)}{72}\left(\frac{251-72}{251}\right)} \Rightarrow .694 \pm .092 \Rightarrow (.602, \quad .786)$$

We are 95% confident that the proportion of all New Jersey Governor's Council business members that have employees with substance abuse problems is between .602 and .786.

5.99   There are a total of 96 channel catfish in the sample. The point estimate of *p* is

$$\hat{p} = \frac{x}{n} = \frac{96}{144} = .667 .$$

The sample size is large enough if both $n\hat{p} \geq 15$ and $n\hat{q} \geq 15$.

$n\hat{p} = 144(.667) = 96$ and $n\hat{q} = 144(.333) = 48$

Since both numbers are greater than or equal to 15, the sample size is sufficiently large to conclude the normal approximation is reasonable.

For confidence coefficient .90, $\alpha = .10$ and $\alpha/2 = .10/2 = .05$. From Table IV, Appendix B, $z_{.05} = 1.645$. The confidence interval is:

$$\hat{p} \pm z_{.05}\sqrt{\frac{\hat{p}\hat{q}}{n}} \Rightarrow .667 \pm 1.645\sqrt{\frac{.667(.333)}{144}} \Rightarrow .667 \pm .065 \Rightarrow (.602, \quad .732)$$

We are 90% confident that the true proportion of channel catfish in the population is between .602 and .732.

5.101 a. For confidence coefficient .99, $\alpha = .01$ and $\alpha/2 = .01/2 = .005$. From Table V, Appendix B, with df $= n - 1 = 3 - 1 = 2$, $t_{.005} = 9.925$. The confidence interval is:

$$\bar{x} \pm t_{.005}\frac{s}{\sqrt{n}} \Rightarrow 49.3 \pm 9.925\frac{1.5}{\sqrt{3}} \Rightarrow 49.3 \pm 8.60 \Rightarrow (40.70, 57.90)$$

b. We are 99% confident that the mean percentage of B(a)p removed from all soil specimens using the poison is between 40.70% and 57.90%.

c. We must assume that the distribution of the percentages of B(a)p removed from all soil specimens using the poison is normal.

d. Since the 99% confidence interval for the mean percent removed contains 50%, this would be a very possible value.

5.103 a. Using MINITAB, the descriptive statistics are:

Descriptive Statistics: IQ25, IQ60

Variable	N	Mean	Median	TrMean	StDev	SE Mean
IQ25	36	66.83	66.50	66.69	14.36	2.39
IQ60	36	45.39	45.00	45.22	12.67	2.11

Variable	Minimum	Maximum	Q1	Q3
IQ25	41.00	94.00	54.25	80.00
IQ60	22.00	73.00	36.25	58.00

For confidence coefficient .99, $\alpha = .01$ and $\alpha/2 = .01/2 = .005$. From Table IV, Appendix B, $z_{.005} = 2.58$. The confidence interval is:

$$\bar{x} \pm z_{\alpha/2}\frac{s}{\sqrt{n}} \Rightarrow 66.83 \pm 2.58\frac{14.36}{\sqrt{36}} \Rightarrow 66.83 \pm 6.17$$
$$\Rightarrow (60.66, \ 73.00)$$

We are 99% confident that the mean raw IQ score for all 25-year-olds is between 60.66 and 73.00.

b. We must assume that the sample is random and that the observations are independent.

c. For confidence coefficient .95, $\alpha = .05$ and $\alpha/2 = .05/2 = .025$. From Table IV, Appendix B, $z_{.025} = 1.96$. The confidence interval is:

$$\bar{x} \pm z_{\alpha/2}\frac{s}{\sqrt{n}} \Rightarrow 45.39 \pm 1.96\frac{12.67}{\sqrt{36}} \Rightarrow 45.39 \pm 4.14$$
$$\Rightarrow (41.25, \ 49.53)$$

We are 95% confident that the mean raw IQ score for all 60-year-olds is between 41.25 and 49.53.

5.105   The bound is $SE = .1$. For confidence coefficient .99, $\alpha = 1 - .99 = .01$ and $\alpha/2 = .01/2 = .005$.
        From Table IV, Appendix B, $z_{.005} = 2.575$.

        We estimate p with from Exercise 5.104 which is $\hat{p} = .636$. Thus,

$$n = \frac{\left(z_{\alpha/2}\right)^2 pq}{(SE)^2} = \frac{2.575^2(.636)(.364)}{.1^2} 1 = 153.5 \Rightarrow 154$$

        The necessary sample size would be 154.

5.107   a.   Of the 24 observations, 20 were 2 weeks of vacation $\Rightarrow \hat{p} = 20/24 = .833$.

             For confidence coefficient .95, $\alpha = .05$ and $\alpha/2 = .05/2 = .025$. From Table IV,
             Appendix B, $z_{.025} = 1.96$. The confidence interval is:

$$\hat{p} \pm z_{.025}\sqrt{\frac{\hat{p}\hat{q}}{n}} \Rightarrow .833 \pm 1.96\sqrt{\frac{.833(.167)}{24}} \Rightarrow .833 \pm .149 \Rightarrow (.683, \ .982)$$

        b.   The sample size is large enough if both $n\hat{p} \geq 15$ and $n\hat{q} \geq 15$.

             $n\hat{p} = 24(.833) = 20$ and $n\hat{q} = 24(.167) = 4$

             Since $n\hat{q}$ is less than 15, the sample size is not sufficiently large to conclude the normal
             approximation is reasonable. The validity of the confidence interval is in question.

        c.   The bound is $SE = .02$. For confidence coefficient .95, $\alpha = .05$ and $\alpha/2 = .05/2 = .025$. From Table
             IV, Appendix B, $z_{.025} = 1.96$. Thus,

$$n = \frac{\left(z_{\alpha/2}\right)^2 pq}{(SE)^2} = \frac{1.96^2(.833)(.167)}{.02^2} = 1,336.02 \approx 1,337.$$

        Thus, we would need a sample size of 1,337.

5.109   Sampling error has to do with chance. In a population, there is variation – not all observations are the
        same. The sampling error has to do with the variation within a sample. By chance, one might get a sample
        that overestimates the mean just because all the observations in the sample happen to be high.
        Nonsampling error has to do with errors that have nothing to do with the sampling. These errors could be
        due to misunderstanding the question being asked, asking a question that the respondent does not know
        how to answer, etc.

5.111   For confidence coefficient .95, $\alpha = .05$ and $\alpha/2 = .025$. From Table IV, Appendix B, $z_{.025} = 1.96$. From Exercise 5.110, a good approximation for p is .094. Also, $SE = .02$.

The sample size is $n = \dfrac{(z_{\alpha/2})^2\, pq}{(SE)^2} = \dfrac{(1.96)^2(.094)(.906)}{.02^2} = 817.9 \approx 818$

You would need to take $n = 818$ samples.

5.113   Solution will vary. See page 488 for Guided Solutions.

5.115   a.   As long as the sample is random (and thus representative), a reliable estimate of the mean weight of all the scallops can be obtained.

b.   The government is using only the sample mean to make a decision. Rather than using a point estimate, they should probably use a confidence interval to estimate the true mean weight of the scallops so they can include a measure of reliability.

c.   We will form a 95% confidence interval for the mean weight of the scallops. Using MINITAB, the descriptive statistics are:

Descriptive Statistics: Weight

```
Variable    N   N*     Mean   SE Mean    StDev   Minimum      Q1   Median     Q3
Weight     18   0    0.9317    0.0178   0.0753    0.8400  0.8800   0.9100   9800

Variable  Maximum
Weight     1.1400
```

For confidence coefficient .95, $\alpha = .05$ and $\alpha/2 = .05/2 = .025$. From Table V, Appendix A, with df $= n - 1 = 18 - 1 = 17$, $t_{.025} = 2.110$.

The 95% confidence interval is:

$$\bar{x} \pm t_{.025}\, \frac{s}{\sqrt{n}} \Rightarrow .932 \pm 2.110\, \frac{.0753}{\sqrt{18}} \Rightarrow .932 \pm .037 \Rightarrow (.895, \ .969)$$

We are 95% confident that the true mean weight of the scallops is between .8943 and .9691. Recall that the weights have been scaled so that a mean weight of 1 corresponds to 1/36 of a pound. Since the above confidence interval does not include 1, we have sufficient evidence to indicate that the minimum weight restriction was violated.

Chapter 6
Inferences Based on a Single Sample:
Tests of Hypothesis

6.1   The null hypothesis is the "status quo" hypothesis, while the alternative hypothesis is the research hypothesis.

6.3   The "level of significance" of a test is α. This is the probability that the test statistic will fall in the rejection region when the null hypothesis is true.

6.5   The four possible results are:
1.   Rejecting the null hypothesis when it is true. This would be a Type I error.
2.   Accepting the null hypothesis when it is true. This would be a correct decision.
3.   Rejecting the null hypothesis when it is false. This would be a correct decision.
4.   Accepting the null hypothesis when it is false. This would be a Type II error.

6.7   When you reject the null hypothesis in favor of the alternative hypothesis, this does not prove the alternative hypothesis is correct. We are $100(1 - \alpha)\%$ confident that there is sufficient evidence to conclude that the alternative hypothesis is correct.

        If we were to repeatedly draw samples from the population and perform the test each time, approximately $100(1 - \alpha)\%$ of the tests performed would yield the correct decision.

6.9   a.   Let p = proportion of college presidents who believe that their online education courses are as good as or superior to courses that utilize traditional face-to-face instruction. The null hypothesis would be:

                H_0: $p = .60$

        b.   The rejection region requires $\alpha/2 = .01/2 = .005$ in each tail if the z-distribution. From Table IV, Appendix B, $z_{.005} = 2.575$. The rejection region for a two-tailed test is $z < -2.575$ or $z > 2.575$.

6.11   Let p = student loan default rate in this year. To see if the student loan default rate is less than .045, we test:

        H_0: $p = .045$
        H_a: $p < .045$

6.13   Let μ = mean caloric content of Virginia school lunches. To test the claim that after the testing period ended, the average caloric content dropped, we test:

        H_0: $\mu = 863$
        H_a: $\mu < 863$

6.15   a.   Since the company must give proof the drug is safe, the null hypothesis would be the drug is unsafe. The alternative hypothesis would be the drug is safe.

        b.   A Type I error would be concluding the drug is safe when it is not safe. A Type II error would be concluding the drug is not safe when it is. α is the probability of concluding the drug is safe when it is not. β is the probability of concluding the drug is not safe when it is.

        c.   In this problem, it would be more important for α to be small. We would want the probability of concluding the drug is safe when it is not to be as small as possible.

152

6.17   a.   A Type I error is rejecting the null hypothesis when it is true. In a murder trial, we would be concluding that the accused is guilty when, in fact, he/she is innocent.

             A Type II error is accepting the null hypothesis when it is false. In this case, we would be concluding that the accused is innocent when, in fact, he/she is guilty.

      b.   Both errors are bad. However, if an innocent person is found guilty of murder and is put to death, there is no way to correct the error. On the other hand, if a guilty person is set free, he/she could murder again.

      c.   In a jury trial, α is assumed to be smaller than β. The only way to convict the accused is for a unanimous decision of guilt. Thus, the probability of convicting an innocent person is set to be small.

      d.   In order to get a unanimous vote to convict, there has to be overwhelming evidence of guilt. The probability of getting a unanimous vote of guilt if the person is really innocent will be very small.

      e.   If a jury is predjuced against a guilty verdict, the value of α will decrease. The probability of convicting an innocent person will be even smaller if the jury if predjudiced against a guilty verdict.

      f.   If a jury is predjudiced against a guilty verdict, the value of β will increase. The probability of declaring a guilty person innocent will be larger if the jury is prejudiced against a guilty verdict.

6.19   a.   The decision rule is to reject H_0 if $\bar{x} > 270$. Recall that

$$z = \frac{\bar{x} - \mu_0}{\sigma_{\bar{x}}}$$

Therefore,   reject H_0 if $\bar{x} > 270$

can be written reject H_0 if $z > \dfrac{\bar{x} - \mu_0}{\sigma_{\bar{x}}}$

$$z > \frac{270 - 255}{63 / \sqrt{81}}$$

$$z > 2.14$$

The decision rule in terms of z is to reject H_0 if $z > 2.14$.

      b. $P(z > 2.14) = .5 - P(0 < z < 2.14)$

$$= .5 - .4838$$

$$= .0162$$

6.21   a. H_0: $\mu = .36$
            H_a: $\mu < .36$

The test statistic is $z = \dfrac{\bar{x} - \mu_0}{\sigma_{\bar{x}}} \approx \dfrac{.323 - .36}{\sqrt{.034} / \sqrt{64}} = -1.61$

The rejection region requires $\alpha = .10$ in the lower tail of the z-distribution. From Table IV, Appendix B, $z_{.10} = 1.28$. The rejection region is $z < -1.28$.

Since the observed value of the test statistic falls in the rejection region ($z = -1.61 < -1.28$), H_0 is rejected. There is sufficient evidence to indicate the mean is less than .36 at $\alpha = .10$.

b.　H_0: $\mu = .36$
　　H_a: $\mu \neq .36$

The test statistic is $z = -1.61$ (see part **a**).

The rejection region requires $\alpha/2 = .10/2 = .05$ in the each tail of the z-distribution. From Table IV, Appendix B, $z_{.05} = 1.645$. The rejection region is $z < -1.645$ or $z > 1.645$.

Since the observed value of the test statistic does not fall in the rejection region ($z = -1.61 \not< -1.645$), H_0 is not rejected. There is insufficient evidence to indicate the mean is different from .36 at $\alpha = .10$.

6.23　a.　The rejection region requires $\alpha = .01$ in the lower tail of the z-distribution. From Table IV, Appendix B, $z_{.01} = 2.33$. The rejection region is $z < -2.33$.

　　b.　The test statistic is $z = \dfrac{\bar{x} - \mu_o}{\sigma_{\bar{x}}} \approx \dfrac{19.3 - 20}{11.9/\sqrt{46}} = -.40$

　　c.　Since the observed value of the test statistics does not fall in the rejection region ($z = -.40 \not< -2.33$), H_0 is not rejected. There is insufficient evidence to indicate the true mean number of latex gloves used per week by all hospital employees is less than 20 at $\alpha = .01$.

6.25　Let $\mu =$ mean lacunarity measurement for all grassland pixels. To determine if the area sampled is grassland, we test:

H_0: $\mu = 220$

H_a: $\mu \neq 220$

The test statistic is $z = \dfrac{\bar{x} - \mu_o}{\sigma_{\bar{x}}} \approx \dfrac{225 - 220}{20/\sqrt{100}} = 2.50$.

The rejection region requires $\alpha/2 = .01/2 = .005$ in each tail of the z-distribution. From Table IV, Appendix B, $z_{.005} = 2.575$. The rejection region is $z < -2.575$ or $z > 2.575$.

Since the observed value of the test statistic does not fall in the rejection region ($z = 2.50 \not> 2.575$), H_0 is not rejected. There is insufficient evidence to conclude that the area sampled is not grassland at $\alpha = .01$.

6.27　a.　To determine if the process is not operating satisfactorily, we test:

　　　　H_0: $\mu = .250$
　　　　H_a: $\mu \neq .250$

　　b.　Using MINITAB, the descriptive statistics are:

Descriptive Statistics: Tees

Variable	N	Mean	Median	TrMean	StDev	SE Mean
Tees	40	0.25248	0.25300	0.25256	0.00223	0.00035

Variable	Minimum	Maximum	Q1	Q3
Tees	0.24700	0.25600	0.25100	0.25400

The test statistic is $z = \dfrac{\bar{x} - \mu_0}{\sigma_{\bar{x}}} \approx \dfrac{.25248 - .250}{.00223/\sqrt{40}} = 7.03$

The rejection region requires $\alpha/2 = .01/2 = .005$ in each tail of the z-distribution. From Table IV, Appendix B, $z_{.005} = 2.575$. The rejection region is $z < -2.575$ or $z > 2.575$.

Since the observed value of the test statistic falls in the rejection region ($z = 7.03 > 2.575$), H_0 is rejected. There is sufficient information to indicate the process is performing in an unsatisfactory manner at $\alpha = .01$.

c. α is the probability of a Type I error. A Type I error, in this case, is to say the process is unsatisfactory when, in fact, it is satisfactory. The risk, then, is to the producer since he will be spending time and money to repair a process that is not in error.

β is the probability of a Type II error. A Type II error, in this case, is to say the process is satisfactory when it, in fact, is not. This is the consumer's risk since he could unknowingly purchase a defective product.

6.29   To determine if the mean point-spread error is different from 0, we test:

H_0: $\mu = 0$
H_a: $\mu \neq 0$

The test statistic is $z = \dfrac{\bar{x} - \mu_0}{\sigma_{\bar{x}}} \approx \dfrac{-1.6 - 0}{13.3/\sqrt{240}} = -1.86$

The rejection region requires $\alpha/2 = .01/2 = .005$ in each tail of the z distribution. From Table IV, Appendix B, $z_{.005} = 2.575$. The rejection region is $z > 2.575$ or $z < -2.575$.

Since the observed value of the test statistic does not fall in the rejection region ($z = -1.86 \not< 2.575$), H_0 is not rejected. There is insufficient evidence to indicate that the true mean point-spread error is different from 0 at $\alpha = .01$.

6.31   a. No. Since the hypothesized value of μ_M (60,000) falls in the 95% confidence interval, it is a likely candidate for the true mean. Thus, we would not reject H_0. There is no evidence that the mean salary for males differs from $60,000.

b. To determine if the true mean salary of males with post-graduate degrees differs from $60,000, we test:

H_0: $\mu = 60,000$
H_a: $\mu \neq 60,000$

The test statistic is $z = \dfrac{\bar{x} - \mu_0}{\sigma_{\bar{x}}} \approx \dfrac{61,340 - 60,000}{2,185} = 0.61$

The rejection region requires $\alpha/2 = .05/2 = .025$ in each tail of the z-distribution. From Table IV, Appendix B, $z_{.025} = 1.96$. The rejection region is $z > 1.96$ or $z < -1.96$.

Since the observed value of the test statistic does not fall in the rejection region ($z = 0.61 \not> 1.96$), H_0 is not rejected. There is insufficient evidence to indicate the true mean salary of males with post-graduate degrees differs from $60,000 at $\alpha = .05$.

c.   Parts a and b must agree. In both cases, a two-sided test / confidence interval is used. The z-score used in both parts is the same, as are $\overline{x}$ and $s_{\overline{x}}$.

d.   No. Since the hypothesized value of μ_F (33,000) falls in the 95% confidence interval, it is a likely candidate for the true mean. Thus, we would not reject H_0. There is no evidence that the mean salary for females differs from \$33,000.

e.   To determine if the true mean salary of females with post-graduate degrees differs from \$33,000, we test:

H_0: $\mu = 33,000$
H_a: $\mu \neq 33,000$

The test statistic is $z = \dfrac{\overline{x} - \mu_0}{\sigma_{\overline{x}}} \approx \dfrac{32,227 - 33,000}{932} = -0.83$

The rejection region requires $\alpha/2 = .05/2 = .025$ in each tail of the z-distribution. From Table IV, Appendix B, $z_{.025} = 1.96$. The rejection region is $z > 1.96$ or $z < -1.96$.

Since the observed value of the test statistic does not fall in the rejection region $(z = -0.83 \not< -1.96)$, H_0 is not rejected. There is insufficient evidence to indicate the true mean salary of females with post-graduate degrees differs from \$33,000 at $\alpha = .05$.

f.   Parts d and e must agree. In both cases, a two-sided test / confidence interval is used. The z-score used in both parts is the same, as are $\overline{x}$ and $s_{\overline{x}}$.

6.33   a.   To determine if CEOs at all California small firms generally agree with the statement, we test:
H_0: $\mu = 3.5$
H_a: $\mu > 3.5$

The test statistic is $z = \dfrac{\overline{x} - \mu_o}{\sigma_{\overline{x}}} \approx \dfrac{3.85 - 3.5}{1.5/\sqrt{137}} = 2.73$

The rejection region requires $\alpha = .05$ in the upper tail of the z-distribution. From Table IV, Appendix B, $z_{.05} = 1.645$. The rejection region is $z > 1.645$.

Since the observed value of the test statistics falls in the rejection region $(z = 2.73 > 1.645)$, H_0 is rejected. There is sufficient evidence to indicate CEOs at all California small firms generally agree with the statement (true mean scale score exceeds 3.5) at $\alpha = .05$.

b.   Although the sample mean of 3.85 is far enough away from 3.5 to statistically conclude the population mean score is greater than 3.5, a score of 3.85 may not be practically different from 3.5 to make any difference.

c.   No. Since the sample size ($n = 137$) is greater than 30, the Central Limit Theorem applies. The distribution of $\overline{x}$ is approximately normal regardless of the population distribution.

6.35   a.   Since the p-value = .10 is greater than $\alpha = .05$, H_0 is not rejected.

b.   Since the p-value = .05 is less than $\alpha = .10$, H_0 is rejected.

c.   Since the p-value = .001 is less than $\alpha = .01$, H_0 is rejected.

d.   Since the p-value = .05 is greater than $\alpha = .025$, H_0 is not rejected.

e.   Since the p-value = .45 is greater than $\alpha = .10$, H_0 is not rejected.

6.37 p-value $= P(z \geq 2.17) = .5 - P(0 < z < 2.17) = .5 - .4850 = .0150$ (using Table IV, Appendix B)

The probability of observing a test statistic of 2.17 or anything more unusual if the true mean is 100 is .0150. Since this probability is so small, there is evidence that the true mean is greater than 100.

6.39 p-value $= P(z \geq 2.17) + P(z \leq -2.17) = (.5 - .4850)2 = .0300$ (using Table IV, Appendix B)

6.41   The smallest value of α for which the null hypothesis would be rejected is just greater than .06.

6.43   a.   Using MINITAB and the data sampled from Exercise 5.18, we get the following:

One-Sample Z: carats-samp

```
Test of mu = 0.6 vs mu not = 0.6
The assumed sigma = 0.262

Variable          N        Mean      StDev    SE Mean
carats-samp       30       0.6910    0.2620   0.0478

Variable               95.0% CI               Z       P
carats-samp      (  0.5972,  0.7848)         1.90   0.057
```

From the printout, the p-value is $p = .057$.

b.   Since the p-value is greater than $\alpha (.057 > .05)$, H_0 is not rejected. There is insufficient evidence to indicate the mean number of carats per diamond is different from .6 at $\alpha = .05$.

6.45   a.   The p-value from the printout is .0693.

b.   From the printout, the set of hypotheses used are:

H_0: $\mu = 6.5$
H_a: $\mu > 6.5$

Since the p-value is not small (.0693), H_0 is not rejected. There is insufficient evidence to indicate the true mean full-service fee of U.S. funeral homes in 2009 exceeds \$6,500 at $\alpha = .05$. This agrees with the decision in Exercise 6.30.

6.47   a.   To determine if the true mean forecast error for buy-side analysts is positive, we test:

H_o: $\mu = 0$
H_a: $\mu > 0$

The test statistic is $z = \dfrac{\bar{x} - \mu_o}{\sigma_{\bar{x}}} \approx \dfrac{.85 - 0}{1.93 / \sqrt{3,526}} = 26.15$.

The observed p-value of the test is $p = P(z > 26.15) \approx 0$ (Using Table IV, Appendix B)

Since the p-value is less than $\alpha (p \approx 0 < .01)$, H_0 is rejected. There is sufficient evidence to indicate that the true mean forecast error for buy-side analysts is positive at $\alpha = .01$. This means that the buy-side analysts are overestimating earnings.

b.   To determine if the true mean forecast error for sell-side analysts is negative; we test:

H_0: $\mu = 0$
H_a: $\mu < 0$

The test statistic is $z = \dfrac{\bar{x} - \mu_o}{\sigma_{\bar{x}}} \approx \dfrac{-.05 - 0}{.85/\sqrt{58,562}} = -14.24$.

The observed *p*-value of the test is $p = P(z < -14.24) \approx 0$ (using Table IV, Appendix B)

Since the p-value is less than α ($p \approx 0 < .01$), H_0 is rejected. There is sufficient evidence to indicate that the true mean forecast error for sell-side analysts is negative at $\alpha = .01$. This means that the sell-side analysts are not underestimating earnings.

6.49   a.   We should use the *t*-distribution in testing a hypothesis about a population mean if the sample size is small, the population being sampled from is normal, and the variance of the population is unknown.

b.   Both distributions are mound-shaped and symmetric. The *t*-distribution is flatter than the *z*-distribution.

6.51   a.   The rejection region requires $\alpha/2 = .05/2 = .025$ in each tail of the *t*-distribution with df $= n - 1 = 14 - 1 = 13$. From Table V, Appendix B, $t_{.025} = 2.160$. The rejection region is $t < -2.160$ or $t > 2.160$.

b.   The rejection region requires $\alpha = .01$ in the upper tail of the *t*-distribution with df $= n - 1 = 24 - 1 = 23$. From Table V, Appendix B, $t_{.01} = 2.500$. The rejection region is $t > 2.500$.

c.   The rejection region requires $\alpha = .10$ in the upper tail of the *t*-distribution with df $= n - 1 = 9 - 1 = 8$. From Table V, Appendix B, $t_{.10} = 1.397$. The rejection region is $t > 1.397$.

d.   The rejection region requires $\alpha = .01$ in the lower tail of the *t*-distribution with df $= n - 1 = 12 - 1 = 11$. From Table V, Appendix B, $t_{.01} = 2.718$. The rejection region is $t < -2.718$.

e.   The rejection region requires $\alpha/2 = .10/2 = .05$ in each tail of the *t*-distribution with df $= n - 1 = 20 - 1 = 19$. From Table V, Appendix B, $t_{.05} = 1.729$. The rejection region is $t < -1.729$ or $t > 1.729$.

f.   The rejection region requires $\alpha = .05$ in the lower tail of the *t*-distribution with df $= n - 1 = 4 - 1 = 3$. From Table V, Appendix B, $t_{.05} = 2.353$. The rejection region is $t < -2.353$.

6.53   a.   We must assume that a random sample was drawn from a normal population.

b.   The hypotheses are:

H_0: $\mu = 1000$
H_a: $\mu > 1000$

The test statistic is $t = 1.89$.

The *p*-value is .038.

There is evidence to reject H_0 for $\alpha > .038$. There is evidence to indicate the mean is greater than 1000 for $\alpha > .038$.

c.   The hypotheses are:

H_0: $\mu = 1000$
H_a: $\mu \neq 1000$

The test statistic is $t = 1.89$.

The p-value is $2(.038) = .076$.

There is no evidence to reject H_0 for $\alpha = .05$. There is insufficient evidence to indicate the mean is different than 1000 for $\alpha = .05$.

There is evidence to reject H_0 for $\alpha > .076$. There is evidence to indicate the mean is different than 1000 for $\alpha > .076$.

6.55   a.   To determine if the mean surface roughness of coated interior pipe differs from 2 micrometers, we test:

H_0: $\mu = 2$
H_a: $\mu \neq 2$

b.   From the printout, the test statistic is $t = -1.02$.

c.   The rejection region requires $\alpha/2 = .05/2 = .025$ in each tail of the t-distribution with df $= n - 1 = 20 - 1 = 19$. From Table V, Appendix B, $t_{.025} = 2.093$. The rejection region is $t < -2.093$ or $t > 2.093$.

d.   Since the observed value of the test statistic does not fall in the rejection region $(t = -1.02 \not< -2.093)$, H_0 is not rejected. There is insufficient evidence to indicate the true mean surface roughness of coated interior pipe differs from 2 micrometers at $\alpha = .05$.

e.   The p-value is $p = .322$. Since the p-value is not less than $\alpha = .05$, H_0 is not rejected. There is insufficient evidence to indicate the true mean surface roughness of coated interior pipe differs from 2 micrometers at $\alpha = .05$.

f.   From Exercise 5.30, we found the 95% confidence interval for the mean surface roughness of coated interior pipe to be $(1.636, 2.126)$. Since the hypothesized value of μ $(\mu = 2)$ falls in the confidence interval, it is a likely value. We cannot reject it. The confidence interval and the test of hypothesis lead to the same conclusion because the critical values for the 2 techniques are the same.

6.57   a.   To determine if the mean number of suicide bombings for all Al Qaeda attacks against the U.S. differs from 2.5, we test:

H_0: $\mu = 2.5$
H_a: $\mu \neq 2.5$

From the printout, the test statistic is $t = -2.46$.

The rejection requires $\alpha/2 = .10/2 = .05$ in each tail of the t-distribution with df $= n - 1 = 21 - 1 = 20$. From Table V, Appendix B, $t_{.05} = 1.725$. The rejection region is $t < -1.725$ or $t > 1.725$.

Since the observed value of the test statistic falls in the rejection region $(t = -2.46 < -1.725)$, H_0 is rejected. There is sufficient evidence to indicate that the true mean number of suicide bombings for all Al Qaeda attacks against the US differs from 2.5 at $\alpha = .10$.

In addition, we could make our decision based on the *p*-value given in the printout. The *p*-value for the test is $p = .0229$. Since the *p*-value is less than $\alpha = .10$, we reject H_0.

b.   From Exercise 5.33, we found the 90% confidence interval for the mean number of suicide bombings for all Al Qaeda attacks against the US to be (1.41, 2.31). Since the hypothesized value of μ ($\mu = 2.5$) does not fall in the confidence interval, it is an unlikely value. We reject it. Therefore, we conclude that the true mean differs from 2.5 at $\alpha = .10$.

c.   The confidence interval and the test of hypothesis lead to the same conclusion because the critical values for 2 techniques are the same.

d.   Since the sample size is small, we must assume that the population being sampled is normal. In addition, we must assume that the sample is random.

e.   Using MINITAB, a histogram of the data is:

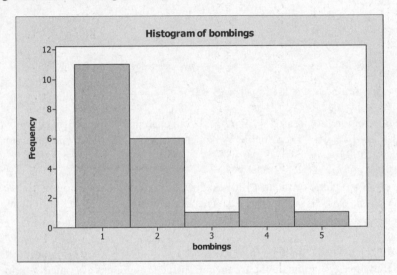

Based on the histogram, the data do not look like they are from a normal distribution. Thus, the validity of the inference in part **a** is questionable.

6.59   Using MINITAB, the descriptive statistics are:

One-Sample T: Skid

```
Test of mu = 425 vs < 425


                                         95%
                                       Upper
Variable    N      Mean    StDev  SE Mean   Bound      T      P
Skid       20   358.450  117.817   26.345  404.004  -2.53  0.010
```

To determine if the mean skidding distance is less than 425 meters, we test:

H_0: $\mu = 425$
H_a: $\mu < 425$

The test statistics is $t = \dfrac{\bar{x} - \mu_o}{s/\sqrt{n}} = \dfrac{358.45 - 425}{117.817/\sqrt{20}} = -2.53$.

The rejection region requires $\alpha = .10$ in the lower tail of the t-distribution with df $= n - 1 = 20 - 1 = 19$. From Table V, Appendix B, $t_{.10} = 1.328$. The rejection region is $t < -1.328$.

Since the observed value of the test statistic falls in the rejection region ($t = -2.53 < -1.328$), H_0 is rejected. There is sufficient evidence to indicate the true mean skidding distance is less than 425 meters at $\alpha = .10$. There is sufficient evidence to refute the claim.

6.61   To determine if the true mean crack intensity of the Mississippi highway exceeds the AASHTO recommended maximum, we test:

H_0: $\mu = .100$
H_a: $\mu > .100$

The test statistic is $t = \dfrac{\bar{x} - \mu_0}{s / \sqrt{n}} = \dfrac{.210 - .100}{\sqrt{.011} / \sqrt{8}} = 2.97$

The rejection region requires $\alpha = .01$ in the upper tail of the t-distribution with df $= n - 1 = 8 - 1 = 7$. From Table V, Appendix B, $t_{.01} = 2.998$. The rejection region is $t > 2.998$.

Since the observed value of the test statistic does not fall in the rejection region ($t = 2.97 \not> 2.998$), H_0 is not rejected. There is insufficient evidence to indicate that the true mean crack intensity of the Mississippi highway exceeds the AASHTO recommended maximum at $\alpha = .01$.

6.63   Using MINITAB, the descriptive statistics for the 2 plants are:

Descriptive Statistics: AL1, AL2

```
Variable   N   N*     Mean    SE Mean     StDev   Minimum   Q1    Median   Q3   Maximum
AL1        2   0   0.00750   0.00250   0.00354   0.00500    *   0.00750    *   0.01000
AL2        2   0    0.0700    0.0200    0.0283    0.0500    *    0.0700    *    0.0900
```

To determine if **plant 1** is violating the OSHA standard, we test:

H_0: $\mu = .004$
H_a: $\mu > .004$

The test statistic is $t = \dfrac{\bar{x} - \mu_o}{s / \sqrt{n}} = \dfrac{.0075 - .004}{.00354 / \sqrt{2}} = 1.40$

Since no α level was given, we will use $\alpha = .10$. The rejection region requires $\alpha = .05$ in the upper tail of the t-distribution with df $= n - 1 = 2 - 1 = 1$. From Table V, Appendix B, $t_{.10} = 3.078$. The rejection region is $t > 3.078$.

Since the observed value of the test statistic does not fall in the rejection region ($t = 1.40 \not> 3.078$), H_0 is not rejected. There is insufficient evidence to indicate the OSHA standard is violated by plant 1 at $\alpha = .10$.

To determine if **plant 2** is violating the OSHA standard, we test:

H_0: $\mu = .004$
H_a: $\mu > .004$

The test statistic is $t = \dfrac{\bar{x} - \mu_o}{s / \sqrt{n}} = \dfrac{.07 - .004}{.0283 / \sqrt{2}} = 3.30$

Since no α level was given, we will use $\alpha = .10$. The rejection region requires $\alpha = .10$ in the upper tail of the t-distribution with df $= n - 1 = 2 - 1 = 1$. From Table V, Appendix B, $t_{.10} = 3.078$. The rejection region is $t > 3.078$.

Since the observed value of the test statistic falls in the rejection region ($t = 3.30 > 3.078$), H_0 is rejected. There is sufficient evidence to indicate the OSHA standard is violated by plant 2 at $\alpha = .10$.

6.65   a. $z = \dfrac{\hat{p} - p_0}{\sqrt{\dfrac{p_0 q_0}{n}}} = \dfrac{.83 - .9}{\sqrt{\dfrac{.9(.1)}{100}}} = -2.33$

       b.   The denominator in Exercise 6.64 is $\sqrt{\dfrac{.7(.3)}{100}} = .0458$ as compared to $\sqrt{\dfrac{.9(.1)}{100}} = .03$ in part **a**. Since the denominator in this problem is smaller, the absolute value of z is larger.

       c.   The rejection region requires $\alpha = .05$ in the lower tail of the z-distribution. From Table IV, Appendix B, $z_{.05} = 1.645$. The rejection region is $z < -1.645$.

            Since the observed value of the test statistic falls in the rejection region ($z = -2.33 < -1.645$), H_0 is rejected. There is sufficient evidence to indicate the population proportion is less than .9 at $\alpha = .05$.

       d.   The p-value $= P(z \le -2.33) = .5 - .4901 = .0099$ (from Table IV, Appendix B). Since the p-value is less than $\alpha = .05$, H_0 is rejected.

6.67   From Exercise 5.40, $n = 50$ and since p is the proportion of consumers who do not like the snack food, $\hat{p}$ will be:

$$\hat{p} = \frac{\text{Number of 0's in sample}}{n} = \frac{29}{50} = .58$$

First, check to see if the normal approximation will be adequate:

$np_0 = 50(.5) = 25$ $\qquad\qquad$ $nq_0 = 50(.5) = 25$

Since both $np_0 \ge 15$ and $nq_0 \ge 15$, the normal distribution will be adequate.

       a. $H_0: p = .5$
            $H_a: p > .5$

            The test statistic is $z = \dfrac{\hat{p} - p_0}{\sigma_{\hat{p}}} = \dfrac{\hat{p} - p_0}{\sqrt{\dfrac{p_0 q_0}{n}}} = \dfrac{.58 - .5}{\sqrt{\dfrac{.5(1 - .5)}{50}}} = 1.13$

            The rejection region requires $\alpha = .10$ in the upper tail of the z-distribution. From Table IV, Appendix B, $z_{.10} = 1.28$. The rejection region is $z > 1.28$.

            Since the observed value of the test statistic does not fall in the rejection region ($z = 1.13 \not> 1.28$), H_0 is not rejected. There is insufficient evidence to indicate the proportion of customers who do not like the snack food is greater than .5 at $\alpha = .10$.

       b. p-value $= P(z \ge 1.13) = .5 - .3708 = .1292$

6.69   a.   The point estimate is $\hat{p} = .42$.

b.   To determine if whether the p has increased since 2005, we test:

H_0: $p = .30$
H_a: $p > .30$

c.   The test statistics is $z = \dfrac{\hat{p} - p_o}{\sqrt{\dfrac{p_o q_o}{n}}} = \dfrac{.42 - .30}{\sqrt{\dfrac{.30(.70)}{4,000}}} = 16.56$

d.   The rejection region requires $\alpha = .01$ in the upper tail of the z-distribution. From Table IV, Appendix B, $z_{.01} = 2.33$. The rejection region is $z > 2.33$.

e.   Since the observed value of the test statistic falls in the rejection region ($z = 16.56 > 2.33$), H_0 is rejected. There is sufficient evidence to conclude that p has increased since 2005 at $\alpha = .01$.

f.   The p-value $= P(z \geq 16.56) = .5 - .5 \approx 0$ is less than .01, H_0 is rejected. The conclusion is the same as that in part **e**.

6.71   To determine if the sample provides sufficient evidence to indicate that the true percentage of all firms that announced one or more acquisitions during the year 2000 is less than 30%, we test:

H_0: $p = .30$
H_a: $p < .30$

The point estimate is $\hat{p} = \dfrac{x}{n} = \dfrac{748}{2,778} = .269$

The test statistic is $z = \dfrac{\hat{p} - p_o}{\sqrt{\dfrac{p_o q_o}{n}}} = \dfrac{.269 - .30}{\sqrt{\dfrac{.30(.70)}{2,778}}} = -3.57$

The rejection region requires $\alpha = .05$ in the lower tail of the z-distribution. From Table IV, Appendix B, $z_{.05} = 1.645$. The rejection region is $z < -1.645$.

Since the observed value of the test statistic falls in the rejection region ($z = -3.57 < -1.645$), H_0 is rejected. There is sufficient evidence to indicate that the true percentage of all firms that announced one or more acquisitions during the year 2000 is less than 30% at $\alpha = .05$.

6.73   a.   To determine whether the true proportion of toothpaste brands with the ADA seal of verifying effective decay prevention is less than .5, we test:

H_0: $p = .5$
H_a: $p < .5$

b.   From the printout, the p-value is $p = .231$.

c.   Since the observed value of p is greater than $\alpha = .10$, H_0 is not rejected. There is insufficient evidence to indicate the true proportion of toothpaste brands with the ADA seal of verifying effective decay prevention is less than .5 at $\alpha = .10$.

6.75   a.   Let p = proportion of middle-aged women who exhibit skin improvement after using the cream. For this problem, $\hat{p} = \dfrac{x}{n} = \dfrac{24}{33} = .727$.

First we check to see if the normal approximation is adequate:

$$np_0 = 33(.6) = 19.8 \quad nq_0 = 33(.4) = 13.2$$

Since $nq_0 = 13.2$ is less than 15, the assumption of normality may not be valid. We will will go ahead and perform the test.

To determine if the cream will improve the skin of more than 60% of middle-aged women, we test:

H_0: $p = .60$
H_a: $p > .60$

The test statistic is $z = \dfrac{\hat{p} - p_0}{\sqrt{\dfrac{p_0 q_0}{n}}} = \dfrac{.727 - .60}{\sqrt{\dfrac{.60(.40)}{33}}} = 1.49$

The rejection region requires $\alpha = .05$ in the upper tail of the z-distribution. From Table IV, Appendix B, $z_{.05} = 1.645$. The rejection region is $z > 1.645$.

Since the observed value of the test statistic does not fall in the rejection region ($z = 1.49 \not> -1.645$), H_0 is not rejected. There is insufficient evidence to indicate the cream will improve the skin of more than 60% of middle-aged women at $\alpha = .05$.

    b.   The *p*-value is $p = P(z \geq 1.49) = (.5 - .4319) = .0681$. (Using Table IV, Appendix B.) Since the *p*-value is greater than $\alpha = .05$, H_0 is not rejected. There is insufficient evidence to indicate the cream will improve the skin of more than 60% of middle-aged women at $\alpha = .05$.

6.77   a.   To determine if the GSR for all scholarship athletes at Division I institutions differs from 60%, we test:

H_0: $p = .60$
H_a: $p \neq .60$

The point estimate is $\hat{p} = \dfrac{x}{n} = \dfrac{315}{500} = .63$

The test statistic is $z = \dfrac{\hat{p} - p_o}{\sqrt{\dfrac{p_o q_o}{n}}} = \dfrac{.63 - .60}{\sqrt{\dfrac{.60(.40)}{500}}} = 1.37$

The rejection region requires $\alpha/2 = .01/2 = .005$ in each tail of the *z*-distribution. From Table IV, Appendix B, $z_{.005} = 2.575$. The rejection region is $z < -2.575$ or $z > 2.575$.

Since the observed value does not fall in the rejection region ($z = 1.37 \not> 2.575$), H_0 is not rejected. There is insufficient evidence to conclude that the GSR for all scholarship athletes at Division I institution differs from 60% at $\alpha = .01$.

b.   To determine if the GSR for all male basketball players at Division I institutions differs from 58%, we test:

H_0: $p = .58$
H_a: $p \neq .58$

The point estimate is $\hat{p} = \dfrac{x}{n} = \dfrac{84}{200} = .42$

The test statistic is $z = \dfrac{\hat{p} - p_o}{\sqrt{\dfrac{p_o q_o}{n}}} = \dfrac{.42 - .58}{\sqrt{\dfrac{.58(.42)}{200}}} = -4.58$

The rejection region requires $\alpha/2 = .01/2 = .005$ in each tail of the z-distribution. From Table IV, Appendix B, $z_{.005} = 2.575$. The rejection region is $z < -2.575$ or $z > 2.575$.

Since the observed value falls in the rejection region ($z = -4.58 < -2.575$), H_0 is rejected. There is sufficient evidence to conclude that the GSR for all male basketball players at Division I institutions differs from 58% $\alpha = .01$.

6.79   To minimize the probability of a Type I error, we will select $\alpha = .01$.

First, check to see if the normal approximation is adequate:

$np_0 = 100(.5) = 50$ $nq_0 = 100(.5) = 50$

Since both $np_0 \geq .15$ and $nq_0 \geq .15$, the normal distribution will be adequate

$\hat{p} = \dfrac{x}{n} = \dfrac{56}{100} = .56$

To determine if more than half of all Diet Coke drinkers prefer Diet Pepsi, we test:

H_0: $p = .5$
H_a: $p > .5$

The test statistic is $z = \dfrac{\hat{p} - p_0}{\sqrt{\dfrac{p_0 q_0}{n}}} = \dfrac{.56 - .5}{\sqrt{\dfrac{.5(.5)}{100}}} = 1.20$

The rejection region requires $\alpha = .01$ in the upper tail of the z-distribution. From Table IV, Appendix B, $z_{.01} = 2.33$. The rejection region is $z > 2.33$.

Since the observed value of the test statistic does not fall in the rejection region ($z = 1.20 \not> 2.33$), H_0 is not rejected. There is insufficient evidence to indicate that more than half of all Diet Coke drinkers prefer Diet Pepsi at $\alpha = .01$.

Since H_0 was not rejected, there is no evidence that Diet Coke drinkers prefer Diet Pepsi.

6.81   a.   By the Central Limit Theorem, the sampling distribution of $\bar{x}$ is
           approximately normal with

           $\mu_{\bar{x}} = \mu = 500$ and

           $\sigma_{\bar{x}} = \dfrac{\sigma}{\sqrt{n}} = \dfrac{100}{\sqrt{25}} = 20.$

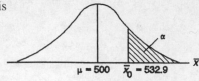

       b. $\bar{x}_0 = \mu_0 + z_\alpha \sigma_{\bar{x}} = \mu_0 + z_\alpha \dfrac{\sigma}{\sqrt{n}}$ where $z_\alpha = z_{.05} = 1.645$ from Table IV, Appendix B.

           Thus, $\bar{x}_0 = 500 + 1.645\dfrac{100}{\sqrt{25}} = 532.9$

       c.   The sampling distribution of $\bar{x}$ is approximately normal by the
           Central Limit Theorem with $\mu_{\bar{x}} = \mu = 550$ and

           $\sigma_{\bar{x}} = \dfrac{\sigma}{\sqrt{n}} = \dfrac{100}{\sqrt{25}} = 20.$

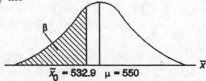

       d. $\beta = P(\bar{x}_0 < 532.9 \text{ when } \mu = 550) = P\left(z < \dfrac{532.9 - 550}{100/\sqrt{25}}\right) = P(z < -.86)$

           $= .5 - .3051 = .1949$

       e. $\text{Power} = 1 - \beta = 1 - .1949 = .8051$

6.83   a.   The sampling distribution of $\bar{x}$ will be approximately normal (by the Central Limit Theorem) with

           $\mu_{\bar{x}} = \mu = 75$ and $\sigma_{\bar{x}} = \dfrac{\sigma}{\sqrt{n}} = \dfrac{15}{\sqrt{49}} = 2.143.$

       b.   The sampling distribution of $\bar{x}$ will be approximately normal (by the Central Limit Theorem) with

           $\mu_{\bar{x}} = \mu = 70$ and $\sigma_{\bar{x}} = \dfrac{\sigma}{\sqrt{n}} = \dfrac{15}{\sqrt{49}} = 2.143.$

       c.   First, find $\bar{x}_0 = \mu_0 - z_\alpha \sigma_{\bar{x}} = \mu_0 - z_\alpha \dfrac{\sigma}{\sqrt{n}}$ where $z_{.10} = 1.28$ from Table IV, Appendix B.

           Thus, $\bar{x}_0 = 75 - 1.28\dfrac{15}{\sqrt{49}} = 72.257$

           Now, find $\beta = P(\bar{x}_0 > 72.257 \text{ when } \mu = 70) = P\left(z > \dfrac{72.257 - 70}{15/\sqrt{49}}\right)$

           $= P(z > 1.05) = .5 - .3531 = .1469$

       d. $\text{Power} = 1 - \beta = 1 - .1469 = .8531$

6.85   a.   The sampling distribution of $\bar{x}$ will be approximately normal (by the Central Limit Theorem) with

$$\mu_{\bar{x}} = \mu = 30 \text{ and } \sigma_{\bar{x}} = \frac{\sigma}{\sqrt{n}} = \frac{1.2}{\sqrt{121}} = .109.$$

b.   The sampling distribution of will be approximately normal (CLT) with $\mu_{\bar{x}} = \mu = 29.8$

and $\sigma_{\bar{x}} = \frac{\sigma}{\sqrt{n}} = \frac{1.2}{\sqrt{121}} = .109.$

c.   First, find $\bar{x}_{O,L} = \mu_0 - z_{\alpha/2}\,\sigma_{\bar{x}} = \mu_0 - z_{\alpha/2}\dfrac{\sigma}{\sqrt{n}}$

where $z_{.05/2} = z_{.025} = 1.96$ from Table IV, Appendix B.

Thus, $\bar{x}_{O,L} = 30 - 1.96\dfrac{1.2}{\sqrt{121}} = 29.79$

$$\bar{x}_{O,U} = \mu_0 + z_{\alpha/2}\,\sigma_{\bar{x}} = \mu_0 + z_{\alpha/2}\frac{\sigma}{\sqrt{n}} = 30 + 1.96\frac{1.2}{\sqrt{121}} = 30.21$$

Now, find $\beta = P(29.79 < \bar{x} < 30.21 \text{ when } \mu = 29.8)$

$$= P\left(\frac{29.79 - 29.8}{1.2/\sqrt{121}} < z < \frac{30.21 - 29.8}{1.2/\sqrt{121}}\right)$$
$$= P(-.09 < z < 3.76)$$
$$= .0359 + .5 = .5359$$

d. $\beta = P(29.79 < \bar{x} < 30.21 \text{ when } \mu = 30.4) = P\left(\dfrac{29.79 - 30.4}{1.2/\sqrt{121}} < z < \dfrac{30.21 - 30.4}{1.2/\sqrt{121}}\right)$

$$= P(-5.59 < z < -1.74)$$
$$= .5 - .4591 = .0409$$

6.87   a.   We have failed to reject H_0 when it is not true. This is a Type II error.

To compute β, first find:

$$\bar{x}_0 = \mu_0 - z_\alpha\sigma_{\bar{x}} = \mu_0 - z_\alpha\frac{\sigma}{\sqrt{n}} \text{ where } z_{.05} = 1.645 \text{ from Table IV, Appendix B.}$$

Thus, $\bar{x}_0 = 5.0 - 1.645\dfrac{.01}{\sqrt{100}} = 4.998355$

Then find:

$$\beta = P(\bar{x}_0 > 4.998355 \text{ when } \mu = 4.9975) = P\left(z > \frac{4.998355 - 4.9975}{.01/\sqrt{100}}\right)$$

$$= P(z > .86) = .5 - .3051 = .1949$$

b.   We have rejected H_0 when it is true. This is a Type I error. The probability of a Type I error is $\alpha = .05$.

c.   A departure of .0025 below 5.0 is $\mu = 4.9975$. Using **a**, β when $\mu = 4.9975$ is .1949. The power of the test is $1 - \beta = 1 - .1949 = .8051$

6.89   First, find $\overline{x}_0$ such that $P(\overline{x} < \overline{x}_0) = .05$.

$$P(\overline{x} < \overline{x}_0) = P\left(z < \frac{\overline{x}_0 - 10}{1.2/\sqrt{48}}\right) = P(z < z_0) = .05.$$

From Table IV, Appendix B, $z_0 = -1.645$.

Thus, $z_0 = \dfrac{\overline{x}_0 - 10}{1.2/\sqrt{48}} \Rightarrow \overline{x}_0 = -1.645(.173) + 10 = 9.715$

The probability of a Type II error is:

$$\beta = P(\overline{x} \geq 9.715 \mid \mu = 9.5) = P\left(z \geq \frac{9.715 - 9.5}{1.2/\sqrt{48}}\right) = P(z \geq 1.24) = .5 - .3925 = .1075$$

6.91   a. $df = n - 1 = 16 - 1 = 15$; reject H_0 if $\chi^2 < 6.26214$ or $\chi^2 > 27.4884$

b. $df = n - 1 = 23 - 1 = 22$; reject H_0 if $\chi^2 > 40.2894$

c. $df = n - 1 = 15 - 1 = 14$; reject H_0 if $\chi^2 > 21.0642$

d. $df = n - 1 = 13 - 1 = 12$; reject H_0 if $\chi^2 < 3.57056$

e. $df = n - 1 = 7 - 1 = 6$; reject H_0 if $\chi^2 < 1.63539$ or $\chi^2 > 12.5916$

f. $df = n - 1 = 25 - 1 = 24$; reject H_0 if $\chi^2 < 13.8484$

6.93   a. H_0: $\sigma^2 = 1$
H_a: $\sigma^2 > 1$

The test statistic is $\chi^2 = \dfrac{(n-1)s^2}{\sigma_0^2} = \dfrac{(100-1)4.84}{1} = 479.16$

The rejection region requires $\alpha = .05$ in the upper tail of the χ^2 distribution with $df = n - 1 = 100 - 1 = 99$. From Table VI, Appendix B, $\chi^2_{.05} \approx 124.324$. The rejection region is $\chi^2 > 124.324$.

Since the observed value of the test statistic falls in the rejection region ($\chi^2 = 479.16 > 124.324$), H_0 is rejected. There is sufficient evidence to indicate the variance is larger than 1 at $\alpha = .05$.

b.   In part **b** of Exercise 6.92, the test statistic was $\chi^2 = 29.04$. The conclusion was to reject H_0 as it was in this problem.

6.95   a.   The rejection region requires $\alpha/2 = .01/2 = .005$ in each tail of the χ^2 distribution with $df = n - 1 = 46 - 1 = 45$. From Table VI, Appendix B, $\chi^2_{.005} \approx 73.12795$ and $\chi^2_{.995} \approx 24.3486$. The rejection region is $\chi^2 < 24.3486$ or $\chi^2 > 73.12795$.

b.   The test statistic is $\chi^2 = \dfrac{(n-1)s^2}{\sigma_o^2} = \dfrac{(46-1)11.9^2}{100} = 63.7245$.

c.   Since the observed value of the test statistic does not fall in the rejection region
($\chi^2 = 63.7245 \not< 24.3486$ and $\chi^2 = 63.7245 \not> 73.12795$), H_0 is not rejected. There is
insufficient evidence to indicate the variance is different from 100 at $\alpha = .01$.

6.97   a.   Let σ^2 = weight variance of tees. To determine if the weight variance differs from .000004 (injection
mold process is out-of-control), we test:

H_0: $\sigma^2 = .000004$
H_a: $\sigma^2 \neq .000004$

b.   Using MINITAB, the descriptive statistics are:

Descriptive Statistics: Tees

Variable	N	Mean	Median	TrMean	StDev	SE Mean
Tees	40	0.25248	0.25300	0.25256	0.00223	0.00035

Variable	Minimum	Maximum	Q1	Q3
Tees	0.24700	0.25600	0.25100	0.25400

The test statistic is $\chi^2 = \dfrac{(n-1)s^2}{\sigma_0^2} = \dfrac{(40-1)(.00223)^2}{.000004} = 48.49$

The rejection region requires $\alpha/2 = .01/2 = .005$ in each tail of the χ^2 distribution with df $= n - 1 =$
$40 - 1 = 39$. From Table VI, Appendix B, $\chi^2_{.005} \approx 66.7659$ and $\chi^2_{.995} \approx 20.7065$. The rejection
region is $\chi^2 > 66.7659$ or $\chi^2 < 20.7065$.

Since the observed value of the test statistic does not fall in the rejection region ($\chi^2 = 49.49 \not>$
66.7659 and $\chi^2 = 49.49 \not< 20.7065$), H_0 is not rejected. There is insufficient evidence to indicate
the injection mold process is out-of-control at $\alpha = .01$.

c.   We must assume that the distributions of the weights of tees is approximately normal. Using
MINITAB, a histogram of the data is:

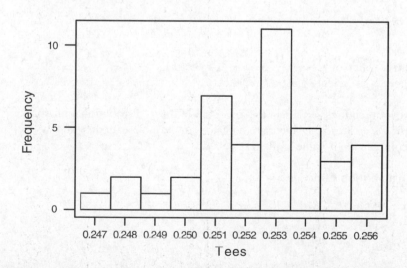

The data look fairly mound-shaped, so the assumption of normality seems to be reasonably satisfied.

6.99   To determine if the diameters of the ball bearings are more variable when produced by the new process, test:

H_0: $\sigma^2 = .00156$
H_a: $\sigma^2 > .00156$

The test statistic is $\chi^2 = \dfrac{(n-1)s^2}{\sigma_0^2} = \dfrac{99(.00211)}{.00156} = 133.90$

The rejection region requires use of the upper tail of the χ^2 distribution with df $= n - 1 = 100 - 1 = 99$. We will use df $= 100 \approx 99$ due to the limitations of the table. From Table VI, Appendix B, $\chi^2_{.025} = 129.561 < 133.90 < 135.807 = \chi^2_{.010}$. The p-value of the test is between .010 and .025. The decision made depends on the desired α. For $\alpha < .010$, there is not enough evidence to show that the variance in the diameters is greater than .00156; the reverse decision would be made for $\alpha \geq .025$.

6.101   a.   Since the sample mean of 3.85 is not that far from the value of 3.5, a large standard deviation would indicate that the value 3.85 is not very many standard deviations from 3.5.

        b.   The rejection region requires $\alpha = .01$ in the upper tail of the z-distribution. From Table IV, Appendix B, $z_{.01} = 2.33$. The rejection region is $z > 2.33$.

              The test statistic is $z = \dfrac{\bar{x} - \mu_o}{\sigma_{\bar{x}}} = \dfrac{3.85 - 3.5}{\sigma/\sqrt{137}}$

              To reject H_0, $z > 2.33$. Thus, we need to find σ so $z > 2.33$.

              $z = \dfrac{3.85 - 3.5}{\sigma/\sqrt{137}} > 2.33 \Rightarrow 3.85 - 3.5 > 2.33\dfrac{\sigma}{\sqrt{137}} \Rightarrow .35 > .199065\sigma \Rightarrow 1.758 < \sigma$

              Thus, the largest value of σ for which we will reject H_0 is 1.758.

        c.   To determine if $\sigma < 1.758$, we test:

              H_0: $\sigma^2 = 1.758^2$
              H_a: $\sigma^2 < 1.758^2$

              The test statistic is $\chi^2 = \dfrac{(n-1)s^2}{\sigma_o^2} = \dfrac{(137-1)1.5^2}{1.758^2} = 99.011$.

              The rejection region requires $\alpha = .01$ in the lower tail of the χ^2 distribution with df $= n - 1 = 137 - 1 = 136$. Since there are no values in the table with df > 100, we will use MINITAB to compute the p-value of the test statistic.

              Cumulative Distribution Function

              ```
              Chi-Square with 136 DF

                        x   P( X <= x )
                   99.011     0.0072496
              ```

              Since the p-value is less than α (p-value $= 0.0072496 < \alpha = .01$), H_0 is rejected. There is sufficient evidence to indicate the standard deviation of the scores is less than 1.758 at $\alpha = .01$.

6.103   The smaller the *p*-value associated with a test of hypothesis, the stronger the support for the **alternative** hypothesis. The *p*-value is the probability of observing your test statistic or anything more unusual, given the null hypothesis is true. If this value is small, it would be very unusual to observe this test statistic if the null hypothesis were true. Thus, it would indicate the alternative hypothesis is true.

6.105   There is not a direct relationship between α and β. That is, if α is known, it does not mean β is known because β depends on the value of the parameter in the alternative hypothesis and the sample size. However, as α decreases, β increases for a fixed value of the parameter and a fixed sample size. Thus if α is very small, β will tend to be large.

6.107   a. H_0: $\mu = 80$
               H_a: $\mu < 80$

The test statistic is $t = \dfrac{\bar{x} - \mu_0}{s / \sqrt{n}} = \dfrac{72.6 - 80}{\sqrt{19.4} / \sqrt{20}} = -7.51$

The rejection region requires $\alpha = .05$ in the lower tail of the *t*-distribution with df $= n - 1 = 20 - 1 = 19$. From Table V, Appendix B, $t_{.05} = 1.729$. The rejection region is $t < -1.729$.

Since the observed value of the test statistic falls in the rejection region ($-7.51 < -1.729$), H_0 is rejected. There is sufficient evidence to indicate that the mean is less than 80 at $\alpha = .05$.

         b. H_0: $\mu = 80$
               H_a: $\mu \neq 80$

The test statistic is $t = \dfrac{\bar{x} - \mu_0}{s / \sqrt{n}} = \dfrac{72.6 - 80}{\sqrt{19.4} / \sqrt{20}} = -7.51$

The rejection region requires $\alpha/2 = .01/2 = .005$ in each tail of the *t*-distribution with df $= n - 1 = 20 - 1 = 19$. From Table V, Appendix B, $t_{.005} = 2.861$. The rejection region is $t < -2.861$ or $t > 2.861$.

Since the observed value of the test statistic falls in the rejection region ($-7.51 < -2.861$), H_0 is rejected. There is sufficient evidence to indicate that the mean is different from 80 at $\alpha = .01$.

6.109   a. H_0: $p = .35$
               H_a: $p < .35$

The test statistic is $z = \dfrac{\hat{p} - p_0}{\sqrt{\dfrac{p_0 q_0}{n}}} = \dfrac{.29 - .35}{\sqrt{\dfrac{.35(.65)}{200}}} = -1.78$

The rejection region requires $\alpha = .05$ in the lower tail of the *z*-distribution. From Table IV, Appendix B, $z_{.05} = 1.645$. The rejection region is $z < -1.645$.

Once the observed value of the test statistic falls in the rejection region ($z = -1.78 < -1.645$), H_0 is rejected. There is sufficient evidence to indicate $p < .35$ at $\alpha = .05$.

b. H_0: $p = .35$
H_a: $p \neq .35$

The test statistic is $z = -1.78$ (from **a**).

The rejection region requires $\alpha/2 = .05/2 = .025$ in each tail of the z-distribution. From Table IV, Appendix B, $t_{.025} = 1.96$. The rejection region is $z < -1.96$ or $z > 1.96$.

Since the observed value of the test statistic does not fall in the rejection region ($z = -1.78 \not< -1.96$), H_0 is not rejected. There is insufficient evidence to indicate p is different from .35 at $\alpha = .05$.

6.111   a. H_0: $\sigma^2 = 30$
H_a: $\sigma^2 > 30$

The test statistic is $\chi^2 = \dfrac{(n-1)s^2}{\sigma_0^2} = \dfrac{(41-1)(6.9)^2}{30} = 63.48$

The rejection region requires $\alpha = .05$ in the upper tail of the χ^2 distribution with df $= n - 1 = 40$. From Table VI, Appendix B, $\chi^2_{.05} = 55.7585$. The rejection region is $\chi^2 > 55.7585$.

Since the observed value of the test statistic falls in the rejection region ($\chi^2 = 63.48 > 55.7585$), H_0 is rejected. There is sufficient evidence to indicate the variance is larger than 30 at $\alpha = .05$.

b. H_0: $\sigma^2 = 30$
H_a: $\sigma^2 \neq 30$

The test statistic is $\chi^2 = 63.48$ (from part a).

The rejection region requires $\alpha/2 = .05/2 = .025$ in each tail of the χ^2 distribution with df $= n - 1 = 40$. From Table VI, Appendix B, $\chi^2_{.025} = 59.3417$ and $\chi^2_{.975} = 24.4331$. The rejection region is $\chi^2 < 24.4331$ or $\chi^2 > 59.3417$.

Since the observed value of the test statistic falls in the rejection region ($\chi^2 = 63.48 > 59.3417$), H_0 is rejected. There is sufficient evidence to indicate the variance is not 30 at $\alpha = .05$.

6.113   a. $\hat{p} = \dfrac{x}{n} = \dfrac{320}{616} = .519$

b.   To determine whether the value of p has changed since 1999, we test:

H_0: $p = .62$
H_a: $p \neq .62$

c.   The test statistic is $z = \dfrac{\hat{p} - p_o}{\sqrt{\dfrac{p_o q_o}{n}}} = \dfrac{.519 - .62}{\sqrt{\dfrac{.62(.38)}{616}}} = -5.16$

d.   The rejection region requires $\alpha/2 = .05/2 = .025$ in each tail of the z-distribution. From Table IV, Appendix B, $z_{.025} = 1.96$. The rejection region is $z < -1.96$ or $z > 1.96$.

e. Since the observed value of the test statistic falls in the rejection region ($z = -5.16 < -1.96$), H_0 is rejected. There is sufficient evidence to indicate the true proportion of businesses that suffered unauthorized use of computer systems in 2006 is different than .62 at $\alpha = .05$.

f. The *p*-value is

$p = P(z \le -5.16) + P(z \ge 5.16) = (.5 - .5) + (.5 - .5) = 0 + 0 = 0$
(Using Table IV, Appendix B)

Since the observed value of *p* is less than $\alpha = .05$, H_0 is rejected. This is the same conclusion as in part **e**.

6.115 a. To determine if the average high technology stock is riskier than the market as a whole, we test:

H_0: $\mu = 1$
H_a: $\mu > 1$

b. The test statistic is $t = \dfrac{\bar{x} - \mu_0}{s / \sqrt{n}}$

The rejection region requires $\alpha = .10$ in the upper tail of the *t*-distribution with df $= n - 1 = 15 - 1 = 14$. From Table V, Appendix B, $t_{.10} = 1.345$. The rejection region is $t > 1.345$.

c. We must assume the population of beta coefficients of technology stocks is normally distributed.

d. The test statistic is $t = \dfrac{\bar{x} - \mu_0}{s / \sqrt{n}} = \dfrac{1.23 - 1}{.37 / \sqrt{15}} = 2.41$

Since the observed value of the test statistic falls in the rejection region ($t = 2.41 > 1.345$), H_0 is rejected. There is sufficient evidence to indicate the mean high technology stock is riskier than the market as a whole at $\alpha = .10$.

e. From Table V, Appendix B, with df $= n - 1 = 15 - 1 = 14$, $.01 < P(t \ge 2.41) < .025$. Thus, $.01 < p$-value $< .025$. The probability of observing this test statistic, $t = 2.41$, or anything more unusual is between .01 and .025. Since this probability is small, there is evidence to indicate the null hypothesis is false for $\alpha = .05$.

f. To determine if the variance of the stock beta values differs from .15, we test:

H_0: $\sigma^2 = .15$
H_a: $\sigma^2 \ne .15$

The test statistic is $\chi^2 = \dfrac{(n-1)s^2}{\sigma_o^2} = \dfrac{(15-1).37^2}{.15} = 12.7773$.

The rejection region requires $\alpha/2 = .05/2 = .025$ in each tail of the χ^2 distribution with df $= n - 1 = 15 - 1 = 14$. From Table VI, Appendix B, $\chi^2_{.975} = 5.62872$ and $\chi^2_{.025} = 26.1190$. The rejection region is $\chi^2 > 26.1190$ or $\chi^2 < 5.62872$.

Since the observed value of the test statistic does not fall in the rejection region ($\chi^2 = 12.7773 \not> 26.1190$ and $\chi^2 = 12.7773 \not< 5.62875$), H_0 is not rejected. There is insufficient evidence to indicate the variance of the stock beta values differs from .15 at $\alpha = .05$.

6.117   To determine whether the true mean pouring temperature differs from the target setting, we test:

H_0: $\mu = 2,550$
H_a: $\mu \neq 2,550$

From the printout, the test statistic is $t = 1.210$ and the p-value is .257.

Since the p-value is greater than $\alpha = .01$, H_0 is not rejected. There is insufficient evidence to indicate the true mean pouring temperature is different from 2,550 degrees at $\alpha = .01$.

6.119   a.   The hypotheses would be:

H_0: Individual does not have the disease
H_a: Individual does have the disease

b.   A Type I error would be: Conclude the individual has the disease when in fact he/she does not. This would be a false positive test.

A Type II error would be: Conclude the individual does not have the disease when in fact he/she does. This would be a false negative test.

c.   If the disease is serious, either error would be grave. Arguments could be made for either error being more grave. However, I believe a Type II error would be more grave: Concluding the individual does not have the disease when he/she does. This person would not receive critical treatment, and may suffer very serious consequences. Thus, it is more important to minimize β.

6.121   To determine if the true standard deviation of the point-spread errors exceed 15 (variance exceeds 225), we test:

H_0: $\sigma^2 = 225$
H_a: $\sigma^2 > 225$

The test statistic is $\chi^2 = \dfrac{(n-1)s^2}{\sigma_0^2} = \dfrac{(240-1)13.3^2}{225} = 187.896$

The rejection region requires α in the upper tail of the χ^2 distribution with df $= n - 1 = 240 - 1 = 239$. The maximum value of df in Table VI is 100. Thus, we cannot find the rejection region using Table VII. Using a statistical package, the p-value associated with $\chi^2 = 187.896$ is .9938.

Since the p-value is so large, there is no evidence to reject H_0. There is insufficient evidence to indicate that the true standard deviation of the point-spread errors exceeds 15 for any reasonable value of α.

(Since the observed variance (or standard deviation) is less than the hypothesized value of the variance (or standard deviation) under H_0, there is no way H_0 will be rejected for any reasonable value of α.)

6.123 a.   First, check to see if n is large enough:

$$np_0 = 132(.5) = 66 \quad nq_0 = 132(.5) = 66$$

Since both $np_0 \ge 15$ and $nq_0 \ge 15$, the normal distribution will be adequate.

To determine if there is evidence to reject the claim that no more than half of all manufacturers are dissatisfied with their trade promotion spending, we test:

H_0: $p = .5$
H_a: $p > .5$

The test statistic is $z = \dfrac{\hat{p} - p_0}{\sqrt{\dfrac{p_0 q_0}{n}}} = \dfrac{.36 - .5}{\sqrt{\dfrac{.5(.5)}{132}}} = -3.22$

The rejection region requires $\alpha = .02$ in the upper tail of the z-distribution. From Table IV, Appendix B, $z_{.02} = 2.05$. The rejection region is $z > 2.05$.

Since the observed value of the test statistic does not fall in the rejection region ($z = -3.22 \not> 2.05$), H_0 is not rejected. There is insufficient evidence to reject the claim that no more than half of all manufacturers are dissatisfied with their trade promotion spending at $\alpha = .02$.

b.   The observed significance level is p-value $= P(z \ge -3.22) \approx .5 + .5 = 1$. Since this p-value is so large, H_0 will not be rejected for any reasonable value of α.

c.   First, we must define the rejection region in terms of $\hat{p}$.

$$\hat{p} = p_0 + z_\alpha\, \sigma_{\hat{p}} = .5 + 2.05\sqrt{\dfrac{.5(.5)}{132}} = .589$$

$$\beta = P(\hat{p} < .589 \,|\, p = .55) = P\left(z < \dfrac{.589 - .55}{\sqrt{\dfrac{.55(.45)}{132}}} \right) = P(z < .90) = .5 + .3159 = .8159$$

6.125 a.   A Type II error is concluding the percentage of shoplifters turned over to police is   50% when in fact, the percentage is higher than 50%.

b.   First, calculate the value of $\hat{p}$ that corresponds to the border between the acceptance region and the rejection region.

$$P(\hat{p} > p_o) = P(z > z_o) = .05. \quad \text{From Table IV, Appendix B, } z_o = 1.645$$

$$\hat{p} = p_o + 1.645\sigma_{\hat{p}} = .5 + 1.645\sqrt{\dfrac{.5(.5)}{40}} = .5 + .1300 = .6300$$

$$\beta = P(\hat{p} \le .6300 \text{ when } p = .55)$$

$$= P\left(z \le \frac{.6300 - .55}{\sqrt{\dfrac{.55(.45)}{40}}} \right) = P(z \le 1.02) = .5 + .3461 = .8461$$

c. If n increases, the probability of a Type II error would decrease.

First, calculate the value of $\hat{p}$ that corresponds to the border between the acceptance region and the rejection region.

$$P(\hat{p} > p_o) = P(z > z_o) = .05. \quad \text{From Table IV, Appendix B, } z_o = 1.645$$

$$\hat{p} = p_o + 1.645\sigma_{\hat{p}} = .5 + 1.645\sqrt{\frac{.5(.5)}{100}} = .5 + .082 = .582$$

$$\beta = P(\hat{p} \le .582 \text{ when } p = .55)$$

$$= P\left(z \le \frac{.582 - .55}{\sqrt{\dfrac{.55(.45)}{100}}} \right) = P(z \le 0.64) = .5 + .2389 = .7389$$

6.127   a.   To determine if the production process should be halted, we test:

H_0: $\mu = 3$
H_a: $\mu > 3$

where μ = mean amount of PCB in the effluent.

The test statistic is $z = \dfrac{\bar{x} - \mu_0}{\sigma_{\bar{x}}} = \dfrac{3.1 - 3}{.5 / \sqrt{50}} = 1.41$

The rejection region requires $\alpha = .01$ in the upper tail of the z-distribution. From Table IV, Appendix B, $z_{.01} = 2.33$. The rejection region is $z > 2.33$.
Since the observed value of the test statistic does not fall in the rejection region, ($z = 1.41 \not> 2.33$), H_0 is not rejected. There is insufficient evidence to indicate the mean amount of PCB in the effluent is more than 3 parts per million at $\alpha = .01$. Do not halt the manufacturing process.

b.   As plant manager, I do not want to shut down the plant unnecessarily. Therefore, I want $\alpha = P$(shut down plant when $\mu = 3$) to be small.

c.   The p-value is $p = P(z \ge 1.41) = .5 - .4207 = .0793$. Since the p-value is not less than $\alpha = .01$, H_0 is not rejected.

6.129   a.   No, it increases the risk of falsely rejecting H_0, i.e., closing the plant unnecessarily.

       b.   First, find $\bar{x}_0$ such that $P(\bar{x} > \bar{x}_0) = P(z > z_0) = .05$.

From Table IV, Appendix B, $z_0 = 1.645$

$$z = \frac{\bar{x}_0 - \mu}{\sigma / \sqrt{n}} \Rightarrow 1.645 = \frac{\bar{x}_0 - 3}{.5 / \sqrt{50}} \Rightarrow \bar{x}_0 = 3.116$$

Then, compute:

$$\beta = P(\bar{x}_0 \le 3.116 \text{ when } \mu = 3.1) = P\left(z \le \frac{3.116 - 3.1}{.5 / \sqrt{50}}\right) = P(z \le .23)$$

$$= .5 + .0910 = .5910$$

$$\text{Power} = 1 - \beta = 1 - .5910 = .4090$$

       c.   The power of the test increases as α increases.

6.131   a.   To determine if the product brings pain relief to headache sufferers in less than 3.5 minutes, on average, we test:

H_0: $\mu = 3.5$
H_a: $\mu < 3.5$

The test statistic is $z = \dfrac{\bar{x} - \mu_0}{\sigma_{\bar{x}}} \approx \dfrac{3.3 - 3.5}{1.1 / \sqrt{50}} = -1.29$

The rejection region requires $\alpha = .05$ in the lower tail of the z-distribution. From Table IV, Appendix B, $z_{.05} = 1.645$. The rejection region is $z < -1.645$.

Since the observed value of the test statistic does not fall in the rejection region ($z = -1.29 \not< -1.645$), H_0 is not rejected. There is insufficient evidence to indicate that the product brings pain relief to headache sufferers in less than 3.5 minutes, on average, at $\alpha = .05$.

       b.   The p-value is $p = P(z \le -1.29) = .5 - .4015 = .0985$.

       c.   If we are conducting a test of hypothesis where the manufacturer's claim is stated in the alternative hypothesis (H_a), then small p-values would support the manufacturer's claim. On the other hand, if we are conducting a test of hypothesis where the manufacturer's claim is stated in the null hypothesis (H_0), then large p-values would support the manufacturer's claim.

6.133   a.   To determine whether the true mean rating for this instructor-related factor exceeds 4, we test:

H_0: $\mu = 4$
H_a: $\mu > 4$

The test statistic is $z = \dfrac{\bar{x} - \mu_0}{\sigma_{\bar{x}}} \approx \dfrac{4.7 - 4}{1.62 / \sqrt{40}} = 2.73$

The rejection region requires $\alpha = .05$ in the upper tail of the z-distribution. From Table IV, Appendix B, $z_{.05} = 1.645$. The rejection region is $z > 1.645$.

Since the observed value of the test statistic falls in the rejection region ($z = 2.73 > 1.645$), H_0 is rejected. There is sufficient evidence to indicate that the true mean rating for this instructor-related factor exceeds 4 at $\alpha = .05$.

b. If the sample size is large enough, one could almost always reject H_0. Thus, we might be able to detect very small differences if the sample size is large enough. This would be statistical significance. However, even though statistical significance is found, it does not necessarily mean that there is practical significance. A statistical significance can sometimes be found between the hypothesized value of a mean and the estimated value of the mean, but, in practice, this difference would mean nothing. This would be practical significance.

c. Since the sample size is sufficiently large ($n = 40$), the Central Limit Theorem indicates that the sampling distribution of is approximately normal. Also, since the sample size is large, s is a good estimator of σ. Thus, the analysis used is appropriate.

6.135 Using MINITAB, the descriptive statistics are:

Descriptive Statistics: Candy

```
Variable  N    Mean  SE Mean  StDev  Minimum      Q1  Median      Q3  Maximum
Candy     5  22.000    0.894  2.000   20.000  20.500  21.000  24.000   25.000
```

To give the benefit of the doubt to the students we will use a small value of α. (We do not want to reject H_0 when it is true to favor the students.) Thus, we will use $\alpha = .001$.

We must also assume that the sample comes from a normal distribution. To determine if the mean number of candies exceeds 15, we test:

H_0: $\mu = 15$
H_a: $\mu > 15$

The test statistic is $\quad z = \dfrac{\bar{x} - \mu_o}{\sigma / \sqrt{n}} = \dfrac{22 - 15}{2 / \sqrt{5}} = 7.83$

The rejection region requires $\alpha = .001$ in the upper tail of the z-distribution. From Table IV, Appendix B, $z_{.001} = 3.08$. The rejection region is $z > 3.08$.

Since the observed value of the test statistic falls in the rejection region ($z = 7.83 > 3.08$), H_0 is rejected. There is sufficient evidence to indicate the mean number of candies exceeds 15 at $\alpha = .001$.

Chapter 7
Inferences Based on Two Samples: Confidence Intervals and Tests of Hypotheses

7.1   a. $\mu_1 \pm 2\sigma_{\bar{x}_1} \Rightarrow \mu_1 \pm 2\dfrac{\sigma_1}{\sqrt{n_1}} \Rightarrow 150 \pm 2\dfrac{\sqrt{900}}{\sqrt{100}} \Rightarrow 150 \pm 6 \Rightarrow (144,\ 156)$

      b. $\mu_2 \pm 2\sigma_{\bar{x}_2} \Rightarrow \mu_2 \pm 2\dfrac{\sigma_2}{\sqrt{n_2}} \Rightarrow 150 \pm 2\dfrac{\sqrt{1600}}{\sqrt{100}} \Rightarrow 150 \pm 8 \Rightarrow (142,\ 158)$

      c. $\mu_{\bar{x}_1 - \bar{x}_2} = \mu_1 - \mu_2 = 150 - 150 = 0$

            $\sigma_{\bar{x}_1 - \bar{x}_2} = \sqrt{\dfrac{\sigma_1^2}{n_1} + \dfrac{\sigma_2^2}{n_2}} = \sqrt{\dfrac{900}{100} + \dfrac{1600}{100}} = \sqrt{\dfrac{2500}{100}} = 5$

      d. $(\mu_1 - \mu_2) \pm 2\sqrt{\dfrac{\sigma_1^2}{n_1} + \dfrac{\sigma_2^2}{n_2}} \Rightarrow (150 - 150) \pm 2\sqrt{\dfrac{900}{100} + \dfrac{1600}{100}} \Rightarrow 0 \pm 10 \Rightarrow (-10,\ 10)$

      e.   The variability of the difference between the sample means is greater than the variability of the individual sample means.

7.3   a.   For confidence coefficient .95, $\alpha = .05$ and $\alpha/2 = .025$. From Table IV, Appendix B, $z_{.025} = 1.96$. The confidence interval is:

$$(\bar{x}_1 - \bar{x}_2) \pm z_{.025}\sqrt{\dfrac{\sigma_1^2}{n_1} + \dfrac{\sigma_2^2}{n_2}} \Rightarrow (5{,}275 - 5{,}240) \pm 1.96\sqrt{\dfrac{150^2}{400} + \dfrac{200^2}{400}}$$

$$\Rightarrow 35 \pm 24.5 \Rightarrow (10.5,\ 59.5)$$

         We are 95% confident that the difference between the population means is between 10.5 and 59.5.

      b.   The test statistic is $z = \dfrac{(\bar{x}_1 - \bar{x}_2) - (\mu_1 - \mu_2)}{\sqrt{\dfrac{\sigma_1^2}{n_1} + \dfrac{\sigma_2^2}{n_2}}} = \dfrac{(5275 - 5240) - 0}{\sqrt{\dfrac{150^2}{400} + \dfrac{200^2}{400}}} = 2.8$

         The p-value of the test is $P(z \le -2.8) + P(z \ge 2.8) = 2P(z \ge 2.8) = 2(.5 - .4974)$

                                              $= 2(.0026) = .0052$

         Since the p-value is so small, there is evidence to reject H_0. There is evidence to indicate the two population means are different for $\alpha > .0052$.

      c.   The p-value would be half of the p-value in part **b**. The p-value $= P(z \ge 2.8) = .5 - .4974 = .0026$. Since the p-value is so small, there is evidence to reject H_0. There is evidence to indicate the mean for population 1 is larger than the mean for population 2 for $\alpha > .0026$.

d.   The test statistic is $z = \dfrac{(\bar{x}_1 - \bar{x}_2) - (\mu_1 - \mu_2)}{\sqrt{\dfrac{\sigma_1^2}{n_1} + \dfrac{\sigma_2^2}{n_2}}} = \dfrac{(5275 - 5240) - 25}{\sqrt{\dfrac{150^2}{400} + \dfrac{200^2}{400}}} = .8$

The p-value of the test is $P(z \leq -.8) + P(z \geq .8) = 2P(z \geq .8) = 2(.5 - .2881) = 2(.2119) = .4238$

Since the p-value is so large, there is no evidence to reject H_0. There is no evidence to indicate that the difference in the 2 population means is different from 25 for $\alpha \leq .10$.

e.   We must assume that we have two independent random samples.

7.5   a.   No. Both populations must be normal.

b.   No. Both populations variances must be equal.

c.   No. Both populations must be normal.

d.   Yes.

e.   No. Both populations must be normal.

7.7   Some preliminary calculations are:

$\bar{x}_1 = \dfrac{\sum x_1}{n_1} = \dfrac{11.8}{5} = 2.36$ $s_1^2 = \dfrac{\sum x_1^2 - \dfrac{\left(\sum x_1\right)^2}{n_1}}{n_1 - 1} = \dfrac{30.78 - \dfrac{(11.8)^2}{5}}{5 - 1} = .733$

$\bar{x}_2 = \dfrac{\sum x_2}{n_2} = \dfrac{14.4}{4} = 3.6$ $s_2^2 = \dfrac{\sum x_2^2 - \dfrac{\left(\sum x_2\right)^2}{n_2}}{n_2 - 1} = \dfrac{53.1 - \dfrac{(14.4)^2}{4}}{4 - 1} = .42$

a. $s_p^2 = \dfrac{(n_1 - 1)s_1^2 + (n_2 - 1)s_2^2}{n_1 + n_2 - 2} = \dfrac{(5 - 1).773 + (4 - 1).42}{5 + 4 - 2} = \dfrac{4.192}{7} = .5989$

b. $H_0: \mu_1 - \mu_2 = 0$
      $H_a: \mu_1 - \mu_2 < 0$

The test statistic is $t = \dfrac{(\bar{x}_1 - \bar{x}_2) - D_0}{\sqrt{s_p^2\left(\dfrac{1}{n_1} + \dfrac{1}{n_2}\right)}} = \dfrac{(2.36 - 3.6) - 0}{\sqrt{.5989\left(\dfrac{1}{5} + \dfrac{1}{4}\right)}} = \dfrac{-1.24}{.5191} = -2.39$

The rejection region *requires* $\alpha = .10$ in the lower tail of the t-distribution with df = $n_1 + n_2 - 2 = 5 + 4 - 2 = 7$. From Table V, Appendix B, $t_{.10} = 1.415$. The rejection region is $t < -1.415$.

Since the test statistic falls in the rejection region ($t = -2.39 < -1.415$), H_0 is rejected. There is sufficient evidence to indicate that $\mu_2 > \mu_1$ at $\alpha = .10$.

c. A small sample confidence interval is needed because $n_1 = 5 < 30$ and $n_2 = 4 < 30$.

For confidence coefficient .90, $\alpha = .10$ and $\alpha/2 = .05$. From Table V, Appendix B, with df $= n_1 + n_2 - 2 = 5 + 4 - 2 = 7$, $t_{.05} = 1.895$. The 90% confidence interval for $(\mu_1 - \mu_2)$ is:

$$(\bar{x}_1 - x_2) \pm t_{.05}\sqrt{s_p^2\left(\frac{1}{n_1} + \frac{1}{n_2}\right)} \Rightarrow (2.36 - 3.6) \pm 1.895\sqrt{.5989\left(\frac{1}{5} + \frac{1}{4}\right)}$$

$$\Rightarrow -1.24 \pm .98 \Rightarrow (-2.22, -0.26)$$

d. The confidence interval in part **c** provides more information about $(\mu_1 - \mu_2)$ than the test of hypothesis in part **b**. The test in part **b** only tells us that μ_2 is greater than μ_1. However, the confidence interval estimates what the difference is between μ_1 and μ_2.

7.9   a. The *p*-value $= .1150$. Since the *p*-value is not small, there is no evidence to reject H_0 for $\alpha \le .10$. There is insufficient evidence to indicate the two population means differ for $\alpha \le .10$.

b. If the alternative hypothesis had been one-tailed, the *p*-value would be half of the value for the two-tailed test. Here, *p*-value $= .1150/2 = .0575$.

There is no evidence to reject H_0 for $\alpha = .05$. There is insufficient evidence to indicate the mean for population 1 is less than the mean for population 2 at $\alpha = .05$.

There is evidence to reject H_0 for $\alpha > .0575$. There is sufficient evidence to indicate the mean for population 1 is less than the mean for population 2 at $\alpha > .0575$.

7.11   a. $s_p^2 = \dfrac{(n_1-1)s_1^2 + (n_2-1)s_2^2}{n_1 + n_2 - 2} = \dfrac{(17-1)3.4^2 + (12-1)4.8^2}{17 + 12 - 2} = 16.237$

H_0: $(\mu_1 - \mu_2) = 0$
H_a: $(\mu_1 - \mu_2) \ne 0$

The test statistic is $t = \dfrac{(\bar{x}_1 - \bar{x}_2) - 0}{\sqrt{s_p^2\left(\dfrac{1}{n_1} + \dfrac{1}{n_2}\right)}} = \dfrac{(5.4 - 7.9) - 0}{\sqrt{16.237\left(\dfrac{1}{17} + \dfrac{1}{12}\right)}} = -1.646$

Since no α was given, we will use $\alpha = .05$. The rejection region requires $\alpha/2 = .05/2 = .025$ in each tail of the *t*-distribution with df $= n_1 + n_2 - 2 = 17 + 12 - 2 = 27$. From Table V, Appendix B, $t_{.025} = 2.052$. The rejection region is $t < -2.052$ or $t > 2.052$.

Since the observed value of the test statistic does not fall in the rejection region ($t = -1.646 \not< -2.052$), H_0 is not rejected. There is insufficient evidence to indicate $\mu_1 - \mu_2$ is different from 0 at $\alpha = .05$.

b. For confidence coefficient .95, $\alpha = .05$ and $\alpha/2 = .025$. From Table V, Appendix B, with df $= n_1 + n_2 - 2 = 17 + 12 - 2 = 27$, $t_{.025} = 2.052$. The confidence interval is:

$$(\bar{x}_1 - \bar{x}_2) \pm t_{.025}\sqrt{s_p^2\left(\frac{1}{n_1} + \frac{1}{n_2}\right)} \text{ where } t \text{ has 27 df}$$

$$\Rightarrow (5.4 - 7.9) - 2.052\sqrt{16.237\left(\frac{1}{17} + \frac{1}{12}\right)} \Rightarrow -2.50 \pm 3.12 \Rightarrow (-5.62, 0.62)$$

7.13   a.   Let μ_1 = mean number of items recalled by those in the video only group and μ_2 = mean number of items recalled by those in the audio and video group. To determine if the mean number of items recalled by the two groups is the same, we test:

$$H_o: \ \mu_1 - \mu_2 = 0$$
$$H_a: \ \mu_1 - \mu_2 \neq 0$$

b. $$s_p^2 = \frac{(n_1-1)s_1^2 + (n_2-1)s_2^2}{n_1 + n_2 - 2} = \frac{(20-1)1.98^2 + (20-1)2.13^2}{20 + 20 - 2} = 4.22865$$

The test statistic is $t = \dfrac{(\overline{x}_1 - \overline{x}_2) - D_o}{\sqrt{s_p^2 \left(\dfrac{1}{n_1} + \dfrac{1}{n_2} \right)}} = \dfrac{(3.70 - 3.30) - 0}{\sqrt{4.22865 \left(\dfrac{1}{20} + \dfrac{1}{20} \right)}} = \dfrac{0.4}{.65028} = 0.62$

c.   The rejection region requires $\alpha/2 = .10/2 = .05$ in each tail of the t-distribution with df $= n_1 + n_2 - 2 = 20 + 20 - 2 = 38$. From Table V, Appendix B, $t_{.05} \approx 1.684$. The rejection region is $t < -1.684$ or $t > 1.684$.

d.   Since the observed value of the test statistic does not fall in the rejection region $(t = 0.62 \not> 1.684)$, H_o is not rejected. There is insufficient evidence to indicate a difference in the mean number of items recalled by the two groups at $\alpha = .10$.

e.   The p-value is $p = .542$. This is the probability of observing our test statistic or anything more unusual if H_0 is true. Since the p-value is not less than $\alpha = .10$, there is no evidence to reject H_0. There is insufficient evidence to indicate a difference in the mean number of items recalled by the two groups at $\alpha = .10$.

f.   We must assume:

1.   Both populations are normal
2.   Random and independent samples
3. $\sigma_1^2 = \sigma_2^2$

7.15   a.   Let μ_1 = mean forecast error of buy-side analysts and μ_2 = mean forecast error of sell-side analysts. For confidence coefficient 0.95, $\alpha = .05$ and $\alpha/2 = .05/2 = .025$. From Table IV, Appendix B, $z_{.025} = 1.96$. The 95% confidence interval is:

$$(\overline{x}_1 - \overline{x}_2) \pm z_{.025} \sqrt{\frac{\sigma_1^2}{n_1} + \frac{\sigma_2^2}{n_2}} \Rightarrow (.85 - (-.05)) \pm 1.96 \sqrt{\frac{1.93^2}{3,526} + \frac{.85^2}{58,562}} \Rightarrow .90 \pm .064 \Rightarrow (.836, \ .964)$$

We are 95% confident that the difference in the mean forecast error of buy-side analysts and sell-side analysts is between .836 and .964.

b.   Based on 95% confidence interval in part **a**, the buy-side analysts has the greater mean forecast error because our interval contains positive numbers.

c.   The assumptions about the underlying populations of forecast errors that are necessary for the validity of the inference are:

1.   The samples are randomly and independently sampled.
2.   The sample sizes are sufficiently large.

7.17   a.   The descriptive statistics are:

Descriptive Statistics: Text-line, Witness-line, Intersection

Variable	N	Mean	Median	TrMean	StDev	SE Mean
Text-lin	3	0.3830	0.3740	0.3830	0.0531	0.0306
Witness-	6	0.3042	0.2955	0.3042	0.1015	0.0415
Intersec	5	0.3290	0.3190	0.3290	0.0443	0.0198

Variable	Minimum	Maximum	Q1	Q3
Text-lin	0.3350	0.4400	0.3350	0.4400
Witness-	0.1880	0.4390	0.2045	0.4075
Intersec	0.2850	0.3930	0.2900	0.3730

Let μ_1 = mean zinc measurement for the text-line, μ_2 = mean zinc measurement for the witness-line, and μ_3 = mean zinc measurement for the intersection.

$$s_p^2 = \frac{(n_1-1)s_1^2 + (n_3-1)s_3^2}{n_1 + n_3 - 2} = \frac{(3-1).0531^2 + (5-1).0443^2}{3+5-2} = .00225$$

For $\alpha = .05$, $\alpha/2 = .05/2 = .025$. Using Table V, Appendix B, with df $= n_1 + n_2 - 2 = 3 + 5 - 2 = 6$, $t_{.025} = 2.447$. The 95% confidence interval is:

$$(\bar{x}_1 - \bar{x}_3) \pm t_{\alpha/2}\sqrt{s_p^2\left(\frac{1}{n_1} + \frac{1}{n_3}\right)} \Rightarrow (.3830 - .3290) \pm 2.447\sqrt{.00225\left(\frac{1}{3} + \frac{1}{5}\right)}$$

$$\Rightarrow 0.0540 \pm .0848 \Rightarrow (-0.0308,\ 0.1388)$$

We are 95% confident that the difference in mean zinc level between text-line and intersection is between −0.0308 and 0.1388.

To determine if there is a difference in the mean zinc measurement between text-line and intersection, we test:

H_0: $\mu_1 = \mu_3$
H_a: $\mu_1 \neq \mu_3$

The test statistic is $t = \dfrac{(\bar{x}_1 - \bar{x}_3) - D_o}{\sqrt{s_p^2\left(\dfrac{1}{n_1} + \dfrac{1}{n_3}\right)}} = \dfrac{(.3830 - .3290) - 0}{\sqrt{.00225\left(\dfrac{1}{3} + \dfrac{1}{5}\right)}} = 1.56$

The rejection region requires $\alpha/2 = .05/2 = .025$ in each tail of the t-distribution with df $= n_1 + n_2 - 2 = 3 + 5 - 2 = 6$. From Table V, Appendix B, $t_{.025} = 2.447$. The rejection region is $t < -2.447$ or t > 2.447.

Since the observed value of the test statistic does not fall in the rejection region ($t = 1.56 \not> 2.365$), H_0 is not rejected. There is insufficient evidence to indicate a difference in the mean zinc measurement between text-line and intersection at $\alpha = .05$.

b. $$s_p^2 = \frac{(n_2-1)s_2^2 + (n_3-1)s_3^2}{n_2+n_3-2} = \frac{(6-1).1015^2 + (5-1).0443^2}{6+5-2} = .006596$$

For $\alpha = .05$, $\alpha/2 = .05/2 = .025$. Using Table V, Appendix B, with df $= n_1 + n_2 - 2 = 6 + 5 - 2 = 9$, $t_{.025} = 2.262$. The 95% confidence interval is:

$$(\bar{x}_2 - \bar{x}_3) \pm t_{\alpha/2}\sqrt{s_p^2\left(\frac{1}{n_2} + \frac{1}{n_3}\right)} \Rightarrow (.3042 - .3290) \pm 2.262\sqrt{.006596\left(\frac{1}{6} + \frac{1}{5}\right)}$$

$$\Rightarrow -.0248 \pm .1112 \Rightarrow (-.1361, \ .0864)$$

We are 95% confident that the difference in mean zinc level between witness-line and intersection is between -0.1361 and 0.0864.

To determine if the difference in mean zinc measurement between the witness-line and the intersection, we test:

H_0: $\mu_2 = \mu_3$
H_a: $\mu_2 \neq \mu_3$

The test statistic is $t = \dfrac{(\bar{x}_2 - \bar{x}_3) - D_o}{\sqrt{s_p^2\left(\dfrac{1}{n_2} + \dfrac{1}{n_3}\right)}} = \dfrac{(.3042 - .3290) - 0}{\sqrt{.006596\left(\dfrac{1}{6} + \dfrac{1}{5}\right)}} = -.50$

The rejection region requires $\alpha/2 = .05/2 = .025$ in each tail of the t-distribution. From Table V, Appendix B, with df $= n_1 + n_2 - 2 = 6 + 5 - 2 = 9$, $t_{.025} = 2.262$. The rejection region is $t < -2.262$ or $t > 2.262$.

Since the observed value of the test statistic does not fall in the rejection region ($t = -.50 \not< -2.262$), H_0 is not rejected. There is insufficient evidence to indicate a difference in mean zinc measurement between witness-line and intersection at $\alpha = .05$.

c.   If we order the sample means, the largest is Text-line, the next largest is intersection and the smallest is witness-line. In parts **a** and **b**, we found that text-line is not different from the intersection and that the witness-line is not different from the intersection. However, we cannot make any decisions about the difference between the witness-line and the text-line.

d.   In order for the above inferences to be valid, we must assume:

1.   The three samples are randomly selected in an independent manner from the three target populations.

2.   All three sampled populations have distributions that are approximately normal.

3.   All three population variances are equal (i.e. $\sigma_1^2 = \sigma_2^2 = \sigma_3^2$)

7.19   Using MINITAB, the descriptive statistics are:

Descriptive Statistics: Control, Rude

```
Variable    N    Mean   StDev  Minimum     Q1   Median      Q3  Maximum
Rude       45   8.511   3.992    0.000  5.500    9.000  11.000   18.000
Control    53   11.81    7.38     0.00   5.50    12.00   17.50    30.00
```

Let μ_1 = mean performance level of students in the rudeness group and μ_2 = mean performance level of students in the control group. To determine if the true performance level for students in the rudeness condition is lower than the true mean performance level for students in the control group, we test:

H_0: $\mu_1 - \mu_2 = 0$
H_a: $\mu_1 - \mu_2 < 0$

The test statistic is $z = \dfrac{(\bar{x}_1 - \bar{x}_2) - 0}{\sqrt{\dfrac{\sigma_1^2}{n_1} + \dfrac{\sigma_2^2}{n_2}}} \approx \dfrac{(8.511 - 11.81) - 0}{\sqrt{\dfrac{3.922^2}{45} + \dfrac{7.38^2}{53}}} = -2.81$

The rejection region requires $\alpha = .01$ in the lower tail of the z-distribution. From Table IV, Appendix B, $z_{.01} = 2.33$. The rejection region is $z < -2.33$.

Since the observed value of the test statistic falls in the rejection region ($z = -2.81 < -2.33$), H_0 is rejected. There is sufficient evidence to indicate the true mean performance level for students in the rudeness condition is lower than the true mean performance level for students in the control group at $\alpha = .01$.

7.21   Using MINITAB, the descriptive statistics are:

Descriptive Statistics: Honey, DM

```
Variable    N    Mean   StDev  Minimum     Q1   Median      Q3  Maximum
Honey      35  10.714   2.855    4.000  9.000   11.000  12.000   16.000
DM         33   8.333   3.256    3.000  6.000    9.000  11.500   15.000
```

Let μ_1 = mean improvement in total cough symptoms score for children receiving the Honey dosage and μ_2 = mean improvement in total cough symptoms score for children receiving the DM dosage. To test if honey may be a preferable treatment for the cough and sleep difficulty associated with childhood upper respiratory tract infection, we test:

H_0: $\mu_1 - \mu_2 = 0$
H_a: $\mu_1 - \mu_2 > 0$

The test statistic is $z = \dfrac{(\bar{x}_1 - \bar{x}_2) - 0}{\sqrt{\dfrac{\sigma_1^2}{n_1} + \dfrac{\sigma_2^2}{n_2}}} \approx \dfrac{(10.714 - 8.333) - 0}{\sqrt{\dfrac{2.855^2}{35} + \dfrac{3.256^2}{33}}} = 3.20$

Since no α was given, we will use $\alpha = .05$. The rejection region requires $\alpha = .05$ in the upper tail of the z-distribution. From Table IV, Appendix B, $z_{.05} = 1.645$. The rejection region is $z > 1.645$.

Since the observed value of the test statistic falls in the rejection region ($z = 3.20 > 1.645$), H_0 is rejected. There is sufficient evidence to indicate that honey may be a preferable treatment for the cough and sleep difficulty associated with childhood upper respiratory tract infection at $\alpha = .05$.

7.23   a.   Let μ_1 = the mean heat rates of traditional augmented gas turbines and μ_2 = the mean heat rates of aeroderivative augmented gas turbines.

Some preliminary calculations are:

$$s_p^2 = \frac{(n_1-1)s_1^2 + (n_2-1)s_2^2}{n_1 + n_2 - 2} = \frac{(39-1)1279^2 + (7-1)2652^2}{39+7-2} = 2,371,831.409$$

To determine if there is a difference in the mean heat rates for traditional augmented gas turbines and the mean heat rates of aeroderivative augmented gas turbines, we test:

$H_o: \mu_1 - \mu_2 = 0$
$H_a: \mu_1 - \mu_2 \neq 0$

The test statistic is

$$t = \frac{(\bar{x}_1 - \bar{x}_2) - D_o}{\sqrt{s_p^2 \left(\frac{1}{n_1} + \frac{1}{n_2}\right)}} = \frac{(11,544 - 12,312) - 0}{\sqrt{2,371,831.409 \left(\frac{1}{39} + \frac{1}{7}\right)}} = \frac{-768}{632.1782} = -1.21$$

The rejection region requires $\alpha/2 = .05/2 = .025$ in each tail of the t-distribution with df $= n_1 + n_2 - 2 = 39 + 7 - 2 = 44$. From Table V, Appendix B, $t_{.025} \approx 2.021$. The rejection region is $t < -2.021$ or $t > 2.021$.

Since the observed value of the test statistic does not fall in the rejection region ($t = -1.20 \not< -2.021$), H_0 is not rejected. There is insufficient evidence to indicate that there is a difference in the mean heat rates for traditional augmented gas turbines and the mean heat rates of aeroderivative augmented gas turbines at $\alpha = .05$.

b.   Let μ_3 = the mean heat rates of advanced augmented gas turbines and μ_2 = the mean heat rates of aeroderivative augmented gas turbines.

Some preliminary calculations are:

$$s_p^2 = \frac{(n_3-1)s_3^2 + (n_2-1)s_2^2}{n_3 + n_2 - 2} = \frac{(21-1)639^2 + (7-1)2652^2}{21+7-2} = 1,937,117.077$$

To determine if there is a difference in the mean heat rates for traditional augmented gas turbines and the mean heat rates of aeroderivative augmented gas turbines, we test:

$H_0: \mu_3 - \mu_2 = 0$
$H_a: \mu_3 - \mu_2 \neq 0$

The test statistic is

$$t = \frac{(\bar{x}_3 - \bar{x}_2) - D_o}{\sqrt{s_p^2 \left(\frac{1}{n_3} + \frac{1}{n_2}\right)}} = \frac{(9,764 - 12,312) - 0}{\sqrt{1,937,117.077 \left(\frac{1}{21} + \frac{1}{7}\right)}} = \frac{-2,548}{607.4329} = -4.19$$

The rejection region requires $\alpha/2 = .05/2 = .025$ in each tail of the t-distribution with df $= n_1 + n_2 - 2 = 21 + 7 - 2 = 26$. From Table V, Appendix B, $t_{.025} \approx 2.056$. The rejection region is $t < -2.056$ or $t > 2.056$.

Since the observed value of the test statistic falls in the rejection region ($t = -4.19 < -2.021$), H_0 is rejected. There is sufficient evidence to indicate that there is a difference in the mean heat rates for advanced augmented gas turbines and the mean heat rates of aeroderivative augmented gas turbines at $\alpha = .05$.

7.25   a.   The rejection region requires $\alpha = .05$ in the upper tail of the t-distribution with df $= n_d - 1 = 12 - 1 = 11$. From Table V, Appendix B, $t_{.05} = 1.796$. The rejection region is $t > 1.796$.

       b.   From Table V, with df $= n_d - 1 = 24 - 1 = 23$, $t_{.10} = 1.319$. The rejection region is $t > 1.319$.

       c.   From Table V, with df $= n_d - 1 = 4 - 1 = 3$, $t_{.025} = 3.182$. The rejection region is $t > 3.182$.

       d.   Using Minitab, with df $= n_d - 1 = 80 - 1 = 79$, $t_{.01} = 2.374$. The rejection region is $t > 2.374$.

7.27   Let μ_1 = mean of population 1 and μ_2 = mean of population 2.

       a. H_0: $\mu_d = 0$
            H_a: $\mu_d < 0$ where $\mu_d = \mu_1 - \mu_2$

       b.   Some preliminary calculations are:

Pair	Population 1	Population 2	Difference, d
1	19	24	−5
2	25	27	−2
3	31	36	−5
4	52	53	−1
5	49	55	−6
6	34	34	0
7	59	66	−7
8	47	51	−4
9	17	20	−3
10	51	55	−4

$$\bar{d} = \frac{\sum_{i=1}^{n_d} d_i}{n_d} = \frac{-37}{10} = -3.7 \qquad s_d^2 = \frac{\sum_{i=1}^{n_d} d_i^2 - \frac{\left(\sum_{i=1}^{n_d} d_i\right)^2}{n_d}}{n_d - 1} = \frac{181 - \frac{(-37)^2}{10}}{10 - 1} = 4.9$$

The test statistic is $t = \dfrac{\bar{d}}{s_d / \sqrt{n_d}} = \dfrac{-3.7}{\sqrt{4.9} / \sqrt{10}} = -5.29$

The rejection region requires $\alpha = .10$ in the lower tail of the t-distribution with df $= n_d - 1 = 10 - 1 = 9$. From Table V, Appendix B, $t_{.10} = 1.383$. The rejection region is $t < -1.383$.

Since the observed value of the test statistic falls in the rejection region ($t = -5.29 < -1.383$), H_0 is rejected. There is sufficient evidence to indicate the mean of population 1 is less than the mean for population 2 at $\alpha = .10$.

b.   For confidence coefficient .90, $\alpha = .10$ and $\alpha/2 = .10/2 = .05$. From Table V, Appendix B, with df $= n_d - 1 = 10 - 1 = 9$, $t_{.05} = 1.833$. The 90% confidence interval is:

$$\bar{d} \pm t_{\alpha/2} \frac{s_d}{\sqrt{n_d}} \Rightarrow -3.7 \pm 1.833 \frac{\sqrt{4.9}}{\sqrt{10}} \Rightarrow -3.7 \pm 1.28 \Rightarrow (-4.98, \; -2.42)$$

We are 90% confident that the difference in the two population means is between -4.98 and -2.42.

d.   We must assume that the population of differences is normal, and the sample of differences is randomly selected.

7.29   a.   Some preliminary calculations:

$$\bar{d} = \frac{\sum_{i=1}^{n_d} d_i}{n_d} = \frac{468}{40} = 11.7$$

$$s_d^2 = \frac{\sum_{i=1}^{n_d} d_i^2 - \frac{\left(\sum_{i=1}^{n_d} d_i\right)^2}{n_d}}{n_d - 1} = \frac{6,880 - \frac{468^2}{40}}{40 - 1} = 36.0103$$

To determine if $(\mu_1 - \mu_2) = \mu_d$ is different from 10, we test:

$H_0: \mu_d = 10$
$H_a: \mu_d \neq 10$

The test statistic is $z = \dfrac{\bar{d} - D_0}{\frac{s_d}{\sqrt{n_d}}} = \dfrac{11.7 - 10}{\frac{\sqrt{36.0103}}{\sqrt{40}}} = 1.79$

The rejection region requires $\alpha/2 = .05/2 = .025$ in each tail of the z-distribution. From Table IV, Appendix B, $z_{.025} = 1.96$. The rejection region is $z < -1.96$ or $z > 1.96$.

Since the observed value of the test statistic does not fall in the rejection region ($z = 1.79 \not> 1.96$), H_0 is not rejected. There is insufficient evidence to indicate $(\mu_1 - \mu_2) = \mu_d$ is different from 10 at $\alpha = .05$.

b.   The p-value is $p = P(z \leq -1.79) + P(z \geq 1.79) = (.5 - .4633) + (.5 - .4633) = .0367 + .0367 = .0734$. The probability of observing our test statistic or anything more unusual if H_0 is true is .0734. Since this p-value is not small, there is no evidence to indicate $(\mu_1 - \mu_2) = \mu_d$ is different from 10 at $\alpha = .05$.

c.   No, we do not need to assume that the population of differences is normally distributed. Because our sample size is 40, the Central Limit Theorem applies.

7.31   a.   Let μ_1 = the mean salary of technology professionals in 2003 and μ_2 = the mean salary of technology professionals in 2005. Let $\mu_d = \mu_1 - \mu_2$.

To determine if the mean salary of technology professionals at all U.S. metropolitan areas has increased between 2003 and 2005, we test:

H_0: $\mu_1 - \mu_2 = 0$ H_0: $\mu_d = 0$

                            OR

H_a: $\mu_1 - \mu_2 < 0$ H_a: $\mu_d < 0$

b.

Metro Area	2003 Salary ($ thousands)	2005 Salary ($ thousands)	Difference (2003 – 2005)
Silicon Valley	87.7	85.9	1.8
New York	78.6	80.3	−1.7
Washington, D.C.	71.4	77.4	−6.0
Los Angeles	70.8	77.1	−6.3
Denver	73.0	77.1	−4.1
Boston	76.3	80.1	−3.8
Atlanta	73.6	73.2	0.4
Chicago	71.1	73.0	−1.9
Philadelphia	69.5	69.8	−0.3
San Diego	69.0	77.1	−8.1
Seattle	71.0	66.9	4.1
Dallas-Ft. Worth	73.0	71.0	2.0
Detroit	62.3	64.1	−1.8

c. $\bar{d} = \dfrac{\sum\limits_{1}^{n_d} d_i}{n_d} = \dfrac{-25.7}{13} = -1.98$

$s_d^2 = \dfrac{\sum\limits_{1}^{n_d} d_i^2 - \dfrac{\left(\sum\limits_{1}^{n_d} d_i\right)^2}{n_d}}{n_d - 1} = \dfrac{206.59 - \dfrac{(-25.7)^2}{13}}{13 - 1} = 12.9819$

$s_d = \sqrt{s_d^2} = \sqrt{12.9819} = 3.6$

d.   The test statistic is $t = \dfrac{\bar{d} - \mu_o}{s_d / \sqrt{n_d}} = \dfrac{-1.98 - 0}{3.6 / \sqrt{13}} = -1.98$

b.   The rejection region requires $\alpha = .10$ in the lower tail of the t-distribution with df = $n_d - 1 = 13 - 1 = 12$. From Table V, Appendix B, $t_{.10} = 1.356$. The rejection region is $t < -1.356$.

f.   Since the observed value of the test statistic falls in the rejection region ($t = -1.98 < -1.356$), H_0 is rejected. There is sufficient evidence to indicate the mean salary of technology professionals at all U.S. metropolitan areas has increased between 2003 and 2005 at $\alpha = .10$.

g.   In order for the inference to be valid, we must assume that the population of differences is normal and that we have a random sample.

Using MINITAB, the histogram of the differences is:

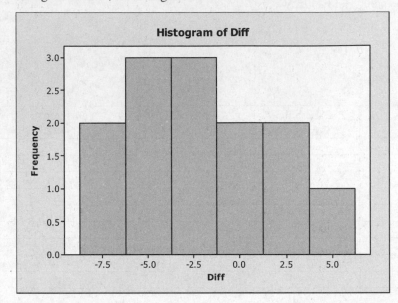

The graph is fairly mound-shaped although it is somewhat skewed to the right. Since there are only 13 observations, this graph is close enough to being mound-shaped to indicate the normal assumption is reasonable.

7.33   a.   The data should be analyzed using a paired-difference test because that is how the data were collected. Response rates were observed twice from each survey using the "not selling" introduction method and the standard introduction method. Since the two sets of data are not independent, they cannot be analyzed using independent samples.

b.   Some preliminary calculations are:

$$s_p^2 = \frac{(n_1 - 1)s_1^2 + (n_2 - 1)s_2^2}{n_1 + n_2 - 2} = \frac{(29 - 1)(.12)^2 + (29 - 1)(.11)^2}{29 + 29 - 2} = .01325$$

Let μ_1 = mean response rate for those using the "not selling" introduction and μ_2 = mean response rate for those using the standard introduction. Using the independent-samples t-test to determine if the mean response rate for "not selling" is higher than that for the standard introduction, we test:

H_0: $\mu_1 - \mu_2 = 0$
H_a: $\mu_1 - \mu_2 > 0$

The test statistic is $t = \dfrac{(\bar{x}_1 - \bar{x}_2) - 0}{\sqrt{s_p^2\left(\dfrac{1}{n_1} + \dfrac{1}{n_2}\right)}} = \dfrac{(.262 - .246) - 0}{\sqrt{.01325\left(\dfrac{1}{29} + \dfrac{1}{29}\right)}} = .53$

The rejection region requires $\alpha = .05$ in the upper tail of the t-distribution with df = $n_1 + n_2 - 2 = 29 + 29 - 2 = 56$. From Table V, Appendix B, $t_{.05} \approx 1.671$. The rejection region is $t > 1.671$.

Since the observed value of the test statistic does not fall in the rejection region ($t = .53 \not> 1.671$), H_0 is not rejected. There is insufficient evidence to indicate the mean response rate for "not selling" is higher than that for the standard introduction at $\alpha = .05$.

c. Since *p*-value is less than $\alpha = .05$ ($p = .001 < .05$), H_0 is rejected. There is sufficient evidence to indicate the mean response rate for "not selling" is higher than that for the standard introduction at $\alpha = .05$.

d. The two inferences in parts **b** and **c** have different results because using the independent samples *t*-test is not appropriate for this study. The paired-difference design is better. There is much variation in response rates from survey to survey. By using the paired difference design, we can eliminate the survey to survey differences.

7.35   Some preliminary calculations are:

Operator	Difference (Before - After)
1	5
2	3
3	9
4	7
5	2
6	–2
7	–1
8	11
9	0
10	5

$$\bar{d} = \frac{\sum d}{n_d} = \frac{39}{10} - 3.9$$

$$s_d^2 = \frac{\sum d^2 - \frac{\left(\sum d\right)^2}{n_F}}{n_d - 1} = \frac{319 - \frac{39^2}{10}}{10 - 1} = 18.5444$$

$$s_d = \sqrt{18.5444} = 4.3063$$

a. To determine if the new napping policy reduced the mean number of customer complaints, we test:

H_0: $\mu_d = 0$
H_a: $\mu_d > 0$

The test statistic is $t = \dfrac{\bar{d} - 0}{\dfrac{s_d}{\sqrt{n_d}}} = \dfrac{3.9 - 0}{\dfrac{4.3063}{\sqrt{10}}} = 2.864$

The rejection region requires $\alpha = .05$ in the upper tail of the *t*-distribution with df $= n_d - 1 = 10 - 1 = 9$. From Table V, Appendix B, $t_{.05} = 1.833$. The rejection region is $t > 1.833$.

Since the observed value of the test statistic falls in the rejection region ($t = 2.864 > 1.833$), H_0 is rejected. There is sufficient evidence to indicate the new napping policy reduced the mean number of customer complaints at $\alpha = .05$.

b.   In order for the above test to be valid, we must assume that

1. The population of differences is normal
2. The differences are randomly selected

7.37   Some preliminary calculations are:

Circuit	Standard Method	Huffman-coding Method	Difference
1	.80	.78	.02
2	.80	.80	.00
3	.83	.86	-.03
4	.53	.53	.00
5	.50	.51	-.01
6	.96	.68	.28
7	.99	.82	.17
8	.98	.72	.26
9	.81	.45	.36
10	.95	.79	.16
11	.99	.77	.22

$$\bar{d} = \frac{\sum_{1}^{n_d} d_i}{n_d} = \frac{1.43}{11} = 0.13$$

$$s_d^2 = \frac{\sum_{1}^{n_d} d_i^2 - \frac{\left(\sum_{1}^{n_d} d_i\right)^2}{n_d}}{n_d - 1} = \frac{0.3799 - \frac{(1.43)^2}{11}}{11 - 1} = 0.0194$$

$$s_d = \sqrt{s_d^2} = \sqrt{0.0194} = 0.1393$$

For confidence coefficient .95, $\alpha = .05$ and $\alpha/2 = .05/2 = .025$. From Table V, Appendix B, with df $= n_d - 1 = 11 - 1 = 10$, $t_{.025} = 2.228$. The 95% confidence interval is:

$$\bar{d} \pm t_{.025} \frac{s_d}{\sqrt{n}} \Rightarrow .13 \pm 2.228 \frac{.1393}{\sqrt{11}} \Rightarrow .13 \pm .094 \Rightarrow (0.036, \quad 0.224)$$

We are 95% confident that the true difference in mean compression ratio between the standard method and the Huffman-based coding method is between 0.036 and 0.224. Since 0 is not contained in the interval, we can conclude there is a difference in mean compression ratios between the two methods. Since the values of the confidence interval are positive, we can conclude that the mean compression ratio for the Huffman-based method is smaller than the standard method.

7.39   Using MINITAB, the descriptive statistics are:

Descriptive Statistics: Male, Female, Diff

Variable	N	Mean	Median	TrMean	StDev	SE Mean
Male	19	5.895	6.000	5.706	2.378	0.546
Female	19	5.526	5.000	5.294	2.458	0.564
Diff	19	0.368	1.000	0.294	3.515	0.806

Variable	Minimum	Maximum	Q1	Q3
Male	3.000	12.000	4.000	8.000
Female	3.000	12.000	4.000	7.000
Diff	-5.000	7.000	-3.000	3.000

Let μ_1 = mean number of swims by male rat pups and μ_2 = mean number of swims by female rat pups. Then $\mu_d = \mu_1 - \mu_2$. To determine if there is a difference in the mean number of swims required by male and female rat pups, we test:

H_0: $\mu_d = 0$
H_a: $\mu_d \neq 0$

The test statistic is $t = \dfrac{\bar{d} - D_o}{\dfrac{s_d}{\sqrt{n_d}}} = \dfrac{.368 - 0}{\dfrac{3.515}{\sqrt{19}}} = 0.46$

The rejection region requires $\alpha/2 = .10/2 = .05$ in each tail of the t-distribution with df $= n_d - 1 = 19 - 1 = 18$. From Table V, Appendix B, $t_{.05} = 1.734$. The rejection region is $t < -1.734$ or $t > 1.734$.

Since the observed value of the test statistic does not fall in the rejection region ($t = 0.46 \not> 1.734$), H_0 is not rejected. There is insufficient evidence to indicate that there is a difference in the mean number of swims required by male and female rat pups at $\alpha = .10$.
(using Minitab, the p-value $\approx .653$.)

Since the sample size is not large, we must assume that the population of differences is normally distributed and that the sample of differences is random. There is no indication that the sample differences are not from a random sample. However, because the number of swims is discrete, the differences are probably not normal.

7.41   a.   From the exercise, we know that x_1 and x_2 are binomial random variables with the number of trials equal to n_1 and n_2. From Chapter 7, we know that for large n, the distribution of $\hat{p}_1 = \dfrac{x_1}{n_1}$ is approximately normal. Since x_1 is simply $\hat{p}_1$ multiplied by a constant, x_1 will also have an approximate normal distribution. Similarly, the distribution of $\hat{p}_2 = \dfrac{x_2}{n_2}$ is approximately normal, and thus, the distribution of x_2 is approximately normal.

b.   The Central Limit Theorem is necessary to find the sampling distributions of $\hat{p}_1$ and $\hat{p}_2$ when n_1 and n_2 are large. Once we have established that both $\hat{p}_1$ and $\hat{p}_2$ have normal distributions, then the distribution of their difference will also be normal.

7.43   From Section 5.4, it was given that the distribution of $\hat{p}$ is approximately normal if $n\hat{p} \geq 15$ and $n\hat{q} \geq 15$.

a. $n_1\hat{p}_1 = 12(.42) = 5.04 < 15$ and $n_1\hat{q}_1 = 12(.58) = 6.96 < 15$
       $n_2\hat{p}_2 = 14(.57) = 7.98 < 15$ and $n_2\hat{q}_2 = 14(.43) = 6.02 < 15$
       Thus, the sample sizes are not large enough to conclude the sampling distribution of $(\hat{p}_1 - \hat{p}_2)$ is approximately normal.

b. $n_1\hat{p}_1 = 12(.92) = 11.04 < 15$ and $n_1\hat{q}_1 = 12(.08) = 0.96 < 15$
       $n_2\hat{p}_2 = 14(.86) = 12.04 < 15$ and $n_2\hat{q}_2 = 14(.14) = 1.96 < 15$
       Thus, the sample sizes are not large enough to conclude the sampling distribution of $(\hat{p}_1 - \hat{p}_2)$ is approximately normal.

c. $n_1\hat{p}_1 = 30(.70) = 21 > 15$ and $n_1\hat{q}_1 = 30(.30) = 9 < 15$
       $n_2\hat{p}_2 = 30(.73) = 21.9 > 15$ and $n_2\hat{q}_2 = 30(.27) = 8.1 < 15$
       Thus, the sample sizes are not large enough to conclude the sampling distribution of $(\hat{p}_1 - \hat{p}_2)$ is approximately normal.

d. $n_1\hat{p}_1 = 100(.93) = 93 > 15$ and $n_1\hat{q}_1 = 100(.07) = 7 < 15$
       $n_2\hat{p}_2 = 250(.97) = 242.5 > 15$ and $n_2\hat{q}_2 = 250(.03) = 7.5 < 15$
       Thus, the sample sizes are not large enough to conclude the sampling distribution of $(\hat{p}_1 - \hat{p}_2)$ is approximately normal.

e. $n_1\hat{p}_1 = 125(.08) = 10 < 15$ and $n_1\hat{q}_1 = 125(.92) = 115 > 15$
       $n_2\hat{p}_2 = 200(.12) = 24 > 15$ and $n_2\hat{q}_2 = 200(.88) = 176 > 15$
       Thus, the sample sizes are not large enough to conclude the sampling distribution of $(\hat{p}_1 - \hat{p}_2)$ is approximately normal.

7.45   a. H_0: $(p_1 - p_2) = 0$
              H_a: $(p_1 - p_2) \neq 0$

              Will need to calculate the following:

              $$\hat{p}_1 = \frac{320}{800} = .40 \quad \hat{p}_2 = \frac{400}{800} = .50 \quad \hat{p} = \frac{320 + 400}{800 + 800} = .45$$

              The test statistic is $z = \dfrac{(\hat{p}_1 - \hat{p}_2) - 0}{\sqrt{\hat{p}\hat{q}\left(\dfrac{1}{n_1} + \dfrac{1}{n_2}\right)}} = \dfrac{(.40 - .50) - 0}{\sqrt{(.45)(.55)\left(\dfrac{1}{800} + \dfrac{1}{800}\right)}} = -4.02$

              The rejection region requires $\alpha/2 = .05/2 = .025$ in each tail of the z-distribution. From Table IV, Appendix B, $z_{.025} = 1.96$. The rejection region is $z < -1.96$ or $z > 1.96$.

              Since the observed value of the test statistic falls in the rejection region ($z = -4.02 < -1.96$), H_0 is rejected. There is sufficient evidence to indicate that the proportions are unequal at $\alpha = .05$.

b. The problem is identical to part **a** until the rejection region. The rejection region requires $\alpha/2 = .01/2 = .005$ in each tail of the z-distribution. From Table IV, Appendix B, $z_{.005} = 2.58$. The rejection region is $z < -2.58$ or $z > 2.58$.

Since the observed value of the test statistic falls in the rejection region ($z = -4.02 < -2.58$), H_0 is rejected. There is sufficient evidence to indicate that the proportions are unequal at $\alpha = .01$.

c. H_0: $p_1 - p_2 = 0$
    H_a: $p_1 - p_2 < 0$

Test statistic as above: $z = -4.02$

The rejection region requires $\alpha = .01$ in the lower tail of the z-distribution. From Table IV, Appendix B, $z_{.01} = 2.33$. The rejection region is $z < -2.33$.

Since the observed value of the test statistic falls in the rejection region ($z = -4.02 < -2.33$), H_0 is rejected. There is sufficient evidence to indicate that $p_1 < p_2$ at $\alpha = .01$.

d. For confidence coefficient .90, $\alpha = .10$ and $\alpha/2 = .10/2 = .05$. From Table IV, Appendix B, $z_{.05} = 1.645$. The confidence interval is:

$$(\hat{p}_1 - \hat{p}_2) \pm z_{.05} \sqrt{\frac{\hat{p}_1 \hat{q}_1}{n_1} + \frac{\hat{p}_2 \hat{p}_2}{n_2}} \Rightarrow (.4 - .5) \pm (1.645) \sqrt{\frac{(.4)(.6)}{800} + \frac{(.5)(.5)}{800}}$$

$$\Rightarrow -.10 \pm .04 \Rightarrow (-.14, -.06)$$

We are 90% confident that the difference between p_1 and p_2 is between $-.14$ and $-.06$.

7.47   a. $\hat{p}_1 = \dfrac{x_1}{n_1} = \dfrac{29}{189} = .153$

b. $\hat{p}_2 = \dfrac{x_2}{n_2} = \dfrac{32}{149} = .215$

c.   For confidence coefficient .90, $\alpha = .10$ and $\alpha/2 = .10/2 = .05$. From Table IV, Appendix B, $z_{.05} = 1.645$. The 90% confidence interval is:

$$(\hat{p}_1 - \hat{p}_2) \pm z_{\alpha/2} \sqrt{\frac{\hat{p}_1 \hat{q}_1}{n_1} + \frac{\hat{p}_2 \hat{q}_2}{n_2}} \Rightarrow (.153 - .215) \pm 1.645 \sqrt{\frac{.153(.847)}{189} + \frac{.215(.785)}{149}}$$

$$\Rightarrow -.062 \pm .070 \Rightarrow (-.132, \quad .008)$$

d.   We are 90% confident that the difference in the proportion of bidders who fall prey to the winner's curse between super-experienced bidders and less-experienced bidders is between $-.132$ and $.008$. Since this interval contains 0, there is no evidence to indicate that there is a difference in the proportion of bidders who fall prey to the winner's curse between super-experienced bidders and less-experienced bidders.

7.49   a.   Let p_1 = proportion of employed individuals who had a routine checkup in the past year and p_2 = proportion of unemployed individuals who had a routine checkup in the past year. The researchers are interested in whether there is a difference in these two proportions, so the parameter of interest is $p_1 - p_2$.

b. To determine if there is a difference in the proportions of employed and unemployed individuals who had a routine checkup in the past year, we test:

H_0: $p_1 - p_2 = 0$
H_a: $p_1 - p_2 \neq 0$

c. Some preliminary calculations are:

$$\hat{p}_1 = \frac{x_1}{n_1} = \frac{642}{1,140} = .563 \qquad\qquad \hat{p}_2 = \frac{x_2}{n_2} = \frac{740}{1,106} = .669$$

$$\hat{p} = \frac{x_1 + x_2}{n_1 + n_2} = \frac{642 + 740}{1,140 + 1,106} = \frac{1,382}{2,246} = .615 \qquad\qquad \hat{q} = 1 - \hat{p} = 1 - .615 = .385$$

The test statistic is $\quad z = \dfrac{(\hat{p}_1 - \hat{p}_2) - 0}{\sqrt{\hat{p}\hat{q}\left(\dfrac{1}{n_1} + \dfrac{1}{n_2}\right)}} = \dfrac{(.563 - .669) - 0}{\sqrt{.615(.385)\left(\dfrac{1}{1,140} + \dfrac{1}{1,106}\right)}} = -5.16$

d. The rejection region requires $\alpha/2 = .01/2 = .005$ in each tail of the z-distribution. From Table IV, Appendix B, $z_{.005} = 2.58$. The rejection region is $z < -2.58$ or $z > 2.58$.

e. The p-value is $P(z \leq -5.16) + P(z \geq 5.16) \approx (.5 - .5) + (.5 - .5) = 0$. This agrees with what was reported.

f. Since the observed value of the test statistic falls in the rejection region ($z = -5.16 < -2.58$), H_0 is rejected. There is sufficient evidence to indicate a difference in the proportion of employed and unemployed individuals who had routine checkups in the past year at $\alpha = .01$.

7.51 a. The two populations of interest are all male cell phone users and all female cell phone users.

b. The estimate of the proportion of men who sometimes do not drive safely while talking or texting on a cell phone is $\hat{p}_1 = .32$. The estimate of the proportion of women is $\hat{p}_2 = .25$.

c. For confidence coefficient .90, $\alpha = .10$ and $\alpha/2 = .10/2 = .05$. From Table IV, Appendix B, $z_{.05} = 1.645$. A 90% confidence interval for the difference between the proportions of men and women who sometimes do not drive safely while talking or texting on a cell phone is:

$$(\hat{p}_1 - \hat{p}_2) \pm z_{.05}\sqrt{\frac{\hat{p}_1\hat{q}_1}{n_1} + \frac{\hat{p}_2\hat{q}_2}{n_2}} \Rightarrow (.32 - .25) \pm 1.645\sqrt{\frac{.32(.68)}{643} + \frac{.25(.75)}{643}}$$

$$\Rightarrow .07 \pm .041 \Rightarrow (.029, \ .111)$$

d. Since the interval does not contain 0, then there is a sufficient evidence to indicate that there is a difference between the proportions of men and women who sometimes do not drive safely while talking or texting on a cell phone. Also, the interval contains all positive values so we can conclude that men are more likely than women to sometimes not drive safely while talking or texting on a cell phone.

e. The estimate of the proportion of men who used their cell phone in an emergency is $\hat{p}_1 = .71$. The estimate of the proportion of women is $\hat{p}_2 = .77$.

     f.   Let p_1 = proportion of men who used their cell phone in an emergency and p_2 = the proportion of women who used their cell phone in an emergency.
Some preliminary calculations are:

$$\hat{p}_1 = \frac{x_1}{n_1} \Rightarrow x_1 = n_1\hat{p}_1 = 643(.71) = 456.53 \qquad \hat{p}_2 = \frac{x_2}{n_2} \Rightarrow x_2 = n_2\hat{p}_2 = 643(.77) = 495.11$$

$$\hat{p} = \frac{x_1 + x_2}{n_1 + n_2} = \frac{456.53 + 495.11}{643 + 643} = .74 \qquad \hat{q} = 1 - \hat{p} = 1 - .74 = .26$$

To determine whether the proportions of men and women who used their cell phones in an emergency differ, we test:

$H_0: p_1 - p_2 = 0$
$H_a: p_1 - p_2 \neq 0$

The test statistic is $z = \dfrac{(\hat{p}_1 - \hat{p}_2) - 0}{\sqrt{\hat{p}\hat{q}\left(\dfrac{1}{n_1} + \dfrac{1}{n_2}\right)}} = \dfrac{(.71 - .77) - 0}{\sqrt{.74(.26)\left(\dfrac{1}{643} + \dfrac{1}{643}\right)}} = -2.45$.

The rejection region requires $\alpha/2 = .10/2 = .05$ in each tail of the z-distribution. From Table IV, Appendix B, $z_{.05} = 1.645$. The rejection region is $z < -1.645$ or $z > 1.645$.

Since the observed value of the test statistic falls in the rejection region ($z = -2.45 < -1.645$), H_0 is rejected. There is sufficient evidence to indicate the proportions of men and women who used their cell phone in an emergency differ at $\alpha = .10$.

7.53   a.   Let p_1 = proportion of African-American drivers searched by the LAPD and p_2 = proportion of white drivers searched by the LAPD.

Some preliminary calculations are:

$$\hat{p}_1 = \frac{x_1}{n_1} = \frac{12,016}{61,688} = .195 \qquad\qquad \hat{p}_2 = \frac{x_2}{n_2} = \frac{5,312}{106,892} = .050$$

$$\hat{p} = \frac{x_1 + x_2}{n_1 + n_2} = \frac{12,016 + 5,312}{61,688 + 106,892} = \frac{17,328}{168,580} = .103$$

To determine if the proportions of African-American and white drivers searched differs, we test:

$H_0: p_1 - p_2 = 0$
$H_a: p_1 - p_2 \neq 0$

The test statistic is $z = \dfrac{(\hat{p}_1 - \hat{p}_2) - 0}{\sqrt{\hat{p}\hat{q}\left(\dfrac{1}{n_1} + \dfrac{1}{n_2}\right)}} = \dfrac{.195 - .050}{\sqrt{.103(.897)\left(\dfrac{1}{61,688} + \dfrac{1}{106,892}\right)}} = 94.35$

The rejection region requires $\alpha/2 = .05/2 = .025$ in each tail of the z-distribution. From Table IV, Appendix B, $z_{.025} = 1.96$. The rejection region is $z < -1.96$ or $z > 1.96$.

Since the observed value of the test statistic falls in the rejection region ($z = 94.35 > 1.96$), H_0 is rejected. There is sufficient evidence to indicate the proportions of African-American drivers and white drivers searched differs at $\alpha = .05$.

b.   Let p_1 = proportion of 'hits' for African-American drivers searched by the LAPD and p_2 = proportion of 'hits' for white drivers searched by the LAPD.

Some preliminary calculations are:

$$\hat{p}_1 = \frac{x_1}{n_1} = \frac{5,134}{12;016} = .427 \qquad\qquad \hat{p}_2 = \frac{x_2}{n_2} = \frac{3,006}{5,312} = .566$$

$$\hat{p} = \frac{x_1 + x_2}{n_1 + n_2} = \frac{5,134 + 3,006}{12,016 + 5,312} = \frac{8,140}{17,328} = .470$$

For confidence coefficient .95, $\alpha = .05$ and $\alpha/2 = .05/2 = .025$. From Table IV, Appendix B, $z_{.025} = 1.96$. The 95% confidence interval is:

$$(\hat{p}_1 - \hat{p}_2) \pm z_{.025} \sqrt{\frac{\hat{p}_1 \hat{q}_1}{n_1} + \frac{\hat{p}_2 \hat{q}_2}{n_2}} \Rightarrow (.427 - .566) \pm 1.96 \sqrt{\frac{.427(.573)}{12,016} + \frac{.566(.434)}{5,312}}$$

$$\Rightarrow -.139 \pm .016 \Rightarrow (-.155, \ -.123)$$

We are 95% confident that the difference in 'hit' rates between African-American drivers and white drivers searched by the LAPD is between $-.155$ and $-.123$.

7.55   Let p_1 = proportion of African American MBA students who begin their career as entrepreneurs and p_2 = proportion of white MBA students who begin their career as entrepreneurs.

Some preliminary calculations:

$$\hat{p}_1 = \frac{x_1}{n_1} = \frac{209}{1,304} = .16 \qquad\qquad \hat{q}_1 = 1 - \hat{p}_1 = 1 - .160 = .84$$

$$\hat{p}_2 = \frac{x_2}{n_2} = \frac{356}{7,120} = .05 \qquad\qquad \hat{q}_2 = 1 - \hat{p}_2 = 1 - .05 = .95$$

We can answer the question by using either a confidence interval or a test of hypothesis. We will use the confidence interval. Since no α was given, we will us a 95% confidence interval. For confidence coefficient .95, $\alpha = .05$ and $\alpha/2 = .05/2 = .025$. From Table IV, Appendix B, $z_{.025} = 1.96$. A 95% confidence interval for the difference in the proportions of two groups is:

$$(\hat{p}_1 - \hat{p}_2) \pm z_{.025} \sqrt{\frac{\hat{p}_1 \hat{q}_1}{n_1} + \frac{\hat{p}_2 \hat{q}_2}{n_2}} \Rightarrow (.16 - .05) \pm 1.96 \sqrt{\frac{.16(.84)}{1,304} + \frac{.05(.95)}{7,120}}$$

$$\Rightarrow .11 \pm .021 \Rightarrow (.089, \ .131)$$

Since this interval does not contain 0, then there is sufficient evidence to indicate that the proportion of African American MBA students who begin their career as entrepreneurs is significantly different than the proportion of White MBA students who begin their career as entrepreneurs. The positive values in the interval mean that the African American MBA students are more likely to begin their career as entrepreneurs than the White MBA students.

7.57   a.   Let p_1 = proportion of women who have food cravings and p_2 = proportion of men who have food cravings.

We know that $\hat{p}_1 = .97$ and $\hat{p}_2 = .67$.

We know that $n_1 p_1 > 15$ and $n_1 q_1 > 15$ in order for the test to be valid. Thus, $n_1(.97) > 15 \Rightarrow n_1 > 15/.97 \approx 16$ and $n_1(.03) > 15 \Rightarrow n_1 > 15/.03 = 500$.

Also, $n_2 p_2 > 15$ and $n_2 q_2 > 15$. Thus, $n_2(.67) > 15 \Rightarrow n_2 > 15/.67 \approx 23$ and $n_2(.33) > . 15 \Rightarrow n_2 > 15/.33 \approx 46$.

b.   This study involved 1,000 McMaster University students. It is very dangerous to generalize the results of this study to the general adult population of North America. The sample of students used may not be representative of the population of interest.

7.59   a.   For confidence coefficient .99, $\alpha = 1 - .99 = .01$ and $\alpha/2 = .01/2 = .005$. From Table IV, Appendix B, $z_{.005} = 2.58$.

$$n_1 = n_2 = \frac{(z_{\alpha/2})^2 (p_1 q_1 + p_2 q_2)}{(ME)^2} = \frac{2.58^2 \left(.4(1-.4) + .7(1-.7)\right)}{.01^2} = \frac{2.99538}{.0001} = 29{,}953.8 \approx 29{,}954$$

b.   For confidence coefficient .90, $\alpha = 1 - .90 = .10$ and $\alpha/2 = .10/2 = .05$. From Table IV, Appendix B, $z_{.05} = 1.645$. Since we have no prior information about the proportions, we use $p_1 = p_2 = .5$ to get a conservative estimate. For a width of .05, the margin of error is .025.

$$n_1 = n_2 = \frac{(z_{\alpha/2})^2 (p_1 q_1 + p_2 q_2)}{(ME)^2} = \frac{(1.645)^2 \left(.5(1-.5) + .5(1-.5)\right)}{.025^2} = 2164.82 \approx 2165$$

c.   From part **b**, $z_{.05} = 1.645$.

$$n_1 = n_2 = \frac{(z_{\alpha/2})^2 (p_1 q_1 + p_2 q_2)}{(ME)^2} = \frac{(1.645)^2 \left(.2(1-.2) + .3(1-.3)\right)}{.03^2} = \frac{1.00123}{.0009} = 1112.48 \approx 1113$$

7.61 $$n_1 = n_2 = \frac{(z_{\alpha/2})^2 (\sigma_1^2 + \sigma_2^2)}{(ME)^2}$$

For confidence coefficient .95, $\alpha = 1 - .95 = .05$ and $\alpha/2 = .05/2 = .025$. From Table IV, Appendix B, $z_{.025} = 1.96$.

$$n_1 = n_2 = \frac{1.96^2 (14 + 14)}{1.8^2} = 33.2 \approx 34$$

7.63   For confidence coefficient 0.99, $\alpha = 1 - .99 = .01$ and $\alpha/2 = .01/2 = 005$. From the Table IV, Appendix B, $z_{.005} = 2.58$.

$$n_1 = n_1 = \frac{(z_{\alpha/2})^2 (\sigma_1^2 + \sigma_2^2)}{(ME)^2} = \frac{2.58^2 (1^2 + 1^2)}{.5^2} = 53.25 \approx 54$$

7.65   For confidence coefficient .90, $\alpha = .10$ and $\alpha/2 = .10/2 = .05$. From Table IV, Appendix B, $z_{.05} = 1.645$. If we assume that we do not know the return rates,

$$n_1 = n_2 = \frac{(z_{.05})^2 (p_1 q_1 + p_2 q_2)}{ME^2} = \frac{1.645^2 (.5(.5) + .5(.5))}{.01^2} = 13,530.1 \approx 13,531$$

7.67   For confidence coefficient .95, $\alpha = .05$ and $\alpha/2 = .025$. From Table IV, Appendix B, $z_{.025} = 1.96$.

$$n_1 = n_2 = \frac{(z_{\alpha/2})^2 (\sigma_1^2 + \sigma_2^2)}{(ME)^2} = \frac{1.96^2 (15^2 + 15^2)}{1^2} = 1728.72 \approx 1729$$

7.69   a.   For confidence coefficient .95, $\alpha = 1 - .95 = .05$ and $\alpha/2 = .05/2 = .025$. From Table IV, Appendix B, $z_{.025} = 1.96$.

$$n_1 = n_2 = \frac{(z_{\alpha/2})^2 (p_1 q_1 + p_2 q_2)}{(ME)^2} = \frac{1.96^2 (.184(.816) + .177(.823))}{.015^2} = 5,050.7 \approx 5,051$$

        b.   The study would involve $5,051 \times 2 = 10,102$ patients. A study this large would be extremely time consuming and expensive.

        c.   Since a difference of .015 is so small, the practical significance detecting a 0.015 difference may not be very worthwhile. A difference of .015 is so close to 0, that it might not make any difference.

7.71   a.   With $v_1 = 9$ and $v_2 = 6$, $F_{.05} = 4.10$.

        b.   With $v_1 = 18$ and $v_2 = 14$, $F_{.01} \approx 3.57$. (Since $v_1 = 18$ is not given, we estimate the value between those for $v_1 = 15$ and $v_1 = 20$.)

        c.   With $v_1 = 11$ and $v_2 = 4$, $F_{.025} \approx 8.81$. (Since $v_1 = 11$ is not given, we estimate the value by averaging those given for $v_1 = 10$ and $v_1 = 12$.)

        d.   With $v_1 = 20$ and $v_2 = 5$, $F_{.10} = 3.21$.

7.73   a.   Reject H_0 if $F > F_{.10} = 1.74$. (From Table VII, Appendix B, with $v_1 = 30$ and $v_2 = 20$.)

        b.   Reject H_0 if $F > F_{.05} = 2.04$. (From Table VIII, Appendix B, with $v_1 = 30$ and $v_2 = 20$.)

        c.   Reject H_0 if $F > F_{.025} = 2.35$. (From Table IX.)

        d.   Reject H_0 if $F > F_{.01} = 2.78$. (From Table X.)

7.75   a.   The rejection region requires $\alpha = .05$ in the upper tail of the F-distribution with $v_1 = n_1 - 1 = 25 - 1 = 24$ and $v_2 = n_2 - 1 = 20 - 1 = 19$. From Table VIII, Appendix B, $F_{.05} = 2.11$. The rejection region is $F > 2.11$ (if $s_1^2 > s_2^2$).

        b.   The rejection region requires $\alpha = .05$ in the upper tail of the F-distribution with $v_1 = n_2 - 1 = 15 - 1 = 14$ and $v_2 = n_1 - 1 = 10 - 1 = 9$. From Table VIII, Appendix B, $F_{.05} \approx 3.01$. The rejection region is $F > 3.01$ (if $s_2^2 > s_1^2$).

c. The rejection region requires $\alpha/2 = .10/2 = .05$ in the upper tail of the F-distribution. If $s_1^2 > s_2^2$, $v_1 = n_1 - 1 = 21 - 1 = 20$ and $v_2 = n_2 - 1 = 31 - 1 = 30$. From Table VIII, Appendix B, $F_{.05} = 1.93$. The rejection region is $F > 1.93$. If $s_1^2 < s_2^2$, $v_1 = n_2 - 1 = 30$ and $v_2 = n_1 - 1 = 20$. From Table VIII, $F_{.05} = 2.04$. The rejection region is $F > 2.04$.

d. The rejection region requires $\alpha = .01$ in the upper tail of the F-distribution with $v_1 = n_2 - 1 = 41 - 1 = 40$ and $v_2 = n_1 - 1 = 31 - 1 = 30$. From Table X, Appendix B, $F_{.01} = 2.30$. The rejection region is $F > 2.30$ (if $s_2^2 > s_1^2$).

e. The rejection region requires $\alpha/2 = .05/2 = .025$ in the upper tail of the F-distribution. If $s_1^2 > s_2^2$, $v_1 = n_1 - 1 = 7 - 1 = 6$ and $v_2 = n_2 - 1 = 16 - 1 = 15$. From Table IX, Appendix B, $F_{.025} = 3.41$. The rejection region is $F > 3.41$. If $s_1^2 < s_2^2$, $v_1 = n_2 - 1 = 15$ and $v_2 = n_1 - 1 = 6$. From Table IX, Appendix B, $F_{.025} = 5.27$. The rejection region is $F > 5.27$.

7.77 a. Using MINITAB, the descriptive statistics are:

Descriptive Statistics: Sample 1, Sample 2

Variable	N	Mean	Median	TrMean	StDev	SE Mean
Sample 1	6	2.417	2.400	2.417	1.436	0.586
Sample 2	5	4.36	3.70	4.36	2.97	1.33

Variable	Minimum	Maximum	Q1	Q3
Sample 1	0.700	4.400	1.075	3.650
Sample 2	1.40	8.90	1.84	7.20

To determine if the variance for population 2 is greater than that for population 1, we test:

H_0: $\sigma_1^2 = \sigma_2^2$

H_a: $\sigma_1^2 < \sigma_2^2$

The test statistic is $F = \dfrac{s_2^2}{s_1^2} = \dfrac{2.97^2}{1.436^2} = 4.28$

The rejection region requires $\alpha = .05$ in the upper tail of the F-distribution with $v_1 = n_2 - 1 = 5 - 1 = 4$ and $v_2 = n_1 - 1 = 6 - 1 = 5$. From Table VIII, Appendix B, $F_{.05} = 5.19$. The rejection region is $F > 5.19$.

Since the observed value of the test statistic does not fall in the rejection region ($F = 4.29 \not> 5.19$), H_0 is not rejected. There is insufficient evidence to indicate the variance for population 2 is greater than that for population 1 at $\alpha = .05$.

b. The p-value is $P(F \geq 4.28)$. From Tables VII and VIII, with $v_1 = 4$ and $v_2 = 5$,

$.05 < P(F \geq 4.28) < .10$

There is no evidence to reject H_0 for $\alpha < .05$ but there is evidence to reject H_0 for $\alpha = .10$.

7.79   a.   To determine if σ_M^2 is less than σ_F^2, we test:

H_0: $\sigma_M^2 = \sigma_F^2$

H_a: $\sigma_M^2 < \sigma_F^2$

b.   The test statistic is $F = \dfrac{\text{Larger sample variance}}{\text{Smaller sample variance}} = \dfrac{s_F^2}{s_M^2} = \dfrac{6.94^2}{6.73^2} = 1.06$

c.   The rejection region requires $\alpha = .10$ in the upper tail of the F-distribution with $v_1 = n_F - 1 = 114 - 1 = 113$ and $v_2 = n_M - 1 = 127 - 1 = 126$. From Table VII, Appendix B, $F_{.10} \approx 1.26$. The rejection region is $F > 1.26$.

d.   The p-value is $P(F \geq 1.06)$. From Table VII, Appendix B, with $v_1 = 113$ and $v_2 = 126$, $.10 < P(F \geq 1.06)$ or $p > .10$

e.   Since the observed value of the test statistic does not fall in the rejection region ($F = 1.063 \not> 1.26$), H_0 is not rejected. There is insufficient evidence to indicate the variation in the male perception scores is less than that for females at $\alpha = .10$.

f.   We must assume that we have two random and independent samples drawn from normal populations.

7.81   Using MINITAB, the descriptive statistics are:

Descriptive Statistics: Novice, Experienced

Variable	N	Mean	Median	TrMean	StDev	SE Mean
Novice	12	32.83	32.00	32.60	8.64	2.49
Experien	12	20.58	19.50	20.60	5.74	1.66

Variable	Minimum	Maximum	Q1	Q3
Novice	20.00	48.00	26.75	39.00
Experien	10.00	31.00	17.25	24.75

a.   Let σ_1^2 = variance in inspection errors for novice inspectors and σ_2^2 = variance in inspection errors for experienced inspectors. Since we wish to determine if the data support the belief that the variance is lower for experienced inspectors than for novice inspectors, we test:

H_0: $\sigma_1^2 = \sigma_2^2$

H_a: $\sigma_1^2 < \sigma_2^2$

The test statistic is $F = \dfrac{\text{Larger sample variance}}{\text{Smaller sample variance}} = \dfrac{s_1^2}{s_2^2} = \dfrac{8.64^2}{5.74^2} = 2.27$

The rejection region requires $\alpha = .05$ in the upper tail of the F-distribution with $v_1 = n_1 - 1 = 12 - 1 = 11$ and $v_2 = n_2 - 1 = 12 - 1 = 11$. From Table VIII, Appendix B, $F_{.05} \approx 2.82$ (using interpolation). The rejection region is $F > 2.82$.

Since the observed value of the test statistic does not fall in the rejection region ($F = 2.27 \not> 2.82$), H_0 is not rejected. The sample data do not support her belief at $\alpha = .05$.

b.   The p-value $= P(F \geq 2.27)$ with $v_1 = 11$ and $v_2 = 11$. Checking Tables VII, VIII, IX, and X in Appendix B, we find $F_{.10} = 2.23$ and $F_{.05} = 2.82$. Since the observed value of F exceeds $F_{.10}$ but is less than $F_{.05}$, the observed significance level for the test is less than .10. So $.05 < p\text{-value} < .10$.

7.83   a.   Let σ_1^2 = variance of the order-to-delivery times for the Persian Gulf War and σ_2^2 = variance of the order-to-delivery times for Bosnia.

Descriptive Statistics: Gulf, Bosnia

Variable	N	Mean	Median	TrMean	StDev	SE Mean
Gulf	9	25.24	27.50	25.24	10.5204	3.51
Bosnia	9	7.38	6.50	7.38	3.6537	1.22

Variable	Minimum	Maximum	Q1	Q3
Gulf	9.10	41.20	15.30	32.15
Bosnia	3.00	15.10	5.25	9.20

To determine if the variances of the order-to-delivery times for the Persian Gulf and Bosnia shipments are equal, we test:

H_0: $\dfrac{\sigma_1^2}{\sigma_2^2} = 1$

H_a: $\dfrac{\sigma_1^2}{\sigma_2^2} \neq 1$

The test statistic is $F = \dfrac{\text{Larger sample variance}}{\text{Smaller sample variance}} = \dfrac{s_1^2}{s_2^2} = \dfrac{10.5204^2}{3.6537^2} = 8.29$

The rejection region requires $\alpha/2 = .05/2 = .025$ in the upper tail of the F-distribution with $v_1 = n_1 - 1 = 9 - 1 = 8$ and $v_2 = n_2 - 1 = 9 - 1 = 8$. From Table IX, Appendix B, $F_{.025} = 4.43$. The rejection region is $F > 4.43$.

Since the observed value of the test statistic falls in the rejection region ($F = 8.29 > 4.43$), H_0 is rejected. There is sufficient evidence to indicate the variances of the order-to-delivery times for the Persian Gulf and Bosnia shipments differ at $\alpha = .05$.

a.   No. One assumption necessary for the small sample confidence interval for $(\mu_1 - \mu_2)$ is that $\sigma_1^2 = \sigma_2^2$. For this problem, there is evidence to indicate that $\sigma_1^2 \neq \sigma_2^2$.

7.85   Let σ_1^2 = variance of improvement scores in the honey dosage group and σ_2^2 = variance of improvement scores in the DM dosage group. From Exercise 7.21, $s_1 = 2.855$ and $s_2 = 3.256$.

To determine if the variability in coughing improvement scores differs for the two groups, we test:

$$H_0:\ \sigma_1^2 = \sigma_2^2$$
$$H_a:\ \sigma_1^2 \neq \sigma_2^2$$

The test statistic is $F = \dfrac{\text{larger sample variance}}{\text{smaller sample variance}} = \dfrac{s_2^2}{s_1^2} = \dfrac{3.256^2}{2.855^2} = 1.30$

The rejection region requires $\alpha/2 = .10/2 = .05$ in the upper tail of the F-distribution with $v_2 = n_2 - 1 = 33 - 1 = 32$ and $v_1 = n_1 - 1 = 35 - 1 = 34$. From Table VIII, Appendix B, $F_{.05} \approx 1.84$. The rejection region is $F > 1.84$.

Since the observed value of the test statistic does not fall in the rejection region ($F = 1.3 \not> 1.84$), H_0 is not rejected. There is insufficient evidence to indicate the variability in the coughing improvement scores differs for the two groups at $\alpha = .10$.

7.87   a. $s_p^2 = \dfrac{(n_1-1)s_1^2 + (n_1-1)s_2^2}{n_1+n_2-2} = \dfrac{11(74.2)+13(60.5)}{12+14-2} = 66.7792$

$$H_0:\ \mu_1 - \mu_2 = 0$$
$$H_a:\ \mu_1 - \mu_2 > 0$$

The test statistic is $t = \dfrac{(\bar{x}_1 - \bar{x}_2) - 0}{\sqrt{s_p^2\left(\frac{1}{n_1}+\frac{1}{n_2}\right)}} = \dfrac{(17.8-15.3)-0}{\sqrt{66.7792\left(\frac{1}{12}+\frac{1}{14}\right)}} = .78$

The rejection region requires $\alpha = .05$ in the upper tail of the t-distribution with df $= n_1 + n_2 - 2 = 12 + 14 - 2 = 24$. From Table V, Appendix B, for df = 24, $t_{.05} = 1.711$. The rejection region is $t > 1.711$.

Since the observed value of the test statistic does not fall in the rejection region ($0.78 \not> 1.711$), H_0 is not rejected. There is insufficient evidence to indicate that $\mu_1 > \mu_2$ at $\alpha = .05$.

b.   For confidence coefficient .99, $\alpha = .01$ and $\alpha/2 = .01/2 = .005$. From Table V, Appendix B, with df $= n_1 + n_2 - 2 = 12 + 14 - 2 = 24$, $t_{.005} = 2.797$. The confidence interval is:

$$(\bar{x}_1 - \bar{x}_2) \pm t_{.005}\sqrt{s_p^2\left(\frac{1}{n_1}+\frac{1}{n_2}\right)} \Rightarrow (17.8-15.3) \pm 2.797\sqrt{66.7792\left(\frac{1}{12}+\frac{1}{14}\right)}$$
$$\Rightarrow 2.50 \pm 8.99 \Rightarrow (-6.49, 11.49)$$

c.   For confidence coefficient .99, $\alpha = .01$ and $\alpha/2 = .01/2 = .005$. From Table IV, Appendix B, $z_{.005} = 2.58$.

$$n_1 = n_2 = \dfrac{(z_{\alpha/2})\left(\sigma_1^2 + \sigma_2^2\right)}{(ME)^2} = \dfrac{(2.58)^2(74.2+60.5)}{2^2} = 224.15 \approx 225$$

7.89   a.   For confidence coefficient .90, $\alpha = .10$ and $\alpha/2 = .05$. From Table IV, Appendix B, $z_{.05} = 1.645$. The confidence interval is:

$$(\bar{x}_1 - \bar{x}_2) \pm z_{.05}\sqrt{\frac{s_1^2}{n_1} + \frac{s_2^2}{n_2}} \Rightarrow (12.2 - 8.3) \pm 1.645\sqrt{\frac{2.1}{135} + \frac{3.0}{148}}$$

$$\Rightarrow 3.90 \pm .31 \Rightarrow (3.59, 4.21)$$

   b. $H_0: \mu_1 - \mu_2 = 0$
        $H_a: \mu_1 - \mu_2 \neq 0$

The test statistic is $z = \dfrac{(\bar{x}_1 - \bar{x}_2)}{\sqrt{\dfrac{s_1^2}{n_1} + \dfrac{s_2^2}{n_2}}} = \dfrac{(12.2 - 8.3) - 0}{\sqrt{\dfrac{2.1}{135} + \dfrac{3.0}{148}}} = 20.60$

The rejection region requires $\alpha/2 = .01/2 = .005$ in each tail of the z-distribution. From Table IV, Appendix B, $z_{.005} = 2.58$. The rejection region is $z < -2.58$ or $z > 2.58$.

Since the observed value of the test statistic falls in the rejection region ($20.60 > 2.58$), H_0 is rejected. There is sufficient evidence to indicate that $\mu_1 \neq \mu_2$ at $\alpha = .01$.

   c.   For confidence coefficient .90, $\alpha = .10$ and $\alpha/2 = .05$. From Table IV, Appendix B, $z_{.05} = 1.645$.

$$n_1 = n_2 = \frac{(z_{\alpha/2})(\sigma_1^2 + \sigma_2^2)}{(ME)^2} = \frac{(1.645)^2(2.1 + 3.0)}{.2^2} = 345.02 \approx 346$$

7.91   a.   This is a paired difference experiment.

Pair	Difference (Pop. 1 - Pop. 2)
1	6
2	4
3	4
4	3
5	2

$$\bar{d} = \frac{\sum_{i=1}^{n_d} d_i}{n_d} = \frac{19}{5} = 3.8 \qquad s_d^2 = \frac{\sum_{i=1}^{n_d} d_i^2 - \frac{\left(\sum_{i=1}^{n_d} d_i\right)^2}{n_d}}{n_d - 1} = \frac{81 - \frac{19^2}{5}}{5 - 1} = 2.2$$

$$s_d = \sqrt{2.2} = 1.4832$$

$H_0: \mu_d = 0$
$H_a: \mu_d \neq 0$

The test statistic is $t = \dfrac{\bar{d} - 0}{s_d/\sqrt{n_d}} = \dfrac{3.8 - 0}{1.4832/\sqrt{5}} = 5.73$

The rejection region requires $\alpha/2 = .05/2 = .025$ in each tail of the t-distribution with df $= n - 1 = 5 - 1 = 4$. From Table V, Appendix B, $t_{.025} = 2.776$. The rejection region is $t < -2.776$ or $t > 2.776$.

Since the observed value of the test statistic falls in the rejection region ($5.73 > 2.776$), H_0 is rejected. There is sufficient evidence to indicate that the population means are different at $\alpha = .05$.

b. For confidence coefficient .95, $\alpha = .05$ and $\alpha/2 = .025$. Therefore, we would use the same t value as above, $t_{.025} = 2.776$. The confidence interval is:

$$\bar{x}_d \pm t_{\alpha/2} \frac{s_d}{\sqrt{n_d}} \Rightarrow 3.8 \pm 3.8 \pm 2.776 \frac{1.4832}{\sqrt{5}} \Rightarrow 3.8 \pm 1.84 \Rightarrow (1.96, 5.64)$$

c. The sample of differences must be randomly selected from a population of differences which has a normal distribution.

7.93   a. Let $\mu_1 =$ average size of the right temporal lobe of the brain for the short-recovery group and $\mu_2 =$ average size of the right temporal lobe of the brain for the long-recovery group.

The target parameter is $\mu_1 - \mu_2$. We must assume that the two samples are random and independent, the two populations being sampled from are approximately normal, and the two population variances are equal.

b. Let $p_1 =$ proportion of athletes who have a good self-image of their body and $p_2 =$ proportion of non-athletes who have a good self-image of their body.

The target parameter for this comparison is $p_1 - p_2$. We must assume that the two samples are random and independent and that the sample sizes are sufficiently large.

c. Let $\mu_1 =$ average weight of eggs produced by a sample of chickens on regular feed and $\mu_2 =$ average weight of eggs produced by a sample of chickens fed a diet supplemented by corn oil. Let $\mu_d =$ average difference in weight between eggs produced by the chickens on regular feed and then on a diet supplemented with corn oil.

The target parameter is μ_d. We must assume that we have a random sample of differences and that the population of differences is approximately normal.

7.95   a. Yes. The sample mean of the virtual-reality group is 10.67 points higher than the sample mean of the simple user interface group.

b. Let $\mu_1 =$ mean improvement score for the virtual-reality group and $\mu_2 =$ mean improvement score for the simple user interface group.

To determine if the mean improvement scores for the virtual-reality group is higher than that for the simple user interface group, we test:

H_0: $\mu_1 - \mu_2 = 0$
H_a: $\mu_1 - \mu_2 > 0$

The test statistic is $z = \dfrac{(\bar{x}_1 - \bar{x}_2) - D_o}{\sqrt{\left(\dfrac{\sigma_1^2}{n_1} + \dfrac{\sigma_2^2}{n_2}\right)}} = \dfrac{(43.15 - 32.48) - 0}{\sqrt{\left(\dfrac{12.57^2}{45} + \dfrac{9.26^2}{45}\right)}} = \dfrac{10.67}{2.3274} = 4.58$

The rejection region requires $\alpha = .05$ in the upper tail of the z-distribution. From Table IV, Appendix B, $z_{.05} = 1.645$. The rejection region is $z > 1.645$.

Since the observed value of the test statistic falls in the rejection region ($z = 4.58 > 1.645$), H_0 is rejected. There is sufficient evidence to indicate the mean improvement scores for the virtual-reality group is higher than that for the simple user interface group $\alpha = .05$.

7.97   a.   The data should be analyzed using a paired-difference analysis because that is how the data were collected. Reaction times were collected twice from each subject, once under the random condition and once under the static condition. Since the two sets of data are not independent, they cannot be analyzed using independent samples analyses.

  b.   Let μ_1 = mean reaction time under the random condition and μ_2 = mean reaction time under the static condition. Let $\mu_d = \mu_1 - \mu_2$. To determine if there is a difference in mean reaction time between the two conditions, we test:

$$H_0: \ \mu_d = 0$$
$$H_a: \ \mu_d \neq 0$$

  c.   The test statistic is $t = 1.52$ with a p-value of .15. Since the p-value is not small, there is no evidence to reject H_0 for any reasonable value of α. There is insufficient evidence to indicate a difference in the mean reaction times between the two conditions. This supports the researchers' claim that visual search has no memory.

7.99   a.   Let μ_1 = mean response by noontime watchers and μ_2 = mean response by non-noontime watchers. To determine if the mean response differs for noontime and non-noontime watchers, we test:

$$H_0: \ \mu_1 = \mu_2$$
$$H_a: \ \mu_1 \neq \mu_2$$

  b.   Since the p-value ($p = .02$) is less than $\alpha = .05$, H_0 is rejected. There is sufficient evidence to indicate the mean response differs for noontime and non-noontime watchers at $\alpha = .05$.

  c.   Since the p-value ($p = .02$) is greater than $\alpha = .01$, H_0 is not rejected. There is insufficient evidence to indicate the mean response differs for noontime and non-noontime watchers at $\alpha = .01$.

  d.   Since the two sample means are so close together, there appears to be no "practical" difference between the two means. Even if there is a statistically significant difference between the two means, there is no practical difference.

7.101   To determine if there is a difference in the proportions of consumer/commercial and industrial product managers who are at least 40 years old, we could use either a test of hypothesis or a confidence interval. Since we are asked only to determine if there is a difference in the proportions, we will use a test of hypothesis.

Let p_1 = proportion of consumer/commercial product managers at least 40 years old and p_2 = proportion of industrial product managers at least 40 years old.

$$\hat{p}_1 = .40 \qquad \hat{q}_1 = 1 - \hat{p}_1 = 1 - .40 = .60$$

$$\hat{p}_2 = .54 \qquad \hat{q}_2 = 1 - \hat{p}_1 = 1 - .54 = .46$$

$$\hat{p} = \frac{n_1 \hat{p}_1 + n_2 \hat{p}_2}{n_1 + n_2} = \frac{93(.40) + 212(.54)}{93 + 212} = .497 \qquad \hat{q} = 1 - \hat{p} = 1 - .497 = .503$$

To see if the samples are sufficiently large:

$$n_1\hat{p}_1 = 93(.4) = 37.2 \text{ and } n_1\hat{q}_1 = 93.6(.6) = 55.8$$

$$n_2\hat{p}_2 = 212(.54) = 114.48 \text{ and } n_2\hat{q}_2 = 212(.46) = 97.52$$

Since all values are greater than 15, the normal approximation will be adequate.

To determine if there is a difference in the proportions of consumer/commercial and industrial product managers who are at least 40 years old, we test:

H_0: $p_1 - p_2 = 0$
H_a: $p_1 - p_2 \neq 0$

The test statistic is $z = \dfrac{(\hat{p}_1 - \hat{p}_2) - 0}{\sqrt{\hat{p}\hat{q}\left(\dfrac{1}{n_1} + \dfrac{1}{n_2}\right)}} = \dfrac{(.40 - .54) - 0}{\sqrt{.497(.503)\left(\dfrac{1}{93} + \dfrac{1}{212}\right)}} = -2.25$

We will use $\alpha = .05$. The rejection region requires $\alpha/2 = .05/2 = .025$ in each tail of the z-distribution. From Table IV, Appendix B, $z_{.025} = 1.96$. The rejection region is $z < -1.96$ or $z > 1.96$.

Since the observed value of the test statistic falls in the rejection region ($z = -2.25 < -1.96$), H_0 is rejected. There is sufficient evidence to indicate that there is a difference in the proportions of consumer/commercial and industrial product managers who are at least 40 years old at $\alpha = .05$.

Since the test statistic is negative, there is evidence to indicate that the industrial product managers tend to be older than the consumer/commercial product managers.

7.103   Let p_1 = unemployment rate for the urban industrial community and p_2 = unemployment rate for the university community.

Some preliminary calculations are:

$$\hat{p}_1 = \frac{x_1}{n_1} = \frac{47}{525} = .0895 \qquad \hat{p}_2 = \frac{x_2}{n_2} = \frac{22}{375} = .0587$$

For confidence coefficient .95, $\alpha = 1 - .95 = .05$ and $\alpha/2 = .05/2 = .025$. From Table IV, Appendix B, $z_{.025} = 1.96$. The confidence interval is:

$$(\hat{p}_1 - \hat{p}_2) \pm z_{.025}\sqrt{\frac{\hat{p}_1\hat{q}_1}{n_1} + \frac{\hat{p}_2\hat{q}_2}{n_2}}$$

$$\Rightarrow (.0895 - .0587) \pm 1.96\sqrt{\frac{.0895(.9105)}{525} + \frac{.0587(.9413)}{375}}$$

$$\Rightarrow .0308 \pm .0341 \Rightarrow (-.0033, .0649)$$

We are 95% confident the difference in unemployment rates in the two communities is between $-.0033$ and .0649.

7.105   a.   Let μ_1 = mean ingratiatory score for managers and μ_2 = mean ingratiatory score for clerical personnel. To determine if there is a difference in ingratiatory behavior between managers and clerical personnel, we test:

$H_0: \mu_1 = \mu_2$
$H_a: \mu_1 \neq \mu_2$

   b.   The test statistic is $z = \dfrac{(\bar{x}_1 - \bar{x}_2) - D_0}{\sqrt{\dfrac{s_1^2}{n_1} + \dfrac{s_2^2}{n_2}}} = \dfrac{(2.41 - 1.90) - 0}{\sqrt{\dfrac{(.74)^2}{288} + \dfrac{(.59)^2}{110}}} = 7.17$

The rejection region requires $\alpha/2 = .05/2 = .025$ in each tail of the z-distribution. From Table IV, Appendix B, $z_{.025} = 1.96$. The rejection region is $z < -1.96$ or $z > 1.96$.

Since the observed value of the test statistic falls in the rejection region ($z = 7.17 > 1.96$), H_0 is rejected. There is sufficient evidence to indicate a difference in ingratiatory behavior between managers and clerical personnel at $\alpha = .05$.

   c.   For confidence coefficient .95, $\alpha = .05$ and $\alpha/2 = .05/2 = .025$. From Table IV, Appendix B, $z_{.025} = 1.96$. The 95% confidence interval is:

$$(\bar{x}_1 - \bar{x}_2) \pm z_{.025} \sqrt{\frac{s_1^2}{n_1} + \frac{s_2^2}{n_2}} \Rightarrow (2.41 - 1.90) \pm 1.96 \sqrt{\frac{.74^2}{288} + \frac{.59^2}{110}}$$

$$\Rightarrow .51 \pm .14 \Rightarrow (.37, .65)$$

We are 95% confident that the difference in mean ingratiatory scores between managers and clerical personnel is between .37 and .65. Since this interval does not contain 0, it is consistent with the test of hypothesis which rejected the hypothesis that there was no difference in mean scores for the two groups.

7.107   a.   Using MINITAB, the descriptive statistics are:

Descriptive Statistics: Purchasers, Nonpurchasers

Variable	N	Mean	Median	TrMean	StDev	SE Mean
Purchase	20	39.80	38.00	39.67	10.04	2.24
Nonpurch	20	47.20	52.00	47.56	13.62	3.05

Variable	Minimum	Maximum	Q1	Q3
Purchase	23.00	59.00	32.25	48.75
Nonpurch	22.00	66.00	33.50	58.75

$$s_p^2 = \frac{(n_1 - 1)s_1^2 + (n_2 - 1)s_2^2}{n_1 + n_2 - 2} = \frac{(20 - 1)10.04^2 + (20 - 1)13.62^2}{20 + 20 - 2} = 143.153$$

Let μ_1 = mean age of nonpurchasers and μ_2 = mean age of purchasers.

To determine if there is a difference in the mean age of purchasers and nonpurchasers, we test:

H_0: $\mu_1 - \mu_2 = 0$
H_a: $\mu_1 - \mu_2 \neq 0$

The test statistic is $t = \dfrac{(\bar{x}_1 - \bar{x}_2) - 0}{\sqrt{s_p^2\left(\dfrac{1}{n_1} + \dfrac{1}{n_2}\right)}} = \dfrac{(47.20 - 39.80) - 0}{\sqrt{143.153\left(\dfrac{1}{20} + \dfrac{1}{20}\right)}} = 1.956$

The rejection region requires $\alpha/2 = .10/2 = .05$ in each tail of the *t*-distribution with df $= n_1 + n_2 - 2 = 20 + 20 - 2 = 38$. From Table V, Appendix B, $t_{.05} \approx 1.684$. The rejection region is $t < -1.684$ or $t > 1.684$.

Since the observed value of the test statistic falls in the rejection region ($t = 1.956 > 1.684$), H_0 is rejected. There is sufficient evidence to indicate the mean age of purchasers and nonpurchasers differ at $\alpha = .10$.

b. The necessary assumptions are:

1. Both sampled populations are approximately normal.
2. The population variances are equal.
3. The samples are randomly and independently sampled.

c. The *p*-value is $P(z \leq -1.956) + P(z \geq 1.956) = (.5 - .4748) + (.5 - .4748) = .0504$. The probability of observing a test statistic of this value or more unusual if H_0 is true is .0504. Since this value is less than $\alpha = .10$, H_0 is rejected. There is sufficient evidence to indicate there is a difference in the mean age of purchasers and nonpurchasers.

d. For confidence coefficient .90, $\alpha = 1 - .90 = .10$ and $\alpha/2 = .10/2 = .05$. From Table V, Appendix B, with df $= 38$, $t_{.05} \approx 1.684$. The confidence interval is:

$$(\bar{x}_2 - \bar{x}_1) \pm t_{.05}\sqrt{s_p^2\left(\frac{1}{n_1} + \frac{1}{n_2}\right)} \Rightarrow (39.8 - 47.2) \pm 1.684\sqrt{143.1684\left(\frac{1}{20} + \frac{1}{20}\right)}$$
$$\Rightarrow -7.4 \pm 6.38 \Rightarrow (-13.77, -1.03)$$

We are 90% confident that the difference in mean ages between purchasers and nonpurchasers is between −13.77 and −1.03.

7.109 a. $\mu_d = \dfrac{\sum_{i=1}^{51} d_i}{51} = \dfrac{335}{51} = 6.57$

b. We do not need to estimate anything – we know the parameter's value.

c. Using MINITAB, the descriptive statistics are:

Descriptive Statistics: SAT2007, SAT2000, Difference

```
Variable      N    Mean   StDev  Minimum      Q1   Median      Q3  Maximum
SAT2007      51  1072.7   78.1    931.0   1004.0   1048.0  1143.0   1221.0
SAT2000      51  1066.1   65.9    966.0   1007.0   1054.0  1120.0   1197.0
Difference   51    6.57   22.41   -73.00    -5.00     5.00   19.00    54.00
```

Let μ_1 = mean SAT score in 2007 and μ_2 = mean SAT score in 2000. Then $\mu_d = \mu_1 - \mu_2$.   To determine if the true mean SAT score in 2007 differs from that in 2000, we test:

H_0: $\mu_d = 0$
H_a: $\mu_d \neq 0$

The test statistic is $z = \dfrac{\bar{d} - D_o}{\dfrac{s_d}{\sqrt{n_d}}} = \dfrac{6.57 - 0}{\dfrac{22.41}{\sqrt{51}}} = 2.09$

The rejection region requires $\alpha/2 = .10/2 = .05$ in each tail of the z-distribution. From Table IV, Appendix B, $z_{.05} = 1.645$. The rejection region is $z < -1.645$ or $z > 1.645$.

Since the observed value of the test statistic falls in the rejection region ($z = 2.09 > 1.645$), H_0 is rejected. There is sufficient evidence to indicate the true mean SAT score in 2007 is different than that in 2000 at $\alpha = .10$.

7.111 For probability .95, $\alpha = 1 - .95 = .05$ and $\alpha/2 = .05/2 = .025$. From Table IV, Appendix B, $z_{.025} = 1.96$. Since we have no prior information about the proportions, we use $p_1 = p_2 = .5$ to get a conservative estimate.

$$n_1 = n_2 = \frac{(z_{\alpha/2})^2 (p_1 q_1 + p_2 q_2)}{(ME)^2} = \frac{(1.96)^2 (.5(1-.5) + .5(1-.5))}{.02^2} = \frac{1.9208}{.0004} = 4,802$$

7.113 a. Let μ_d = mean difference in pupil dilation between pattern 1 and pattern 2.

To determine if the pupil dilation differs for the two patterns, we test:

H_0: $\mu_d = 0$
H_a: $\mu_d \neq 0$

b. Using MINITAB, the descriptive statistics are:

Descriptive Statistics: Pattern1, Pattern2, Diff

```
Variable        N      Mean    Median    TrMean     StDev   SE Mean
Pattern1       15     1.122     1.000     1.141     0.505     0.130
Pattern2       15     0.883     0.910     0.892     0.453     0.117
Diff           15    0.2393    0.2100    0.2338    0.1608    0.0415

Variable   Minimum   Maximum        Q1        Q3
Pattern1     0.150     1.850     0.850     1.460
Pattern2     0.050     1.600     0.650     1.220
Diff       -0.0400    0.5900    0.1200    0.3100
```

The test statistic is $t = \dfrac{\bar{d} - D_0}{\dfrac{s_d}{\sqrt{n_d}}} = \dfrac{.2393 - 0}{\dfrac{0.1608}{\sqrt{15}}} = 5.76$

Since no α is given, we will use $\alpha = .05$. The rejection region requires $\alpha/2 = .05/2 = .025$ in each tail of the t-distribution with df $= n_d - 1 = 15 - 1 = 14$. From Table V, Appendix B, $t_{.025} = 2.145$. The rejection region is $t < -2.145$ or $t > 2.145$.

Since the observed value of the test statistic falls in the rejection region ($t = 5.76 > 2.145$), H_0 is rejected. There is sufficient evidence to indicate that there is a difference in the mean pupil dilation between pattern 1 and pattern 2 at $\alpha = .05$.

c.   The paired difference design is better. There is much variation in pupil dilation from person to person. By using the paired difference design, we can eliminate the person to person differences.

7.115   Attitude towards the Advertisement:

The p-value $= .091$. There is no evidence to reject H_0 for $\alpha = .05$. There is no evidence to indicate the first ad will be more effective when shown to males for $\alpha = .05$. There is evidence to reject H_0 for $\alpha = .10$. There is evidence to indicate the first ad will be more effective when shown to males for $\alpha = .10$.

Attitude toward Brand of Soft Drink:

The p-value $= .032$. There is evidence to reject H_0 for $\alpha > .032$. There is evidence to indicate the first ad will be more effective when shown to males for $\alpha > .032$.

Intention to Purchase the Soft Drink:

The p-value $= .050$. There is no evidence to reject H_0 for $\alpha = .05$. There is no evidence to indicate the first ad will be more effective when shown to males for $\alpha = .05$. There is evidence to reject H_0 for $\alpha > .050$. There is evidence to indicate the first ad will be more effective when shown to males for $\alpha > .050$.

No, I do not agree with the author's hypothesis. The results agree with the author's hypothesis for only the attitude toward the advertisement id using $\alpha = .05$. If we want to use $\alpha = .10$, then the author's hypotheses are all supported.

7.117   Some preliminary calculations are:

Working Days	Difference (Design 1 - Design 2)
8/16	−53
8/17	−271
8/18	−206
8/19	−266
8/20	−213
8/23	−183
8/24	−118
8/25	−87

$\bar{d} = \dfrac{\sum d}{n_d} = \dfrac{-1,397}{8} = -174.625$

$$s_d^2 = \frac{\sum d^2 - \frac{\left(\sum d\right)^2}{n_d}}{n_d - 1} = \frac{289,793 - \frac{(-1,397)^2}{8}}{8 - 1} = 6,548.839$$

$$s_d = \sqrt{s_d^2} = \sqrt{6,548.839} = 80.925$$

To determine if Design 2 is superior to Design 1, we test:

H_0: $\mu_d = 0$
H_a: $\mu_d < 0$

The test statistic is $t = \dfrac{\bar{d} - \mu_o}{s_d / \sqrt{n_d}} = \dfrac{-174.625 - 0}{80.925 / \sqrt{8}} = -6.103$

Since no α value was given, we will use $\alpha = .05$. The rejection region requires $\alpha = .05$ in the lower tail of the t-distribution with df $= n_d - 1 = 8 - 1 = 7$. From Table V, Appendix B, $t_{.05} = 1.895$. The rejection region is $t < -1.895$.

Since the observed value of the test statistic falls in the rejection region ($t = -6.103 < -1.895$), H_0 is rejected. There is sufficient evidence to indicate Design 2 is superior to Design 1 at $\alpha = .05$.

For confidence coefficient .95, $\alpha = .05$ and $\alpha/2 = .025$. From Table V, Appendix B, with df $= n_d - 1 = 8 - 1 = 7$, $t_{.025} = 2.365$. A 95% confidence interval for μ_d is:

$$\bar{d} \pm t_{.025} \frac{s_d}{\sqrt{n_d}} \rightarrow -174.625 \pm 2.365 \frac{80.925}{\sqrt{8}} \rightarrow -174.625 \pm 67.666 \Rightarrow (-242.29, \; -106.96)$$

Since this interval does not contain 0, there is evidence to indicate Design 2 is superior to Design 1.

Chapter 8
Design of Experiments and
Analysis of Variance

8.1   Since only one factor is utilized, the treatments are the four levels (A, B, C, D) of the qualitative factor.

8.3   One has no control over the levels of the factors in an observational experiment. One does have control of the levels of the factors in a designed experiment.

8.5   a.   This is an observational experiment. The economist has no control over the factor levels or unemployment rates.

       b.   This is a designed experiment. The manager chooses only three different incentive programs to compare, and randomly assigns an incentive program to each of nine plants.

       c.   This is an observational experiment. Even though the marketer chooses the publication, he has no control over who responds to the ads.

       d.   This is an observational experiment. The load on the facility's generators is only observed, not controlled.

       e.   This is an observational experiment. One has no control over the distance of the haul, the goods hauled, or the price of diesel fuel.

8.7   a.   The response variable is the age when the tumor was first detected.

       b.   The experimental units are the smokers.

       c.   There is one factor in this problem: screening method.

       d.   There are 2 treatments in this problem, corresponding to the 2 levels of the factor. The treatments are CT and chest X-ray.

8.9   a.   The experimental units for this study are the students in the introductory psychology class.

       b.   The study is a designed experiment because the students are randomly assigned to a particular study group.

       c.   There are 2 factors in this problem: Class standing and study group.

       d.   Class standing has 3 levels: Low, Medium, and High. Study group has 2 levels: practice test and review.

       e.   There are a total of $3 \times 2 = 6$ treatments. They are: (Low, Review), (Low, Practice exam), (Medium, Review), (Medium, Practice exam), (High, Review), and (High, Practice exam).

       f.   The response variable is the final exam score.

214

8.11   a.   There are 2 factors in this problem, each with 2 levels. Thus, there are a total of $2 \times 2 = 4$ treatments.

  b.   The 4 treatments are: (Within-store, home), (Within-store, in store), (Between-store,home), and (Between-store, in store).

8.13   a.   The dependent variable is the dissolution time.

  b.   There are 3 factors in this experiment: Binding agent, binding concentration, and relative density. Binding agent has 2 levels – khaya gum and PVP. Binding concentration has 2 levels – .5% and 4.0%. Relative density has 2 levels – high and low.

  c.   There could be a total of $2 \times 2 \times 2 = 8$ treatments for this experiment. They are:

khaya gum, .5%, high   PVP, .5%, high
khaya gum, .5%, low   PVP, .5%, low
khaya gum, 4.0%, high   PVP, 4.0%, high
khaya gum, 4.0%, low   PVP, 4.0%, low

8.15   a.   From Table VIII with $v_1 = 4$ and $v_2 = 4$, $F_{.05} = 6.39$.

  b.   From Table X with $v_1 = 4$ and $v_2 = 4$, $F_{.01} = 15.98$.

  c.   From Table VII with $v_1 = 30$ and $v_2 = 40$, $F_{.10} = 1.54$.

  d.   From Table IX with $v_1 = 15$, and $v_2 = 12$, $F_{.025} = 3.18$.

8.17   a.   In the second dot diagram **#2**, the difference between the sample means is small relative to the variability within the sample observations. In the first dot diagram **#1**, the values in each of the samples are grouped together with a range of 4, while in the second diagram **#2**, the range of values is 8.

  b.   For diagram **#1**,

$$\bar{x}_1 = \frac{\sum x_1}{n} = \frac{7+8+9+9+10+11}{6} = \frac{54}{6} = 9$$

$$\bar{x}_2 = \frac{\sum x_2}{n} = \frac{12+13+14+14+15+16}{6} = \frac{84}{6} = 14$$

For diagram **#2**,

$$\bar{x}_1 = \frac{\sum x_1}{n} = \frac{5+5+7+11+13+13}{6} = \frac{54}{6} = 9$$

$$\bar{x}_2 = \frac{\sum x_2}{n} = \frac{10+10+12+16+18+18}{6} = \frac{84}{6} = 14$$

c.   For diagram **#1**,

$$SST = \sum_{i=1}^{2} n_i (\bar{x}_i - \bar{x})^2 \ 1 = 6(9 - 11.5)^2 + 6(14 - 11.5)^2 = 75$$

$$\left(\bar{x} = \frac{\sum x}{n} = \frac{54 + 84}{12} = 11.5 \right)$$

For diagram **#2**,

$$SST = \sum_{i=1}^{2} n_i (\bar{x}_i - \bar{x})^2 = 6(9 - 11.5)^2 + 6(14 - 11.5)^2 = 75$$

d.   For diagram **#1**,

$$s_1^2 = \frac{\sum x_1^2 - \frac{\left(\sum x_1\right)^2}{n_1}}{n_1 - 1} = \frac{496 - \frac{54^2}{6}}{6 - 1} = \frac{496 - \frac{54^2}{6}}{6 - 1} = 2$$

$$s_2^2 = \frac{\sum x_2^2 - \frac{\left(\sum x_2\right)^2}{n_2}}{n_2 - 1} = \frac{1186 - \frac{84^2}{6}}{6 - 1} = 2$$

$$SSE = (n_1 - 1) s_1^2 + (n_2 - 1) s_2^2 = (6 - 1)2 + (6 - 1)2 = 20$$

For diagram **#2**,

$$s_1^2 = \frac{\sum x_1^2 - \frac{\left(\sum x_1\right)^2}{n_1}}{n_1 - 1} = \frac{558 - \frac{54^2}{6}}{6 - 1} = 14.4$$

$$s_2^2 = \frac{\sum x_2^2 - \frac{\left(\sum x_2\right)^2}{n_2}}{n_2 - 1} = \frac{1248 - \frac{84^2}{6}}{6 - 1} = 14.4$$

$$SSE = (n_1 - 1) s_1^2 + (n_2 - 1) s_2^2 = (6 - 1)14.4 + (6 - 1)14.4 = 144$$

e.   For diagram **#1**, SS(Total) = SST + SSE = 75 + 20 = 95

$$SST \ is \ \frac{SST}{SS(Total)} \times 100\% = \frac{75}{95} \times 100\% = 78.95\% \ of \ SS(Total)$$

For diagram **#2**, SS(Total) = SST + SSE = 75 + 144 = 219

$$SST \ is \ \frac{SST}{SS(Total)} \times 100\% = \frac{75}{219} \times 100\% = 34.25\% \ of \ SS(Total)$$

f. For diagram #1, MST $= \dfrac{SST}{k-1} = \dfrac{75}{2-1} = 75$

$$MSE = \dfrac{SSE}{n-k} = \dfrac{20}{12-2} = 2 \qquad F = \dfrac{MST}{MSE} = \dfrac{75}{2} = 37.5$$

For diagram #2, MST $= \dfrac{SST}{k-1} = \dfrac{75}{2-1} = 75$

$$MSE = \dfrac{SSE}{n-k} = \dfrac{144}{12-2} = 14.4 \quad F = \dfrac{MST}{MSE} = \dfrac{75}{14.4} = 5.21$$

g. The rejection region for both diagrams requires $\alpha = .05$ in the upper tail of the F-distribution with $v_1 = p - 1 = 2 - 1 = 1$ and $v_2 = n - p = 12 - 2 = 10$. From Table VIII, Appendix B, $F_{.05} = 4.96$. The rejection region is $F > 4.96$.

For diagram #1, the observed value of the test statistic falls in the rejection region ($F = 37.5 > 4.96$). Thus, H_0 is rejected. There is sufficient evidence to indicate the samples were drawn from populations with different means at $\alpha = .05$.

For diagram #2, the observed value of the test statistic falls in the rejection region ($F = 5.21 > 4.96$). Thus, H_0 is rejected. There is sufficient evidence to indicate the samples were drawn from populations with different means at $\alpha = .05$.

h. We must assume both populations are normally distributed with common variances.

8.19 Refer to Exercise 8.17, the ANOVA table is:

For diagram #1:

Source	Df	SS	MS	F
Treatment	1	75	75	37.5
Error	10	20	2	
Total	11	95		

For diagram #2:

Source	Df	SS	MS	F
Treatment	1	75	75	5.21
Error	10	144	14.4	
Total	11	219		

8.21 a. Some preliminary calculations are:

$$CM = \dfrac{\left(\sum y_i\right)^2}{n} = \dfrac{37.1^2}{12} = 114.701$$

$$SS(Total) = \sum y_i^2 - CM = 145.89 - 114.701 = 31.189$$

$$SST = \sum \dfrac{T_i^2}{n_i} - CM = \dfrac{16.9^2}{5} + \dfrac{16.0^2}{4} + \dfrac{4.2^2}{3} - 114.701$$

$$= 127.002 - 114.701 = 12.301$$

$$SSE = SS(Total) - SST = 31.189 - 12.301 = 18.888$$

$$MST = \frac{SST}{k-1} = \frac{12.301}{3-1} = 6.1505 \qquad MSE = \frac{SSE}{n-k} = \frac{18.888}{12-3} = 2.0987$$

$$F = \frac{MST}{MSE} = \frac{6.1505}{2.0987} = 2.931$$

Source	df	SS	MS	F
Treatments	2	12.30	6.15	2.93
Error	9	18.89	2.10	
Total	11	31.19		

b. H_0: $\mu_1 = \mu_2 = \mu_3$
H_a: At least two treatment means differ

The test statistic is $F = 2.931$.

The rejection region requires $\alpha = .01$ in the upper tail of the F-distribution with $v_1 = k - 1 = 3 - 1 = 2$ and $v_2 = n - k = 12 - 3 = 9$. From Table X, Appendix B, $F_{.01} = 8.02$. The rejection region is $F > 8.02$.

Since the observed value of the test statistic does not fall in the rejection region ($F = 2.93 \not> 8.02$), H_0 is not rejected. There is insufficient evidence to indicate a difference in the treatment means at $\alpha = .01$.

8.23   a.   To determine if the mean LUST discount percentages across the seven states differ, we test:
H_0: $\mu_1 = \mu_2 = \mu_3 = \mu_4 = \mu_5 = \mu_6 = \mu_7$
H_a: At least two treatment means differ

b.   From the ANOVA table, the test statistic is F = 1.60 and the p-value = 0.174.

Since the observed p-value ($p = 0.174$) is not less than $\alpha = .10$, H_0 is not rejected. There is insufficient evidence to indicate a difference in the mean LUST discount percentages among the seven states at $\alpha = .10$.

8.25   a.   A completely randomized design was used.

b.   There are 4 treatments: 3 robots/colony, 6 robots/colony, 9 robots/colony, and 12 robots/colony.

c.   To determine if there was a difference in the mean energy expended (per robot) among the 4 colony sizes, we test:

H_0: $\mu_1 = \mu_2 = \mu_3 = \mu_4$
H_a: At least two means differ

d.   Since the p-value ($<.001$) is less than $\alpha(.05)$, H_0 is rejected. There is sufficient evidence to indicate a difference in mean energy expended per robot among the 4 colony sizes at $\alpha = .05$.

8.27   To determine if a driver's propensity to engage in road rage is related to his/her income, we test:

H_0: $\mu_1 = \mu_2 = \mu_3$
H_a: At least two means differ

The test statistic is $F = 3.90$ and the p-value is $p < .01$. Since the p-value is less than $\alpha = .05$, H_0 is rejected. There is sufficient evidence to indicate a driver's propensity to engage in road rage is related to his/her income for $\alpha > .01$. Since the sample means increase as the income increases, it appears that road rage increases as income increases.

8.29   a.   There is one factor in this problem which is Group. There are 5 treatments in this problem, corresponding to the 5 levels of Group: Casualties, Survivors, Implementers/casualties, Implementers/survivors, and Formulators. The response variable is the ethics score. The experimental units are the employees enrolled in an Executive MBA program.

        b.   To determine if there are any differences among the mean ethics scores for the five groups, we test:

H_0: $\mu_1 = \mu_2 = \mu_3 = \mu_4 = \mu_5$
H_a: At least one of the population means differs from the rest

        c.   The test statistic is $F = 9.85$ and the p-value is $p = 0.000$. Since the p-value (0.000) is less than any reasonable significance level α, H_0 is rejected. There is sufficient evidence to indicate a difference in the mean ethics scores among the five groups of employees for any reasonable value of α

        d.   We will check the assumptions of normality and equal variances. Using MINITAB, the histograms are:

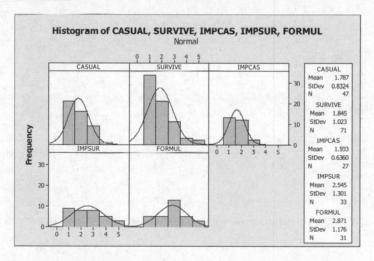

The data for some of the 5 groups do not look particularly mound-shaped, so the assumption of normality is probably not valid.

Using MINITAB, the boxplots are:

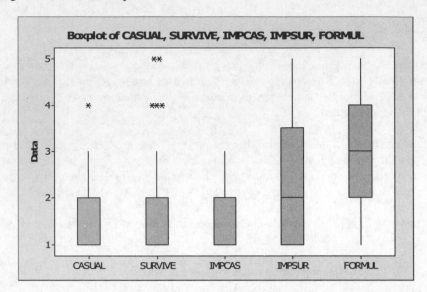

The spreads of responses do not appear to be about the same. The groups Implementers/survivors and Formulators have more variability than the other three groups. Thus, the assumption of constant variance is probably not valid.

The assumptions required for the ANOVA F-test do not appear to be reasonably satisfied.

8.31   a.   To determine if the mean level of trust differs among the six treatments, we test:

H_0: $\mu_1 = \mu_2 = \mu_3 = \mu_4 = \mu_5 = \mu_6$
H_a: At least one μ_i differs

b.   The test statistic is $F = 2.21$.

The rejection region requires α in the upper tail of the F-distribution with $v_1 = k - 1 = 6 - 1 = 5$ and $v_2 = n - k = 237 - 6 = 231$. From Table VII, Appendix B, $F_{.05} \approx 2.21$. The rejection region is $F > 2.21$.

Since the observed value of the test statistic does not fall in the rejection region ($F = 2.21 \not> 2.21$), H_0 is not rejected. There is insufficient evidence to indicate that at least two mean trusts differ at $\alpha = .05$.

c.   We must assume that all six samples are drawn from normal populations, the six population variances are the same, and that the samples are independent.

d.   I would classify this experiment as designed. Each subject was randomly assigned to receive one of the six scenarios.

8.33   To determine if the mean THICKNESS differs among the 4 types of housing, we test:

$H_0: \mu_1 = \mu_2 = \mu_3 = \mu_4$
H_a: At least two treatment means differ

The test statistic is F = 11.74 and the *p*-value = 0.000. Since the observed *p*-value (0.000) is less than any reasonable significance level, H_o is rejected. There is sufficient evidence to indicate a difference in the mean thickness among the four levels of housing for any reasonable value of α.

To determine if the mean WHIPPING CAPACITY differs among the 4 types of housing, we test:

$H_0: \mu_1 = \mu_2 = \mu_3 = \mu_4$
H_a: At least two treatment means differ

The test statistic is F = 31.36 and the *p*-value = 0.000. Since the observed p-value (0.000) is less than any reasonable significance level, H_o is rejected. There is sufficient evidence to indicate a difference in the mean whipping capacity among the four levels of housing for any reasonable value of α.

To determine if the mean STRENGTH differs among the 4 types of housing, we test:

$H_0: \mu_1 = \mu_2 = \mu_3 = \mu_4$
H_a: At least two treatment means differ

The test statistic is F = 1.70 and the *p*-value = 0.193. Since the observed *p*-value (0.193) is higher than any reasonable significance level, H_0 is not rejected. There is insufficient evidence to indicate a difference in the mean strength among the four levels of housing for any reasonable value of α.
Thus, the mean thickness and the mean percent overrun differ among the 4 housing systems.

8.35   The number of pairwise comparisons is equal to $k(k-1)/2$.

    a.   For $k = 3$, the number of comparisons is $3(3-1)/2 = 3$.

    b.   For $k = 5$, the number of comparisons is $5(5-1)/2 = 10$.

    c.   For $k = 4$, the number of comparisons is $4(4-1)/2 = 6$.

    d.   For $k = 10$, the number of comparisons is $10(10-1)/2 = 45$.

8.37   A comparisonwise error rate is the error rate (or the probability of declaring the means different when, in fact, they are not different, which is also the probability of a Type I error) for each individual comparison. That is, if each comparison is run using $\alpha = .05$, then the comparisonwise error rate is .05.

8.39 $(\mu_1 - \mu_2)$: (2, 15)   Since all values in the interval are positive, μ_1 is significantly greater than μ_2.

       $(\mu_1 - \mu_3)$: (4, 7)   Since all values in the interval are positive, μ_1 is significantly greater than μ_3.

       $(\mu_1 - \mu_4)$: (-10, 3)   Since 0 is in the interval, μ_1 is not significantly different from μ_4. However, since the center of the interval is less than 0, μ_4 is larger than μ_1.

       $(\mu_2 - \mu_3)$: (-5, 11)   Since 0 is in the interval, μ_2 is not significantly different from μ_3. However, since the center of the interval is greater than 0, μ_2 is larger than μ_3.

       $(\mu_2 - \mu_4)$: $(-12, -6)$ Since all values in the interval are negative, μ_4 is significantly greater than μ_2.

       $(\mu_3 - \mu_4)$: $(-8, -5)$ Since all values in the interval are negative, μ_4 is significantly greater than μ_3.

Thus, the largest mean is μ_4 followed by μ_1, μ_2, and μ_3.

8.41   The mean response for Division I coaches is significantly higher than the mean responses for the Division II and Division III coaches. There is no difference in the mean responses between Division II and Division III coaches.

8.43   a.   Tukey's multiple comparison method is preferred over other methods because it controls experimental error at the chosen α level. It is more powerful than the other methods.

     b.   From the confidence interval comparing large-cap and medium-cap mutual funds, we find that 0 is in the interval. Thus, 0 is not an unusual value for the difference in the mean rates of return between large-cap and medium-cap mutual funds. This means we would not reject H_0. There is insufficient evidence of a difference in mean rates of return between large-cap and medium-cap mutual funds at $\alpha = .05$.

     c.   From the confidence interval comparing large-cap and small-cap mutual funds, we find that 0 is not in the interval. Thus, 0 is an unusual value for the difference in the mean rates of return between large-cap and small-cap mutual funds. This means we would reject H_0. There is sufficient evidence of a difference in mean rates of return between large-cap and small-cap mutual funds at $\alpha = .05$.

     d.   From the confidence interval comparing medium-cap and small-cap mutual funds, we find that 0 is in the interval. Thus, 0 is not an unusual value for the difference in the mean rates of return between medium-cap and small-cap mutual funds. This means we would not reject H_0. There is insufficient evidence of a difference in mean rates of return between medium-cap and small-cap mutual funds at $\alpha = .05$.

     e.   From the above, the mean rate of return for large-cap mutual funds is the largest, followed by medium-cap, followed by small-cap mutual funds. The mean rate of return for large-cap funds is significantly larger than that for small-cap funds. No other differences exist.

     f.   We are 95% confident of this decision.

8.45   a.   The probability of declaring at least one pair of means different when they are not is .01.

       b.   There are a total of $\frac{k(k-1)}{2} = \frac{3(3-1)}{2} = 3$ pair-wise comparisons. They are:

            'Under $30 thousand' to 'Between $30 and $60 thousand'
            'Under $30 thousand' to 'Over $60 thousand'
            'Between $30 and $60 thousand' to 'Over $60 thousand'

       c.   Means for groups in homogeneous subsets are displayed in the table:

Income		Subsets	
Group	N	1	2
Under $30,000	379	4.60	
$30,000-$60,000	392		5.08
Over $60,000	267		5.15

       d.   Two of the comparisons in part b will yield confidence intervals that do not contain 0. They are:

            'Under $30 thousand' to 'Between $30 and $60 thousand'
            'Under $30 thousand' to 'Over $60 thousand'

8.47   The mean level of trust for the "no close" technique is significantly higher than that for the "assumed close" and the "either-or" techniques. The mean level of trust for the "impending event" technique is significantly higher than that for the "either-or" technique. No other significant differences exist.

8.49   a.   The confidence interval for $(\mu_{CAGE} - \mu_{BARN})$ is $(-.1250, -.0323)$. Since 0 is not contained in this interval, there is sufficient evidence of a difference in the mean thickness between cage and barn egg housing systems. Since this interval is negative, this implies that the thickness is larger for the barn egg housing system.

       b.   The confidence interval for $(\mu_{CAGE} - \mu_{FREE})$ is $(-.1233, -.0307)$. Since 0 is not contained in this interval, there is sufficient evidence of a difference in the mean thickness between cage and free range egg housing systems. Since this interval is negative, this implies that the thickness is larger for the free range egg housing system.

       c.   The confidence interval for $(\mu_{CAGE} - \mu_{ORGANIC})$ is $(-.1050, -.0123)$. Since 0 is not contained in this interval, there is sufficient evidence of a difference in the mean thickness between cage and organic egg housing systems. Since this interval is negative, this implies that the thickness is larger for the organic egg housing system.

       d.   The confidence interval for $(\mu_{BARN} - \mu_{FREE})$ is $(-.0501, .0535)$. Since 0 is contained in this interval, there is insufficient evidence of a difference in the mean thickness between barn and free range egg housing systems. Since the center of the interval is greater than 0, the sample mean for barn is greater than that for free range.

       e.   The confidence interval for $(\mu_{BARN} - \mu_{ORGANIC})$ is $(-.0318, .0718)$. Since 0 is contained in this interval, there is insufficient evidence of a difference in the mean thickness between barn and organic egg housing systems. Since the center of the interval is greater than 0, the sample mean for barn is greater than that for organic.

f.   The confidence interval for ($\mu_{FREE} - \mu_{ORGANIC}$) is ($-.0335, .0701$). Since 0 is contained in this interval, there is insufficient evidence of a difference in the mean thickness between free range and organic egg housing systems. Since the center of the interval is greater than 0, the sample mean for free range is greater than that for organic.

g.   We rank the housing system means as follows:
Housing System: Cage < <u>Organic < Free < Barn</u>
We are 95% confident that the mean shell thickness for the cage housing system is significantly less than the mean thickness for the other three housing systems. There is no significant difference in the mean shell thicknesses among the barn, free range and organic housing systems.

8.51   a.   Treatment $df = k - 1 = 3 - 1 = 2$
Block $df = b - 1 = 3 - 1 = 2$
Error $df = n - k - b + 1 = 9\ 3 - 3 + 1 = 4$
Total $df = n - 1 = 9 - 1 = 8$

$$SSB = \sum_{i=1}^{b} \frac{B_i^2}{k} - CM \quad \text{from Appendix B}$$

where $CM = \dfrac{\left(\sum x_i\right)^2}{n} = \dfrac{49^2}{9} = 266.7778$

$SSB = \dfrac{17^2}{3} + \dfrac{15^2}{3} + \dfrac{17^2}{3} - 266.7778 = .8889$

$SSE = SS(Total) - SST - SSB = 30.2222 - 21.5555 - .8889 = 7.7778$

$MST = \dfrac{SST}{k-1} = \dfrac{21.5555}{2} = 10.7778 \quad MSB = \dfrac{SSB}{b-1} = \dfrac{.8889}{2} = .4445$

$MSE = \dfrac{SSE}{n-k-b+1} = \dfrac{7.7778}{4} = 1.9445$

$F_T = \dfrac{MST}{MSE} = \dfrac{10.7778}{1.9445} = 5.54 \qquad F_B = \dfrac{MSB}{MSE} = \dfrac{.4445}{1.9445} = .23$

The ANOVA table is:

Source	df	SS	MS	F
Treatment	2	21.5555	10.7778	5.54
Block	2	.8889	.4445	.23
Error	4	7.7778	1.9445	
Total	8	30.2222		

b. H_0: $\mu_1 = \mu_2 = \mu_3$ vs H_a: At least two treatment means differ

c.   The test statistic is $F = \dfrac{MST}{MSE} = 5.54$

d.   A Type I error would be concluding at least two treatment means differ when they do not.

A Type II error would be concluding all the treatment means are the same when at least two differ.

e. The rejection region requires $\alpha = .05$ in the upper tail of the F distribution with $v_1 = k - 1 = 3 - 1 = 2$ and $v_2 = n - k - b + 1 = 9 - 3 - 3 + 1 = 4$. From Table VIII, Appendix A, $F_{.05} = 6.94$. The rejection region is $F > 6.94$.

Since the observed value of the test statistic does not fall in the rejection region ($F = 5.54 \not> 6.94$), H_0 is not rejected. There is insufficient evidence to indicate at least two of the treatment means differ at $\alpha = .05$.

8.53   a. $SST = .2(500) = 100 \qquad SSB = .3(500) = 150$
$SSE = SS(Total) - SST - SSB = 500 - 100 - 150 = 250$

$$MST = \frac{SST}{k-1} = \frac{100}{4-1} = 33.3333 \qquad MSB = \frac{SSB}{b-1} = \frac{150}{9-1} = 18.75$$

$$MSE = \frac{SSE}{n-k-b+1} = \frac{250}{36-4-9+1} = \frac{250}{4} = 10.4167$$

$$F_T = \frac{MST}{MSE} = \frac{33.3333}{10.4167} = 3.20 \qquad F_B = \frac{MSB}{MSE} = \frac{18.75}{10.4167} = 1.80$$

To determine if differences exist among the treatment means, we test:

$H_0: \mu_1 = \mu_2 = \mu_3 = \mu_4 = \mu_5$
H_a: At least two treatment means differ

The test statistic is $F = 3.20$.

The rejection region requires $\alpha = .05$ in the upper tail of the F distribution with $v_1 = k - 1 = 4 - 1 = 3$ and $v_2 = n - k - b + 1 = 36 - 4 - 9 + 1 = 24$. From Table VIII, Appendix B, $F_{.05} = 3.01$. The rejection region is $F > 3.01$.

Since the observed value of the test statistic falls in the rejection region ($F = 3.20 > 3.01$), H_0 is rejected. There is sufficient evidence to indicate differences among the treatment means at $\alpha = .05$.

To determine if differences exist among the block means, we test:

$H_0: \mu_1 = \mu_2 = \cdots = \mu_9$
H_a: At least two block means differ

The test statistic is $F = 1.80$.

The rejection region requires $\alpha = .05$ in the upper tail of the F distribution with $v_1 = b - 1 = 9 - 1 = 8$ and $v_2 = n - b - k + 1 = 36 - 9 - 4 + 1 = 24$. From Table VIII, Appendix B, $F_{.05} = 2.36$. The rejection region is $F > 2.36$.
Since the observed value of the test statistic does not fall in the rejection region ($F = 1.80 \not> 2.36$), H_0 is not rejected. There is insufficient evidence to indicate differences among the block means at $\alpha = .05$.

b. $SST = .5(500) = 250 \qquad SSB = .2(500) = 100$
$SSE = SS(Total) - SST - SSB = 500 - 250 - 100 = 150$

$$MST = \frac{SST}{k-1} = \frac{250}{4-1} = 83.3333 \qquad MSB = \frac{SSB}{b-1} = \frac{100}{9-1} = 12.5$$

$$MSE = \frac{SSE}{n-k-b+1} = \frac{150}{36-4-9+1} = 6.25$$

$$F_T = \frac{MST}{MSE} = \frac{83.3333}{6.25} = 13.33 \qquad\qquad F_B = \frac{MSB}{MSE} = \frac{12.5}{6.25} = 2$$

To determine if differences exist among the treatment means, we test:

H_0: $\mu_1 = \mu_2 = \mu_3 = \mu_4$
H_a: At least two treatment means differ

The test statistic is $F = 13.33$.

The rejection region is $F > 3.01$ (same as above).

Since the observed value of the test statistic falls in the rejection region ($F = 13.33 > 3.01$), H_0 is rejected. There is sufficient evidence to indicate differences exist among the treatment means at $\alpha = .05$.

To determine if differences exist among the block means, we test:

H_0: $\mu_1 = \mu_2 = \cdots = \mu_9$
H_a: At least two block means differ

The test statistic is $F = 2.00$.

The rejection region is $F > 2.36$ (same as above).

Since the observed value of the test statistic does not fall in the rejection region ($F = 2.00 \not> 2.36$), H_0 is not rejected. There is insufficient evidence to indicate differences exist among the block means at $\alpha = .05$.

c. $SST = .2(500) = 100 \qquad\qquad SSB = .5(500) = 250$
$SSE = SS(\text{Total}) - SST - SSB = 500 - 100 - 250 = 150$

$$MST = \frac{SST}{k-1} = \frac{100}{4-1} = 33.3333 \qquad MSB = \frac{SSB}{b-1} = \frac{250}{9-1} = 31.25$$

$$MSE = \frac{SSE}{n-k-b+1} = \frac{150}{36-4-9+1} = 6.25$$

$$F_T = \frac{MST}{MSE} = \frac{33.3333}{6.25} = 5.33 \qquad\qquad F_B = \frac{MSB}{MSE} = \frac{31.25}{6.25} = 5.00$$

To determine if differences exist among the treatment means, we test:

H_0: $\mu_1 = \mu_2 = \mu_3 = \mu_4$
H_a: At least two treatment means differ

The test statistic is $F = 5.33$.
The rejection region is $F > 3.01$ (same as above).

Since the observed value of the test statistic falls in the rejection region ($F = 5.33 > 3.01$), H_0 is rejected. There is sufficient evidence to indicate differences exist among the treatment means at $\alpha = .05$.

To determine if differences exist among the block means, we test:

H_0: $\mu_1 = \mu_2 = \cdots = \mu_9$
H_a: At least two block means differ

The test statistic is $F = 5.00$.

The rejection region is $F > 2.36$ (same as above).

Since the observed value of the test statistic falls in the rejection region ($F = 5.00 > 2.36$), H_0 is rejected. There is sufficient evidence to indicate differences exist among the block means at $\alpha = .05$.

d. $SST = .4(500) = 200 \qquad SSB = .4(500) = 200$

$SSE = SS(Total) - SST - SSB = 500 - 200 - 200 = 100$

$$MST = \frac{SST}{k-1} = \frac{200}{4-1} = 66.6667 \qquad MSB = \frac{SSB}{b-1} = \frac{200}{9-1} = 25$$

$$MSE = \frac{SSE}{n-k-b+1} = \frac{100}{36-4-9+1} = 4.1667$$

$$F_T = \frac{MST}{MSE} = \frac{66.6667}{4.1667} = 16.0 \qquad F_B = \frac{MSB}{MSE} = \frac{25}{4.1667} = 6.00$$

To determine if differences exist among the treatment means, we test:

H_0: $\mu_1 = \mu_2 = \mu_3 = \mu_4$
H_a: At least two treatment means differ

The test statistic is $F = 16.0$.

The rejection region is $F > 3.01$ (same as above).

Since the observed value of the test statistic falls in the rejection region ($F = 16.0 > 3.01$), H_0 is rejected. There is sufficient evidence to indicate differences among the treatment means at $\alpha = .05$.

To determine if differences exist among the block means, we test:

H_0: $\mu_1 = \mu_2 = \cdots = \mu_9$
H_a: At least two block means differ

The test statistic is $F = 6.00$.

The rejection region is $F > 2.36$ (same as above).

Since the observed value of the test statistic falls in the rejection region ($F = 6.00 > 2.36$), H_0 is rejected. There is sufficient evidence to indicate differences exist among the block means at $\alpha = .05$.

e. $SST = .2(500) = 100 \qquad SSB = .2(500) = 100$

$SSE = SS(Total) - SST - SSB = 500 - 100 - 100 = 300$

$$MST = \frac{SST}{k-1} = \frac{100}{4-1} = 33.3333 \qquad MSB = \frac{SSB}{b-1} = \frac{100}{9-1} = 12.5$$

$$MSE = \frac{SSE}{n-k-b+1} = \frac{300}{36-4-9+1} = 12.5$$

$$F_T = \frac{MST}{MSE} = \frac{33.3333}{12.5} = 2.67 \qquad F_B = \frac{MSB}{MSE} = \frac{12.5}{12.5} = 1.00$$

To determine if differences exist among the treatment means, we test:

H_0: $\mu_1 = \mu_2 = \mu_3 = \mu_4$
H_a: At least two treatment means differ

The test statistic is $F = 2.67$.

The rejection region is $F > 3.01$ (same as above).

Since the observed value of the test statistic does not fall in the rejection region ($F = 2.67 \not> 3.01$), H_0 is not rejected. There is insufficient evidence to indicate differences exist among the treatment means at $\alpha = .05$.

To determine if differences exist among the block means, we test:

H_0: $\mu_1 = \mu_2 = \cdots = \mu_9$
H_a: At least two block means differ

The test statistic is $F = 1.00$.

The rejection region is $F > 2.36$ (same as above).

Since the observed value of the test statistic does not fall in the rejection region ($F = 1.00 \not> 2.36$), H_0 is not rejected. There is insufficient evidence to indicate differences among the block means at $\alpha = .05$.

8.55   a.   A randomized block design should be used to analyze the data because the same employees were measured at all three time periods. Thus, the blocks are the employees and the treatments are the three time periods.

        b.   There is still enough information in the table to make a conclusion because the *p*-values are given.

        b.   To determine if there are differences in the mean competence levels among the three time periods, we test:

           H_0: $\mu_1 = \mu_2 = \mu_3$
           H_a: At least two treatment means differ

        d.   The *p*-value is $p = 0.001$. At a significance level $> .001$, we reject H_0. There is sufficient evidence to conclude that there is a difference in the mean competence levels among the three time periods for any value of $\alpha > 0.001$.

        e.   With 90% confidence, the mean competence before the training is significantly less than the mean competence 2-days after and 2-months after. There is no significant difference in the mean competence between 2-days after and 2-months after.

8.57   a.   The time of the year (month) could affect the number of rigs running, so a randomized complete block design was used to "block" out the month to month variation.

        b.   There are 3 treatments in this experiment. They are the three states – California, Utah, and Alaska.

        c.   There are 3 blocks in this experiment – the three months selected: November 2000, October 2001, and November 2001.

d. To determine if there is a difference in the mean number of rigs running among the three states, we test:

H_0: $\mu_1 = \mu_2 = \mu_3$

e. From the printout, the test statistic is $F = 38.07$ and the p-value is $p = 0.002$. Since the p-value is so small, we would reject H_0 for any value of $\alpha > .002$. There is sufficient evidence to indicate a difference in the mean number of oil rigs running among the three states.

f. From the SPSS printout, there is no significant difference in the mean number of oil rigs running in Alaska and Utah. However, both of these states have a significantly smaller number of rigs running than does California. Thus, California has the largest mean number of oil rigs running.

8.59   Using MINITAB, the ANOVA table is:

Two-way ANOVA: Rate versus Week, Day

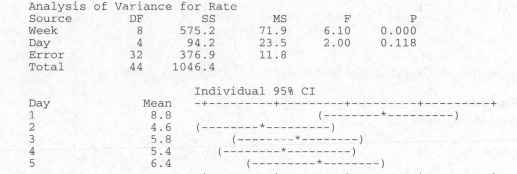

```
Analysis of Variance for Rate
Source       DF        SS        MS        F         P
Week          8     575.2      71.9      6.10     0.000
Day           4      94.2      23.5      2.00     0.118
Error        32     376.9      11.8
Total        44    1046.4

                    Individual 95% CI
Day          Mean   -+---------+---------+---------+---------+
1            8.8                        (--------*---------)
2            4.6     (---------*---------)
3            5.8        (--------*--------)
4            5.4     (--------*--------)
5            6.4        (---------*--------)
                    -+---------+---------+---------+---------+
                    2.5       5.0       7.5      10.0      12.5
```

To determine if there is a difference in mean rate of absenteeism among the 5 days of the week, we test:

H_0: $\mu_1 = \mu_2 = \mu_3 = \mu_4 = \mu_5$
H_a: At least two treatment means differ

The test statistic is $F = 2.00$.

Since no α was given, we will select $\alpha = .05$. The rejection region requires $\alpha = .05$ in the upper tail of the F distribution with $v_1 = k - 1 = 5 - 1 = 4$ and $v_2 = n - k - b + 1 = 45 - 5 - 9 + 1 = 32$. From Table VIII, Appendix B, $F_{.05, 4, 32} \approx 2.69$. The rejection region is $F > 2.69$.
Since the observed value of the test statistic does not fall in the rejection region ($F = 2.00 \not> 2.69$), H_0 is not rejected. There is insufficient evidence to indicate a difference in mean rate of absenteeism among the 5 days of the week at $\alpha = .05$.

To test for the effectiveness of blocking, we test:

H_0: All block means are the same
H_a: At least two block means differ

The test statistic is $F = 6.10$.

The rejection region requires $\alpha = .05$ in the upper tail of the F distribution with $v_1 = b - 1 = 9 - 1 = 8$ and $v_2 = n - k - b + 1 = 45 - 5 - 9 + 1 = 32$. From Table VIII, Appendix B, $F_{.05, 8, 32} \approx 2.27$. The rejection region is $F > 2.27$.

Since the observed value of the test statistic falls in the rejection region ($F = 6.10 > 2.27$), H_0 is rejected. There is sufficient evidence to indicate blocking was effective at $\alpha = .05$.

8.61   Using MINITAB, the ANOVA table is:

Two-way ANOVA: Corrosion versus Time, System

```
Source   DF       SS        MS       F       P
Time      2   63.1050   31.5525   337.06   0.000
System    3    9.5833    3.1944    34.12   0.000
Error     6    0.5617    0.0936
Total    11   73.2500
```

```
S = 0.3060    R-Sq = 99.23%    R-Sq(adj) = 98.59%
```

```
                      Individual 95% CIs For Mean Based on
                      Pooled StDev
System    Mean    ------+---------+---------+---------+---
1        9.0667       (----*-----)
2        9.7333              (-----*----)
3       11.0667                               (----*-----)
4        8.7333   (----*-----)
                  ------+---------+---------+---------+---
                      8.80      9.60     10.40     11.20
```

To determine if there is a difference in mean corrosion rates among the 4 systems, we test:

H_0: $\mu_1 = \mu_2 = \mu_3 = \mu_4$
H_a: At least two treatment means differ

The test statistic is $F = 34.12$.

Since no α level was given, we will select $\alpha = .05$. The rejection region requires $\alpha = .05$ in the upper tail of the F distribution with $\nu_1 = k - 1 = 4 - 1 = 3$ and $\nu_2 = n - k - b + 1 = 12 - 4 - 3 + 1 = 6$. From Table VIII, Appendix B, $F_{.05, 3, 6} = 4.76$. The rejection region is $F > 4.76$.

Since the observed value of the test statistic falls in the rejection region ($F = 34.12 > 4.76$), H_0 is rejected. There is sufficient evidence to indicate a difference in mean corrosion rates among the 4 systems at $\alpha = .05$.

Using SAS, Tukey's multiple comparison results are:

```
          Tukey's Studentized Range (HSD) Test for CORROSION

NOTE: This test controls the Type I experimentwise error rate, but it generally has a higher
Type II error rate than REGWQ.


              Alpha                                    0.05
              Error Degrees of Freedom                    6
              Error Mean Square                     0.093611
              Critical Value of Studentized Range   4.89559
              Minimum Significant Difference          0.8648


        Means with the same letter are not significantly different.


        Tukey Grouping          Mean     N    SYSTEM

                       A      11.0667     3     3

                       B       9.7333     3     2
                       B
                 C     B       9.0667     3     1
                 C
                 C              8.7333     3     4
```

The mean corrosion rate for system 3 is significantly larger than all of the other mean corrosion rates. The mean corrosion rate of system 2 is significantly larger than the mean for system 4. If we want the system (epoxy coating) with the lowest corrosion rate, we would pick either system 1 or system 4. There is no significant difference between these two groups and they are in the lowest corrosion rate group.

8.63   a.   The ANOVA table is:

Source	df	SS	MS	F
A	2	.8	.4000	3.69
B	3	5.3	1.7667	16.31
AB	6	9.6	1.6000	14.77
Error	12	1.3	.1083	
Total	23	17.0		

df for A is $a - 1 = 3 - 1 = 2$
    df for $B = b - 1 = 4 - 1 = 3$
df for AB is $(a - 1)(b - 1) = 2(3) = 6$
    df for Error is $n - ab = 24 - 3(4) = 12$
df for Total is $n - 1 = 24 - 1 = 23$

$$SSE = SS(Total) - SSA - SSB - SSAB = 17.0 - .8 - 5.3 - 9.6 = 1.3$$

$$MSA = \frac{SSA}{a-1} = \frac{.8}{3-1} = .40 \quad MSB = \frac{SSB}{b-1} = \frac{5.3}{4-1} = 1.7667$$

$$MSAB = \frac{SSAB}{(a-1)(b-1)} = \frac{9.6}{(3-1)(4-1)} = 1.60$$

$$MSE = \frac{SSE}{n - ab} = \frac{1.3}{24 - 3(4)} = .1083$$

$$F_A = \frac{MSA}{MSE} = \frac{.4000}{.1083} = 3.69 \quad F_B = \frac{MSB}{MSE} = \frac{1.7667}{.1083} = 16.31$$

$$F_{AB} = \frac{MSAB}{MSE} = \frac{1.6000}{.1083} = 14.77$$

b.   Sum of Squares for Treatment $= SSA + SSB + SSAB = .8 = 5.3 + 2.6 = 15.7$

$$MST = \frac{SST}{ab-1} = \frac{15.7}{3(4)-1} = 1.4273 \quad F_T = \frac{MST}{MSE} = \frac{1.4273}{.1083} = 13.18$$

To determine if the treatment means differ, we test:

H_0: $\mu_1 = \mu_2 = \cdots = \mu_{12}$
H_a: At least two treatments means differ

The test statistic is $F = 13.18$.

The rejection region requires $\alpha = .05$ in the upper tail of the F-distribution with $v_1 = ab - 1 = 3(4) - 1 = 11$ and $v_2 = n - ab = 24 - 3(4) = 12$. From Table VIII, Appendix B, $F_{.05} \approx 2.75$. The rejection region is $F > 2.75$.

Since the observed value of the test statistic falls in the rejection region ($F = 13.18 > 2.75$), H_0 is rejected. There is sufficient evidence to indicate the treatment means differ at $\alpha = .05$.

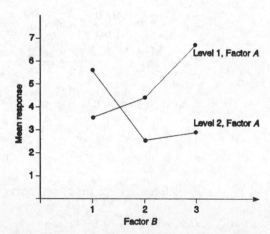

c.   Yes. We need to partition the Treatment Sum of Squares into the Main Effects and Interaction Sum of Squares. Then we test whether factors A and B interact. Depending on the conclusion of the test for interaction, we either test for main effects or compare the treatment means.

d.   Two factors are said to interact if the effect of one factor on the dependent variable is not the same at different levels of the second factor. If the factors interact, then tests for main effects are not necessary. We need to compare the treatment means for one factor at each level of the second.

e.   To determine if the factors interact, we test:

H_0: Factors A and B do not interact to affect the response mean
H_a: Factors A and B do interact to affect the response mean

The test statistic is $F = \dfrac{\text{MS}AB}{\text{MSE}} = 14.77$

The rejection region requires $\alpha = .05$ in the upper tail of the F-distribution with $\nu_1 = (a-1)(b-1) = (3-1)(4-1) = 6$ and $\nu_2 = n - ab = 24 - 3(4) = 12$. From Table VIII, Appendix B, $F_{.05} = 3.00$. The rejection region is $F > 3.00$.

Since the observed value of the test statistic falls in the rejection region ($F = 14.77 > 3.00$), H_0 is rejected. There is sufficient evidence to indicate the two factors interact to affect the response mean at $\alpha = .05$.

f.   No. Testing for main effects is not warranted because interaction is present. Instead, we compare the treatment means of one factor at each level of the second factor.

8.65   a.   The treatments for this experiment consist of a level for factor A and a level for factor B. There are six treatments—(1, 1), (1, 2), (1, 3), (2, 1), (2, 2), and (2, 3) where the first number represents the level of factor A and the second number represents the level of factor B.

The treatment means appear to be different because the sample means are quite different. The factors appear to interact because the lines are not parallel.

b. $\text{SST} = \text{SSA} + \text{SSB} + \text{SSAB} = 4.4408 + 4.1267 + 18.0667 = 26.5742$

$\text{MST} = \dfrac{\text{SST}}{ab-1} = \dfrac{26.5742}{2(3)-1} = 5.315$ $F_{\text{T}} = \dfrac{\text{MST}}{\text{MSE}} = \dfrac{5.315}{.246} = 21.62$

To determine whether the treatment means differ, we test:

H_0: $\mu_1 = \mu_2 = \mu_3 = \mu_4 = \mu_5 = \mu_6$
H_a: At least two treatment means differ

The test statistic is $F = \dfrac{MST}{MSE} = 21.62$

The rejection region requires $\alpha = .05$ in the upper tail of the F-distribution with $v_1 = ab - 1 = 2(3) - 1 = 5$ and $v_2 = n - ab = 12 - 2(3) = 6$. From Table VIII, Appendix B, $F_{.05} = 4.39$. The rejection region is $F > 4.39$.

Since the observed value of the test statistic falls in the rejection region ($F = 21.62 > 4.39$), H_0 is rejected. There is sufficient evidence to indicate that the treatment means differ at $\alpha = .05$. This supports the plot in **a**.

c. Yes. Since there are differences among the treatment means, we test for interaction. To determine whether the factors A and B interact, we test:

H_0: Factors A and B do not interact to affect the mean response
H_a: Factors A and B do interact to affect the mean response

The test statistic is $F = \dfrac{MSAB}{MSE} = \dfrac{9.0033}{.24583} = 36.62$

The rejection region requires $\alpha = .05$ in the upper tail of the F-distribution with $v_1 = (a-1)(b-1) = (2-1)(3-1) = 2$ and $v_2 = n - ab = 12 - 2(3) = 6$. From Table VIII, Appendix B, $F_{.05} = 5.14$. The rejection region is $F > 5.14$.

Since the observed value of the test statistic falls in the rejection region ($F = 36.62 > 5.14$), H_0 is rejected. There is sufficient evidence to indicate that factors A and B interact to affect the response mean at $\alpha = .05$.

d. No. Because interaction is present, the tests for main effects are not warranted.

e. The results of the tests in parts **b** and **c** support the visual interpretation in part **a**.

8.67 a. $SSA = .2(1000) = 200$, $SSB = .1(1000) = 100$, $SSAB = .1(1000) = 100$
$SSE = SS(\text{Total}) - SSA - SSB - SSAB = 1000 - 200 - 100 - 100 = 600$
$SST = SSA + SSB + SSAB = 200 + 100 + 100 = 400$

$MSA = \dfrac{SSA}{a-1} = \dfrac{200}{3-1} = 100$ $\qquad MSB = \dfrac{SSB}{b-1} = \dfrac{100}{3-1} = 50$

$MSAB = \dfrac{SSAB}{(a-1)(b-1)} = \dfrac{100}{(3-1)(3-1)} = 25$

$MSE = \dfrac{SSE}{n-ab} = \dfrac{600}{27-3(3)} = 33.333$ $\qquad MST = \dfrac{SST}{ab-1} = \dfrac{400}{3(3)-1} = 50$

$F_A = \dfrac{MSA}{MSE} = \dfrac{100}{33.333} = 3.00$ $\qquad F_B = \dfrac{MSB}{MSE} = \dfrac{50}{33.333} = 1.50$

$F_{AB} = \dfrac{MSAB}{MSE} = \dfrac{25}{33.333} = .75$ $\qquad F_T = \dfrac{MST}{MSE} = \dfrac{50}{33.333} = 1.50$

Source	df	SS	MS	F
A	2	200	100	3.00
B	2	100	50	1.50
AB	4	100	25	.75
Error	18	600	33.333	
Total	26	1000		

To determine whether the treatment means differ, we test:

H_0: $\mu_1 = \mu_2 = \cdots = \mu_9$
H_a: At least two treatment means differ

The test statistic is $F = \dfrac{\text{MST}}{\text{MSE}} = 1.50$

Suppose $\alpha = .05$. The rejection region requires $\alpha = .05$ in the upper tail of the F-distribution with $v_1 = ab - 1 = 3(3) - 1 = 8$ and $v_2 = n - ab = 27 - 3(3) = 18$. From Table VIII, Appendix B, $F_{.05} = 2.51$. The rejection region is $F > 2.51$.

Since the observed value of the test statistic does not fall in the rejection region ($F = 1.50 \not> 2.51$), H_0 is not rejected. There is insufficient evidence to indicate the treatment means differ at $\alpha = .05$. Since there are no treatment mean differences, we have nothing more to do.

b. $\text{SS}A = .1(1000) = 100$, $\text{SS}B = .1(1000) = 100$, $\text{SS}AB = .5(1000) = 500$
$\text{SSE} = \text{SS(Total)} - \text{SS}A - \text{SS}B - \text{SS}AB = 1000 - 100 - 100 - 500 = 300$
$\text{SST} = \text{SS}A + \text{SS}B + \text{SS}AB = 100 + 100 + 500 = 700$

$$\text{MS}A = \frac{\text{SS}A}{a-1} = \frac{100}{3-1} = 50 \qquad\qquad \text{MS}B = \frac{\text{SS}B}{b-1} = \frac{100}{3-1} = 50$$

$$\text{MS}AB = \frac{\text{SS}AB}{(a-1)(b-1)} = \frac{500}{(3-1)(3-1)} = 125$$

$$\text{MSE} = \frac{\text{SSE}}{n-ab} = \frac{300}{27-3(3)} = 16.667 \qquad \text{MST} = \frac{\text{SST}}{ab-1} = \frac{700}{9-1} = 87.5$$

$$F_A = \frac{\text{MS}A}{\text{MSE}} = \frac{50}{16.667} = 3.00 \qquad\qquad F_B = \frac{\text{MS}B}{\text{MSE}} = \frac{50}{16.667} = 3.00$$

$$F_{AB} = \frac{\text{MS}AB}{\text{MSE}} = \frac{125}{16.667} = 7.50 \qquad\qquad F_T = \frac{\text{MST}}{\text{MSE}} = \frac{87.5}{16.667} = 5.25$$

Source	df	SS	MS	F
A	2	100	50	3.00
B	2	100	50	3.00
AB	4	500	125	7.50
Error	18	300	16.667	
Total	26	1000		

To determine if the treatment means differ, we test:

H_0: $\mu_1 = \mu_2 = \cdots = \mu_9$
H_a: At least two treatment means differ

The test statistic is $F = \dfrac{\text{MST}}{\text{MSE}} = 5.25$

The rejection region requires $\alpha = .05$ in the upper tail of the F-distribution with $v_1 = ab - 1$ $= 3(3) - 1 = 8$ and $v_2 = n - ab = 27 - 3(3) = 18$. From Table VIII, Appendix B, $F_{.05} = 2.51$. The rejection region is $F > 2.51$.

Since the observed value of the test statistic falls in the rejection region ($F = 5.25 > 2.51$), H_0 is rejected. There is sufficient evidence to indicate the treatment means differ at $\alpha = .05$.

Since the treatment means differ, we next test for interaction between factors A and B. To determine if factors A and B interact, we test:

H_0: Factors A and B do not interact to affect the mean response
H_a: Factors A and B do interact to affect the mean response

The test statistic is $F = \dfrac{\text{MS}AB}{\text{MSE}} = 7.50$

The rejection region requires $\alpha = .05$ in the upper tail of the F-distribution with $v_1 = (a-1)(b-1) = (3-1)(3-1) = 4$ and $v_2 = n - ab = 27 - 3(3) = 18$. From Table VIII, Appendix B, $F_{.05} = 2.93$. The rejection region is $F > 2.93$.

Since the observed value of the test statistic falls in the rejection region ($F = 7.50 > 2.93$), H_0 is rejected. There is sufficient evidence to indicate the factors A and B interact at $\alpha = .05$. Since interaction is present, no tests for main effects are necessary.

c. $SSA = .4(1000) = 400$, $SSB = .1(1000) = 100$, $SSAB = .2(1000) = 200$

$SSE = SS(\text{Total}) - SSA - SSB - SSAB = 1000 - 400 - 100 - 200 = 300$

$SST = SSA + SSB + SSAB = 400 + 100 + 200 = 700$

$MSA = \dfrac{SSA}{a-1} = \dfrac{400}{3-1} = 50$ $\qquad$ $MSB = \dfrac{SSB}{b-1} = \dfrac{100}{3-1} = 50$

$MSAB = \dfrac{SSAB}{(a-1)(b-1)} = \dfrac{200}{(3-1)(3-1)} = 50$

$MSE = \dfrac{SSE}{n-ab} = \dfrac{300}{27-3(3)} = 16.667$ $\qquad$ $MST = \dfrac{SST}{ab-1} = \dfrac{700}{3(3)-1} = 87.5$

$F_A = \dfrac{MSA}{MSE} = \dfrac{200}{16.667} = 12.00$ $\qquad$ $F_B = \dfrac{MSB}{MSE} = \dfrac{50}{16.667} = 3.00$

$F_{AB} = \dfrac{MSAB}{MSE} = \dfrac{50}{16.667} = 3.00$ $\qquad$ $F_T = \dfrac{MST}{MSE} = \dfrac{87.5}{16.667} = 5.25$

Source	df	SS	MS	F
A	2	400	200	12.00
B	2	100	50	3.00
AB	4	200	50	3.00
Error	18	300	16.667	
Total	26	1000		

To determine if the treatment means differ, we test:

H_0: $\mu_1 = \mu_2 = \cdots = \mu_9$
H_a: At least two treatment means differ

The test statistic is $F = \dfrac{MST}{MSE} = 5.25$

The rejection region requires $\alpha = .05$ in the upper tail of the F-distribution with $v_1 = ab - 1 = 3(3) - 1 = 8$ and $v_2 = n - ab = 27 - 3(3) = 18$. From Table VIII, Appendix B, $F_{.05} = 2.51$. The rejection region is $F > 2.51$.

Since the observed value of the test statistic falls in the rejection region ($F = 5.25 > 2.51$), H_0 is rejected. There is sufficient evidence to indicate the treatment means differ at $\alpha = .05$.

Since the treatment means differ, we next test for interaction between factors A and B. To determine if factors A and B interact, we test:

H_0: Factors A and B do not interact to affect the mean response
H_a: Factors A and B do interact to affect the mean response

The test statistic is $F = \dfrac{MSAB}{MSE} = 3.00$

The rejection region requires $\alpha = .05$ in the upper tail of the F-distribution with $v_1 = (a - 1)(b - 1) = (3 - 1)(3 - 1) = 4$ and $v_2 = n - ab = 27 - 3(3) = 18$. From Table VIII, Appendix B, $F_{.05} = 2.93$. The rejection region is $F > 2.93$.

Since the observed value of the test statistic falls in the rejection region ($F = 3.00 > 2.93$), H_0 is rejected. There is sufficient evidence to indicate the factors A and B interact at $\alpha = .05$. Since interaction is present, no tests for main effects are necessary.

d. $SSA = .4(1000) = 400$, $SSB = .4(1000) = 400$, $SSAB = .1(1000) = 100$

$SSE = SS(\text{Total}) - SSA - SSB - SSAB = 1000 - 400 - 400 - 100 = 100$

$SST = SSA + SSB + SSAB = 400 + 400 + 100 = 900$

$MSA = \dfrac{SSA}{a-1} = \dfrac{400}{3-1} = 200 \qquad\qquad MSB = \dfrac{SSB}{b-1} = \dfrac{400}{3-1} = 200$

$MSAB = \dfrac{SSAB}{(a-1)(b-1)} = \dfrac{100}{(3-1)(3-1)} = 25$

$MSE = \dfrac{SSE}{n-ab} = \dfrac{100}{27-3(3)} = 5.556 \qquad MST = \dfrac{SST}{ab-1} = \dfrac{900}{3(3)-1} = 112.5$

$F_A = \dfrac{MSA}{MSE} = \dfrac{200}{5.556} = 36.00 \qquad\qquad F_B = \dfrac{MSB}{MSE} = \dfrac{200}{5.556} = 36.00$

$F_{AB} = \dfrac{MSAB}{MSE} = \dfrac{25}{5.556} = 4.50 \qquad\qquad F_T = \dfrac{MST}{MSE} = \dfrac{112.5}{5.556} = 20.25$

Source	df	SS	MS	F
A	2	400	200	36.00
B	2	400	200	36.00
AB	4	100	25	4.50
Error	18	100	5.556	
Total	26	1000		

To determine if the treatment means differ, we test:

H_0: $\mu_1 = \mu_2 = \cdots = \mu_9$
H_a: At least two treatment means differ

The test statistic is $F = \dfrac{\text{MST}}{\text{MSE}} = 20.25$

The rejection region requires $\alpha = .05$ in the upper tail of the F-distribution with $v_1 = ab - 1 = 3(3) - 1 = 8$ and $v_2 = n - ab = 27 - 3(3) = 18$. From Table VIII, Appendix B, $F_{.05} = 2.51$. The rejection region is $F > 2.51$.

Since the observed value of the test statistic falls in the rejection region ($F = 20.25 > 2.51$), H_0 is rejected. There is sufficient evidence to indicate the treatment means differ at $\alpha = .05$.

Since the treatment means differ, we next test for interaction between factors A and B. To determine if factors A and B interact, we test:

H_0: Factors A and B do not interact to affect the mean response
H_a: Factors A and B do interact to affect the mean response

The test statistic is $F = \dfrac{\text{MS}AB}{\text{MSE}} = 4.50$

The rejection region requires $\alpha = .05$ in the upper tail of the F-distribution with $v_1 = (a - 1)(b - 1) = (3 - 1)(3 - 1) = 4$ and $v_2 = n - ab = 27 - 3(3) = 18$. From Table VIII, Appendix B, $F_{.05} = 2.93$. The rejection region is $F > 2.93$.

Since the observed value of the test statistic falls in the rejection region ($F = 4.50 > 2.93$), H_0 is rejected. There is sufficient evidence to indicate the factors A and B interact at $\alpha = .05$. Since interaction is present, no tests for main effects are necessary.

8.69   a.   This is a complete 6×6 factorial design.

b.   There are 2 factors – Coagulant and pH level. There are 6 levels of coagulant: 5, 10, 20, 50, 100, and 200 mg / liter. There are 6 levels of pH: 4.0, 5.0, 6.0, 7.0, 8.0, and 9.0.

There are 6 x 6 = 36 treatments. In the pairs, let the coagulant level be the first number and pH level the second. The 36 treatments are:

(5, 4.0)   (5, 5.0)   (5, 6.0)   (5, 7.0)   (5, 8.0)   (5, 9.0)
(10, 4.0)   (10, 5.0)   (10, 6.0)   (10, 7.0)   (10, 8.0)   (10, 9.0)
(20, 4.0)   (20, 5.0)   (20, 6.0)   (20, 7.0)   (20, 8.0)   (20, 9.0)
(50, 4.0)   (50, 5.0)   (50, 6.0)   (50, 7.0)   (50, 8.0)   (50, 9.0)
(100, 4.0)   (100, 5.0)   (100, 6.0)   (100, 7.0)   (100, 8.0)   (100, 9.0)
(200, 4.0)   (200, 5.0)   (200, 6.0)   (200, 7.0)   (200, 8.0)   (200, 9.0)

8.71   a.   This is a complete 2×2 factorial design. The 2 factors are Color and Question.
There are two levels of color – Blue and Red. There are two levels of question – difficult and simple. The 4 treatments are: blue/difficult, blue/simple, red/difficult, red/simple.

b.   There is a significant interaction between color and question. The effect of color on the mean score is different at each level of question.

c.   Using MINITAB, the graph is:

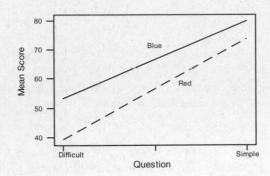

Since the lines are not parallel, it indicates that there is significant interaction between color and question.

8.73   a.   There are two factors for this experiment, housing system and weight class. There are a total of $4 \times 2 = 8$ treatments. The treatments are:

Cage, M   Cage, L   Free, M   Free, L
Barn, M   Barn, L   Organic, M   Organic, L

b.   Using SAS, the results are:

```
The GLM Procedure

Dependent Variable: OVERRUN

                                     Sum of
       Source            DF          Squares      Mean Square   F Value   Pr > F

       Model              7       11364.52381     1623.50340     14.93    <.0001

       Error             20        2175.33333      108.76667

       Corrected Total   27       13539.85714


              R-Square     Coeff Var      Root MSE     OVERRUN Mean

              0.839339     2.061383       10.42913       505.9286


       Source            DF        Type I SS      Mean Square   F Value   Pr > F

       HOUSING            3       10787.79048     3595.93016     33.06    <.0001
       WTCLASS            1         329.14286      329.14286      3.03    0.0973
       HOUSING*WTCLASS    3         247.59048       82.53016      0.76    0.5303


       Source            DF       Type III SS     Mean Square   F Value   Pr > F

       HOUSING            3       10787.79048     3595.93016     33.06    <.0001
       WTCLASS            1         320.47407      320.47407      2.95    0.1015
       HOUSING*WTCLASS    3         247.59048       82.53016      0.76    0.5303
```

c.   To determine if interaction between housing system and weight class exists, we test:

H_0: Housing system and weight class do not interact
H_a: Housing system and weight class do interact

The test statistic is $F = 0.76$ and the p-value is $p = .5303$. Since the p-value is not less than α ($p = .5303 \not< .05$), H_0 is not rejected. There is insufficient evidence to indicate that housing system and weight class interact at $\alpha = .05$.

d. To determine if there is a difference in mean whipping capacity among the 4 housing systems, we test:

H_0: $\mu_1 = \mu_2 = \mu_3 = \mu_4$
H_a: At least two means differ

The test statistic is $F = 33.06$ and the *p*-value is less than .0001. Since the *p*-value is less than α ($p < .0001 < .05$), H_0 is rejected. There is sufficient evidence to indicate a difference in mean whipping capacity among the 4 housing systems at $\alpha = .05$.

e. To determine if there is a difference in mean whipping capacity between the 2 weight classes, we test:
H_0: $\mu_1 = \mu_2$
H_a: $\mu_1 \neq \mu_2$

The test statistic is $F = 2.95$ and the *p*-value is .1015. Since the *p*-value is not less than α ($p = .1015 \nless .05$), H_0 is not rejected. There is insufficient evidence to indicate a difference in mean whipping capacity between the 2 weight classes at $\alpha = .05$.

8.75 Yes. Using MINITAB, a plot of the data is:

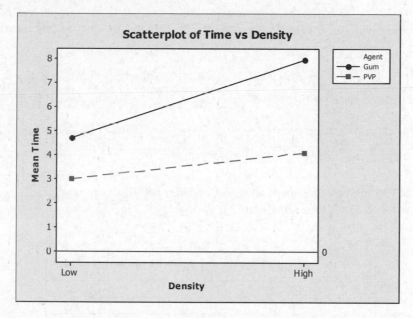

Since the lines are not parallel, this indicates interaction is present. The increase in mean time when density is increased from low to high for PVP is not as great as the increase in mean time when density is increased from low to high for GUM.

8.77 a. Low Load, Ambiguous: $\text{Total}_1 = n_1 \bar{x}_1 = 25(18) = 450$
High Load, Ambiguous: $\text{Total}_2 = n_2 \bar{x}_2 = 25(6.1) = 152.5$
Low Load, Common: $\text{Total}_3 = n_3 \bar{x}_3 = 25(7.8) = 195$
High Load, Common: $\text{Total}_4 = n_4 \bar{x}_4 = 25(6.3) = 157.5$

b. $\text{CM} = \dfrac{(\text{sum of all observations})^2}{n} = \dfrac{(450 + 152.5 + 195 + 157.5)^2}{100} = \dfrac{955^2}{100} = 9{,}120.25$

c. Low Load total is 450 + 195 = 645. High Load total is 152.5 + 157.5 = 310.

$$SS(Load) = \frac{\sum_{i=1}^{a} A_i^2}{br} - CM = \frac{645^2}{2(25)} + \frac{310^2}{2(25)} - 9,120.25 = 10,242.5 - 9,120.25 = 1,122.25$$

Ambiguous total is 450 + 152.5 = 602.5. Common total is 195 + 157.5 = 352.5

$$SS(Name) = \frac{\sum_{j=1}^{b} B_j^2}{ar} - CM = \frac{602.5^2}{2(25)} + \frac{352.5^2}{2(25)} - 7,700.0625 = 9,745.25 - 9,120.25 = 625$$

$$SS(Load \times Name) = \frac{\sum_{i=1}^{a}\sum_{j=1}^{b} AB_{ij}^2}{r} - SS(Load) - SS(Name) - CM$$

$$= \frac{450^2}{25} + \frac{152.5^2}{25} + \frac{195^2}{25} + \frac{157.5^2}{25} - 1,122.25 - 625 - 9,120.25$$

$$= 11,543.5 - 1,122.25 - 625 - 9,120.25 = 676$$

d. Low Load, Ambiguous: $s_1^2 = 15^2 = 225$ $(n_1 - 1)s_1^2 = (25-1)225 = 5,400$

High Load, Ambiguous: $s_2^2 = 9.5^2 = 90.25$ $(n_2 - 1)s_2^2 = (25-1)90.25 = 2,166$

Low Load, Common: $s_3^2 = 9.5^2 = 90.25$ $(n_3 - 1)s_3^2 = (25-1)90.25 = 2,166$

High Load, Common: $s_4^2 = 10^2 = 100$ $(n_4 - 1)s_4^2 = (25-1)100 = 2,400$

e. $SSE = (n_1 - 1)s_1^2 + (n_2 - 1)s_2^2 + (n_3 - 1)s_3^2 + (n_4 - 1)s_4^2$

$= 5,400 + 2,166 + 2,166 + 2,400 = 12,132$

f. SS(Total) = SS(Load) + SS(Name) + SS(Load x Name) + SSE

$= 1,122.25 + 625 + 676 + 12,132 = 14,555.25$

g. The ANOVA table is:

Source	df	SS	MS	F
Load	1	1,122.25	1,122.25	8.88
Name	1	625.00	625.00	4.95
Load x Name	1	676.00	676.00	5.35
Error	96	12,132.00	126.375	
Total	99	14,555.25		

h. Yes. We computed 5.35, which is almost the same as 5.34. The difference could be due to round-off error.

i. To determine if interaction between Load and Name is present, we test:

H_0: Load and Name do not interact
H_a: Load and Name class do interact

The test statistic is $F = 5.35$.

The rejection region requires $\alpha = .05$ in the upper tail of the F distribution with $v_1 = (a-1)(b-1) = (2-1)(2-1) = 1$ and $v_2 = n - ab = 100 - 4 = 96$. From Table VIII, Appendix B, $F_{.05} \approx 3.96$. The rejection region is $F > 3.96$.

Since the observed value of the test statistic falls in the rejection region ($F = 5.35 > 3.96$), H_0 is rejected. There is sufficient evidence to indicate that Load and Name interact at $\alpha = .05$.

Using MINITAB, a graph of the results is:

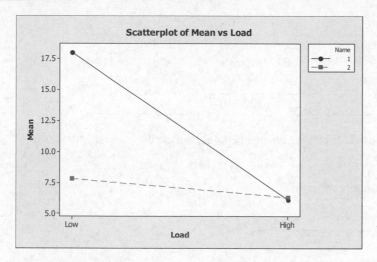

From the graph, the interaction is quite apparent. For Low load, the mean number of jelly beans taken for the ambiguous name is much higher than the mean number taken for the common name. However, for High load, there is essentially no difference in the mean number of jelly beans taken between the two names.

j. We must assume that:
1. The response distributions for each Load-Name combination (treatment) is normal.
2. The response variance is constant for all Load-Name combinations.
3. Random and independent samples of experimental units are associated with each Load-Name combination.

8.79 In a completely randomized design, independent random selection of treatments to be assigned to experimental units is required. In a randomized block design, the experimental units are first grouped into blocks such that within the blocks the experimental units are homogeneous and between the blocks the experimental units are heterogeneous.

8.81 When the overall level of significance of a multiple comparisons procedure is α, the level of significance for each comparison is less than α.

8.83 a. SS(Treatment) = SS(Total) − SS(Block) − SSE = 22.31 − 10.688 - .288 = 11.334

$$\text{MS(Treatment)} = \frac{\text{SS(Treatment)}}{k-1} = \frac{11.334}{4-1} = 3.778, \quad df = k-1 = 4-1 = 3$$

$$\text{MS(Block)} = \frac{\text{SS(Block)}}{b-1} = \frac{10.688}{5-1} = 2.672, \quad df = b-1 = 5-1 = 4$$

$$\text{MSE} = \frac{\text{SSE}}{n-k-b+1} = \frac{.288}{20-4-5+1} = .024, \quad df = n-k-b+1 = 20-4-5+1 = 12$$

$$\text{Treatment F} = \frac{\text{MS(Treatment)}}{\text{MSE}} = \frac{3.778}{.024} = 157.42$$

$$\text{Block F} = \frac{\text{MS(Block)}}{\text{MSE}} = \frac{2.672}{.024} = 111.33$$

The ANOVA Table is:

Source	df	SS	MS	F
Treatment	3	11.334	3.778	157.42
Block	4	10.688	2.672	111.33
Error	12	0.288	0.024	
Total	19	22.310		

b.   To determine if there is a difference among the treatment means, we test:

H_0: $\mu_A = \mu_B = \mu_C = \mu_D$
H_a: At least two treatment means differ

The test statistic is $F = \dfrac{\text{MS(Treatment)}}{\text{MSE}} = 157.42$

The rejection region requires $\alpha = .05$ in the upper tail of the F distribution with $v_1 = k - 1 = 4 - 1 = 3$ and $v_2 = n - k - b + 1 = 20 - 4 - 5 + 1 = 12$. From Table VIII, Appendix B, $F_{.05} = 3.49$. The rejection region is $F > 3.49$.

Since the observed value of the test statistic falls in the rejection region ($F = 157.42 > 3.49$), H_0 is rejected. There is sufficient evidence to indicate a difference among thetreatment means at $\alpha = .05$.

c.   Since there is evidence of differences among the treatment means, we need to compare the treatment means. The number of pairwise comparisons is $\dfrac{k(k-1)}{2} = \dfrac{4(4-1)}{2} = 6$.

d.   To determine if there are difference among the block means, we test:

H_0: All block means are the same
H_a: At least two block means differ

The test statistic is $F = \dfrac{\text{MS(Block)}}{\text{MSE}} = 111.33$

The rejection region requires $\alpha = .05$ in the upper tail of the F distribution with $v_1 = b - 1 = 5 - 1 = 4$ and $v_2 = n - k - b + 1 = 20 - 4 - 5 + 1 = 12$. From Table VIII, Appendix B, $F_{.05} = 3.26$. The rejection region is $F > 3.26$.

Since the observed value of the test statistic falls in the rejection region ($F = 111.33 > 3.26$), H_0 is rejected. There is sufficient evidence that the block means differ at $\alpha = .05$.

8.85   a.   The data are collected as a completely randomized design because five boxes of each size were randomly selected and tested.

b.   Yes. The confidence intervals surrounding each of the means do not overlap. This would indicate that there is a difference in the means for the two sizes.

c.   No. Several of the confidence intervals overlap. This would indicate that the mean compression strengths of the sizes that have intervals that overlap are not significantly different.

8.87   a.   The experimental design used in this example was a randomized block design.

b.   The experimental units in this problem are the electronic commerce and internet-based companies. The response variable is the rate of return for the stock of the companies. The treatments are the 4 categories of companies: e-companies, internet software and service, internet hardware, and internet communication. The blocks are the 3 age categories: 1 year-old, 3 year-old, and 5 year-old.

8.89   a.   To determine if leadership style affects behavior of subordinates, we test:

H_0: All four treatment means are the same
H_a: At least two treatment means differ

The test statistic is $F = 30.4$.

The rejection region requires $\alpha = .05$ in the upper tail of the F-distribution with $v_1 = ab - 1 = 2(2) - 1 = 3$ and $v_2 = n - ab = 257 - 2(2) = 253$. From Table VIII, Appendix B, $F_{.05} \approx 2.60$. The rejection region is $F > 2.60$.
Since the observed value of the test statistic falls in the rejection region ($F = 30.4 > 2.60$), H_0 is rejected. There is sufficient evidence to indicate that leadership style affects behavior of subordinates at $\alpha = .05$.

b.   From the table, the mean response for High control, low consideration is significantly higher than for any other treatment. The mean response for Low control, low consideration is significantly higher than that for High control, high consideration and for Low control, high consideration. No other significant differences exist.

c.   The assumptions for Bonferroni's method are the same as those for the ANOVA. Thus, we must assume that:

i.   The populations sampled from are normal.
ii.   The population variances are the same.
iii.   The samples are independent.

8.91   a.   This is an observational experiment. The researcher recorded the number of users per hour for each of 24 hours per day, 7 days per week, for 7 weeks. The researcher did not manipulate the weeks or days or hours.

b.   The two factors are (1) the day of the week with 7 levels and (2) the hour of the day with 24 levels.

c.   In a factorial experiment, a is the number of levels of factor A and b is the number of levels of factor B. If we let factor A be the day of the week and factor B be the hour of the day, then $a = 7$ and $b = 24$.

d. To determine if the $a \times b = 7 \times 24 = 168$ treatment means differ, we test:

H_0: $\mu_1 = \mu_2 = \mu_3 = \ldots = \mu_{168}$
H_a: At least two means differ

The test statistic is $F = \dfrac{\text{MST}}{\text{MSE}} = \dfrac{1143.99}{45.65} = 25.06$

The rejection region requires $\alpha = .01$ in the upper tail of the F distribution with $v_1 = p - 1 = 168 - 1 = 167$ and $v_2 = n - p = 1172 - 168 = 1004$. From Table X, Appendix B, $F_{.01} \approx 1.00$. The rejection region is $F > 1.00$.

Since the observed value of the test statistic falls in the rejection region ($F = 25.06 > 1.00$), H_0 is rejected. There is sufficient evidence to indicate a difference in mean usage among the day-hour combinations at $\alpha = .01$.

e. The hypotheses used to test if an interaction effect exists are:

H_0: Days and hours do not interact to affect the mean usage
H_a: Days and hours interact do affect the mean usage

f. The test statistic is $F = \dfrac{\text{MSAB}}{\text{MSE}} = \dfrac{55.69}{45.65} = 1.22$

The p-value is $p = .0527$. Since the p-value is not less than $\alpha = .01$, H_0 is not rejected. There is insufficient evidence to indicate days and hours interact to affect usage at $\alpha = .01$.

g. To determine if the mean usage differs among the days of the week, we test:

H_0: $\mu_1 = \mu_2 = \mu_3 = \mu_4 = \mu_5 = \mu_6 = \mu_7$
H_a: At least two means differ

The test statistic is $F = \dfrac{\text{MSA}}{\text{MSE}} = \dfrac{3122.02}{45.65} = 68.39$

The p-value is $p = .0001$. Since the p-value is less than $\alpha = .01$, H_0 is rejected. There is sufficient evidence to indicate the mean usage differs among the days of the week at $\alpha = .01$.

To determine if the mean usage differs among the hours of the day, we test:

H_0: $\mu_1 = \mu_2 = \mu_3 = \ldots = \mu_{24}$
H_a: At least two means differ

The test statistic is $F = \dfrac{\text{MSB}}{\text{MSE}} = \dfrac{7157.82}{45.65} = 156.80$

The p-value is $p = .0001$. Since the p-value is less than $\alpha = .01$, H_0 is rejected. There is sufficient evidence to indicate the mean usage differs among the hours of the day at $\alpha = .01$.

8.93   a.   The df for Groups $= v_1 = k - 1 = 3 - 1 = 2$. The df for Error $= v_2 = n - k = 71 - 3 = 68$.

The completed ANOVA table is:

Source	df	SS	MS	F
Groups	2	128.70	64.35	0.16
Error	68	27,124.52	398.89	

b.   To determine if the total number of activities undertaken differed among the three groups of entrepreneurs, we test:

H_0: $\mu_1 = \mu_2 = \mu_3$
H_a: At least one mean differs

The test statistic is $F = 0.16$.

The rejection region requires $\alpha = .05$ in the upper tail of the F-distribution with $v_1 = k - 1 = 3 - 1 = 2$ and $v_2 = n - k = 71 - 3 = 68$. From Table VIII, Appendix B, $F_{.05} \approx 3.15$. The rejection region is $F > 3.15$.

Since the observed value of the test statistic does not fall in the rejection region ($F = 0.16 \not> 3.15$), H_0 is not rejected. There is insufficient evidence to indicate that the total number of activities differed among the groups of entrepreneurs at $\alpha = .05$.

c.   The p-value of the test is $P(F > 0.16)$. From Table VII, Appendix B, with $v_1 = 2$ and $v_2 = 68$, $P(F > 0.16) > .10$.

d.   No. Since our conclusion was that there was no evidence of a difference in the total number of activities among the groups, there would be no evidence to indicate a difference between two specific groups.

8.95   a.   The quality of the steel ingot.

b.   There are two factors: temperature and pressure. They are quantitative factors since they are numerical.

c.   The treatments are the $3 \times 5 = 15$ factor-level combinations of temperature and pressure.

d.   The steel ingots are the experimental units.

8.97   a.   A completely randomized design was used. There are five treatments. They are the five different educational levels.

b.   To determine if the mean concern ratings differ for at least two education levels, we test:

H_0: $\mu_1 = \mu_2 = \mu_3 = \mu_4 = \mu_5$
H_a: At least two treatment means differ

where μ_i represents the mean concern rating of the ith education level.

The test statistic is $F = 3.298$.

The rejection region requires $\alpha = .05$ in the upper tail of the F-distribution with $v_1 = p - 1 = 5 - 1 = 4$ and $v_2 = n - p = 315 - 5 = 310$. From Table VIII, Appendix B, $F_{.05} \approx 2.37$. The rejection region is $F > 2.37$.

Since the observed value of the test statistic falls in the rejection region ($F = 3.298 > 2.37$), H_0 is rejected. There is sufficient evidence to indicate a difference in the mean concern ratings among the 5 education levels at $\alpha = .05$.

c. The mean concern rating for those with post-graduate education is significantly greater than the mean concern rating for the four other education level groups. There are no other significant differences.

8.99   a. A 6×5 factorial design was used for this experiment. There are 6 cylinders and 5 batches.

    b. The two factors are cylinders with 6 levels and batches with 5 levels.

    c. There are a total of $a \times b = 6 \times 5 = 30$ treatments.

    d. $\sum x_i = 1 + 1 + 2 + \ldots + 2 = 145$

$$CM = \frac{\left(\sum x_i\right)^2}{n} = \frac{(145)^2}{90} = 233.61111$$

$$SS(Batch) = \frac{\sum A_i^2}{br} - CM = \frac{12^2}{6(3)} + \frac{24^2}{6(3)} + \frac{57^2}{6(3)} + \frac{24^2}{6(3)} + \frac{28^2}{6(3)} - 233.61111$$

$$= 296.05556 - 233.61111 = 62.44445$$

$$SS(Cyl) = \frac{\sum B_i^2}{br} - CM = \frac{46^2}{5(3)} + \frac{14^2}{5(3)} + \frac{31^2}{5(3)} + \frac{14^2}{5(3)} + \frac{14^2}{5(3)} + \frac{26^2}{5(3)} - 233.61111$$

$$= 289.4 - 233.61111 = 55.78889$$

$$SS(B \times C) = \frac{\sum \sum AB_{ij}^2}{r} - SS(Batch) - SS(Cyl) - CM$$

$$= \frac{4^2}{3} + \frac{1^2}{3} + \frac{3^2}{3} + \cdots + \frac{6^2}{3} - 62.44445 - 55.78889 - 233.61111$$

$$= \frac{1201}{3} - 62.44445 - 55.78889 - 233.61111 = 48.48888$$

$$SSTot = \sum \sum x_{ij}^2 - CM = 513 - 233.61111 = 279.38889$$

$$SSE = SSTot - SS(Batch) - SS(Cyl) - SS(B \times C)$$

$$= 279.38889 - 62.44445 - 55.78889 - 48.48888 = 112.66667$$

$$MS(Batch) = \quad = 15.6111$$

$$MS(Cyl) = \frac{SS(Cyl)}{b-1} = \frac{55.78889}{6-1} = 11.1578$$

$$MS(B \times C) = \frac{SS(B \times C)}{(a-1)(b-1)} = \frac{48.48888}{(5-1)(6-1)} = 2.4244$$

$$MSE = \frac{SSE}{n-ab} = \frac{112.66667}{90-5(6)} = 1.8778$$

$$F_B = \frac{MS(Batch)}{MSE} = \frac{15.6111}{1.8778} = 8.31 \qquad F_C = \frac{MS(Cyl)}{MSE} = \frac{11.1578}{1.8778} = 5.94$$

$$F_{B \times C} = \frac{MS(B \times C)}{MSE} = \frac{2.4244}{1.8778} = 1.29$$

The ANOVA Table is:

Source	df	SS	MS	F
Batch	4	62.444	15.611	8.31
Cyl	5	55.789	11.158	5.94
B × C	20	48.489	2.424	1.29
Error	60	112.667	1.878	
Total	89	279.389		

$$SST = SS(Batch) + SS(Cyl) + SS(B \times C) = 62.44444 + 55.788889 + 48.48888$$

$$= 166.72221$$

$$MST = \frac{SST}{ab-1} = \frac{166.72221}{5(6)-1} = 5.749 \qquad F_T = \frac{MST}{MSE} = 3.06$$

To determine if differences exist among the treatment means, we test:

H_0: $\mu_1 = \mu_2 = \mu_3 = \ldots = \mu_{30}$
H_a: At least two means differ

The test statistic is $F_T = 3.06$.

Since no α is given, we will use $\alpha = .05$. The rejection region requires $\alpha = .05$ in the upper tail of the F distribution with $\nu_1 = ab - 1 = 5(6) - 1 = 29$ and $\nu_2 = n - ab = 90 - 5(6) = 60$. From Table VIII, Appendix B, $F_{.05} \approx 1.65$. The rejection region is $F > 1.65$.

Since the observed value of the test statistic falls in the rejection region ($F = 3.06 > 1.65$), H_0 is rejected. There is sufficient evidence to indicate differences exist among the treatment means at $\alpha = .05$.

e. If batch and cylinder interact to affect the mean weight, this means that the effect of batch on mean weight depends on the level of cylinder. Batch 1 may have the highest mean weight on cylinder 2, but Batch 4 may have the highest mean weight on cylinder 6.

f.   To determine if Batch and Cylinder interact to affect mean weight, we test:

H_0: Batch and Cylinder do not interact
H_a: Batch and Cylinder interact

The test statistic is $F = \dfrac{MS(B \times C)}{MSE} = 1.29$

The rejection region requires $\alpha = .05$ in the upper tail of the F distribution with $v_1 = (a-1)(b-1) = (5-1)(6-1) = 20$ and $v_2 = n - ab = 90 - 5(6) = 60$. From Table VIII, Appendix B, $F_{.05} = 1.75$. The rejection region is $F > 1.75$.

Since the observed value of the test statistic does not fall in the rejection region ($F = 1.29 \ngtr 1.75$), H_0 is not rejected. There is insufficient evidence to indicate Batch and Cylinder interact to affect the mean weight at $\alpha = .05$.

g.   Since we did not find any evidence of interaction in part **f**, we will test for the main effects.

To determine if the mean weights differ among the batches, we test:

H_0: $\mu_1 = \mu_2 = \mu_3 = \mu_4 = \mu_5$
H_a: At least two means differ

The test statistic is $F_B = 8.31$.

The rejection region requires $\alpha = .05$ in the upper tail of the F distribution with $v_1 = a - 1 = 5 - 1 = 4$ and $v_2 = n - ab = 90 - 5(6) = 60$. From Table VIII, Appendix B, $F_{.05} = 2.53$. The rejection region is $F > 2.53$.

Since the observed value of the test statistic falls in the rejection region ($F = 8.31 > 2.53$), H_0 is rejected. There is sufficient evidence to indicate differences exist among the batches at $\alpha = .05$.

To determine if the mean weights differ among the cylinders, we test:

H_0: $\mu_1 = \mu_2 = \mu_3 = \mu_4 = \mu_5 = \mu_6$
H_a: At least two means differ

The test statistic is $F_C = 5.94$.

The rejection region requires $\alpha = .05$ in the upper tail of the F distribution with $v_1 = b - 1 = 6 - 1 = 5$ and $v_2 = n - ab = 90 - 5(6) = 60$. From Table VIII, Appendix B, $F_{.05} \approx 2.37$. The rejection region is $F > 2.37$.

Since the observed value of the test statistic falls in the rejection region ($F = 5.94 > 2.37$), H_0 is rejected. There is sufficient evidence to indicate differences exist among the cylinders at $\alpha = .05$.

8.101 a.   This is a 2×2 factorial experiment.

b.   The two factors are the tent type (treated or untreated) and location (inside or outside). There are $2 \times 2 = 4$ treatments. The four treatments are (treated, inside), (treated, outside), (untreated, inside), and (untreated, outside).

c.   The response variable is the number of mosquito bites received in a 20 minute interval.

d.   There is sufficient evidence to indicate interaction is present. This indicates that the effect of the tent type on the number of mosquito bites depends on whether the person is inside or outside.

8.103   Using MINITAB, the ANOVA Table is:

General Linear Model: Rating versus Prep, Standing

```
Factor      Type  Levels  Values
Prep        fixed    2    PRACTICE REVIEW
Standing    fixed    3    HI   LOW MED

Analysis of Variance for Rating, using Adjusted SS for Tests

Source            DF     Seq SS     Adj SS     Adj MS      F       P
Prep               1     54.735     54.735     54.735   14.40   0.000
Standing           2     16.500     16.500      8.250    2.17   0.118
Prep*Standing      2     13.470     13.470      6.735    1.77   0.174
Error            126    478.955    478.955      3.801
Total            131    563.659

Tukey 95.0% Simultaneous Confidence Intervals
Response Variable Rating
All Pairwise Comparisons among Levels of Prep

Prep = PRACTICE subtracted from:

Prep        Lower    Center    Upper    ---+---------+---------+---------+---
REVIEW     -1.960    -1.288   -0.6162   (-----------*----------)
                                        ---+---------+---------+---------+---
                                        -1.80     -1.20      -0.60      0.00
```

First, we must test for treatment effects.

$$SST = SS(Prep) + SS(Stand) + SS(PxS) = 54.735 + 16.500 + 13.470 = 84.705.$$

The df = 1 + 2 + 2 = 5.

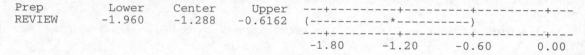

$$MST = \frac{SST}{ab-1} = \frac{84.705}{2(3)-1} = 16.941 \qquad F = \frac{MST}{MSE} = \frac{16.941}{3.801} = 4.46$$

To determine if there are differences in mean ratings among the 6 treatments, we test:

H_0: All treatment means are the same
H_a: At least two treatment means differ

The test statistic is $F = 4.46$.

Since no α was given, we will use $\alpha = .05$. The rejection region requires $\alpha = .05$ in the upper tail of the F distribution with $\nu_1 = ab - 1 = 2(3) - 1 = 5$ and $\nu_2 = n - ab = 132 - 2(3) = 126$. From Table VIII, Appendix B, $F_{.05} \approx 2.29$. The rejection region is $F > 2.29$.

Since the observed value of the test statistic falls in the rejection region ($F = 4.46 > 2.29$), H_0 is rejected. There is sufficient evidence that differences exist among the treatment means at $\alpha = .05$. Since differences exist, we now test for the interaction effect between Preparation and Class Standing.

To determine if Preparation and Class Standing interact, we test:

H_0: Preparation and Class Standing do not interact
H_a: Preparation and Class Standing do interact

The test statistic is $F = 1.77$ and p = .174

Since the *p*-value is greater than α ($p = .174 > .05$), H_0 is not rejected. There is insufficient evidence that Preparation and Class Standing interact at $\alpha = .05$. Since the interaction does not exist, we test for the main effects of Preparation and Class standing.

To determine if there are differences in the mean rating between the three levels of Class standing, we test:

H_0: $\mu_L = \mu_M = \mu_H$
H_a: At least 2 means differ

The test statistics is $F = 2.17$ and $p = 0.118$.

Since the *p*-value is greater than α ($p = .118 > .05$), H_0 is not rejected. There is insufficient evidence that the mean ratings differ among the 3 levels of Class Standing at $\alpha = .05$.

To determine if there are differences in the mean rating between the two levels of Preparation, we test:

H_0: $\mu_P = \mu_S$
H_a: $\mu_P \neq \mu_S$

The test statistics is $F = 14.40$ and $p = 0.000$.

Since the *p*-value is less than α ($p = 0.000 < .05$), H_0 is rejected. There is sufficient evidence that the mean ratings differ between the two levels of preparation at $\alpha = .05$.

There are only 2 levels of Preparation. The mean rating for Practice is higher than the mean rating Review.

Chapter 9
Categorical Data Analysis

9.1   a.   The rejection region requires $\alpha = .05$ in the upper tail of the χ^2 distribution with df $= k - 1 = 3 - 1 = 2$. From Table VI, Appendix B, $\chi^2_{.05} = 5.99147$. The rejection region is $\chi^2 > 5.99147$.

      b.   The rejection region requires $\alpha = .10$ in the upper tail of the χ^2 distribution with df $= k - 1 = 5 - 1 = 4$. From Table VI, Appendix B, $\chi^2_{.10} = 7.77944$. The rejection region is $\chi^2 > 7.77944$.

      c.   The rejection region requires $\alpha = .01$ in the upper tail of the χ^2 distribution with df $= k - 1 = 4 - 1 = 3$. From Table VI, Appendix B, $\chi^2_{.01} = 11.3449$. The rejection region is $\chi^2 > 11.3449$.

9.3   The sample size n will be large enough so that, for every cell, the expected cell count, E_i, will be equal to 5 or more.

9.5   Some preliminary calculations are:

If the probabilities are the same, $p_{1,0} = p_{2,0} = p_{3,0} = p_{4,0} = .25$

$E_1 = np_{1,0} = 205(.25) = 51.25$
$E_2 = E_3 = E_4 = 205(.25) = 51.25$

      a.   To determine if the multinomial probabilities differ, we test:

H_0: $p_1 = p_2 = p_3 = p_4 = .25$
H_a: At least one of the probabilities differs from .25

The test statistic is $\chi^2 = \sum \dfrac{[n_i - E_i]^2}{E_i}$

$$= \frac{(43 - 51.25)^2}{51.25} + \frac{(56 - 51.25)^2}{51.25} + \frac{(59 - 51.25)^2}{51.25} + \frac{(47 - 51.25)^2}{51.25} = 3.293$$

The rejection region requires $\alpha = .05$ in the upper tail of the χ^2 distribution with df $= k - 1 = 4 - 1 = 3$. From Table VI, Appendix B, $\chi^2_{.05} = 7.81473$. The rejection region is $\chi^2 > 7.81473$.

Since the observed value of the test statistic does not fall in the rejection region ($\chi^2 = 3.293 \not> 7.81473$), H_0 is not rejected. There is insufficient evidence to indicate the multinomial probabilities differ at $\alpha = .05$.

      b.   The Type I error is concluding the multinomial probabilities differ when, in fact, they do not.

The Type II error is concluding the multinomial probabilities are equal, when, in fact, they are not.

c. For confidence coefficient .95, $\alpha = .05$ and $\alpha/2 = .05/2 = .025$. From Table IV, Appendix B, $z_{.025} = 1.96$.

$\hat{p}_3 = 59/205 = .288$

The confidence interval is:

$$\hat{p}_3 \pm z_{.025}\sqrt{\frac{\hat{p}\hat{q}}{n}} \Rightarrow .288 \pm 1.96\sqrt{\frac{.288(.712)}{205}} \Rightarrow .288 \pm .062 \Rightarrow (.226, .350)$$

9.7 a. The qualitative variable in this exercise is what "Made in the USA" means. There are 4 levels or categories for this variable: 100% of labor and materials are produced in the US, 75-99% of labor and materials are produced in the US, 50-74% of labor and materials are produced in the US, and less than 50% of labor and materials are produced in the US.

b. The consumer advocate group hypothesized that $p_1 = \frac{1}{2} = .50$, $p_2 = \frac{1}{4} = .25$, $p_3 = 1/5 = .20$, and $p_4 = .05$.

c. To determine if the consumer advocate group's claim is correct, we test:

H_0: $p_1 = .5$, $p_2 = .25$, $p_3 = .20$, and $p_4 = .05$
H_a: At least one of the proportions differs from their hypothesized values

d. Some preliminary calculations are:

$n = 64 + 20 + 18 + 4 = 106$.

$E_1 = np_{1,0} = 106(.50) = 53$; $E_2 = np_{2,0} = 106(.25) = 26.5$;
$E_3 = np_{3,0} = 106(.20) = 21.2$; $E_4 = np_{4,0} = 106(.05) = 5.3$

$$\chi^2 = \sum\frac{[n_i - E_i]^2}{E_i} = \frac{(64-53)^2}{53} + \frac{(20-26.5)^2}{26.5} + \frac{(18-21.2)^2}{21.2} + \frac{(4-5.3)^2}{5.3} = 4.68$$

e. The rejection region requires $\alpha = .10$ in the upper tail of the χ^2 distribution with df = $k - 1 = 4 - 1 = 3$. From Table VI, Appendix B, $\chi^2_{.10} = 6.25139$. The rejection region is $\chi^2 > 6.25139$.

f. Since the observed value of the test statistic does not fall in the rejection region ($\chi^2 = 4.68 \not> 6.25139$), H_0 is not rejected. There is insufficient evidence to indicate the consumer advocate group's claim is incorrect at $\alpha = .10$.

g. $\hat{p}_1 = \frac{n_1}{n} = \frac{64}{106} = .604$

For confidence coefficient .90, $\alpha = 1 - .90 = .10$ and $\alpha/2 = .10/2 = .05$. From Table IV, Appendix B, $z_{.05} = 1.645$. The 90% confidence interval is:

$$\hat{p}_1 \pm z_{.05}\sqrt{\frac{\hat{p}_1(1-\hat{p}_1)}{n}} \Rightarrow .604 \pm 1.645\sqrt{\frac{.604(.396)}{106}} \Rightarrow .604 \pm .078 \Rightarrow (.526,\ .682)$$

We are 90% confident that the proportion of all consumers who believe "Made in the USA" means "100%" of labor and material are produced in the US is between .526 and .682.

9.9   a.   Since there are 10 income groups, we would expect 10% or $1,072(.10) = 107.2$ givers in each of the income categories.

   b.   The null hypothesis for testing whether the true proportions of charitable givers in each income group are the same is:

   H_0: $p_1 = p_2 = \ldots = p_{10} = .10$

   c.   Some preliminary calculations are:

   $\hat{E}_1 = E_2 = \ldots = E_{10} = np_{1,0} = 1,072(.10) = 170.2$

   $$\chi^2 = \sum \frac{[n_i - E_i]^2}{E_i} = \frac{(42-107.2)^2}{107.2} + \frac{(93-107.2)^2}{107.2} + \ldots + \frac{(127-107.2)^2}{107.2} = 93.15$$

   d.   The rejection region requires $\alpha = .10$ in the upper tail of the χ^2 distribution with $df = k - 1 = 10 - 1 = 9$. From Table VI, Appendix B, $\chi^2_{.10} = 14.6837$. The rejection region is $\chi^2 > 14.6837$.

   e.   Since the observed value of the test statistic falls in the rejection region ($\chi^2 = 93.15 > 14.6837$), H_0 is rejected. There is sufficient evidence to indicate that the true proportions of charitable givers in each income group are not all the same at $\alpha = .10$.

9.11   a.   The data come from a multinomial experiment because there are several possible categorical responses to the question.

   b.   To determine if the multinomial probabilities agree with the theory, we test:
   H_0: $p_1 = .50$, $p_2 = p_3 = p_4 = p_5 = .10$, $p_6 = p_7 = .05$

   c.   Using MINITAB, the results are:

   Chi-Square Goodness-of-Fit Test for Observed Counts in Variable: C1

Category	Observed	Test Proportion	Expected	Contribution to Chi-Sq
1	869	0.50	1059.50	34.252
2	339	0.10	211.90	76.236
3	338	0.10	211.90	75.041
4	127	0.10	211.90	34.016
5	85	0.10	211.90	75.996
6	128	0.05	105.95	4.589
7	233	0.05	105.95	152.352

N	DF	Chi-Sq	P-Value
2119	6	452.483	0.000

   To determine if the multinomial probabilities agree with the theory, we test:

   H_0: $p_1 = .50$, $p_2 = p_3 = p_4 = p_5 = .10$, $p_6 = p_7 = .05$
   H_a: At least one of the probabilities differs from its hypothesized value

   The test statistic is $\chi^2 = 452.843$ and the p-value is 0.000. Since the p-value is less that $\alpha = .01$, H_0 is rejected. There is sufficient evidence to indicate that at least one of the proportions differs from its hypothesized value at $\alpha = .01$.

9.13   Some preliminary calculations are:

$E_1 = E_2 = E_3 = E_4 = np_{1,0} = 83(.25) = 20.75$

To determine if there are differences in the percentage of incidents in the four cause categories, we test:

H_0: $p_1 = p_2 = p_3 = p_4 = .25$
H_a: At least one p_i differs from its hypothesized value

The test statistic is

$$\chi^2 = \sum \frac{\left[n_i - E_i\right]^2}{E_i} = \frac{(27-20.75)^2}{20.75} + \frac{(24-20.75)^2}{20.75} + \frac{(22-20.75)^2}{20.75} + \frac{(10-20.75)^2}{20.75}$$
$$= 8.036$$

The rejection region requires $\alpha = .05$ in the upper tail of the χ^2 distribution with df $= k - 1 = 4 - 1 = 3$. From Table VI, Appendix B, $\chi^2_{.05} = 7.81473$. The rejection region is $\chi^2 > 7.81473$.

Since the observed value of the test statistic falls in the rejection region ($\chi^2 = 80.36 > 7.81473$), H_0 is rejected. There is sufficient evidence to indicate there are differences in the percentages of incidents in the four cause categories at $\alpha = .05$.

9.15   To determine if the number of overweight trucks per week is distributed over the 7 days of the week in direct proportion to the volume of truck traffic, we test:

H_0: $p_1 = .191, p_2 = .198, p_3 = .187, p_4 = .180, p_5 = .155, p_6 = .043, p_7 = .046$
H_a: At least one of the probabilities differs from the hypothesized value

$E_1 = np_{1,0} = 414(.191) = 79.074$
$E_2 = np_{2,0} = 414(.198) = 81.972$
$E_3 = np_{3,0} = 414(.187) = 77.418$
$E_4 = np_{4,0} = 414(.180) = 74.520$
$E_5 = np_{5,0} = 414(.155) = 64.170$
$E_6 = np_{6,0} = 414(.043) = 17.802$
$E_7 = np_{7,0} = 414(.046) = 19.044$

The test statistic is $\chi^2 = \sum \frac{[n_i - E_i]^2}{E_i} = \frac{(90-79.074)^2}{79.074} + \frac{(82-81.972)^2}{81.972}$

$$+ \frac{(72-77.418)^2}{77.418} + \frac{(70-74.520)^2}{74.520} + \frac{(51-64.170)^2}{64.170} + \frac{(18-17.802)^2}{17.802} + \frac{(31-19.044)^2}{19.044} = 12.374$$

The rejection region requires $\alpha = .05$ in the upper tail of the χ^2 distribution with df $= k - 1 = 7 - 1 = 6$. From Table VI, Appendix B, $\chi^2_{.05} = 12.5916$. The rejection region is $\chi^2 > 12.5916$.

Since the observed value of the test statistic does not fall in the rejection region ($\chi^2 = 12.374 \not> 12.5916$), H_0 is not rejected. There is insufficient evidence to indicate the number of overweight trucks per week is distributed over the 7 days of the week is not in direct proportion to the volume of truck traffic at $\alpha = .05$.

9.17   a. $df = (r-1)(c-1) = (5-1)(5-1) = 16$. From Table VI, Appendix B, $\chi^2_{.05} = 26.2962$. The rejection region is $\chi^2 > 26.2962$.

b. $df = (r-1)(c-1) = (3-1)(6-1) = 10$. From Table VI, Appendix B, $\chi^2_{.10} = 15.9871$. The rejection region is $\chi^2 > 15.9871$.

c. $df = (r-1)(c-1) = (2-1)(3-1) = 2$. From Table VI, Appendix B, $\chi^2 = 9.21034$. The rejection region is $\chi^2 > 9.21034$.

9.19   a.   To convert the frequencies to percentages, divide the numbers in each column by the column total and multiply by 100. Also, divide the row totals by the overall total and multiply by 100. The column totals are 25, 64, and 78, while the row totals are 96 and 71. The overall sample size is 165. The table of percentages are:

	Column			
	1	**2**	**3**	
Row 1	$\frac{9}{25} \cdot 100 = 36\%$	$\frac{34}{64} \cdot 100 = 53.1\%$	$\frac{53}{78} \cdot 100 = 67.9\%$	$\frac{96}{167} \cdot 100 = 57.5\%$
2	$\frac{16}{25} \cdot 100 = 64\%$	$\frac{30}{64} \cdot 100 = 46.9\%$	$\frac{25}{78} \cdot 100 = 32.1\%$	$\frac{71}{167} \cdot 100 = 42.5\%$

b.   Using MINITAB, the graph is:

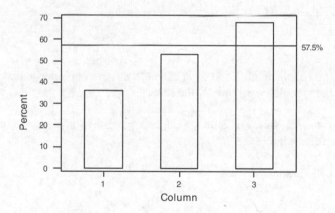

c.   If the rows and columns are independent, the row percentages in each column would be close to the row total percentages. This pattern is not evident in the plot, implying the rows and columns are not independent. In Exercise 9.18, we did not have enough evidence to say the rows and columns were not independent. If the sample sizes were bigger, we would have been able to reject H_0.

9.21   a-b.   To convert the frequencies to percentages, divide the numbers in each column by the column total and multiply by 100. Also, divide the row totals by the overall total and multiply by 100.

	B			
	B_1	B_2	B_3	**Totals**
A_1	$\dfrac{40}{134} \cdot 100 = 29.9\%$	$\dfrac{72}{163} \cdot 100 = 44.2\%$	$\dfrac{42}{142} \cdot 100 = 29.6\%$	$\dfrac{154}{439} \cdot 100 = 35.1\%$
Row A_2	$\dfrac{63}{134} \cdot 100 = 47.0\%$	$\dfrac{53}{163} \cdot 100 = 32.5\%$	$\dfrac{70}{142} \cdot 100 = 49.3\%$	$\dfrac{186}{439} \cdot 100 = 42.4\%$
A_3	$\dfrac{31}{134} \cdot 100 = 23.1\%$	$\dfrac{38}{163} \cdot 100 = 23.3\%$	$\dfrac{30}{142} \cdot 100 = 21.1\%$	$\dfrac{99}{439} \cdot 100 = 22.6\%$

Using MINITAB, the graph is:

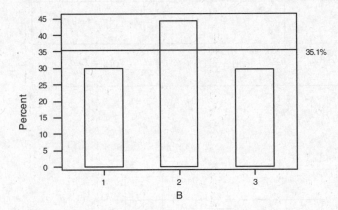

The graph supports the conclusion that the rows and columns are not independent. If they were, then the height of all the bars would be essentially the same.

9.23   a.   To compare the two proportions, we could use either a test of hypothesis or a confidence interval. I will use a 95% confidence interval.

Some preliminary calculations are:

$$\hat{p}_{M1} = \frac{x_{M1}}{n_M} = \frac{29}{103} = .282 \qquad\qquad \hat{p}_{F1} = \frac{x_{F1}}{n_F} = \frac{89}{174} = .511$$

For confidence coefficient .95, $\alpha = .05$ and $\alpha/2 = .05/2 = .025$. From Table IV, Appendix B, $z_{.025} = 1.96$. The 95% confidence interval is:

$$\left(\hat{p}_{M1} - \hat{p}_{F1}\right) \pm z_{.025} \sqrt{\frac{\hat{p}_{M1}\hat{q}_{M1}}{n_M} + \frac{\hat{p}_{F1}\hat{q}_{F1}}{n_F}} \Rightarrow (.282 - .511) \pm 1.96 \sqrt{\frac{.282(.718)}{103} + \frac{.511(.489)}{174}}$$

$$\Rightarrow -.229 \pm .114 \Rightarrow (-.343, \quad -.115)$$

We are 95% confident that the difference in the proportions of male and female professionals who believe their salaries are too low is between $-.343$ and $-.115$. Since 0 is not in this interval, there is evidence that the two proportions are different.

   b.   Some preliminary calculations are:

$$\hat{p}_{M2} = \frac{x_{M2}}{n_M} = \frac{58}{103} = .563 \qquad\qquad \hat{p}_{F2} = \frac{x_{F2}}{n_F} = \frac{64}{174} = .368$$

For confidence coefficient .95, $\alpha = .05$ and $\alpha/2 = .05/2 = .025$. From Table IV, Appendix B, $z_{.025} = 1.96$. The 95% confidence interval is:

$$\left(\hat{p}_{M2} - \hat{p}_{F2}\right) \pm z_{.025}\sqrt{\frac{\hat{p}_{M2}\hat{q}_{M2}}{n_M} + \frac{\hat{p}_{F2}\hat{q}_{F2}}{n_F}} \Rightarrow (.563 - .368) \pm 1.96\sqrt{\frac{.563(.437)}{103} + \frac{.368(.632)}{174}}$$

$$\Rightarrow .195 \pm .120 \Rightarrow (.075, \ .315)$$

We are 95% confident that the difference in the proportions of male and female professionals who believe their salaries are equitable/fair is between .075 and .315. Since 0 is not in this interval, there is evidence that the two proportions are different.

c. Some preliminary calculations are:

$$\hat{p}_{M3} = \frac{x_{M3}}{n_M} = \frac{16}{103} = .155 \qquad\qquad \hat{p}_{F3} = \frac{x_{F3}}{n_F} = \frac{21}{174} = .121$$

For confidence coefficient .95, $\alpha = .05$ and $\alpha/2 = .05/2 = .025$. From Table IV, Appendix B, $z_{.025} = 1.96$. The 95% confidence interval is:

$$\left(\hat{p}_{M3} - \hat{p}_{F3}\right) \pm z_{.025}\sqrt{\frac{\hat{p}_{M3}\hat{q}_{M3}}{n_M} + \frac{\hat{p}_{F3}\hat{q}_{F3}}{n_F}} \Rightarrow (.155 - .121) \pm 1.96\sqrt{\frac{.155(.845)}{103} + \frac{.121(.879)}{174}}$$

$$\Rightarrow .034 \pm .085 \Rightarrow (-.051, \ .119)$$

We are 95% confident that the difference in the proportions of male and female professionals who believe they are well paid is between $-.051$ and $.119$. Since 0 is in this interval, there is no evidence that the two proportions are different.

d. Yes. Since there were differences between the proportions of males and females on 2 of the 3 levels, there is evidence that the opinions of males and females are different.

e. Some preliminary calculations are:

$$\hat{E}_{11} = \frac{R_1 C_1}{n} = \frac{118(103)}{277} = 43.877 \qquad\qquad \hat{E}_{12} = \frac{R_1 C_2}{n} = \frac{118(174)}{277} = 74.123$$

$$\hat{E}_{21} = \frac{R_2 C_1}{n} = \frac{122(103)}{277} = 45.365 \qquad\qquad \hat{E}_{22} = \frac{R_2 C_2}{n} = \frac{122(174)}{277} = 76.635$$

$$\hat{E}_{31} = \frac{R_3 C_1}{n} = \frac{37(103)}{277} = 13.758 \qquad\qquad \hat{E}_{33} = \frac{R_3 C_3}{n} = \frac{37(174)}{277} = 23.242$$

To determine if the opinion on the fairness of a travel professional's salary differ for males and females, we test:

H_0: Opinion and Gender are independent
H_a: Opinion and Gender are dependent

The test statistic is

$$\chi^2 = \sum\sum \frac{\left[n_{ij} - \hat{E}_{ij}\right]^2}{\hat{E}_{ij}} = \frac{(29 - 43.877)^2}{43.877} + \frac{(89 - 74.123)^2}{74.123} + \frac{(58 - 45.365)^2}{45.365}$$

$$+ \frac{(64 - 76.635)^2}{76.635} + \frac{(16 - 13.758)^2}{13.758} + \frac{(21 - 23.242)^2}{23.242} = 14.214$$

The rejection region requires $\alpha = .10$ in the upper tail of the χ^2 distribution with df $= (r - 1)(c - 1)$ $= (3 - 1)(2 - 1) = 2$. From Table VI, Appendix B, $\chi^2_{.10} = 4.60517$. The rejection region is $\chi^2 > 4.60517$.

Since the observed value of the test statistic falls in the rejection region ($\chi^2 = 14.214 > 4.60517$), H_0 is rejected. There is sufficient evidence to indicate that the opinion on the fairness of a travel professional's salary differ for males and females at $\alpha = .10$.

f. For confidence coefficient .90, $\alpha = .10$ and $\alpha/2 = .10/2 = .05$. From Table IV, Appendix B, $z_{.05} = 1.645$. The 90% confidence interval is:

$$\left(\hat{p}_{M1} - \hat{p}_{F1}\right) \pm z_{.05}\sqrt{\frac{\hat{p}_{M1}\hat{q}_{M1}}{n_M} + \frac{\hat{p}_{F1}\hat{q}_{F1}}{n_F}} \Rightarrow (.282 - .511) \pm 1.645\sqrt{\frac{.282(.718)}{103} + \frac{.511(.489)}{174}}$$

$$\Rightarrow -.229 \pm .096 \Rightarrow (-.325, \quad -.133)$$

We are 90% confident that the difference in the proportions of male and female professionals who believe their salaries are too low is between -.325 and -.133. Since 0 is not in this interval, there is evidence that the two proportions are different.

9.25 a. Some preliminary calculations are:

$$\hat{p}_{C1} = \frac{x_{C1}}{n_1} = \frac{175}{6,222} = .028 \qquad\qquad \hat{p}_{C2} = \frac{x_{C2}}{n_2} = \frac{236}{4,692} = .050$$

$$\hat{p}_{C3} = \frac{x_{C3}}{n_3} = \frac{319}{7,140} = .045 \qquad\qquad \hat{p}_{C4} = \frac{x_{C4}}{n_4} = \frac{231}{6,120} = .038$$

$$\hat{p}_{C5} = \frac{x_{C5}}{n_5} = \frac{480}{10,353} = .046 \qquad\qquad \hat{p}_{C6} = \frac{x_{C6}}{n_6} = \frac{187}{4794} = .039$$

The proportions range from .028 to .050. Since .050 is about twice as big as .028, there may be evidence to conclude some of the proportions are different.

b. Some preliminary calculations are:

$$\hat{E}_{11} = \frac{R_1 C_1}{n} = \frac{6,222(37,693)}{39,321} = 5,964.39 \qquad \hat{E}_{12} = \frac{R_1 C_2}{n} = \frac{6,222(1628)}{39,321} = 257.61$$

$$\hat{E}_{21} = \frac{R_2 C_1}{n} = \frac{4,692(37,693)}{39,321} = 4497.74 \qquad \hat{E}_{22} = \frac{R_2 C_2}{n} = \frac{4,692(1,628)}{39,321} = 194.26$$

$$\hat{E}_{31} = \frac{R_3 C_1}{n} = \frac{7,140(37,693)}{39,321} = 6,844.38 \qquad \hat{E}_{32} = \frac{R_3 C_2}{n} = \frac{7,140(1,628)}{39,321} = 295.62$$

$$\hat{E}_{41} = \frac{R_4 C_1}{n} = \frac{6,120(37,693)}{39,321} = 5,866.61 \qquad \hat{E}_{42} = \frac{R_4 C_2}{n} = \frac{6,120(1,628)}{39,321} = 253.39$$

$$\hat{E}_{51} = \frac{R_5 C_1}{n} = \frac{10,353(37,693)}{39,321} = 9,924.36 \qquad \hat{E}_{52} = \frac{R_5 C_2}{n} = \frac{10,353(1,628)}{39,321} = 428.64$$

$$\hat{E}_{61} = \frac{R_6 C_1}{n} = \frac{4,794(37,693)}{39,321} = 4,595.51 \qquad \hat{E}_{62} = \frac{R_6 C_2}{n} = \frac{4,794(1,628)}{39,321} - 198.49$$

To determine if the proportions of censored measurements differ for the six tractor lines, we test:

H_0: Tractor lines and Censored measurements are independent
H_a: Tractor lines and Censored measurements are dependent

The test statistic is

$$\chi^2 = \sum\sum \frac{\left[n_{ij} - \hat{E}_{ij} \right]^2}{\hat{E}_{ij}} = \frac{(6047 - 5964.39)^2}{5964.39} + \frac{(175 - 257.61)^2}{257.61} + \frac{(4456 - 4497.74)^2}{4497.74}$$

$$+ \cdots + \frac{(187 - 198.49)^2}{198.49} = 48.0978$$

The rejection region requires $\alpha = .01$ in the upper tail of the χ^2 distribution with df $= (r-1)(c-1) = (6-1)(2-1) = 5$. From Table VI, Appendix B, $\chi^2_{.01} = 15.0863$. The rejection region is $\chi^2 > 15.0863$.

Since the observed value of the test statistic falls in the rejection region ($\chi^2 = 48.0978 > 15.0863$), H_0 is rejected. There is sufficient evidence to indicate that the proportions of censored measurements differ for the six tractor lines at $\alpha = .01$.

c. Even though there are differences in the proportions of censored data among the 6 tractor lines, these proportions range from .028 to .050. In practice, there is very little difference between .028 and .050.

9.27   To determine if Defect and Pred_EVG are dependent, we test:

H_0: Defect and Pred_EVG are independent
H_a: Defect and Pred_EVG are dependent

The test statistic is $\chi^2 = 1.188$.

Since no α level was given, we will use $\alpha = .05$. The rejection region requires $\alpha = .05$ in the upper tail of the χ^2 distribution with df $= (r-1)(c-1) = (2-1)(2-1) = 1$. From Table VI, Appendix B, $\chi^2_{.05} = 3.84146$. The rejection region is $\chi^2 > 3.84146$.

Since the observed value of the test statistic does not fall in the rejection region ($\chi^2 = 1.188 \not> 3.84146$), H_0 is not rejected. There is insufficient evidence to indicate that Defect and Pred_EVG are dependent at $\alpha = .05$. If Defect and Pred_EVG are independent, then the Pred_EVG is no better predicting defects than just guessing. I would not recommend the essential complexity algorithm be used as a predictor of defective software modules.

9.29   Some preliminary calculations are:

$$\hat{E}_{11} = \frac{R_1 C_1}{n} = \frac{32(32)}{96} = 10.667 \qquad \hat{E}_{12} = \frac{R_1 C_2}{n} = \frac{32(64)}{96} = 21.333$$

$$\hat{E}_{21} = \frac{R_2 C_1}{n} = \frac{32(32)}{96} = 10.667 \qquad \hat{E}_{22} = \frac{R_2 C_2}{n} = \frac{32(64)}{96} = 21.333$$

$$\hat{E}_{31} = \frac{R_3 C_1}{n} = \frac{32(32)}{96} = 10.667 \qquad \hat{E}_{32} = \frac{R_3 C_2}{n} = \frac{32(64)}{96} = 21.333$$

To determine if the proportion of subjects who selected menus consistent with the theory depends on goal condition, we test:

H_0: Goal condition and Consistent with theory are independent
H_a: Goal condition and Consistent with theory are dependent

The test statistic is

$$\chi^2 = \sum\sum \frac{\left[n_{ij} - \hat{E}_{ij}\right]^2}{\hat{E}_{ij}} = \frac{(15-10.667)^2}{10.667} + \frac{(17-21.333)^2}{21.333} + \frac{(14-10.667)^2}{10.667} + \frac{(18-21.333)^2}{21.333}$$

$$+ \frac{(3-10.667)^2}{10.667} + \frac{(29-21.333)^2}{21.333} = 12.469$$

The rejection region requires $\alpha = .01$ in the upper tail of the χ^2 distribution with df $= (r-1)(c-1)$ $= (3-1)(2-1) = 2$. From Table VI, Appendix B, $\chi^2_{.01} = 9.21034$. The rejection region is $\chi^2 > 9.21034$.

Since the observed value of the test statistic falls in the rejection region ($\chi^2 = 12.469 > 9.21034$), H_0 is rejected. There is sufficient evidence to indicate that the proportion of subjects who selected menus consistent with the theory depends on goal   condition at $\alpha = .01$.

9.31   Using MINITAB, the results are:

Tabulated statistics: Instruction, Strategy

```
Rows: Instruction   Columns: Strategy

              Guess    Other    TTBC     All

Cue              5        6       13      24
             20.83    25.00    54.17   100.00
             35.71    35.29    76.47    50.00

Pattern          9       11        4      24
             37.50    45.83    16.67   100.00
             64.29    64.71    23.53    50.00

All             14       17       17      48
             29.17    35.42    35.42   100.00
            100.00   100.00   100.00   100.00

Cell Contents:        Count
                      % of Row
                      % of Column
```

```
Pearson Chi-Square = 7.378, DF = 2, P-Value = 0.025
Likelihood Ratio Chi-Square = 7.668, DF = 2, P-Value = 0.022
```

To determine if the choice of heuristic strategy depends on type of instruction, we test:
H_0: Heuristic strategy and type of instruction are independent
H_a: Heuristic strategy and type of instruction are dependent

From the printout, the test statistic is $\chi^2 = 7.378$ and the p-value is $p = .025$.
Since the p-value is less than $\alpha (p = .025 < .05)$, H_0 is rejected. There is sufficient evidence to indicate the choice of heuristic strategy depends on type of instruction at $\alpha = .05$.

Since the p-value is not less than $\alpha (p = .025 \not< .01)$, H_0 is not rejected. There is insufficient evidence to indicate the choice of heuristic strategy depends on type of instruction at $\alpha = .01$.

9.33   a.   To determine if the vaccine is effective in treating the MN strain of HIV, we test:

H_0: Vaccine status and MN strain are independent
H_a: Vaccine status and MN strain are dependent

The test statistic is $\chi^2 = 4.411$ (from the printout)

The p-value is .036. Since the p-value is less than $\alpha = .05$, H_0 is rejected. There is sufficient evidence to indicate that the vaccine is effective in treating the MN strain of HIV at $\alpha = .05$.

b.   We must assume that we have a random sample from the population of interest. We cannot really check this assumption. The second assumption is that all expected cell counts will be 5 or more. In this case, since there are only 7 observations in the second row, there is no way that the expected cell counts in that row will both be 5 or more (the sum of the expected cell counts in the row must sum to the observed row total).

c. $$\frac{\binom{7}{2}\binom{31}{22}}{\binom{38}{24}} = \frac{\frac{7!}{2!(7-2)!}\cdot\frac{31!}{22!(31-22)!}}{\frac{38!}{24!(38-24)!}} = \frac{\frac{7\cdot6\cdots1}{2\cdot5\cdot4\cdot3\cdot2\cdot1}\cdot\frac{31\cdot30\cdots1}{22\cdot21\cdots1\cdot9\cdot8\cdots1}}{\frac{38\cdot37\cdots1}{24\cdot23\cdots1\cdot14\cdot13\cdots1}} = .04378$$

d.   Table 1:

$$\frac{\binom{7}{1}\binom{31}{23}}{\binom{38}{24}} = \frac{\dfrac{7!}{1!(7-1)!}\dfrac{31!}{23!(31-23)!}}{\dfrac{38!}{24!(38-24)!}} = \frac{\dfrac{7\cdot6\cdots1}{1\cdot6\cdot5\cdot4\cdot3\cdot2\cdot1}\dfrac{31\cdot30\cdots1}{23\cdot22\cdots1\cdot8\cdot7\cdots1}}{\dfrac{38\cdot37\cdots1}{24\cdot23\cdots1\cdot14\cdot13\cdots1}} = .00571$$

Table 2:

$$\frac{\binom{7}{0}\binom{31}{24}}{\binom{38}{24}} = \frac{\dfrac{7!}{0!(7-0)!}\dfrac{31!}{24!(31-24)!}}{\dfrac{38!}{24!(38-24)!}} = \frac{\dfrac{7\cdot6\cdots1}{1\cdot7\cdot6\cdot5\cdot4\cdot3\cdot2\cdot1}\dfrac{31\cdot30\cdots1}{24\cdot23\cdots1\cdot7\cdot6\cdots1}}{\dfrac{38\cdot37\cdots1}{24\cdot23\cdots1\cdot14\cdot13\cdots1}} = .00027$$

e.   The *p*-value is .04378 + .00571 + .00027 = .04976. Since the p-value is less than $\alpha = .05$, H_0 is rejected. There is sufficient evidence to indicate that the vaccine is effective in treating the MN strain of HIV at $\alpha = .05$.

9.35   a.   Some preliminary calculations are:
        If all the categories are equally likely,

$$p_{1,0} = p_{2,0} = p_{3,0} = p_{4,0} = p_{5,0} = .2$$

$$E_1 = E_2 = E_3 = E_4 = E_5 = np_{1,0} = 150(.2) = 30$$

To determine if the categories are not equally likely, we test:

H_0: $p_1 = p_2 = p_3 = p_4 = p_5 = .2$
H_a: At least one probability is different from .2

The test statistic is $\chi^2 = \sum \dfrac{[n_i - E_i]^2}{E_i}$

$$= \frac{(28-30)^2}{30} + \frac{(35-30)^2}{30} + \frac{(33-30)^2}{30} + \frac{(25-30)^2}{30} + \frac{(29-30)^2}{30} = 2.133$$

The rejection region requires $\alpha = .10$ in the upper tail of the χ^2 distribution with df = $k - 1 = 5 - 1 = 4$. From Table VI, Appendix B, $\chi^2_{.10} = 7.77944$. The rejection region is $\chi^2 > 7.77944$.

Since the observed value of the test statistic does not fall in the rejection region ($\chi^2 = 2.133 \not> 7.77944$), H_0 is not rejected. There is insufficient evidence to indicate the categories are not equally likely at $\alpha = .10$.

b. $\hat{p}_2 = \dfrac{35}{150} = .233$

For confidence coefficient .90, $\alpha = .10$ and $\alpha/2 = .05$. From Table IV, Appendix B, $z_{.05} = 1.645$. The confidence interval is:

$$\hat{p}_2 \pm z_{.05}\sqrt{\frac{\hat{p}_2\hat{q}_2}{n_2}} \Rightarrow .233 \pm 1.645\sqrt{\frac{.233(.767)}{150}} \Rightarrow .233 \pm .057 \Rightarrow (.176, .290)$$

9.37   a.   To determine if the opinions are not evenly divided on the issue of national health insurance, we test:

H_0: $p_1 = p_2 = p_3 = 1/3$
H_a: At least one p_i differs from its hypothesized value.

b.   The test statistic is $\chi^2 = 87.74$ (from the printout)

The observed p-value is $p = .0000$. Since the observed p-value is less than α ($p = .0000 < \alpha = .01$), H_0 is rejected. There is sufficient evidence to indicate the opinions are not evenly divided on the issue of national health insurance at $\alpha = .01$.

c.   Let p_1 = proportion of heads of household in the U.S. population that favor national health insurance. Some preliminary calculations are:

$$\hat{p}_1 = \frac{n_1}{n} = \frac{234}{434} = .539$$

For confidence coefficient .95, $\alpha = .05$ and $\alpha/2 = .05/2 = .025$. From Table IV, Appendix B, $z_{.025} = 1.96$. The 95% confidence interval is:

$$\hat{p}_1 \pm z_{.025}\sqrt{\frac{\hat{p}_1(1-\hat{p}_1)}{n}} \Rightarrow .539 \pm 1.96\sqrt{\frac{.539(1-.539)}{434}}$$
$$\Rightarrow .539 \pm .047 \Rightarrow (.492, .586)$$

We are 95% confident that the true proportion of heads of household in the U.S. population that favor national health insurance is between .492 and .586.

9.39   Some preliminary calculations:

$$\hat{E}_{11} = \frac{R_1 C_1}{n} = \frac{2,359(1,712)}{5,026} = 803.543 \qquad \hat{E}_{12} = \frac{R_1 C_2}{n} = \frac{2,359(3,314)}{5,026} = 1,555.457$$

$$\hat{E}_{21} = \frac{R_2 C_1}{n} = \frac{2,667(1,712)}{5,026} = 908.457 \qquad \hat{E}_{22} = \frac{R_2 C_2}{n} = \frac{2,667(3,314)}{5,026} = 1,758.543$$

To determine if travelers who use the Internet to search for travel information are likely to be people who are college educated, we test:

H_0: Education and use of Internet for travel information are independent
H_a: Education and use of Internet for travel information are dependent

The test statistic is $\chi^2 = \sum\sum \dfrac{[n_{ij} - \hat{E}_{ij}]^2}{\hat{E}_{ij}}$

$$= \frac{(1,072 - 803.543)^2}{803.543} + \frac{(1,287 - 1,555.457)^2}{1,555.457} + \frac{(640 - 908.547)^2}{908.457} + \frac{(2,027 - 1,758.543)^2}{1,758.543}$$
$$= 256.336$$

The rejection region requires $\alpha = .05$ in the upper tail of the χ^2 distribution with df $= (r-1)(c-1) = (2-1)(2-1) = 1$. From Table VI, Appendix B, $\chi^2_{.05} = 3.84146$. The rejection region is $\chi^2 > 3.84146$.

Since the observed value of the test statistic falls in the rejection region ($\chi^2 = 256.336 > 3.814146$), H_0 is rejected. There is sufficient evidence to indicate that travelers who use the Internet to search for travel information and level of education are dependent at $\alpha = .05$. Since the proportion of college educated who use the Internet to search for travel information ($1072/2359 = .45$) is greater than the proportion of less than college educated ($640/2667 = .24$), the conclusion supports the researchers claim that travelers who use the Internet to search for travel information are likely to be people who are college educated.

The necessary assumptions are
1. The k observed counts are a random sample from the populations of interest.
2. The sample size, n, will be large enough so that, for every cell, the expected count, E_{ij}, will be equal to 5 or more.

9.41   a.   Some preliminary calculations are:

$$\hat{E}_{11} = \frac{R_1 C_1}{n} = \frac{53(35)}{70} = 26.5 \qquad \hat{E}_{13} = \frac{R_1 C_2}{n} = \frac{53(35)}{70} = 26.5$$

$$\hat{E}_{21} = \frac{R_2 C_1}{n} = \frac{17(35)}{70} = 8.5 \qquad \hat{E}_{22} = \frac{R_2 C_2}{n} = \frac{17(35)}{70} = 8.5$$

To determine if the severity of the ethical issue influenced whether the issue was identified or not by the auditors, we test:

H_0: Severity of ethical issue and identification are independent
H_a: Severity of ethical issue and identification are dependent

The test statistic is $\chi^2 = \sum \sum \dfrac{\left[n_{ij} - \hat{E}_{ij} \right]^2}{\hat{E}_{ij}}$

$$= \frac{(27 - 26.5)^2}{26.5} + \frac{(26 - 26.5)^2}{26.5} + \frac{(8 - 8.5)^2}{8.5} + \frac{(9 - 8.5)^2}{8.5} = .078$$

The rejection region requires $\alpha = .05$ in the upper tail of the χ^2 distribution with df $= (r - 1)(c - 1) = (2 - 1)(2 - 1) = 1$. From Table VI, Appendix B, $\chi^2_{.05} = 3.84146$. The rejection region is $\chi^2 > 3.84146$.

Since the observed value of the test statistic does not fall in the rejection region ($\chi^2 = .078 \not> 3.84146$), H_0 is not rejected. There is insufficient evidence to indicate that the severity of the ethical issue influenced whether the issue was identified or not by the auditors at $\alpha = .05$.

b.   No. If there were 0 in the bottom cell of the column, then the expected count for that cell will be less than 5. One of the assumptions necessary for the test statistic to have a χ^2 distribution will not hold.

c.   Suppose we change the numbers in the table to be as follows:

	Severity of Ethical Issue	
	Moderate	**Severe**
Ethical Issue Identified	32	21
Ethical Issue Not Identified	3	14

Since the row and column totals are the same, the expected cell counts are the same as above.

The test statistic is $\chi^2 = \sum \sum \dfrac{\left[n_{ij} - \hat{E}_{ij} \right]^2}{\hat{E}_{ij}}$

$$= \frac{(32-26.5)^2}{26.5} + \frac{(21-26.5)^2}{26.5} + \frac{(3-8.5)^2}{8.5} + \frac{(14-8.5)^2}{8.5} = 9.401$$

Now the test statistic would fall in the rejection region.

9.43 Some preliminary calculations are:

$E_1 = E_2 = E_3 = E_4 = E_5 = np_{1,0} = 95(.20) = 19$

To determine if the true percentages of ADEs in the five "cause" categories are different, we test:

H_0: $p_1 = p_2 = p_3 = p_4 = p_5 = .2$
H_a: At least one proportion differs from .2

The test statistic is

$$\chi^2 = \sum \frac{[n_i - E_i]^2}{E_i} = \frac{(29-19)^2}{19} + \frac{(17-19)^2}{19} + \frac{(17-19)^2}{19} + \frac{(17-19)^2}{19} + \frac{(17-19)^2}{19} = 16$$

The rejection region requires $\alpha = .10$ in the upper tail of the χ^2 distribution with df $= k - 1 = 5 - 1 = 4$. From Table VI, Appendix B, $\chi^2_{.10} = 7.77944$. The rejection region is $\chi^2 > 7.77944$.

Since the observed value of the test statistic falls in the rejection region ($\chi^2 = 16 > 7.77944$), H_0 is rejected. There is sufficient evidence to indicate that the true percentages of ADEs in the five "cause" categories are different at $\alpha = .10$.

9.45 a. The contingency table is:

		Committee		Totals
		Acceptable	Rejected	
Inspector	Acceptable	101	23	124
	Rejected	10	19	29
	Totals	111	42	153

b. Yes. To plot the percentages, first convert frequencies to percentages by dividing the numbers in each column by the column total and multiplying by 100. Also, divide the row totals by the overall total and multiply by 100.

		Acceptable	Rejected	Totals
Inspector	Acceptable	$\frac{101}{111} \cdot 100 = 90.99\%$	$\frac{23}{42} \cdot 100 = 54.76\%$	$\frac{124}{153} \cdot 100 = 81.05\%$
	Rejected	$\frac{10}{111} \cdot 100 = 9.01\%$	$\frac{19}{42} \cdot 100 = 45.23\%$	$\frac{29}{153} \cdot 100 = 18.95\%$

Using MINITAB, the graph of the data is:

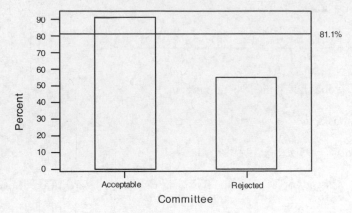

From the plot, it appears there is a relationship.

c. Some preliminary calculations are:

$$\hat{E}_{11} = \frac{R_1 C_1}{n_1} = \frac{124(111)}{153} = 89.691 \qquad \hat{E}_{21} = \frac{R_1 C_2}{n_1} = \frac{124(42)}{153} = 34.039$$

$$\hat{E}_{21} = \frac{R_2 C_1}{n_1} = \frac{29(111)}{153} = 21.039 \qquad \hat{E}_{22} = \frac{R_2 C_2}{n_1} = \frac{29(42)}{153} = 7.961$$

To determine if the inspector's classifications and the committee's classifications are related, we test:

H_0: The inspector's and committee's classification are independent
H_a: The inspector's and committee's classifications are dependent

The test statistic is $\chi^2 = \sum \sum \dfrac{\left[n_{ij} - \hat{E}_{ij} \right]^2}{\hat{E}_{ij}}$

$$= \frac{(101 - 89.961)^2}{89.961} + \frac{(23 - 34.039)^2}{34.039} + \frac{(10 - 21.039)^2}{21.039} + \frac{(19 - 7.961)^2}{7.961}$$
$$= 26.034$$

The rejection region requires $\alpha = .05$ in the upper tail of the χ^2 distribution with df = $(r-1)(c-1) = (2-1)(2-1) = 1$. From Table VI, Appendix B, $\chi^2_{.05} = 3.84146$. The rejection region is $\chi^2 > 3.84146$.

Since the observed value of the test statistic falls in the rejection region ($\chi^2 = 26.034 > 3.84146$), H_0 is rejected. There is sufficient evidence to indicate the inspector's and committee's classifications are related at $\alpha = .05$. This indicates that the inspector and committee tend to make the same decisions.

9.47 a. Some preliminary calculations are:

$E_1 = np_{1,0} = 19,115(.2010) = 3,842.115$
$En_2 = np_{2,0} = 19,115(.1010) = 1,930.615$
$En_3 = np_{3,0} = 19,115(.0542) = 1,036.033$
$En_4 = np_{4,0} = 19,115(.1601) = 3,060.3115$
$En_5 = np_{5,0} = 19,115(.2865) = 5,476.4475$
$En_6 = np_{6,0} = 19,115(.1238) = 2,366.437$
$En_7 = np_{7,0} = 19,115(.0732) = 1,399.218$

To determine if there is evidence to conclude that the purchases of the household panel is representative of the population of households, we test:

H_0: $p_1 = .201, p_2 = .101, p_3 = .0542, p_4 = .1601, p_5 = .2865, p_6 = .1238, p_7 = .0732$
H_a: At least one p_i does not equal its hypothesized value

The test statistic is $\chi^2 = \sum \dfrac{[n_i - E_i]^2}{E_i}$

$$= \frac{(3,165 - 3,842.115)^2}{3,842.115} + \frac{(1,892 - 1,930.615)^2}{1,930.615} + \frac{(726 - 1,036.033)^2}{1,036.033}$$

$$+ \frac{(4,079 - 3,060.3115)^2}{3,060.3115} + \frac{(6,206 - 5,476.4475)^2}{5,476.4475} + \frac{(1,627 - 2,366.437)^2}{2,366.437}$$

$$+ \frac{(1,420 - 1,399.218)^2}{1,399.218} = 880.521$$

The rejection region requires $\alpha = .05$ in the upper tail of the χ^2 distribution with df = $k - 1 = 7 - 1 = 6$. From Table VI, Appendix B, $\chi^2_{.05} = 12.5916$. The rejection region is $\chi^2 > 12.5916$.

Since the observed value of the test statistic falls in the rejection region ($\chi^2 = 880.521 > 12.5916$), H_0 is rejected. There is sufficient evidence to indicate that the purchases of the household panel is not representative of the population of households at $\alpha = .05$.

b. We must assume that:

1. A multinomial experiment was conducted. This is generally satisfied by taking a random sample from the population of interest.
2. The sample size n will be large enough so that, for every cell, the expected cell count, $E(n_i)$, will be equal to 5 or more.

c. From Table VI, Appendix B, with df = 6, the p-value = $P(\chi^2 > 880.521) < .005$.

9.49 a. The contingency table is:

Altitude	Flight Response		Totals
	Low	High	
< 300	85	105	190
300-600	77	121	198
≥ 600	17	59	76
Totals	179	285	464

b.   Some preliminary calculations are:

$$\hat{E}_{11} = \frac{R_1 C_1}{n} = \frac{190(179)}{464} = 73.297 \qquad \hat{E}_{12} = \frac{R_1 C_2}{n} = \frac{190(285)}{464} = 116.703$$

$$\hat{E}_{21} = \frac{R_2 C_1}{n} = \frac{198(179)}{464} = 76.384 \qquad \hat{E}_{22} = \frac{R_2 C_2}{n} = \frac{198(285)}{464} = 121.616$$

$$\hat{E}_{31} = \frac{R_3 C_1}{n} = \frac{76(179)}{464} = 29.319 \qquad \hat{E}_{32} = \frac{R_3 C_2}{n} = \frac{76(285)}{464} = 46.681$$

To determine if flight response of the geese depends on the altitude of the helicopter, we test:

H_0: Flight response and Altitude of helicopter are independent
H_a: Flight response and Altitude of helicopter are dependent

The test statistic is

$$\chi^2 = \sum \sum \frac{\left[n_{ij} - \hat{E}_{ij} \right]^2}{\hat{E}_{ij}}$$

$$= \frac{(85 - 73.297)^2}{73.297} + \frac{(105 - 116.703)^2}{116.703} + \frac{(77 - 76.384)^2}{76.384} + \frac{(121 - 121.616)^2}{121.616}$$

$$+ \frac{(17 - 29.319)^2}{29.319} + \frac{(59 - 46.681)^2}{46.681}$$

$$= 11.477$$

The rejection region requires $\alpha = .01$ in the upper tail of the χ^2 distribution with df $= (r - 1)(c - 1) = (3 - 1)(2 - 1) = 2$. From Table VI, Appendix B, $\chi^2_{.01} = 9.21034$. The rejection region is $\chi^2 > 9.21034$.

Since the observed value of the test statistic falls in the rejection region ($\chi^2 = 11.477 > 9.21034$), H_0 is rejected. There is sufficient evidence to indicate that the flight response of the geese depends on the altitude of the helicopter at $\alpha = .01$.

c.   The contingency table is:

Lateral Distance	Flight Response		Totals
	Low	High	
< 1000	37	243	280
1000-2000	68	37	105
2000-3000	44	4	48
≥ 3000	30	1	31
Totals	179	285	464

d.   Some preliminary calculations are:

$$\hat{E}_{11} = \frac{R_1 C_1}{n} = \frac{280(179)}{464} = 108.017 \qquad \hat{E}_{12} = \frac{R_1 C_2}{n} = \frac{280(285)}{464} = 171.983$$

$$\hat{E}_{21} = \frac{R_2 C_1}{n} = \frac{105(179)}{464} = 40.506 \qquad \hat{E}_{22} = \frac{R_2 C_2}{n} = \frac{105(285)}{464} = 64.494$$

$$\hat{E}_{31} = \frac{R_3 C_1}{n} = \frac{48(179)}{464} = 18.517 \qquad \hat{E}_{32} = \frac{R_3 C_2}{n} = \frac{48(285)}{464} = 29.483$$

$$\hat{E}_{41} = \frac{R_4 C_1}{n} = \frac{31(179)}{464} = 11.959 \qquad \hat{E}_{42} = \frac{R_4 C_2}{n} = \frac{31(285)}{464} = 19.041$$

To determine if flight response of the geese depends on the lateral distance of the helicopter, we test:

H_0: Flight response and Lateral distance of the helicopter are independent
H_a: Flight response and Lateral distance of the helicopter are dependent

The test statistic is

$$\chi^2 = \sum\sum \frac{\left[n_{ij} - \hat{E}_{ij} \right]^2}{\hat{E}_{ij}}$$

$$= \frac{(37 - 108.017)^2}{108.017} + \frac{(243 - 171.983)^2}{171.983} + \frac{(68 - 40.506)^2}{40.506} + \frac{(37 - 64.494)^2}{64.494}$$

$$+ \frac{(44 - 18.517)^2}{18.517} + \frac{(4 - 29.494)^2}{29.494} + \frac{(30 - 11.959)^2}{11.959} + \frac{(1 - 19.041)^2}{19.041}$$

$$= 207.814$$

The rejection region requires $\alpha = .01$ in the upper tail of the χ^2 distribution with $df = (r - 1)(c - 1) = (4 - 1)(2 - 1) = 3$. From Table VI, Appendix B, $\chi^2_{.01} = 11.3449$. The rejection region is $\chi^2 > 11.3449$.

Since the observed value of the test statistic falls in the rejection region ($\chi^2 = 207.814 > 11.3449$), H_0 is rejected. There is sufficient evidence to indicate that the flight response of the geese depends on the lateral distance of the helicopter at $\alpha = .01$.

e.   Using SAS, the contingency table for altitude by response with the column percents is:

```
                        Table of ALTGRP by RESPONSE

             ALTGRP      RESPONSE

             Frequency|
             Percent  |
             Row Pct  |
             Col Pct  | LOW     |HIGH     |  Total
             ---------+---------+---------+
             <300     |      85 |     105 |     190
                      |   18.32 |   22.63 |   40.95
                      |   44.74 |   55.26 |
                      |   47.49 |   36.84 |
             ---------+---------+---------+
             300-600  |      77 |     121 |     198
                      |   16.59 |   26.08 |   42.67
                      |   38.89 |   61.11 |
                      |   43.02 |   42.46 |
             ---------+---------+---------+
             600+     |      17 |      59 |      76
                      |    3.66 |   12.72 |   16.38
                      |   22.37 |   77.63 |
                      |    9.50 |   20.70 |
             ---------+---------+---------+
             Total           179       285       464
                           38.58     61.42    100.00


        Statistics for Table of ALTGRP by RESPONSE

          Statistic                     DF       Value      Prob
          ------------------------------------------------------
          Chi-Square                     2     11.4770    0.0032
          Likelihood Ratio Chi-Square    2     12.1040    0.0024
          Mantel-Haenszel Chi-Square     1     10.2104    0.0014
          Phi Coefficient                       0.1573
          Contingency Coefficient               0.1554
          Cramer's V                            0.1573

                     Sample Size = 464
```

From the row percents, it appears that the lower the plane, the lower the response. For altitude <300m, 55.26% of the geese had a high response. For altitude 300-600m, 61.11% of the geese had a high response. For altitude 600+m, 77.63% of the geese had a high response. Thus, instead of setting a minimum altitude for the planes, we need to set a maximum altitude. For this data, the lowest response is at an altitude of < 300 meters.

Using SAS, the contingency table for lateral distance by response with the column percents is:

```
                     The FREQ Procedure

                 Table of LATGRP by RESPONSE

         LATGRP      RESPONSE

         Frequency |
         Percent   |
         Row Pct   |
         Col Pct   |LOW      |HIGH     |  Total
         ----------+---------+---------+
         <1000     |      37 |     242 |     279
                   |    7.99 |   52.27 |   60.26
                   |   13.26 |   86.74 |
                   |   20.67 |   85.21 |
         ----------+---------+---------+
         1000-2000 |      68 |      37 |     105
                   |   14.69 |    7.99 |   22.68
                   |   64.76 |   35.24 |
                   |   37.99 |   13.03 |
         ----------+---------+---------+
         2000-3000 |      44 |       4 |      48
                   |    9.50 |    0.86 |   10.37
                   |   91.67 |    8.33 |
                   |   24.58 |    1.41 |
         ----------+---------+---------+
         3000+     |      30 |       1 |      31
                   |    6.48 |    0.22 |    6.70
                   |   96.77 |    3.23 |
                   |   16.76 |    0.35 |
         ----------+---------+---------+
         Total            179       284       463
                        38.66     61.34    100.00

                     Frequency Missing = 1


             Statistics for Table of LATGRP by RESPONSE

         Statistic                      DF      Value       Prob
         ------------------------------------------------------------
         Chi-Square                      3     207.0800    <.0001
         Likelihood Ratio Chi-Square     3     226.8291    <.0001
         Mantel-Haenszel Chi-Square      1     189.2843    <.0001
         Phi Coefficient                        0.6688
         Contingency Coefficient                0.5559
         Cramer's V                             0.6688

                 Effective Sample Size = 463
                     Frequency Missing = 1
```

From the row percents, it appears that the greater the lateral distance, the lower the response. For a lateral distance of 3000+m only 3.23% of the geese had a high response. Thus, the further away the plane is laterally, the lower the response. For this data, the lowest response is when the plane is further than 3000 meters.

Thus the recommendation would be a maximum height of 300 m and a minimum lateral distance of 3000 m.

9.51   a. $\chi^2 = \sum \dfrac{[n_i - E_i]^2}{E_i}$

$$= \frac{(26-23)^2}{23} + \frac{(146-136)^2}{136} + \frac{(361-341)^2}{341} + \frac{(143-136)^2}{136} + \frac{(13-23)^2}{23}$$

$$= 9.647$$

   b.   From Table VI, Appendix B, with df $= 5$, $\chi^2_{.05} = 11.0705$

c.   No. $\chi^2 = 9.647 \not> 11.0705$. Do not reject H_0. There is insufficient evidence to indicate the salary distribution is nonnormal for $\alpha = .05$.

d.   The p-value $= P(\chi^2 \geq 9.647)$.

Using Table VI, Appendix B, with df = 5,

$.05 < P(\chi^2 \geq 9.647) < .10$.

9.53   Using SAS, the output is:

```
                            The FREQ Procedure

                        Table of CANDIDATE by TIME

            CANDIDATE      TIME

            Frequency|
            Col Pct  |       1|       2|       3|       4|       5|       6| Total
            ---------+--------+--------+--------+--------+--------+--------+
            SMITH    |     208|     208|     451|     392|     351|     410|  2020
                     |   52.53|   55.32|   55.34|   55.92|   56.16|   55.33|
            ---------+--------+--------+--------+--------+--------+--------+
            COPPIN   |      55|      51|     109|      98|      88|     104|   505
                     |   13.89|   13.56|   13.37|   13.98|   14.08|   14.04|
            ---------+--------+--------+--------+--------+--------+--------+
            MONTES   |     133|     117|     255|     211|     186|     227|  1129
                     |   33.59|   31.12|   31.29|   30.10|   29.76|   30.63|
            ---------+--------+--------+--------+--------+--------+--------+
            Total         396      376      815      701      625      741   3654


                 Statistics for Table of CANDIDATE by TIME

            Statistic                     DF       Value      Prob
            ------------------------------------------------------------
            Chi-Square                    10      2.2839    0.9937
            Likelihood Ratio Chi-Square   10      2.2722    0.9938
            Mantel-Haenszel Chi-Square     1      0.9851    0.3209
            Phi Coefficient                       0.0250
            Contingency Coefficient               0.0250
            Cramer's V                            0.0177

                         Sample Size = 3654

    To determine if candidates received votes independent of time period, we test:
```

H_0: Voting and Time period are independent
H_a: Voting and Time period are dependent

The test statistic is $\chi^2 = 2.2839$.

Since no value of α was given, we will use $\alpha = .05$. The rejection region requires $\alpha = .05$ in the upper tail of the χ^2 distribution with df $= (r-1)(c-1) = (3-1)(6-1) = 10$. From Table VI, Appendix B, $\chi^2_{.05} = 18.3070$. The rejection region is $\chi^2 > 18.3070$.

Since the observed value of the test statistic does not fall in the rejection region ($\chi^2 = 2.2839 \not> 18.3070$), H_0 is not rejected. There is insufficient evidence to indicate Voting and Time period are dependent at $\alpha = .05$. Thus, we can conclude that voting and time period are independent. This means that regardless of time period, the percentage of votes received by each candidate is the same. In the table created by SAS, the bottom number in each cell is the column percent. This is the percent of votes received by the candidate in each time period. An inspection of these percents indicates that candidate Smith received approximately 55.3% of the votes each time period, candidate Coppin received approximately 13.8% of the vote, and candidate Montes received approximately 30.9% of the vote. All of this indicates that the election was rigged.

Chapter 10
Simple Linear Regression

10.1   a.

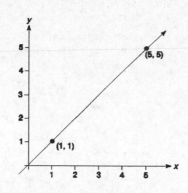

b.

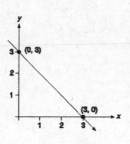

c.

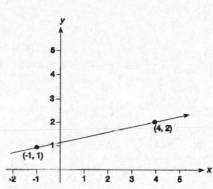

d.

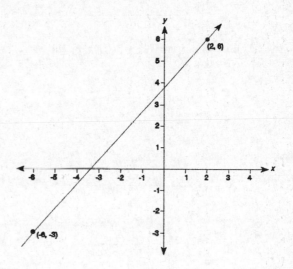

10.3   The two equations are:

$$4 = \beta_0 + \beta_1(-2) \text{ and } 6 = \beta_0 + \beta_1(4)$$

Subtracting the first equation from the second, we get

$$6 = \beta_0 + 4\beta_1$$
$$-(4 = \beta_0 - 2\beta_1)$$
$$\overline{}$$
$$2 = \quad 6\beta_1 \;\Rightarrow\; \beta_1 = \frac{1}{3}$$

Substituting $\beta_1 = $ into the first equation, we get:

$$4 = \beta_0 + \;\Rightarrow\; \beta_0 = 4 + \frac{2}{3} = \frac{14}{3}$$

The equation for the line is $y = \dfrac{14}{3} + \dfrac{1}{3}x$.

10.5   To graph a line, we need two points. Pick two values for x, and find the corresponding y values by substituting the values of x into the equation.

a.   Let $x = 0 \Rightarrow y = 4 + (0) = 4$
and $x = 2 \Rightarrow y = 4 + (2) = 6$

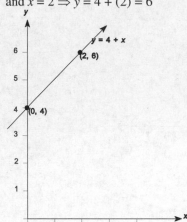

b.   Let $x = 0 \Rightarrow y = 5 - 2(0) = 5$
and $x = 2 \Rightarrow y = 5 - 2(2) = 1$

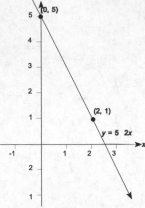

c.   Let $x = 0 \Rightarrow y = -4 + 3(0) = -4$ and $x = 2 \Rightarrow$
$y = -4 + 3(2) = 2$

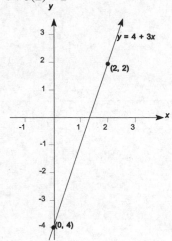

d.   Let $x = 0 \Rightarrow y = -2(0) = 0$
and $x = 2 \Rightarrow y = -2(2) = -4$

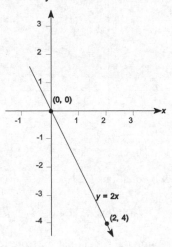

e.   Let $x = 0 \Rightarrow y = 0$
and $x = 2 \Rightarrow y = 2$

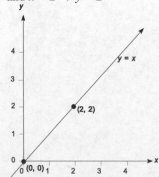

f.   Let $x = 0 \Rightarrow y = .5 + 1.5(0) = .5$
and $x = 2 \Rightarrow y = .5 + 1.5(2) = 3.5$

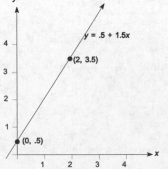

10.7   A deterministic model does not allow for random error or variation, whereas a probabilistic model does. An example where a deterministic model would be appropriate is:

Let y = cost of a 2×4 piece of lumber and
  x = length (in feet)

The model would be $y = \beta_1 x$. There should be no variation in price for the same length of wood.

An example where a probabilistic model would be appropriate is:

Let y = sales per month of a commodity and
  x = amount of money spent advertising

The model would be $y = \beta_0 + \beta_1 x + \varepsilon$. The sales per month will probably vary even if the amount of money spent on advertising remains the same.

10.9   No. The random error component, ε, allows the values of the variable to fall above or below the line.

10.11   From Exercise 10.10, $\hat{\beta}_0 = 7.10$ and $\hat{\beta}_1 = -.78$.

The fitted line is $\hat{y} = 7.10 - .78x$. To obtain values for , we substitute values of x into the equation and solve for $\hat{y}$.

a.

x	y	$\hat{y} = 7.10 - .78x$	$(y - \hat{y})$	$(y - \hat{y})^2$
7	2	1.64	.36	.1296
4	4	3.98	.02	.0004
6	2	2.42	−.42	.1764
2	5	5.54	−.54	.2916
1	7	6.32	.68	.4624
1	6	6.32	−.32	.1024
3	5	4.76	.24	.0576

$$\sum (y - \hat{y}) = 0.02 \qquad \text{SSE} = \sum (y - \hat{y})^2 = 1.2204$$

b.

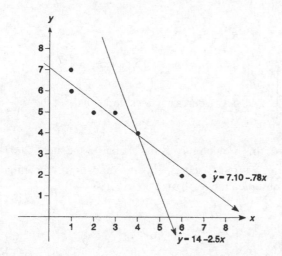

c.

x	y	$\hat{y} = 14 - 2.5x$	$(y - \hat{y})$	$(y - \hat{y})^2$
7	2	−3.5	5.5	30.25
4	4	4	0	0
6	2	−1	3	9
2	5	9	−4	16
1	7	11.5	−4.5	20.25
1	6	11.5	−5.5	30.25
3	5	6.5	−1.5	2.25

$$\sum (y - \hat{y}) = -7 \qquad SSE = 108.00$$

10.13   a.

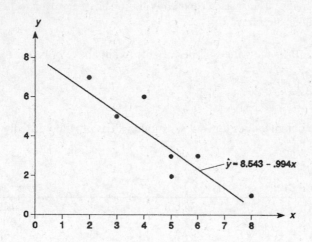

b.   Looking at the scattergram, x and y appear to have a negative linear relationship.

c.   From the printout, $\hat{\beta}_1 = -.9939$ and $\hat{\beta}_0 = 8.543$

d.   The least squares line is $\hat{y} = 8.543 - .994x$. The line is plotted in part **a**. It appears to fit the data well.

10.15   a.   The straight-line model would be: $y = \beta_o + \beta_1 x + \varepsilon$

b.   From the printout, the least squares line is: $\hat{y} = -146.856 + 1.144x$.

c.   Since range of observed values for the 2000 SAT scores (x) does not include 0, the y-intercept has no meaning.

d.   The slope of the line is β_1. In terms of this problem, β_1 is the change in the mean 2007 SAT score for each additional point increase in the 2000 SAT score. This interpretation is meaningful for values of x within the observed range. The observed range of x is 966 to 1,197.

10.17   a.   Some preliminary calculations are:

$$\sum x = 5.45 \qquad\qquad \sum y = 239 \qquad\qquad \sum xy = 237.1$$

$$\sum x^2 = 5.5075 \qquad\qquad \sum y^2 = 10,255$$

$$\bar{x} = \frac{\sum x}{n} = \frac{5.45}{6} = .908333333 \qquad\qquad \bar{y} = \frac{\sum y}{n} = \frac{239}{6} = 39.83333333$$

$$SS_{xy} = \sum xy - \frac{\left(\sum x\right)\left(\sum y\right)}{n} = 237.1 - \frac{5.45(239)}{6}$$
$$= 237.1 - 217.09166667 = 20.0083333$$

$$SS_{xx} = \sum x^2 - \frac{\left(\sum x\right)^2}{n} = 5.5075 - \frac{(5.45)^2}{6} = 5.5075 - 4.950416667 = .5570833333$$

$$\hat{\beta}_1 = \frac{SS_{xy}}{SS_{xx}} = \frac{20.0083333}{.5570833333} = 35.91623038 \approx 35.92$$

$$\hat{\beta}_o = \bar{y} - \hat{\beta}_1 \bar{x} = 39.8333333 - 35.91623038(.90833333) = 7.20942408 \approx 7.21$$

$$\hat{y} = 7.21 + 35.92x$$

     b.   Since 0 is not in the observed range of x (Surface Area to Volume), $\hat{\beta}_o$ has not meaning. $\hat{\beta}_1 = 35.92$. For each unit change in Surface Area to Volume, the mean Drug Release Rate is estimated to increase by 35.92.

     c.   For $x = .50$, $\hat{y} = 7.21 + 35.92(.50) = 25.17$

     d.   The reliability of the estimate in part c is in question. The value of x, .50, is outside the observed range of x. We have no idea what the relationship between y and x is outside the observed range.

10.19   a.   The straight line model would be: $E(y) = \beta_0 + \beta_1 x$

     b.   Some preliminary calculations are:

$$\sum x = 11,958 \qquad\qquad \sum y = 2,478.8 \qquad\qquad \sum xy = 739,647.16$$

$$\sum x^2 = 3,577,052.56 \qquad\qquad \sum y^2 = 154,676.28$$

$$\bar{x} = \frac{\sum x}{n} = \frac{11,958}{40} = 298.95 \qquad\qquad \bar{y} = \frac{\sum y}{n} = \frac{2,478.8}{40} = 61.97$$

$$SS_{xy} = \sum xy - \frac{\left(\sum x\right)\left(\sum y\right)}{n} = 739,647.16 - \frac{11,958(2,478.8)}{40} = -1,390.16$$

$$SS_{xx} = \sum x^2 - \frac{\left(\sum x\right)^2}{n} = 3,577,052.56 - \frac{11,958^2}{40} = 2,208.46$$

$$\hat{\beta}_1 = \frac{SS_{xy}}{SS_{xx}} = \frac{-1,390.16}{2,208.46} = -0.629443141 \approx -0.629$$

$$\hat{\beta}_0 = \bar{y} - \hat{\beta}_1 \bar{x} = 61.97 - (-0.629443141)(298.95) = 250.142027 \approx 250.14$$

$$\hat{y} = 250.14 - 0.629x$$

c. Since 0 is not in the observed range of x (distance), $\hat{\beta}_0$ has no meaning.

d. $\hat{\beta}_1 = -0.629$. For each unit increase in a golfer's average driving distance, the mean driving accuracy is estimated to decrease by 0.629.

e. The estimate of the slope will help determine if the golfer's concern is valid since it tells us the change in driving accuracy per unit change in driving distance.

10.21   a.   A proposed model is $E(y) = \beta_0 + \beta_1 x$.

b. (Note: There are 3 observations that have missing values on the Net Worth variable. Thus, only 47 observations are used.) Some preliminary calculations are:

$$\sum x = 337,059 \qquad \sum y = 34,290 \qquad \sum xy = 593,034,746$$

$$\sum x^2 = 12,725,850,505 \qquad \sum y^2 = 102,624,918$$

$$\bar{x} = \frac{\sum x}{n} = \frac{337,059}{47} = 7,171.468085 \qquad \bar{y} = \frac{\sum y}{n} = \frac{34,290}{47} = 729.5744681$$

$$SS_{xy} = \sum xy - \frac{\left(\sum x\right)\left(\sum y\right)}{n} = 593,034,746 - \frac{337,059(34,290)}{47}$$
$$= 593,034,746 - 245,909,640.6 = 347,124,105.4$$

$$SS_{xx} = \sum x^2 - \frac{\left(\sum x\right)^2}{n} = 12,725,850,505 - \frac{(337,059)^2}{47}$$
$$= 12,725,850,505 - 2,417,207,861 = 10,308,642,644$$

$$\hat{\beta}_1 = \frac{SS_{xy}}{SS_{xx}} = \frac{347,124,105.4}{10,308,642,644} = 0.033673212 \approx 0.034$$

$$\hat{\beta}_o = \bar{y} - \hat{\beta}_1 \bar{x} = 729.5744681 - (0.033673212)(7171.468085)$$
$$= 488.0881029 \approx 488.09$$

The fitted regression line is: $\hat{y} = 488.09 + 0.034x$

c. Using MINITAB, the fitted regression line is:

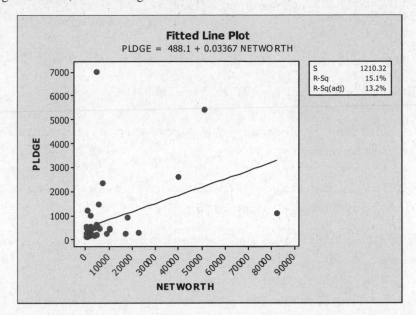

There does not appear to be much of a relationship between Net Worth and Amount Pledged. There is a very weak positive linear relationship between Net Worth and Amount Pledged.

d. $\hat{\beta}_o = 488.09$.   Since 0 is not in the range of observed values of Net Worth, the y-intercept has no meaning.

$\hat{\beta}_1 = 0.034$. For each additional million dollars of Net Worth, the mean Amount Pledged is estimated to increase by .034 million dollars.

10.23 a. We will select Average Salary as the dependent variable and Mean GMAT as the independent variable.

b. Some preliminary calculations are:

$$\sum x = 6,944 \qquad \sum y = 1,080,288 \qquad \sum xy = 751,698,490$$

$$\sum x^2 = 4,824,680 \qquad \sum y^2 = 118,151,669,430$$

$$\bar{x} = \frac{\sum x}{n} = \frac{6,944}{10} = 694.4 \qquad \bar{y} = \frac{\sum y}{n} = \frac{1,080,288}{10} = 108,028.8$$

$$SS_{xy} = \sum xy - \frac{\left(\sum x\right)\left(\sum y\right)}{n} = 751,698,490 - \frac{6,944(1,080,288)}{10}$$
$$= 751,698,490 - 75,015,987.2 = 1,546,502.8$$

$$SS_{xx} = \sum x^2 - \frac{\left(\sum x\right)^2}{n} = 4,824,680 - \frac{(6,944)^2}{10}$$
$$= 4,824,680 - 4,821,913.6 = 2,766.4$$

$$\hat{\beta_1} = \frac{SS_{xy}}{SS_{xx}} = \frac{1,546,502.8}{2,766.4} = 559.0307981 \approx 559.031$$

$$\hat{\beta_o} = \bar{y} - \hat{\beta_1}\bar{x} = 108,028.8 - (559.0307981)(694.4) = -280,162.1862 \approx -280,162.186$$

The fitted regression line is: $\hat{y} = -280,162.186 + 559.031x$

$\hat{\beta_o} = -280,162.186$.   Since 0 is not in the range of observed values of the variable Mean GMAT, the y-intercept has no meaning.

$\hat{\beta_1} = -0.271$.   For each additional point increase in the mean GMAT score, the mean value of Average Salary is estimated to increase by $559.031.

10.25   The graph in **b** would have the smallest s^2 because the width of the data points is the smallest.

10.27   a. $s^2 = \dfrac{SSE}{n-2} = \dfrac{8.34}{26-2} = .3475$

b.   We would expect most of the observations to be within $2s$ of the least squares line. This is:
$$2s = 2\sqrt{.3475} \approx 1.179$$

10.29   a.   From the printout, SSE = 20,608.39, s^2 = MSE = 420.58, and s = 20.51.

b. s = 20.51. We would expect approximately 95% of the observed values of y (2007 SAT Score) to fall within $2s$ or $2(20.51) = 41$ units of their least squares predicted values.

10.31   a.   From part **a** of Exercise 10.17, $SS_{xy} = 20.00833333$, $\sum y = 239$, $\sum y^2 = 10,255$, and $\hat{\beta_1} = 35.91623038$.

$$SS_{yy} = \sum y^2 - \frac{\left(\sum y\right)^2}{n} = 10,255 - \frac{(239)^2}{6}$$
$$= 10,255 - 9520.166667 = 734.8333333$$

$$SSE = SS_{yy} - \hat{\beta_1}SS_{xy} = 734.833333 - 35.91623068(20.00833333) = 16.2094179$$

$$s^2 = MSE = \frac{SSE}{n-2} = \frac{16.2094179}{6-2} = 4.052354475 \text{ and } s = \sqrt{4.052354475} = 2.01$$

b. s = 2.01. We would expect approximately 95% of the observed values of y (Drug release rate) to fall within $2s$ or $2(2.01) = 4.02$ units of their least squares predicted values.

10.33 a. From Exercise 10.20, $SS_{xy} = -130.44167$, $\hat{\beta}_1 = -.002310625$, $\sum y = 135.8$, and $\sum y^2 = 769.72$.

$$SS_{yy} = \sum y^2 - \frac{\left(\sum y\right)^2}{n} = 769.72 - \frac{(135.8)^2}{24}$$
$$= 769.72 - 768.4016667 = 1.3183333$$

$$SSE = SS_{yy} - \hat{\beta}_1 SS_{xy} = 1.3183333 - (-.002310625)(-130.44167) = 1.016931516 \approx 1.017$$

$$s^2 = MSE = \frac{SSE}{n-2} = \frac{1.016931516}{24-2} = 0.046224159 \approx .0462 \text{ and}$$

$$s = \sqrt{0.046224159} = 0.215$$

b. s^2 is measured in square units. It is very difficult to explain something measured in square units.

c. $s = 0.215$. We would expect approximately 95% of the observed values of y (sweetness index) to fall within $2s$ or $2(0.215) = 0.43$ units of their least squares predicted values.

10.35 a. From Exercise 10.22, $SS_{xy} = -3,881.9986$, $\sum y = 3,781.1$, $\sum y^2 = 651,612.45$, and $\hat{\beta}_1 = -0.305444503$.

$$SS_{yy} = \sum y^2 - \frac{\left(\sum y\right)^2}{n} = 651,612.45 - \frac{(3,781.1)^2}{22}$$
$$= 651,612.45 - 649,850.7823 = 1,761.6677$$

$$SSE = SS_{yy} - \hat{\beta}_1 SS_{xy} = 1,761.6677 - (-.305444503(-3,882.3686) = 575.8195525$$

$$s^2 = MSE = \frac{SSE}{n-2} = \frac{575.8195525}{22-2} = 28.79097763 \text{ and } s = \sqrt{28.79097763} = 5.37$$

$s = 5.37$. We would expect approximately 95% of the observed values of y (FCAT-Math scores) to fall within $2s$ or $2(5.37) = 10.74$ units of their least squares predicted values.

b. From Exercise 10.22, $SS_{xy} = -3,442.16$, $\sum y = 3,764.2$, $\sum y^2 = 645,221.16$, and $\hat{\beta}_1 = -0.270811187$.

$$SS_{yy} = \sum y^2 - \frac{\left(\sum y\right)^2}{n} = 645,221.16 - \frac{(3,764.2)^2}{22}$$
$$= 645,221.16 - 644,054.62 = 1,166.54$$

$$SSE = SS_{yy} - \hat{\beta}_1 SS_{xy} = 1,166.54 - (-.270811187(-3,442.16) = 234.3645646$$

$$s^2 = MSE = \frac{SSE}{n-2} = \frac{234.3645646}{22-2} = 11.71822823 \text{ and } s = \sqrt{11.71822823} = 3.42$$

$s = 3.42$. We would expect approximately 95% of the observed values of y (FCAT-Reading scores) to fall within $2s$ or $2(3.42) = 6.84$ units of their least squares predicted values.

c.	The sample standard deviation for predicting FCAT-Math scores is $s = 5.3657$. The sample standard deviation for predicting FCAT-Reading scores is $s = 3.4232$. Since the standard deviation for predicting FCAT-Reading scores is smaller than the standard deviation for predicting FCAT-Math scores, we can more accurately predict the FCAT-Reading scores.

10.37	a.	For confidence coefficient .95, $\alpha = 1 - .95 = .05$ and $\alpha/2 = .05/2 = .025$. From Table V, Appendix B, with df $= n - 2 = 10 - 2 = 8$, $t_{.025} = 2.306$.

The 95% confidence interval for β_1 is:

$$\hat{\beta}_1 \pm t_{.025}\, s_{\hat{\beta}_1} \quad \text{where} \quad s_{\hat{\beta}_1} = \frac{s}{\sqrt{SS_{xx}}} = \frac{3}{\sqrt{35}} = .5071$$
$$\Rightarrow 31 \pm 2.306(.5071) \Rightarrow 31 \pm 1.17 \Rightarrow (29.83, 32.17)$$

For confidence coefficient .90, $\alpha = 1 - .90 = .10$ and $\alpha/2 = .10/2 = .05$. From Table V, Appendix B, with df $= 8$, $t_{.05} = 1.860$.

The 90% confidence interval for β_1 is:

$$\hat{\beta}_1 \pm t_{.05}\, s_{\hat{\beta}_1} \Rightarrow 31 \pm 1.860(.5071) \Rightarrow 31 \pm .94 \Rightarrow (30.06, 31.94)$$

b.	$s^2 = \dfrac{SSE}{n-2} = \dfrac{1960}{14-2} = 163.33$, $s = \sqrt{s^2} = 12.7802$

For confidence coefficient, .95, $\alpha = 1 - .95 = .05$ and $\alpha/2 = .05/2 = .025$. From Table V, Appendix B, with df $= n - 2 = 14 - 2 = 12$, $t_{.025} = 2.179$. The 95% confidence interval for β_1 is:

$$\hat{\beta}_1 \pm t_{.025}\, s_{\hat{\beta}_1} \quad \text{where} \quad s_{\hat{\beta}_1} = \frac{s}{\sqrt{SS_{xx}}} = \frac{12.7802}{\sqrt{30}} = 2.3333$$
$$\Rightarrow 64 \pm 2.179(2.3333) \Rightarrow 64 \pm 5.08 \Rightarrow (58.92, 69.08)$$

For confidence coefficient .90, $\alpha = 1 - .90 = .10$ and $\alpha/2 = .10/2 = .05$. From Table V, Appendix B, with df $= 12$, $t_{.05} = 1.782$.

The 90% confidence interval for β_1 is:

$$\hat{\beta}_1 \pm t_{.05}\, s_{\hat{\beta}_1} \Rightarrow 64 \pm 1.782(2.3333) \Rightarrow 64 \pm 4.16 \Rightarrow (59.84, 68.16)$$

c.	$s^2 = \dfrac{SSE}{n-2} = \dfrac{146}{20-2} = 8.1111$, $s = \sqrt{s^2} = 2.848$

For confidence coefficient .95, $\alpha = 1 - .95 = .05$ and $\alpha/2 = .05/2 = .025$. From Table V, Appendix B, with df $= n - 2 = 20 - 2 = 18$, $t_{.025} = 2.101$. The 95% confidence interval for β_1 is:

$$\hat{\beta}_1 \pm t_{.025}\, s_{\hat{\beta}_1} \quad \text{where} \quad s_{\hat{\beta}_1} = \frac{s}{\sqrt{SS_{xx}}} = \frac{2.848}{\sqrt{64}} = .356$$
$$\Rightarrow -8.4 \pm 2.101(.356) \Rightarrow -8.4 \pm .75 \Rightarrow (-9.15, -7.65)$$

For confidence coefficient .90, $\alpha = 1 - .90 = .10$ and $\alpha/2 = .10/2 = .05$. From Table V, Appendix B, with df = 18, $t_{.05} = 1.734$.

The 90% confidence interval for β_1 is:

$$\hat{\beta}_1 \pm t_{.05}\, s_{\hat{\beta}_1} \Rightarrow -8.4 \pm 1.734(.356) \Rightarrow -8.4 \pm .62 \Rightarrow (-9.02, -7.78)$$

10.39   From Exercise 10.38, $\hat{\beta}_1 = .82$, $s = 1.1922$, $SS_{xx} = 28$, and $n = 7$.

For confidence coefficient .80, $\alpha = 1 - .80 = .20$ and $\alpha/2 = .20/2 = .10$. From Table V, Appendix B, with df = $n - 2 = 7 - 2 = 5$, $t_{.10} = 1.476$. The 80% confidence interval for β_1 is:

$$\hat{\beta}_1 \pm t_{.025}\, s_{\hat{\beta}_1} \text{ where } s_{\hat{\beta}_1} = \frac{s}{\sqrt{SS_{xx}}} = \frac{1.1922}{\sqrt{28}} = .2253$$
$$\Rightarrow .82 \pm 1.476(.2253) \Rightarrow .82 \pm .33 \Rightarrow (.49, 1.15)$$

For confidence coefficient .98, $\alpha = 1 - .98 = .02$ and $\alpha/2 = .02/2 = .01$. From Table V, Appendix B, with df = 5, $t_{.01} = 3.365$.

The 98% confidence interval for β_1 is:

$$\hat{\beta}_1 \pm t_{.01}\, s_{\hat{\beta}_1} \Rightarrow .82 \pm 3.365(.2253) \Rightarrow .82 \pm .76 \Rightarrow (.06, 1.58)$$

10.41   a.   To determine if the average state SAT score in 2007 has a positive relationship with the average state SAT score in 2000, we test:

$$H_0: \beta_1 = 0$$
$$H_a: \beta_1 > 0$$

   b.   From the printout in Exercise 10.15, the *p*-value is $p = 0.000$. This is the *p*-value for a 2-tailed test. The *p*-value for this one-tailed test is $0.000/2 = 0.000$. Since the *p*-value is less than $\alpha = .05$, H_0 is rejected. There is sufficient evidence to indicate the average state SAT score in 2007 has a positive relationship with the average state SAT score in 2000 at $\alpha = .05$.

   c.   For confidence coefficient .95, $\alpha = .05$ and $\alpha/2 = .05/2 = .025$. From Table V, Appendix B, with df = $n - 2 = 51 - 2 = 49$, $t_{.025} \approx 2.011$. The 95% confidence interval is:

$$\hat{\beta}_1 \pm t_{.025}\, s_{\hat{\beta}_1} \Rightarrow 1.144 \pm 2.011(.044) \Rightarrow 1.144 \pm .088 \Rightarrow (1.056, \ 1.232) \text{ or } (1.06, 1.23)$$

We are 95% confident that for each additional point in the 2000 average state SAT score, the increase in the 2007 average state SAT score is between 1.06 and 1.23.

10.43   First, we must compute s^2. From Exercise 10.17, $SS_{xy} = 20.00833333$,

$SS_{xx} = 0.5570833333$, $\sum y = 239$, $\sum y^2 = 10,255$, and $\hat{\beta}_1 = 35.91623038$.

$$SS_{yy} = \sum y^2 - \frac{\left(\sum y\right)^2}{n} = 10,255 - \frac{(239)^2}{6}$$
$$= 10,255 - 9,520.1666667 = 734.8333333$$

$$SSE = SS_{yy} - \hat{\beta}_1 SS_{xy} = 734.83333333 - (35.91623038)(20.008333333) = 16.2094236$$

$$s^2 = MSE = \frac{SSE}{n-2} = \frac{16.2094326}{6-2} = 4.0523559 \text{ and } s = \sqrt{4.0523559} = 2.0130$$

$$s_{\hat{\beta}_1} = \frac{\sqrt{MSE}}{\sqrt{SS_{xx}}} = \frac{\sqrt{4.0523559}}{\sqrt{0.55708333}} = 2.6971$$

For confidence coefficient .90, $\alpha = .10$ and $\alpha/2 = .10/2 = .05$. From Table V, Appendix B, with df $= n - 2$ $= 6 - 2 = 4$, $t_{.05} = 2.132$. The 90% confidence interval is:

$$\hat{\beta}_1 \pm t_{.05} s_{\hat{\beta}_1} \Rightarrow 35.916 \pm 2.132(2.6971) \Rightarrow 35.916 \pm 5.7502 \Rightarrow (30.17, \ 41.67)$$

We are 90% confident that for each additional unit increase in Surface Area to Volume, the increase in the Drug release rate is between 30.17 and 41.67.

10.45   a.   To determine if driving accuracy decreases linearly as driving distance increases, we test:

H_0: $\beta_1 = 0$
H_a: $\beta_1 < 0$

b.   From Exercise 10.19:
$$\sum y = 2,478.8 \qquad \sum y^2 = 154,676.28 \qquad SS_{xy} = -1,390.16 \qquad SS_{xx} = 2,208.46$$
$$\hat{\beta}_1 = -0.629443141$$

$$SS_{yy} = \sum y^2 - \frac{\left(\sum y\right)^2}{n} = 154,676.28 - \frac{2,478.8^2}{40} = 1,065.044$$

$$SSE = SS_{yy} - \hat{\beta}_1 SS_{xy} = 1,065.044 - (-.629443141)(-1,390.16) = 190.0173231$$

$$s^2 = MSE = \frac{SSE}{n-2} = \frac{190.0173231}{40-2} = 5.000455871 \qquad s = \sqrt{5.000455871} = 2.236169911$$

$$s_{\hat{\beta}_1} = \frac{s}{\sqrt{SS_{xx}}} = \frac{2.236169911}{\sqrt{2,208.46}} = .04758$$

The test statistic is $t = \dfrac{\hat{\beta}_1}{s_{\hat{\beta}_1}} = \dfrac{-.6294}{.04758} = -13.23$.

Using Table V, with df $= n - 2 = 40 - 2 = 38$, the p-value is approximately 0.000.

c. Since the *p*-value is less than $\alpha = .01$, H_0 is rejected. There is sufficient evidence to indicate driving accuracy decreases linearly as driving distance increases at $\alpha = .01$.

10.47 Some preliminary calculations are:

$$\sum x = 301,713 \qquad \sum y = 811 \qquad \sum xy = 27,261,248$$

$$\sum x^2 = 10,707,042,109 \qquad \sum y^2 = 73,235$$

$$\bar{x} = \frac{\sum x}{n} = \frac{301,713}{9} = 33,523.66667 \qquad \bar{y} = \frac{\sum y}{n} = \frac{811}{9} = 90.1111111$$

$$SS_{xy} = \sum xy - \frac{\left(\sum x\right)\left(\sum y\right)}{n} = 27,261,248 - \frac{301,713(811)}{9}$$
$$= 27,261,248 - 27,187,693.67 = 73,554.33$$

$$SS_{xx} = \sum x^2 - \frac{\left(\sum x\right)^2}{n} = 10,707,042,109 - \frac{(301,713)^2}{9}$$
$$= 10,707,042,109 - 10,114,526,041 = 592,516,068$$

$$SS_{yy} = \sum y^2 - \frac{\left(\sum y\right)^2}{n} = 73,235 - \frac{(811)^2}{9}$$
$$= 73,235 - 73,080.111111 = 154.88889$$

$$\hat{\beta}_1 = \frac{SS_{xy}}{SS_{xx}} = \frac{73,554.33}{592,516,068} = 0.000124138 \approx 0.0001241$$

$$SSE = SS_{yy} - \hat{\beta}_1 SS_{xy} = 154.888889 - (.000124138)(73,554.33) = 145.7580026$$

$$s^2 = MSE = \frac{SSE}{n-2} = \frac{145.7580026}{9-2} = 20.8225718 \quad \text{and} \quad s = \sqrt{20.8225718} = 4.5632$$

$$s_{\hat{\beta}_1} = \frac{\sqrt{MSE}}{\sqrt{SS_{xx}}} = \frac{\sqrt{20.8225718}}{\sqrt{592,516,068}} = 0.0001875$$

To determine if there is a positive linear relationship between the percentage of graduates with job offers and tuition costs, we test:

H_0: $\beta_1 = 0$
H_a: $\beta_1 > 0$

The test statistic is $t = \dfrac{\hat{\beta}_1 - 0}{s_{\hat{\beta}_1}} = \dfrac{.0001243}{.0001875} = .66$

The rejection region requires $\alpha = .10$ in the upper tail of the *t*-distribution with df $= n - 2 = 9 - 2 = 7$. From Table V, Appendix B, $t_{.10} = 1.415$. The rejection region is $t > 1.415$.

Since the observed value of the test statistic does not fall in the rejection region ($t = .66 \not> 1.415$), H_0 is not rejected. There is insufficient evidence to indicate a positive linear relationship between the percentage of graduates with job offers and tuition costs at $\alpha = .10$.

10.49 a. Using MINITAB, the scattergram is:

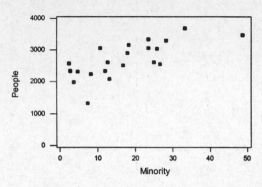

It appears from the plot that as the percentage of the population that is minority increases, the number of people per branch bank tends to increase.

b. The value of β_1 will be positive. As one variable increases, the other tends to increase.

c. $\sum x = 363.8 \qquad \sum y = 56,560 \qquad \sum xy = 1,075,763 \qquad \sum x^2 = 9,020.86$

$\sum y^2 = 158,763,894$

$\bar{x} = \dfrac{\sum x}{n} = \dfrac{363.8}{21} = 17.32380952 \qquad \bar{y} = \dfrac{\sum x}{n} = \dfrac{56,560}{21} = 2,693.33333$

$SS_{xy} = \sum xy - \dfrac{\left(\sum x\right)\left(\sum y\right)}{n} = 1,075,763 - \dfrac{363.8(56,560)}{21}$
$\qquad = 1,075,763 - 979,834.6667 = 95,928.3333$

$SS_{xx} = \sum x^2 - \dfrac{\left(\sum x\right)^2}{n} = 9,020.86 - \dfrac{363.8^2}{21}$
$\qquad = 9,020.86 - 6,302.401905 = 2,718.458095$

$\hat{\beta}_1 = \dfrac{SS_{xy}}{SS_{xx}} = \dfrac{95,928.3333}{2,718.458095} = 35.28777342 \approx 35.288$

$SS_{yy} = \sum y^2 - \dfrac{\left(\sum y\right)^2}{n} = 158,863,894 - \dfrac{56,560^2}{21}$
$\qquad = 158,763,894 - 152,334,933.3 = 6,428,960.7$

$$SSE = SS_{yy} - \hat{\beta}_1 \, SS_{xy} = 6,428,960.7 - 35.28777342(95,928.3333)$$

$$= 6,428,960.7 - 3,385,097.29 = 3,043,863.41$$

$$s^2 = \frac{SSE}{n-2} = \frac{3,043,863.41}{21-2} = 160,203.3374$$

$$s = \sqrt{s^2} = \sqrt{160,203.3374} = 400.2541$$

To determine if the data support the charge made against the New Jersey banking community, we test:

$H_0: \; \beta_1 = 0$

$H_a: \; \beta_1 \neq 0$

The test statistic is $t = \dfrac{\hat{\beta}_1 - 0}{s_{\hat{\beta}_1}} = \dfrac{35.288 - 0}{\dfrac{400.2541}{\sqrt{2,718.458095}}} = 4.60$

The rejection region requires $\alpha/2 = .01/2 = .005$ in each tail of the t-distribution with df $= n - 2 = 21 - 2 = 19$. From Table V, Appendix B, $t_{.005} = 2.861$. The rejection region is $t < -2.861$ or $t > 2.861$.

Since the observed value of the test statistic falls in the rejection region ($t = 4.60 > 2.861$), H_0 is rejected. There is sufficient evidence to support the charge made against the New Jersey banking community at $\alpha = .01$.

10.51 The estimates are: $\hat{\beta}_o = .51514$ and $\hat{\beta}_1 = .00002074$. Thus, $\hat{y} = .515 + .00002074x$.

b. To determine if a positive linear relationship exists between elevation and slugging percentage, we test:

$H_0: \; \beta_1 = 0$

$H_a: \; \beta_1 > 0$

The test statistic is $t = 2.89$ and the p-value is $p = 0.008/2 = .004$. Since the p-value is less than $\alpha = .01$, H_0 is rejected. There is sufficient evidence to indicate that a positive linear relationship exists between elevation and slugging percentage at $\alpha = .01$.

c.   The scatterplot for the data is:

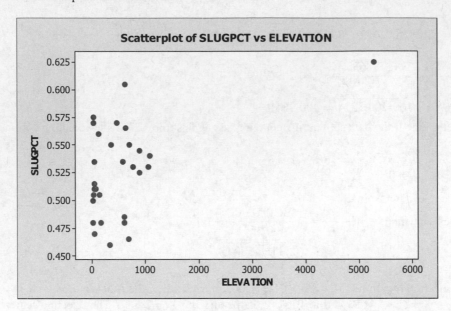

The data point for Denver is very far from the rest. This point looks to be an outlier. It is much different than all of the rest of the points.

d.   Removing the data point for Denver, the Minitab output is:

Regression Analysis: SLUGPCT versus ELEVATION

```
The regression equation is
SLUGPCT = 0.515 + 0.000020 ELEVATION


Predictor         Coef      SE Coef        T       P
Constant       0.51537      0.01066    48.33   0.000
ELEVATION   0.00002012   0.00002034     0.99   0.332


S = 0.0376839    R-Sq = 3.6%    R-Sq(adj) = 0.0%


Analysis of Variance

Source          DF         SS          MS       F       P
Regression       1   0.001389    0.001389    0.98   0.332
Residual Error  26   0.036922    0.001420
Total           27   0.038311
```

The estimates are: $\hat{\beta}_o = .51537$ and $\hat{\beta}_1 = .00002012$

To determine if a positive linear relationship exists between elevation and slugging percentage, we test:

H_0: $\beta_1 = 0$
H_a: $\beta_1 > 0$

The test statistic is $t = 0.99$ and the p-value is $p = 0.332/2 = .166$. Since the p-value is not less than $\alpha = .01$, H_0 is not rejected. There is insufficient evidence to indicate that a positive linear relationship exists between elevation and slugging percentage when Denver is removed form the data at $\alpha = .01$.

10.53   a.   If $r = .7$, there is a positive relationship between x and y. As x increases, y tends to increase. The slope is positive.

   b.   If $r = -.7$, there is a negative relationship between x and y. As x increases, y tends to decrease. The slope is negative.

   c.   If $r = 0$, there is a 0 slope. There is no relationship between x and y.

   d.   If $r^2 = .64$, then r is either .8 or $-.8$. The relationship between x and y could be either positive or negative.

10.55   a.   From Exercises 10.10 and 10.28,

$$r^2 = 1 - \frac{SSE}{SS_{yy}} = 1 - \frac{1.22033896}{21.7142857} = 1 - .0562 = .9438$$

94.38% of the total sample variability around the sample mean response is explained by the linear relationship between y and x.

   b.   Some preliminary calculations are:

$$\sum x = 33 \qquad \sum y = 27 \qquad \sum xy = 104$$

$$\sum x^2 = 179 \qquad \sum y^2 = 133$$

$$SS_{xy} = \sum xy - \frac{\left(\sum x\right)\left(\sum y\right)}{n} = 104 - \frac{33(27)}{7} = -23.2857143$$

$$SS_{xx} = \sum x^2 - \frac{\left(\sum x\right)^2}{n} = 179 - \frac{33^2}{7} = 23.4285714$$

$$\hat{\beta}_1 = \frac{SS_{xy}}{SS_{xx}} = \frac{-23.2857143}{23.4285714} = -.99390244$$

$$SS_{yy} = \sum y^2 - \frac{\left(\sum y\right)^2}{n} = 133 - \frac{27^2}{7} = 28.8571429$$

$$SSE = SS_{yy} - \hat{\beta}_1 SS_{xy} = 28.8571429 - (-.99390244)(-23.2857143) = 5.71341462$$

$$r^2 = 1 - \frac{SSE}{SS_{yy}} = 1 - \frac{5.71341462}{28.8571429} = 1 - .1980 = .802$$

80.2% of the total sample variability around the sample mean response is explained by the linear relationship between y and x.

10.57   a.   The linear model would be: $E(y) = \beta_o + \beta_1 x$

        b. $r = .68$. There is a moderate positive linear relationship between RMP and SET.

        c.   Since $r = .68$ is positive, the slope of the line will also be positive.

        d.   The p-value is $p = .001$. Since this value is so small, we would reject H_0. There is sufficient evidence of a linear relationship between RMP and SET for any value of $\alpha > .001$.

        e. $r^2 = .68^2 = .4624$. 46.24% of the total sample variability around the sample mean SET values is explained by the linear relationship between SET and RMP.

10.59   a.   The value of r is .70. Since this number is fairly large, there is a moderately strong positive linear relationship between self-knowledge skill level and goal-setting ability.

        b.   Since the p-value is so small ($p = .001$), there is evidence to reject H_0. There is sufficient evidence to indicate a significant positive linear relationship between self-knowledge skill level and goal-setting ability for any value of $\alpha > .001$.

        c. $r^2 = .70^2 = .49$. 49% of the total sample variability around the sample mean goal-setting ability is explained by the linear relationship between self-knowledge skill level and goal-setting ability.

10.61   a. $r = .983$. There is a strong positive linear relationship between the number of females in managerial positions and the number of females with college degrees.

        b. $r = .074$. There is a very weak positive linear relationship between the number of females in managerial positions and the number of female high school graduates with no college degree.

        c. $r = .722$. There is a moderately strong positive linear relationship between the number of males in managerial positions and the number of males with college degrees.

        d. $r = .528$. There is a moderately weak positive linear relationship between the number of males in managerial positions and the number of male high school graduates with no college degree.

10.63   Some preliminary calculations are:

$$\sum x = 6,167 \qquad \sum x^2 = 1,641,115 \qquad \sum xy = 34,764.5 \qquad \sum y = 135.8$$
$$\sum y^2 = 769.72$$

$$SS_{xy} = \sum xy - \frac{\sum x \sum y}{n} = 34,764.5 - \frac{6167(135.8)}{24} = -130.44167$$

$$SS_{xx} = \sum x^2 - \frac{\left(\sum x\right)^2}{n} = 1,641,115 - \frac{(6,167)^2}{24} = 56,452.95833$$

$$SS_{yy} = \sum y^2 - \frac{\left(\sum y\right)^2}{n} = 769.72 - \frac{135.8^2}{24} = 1.3183333$$

$$\hat{\beta}_1 = \frac{SS_{xy}}{SS_{xx}} = \frac{-130.44167}{56,452.95833} = -0.002310625$$

$$SSE = SS_{yy} - \hat{\beta}_1 SS_{xy} = 1.3183333 - (-0.002310625)(-130.44167) = 1.016931516$$

$$r^2 = \frac{SS_{yy} - SSE}{SS_{yy}} = \frac{1.3183333 - 1.016931516}{1.3183333} = .2286$$

22.86% of the total sample variability around the sample mean sweetness index is explained by the linear relationship between the sweetness index and the amount of water soluble pectin.

$$r = -\sqrt{.2286} = -.478 \quad \text{(The value of r is negative because } \hat{\beta}_1 \text{ is negative.)}$$

Since this value is not close to one, there is a rather weak negative linear relationship between the sweetness index and the amount of water soluble pectin.

10.65   a.   Since $r = .41$, there is a fairly weak positive linear relationship between height and average earnings from 1985-2000 for those whose occupation is in Sales.

       b. $r^2 = .41^2 = .168$. Since $r^2 = .168$, 16.8% of the total sample variability around the sample mean average earnings from 1985-2000 for those who are in Sales is explained by the linear relationship between average earnings and height.

       c.   To determine whether average earnings and height are positively correlated for those in Sales, we test:

            H_0: $\rho = 0$
            H_a: $\rho > 0$

       d. $t = \dfrac{r\sqrt{n-2}}{\sqrt{1-r^2}} = \dfrac{.41\sqrt{117-2}}{\sqrt{1-.41^2}} = 4.82$

       e.   The rejection region requires $\alpha = .01$ in the upper tail of the t-distribution with $df = n - 2 = 117 - 2 = 115$. From Table V, Appendix B, $t_{.01} \approx 2.358$. The rejection region is $t > 2.358$.

            Since the observed value of the test statistic falls in the rejection region ($t = 4.82 > 2.358$), H_0 is rejected. There is sufficient evidence to indicate the average earnings and height for those in Sales are positively correlated at $\alpha = .01$.

       f.   Suppose we pick managers.

            Since $r = .35$, there is a fairly weak positive linear relationship between height and average earnings from 1985-2000 for those whose occupation is Managers.
            $r^2 = .35^2 = .1225$. Since $r^2 = .1225$, 12.25% of the total sample variability around the sample mean average earnings from 1985-2000 for Managers is explained by the linear relationship between average earnings and height.

            To determine whether average earnings and height are positively correlated for Managers, we test:

            H_0: $\rho = 0$
            H_a: $\rho > 0$

$$t = \frac{r\sqrt{n-2}}{\sqrt{1-r^2}} = \frac{.35\sqrt{455-2}}{\sqrt{1-.35^2}} = 7.95$$

The rejection region requires $\alpha = .01$ in the upper tail of the t-distribution with df $= n - 2 = 455 - 2 = 453$. From Table V, Appendix B, $t_{.01} \approx 2.326$. The rejection region is $t > 2.326$.

Since the observed value of the test statistic falls in the rejection region ($t = 7.95 > 2.326$), H_0 is rejected. There is sufficient evidence to indicate the average earnings and height for Managers are positively correlated at $\alpha = .01$.

10.67 From Exercise 10.23, $SS_{xy} = 73,554.33$, $SS_{xx} = 592,516,068$, $SS_{yy} = 154.888889$, $\hat{\beta}_1 = 0.000124138 \approx 0.0001241$, $\sum y = 811$ and $\sum x = 301,713$

$$r = \frac{SS_{xy}}{\sqrt{SS_{xx}}\sqrt{SS_{yy}}} = \frac{73,554.33}{\sqrt{592,516,068}\sqrt{154.888889}} = .243$$

There is a weak positive linear relationship between the percentage of graduates with job offers and the tuition cost.

$r^2 = .243^2 = .059$ Approximately 5.9% of the variability in the percentage of graduates with job offers around the sample mean is explained by the linear relationship between percentage of graduates with job offers and tuition cost.

$$\hat{\beta}_o = \bar{y} - \hat{\beta}_1\bar{x} = \frac{811}{9} - (0.000124138)(\frac{301,713}{9}) = 85.94955018 \approx 85.9496$$

The fitted regression line is: $\hat{y} = 85.9496 + .0001241x$.

10.69 a. From the printout, $r = .570$.

b. Since the coefficient of correlation is close to .5, there is a weak positive linear relationship between the agreement of American managers and Asian managers. Since the coefficient of correlation is not very close to 1, this indicates that there is a trend in views between American managers and Asian managers, but it is not very strong. Thus, the attitudes of these two groups are only somewhat similar.

c. Some preliminary calculations:

$$\sum x = 195 \quad \sum x^2 = 8,425 \quad \sum xy = 14,700 \quad \sum y = 355 \quad \sum y^2 = 26,125$$

$$SS_{xy} = \sum xy - \frac{(\sum x)(\sum y)}{n} = 14,700 - \frac{195(355)}{5} = 855$$

$$SS_{xx} = \sum x^2 - \frac{(\sum x)^2}{n} = 8,425 - \frac{195^2}{5} = 820$$

$$SS_{yy} = \sum y^2 - \frac{(\sum y)^2}{n} = 26,125 - \frac{355^2}{5} = 920$$

$$r = \frac{SS_{xy}}{\sqrt{SS_{xx}SS_{yy}}} = \frac{855}{\sqrt{820(920)}} = .9844$$

The coefficient of correlation is .9844. There is a very strong positive linear relationship between views of American and Asian managers. Even though the coefficient of correlation is close to one, the values of the Asian managers are approximately 30 points higher in each case than the values of the American managers. We would conclude that the attitudes of America and Asian managers are different.

10.71   a.,b.   The scattergram is:

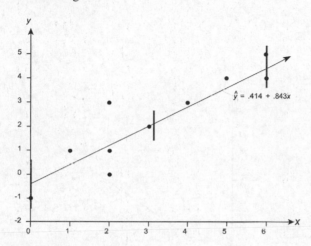

c. $SSE = SS_{yy} - \hat{\beta}_1 SS_{xy} = 33.6 - .84318766(32.8) = 5.94344473$

$s^2 = \dfrac{SSE}{n-2} = \dfrac{5.94344473}{10-2} = .742930591$ $\qquad$ $s = \sqrt{.742930591} = .8619$

$\bar{x} = \dfrac{31}{10} = 3.1$

The form of the confidence interval is $\hat{y} \pm t_{\alpha/2}\, s \sqrt{\dfrac{1}{n} + \dfrac{\left(x_p - \bar{x}\right)^2}{SS_{xx}}}$

For $x_p = 6$, $\hat{y} = -.414 + .843(6) = 4.64$

For confidence coefficient .95, $\alpha = .05$ and $\alpha/2 = .025$. From Table V, Appendix B, with df $= n - 2 = 10 - 2 = 8$, $t_{.025} = 2.306$. The confidence interval is:

$$4.64 \pm 2.306(.8619)\sqrt{\frac{1}{10} + \frac{(6-3.1)^2}{38.9}} \Rightarrow 4.64 \pm 1.12 \Rightarrow (3.52, 5.76)$$

d.   For $x_p = 3.2$, $\hat{y} = -.414 + .843(3.2) = 2.28$

The confidence interval is:

$$2.28 \pm 2.306(.8619)\sqrt{\frac{1}{10} + \frac{(3.2-3.1)^2}{38.9}} \Rightarrow 2.28 \pm .63 \Rightarrow (1.65, 2.91)$$

For $x_p = 0$, $\hat{y} = -.414 + .843(0) = -.41$

The confidence interval is:

$$-.41 \pm 2.306(.8619)\sqrt{\frac{1}{10} + \frac{(0-3.1)^2}{38.9}} \Rightarrow -.41 \pm 1.17 \Rightarrow (-1.58, .76)$$

e. The width of the confidence interval for the mean value of y depends on the distance x_p is from $\bar{x}$. The width of the interval for $x_p = 3.2$ is the smallest because 3.2 is the closest to $\bar{x} = 3.1$. The width of the interval for $x_p = 0$ is the widest because 0 is the farthest from $\bar{x} = 3.1$.

10.73 a. $\hat{\beta}_1 = \dfrac{SS_{xy}}{SS_{xx}} = \dfrac{28}{32} = .875$

$\hat{\beta}_0 - \bar{y} - \hat{\beta}_1\bar{x} = 4 - .875(3) = 1.375$

The least squares line is $\hat{y} = 1.375 + .875x$.

b. The least squares line is:

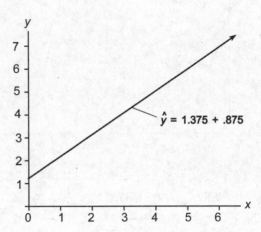

$\hat{y} = 1.375 + .875$

c. $SSE = SS_{yy} - \hat{\beta}_1 SS_{xy} = 26 - .875(28) = 1.5$

d. $s^2 = \dfrac{SSE}{n-2} = \dfrac{1.5}{10-2} = .1875$

e. $s = \sqrt{.1875} = .4330$

The form of the confidence interval is $\hat{y} \pm t_{\alpha/2}\, s \sqrt{\dfrac{1}{n} + \dfrac{\left(x_p - \bar{x}\right)^2}{SS_{xx}}}$

For $x_p = 2.5$, $\hat{y} = 1.375 + .875(2.5) = 3.56$

For confidence coefficient .95, $\alpha = .05$ and $\alpha/2 = .025$. From Table V, Appendix B, with df $= n - 2 = 10 - 2 = 8$, $t_{.025} = 2.306$. The confidence interval is:

$$3.56 \pm 2.306(.4330)\sqrt{\frac{1}{10} + \frac{(2.5-3)^2}{32}} \Rightarrow 3.56 \pm .33 \Rightarrow (3.23, 3.89)$$

f.   The form of the prediction interval is $\hat{y} \pm t_{\alpha/2} s \sqrt{1 + \dfrac{1}{n} + \dfrac{\left(x_p - \bar{x}\right)^2}{SS_{xx}}}$

For $x_p = 4$, $\hat{y} = 1.375 + .875(4) = 4.875$

For confidence coefficient .95, $\alpha = .05$ and $\alpha/2 = .025$. From Table V, Appendix B, with $df = n - 2 = 10 - 2 = 8$, $t_{.025} = 2.306$. The prediction interval is:

$$4.875 \pm 2.306(.4330)\sqrt{1 + \frac{1}{10} + \frac{(4-3)^2}{32}} \Rightarrow 4.875 \pm 1.062 \Rightarrow (3.81, 5.94)$$

10.75 a.   The 95% confidence interval for $E(y)$ when $y = .52$ is (3,598.1, 3,868.1). We are 95% confident that the mean asking price for a diamond weighing .52 carats is between \$3,598.10 and \$3,868.10.

b.   The 95% prediction interval for y when $y = .52$ is (1,529.8, 5,936.3). We are 95% confident that the actual asking price for a diamond weighing .52 carats is between \$1,529.80 and \$5,936.30.

10.77 Answers may vary. One possible answer is:

For run 1, the 90% confidence interval for $x = 220.00$ is (5.65, 5.84). We are 90% confident that the mean sweetness index of all orange juice samples will be between 5.65 and 5.84 parts per million when the pectin value is 220.00.

10.79 a.   Using MINITAB, the prediction interval for the acatual value and confidence interval for the mean are:

```
Predicted Values for New Observations

New
Obs    Fit   SE Fit      99% CI          99% PI
  1  3.510   0.196   (2.955, 4.066)  (1.020, 6.000)

Values of Predictors for New Observations

New
Obs  Time
  1  15.0
```

The 99% confidence interval for the mean mass of all spills with an elapsed time of 15 minutes is (2.955, 4.066). We are 99% confident that the mean mass of all spills will be between 2.995 and 4.066 when the elapsed time is 15 minutes.

b.   The 99% prediction interval for the actual mass of a spill with an elapsed time of 15 minutes is (1.020, 6.000). We are 99% confident that the actual mass of a spill will be between 1.020 and 6.000 when the elapsed time is 15 minutes.

c.   The prediction interval for the actual value is larger than the confidence interval for the mean. This will always be true. The prediction interval for the actual value contains 2 errors. First, we must locate the true mean of the distribution. Once this mean is located, the actual values of the variables can still vary around this mean. There is variance in locating the mean and then variance of the actual observations around the mean.

10.81   a.   Using MINITAB, the results of the regression analysis are:

Regression Analysis: QuitRate versus AvgWage

```
The regression equation is
QuitRate = 4.86 - 0.347 AvgWage

Predictor          Coef       SE Coef           T          P
Constant         4.8615        0.5201        9.35      0.000
AvgWage         -0.34655       0.05866       -5.91      0.000

S = 0.4862       R-Sq = 72.9%      R-Sq(adj) = 70.8%

Analysis of Variance

Source             DF            SS           MS          F          P
Regression          1        8.2507       8.2507      34.90      0.000
Residual Error     13        3.0733       0.2364
Total              14       11.3240
```

To determine if the average hourly wage rate contributes information to predict quit rates, we test:

$H_0: \ \beta_1 = 0$
$H_a: \ \beta_1 \neq 0$

The test statistic is $t = \dfrac{\hat{\beta}_1 - 0}{s_{\hat{\beta}_1}} = -5.91$ (from printout).

The rejection region requires $\alpha/2 = .05/2 = .025$ in each tail of the t-distribution with df $= n - 2 = 15 - 2 = 13$. From Table V, Appendix B, $t_{.025} = 2.160$. The rejection region is $t < -2.160$ or $t > 2.160$.

Since the observed value of the test statistic falls in the rejection region ($t = -5.91 < -2.160$), H_0 is rejected. There is sufficient evidence to indicate that the average hourly wage rate contributes information to predict quit ratio at $\alpha = .05$.

Since the slope is negative ($\hat{\beta}_1 = -.3466$), the model suggests that x and y have a negative relationship. As the average hourly wage rate increases, the quit rate tends to decrease.

b.   Some preliminary calculations are:

$$\sum x = 129.05 \qquad \sum x^2 = 1,179 \qquad \bar{x} = \frac{\sum x}{n} = \frac{129.05}{15} = 8.6033$$

$$\hat{y} = 4.8615 - 0.34655(9) = 1.743$$

$$SS_{xx} = \sum x^2 - \frac{\left(\sum x\right)^2}{n} = 1,179 - \frac{(129.05)^2}{15} = 68.739833$$

For confidence level .95, $\alpha = .05$ and $\alpha/2 = .05/2 = .025$. From Table V, Appendix B, with df $= n - 2 = 15 - 2 = 13$, $t_{.025} = 2.160$. The 95% prediction interval is:

$$\hat{y} \pm t_{\alpha/2} s \sqrt{1 + \frac{1}{n} + \frac{\left(x_p - \bar{x}\right)^2}{SS_{xx}}} \Rightarrow 1.743 \pm 2.160(.4862)\sqrt{1 + \frac{1}{15} + \frac{(9 - 8.6033)^2}{68.739833}}$$

$$\Rightarrow 1.743 \pm 1.086 \Rightarrow (0.657, \quad 2.829)$$

We are 95% confident that the actual quit rate when the average hourly wage is \$9.00 is between 0.657 and 2.829.

c.   The 95% confidence interval is:

$$\hat{y} \pm t_{\alpha/2} s \sqrt{\frac{1}{n} + \frac{\left(x_p - \bar{x}\right)^2}{SS_{xx}}} \Rightarrow 1.743 \pm 2.160(.4862)\sqrt{\frac{1}{15} + \frac{(9 - 8.6033)^2}{68.739833}}$$

$$\Rightarrow 1.743 \pm 0.276 \Rightarrow (1.467, \quad 2.019)$$

We are 95% confident that the mean quit rate when the average hourly wage is $9.00 is between 1.467 and 2.019.

10.83   Using MINITAB, a scattergram of the data is:

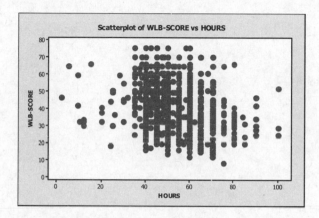

From the plot, it appears that there may be a negative linear relationship between WLB-scores and the average number of hours worked per week.

Using MINITAB, the results are:

Regression Analysis: WLB-SCORE versus HOURS

```
The regression equation is
WLB-SCORE = 62.5 - 0.347 HOURS


Predictor       Coef   SE Coef        T      P
Constant      62.499     1.414    44.22  0.000
HOURS        -0.34673   0.02761   -12.56  0.000


S = 12.2845    R-Sq = 7.0%    R-Sq(adj) = 7.0%


Analysis of Variance

Source          DF       SS      MS       F      P
Regression       1    23803   23803  157.73  0.000
Residual Error  2085  314647     151
Total           2086  338451
```

The fitted straight line model is: $\hat{y} = 62.499 - .34673x$. For each additional hour worked per week, the mean WLB-score is estimated to decrease by .34673.

To determine if the model is adequate, we test:

H_0: $\beta_1 = 0$
H_a: $\beta_1 \neq 0$

From the printout, the test statistic is $t = -12.56$ and the *p*-value is $p = 0.000$. Since the *p*-value is so small, H_0 is rejected. There is sufficient evidence to indicate that there is a linear relationship between the average number of hours worked per week and the WLB-score for any reasonable value of α. Since $\hat{\beta}_1$ is negative, as the average number of hours worked per week increases, the WLB-score decreases.

From the printout, $r^2 = 7\%$ or .07. This means that only 7% of the sample variation of the WLB-scores around their means is explained by the linear relationship between the average number of hours worked per week and the WLB-scores. Even though the p-value for testing whether the model is adequate is extremely small, this model does not explain much of the variation. There is much variation in the WLB-scores that is not explained by the average number of hours worked per week.

10.85 a. $\hat{\beta}_1 = \dfrac{SS_{xy}}{SS_{xx}} = \dfrac{-88}{55} = -1.6$, $\hat{\beta}_0 = \bar{y} - \hat{\beta}_1 \bar{x} = 35 - (-1.6)(1.3) = 37.08$

The least squares line is $\hat{y} = 37.08 - 1.6x$.

   b.

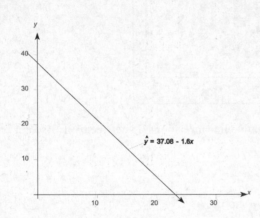

$\hat{y} = 37.08 - 1.6x$

   c. $SSE = SS_{yy} - \hat{\beta}_1 SS_{xy} = 198 - (-1.6)(-88) = 57.2$

   d. $s^2 = \dfrac{SSE}{n-2} = \dfrac{57.2}{15-2} = 4.4$

   e.   For confidence coefficient .90, $\alpha = 1 - .90 = .10$ and $\alpha/2 = .10/2 = .05$. From Table V, Appendix B, with df $= n - 2 = 15 - 2 = 13$, $t_{.05} = 1.771$. The 90% confidence interval for β_1 is:

$$\hat{y} \pm t_{\alpha/2}\dfrac{s}{\sqrt{SS_{xx}}} \Rightarrow -1.6 \pm 1.771\dfrac{\sqrt{4.4}}{\sqrt{55}} \Rightarrow -1.6 \pm .50 \Rightarrow (-2.10, -1.10)$$

We are 90% confident the change in the mean value of *y* for each unit change in *x* is between −2.10 and −1.10.

f. For $x_p = 15$, $\hat{y} = 37.08 - 1.6(15) = 13.08$

The 90% confidence interval is:

$$\hat{y} \pm t_{\alpha/2} s \sqrt{\frac{1}{n} + \frac{\left(x_p - \bar{x}\right)^2}{SS_{xx}}} \Rightarrow 13.08 \pm 1.771\left(\sqrt{4.4}\right)\sqrt{\frac{1}{15} + \frac{(15 - 1.3)^2}{55}}$$

$$\Rightarrow 13.08 \pm 6.93 \Rightarrow (6.15, 20.01)$$

g. The 90% prediction interval is:

$$\hat{y} \pm t_{\alpha/2} s \sqrt{\frac{1}{n} + \frac{\left(x_p - \bar{x}\right)^2}{SS_{xx}}} \Rightarrow 13.08 \pm 1.771\left(\sqrt{4.4}\right)\sqrt{\frac{1}{15} + \frac{(15 - 1.3)^2}{55}}$$

$$\Rightarrow 13.08 \pm 7.86 \Rightarrow (5.22, 20.94)$$

10.87 a. There appears to be a somewhat positive linear relationship.

b. For confidence level .90, $\alpha = .10$ and $\alpha/2 = .10/2 = .05$. From Table V, Appendix B, with df = $n - 2$ = 47 − 2 = 45, $t_{.05} \approx 1.684$. The confidence interval is:

$$\hat{\beta}_1 \pm t_{.05} s_{\hat{\beta}_1} \Rightarrow 1.39 \pm 1.684(.06) \Rightarrow 1.39 \pm .10 \Rightarrow (1.29, 1.49)$$

c. We are 90% confident that the change in the mean McCool winter-adjusted rainfall erosivity index for each one unit change in the once-in-5-year snowmelt runoff amount is between 1.29 and 1.49.

10.89 a. It appears as salary increases, the retaliation index decreases.

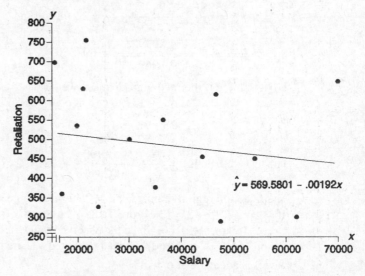

b. $\sum x = 544,100 \qquad \sum y = 7,497 \qquad \sum xy = 263,977,000$

$\sum x^2 = 23,876,290,000 \qquad \sum y^2 = 4,061,063$

$\bar{x} = \dfrac{\sum x}{n} = \dfrac{544,100}{15} = 36,273.333 \qquad \bar{y} = \dfrac{\sum y}{n} = \dfrac{7,497}{15} = 499.8$

$$SS_{xy} = \sum xy - \frac{\left(\sum x\right)\left(\sum y\right)}{n} = 263,977,000 - \frac{(544,100)(7,497)}{15}$$

$$= 263,977,000 - 271,941,180 = -7,964,180$$

$$SS_{xx} = \sum x^2 - \frac{\left(\sum x\right)^2}{n} = 23,876,290,000 - \frac{(544,100)^2}{15}$$
$$= 23,876,290,000 - 19,736,320,670 = 4,139,969,330$$

$$\hat{\beta}_1 = \frac{SS_{xy}}{SS_{xx}} = \frac{-7,964,180}{4,139,969,330} = -.001923729 \approx -.00192$$

$$\hat{\beta}_0 = \bar{y} - \hat{\beta}_1\bar{x} = 499.8 - (-.001923729)(36,273.333)$$
$$= 499.8 + 69.78007144 = 569.5800714 \approx 569.5801$$

$$\hat{y} = 569.5801 - .00192x$$

c. The least squares line supports the answer because the line has a negative slope.

d. $\hat{\beta}_0 = 569.58$ This has no meaning because $x = 0$ is not in the observed range.

e. $\hat{\beta}_1 = -.0019$ When the salary increases by \$1, the mean retaliation index is estimated to decrease by .0019. This is meaningful for the range of x from \$16,900 to \$70,000.

f. Some preliminary calculations are:

$$SS_{yy} = \sum y^2 - \frac{\left(\sum y\right)^2}{n} = 4,061,063 - \frac{7,497^2}{15} = 314,062.4$$

$$SSE = SS_{yy} - \hat{\beta}_1 SS_{xy} = 314,062.4 - (-.001923729)(-7,964,180) = 298,741.476$$

$$s^2 = MSE = \frac{SSE}{n-2} = \frac{298,741.476}{15-2} = 22,980.11354 \qquad s = \sqrt{22,980.11354} = 151.591931$$

$$s_{\hat{\beta}_1} = \frac{s}{\sqrt{SS_{xx}}} = \frac{151.591931}{\sqrt{4,139,969,330}} = .002356$$

To determine if the model is adequate, we test:

H_0: $\beta_1 = 0$
H_a: $\beta_1 \neq 0$

The test statistic is $t = \dfrac{\hat{\beta}_1}{s_{\hat{\beta}_1}} = \dfrac{-.00192}{.002356} = -.82$.

The rejection region requires $\alpha/2 = .05/2 = .025$ in each tail of the t-distribution with df $= n - 2 = 15 - 2 = 13$. From Table V, Appendix B, $t_{.025} = 2.160$. The rejection region is $t < -2.160$ or $t > 2.160$. Since the observed value of the test statistic does not fall in the rejection region ($t = -.82 \not< -2.160$), H_0 is not rejected. There is insufficient evidence to indicate that the model is adequate at $\alpha = .05$.

10.91 a. The correlation between Australia and the U.S. is .48. There is a moderately weak positive linear relationship between the returns on stocks of Australia and the U.S.

c. These correlation coefficients are measuring the strength of the linear relationship between the returns on stocks of a country and the U.S. The actual relationship could be something other than linear.

10.93 a. Using MINITAB, the regression analysis is:

Regression Analysis: Index versus Interactions

```
The regression equation is
Index = 44.1 + 0.237 Interactions

Predictor        Coef      SE Coef         T         P
Constant       44.130        9.362      4.71     0.000
Interact       0.2366       0.1865      1.27     0.222

S = 19.40        R-Sq = 8.6%       R-Sq(adj) = 3.3%

Analysis of Variance

Source            DF          SS         MS        F        P
Regression         1       606.0      606.0     1.61    0.222
Residual Error    17      6400.6      376.5
Total             18      7006.6
```

For confidence coefficient .90, $\alpha = 1 - .90 = .10$ and $\alpha/2 = .10/2 = .05$. From Table VI, Appendix B, $t_{.05} = 1.740$ with df $= n - 2 = 19 - 2 = 17$.

The prediction interval is:

$$\hat{y} \pm t_{\alpha/2}\, s \sqrt{1 + \frac{1}{n} + \frac{(x_p - \bar{x})^2}{SS_{xx}}} \quad \text{where } \hat{y} = 44.13 + .2366(55) = 57.14$$

$$\Rightarrow 57.14 \pm 1.74(19.40)\sqrt{1 + \frac{1}{19} + \frac{(55 - 44.1579)^2}{10,824.5263}} \Rightarrow 57.14 \pm 34.82$$

$$\Rightarrow (22.32, 91.96)$$

b. The number of interactions with outsiders in the study went from 10 to 82. The value 110 is not within this interval. We do not know if the relationship between *x* and *y* is the same outside the observed range. Also, the farther x_p lies from the larger will be the error of prediction. The prediction interval for a particular value of *y* will be very wide when $x_p = 110$.

c. The prediction interval for a manager's success index will be narrowest when the number of contacts with people outside her work unit is $\bar{x} = 44.1579$ (44).

10.95 Using MINITAB, the regression analysis is:

Regression Analysis: Value versus Age

```
The regression equation is
Value = - 92.5 + 8.35 Age

Predictor        Coef      SE Coef         T         P
Constant       -92.46        79.29     -1.17     0.249
Age             8.347         2.570      3.25     0.002

S = 286.5        R-Sq = 18.0%      R-Sq(adj) = 16.3%

Analysis of Variance

Source            DF          SS         MS        F        P
Regression         1      865746     865746    10.55    0.002
Residual Error    48     3939797      82079
Total             49     4805542
```

The fitted regression line is: $\hat{y} = -92.46 + 8.347x$

A scattergram of the data is:

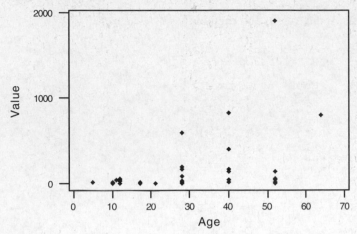

It appears that there is a positive linear relationship between age and market value, but it does not appear to be very strong.

To determine if age and market value are linearly related, we test:

H_0: $\beta_1 = 0$
H_0: $\beta_1 \neq 0$

From the printout, the test statistic is $t = 3.25$.

The p-value is $p = .002$. Since the p-value is so small, we will reject H_0. There is sufficient evidence to indicate a linear relationship between age and market value at $\alpha > .002$.

$r^2 = .18$. 18% of the total sample variability around the sample mean market value is explained by the linear relationship between market value and age.

10.97   a.

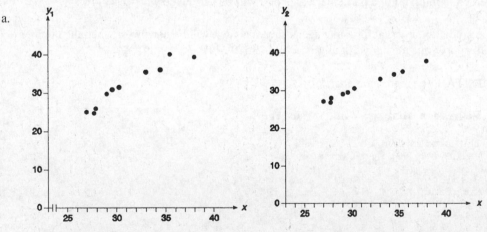

     b.   It appears that the weigh-in-motion reading after calibration adjustment is more highly correlated with the static weight of trucks than prior to calibration adjustment. The scattergram is closer to a straight line.

c. Some preliminary calculations are:

$$\sum x = 312.8 \qquad \sum y = 9911.42 \qquad \sum xy_1 = 10{,}201.41$$

$$\sum y_1 = 320.2 \qquad \sum y_1^2 = 10{,}543.68 \qquad n = 10$$

$$\sum y_2 = 311.2 \qquad \sum y_2^2 = 9809.52 \qquad \sum xy_2 = 9859.84$$

$$SS_{xy_1} = \sum xy_1 - \frac{\sum x \sum y_1}{n} = 10{,}201.41 - \frac{312.8(320.2)}{10} = 185.554$$

$$SS_{xx} = \sum x^2 - \frac{\left(\sum x\right)^2}{n} = 9911.42 - \frac{312.8^2}{10} = 127.036$$

$$SS_{y_1y_1} = \sum y_1^2 - \frac{\left(\sum y_1\right)^2}{n} = 10{,}543.68 - \frac{320.2^2}{10} = 290.876$$

$$SS_{xy_2} = \sum xy_2 - \frac{\sum x \sum y_2}{n} = 9859.84 - \frac{312.8(311.2)}{10} = 125.504$$

$$SS_{y_2y_2} = \sum y_2^2 - \frac{\left(\sum y_2\right)^2}{n} = 9809.52 \quad \frac{311.2^2}{10} = 124.976$$

$$r_1 = \frac{SS_{xy_1}}{\sqrt{SS_{xx}SS_{y_1y_1}}} = \frac{185.554}{\sqrt{127.036(290.876)}} = .965$$

$$r_2 = \frac{SS_{xy_2}}{\sqrt{SS_{xx}SS_{y_2y_2}}} = \frac{125.504}{\sqrt{127.036(124.976)}} = .996$$

$r_1 = .956$ implies the static weight of trucks and weigh-in-motion prior to calibration adjustment have a strong positive linear relationship.

$r_2 = .996$ implies the static weight of trucks and weigh-in-motion after calibration adjustment have a stronger positive linear relationship.

The closer r is to 1 indicates the more accurate the weigh-in-motion readings are.

d. Yes. If the weigh-in-motion readings were all exactly the same distance below (or above) the actual readings, r would be 1.

10.99   a.   Using MINITAB, the results of fitting the regression line are:

Regression Analysis: Offices versus Lawyers

```
The regression equation is
Offices = 2.78 + 0.0170 Lawyers


Predictor       Coef    SE Coef      T       P
Constant      2.7803     0.7522    3.70   0.001
Lawyers     0.016958   0.004219    4.02   0.001


S = 2.24627    R-Sq = 40.2%    R-Sq(adj) = 37.7%


Analysis of Variance

Source          DF        SS       MS      F       P
Regression       1    81.518   81.518  16.16   0.001
Residual Error  24   121.097    5.046
Total           25   202.615


Unusual Observations

Obs   Lawyers   Offices      Fit   SE Fit   Residual   St Resid
  1       529    11.000   11.751    1.681     -0.751      -0.50 X
 14       100    12.000    4.476    0.479      7.524       3.43R


R denotes an observation with a large standardized residual.
X denotes an observation whose X value gives it large influence.
```

The least squares regression lie is: $\hat{y} = 2.7803 + 0.01696x$.

b.   To determine if there is a significant linear relationship between the number of law offices and the number of lawyers, we test:

H_0: $\beta = 0$
H_a: $\beta \neq 0$

From the printout, the test statistic is $t = 4.02$ and the p-value is $p = 0.001$. Since the p-value is very small, we would reject H_0 for any reasonable value of α. There is sufficient evidence to indicate that there is a linear relationship between the number of law offices and the number of lawyers at any value of $\alpha > 0.001$.

From the printout, the value of r^2 is R-Sq = 40.2% or .402. Thus, 40.2% of the total sample variability around the sample mean number of law offices is explained by the linear relationship between the number of law offices and the number of lawyers. Thus, there is a significant linear relationship between the number of law offices and the number of lawyers, but less than half of the variability is being explained by the model. This model may not be real good for predicting the number of law offices based on the number of lawyers.

c.   For $x = 300$, $\hat{y} = 2.7803 + 0.01696(300) = 7.8683$. Thus, if a firm has 300 lawyers, they build 8 law offices.

10.101   Using MINITAB, the two regression analyses are:

Regression Analysis

```
The regression equation is
Ind.Costs = 301 + 10.3 Mach-Hours

Predictor      Coef      StDev         T       P
Constant      301.0      229.8      1.31    0.219
Mach-Hou     10.312      3.124      3.30    0.008

S = 170.5      R-Sq = 52.1%      R-Sq(adj) = 47.4%

Analysis of Variance

Source           DF         SS        MS       F       P
Regression        1     316874    316874   10.90   0.008
Residual Error   10     290824     29082
Total            11     607698
```

Regression Analysis

```
The regression equation is
Ind.Costs = 745 + 7.72 Direct-Hours
Predictor      Coef      StDev         T       P
Constant      744.7      217.6      3.42    0.007
Direct-H      7.716      5.396      1.43    0.183
S = 224.6      R-Sq = 17.0%      R-Sq(adj) = 8.7%

Analysis of Variance

Source           DF         SS        MS       F       P
Regression        1     103187    103187    2.05   0.183
Residual Error   10     504511     50451
Total            11     607698

Unusual Observations
Obs    Direct-H    Ind.Cost       Fit   StDev Fit   Residual   St  Resid
  9        70.0      1316.0    1284.8      181.9       31.2         0.24 X

X denotes an observation whose X value gives it large influence.
```

From these two cost functions, the model containing Machine-Hours should be used to predict Indirect Manufacturing Labor Costs. There is a significant linear relationship between Indirect Manufacturing Labor Costs and Machine-Hours $(t = 3.30, p = 0.008)$. There is not a significant linear relationship between Indirect Manufacturing Labor Costs and Direct Manufacturing Labor-Hours $(t = 1.43, p = 0.183)$. The r^2 for the first model is .521 while the r^2 for the second model is .170. In addition, the standard deviation for the first model is 170.5 while the standard deviation for the second model is 224.6. All of these lead to the better model as the model containing Machine-Hours as the independent variable.

Chapter 11
Multiple Regression and Model Building

11.1 a. $E(y) = \beta_0 + \beta_1 x_1 + \beta_2 x_2$

  b. $E(y) = \beta_0 + \beta_1 x_1 + \beta_2 x_2 + \beta_3 x_3 + \beta_4 x_4$

  c. $E(y) = \beta_0 + \beta_1 x_1 + \beta_2 x_2 + \beta_3 x_3 + \beta_4 x_4 + \beta_5 x_5$

11.3 a. We are given $\hat{\beta}_2 = 2.7$, $s_{\hat{\beta}_1} = 1.86$, and $n = 30$.

H_0: $\beta_2 = 0$
H_a: $\beta_2 \neq 0$

The test statistic is $t = \dfrac{\hat{\beta}_2 - 0}{s_{\hat{\beta}_2}} = \dfrac{2.7}{1.86} = 1.45$

The rejection region requires $\alpha/2 = .05/2 = .025$ in each tail of the t distribution with df $= n - (k + 1)$ $= 30 - (3 + 1) = 26$. From Table V, Appendix B, $t_{.025} = 2.056$. The rejection region is $t < -2.056$ or $t > 2.056$.

Since the observed value of the test statistic does not fall in the rejection region ($t = 1.45 \ngtr 2.056$), H_0 is not rejected. There is insufficient evidence to indicate $\beta_2 \neq 0$ at $\alpha = .05$.

  b. We are given $\beta_3 = .93$, $s_{\hat{\beta}_3} = .29$, and $n = 30$.

Test H_0: $\beta_3 = 0$
      H_a: $\beta_3 \neq 0$

The test statistic is $t = \dfrac{\hat{\beta}_3 - 0}{s_{\hat{\beta}_3}} = \dfrac{.93}{.29} = 3.21$

The rejection region is the same as part **a**, $t < -2.056$ or $t > 2.056$.

Since the observed value of the test statistic falls in the rejection region ($t = 3.21 > 2.056$), H_0 is rejected. There is sufficient evidence to indicate $\beta_3 \neq 0$ at $\alpha = .05$.

  c. $\hat{\beta}_3$ has a smaller estimated standard error than $\hat{\beta}_2$. Therefore, the test statistic is larger for $\hat{\beta}_3$ even though $\hat{\beta}_3$ is smaller than $\hat{\beta}_2$.

11.5 The number of degrees of freedom available for estimating σ^2 is $n - (k + 1)$ where k is the number of independent variables in the regression model. Each additional independent variable placed in the model causes a corresponding decrease in the degrees of freedom.

11.7   a.   Yes. Since $R^2 = .92$ is close to 1, this indicates the model provides a good fit. Without knowledge of the units of the dependent variable, the value of SSE cannot be used to determine how well the model fits.

b. $H_0: \beta_1 = \beta_2 = \cdots = \beta_5 = 0$
$H_a:$ At least one of the parameters is not 0

The test statistic is $F = \dfrac{R^2 / k}{(1 - R^2)/[n - (k+1)]} = \dfrac{.92/5}{(1 - .92)/[30 - (5+1)]} = 55.2$

The rejection region requires $\alpha = .05$ in the upper tail of the F distribution with $v_1 = k = 5$ and $v_2 = n - (k + 1) = 30 - (5 + 1) = 24$. From Table VIII, Appendix B, $F_{.05} = 2.62$. The rejection region is $F > 2.62$.

Since the observed value of the test statistic falls in the rejection region ($F = 55.2 > 2.62$), H_0 is rejected. There is sufficient evidence to indicate the model is useful in predicting y at $\alpha = .05$.

11.9   a.   To determine if the model is useful, we test:

$H_0: \beta_1 = \beta_2 = \beta_3 = \beta_4 = 0$
$H_a:$ At least 1 $\beta_i \neq 0$

From the problem, the test statistic is $F = 4.74$ and the p-value is less than .01.
Since the p-value is less than $\alpha = .05$ ($p < .01$), H_0 is rejected. There is sufficient evidence to indicate the model is useful for predicting accountant's Mach scores at $\alpha = .05$

b. $R^2 = .13$. 13% of the total sample variation of the accountant's Mach scores around their means is explained by the model containing age, gender, education, and income.

c.   To determine if income is a useful predictor of Mach score, we test:

$H_0: \beta_4 = 0$
$H_a: \beta_4 \neq 0$

From the printout, $t = 0.52$ and the p-value is $p > .10$. Since the p-value is greater than $\alpha = .05$ ($p > .10$), H_0 is not rejected. There is insufficient evidence to indicate that income is a useful predictor of Mach score at $\alpha = .05$.

11.11   a.   The least squares prediction equation is: $\hat{y} = 1.81231 + 0.10875x_1 + 0.00017x_2$

b. $\hat{\beta}_o = 1.81231$. Since $x_1 = 0$ and $x_2 = 0$ are not in the observed range, $\hat{\beta}_o$ has no meaning.

$\hat{\beta}_1 = 0.10875$. For each additional mile of roadway length, the mean number of crashes per three years is estimated to increase by .10875 when average annual daily traffic is held constant.

$\hat{\beta}_2 = 0.00017$. For each additional unit increase in average annual daily traffic, the mean number of crashes per three years is estimated to increase by .00017 when miles of roadway length is held constant.

c.   For confidence coefficient .99, $\alpha = .01$ and $\alpha/2 = .01/2 = .005$. From Table V, Appendix B, with df $= n - (k+1) = 100 - (2+1) = 97$, $t_{.005} \approx 2.63$. The 99% confidence interval is:

$$\hat{\beta}_1 \pm t_{.005}s_{\hat{\beta}_1} \Rightarrow 0.10875 \pm 2.63(0.03166) \Rightarrow 0.10875 \pm 0.08327$$
$$\Rightarrow (0.02548, \ 0.19202)$$

We are 99% confident that the increase in the mean number of crashes per three years will be between 0.02548 and 0.19202 for each additional mile of roadway length, holding average annual daily traffic constant.

d.   The 99% confidence interval is:

$$\hat{\beta}_2 \pm t_{.005}s_{\hat{\beta}_2} \Rightarrow 0.00017 \pm 2.63(0.00003) \Rightarrow 0.00017 \pm 0.00008$$
$$\Rightarrow (0.00009, \ 0.00025)$$

We are 99% confident that the increase in the mean number of crashes per three years will be between 0.00009 and 0.00025 for each additional unit increase in average annual daily traffic, holding mile of roadway length constant.

e.   The least squares prediction equation is: $\hat{y} = 1.20785 + 0.06343x_1 + 0.00056x_2$

$\hat{\beta}_o = 1.20785$. Since $x_1 = 0$ and $x_2 = 0$ are not in the observed range, $\hat{\beta}_o$ has no meaning.

$\hat{\beta}_1 = 0.06343$. For each additional mile of roadway length, the mean number of crashes per three years is estimated to increase by 0.06343 when average annual daily traffic is held constant.

$\hat{\beta}_2 = 0.00056$. For each additional unit increase in average annual daily traffic, the mean number of crashes per three years is estimated to increase by 0.00056 when miles of roadway length is held constant.

The 99% confidence interval is:

$$\hat{\beta}_1 \pm t_{.005}s_{\hat{\beta}_1} \Rightarrow 0.06343 \pm 2.63(0.01809) \Rightarrow 0.06343 \pm 0.04758$$
$$\Rightarrow (0.01585, \ 0.11101)$$

We are 99% confident that the increase in the mean number of crashes per three years will be between 0.01585 and 0.11101 for each additional mile of roadway length, holding average annual daily traffic constant.

The 99% confidence interval is:

$$\hat{\beta}_2 \pm t_{.005}s_{\hat{\beta}_2} \Rightarrow 0.00056 \pm 2.63(0.00012) \Rightarrow 0.00056 \pm 0.00032$$
$$\Rightarrow (0.00024, \ 0.00088)$$

We are 99% confident that the increase in the mean number of crashes per three years will be between 0.00024 and 0.00088 for each additional unit increase in average annual daily traffic, holding mile of roadway length constant.

11.13   a. $\hat{\beta}_1 = 2.006$. For each unit increase in the proportion of block with low-density residential areas, the mean population density is estimated to increase by 2.006, holding proportion of block with high-density residential areas constant. Since x_1 is a proportion, it is unlikely that it can increase by one unit. A better interpretation is: For each increase of .1 in the proportion of block with low-density residential areas, the mean population density is estimated to increase by .2006, holding proportion of block with high-density residential areas constant.

$\hat{\beta}_2 = 5.006$. For each unit increase in the proportion of block with high-density residential areas, the mean population density is estimated to increase by 5.006, holding proportion of block with low-density residential areas constant. Since x_2 is a proportion, it is unlikely that it can increase by one unit. A better interpretation is: For each increase of .1 in the proportion of block with high-density residential areas, the mean population density is estimated to increase by .5006, holding proportion of block with low-density residential areas constant.

   b. $R^2 = .686$. 68.6% of the total sample variation of the population densities is explained by the linear relationship between population density and the independent variables proportion of block with low-density residential areas and the proportion of block with high-density residential areas.

   c.   To determine if the overall model is adequate, we test:

H_0: $\beta_1 = \beta_2 = 0$
H_a: At least one $\beta_i \neq 0$

   d.   The test statistic is $F = \dfrac{R^2 / k}{(1 - R^2) / [n - (k+1)]} = \dfrac{.686 / 2}{(1 - .686) / [125 - (2+1)]} = 133.27$

   d.   The rejection region requires $\alpha = .01$ in the upper tail of the F distribution with $\upsilon_1 = k = 2$ and $\upsilon_2 = n - (k + 1) = 125 - (2 + 1) = 122$. From Table X, Appendix B, $F_{.01} \approx 4.79$. The rejection region is $F > 4.79$.

Since the observed value of the test statistic falls in the rejection region ($F = 133.27 > 4.79$), H_0 is rejected. There is sufficient evidence to indicate the model is adequate at $\alpha = .01$.

11.15   a.   The first order model would be

$$E(y) = \beta_0 + \beta_1 x_1 + \beta_2 x_2 + \beta_3 x_3 + \beta_4 x_4$$

   b.   Since the p-value is less than α ($p = .005 < .01$), H_0 is rejected. There is sufficient evidence to indicate that there is a negative linear relationship between change from routine and the number of years played golf, holding number of rounds of golf per year, total number of golf vacations, and average golf score constant.

   c.   The statement would be correct if the independent variables are not correlated. However, if the independent variables are correlated, then this interpretation would not necessarily hold.

   d.   To determine if the overall first-order regression model is adequate, we test:

H_0: $\beta_1 = \beta_2 = \beta_3 = \beta_4 = 0$

   e.   For all dependent variables, the rejection region requires $\alpha = .01$ in the upper tail of the F-distribution with $\nu_1 = k = 4$ and $\nu_2 = n - (k + 1) = 393 - (4 + 1) = 388$. From Table X, Appendix B, $F_{.01} \approx 3.32$. The rejection region is $F > 3.32$. Using MINITAB, the exact $F_{.01, 4, 388}$ is 3.67. The true rejection region is $F > 3.67$.

f.   For **Thrill**: Since the observed value of the test statistic falls in the rejection region
     ($F = 5.56 > 3.67$), H_0 is rejected. There is sufficient evidence to indicate at least one of the 4
     independent variables is linearly related to Thrill at $\alpha = .01$.

     For **Change from Routine**: Since the observed value of the test statistic does not fall in the rejection
     region ($F = 3.02 \not> 3.67$), H_0 is not rejected. There is insufficient evidence to indicate at least one of
     the 4 independent variables is linearly related to Change from Routine at $\alpha = .01$.

     For **Surprise**: Since the observed value of the test statistic does not fall in the rejection region ($F =
     3.33 \not> 3.67$), H_0 is not rejected. There is insufficient evidence to indicate at least one of the 4
     independent variables is linearly related to Surprise at $\alpha = .01$.

e.   For Thrill: Since the p-value is less than α ($p < .001 < .01$), H_0 is rejected. There is sufficient evidence
     to indicate that at least one of the independent variables is linearly related to Thrill at $\alpha = .01$.

     For Change from Routine: Since the p-value is not less than α ($p = .018 > .01$), H_0 is not rejected.
     There is insufficient evidence to indicate that at least one of the independent variables is linearly
     related to Change from Routine at $\alpha = .01$.

     For Surprise: Since the p-value is not less than α ($p = .011 > .01$), H_0 is not rejected. There is
     insufficient evidence to indicate that at least one of the independent variables is linearly related to
     Surprise at $\alpha = .01$.

h.   For Thrill: $R^2 = .055$. 5.5% of the total variability around the mean thrill values can be explained by
     the model containing the 4 independent variables: x_1 = number of rounds of golf per year, x_2 = total
     number of golf vacations taken, x_3 = number of years played golf, and x_4 = average golf score.

     For Change from Routine: $R^2 = .030$. 3.0% of the total variability around the mean change from
     routine values can be explained by the model containing the 4 independent variables: x_1 = number of
     rounds of golf per year, x_2 = total number of golf vacations taken, x_3 = number of years played golf,
     and x_4 = average golf score.

     For Surprise: $R^2 = .023$. 2.3% of the total variability around the mean surprise values can be
     explained by the model containing the 4 independent variables: x_1 = number of rounds of golf per
     year, x_2 = total number of golf vacations taken, x_3 = number of years played golf, and x_4 = average
     golf score.

11.17   a.   The first-order model is: $E(y) = \beta_0 + \beta_1 x_1 + \beta_2 x_2$

     b.   Using MINITAB, the results of fitting the model are:

Regression Analysis: Earnings versus Age, Hours

```
The regression equation is
Earnings = - 20 + 13.4 Age + 244 Hours


Predictor    Coef   SE Coef      T       P
Constant    -20.4     652.7   -0.03   0.976
Age        13.350     7.672    1.74   0.107
Hours      243.71     63.51    3.84   0.002


S = 547.737   R-Sq = 58.2%   R-Sq(adj) = 51.3%

Analysis of Variance

Source          DF        SS       MS      F      P
Regression       2   5018232  2509116   8.36  0.005
Residual Error  12   3600196   300016
Total           14   8618428

Source   DF   Seq SS
Age       1    600498
Hours     1   4417734


Unusual Observations

Obs   Age   Earnings    Fit   SE Fit   Residual   St Resid
  4  18.0       1552   2657      205      -1105      -2.18R

R denotes an observation with a large standardized residual.
```

The least squares prediction equation is: $\hat{y} = -20.4 + 13.350 x_1 + 243.71 x_2$

     c. $\hat{\beta}_0 = -20.4$. This has no meaning since $x_1 = 0$ and $x_2 = 0$ are not in the observed range.

         $\hat{\beta}_1 = 13.350$. For each additional year of age, the mean annual earnings is predicted to increase by $13.350, holding hours worked per day constant.

         $\hat{\beta}_2 = 243.71$. For each additional hour worked per day, the mean annual earnings is predicted to increase by $243.71, holding age constant.

     d.   To determine if age is a useful predictor of annual earnings, we test:

$H_0: \beta_1 = 0$
$H_a: \beta_1 \neq 0$

The test statistic is $t = 1.74$.

The p-value is $p = .107$. Since the p-value is greater than $\alpha = .01$ ($p = .107 > \alpha = .01$), H_0 is not rejected. There is insufficient evidence to indicate that age is a useful predictor of annual earnings, adjusted for hours worked per day, at $\alpha = .01$.

e.   For confidence coefficient .95, $\alpha = .05$ and $\alpha/2 = .05/2 = .025$. From Table V, Appendix B, with df $= n - (k + 1) = 15 - (2 + 1) = 12$, $t_{.025} = 2.179$. The 95% confidence interval is:

$$\hat{\beta}_2 \pm t_{.005} s_{\hat{\beta}_2} \Rightarrow 243.71 \pm 2.179(63.51) \Rightarrow 243.71 \pm 138.388$$

$$\Rightarrow (105.322, \quad 382.098)$$

We are 95% confident that the change in the mean annual earnings for each additional hour worked per day will be somewhere between \$105.322 and \$382.098, holding age constant.

f.   From the printout, $R^2 = R\text{-Sq} = 58.2\%$ or $.582$. 58.2% of the total sample variance of annual earnings is explained by the model containing age and hours worked per day.

g. $R^2_a = R\text{-Sq(adj)} = 51.3\%$ or $.513$.   51.3% of the total sample variance of annual earnings is explained by the model containing age and hours worked per day, adjusted for the sample size and the number of parameters in the model.

h.   To determine if at least one of the variables is useful in predicting the annual earnings, we test:

H_0: $\beta_1 = \beta_2 = 0$
H_a: At least 1 $\beta_i \neq 0$

The test statistic is $F = 8.36$ and the p-value is $p = .005$. Since the p-value is less than $\alpha = .01$ $(p = .005 < .01)$, H_0 is rejected. There is sufficient evidence to indicate at least one of the variables is useful in predicting the annual earnings at $\alpha = .01$.

11.19   a.   The 1st-order model is $E(y) = \beta_0 + \beta_1 x_1 + \beta_2 x_2 + \beta_3 x_3 + \beta_4 x_4 + \beta_5 x_5$.

b.   Using MINITAB, the results are:

Regression Analysis: HEATRATE versus RPM, INLET-TEMP, ...

```
The regression equation is
HEATRATE = 13614 + 0.0888 RPM - 9.20 INLET-TEMP + 14.4 EXH-TEMP + 0.4 CPRATIO
           - 0.848 AIRFLOW


Predictor      Coef   SE Coef       T      P
Constant    13614.5     870.0   15.65  0.000
RPM         0.08879   0.01391    6.38  0.000
INLET-TEMP   -9.201     1.499   -6.14  0.000
EXH-TEMP     14.394     3.461    4.16  0.000
CPRATIO        0.35     29.56    0.01  0.991
AIRFLOW     -0.8480    0.4421   -1.92  0.060


S = 458.828   R-Sq = 92.4%   R-Sq(adj) = 91.7%
```

```
Analysis of Variance

Source           DF         SS        MS       F       P
Regression        5   155055273  31011055  147.30   0.000
Residual Error   61    12841935    210524
Total            66   167897208


Source       DF     Seq SS
RPM           1  119598530
INLET-TEMP    1   26893467
EXH-TEMP      1    7784225
CPRATIO       1       4623
AIRFLOW       1     774427


Unusual Observations

Obs     RPM   HEATRATE      Fit  SE Fit  Residual  St Resid
 11   18000    14628.0  13214.0   117.9    1414.0     3.19R
 32   14950    10656.0  11663.0   132.5   -1007.0    -2.29R
 36    4473    13523.0  12489.5   195.1    1033.5     2.49R
 47    7280    11588.0  10533.0   154.7    1055.0     2.44R
 61   33000    16243.0  15758.0   246.5     485.0     1.25 X
 64    3600     8714.0   8415.2   340.9     298.8     0.97 X

R denotes an observation with a large standardized residual.
X denotes an observation whose X value gives it large influence.
```

The least squares prediction equation is:

$$\hat{y} = 13,614.5 + 0.0888x_1 - 9.201x_2 + 14.394x_3 + 0.35x_4 - 0.848x_5$$

c. $\hat{\beta}_o = 13,614.5$. Since 0 is not within the range of all the independent variables, this value has no meaning.

$\hat{\beta}_1 = 0.0888$. For each unit increase in RPM, the mean heat rate is estimated to increase by .0888, holding all the other 4 variables constant.

$\hat{\beta}_2 = -9.201$. For each unit increase in inlet temperature, the mean heat rate is estimated to decrease by 9.201, holding all the other 4 variables constant.

$\hat{\beta}_3 = 14.394$. For each unit increase in exhaust temperature, the mean heat rate is estimated to increase by 14.394, holding all the other 4 variables constant.

$\hat{\beta}_4 = 0.35$. For each unit increase in cycle pressure ratio, the mean heat rate is estimated to increase by 0.35, holding all the other 4 variables constant.

$\hat{\beta}_5 = -0.8480$. For each unit increase in air flow rate, the mean heat rate is estimated to decrease by .848, holding all the other 4 variables constant.

d.   From the printout, $s = 458.828$. We would expect to see most of the heat rate values within $2s$ or $2(458.828) = 917.656$ units of the least squares line.

e. To determine if at least one of the variables is useful in predicting the heat rate values, we test:

H_0: $\beta_1 = \beta_2 = \beta_3 = \beta_4 = \beta_5 = 0$
H_a: At least 1 $\beta_i \neq 0$

The test statistic is $F = 147.30$ and the p-value is $p = .000$. Since the p-value is less than $\alpha = .01$ $(p = .000 < .01)$, H_0 is rejected. There is sufficient evidence to indicate at least one of the variables is useful in predicting the heat rate values at $\alpha = .01$.

f. $R^2_a = R\text{-Sq(adj)} = 91.7\%$ or $.917$. 91.7% of the total sample variance of the heat rate values is explained by the model containing the 5 independent variables.

g. To determine if there is evidence to indicate heat rate is linearly related to inlet temperature, we test:

H_0: $\beta_2 = 0$
H_a: $\beta_2 \neq 0$

The test statistic is t = -6.14 and the p-value is $p = 0.000$. Since the p-value is less than $\alpha = .01$ $(p = .000 < .01)$, H_0 is rejected. There is sufficient evidence to indicate heat rate is linearly related to inlet temperature at $\alpha = .01$.

11.21 a. $R^2 = .362$. 36.2% of the variability in the AC scores can be explained by the model containing the variables self-esteem score, optimism score, and group cohesion score.

b. To test the utility of the model, we test:

H_0: $\beta_1 = \beta_2 = \beta_3 = 0$
H_a: At least one $\beta_i \neq 0$, $i = 1, 2, 3$

The test statistic is:

$$F = \frac{R^2 / k}{(1 - R^2)/[n - (k+1)]} = \frac{.362/3}{(1 - .362)/[31 - (3+1)]} = 5.11$$

The rejection region requires $\alpha = .05$ in the upper tail of the F distribution with $v_1 = k = 3$ and $v_2 = n - (k+1) = 31 - (3+1) = 27$. From Table VIII, Appendix B, $F_{.05} = 2.96$. The rejection region is $F > 2.96$.

Since the observed value of the test statistic falls in the rejection region $(F = 5.11 > 2.96)$, H_0 is rejected. There is sufficient evidence that the model is useful in predicting AC score at $\alpha = .05$.

11.23 a. **Model 1:**

H_0: $\beta_1 = 0$
H_a: $\beta_1 \neq 0$

The test statistic is $t = \dfrac{\hat{\beta}_1 - 0}{s_{\hat{\beta}_1}} = \dfrac{.0354}{.0137} = 2.58$.

Since no α was given, we will use $\alpha = .05$. The rejection region requires $\alpha/2 = .05/2 = .025$ in each tail of the t distribution. From Table V, Appendix B, with df = $n - (k+1) = 12 - (1+1) = 10$, $t_{.025} = 2.228$. The rejection region is $t < -2.228$ or $t > 2.228$.

Since the observed value of the test statistic falls in the rejection region ($t = 2.58 > 2.228$), H_0 is rejected. There is sufficient evidence to indicate that there is a linear relationship between vintage and the logarithm of price.

Model 2:

H_0: $\beta_1 = 0$
H_a: $\beta_1 \neq 0$

The test statistic is $t = \dfrac{\hat{\beta}_1 - 0}{s_{\hat{\beta}_1}} = \dfrac{.0238}{.00717} = 3.32$

Since no α was given, we will use $\alpha = .05$. The rejection region requires $\alpha/2 = .05/2 = .025$ in each tail of the t distribution. From Table V, Appendix B, with df $= n - (k + 1) = 12 - (4 + 1) = 7$, $t_{.025} = 2.365$. The rejection region is $t < -2.365$ or $t > 2.365$.

Since the observed value of the test statistic falls in the rejection region ($t = 3.32 > 2.365$), H_0 is rejected. There is sufficient evidence to indicate that there is a linear relationship between vintage and the logarithm of price, adjusting for all other variables.

H_0: $\beta_2 = 0$
H_a: $\beta_2 \neq 0$

The test statistic is $t = \dfrac{\hat{\beta}_2 - 0}{s_{\hat{\beta}_2}} = \dfrac{.616}{.0952} = 6.47$

The rejection region is $t < -2.365$ or $t > 2.365$.

Since the observed value of the test statistic falls in the rejection region ($t = 6.47 > 2.365$), H_0 is rejected. There is sufficient evidence to indicate that there is a linear relationship between average growing season temperature and the logarithm of price, adjusting for all other variables.

H_0: $\beta_3 = 0$
H_a: $\beta_3 \neq 0$

The test statistic is $t = \dfrac{\hat{\beta}_3 - 0}{s_{\hat{\beta}_3}} = \dfrac{-.00386}{.00081} = -4.77$

The rejection region is $t < -2.365$ or $t > 2.365$.

Since the observed value of the test statistic falls in the rejection region ($t = -4.77 < -2.365$), H_0 is rejected. There is sufficient evidence to indicate that there is a linear relationship between Sept./Aug. rainfall and the logarithm of price, adjusting for all other variables.

H_0: $\beta_4 = 0$
H_a: $\beta_4 \neq 0$

The test statistic is $t = \dfrac{\hat{\beta}_4 - 0}{s_{\hat{\beta}_4}} = \dfrac{.0001173}{.000482} = 0.24$.

The rejection region is $t < -2.365$ or $t > 2.365$.

Since the observed value of the test statistic does not fall in the rejection region ($t = 0.24 \not> 2.365$), H_0 is not rejected. There is insufficient evidence to indicate that there is a linear relationship between rainfall in months preceding vintage and the logarithm of price, adjusting for all other variables.

Model 3:

H_0: $\beta_1 = 0$
H_a: $\beta_1 \neq 0$

The test statistic is $t = \dfrac{\hat{\beta}_1 - 0}{s_{\hat{\beta}_1}} = \dfrac{.0240}{.00747} = 3.21$

Since no α was given, we will use $\alpha = .05$. The rejection region requires $\alpha/2 = .05/2 = .025$ in each tail of the t distribution. From Table V, Appendix B, with df $= n - (k + 1) = 12 - (5 + 1) = 7$, $t_{.025} = 2.447$. The rejection region is $t < -2.447$ or $t > 2.447$.

Since the observed value of the test statistic falls in the rejection region ($t = 3.21 > 2.447$), H_0 is rejected. There is sufficient evidence to indicate that there is a linear relationship between vintage and the logarithm of price, adjusting for all other variables.

H_0: $\beta_2 = 0$
H_a: $\beta_2 \neq 0$

The test statistic is $t = \dfrac{\hat{\beta}_2 - 0}{s_{\hat{\beta}_2}} = \dfrac{.608}{.116} = 5.24$.

The rejection region is $t < -2.447$ or $t > 2.447$.

Since the observed value of the test statistic falls in the rejection region ($t = 5.24 > 2.447$), H_0 is rejected. There is sufficient evidence to indicate that there is a linear relationship between average growing season temperature and the logarithm of price, adjusting for all other variables.

H_0: $\beta_3 = 0$
H_a: $\beta_3 \neq 0$

The test statistic is $t = \dfrac{\hat{\beta}_3 - 0}{s_{\hat{\beta}_3}} = \dfrac{-.00380}{.00095} = -4.00$

The rejection region is $t < -2.447$ or $t > -2.447$.

Since the observed value of the test statistic falls in the rejection region ($t = -4.00 < -2.447$), H_0 is rejected. There is sufficient evidence to indicate that there is a linear relationship between Sept./Aug. rainfall and the logarithm of price, adjusting for all other variables.

H_0: $\beta_4 = 0$
H_a: $\beta_4 \neq 0$

The test statistic is $t = \dfrac{\hat{\beta}_4 - 0}{s_{\hat{\beta}_4}} = \dfrac{.00115}{.000505} = 2.28$

The rejection region is $t < -2.447$ or $t > 2.447$.

Since the observed value of the test statistic does not fall in the rejection region ($t = 2.28 \not> 2.365$), H_0 is not rejected. There is insufficient evidence to indicate that there is a linear relationship between rainfall in months preceding vintage and the logarithm of price, adjusting for all other variables.

H_0: $\beta_5 = 0$
H_a: $\beta_5 \neq 0$

The test statistic is $t = \dfrac{\hat{\beta}_5 - 0}{s_{\hat{\beta}_5}} = \dfrac{.00765}{.0565} = 0.14$.

The rejection region is $t < -2.447$ or $t > 2.447$.

Since the observed value of the test statistic does not fall in the rejection region ($t = 0.14 \not> 2.365$), H_0 is not rejected. There is insufficient evidence to indicate that there is a linear relationship between average September temperature and the logarithm of price, adjusting for all other variables.

b.   **Model 1:**

$\hat{\beta}_1 = .0354$, $e^{.0354} - 1 = .036$

We estimate that the mean price will increase by 3.6% for each additional increase of unit of x_1, vintage year.

Model 2:

$\hat{\beta}_1 = .0238$, $e^{.0238} - 1 = .024$

We estimate that the mean price will increase by 2.4% for each additional increase of 1 unit of x_1, vintage year (with all other variables held constant).

$\hat{\beta}_2 = .616$, $e^{.616} - 1 = .852$

We estimate that the mean price will increase by 85.2% for each additional increase of 1 unit of x_2, average growing season temperature °C (with all other variables held constant).

$\hat{\beta}_3 = -.00386$, $e^{-.00386} - 1 = -.004$

We estimate that the mean price will decrease by .4% for each additional increase of 1 unit of x_3, Sept./Aug. rainfall in cm (with all other variables held constant).

$\hat{\beta}_4 = .0001173$, $e^{.0001173} - 1 = .0001$

We estimate that the mean price will increase by .01% for each additional increase of 1 unit of x_4, rainfall in months preceding vintage in cm (with all other variables held constant).

Model 3:

$$\hat{\beta}_1 = .0240, \; e^{.0240} - 1 = .024$$

We estimate that the mean price will increase by 2.4% for each additional increase of 1 unit of x_1, vintage year (with all other variables held constant).

$$\hat{\beta}_2 = .608, \; e^{.608} - 1 = .837$$

We estimate that the mean price will increase by 83.7% for each additional increase of 1 unit of x_2, average growing season temperatures in °C (with all other variables held constant).

$$\hat{\beta}_3 = -.00380, \; e^{0.00380} - 1 = -.004$$

We estimate that the mean price will decrease by .4% for each additional increase of 1 unit of x_3, Sept./Aug. rainfall in cm, (with all other variables held constant).

$$\hat{\beta}_4 = .00115, \; e^{.00115} - 1 = .001$$

We estimate that the average mean price will increase by .1% for each additional increase of 1 unit of x_4, rainfall in months preceding vintage in cm (with all other variables held constant).

$$\hat{\beta}_5 = .00765, \; e^{.00765} - 1 = .008$$

We estimate that the average mean price will increase by .8% for each additional increase of 1 unit of x_5, average Sept. temperature in °C (with all other variables held constant).

c. I would recommend model 2. Model 1 has only 1 independent variable in the model and it is significant at $\alpha = .05$. The R^2 for this model is $R^2 = .212$ and $s = .575$. Model 2 has 4 independent variables in the model and all terms are significant at $\alpha = .05$ except one. This one variable is significant at $\alpha = .10$. This model has $R^2 = .828$ and $s = .287$. Comparing model 2 to model 1, the R^2 for model 2 is much larger than that for model 1 and the estimate of the standard deviation is much smaller. Model 3 contains all of the independent variables that model 2 has plus one additional variable. This additional variable is not significant at $\alpha = .10$. In addition, the R^2 for this new model = .828, the same as for model 2. However, the estimate of the standard deviation of model 3 is now larger than that of model 2. This indicates that model 2 is better than model 3.

11.25   a.   For $x_1 = 1$, $x_2 = 10$, $x_3 = 5$, and $x_4 = 2$, $\hat{y} = 3.58 + .01(1) - .06(10) - .01(5) + .42(2) = 3.78$

      b.   For $x_1 = 0$, $x_2 = 8$, $x_3 = 10$, and $x_4 = 4$, $\hat{y} = 3.58 + .01(0) - .06(8) - .01(10) + .42(4) = 4.68$

11.27   a.   The 95% prediction interval is (1,759.75, 4,275.38). We are 95% confident that the true actual annual earnings for a vendor who is 45 years old and who works 10 hours per day is between $1,759.75 and $4,275.38.

      b.   The 95% confidence interval is (2,620.25, 3,414.87). We are 95% confident that the true mean annual earnings for vendors who are 45 years old and who work 10 hours per day is between $2,620.25 and $3,414.87.

      c.   Yes. The prediction interval for the ACTUAL value of y is always wider than the confidence interval for the MEAN value of y.

11.29   a.   The 95% prediction interval is (11,599.6, 13,665.5). We are 95% confident that the actual heat rate will be between 11,599.6 and 13.665.5 when the RPM is 7,500, the inlet temperature is 1,000, the exhaust temperature is 525, the cycle pressure ratio is 13.5 and the air flow rate is 10.

       b.   The 95% confidence interval is (12,157.9, 13,107.1). We are 95% confident that the mean heat rate will be between 12,157.9 and 13,107.1 when the RPM is 7,500, the inlet temperature is 1,000, the exhaust temperature is 525, the cycle pressure ratio is 13.5 and the air flow rate is 10.

       c.   Yes. The confidence interval for the mean will always be smaller than the prediction interval for the actual value. This is because there are 2 error terms involved in predicting an actual value and only one error term involved in estimating the mean. First, we have the error in locating the mean of the distribution. Once the mean is located, the actual value can still vary around the mean, thus, the second error. There is only one error term involved when estimating the mean, which is the error in locating the mean.

11.31   a.   Using MINITAB, the results are:

Regression Analysis: PPRatio versus ARTenure, AR6Year, AveSal6

```
The regression equation is
PPRatio = 0.70 + 0.180 ARTenure + 0.0729 AR6Year - 0.120 AveSal6


Predictor        Coef   SE Coef       T       P
Constant        0.704     1.192    0.59   0.556
ARTenure      0.17957   0.08876    2.02   0.045
AR6Year       0.07285   0.07379    0.99   0.325
AveSal6      -0.11981   0.04238   -2.83   0.005


S = 8.89248   R-Sq = 11.2%   R-Sq(adj) = 9.6%


Analysis of Variance

Source           DF        SS       MS      F       P
Regression        3   1704.73   568.24   7.19   0.000
Residual Error  171  13522.03    79.08
Total           174  15226.76


Source       DF   Seq SS
ARTenure      1   994.79
AR6Year       1    78.02
AveSal6       1   631.93
```

The least squares prediction equation is: $\hat{y} = .704 + .180x_1 + .0729x_2 - .120x_3$

       b.   To determine if the model is adequate, we test:

H_0: $\beta_1 = \beta_2 = \beta_3 = 0$
H_a: At least one $\beta_i \neq 0$

From the printout, the test statistic is $F = 7.19$ and the p-value is $p = .000$.
Since the p-value is less than α ($p = .000 < .05$), H_0 is rejected. There is sufficient evidence to indicate the model is adequate at $\alpha = .05$.

c. Using MINITAB, the results are:

Predicted Values for New Observations

```
New
Obs    Fit   SE Fit       95% CI            95% PI
 1   10.098  1.830   (6.486, 13.710)   (-7.822, 28.019)


Values of Predictors for New Observations

New
Obs  ARTenure  AR6Year  AveSal6
 1     40.0     32.0     1.00
```

The 95% confidence interval for the efficiency rating of a CEO with $x_1 = 40\%$, $x_2 = 32\%$, and $x_3 = \$1$ million is $(-7.822, 28.019)$. We are 95% confident that the actual efficiency rating of a CEO with the above values for the independent variables is between -7.822 and 28.019.

11.33 a. From MINITAB, the output is:

Regression Analysis: Man-Hours versus Capacity, Pressure, Type, Drum

```
The regression equation is
Man-Hours = - 3783 + 0.00875 Capacity + 1.93 Pressure + 3444 Type + 2093 Drum

Predictor        Coef      SE Coef        T        P
Constant        -3783         1205     -3.14    0.004
Capacity    0.0087490    0.0009035      9.68    0.000
Pressure       1.9265       0.6489      2.97    0.006
Type           3444.3        911.7      3.78    0.001
Drum           2093.4        305.6      6.85    0.000

S = 894.6      R-Sq = 90.3%     R-Sq(adj) = 89.0%

Analysis of Variance

Source          DF          SS          MS        F        P
Regression       4   230854854    57713714    72.11    0.000
Residual Error  31    24809761      800315
Total           35   255664615

Source       DF      Seq SS
Capacity      1   175007141
Pressure      1      490357
Type          1    17813091
Drum          1    37544266

Predicted Values for New Observations

New Obs    Fit    SE Fit      95.0% CI           95.0% PI
1         1936       239   ( 1449,   2424) (    48,   3825)

Values of Predictors for New Observations

New Obs  Capacity  Pressure    Type    Drum
1          150000       500    1.00  0.000000
```

The fitted regression line is:

$$\hat{y} = -3,783 + 0.00875x_1 + 1.9265x_2 + 3,444.3x_3 + 2,093.4x_4$$

b. To determine if the model is useful for predicting the number of man-hours needed, we test:

H_0: $\beta_1 = \beta_2 = \beta_3 = \beta_4 = 0$
H_a: At least one $\beta_i \neq 0$, $i = 1, 2, 3, 4$

The test statistic is $F = 72.11$ with p-value $= .000$. Since the p-value is less than $\alpha = .01$, we can reject H_0. There is sufficient evidence that the model is useful for predicting man-hours at $\alpha = .01$.

c. The confidence interval is (1449, 2424).

With 95% confidence, we can conclude that the mean number of man-hours for all boilers with characteristics $x_1 = 150,000$, $x_2 = 500$, $x_3 = 1$, $x_4 = 0$ will fall between 1449 hours and 2424 hours.

11.35   a. The response surface is a twisted surface in three-dimensional space.

b. For $x_1 = 0$, $E(y) = 3 + 0 + 2x_2 - 0x_2 = 3 + 2x_2$
    For $x_1 = 1$, $E(y) = 3 + 1 + 2x_2 - 1x_2 = 4 + x_2$
    For $x_1 = 2$, $E(y) = 3 + 2 + 2x_2 - 2x_2 = 5$

The plot of the lines is

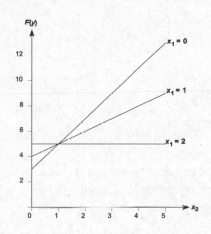

c. The lines are not parallel because interaction between x_1 and x_2 is present. Interaction between x_1 and x_2 means that the effect of x_2 on y depends on what level x_1 takes on.

d. For $x_1 = 0$, as x_2 increases from 0 to 5, $E(y)$ increases from 3 to 13.
    For $x_1 = 1$, as x_2 increases from 0 to 5, $E(y)$ increases from 4 to 9.
    For $x_1 = 2$, as x_2 increases from 0 to 5, $E(y) = 5$.

e. For $x_1 = 2$ and $x_2 = 4$, $E(y) = 5$
    For $x_1 = 0$ and $x_2 = 5$, $E(y) = 13$

Thus, $E(y)$ changes from 5 to 13.

11.37 a. The prediction equation is:

$$\hat{y} = -2.55 + 3.82x_1 + 2.63x_2 - 1.29x_1x_2$$

b. The response surface is a twisted plane, since the equation contains an interaction term.

c. For $x_2 = 1$, $= -2.55 + 3.82x_1 + 2.63(1) - 1.29x_1(1)$
        $= .08 + 2.53x_1$
    For $x_2 = 3$, $= -2.55 + 3.82x_1 + 2.63(3) - 1.29x_1(3)$
        $= 5.34 - .05x_1$
    For $x_2 = 5$, $= -2.55 + 3.82x_1 + 2.63(5) - 1.29x_1(5)$
        $= 10.6 - 2.63x_1$

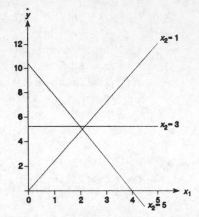

d. If x_1 and x_2 interact, the effect of x_1 on $\hat{y}$ is different at different levels of x_2. When $x_2 = 1$, as x_1 increases, $\hat{y}$ also increases. When $x_2 = 5$, as x_1 increases, $\hat{y}$ decreases.

e. The hypotheses are:

H_0: $\beta_3 = 0$
H_a: $\beta_3 \neq 0$

f. The test statistic is $t = \dfrac{\hat{\beta}_3}{s_{\hat{\beta}_3}} = \dfrac{-1.285}{.159} = -8.06$

The rejection region requires $\alpha/2 = .01/2 = .005$ in each tail of the t distribution with df $= n - (k + 1) = 15 - (3 + 1) = 11$. From Table V, Appendix B, $t_{.005} = 3.106$. The rejection region is $t < -3.106$ or $t > 3.106$.

Since the observed value of the test statistic falls in the rejection region ($t = -8.06 < -3.106$), H_0 is rejected. There is sufficient evidence to indicate that x_1 and x_2 interact at $\alpha = .01$.

11.39 a. A regression model incorporating interaction between x_1 and x_2 would be:

$$E(y) = \beta_o + \beta_1 x_1 + \beta_2 x_2 + \beta_3 x_1 x_2$$

b. If the slope of the relationship between number of defects (y) and turntable speed (x_1) is steeper for lower values of cutting blade speed, then the interaction term must be negative. As the value of cutting speed increases, the steepness gets smaller, thus, the interaction term must get smaller. This implies $\beta_3 < 0$.

11.41   a.   Using MINITAB, the results of fitting the interaction model are:

Regression Analysis: Earnings versus Age, Hours, A_H

```
The regression equation is
Earnings = 1042 - 13.2 Age + 103 Hours + 3.62 A_H


Predictor     Coef   SE Coef      T      P
Constant      1042      1304   0.80  0.441
Age         -13.24     29.23  -0.45  0.659
Hours        103.3     162.0   0.64  0.537
A_H          3.621     3.840   0.94  0.366


S = 550.289   R-Sq = 61.4%   R-Sq(adj) = 50.8%


Analysis of Variance

Source           DF        SS       MS     F      P
Regression        3   5287427  1762476  5.82  0.012
Residual Error   11   3331000   302818
Total            14   8618428


Source  DF    Seq SS
Age      1    600498
Hours    1   4417734
A_H      1    269196
```

The least squares prediction equation is:

$$\hat{y} = 1042 - 13.24x_1 + 103.3x_2 + 3.621x_1 x_2$$

b.   When $x_2 = 10$, the least squares line is:

$$\hat{y} = 1042 - 13.24x_1 + 103.3(10) + 3.621x_1(10)$$
$$= 1042 + 1033 - 13.24x_1 + 36.21x_1 = 2075 + 22.97x_1$$

The estimated slope relating annual earnings to age is 22.97. When hours worked is equal to 10, for each additional year of age, the mean annual earnings is estimated to increase by 22.97.

c.   When $x_1 = 40$, the least squares line is:

$$\hat{y} = 1042 - 13.24(40) + 103.3x_2 + 3.621(40)x_2$$
$$= 1042 - 529.6 + 103.3x_2 + 144.84x_2 = 512.4 + 248.14x_2$$

The estimated slope relating annual earnings to hours worked is 248.14. When age is equal to 40, for each additional hour worked, the mean annual earnings is estimated to increase by 248.14.

d.   To determine if age and hours worked interact, we test:

$$H_0: \ \beta_3 = 0$$

e.   From the printout, the test statistic for the test for interaction is $t = 0.94$ and the p-value is $p = .366$.

f.   Since the p-value is so large ($p = .366$), H_0 is not rejected. There is insufficient evidence to indicate age and hours worked interact to affect annual earnings.

11.43   a.   Let x_1 = latitude, x_2 = longitude, and x_3 = depth. The model is

$$y = \beta_o + \beta_1 x_1 + \beta_2 x_2 + \beta_3 x_3 + \beta_4 x_1 x_3 + \beta_5 x_2 x_3 + \varepsilon.$$

   b.   Using MINITAB, the results are:

Regression Analysis: ARSENIC versus LATITUDE, LONGITUDE, ...

```
The regression equation is
ARSENIC = 10845 - 1280 LATITUDE + 217 LONGITUDE - 1549 DEPTH-FT - 11.0 Lat_d
          + 20.0 Long_d


327 cases used, 1 cases contain missing values


Predictor      Coef   SE Coef       T       P
Constant      10845     67720    0.16   0.873
LATITUDE      -1280      1053   -1.22   0.225
LONGITUDE     217.4     814.5    0.27   0.790
DEPTH-FT    -1549.2     985.6   -1.57   0.117
Lat_D        -11.00     11.86   -0.93   0.355
Long_D        19.98     11.20    1.78   0.076


S = 103.072   R-Sq = 13.7%   R-Sq(adj) = 12.4%


Analysis of Variance

Source           DF        SS      MS      F      P
Regression        5    542303  108461  10.21  0.000
Residual Error  321   3410258   10624
Total           326   3952562


Source       DF   Seq SS
LATITUDE      1   132448
LONGITUDE     1   320144
DEPTH-FT      1    53179
Lat_D         1     2756
Long_D        1    33777
```

The least squares model is:

$$\hat{y} = 10,845 - 1,280 \text{ latitude} + 217.4 \text{ longitude} - 1,549.2 \text{ depth} - 11.00 \text{ lat\_d} + 19.98 \text{ long\_d}$$

   c.   To determine if latitude and depth interact to affect arsenic level, we test:

H_0: $\beta_4 = 0$
H_a: $\beta_4 \neq 0$

From the printout, the test statistic is $F = -.93$ and the p-value is $p = .355$.
Since the p-value is not less than α $(p = .355 \nless .05)$, H_o is not rejected. There is insufficient evidence to indicate latitude and depth interact to affect arsenic level at $\alpha = .05$.

d. To determine if longitude and depth interact to affect arsenic level, we test:

H_0: $\beta_5 = 0$
H_a: $\beta_5 \neq 0$

From the printout, the test statistic is $F = 1.78$ and the p-value is $p = .076$.
Since the p-value is not less than α ($p = .076 \not< .05$), H_o is not rejected. There is insufficient evidence to indicate longitude and depth interact to affect arsenic level at $\alpha = .05$.

e. Because the interactions are not significant, this means that the effect of latitude on the arsenic levels does not depend on the depth and the effect of longitude on the arsenic levels does not depend on the depth.

11.45 a. By including the interaction terms, it implies that the relationship between voltage and volume fraction of the disperse phase depends on the levels of salinity and surfactant concentration.

A possible sketch of the relationship is:

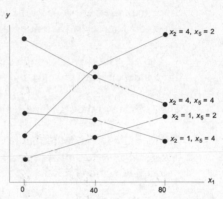

b. From MINITAB, the output is:

Regression Analysis: Voltage versus x1, x2, x5, x1x2, x1x5

```
The regression equation is
Voltage = 0.906 - 0.0228 x1 + 0.305 x2 + 0.275 x5 - 0.00280 x1x2
+ 0.00158 x1x5

Predictor         Coef      SE Coef          T        P
Constant        0.9057       0.2855       3.17    0.007
x1           -0.022753     0.008318      -2.74    0.017
x2              0.3047       0.2366       1.29    0.220
x5              0.2747       0.2270       1.21    0.248
x1x2         -0.002804     0.003790      -0.74    0.473
x1x5          0.001579     0.003947       0.40    0.696

S = 0.5047      R-Sq = 67.9%      R-Sq(adj) = 55.6%

Analysis of Variance

Source           DF           SS          MS        F        P
Regression        5       7.0103      1.4021     5.51    0.006
Residual Error   13       3.3107      0.2547
Total            18      10.3210

Source      DF     Seq SS
x1           1     1.4016
x2           1     1.9263
x5           1     3.5422
x1x2         1     0.0994
x1x5         1     0.0408
```

The fitted regression line is:

$$\hat{y} = .906 - .023x_1 + .305x_2 + .275x_5 - .003x_1x_2 + .002x_1x_5$$

To determine if the model is useful, we test:

H_0: $\beta_1 = \beta_2 = \beta_3 = \beta_4 = \beta_5 = 0$
H_a: At least one $\beta_i \neq 0$, for $i = 1, 2, ..., 5$

The test statistic is $F = 5.51$.

Since no α was given, $\alpha = .05$ will be used. The rejection region requires $\alpha = .05$ in the upper tail of the F-distribution with $v_1 = k = 5$ and $v_2 = n - (k + 1) = 19 - (5 + 1) = 13$. From Table VII, Appendix B, $F_{.05} = 3.03$. The rejection region is $F > 3.03$.

Since the observed value of the test statistic falls in the rejection region ($F = 5.51 > 3.03$), H_0 is rejected. There is sufficient evidence to indicate the model is useful for predicting voltage at $\alpha = .05$.

$R^2 = .679$. Thus, 67.9% of the sample variation of voltage is explained by the model containing the three independent variables and two interaction terms.

The estimate of the standard deviation is $s = .5047$.

Comparing this model to that fit in Exercise 11.20, the model in Exercise 11.20 appears to fit the data better. The model in Exercise 11.20 has a higher R^2 (.771 vs .679) and a smaller estimate of the standard deviation (.4365 vs .5047).

c. $\hat{\beta}_0 = .906$. This is simply the estimate of the y-intercept.

$\hat{\beta}_1 = -.023$. For each unit increase in disperse phase volume, we estimate that the mean voltage will decrease by .023 units, holding salinity and surfactant concentration at 0.

$\hat{\beta}_2 = .305$. For each unit increase in salinity, we estimate that the mean voltage will increase by .305 units, holding disperse phase volume and surfactant concentration at 0.

$\hat{\beta}_3 = .275$. For each unit increase in surfactant concentration, we estimate that the mean voltage will increase by .275 units, holding disperse phase volume and salinity at 0.

$\hat{\beta}_4 = -.003$. This estimates the difference in the slope of the relationship between voltage and disperse phase volume for each unit increase in salinity, holding surfactant concentration constant.

$\hat{\beta}_5 = .002$. This estimates the difference in the slope of the relationship between voltage and disperse phase volume for each unit increase in surfactant concentration, holding salinity constant.

11.47 a. $E(y) = \beta_0 + \beta_1 x + \beta_2 x^2$

  b. $E(y) = \beta_0 + \beta_1 x_1 + \beta_2 x_2 + \beta_3 x_1 x_2 + \beta_4 x_1^2 + \beta_5 x_2^2$

  c. $E(y) = \beta_0 + \beta_1 x_1 + \beta_2 x_2 + \beta_3 x_3 + \beta_4 x_1 x_2 + \beta_5 x_1 x_3 + \beta_6 x_2 x_3 + \beta_7 x_1^2 + \beta_8 x_2^2 + \beta_9 x_3^2$

11.49 a. To determine if the model contributes information for predicting y, we test:

    H_0: $\beta_1 = \beta_2 = 0$
    H_a: At least one $\beta_i \neq 0$, $i = 1, 2$

    The test statistic is $F = \dfrac{R^2 / k}{(1 - R^2)/[n - (k+1)]} = \dfrac{.91/2}{(1-.91)/[20 - (2+1)]} = 85.94$

    The rejection region requires $\alpha = .05$ in the upper tail of the F distribution, with $v_1 = k = 2$, and $v_2 = n - (k+1) = 20 - (2+1) = 17$. From Table VIII, Appendix B, $F_{.05} = 3.59$. The rejection region is $F > 3.59$.

    Since the observed value of the test statistic falls in the rejection region ($F = 85.94 > 3.59$), H_0 is rejected. There is sufficient evidence that the model contributes information for predicting y at $\alpha = .05$.

  b. To determine if upward curvature exists, we test:

    H_0: $\beta_2 = 0$
    H_a: $\beta_2 > 0$

  c. To determine if downward curvature exists, we test:

    H_0: $\beta_2 = 0$
    H_a: $\beta_2 < 0$

11.51 a. To determine if at least one of the parameters is nonzero, we test:

  H_0: $\beta_1 = \beta_2 = \beta_3 = \beta_4 = \beta_5 = 0$
  H_a: At least one $\beta_i \neq 0$, $i = 1, 2, 3, 4, 5$

  The test statistic is $F = 25.93$, with p-value $= 0.000$. Since the p-value is less than $\alpha = .05$, H_0 is rejected. There is sufficient evidence to indicate that at least one of the parameters β_1, β_2, β_3, β_4, and β_5 is nonzero at $\alpha = .05$.

  b. H_0: $\beta_4 = 0$
    H_a: $\beta_4 \neq 0$

  The test statistic is $t = -10.74$ with p-value $= 0.000$. Since the p-value is less than $\alpha = .01$, H_0 is rejected. There is sufficient evidence to indicate that $\beta_4 \neq 0$ at $\alpha = .01$.

  c. H_0: $\beta_5 = 0$
    H_a: $\beta_5 \neq 0$

  The test statistic is $t = .60$ with p-value $= .550$. Since the p-value is greater than $\alpha = .01$, H_0 is not rejected. There is insufficient evidence to indicate that $\beta_5 \neq 0$ at $\alpha = .01$.

  d. Graphs may vary.

11.53   a.

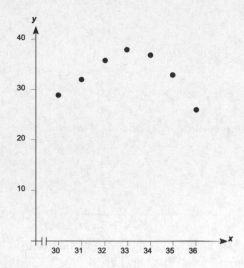

b.   If information were available only for $x = 30$, 31, 32, and 33, we would suggest a first-order model where $\beta_1 > 0$. If information was available only for $x = 33$, 34, 35, and 36, we would again suggest a first-order model where $\beta_1 < 0$. If all the information was available, we would suggest a second-order model.

11.55   a.   The complete 2nd order model is:

$$E(y) = \beta_0 + \beta_1 x_1 + \beta_2 x_2 + \beta_3 x_1 x_2 + \beta_4 x_1^2 + \beta_5 x_2^2$$

b. $R^2 = .14$. 14% of the total variation in the efficiency scores is explained by the complete 2nd order model containing level of CEO leadership and level of congruence between the CEO and the VP.

c.   If the β-coefficient for the x_2^2 term is negative, then as the value of the level of congruence increases, the efficiency will increase at a decreasing rate to some point and then the efficiency will decrease at an increasing rate, holding level of CEO leadership constant.

d.   Since the *p*-value is less than α ($p = .02 < .05$), H_0 is rejected. There is sufficient evidence to indicate that the level of CEO leadership and the level of congruence between the CEO and the VP interact to affect efficiency. This means that the effect of CEO leadership on efficiency depends on the level of congruence between the CEO and the VP.

11.57   a.   A first order model is:

$$E(y) = \beta_0 + \beta_1 x$$

b.   A second order model is:

$$E(y) = \beta_0 + \beta_1 x + \beta_2 x^2$$

c.   Using MINITAB, a scattergram of these data is:

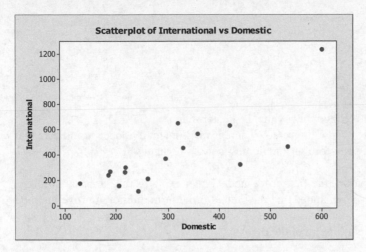

From the plot, it appears that the first order model might fit the data better. There does not appear to be much of a curve to the relationship.

d.   Using MINITAB, the output is:

Regression Analysis: International versus Domestic, Dsq

```
The regression equation is
International = 183 - 0.24 Domestic + 0.00262 Dsq


Predictor        Coef      SE Coef        T       P
Constant        182.9        301.0     0.61   0.554
Domestic       -0.243        1.849    -0.13   0.897
Dsq          0.002625     0.002523     1.04   0.317


S = 175.370    R-Sq = 65.4%    R-Sq(adj) = 60.1%


Analysis of Variance

Source            DF          SS        MS        F       P
Regression         2      755320    377660    12.28   0.001
Residual Error    13      399811     30755
Total             15     1155131


Source      DF   Seq SS
Domestic     1   722025
Dsq          1    33295
```

To investigate the usefulness of the model, we test:

H_0: $\beta_1 = \beta_2 = 0$
H_a: At least one $\beta_i \neq 0$, $i = 1, 2$

The test statistic is $F = 12.28$.

The p-value is $p = 0.001$. Since the p-value is so small, we reject H_0. There is sufficient evidence to indicate the model is useful for predicting foreign gross revenue.

To determine if a curvilinear relationship exists between foreign and domestic gross revenues, we test:

H_0: $\beta_2 = 0$
H_a: $\beta_2 \neq 0$

The test statistic is $t = 1.04$.

The p-value is $p = .317$ Since the p-value is greater than $\alpha = .05$
($p = 0.317 > \alpha = .05$), H_0 is not rejected. There is insufficient evidence to indicate that a curvilinear relationship exists between foreign and domestic gross revenues at $\alpha = .05$.

e.   From the analysis in part **d**, the first-order model better explains the variation in foreign gross revenues. In part **d**, we concluded that the second-order term did not improve the model.

11.59 a.   Using MINITAB, the scattergram of the data is:

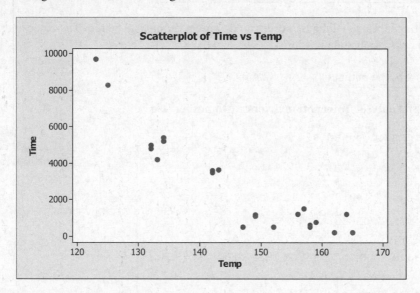

The relationship appears to be curvilinear. As temperature increases, the value of time tends to decrease but at a decreasing rate.

b.   Using MINITAB the results are:

Regression Analysis: Time versus Temp, Tempsq

```
The regression equation is
Time = 154243 - 1909 Temp + 5.93 Tempsq


Predictor      Coef    SE Coef       T       P
Constant     154243      21868    7.05   0.000
Temp        -1908.9      303.7   -6.29   0.000
Tempsq        5.929      1.048    5.66   0.000


S = 688.137    R-Sq = 94.2%    R-Sq(adj) = 93.5%
```

```
Analysis of Variance

Source          DF        SS         MS        F       P
Regression       2   144830280   72415140   152.93   0.000
Residual Error  19     8997107     473532
Total           21   153827386


Source   DF      Seq SS
Temp      1   129663987
Tempsq    1    15166293
```

The fitted regression line is: $\hat{y} = 154{,}243 - 1{,}908.9temp + 5.929temp^2$

c. To determine if there is an upward curvature in the relationship between failure time and solder temperature, we test:

H_o: $\beta_2 = 0$
H_a: $\beta_2 > 0$

From the printout, the test statistic is $t = 5.66$ and the p-value is $p = 0.000$. Since the p-value is less than α ($p = 0.000 < .05$), H_0 is rejected. There is sufficient evidence to indicate an upward curvature in the relationship between failure time and solder temperature at $\alpha = .05$.

11.61 The model would be $E(y) = \beta_0 + \beta_1 x + \beta_2 x^2$. Since the value of y is expected to increase and then decrease as x gets larger, β_2 will be negative. A sketch of the model would be:

11.63 Let $x = \begin{cases} 1 & \text{if qualitative variable assumes 2nd level} \\ 0 & \text{otherwise} \end{cases}$

The model is $E(y) = \beta_0 + \beta_1 x$

β_0 = mean value of y when the qualitative variable assumes the first level
β_1 = difference in the mean values of y between levels 2 and 1 of the qualitative variable

11.65 a. Level 1 implies $x_1 = x_2 = x_3 = 0$. $\hat{y} = 10.2$
   Level 2 implies $x_1 = 1$ and $x_2 = x_3 = 0$. $\hat{y} = 10.2 - 4(1) = 6.2$
   Level 3 implies $x_2 = 1$ and $x_1 = x_3 = 0$. $\hat{y} = 10.2 + 12(1) = 22.2$
   Level 4 implies $x_3 = 1$ and $x_1 = x_2 = 0$. $\hat{y} = 10.2 + 2(1) = 12.2$

b. The hypotheses are:

H_0: $\beta_1 = \beta_2 = \beta_3 = 0$
H_a: At least one $\beta_i \neq 0$, $i = 1, 2, 3$

11.67 a. Let $x_1 = \begin{cases} 1 \text{ if grape-picking method is manual} \\ 0 \text{ otherwise} \end{cases}$ Let $x_2 = \begin{cases} 1 \text{ if soil type is clay} \\ 0 \text{ otherwise} \end{cases}$

Let $x_3 = \begin{cases} 1 \text{ if soil type is gravel} \\ 0 \text{ otherwise} \end{cases}$ Let $x_4 = \begin{cases} 1 \text{ if slope orientation is East} \\ 0 \text{ otherwise} \end{cases}$

Let $x_5 = \begin{cases} 1 \text{ if slope orientation is South} \\ 0 \text{ otherwise} \end{cases}$ Let $x_6 = \begin{cases} 1 \text{ if slope orientation is West} \\ 0 \text{ otherwise} \end{cases}$

Let $x_7 = \begin{cases} 1 \text{ if slope orientation is Southeast} \\ 0 \text{ otherwise} \end{cases}$

b. The model is: $E(y) = \beta_0 + \beta_1 x_1$
β_0 = mean wine quality for grape-picking method automated
β_1 = difference in mean wine quality between grape-picking methods manual and automated

c. The model is: $E(y) = \beta_0 + \beta_1 x_2 + \beta_2 x_3$
β_0 = mean wine quality for soil type sand
β_1 = difference in mean wine quality between soil types clay and sand
β_2 = difference in mean wine quality between soil types gravel and sand

d. The model is: $E(y) = \beta_0 + \beta_1 x_4 + \beta_2 x_5 + \beta_3 x_6 + \beta_4 x_7$
β_0 = mean wine quality for slope orientation Southwest
β_1 = difference in mean wine quality between slope orientations East and Southwest
β_2 = difference in mean wine quality between slope orientations South and Southwest
β_3 = difference in mean wine quality between slope orientations West and Southwest
β_4 = difference in mean wine quality between slope orientations Southeast and Southwest

11.69 a. Let $x = \begin{cases} 1 \text{ if Developer} \\ 0 \text{ otherwise} \end{cases}$

Then the model would be: $E(y) = \beta_0 + \beta_1 x$

β_0 = mean accuracy for the Project Leader

β_1 = difference in mean accuracy between the Developer and the Project Leader

b. Let $x_1 = \begin{cases} 1 \text{ if Low} \\ 0 \text{ otherwise} \end{cases}$ Let $x_2 = \begin{cases} 1 \text{ if Medium} \\ 0 \text{ otherwise} \end{cases}$

Then the model would be: $E(y) = \beta_0 + \beta_1 x_1 + \beta_2 x_2$

β_0 = mean accuracy for the High task complexity

β_1 = difference in mean accuracy between Low and High task complexity

β_2 = difference in mean accuracy between Medium and High task complexity

c. Let $x = \begin{cases} 1 & \text{if Fixed price} \\ 0 & \text{otherwise} \end{cases}$

Then the model would be: $E(y) = \beta_0 + \beta_1 x$

β_0 = mean accuracy for the Hourly rate

β_1 = difference in mean accuracy between the Fixed price and the Hourly rate

d. Let $x_1 = \begin{cases} 1 & \text{if Time-of-delivery} \\ 0 & \text{otherwise} \end{cases}$ 　　 Let $x_2 = \begin{cases} 1 & \text{if Cost} \\ 0 & \text{otherwise} \end{cases}$

Then the model would be: $E(y) = \beta_0 + \beta_1 x_1 + \beta_2 x_2$

β_0 = mean accuracy for the Quality

β_1 = difference in mean accuracy between Time-of-delivery and Quality

β_2 = difference in mean accuracy between Cost and Quality

11.71 a. $R^2_{adj} = .76$. 76% of the total sample variation of SAT-Math scores is explained by the regression model including score on PSAT and whether the student was coached or not, adjusting for the sample size and the number of independent variables in the model.

b. For confidence level .95, $\alpha = .05$ and $\alpha/2 = .05/2 = .025$. From Table V, Appendix B, with df $= n - (k + 1) = 3,492 - (2 + 1) = 3,489$, $t_{.025} = 1.96$. The 95% confidence interval is:

$$\hat{\beta}_2 \pm t_{\alpha/2} s_{\hat{\beta}_2} \Rightarrow 19 \pm 1.96(3) \Rightarrow 19 \pm 5.88 \Rightarrow (13.12, \ 24.88)$$

We are 95% confident that the mean SAT-Math score for those who were coached was anywhere from 13.12 to 24.88 points higher than the mean for those who were not coached, holding PSAT scores constant.

c. Since 0 is not contained in the confidence interval for β_2, we can conclude that the coaching effect was present. Those who received coaching scored higher on the SAT-Math than those who did not, holding PSAT scores constant.

11.73 a. To determine if there is a difference in the mean monthly rate of return for T-Bills between an expansive Fed monetary policy and a restrictive Fed monetary policy, we test:

$H_0: \beta_1 = 0$
$H_a: \beta_1 \neq 0$

The test statistic is $t = 8.14$.

Since no n nor α is given, we cannot determine the exact rejection region. However, we can assume that n is greater than 2 since the data used are from 1972 and 1997. With $\alpha = .05$, the critical value of t for the rejection region will be smaller than 4.303. Thus, with $\alpha = .05$, $t = 8.14$ will fall in the rejection region. There is sufficient evidence to indicate a difference in the mean monthly rate of return for T-Bills between an expansive Fed monetary policy and a restrictive Fed monetary policy at $\alpha = .05$.

However, the value of R^2 is .1818. The model used is explaining only 18.18% of the variability in the monthly rate of return. This is not a particularly large value.

To determine if there is a difference in the mean monthly rate of return for Equity REIT between an expansive Fed monetary policy and a restrictive Fed monetary policy, we test:

H_0: $\beta_1 = 0$
H_a: $\beta_1 \neq 0$

The test statistic is $t = -3.46$.
Since no n nor α is given, we cannot determine the exact rejection region. However, we can assume that n is greater than 4 since the data used are from 1972 and 1997. With $\alpha = .05$, the critical value of t for the rejection region will be smaller than -3.182. Thus, with $\alpha = .05$, $t = -3.46$ will fall in the rejection region. There is sufficient evidence to indicate a difference in the mean monthly rate of return for Equity REIT between an expansive Fed monetary policy and a restrictive Fed monetary policy at $\alpha = .05$.

However, the value of R^2 is .0387. The model used is explaining only 3.87% of the variability in the monthly rate of return. This is a very small value.

b.   For the first model, β_1 is the difference in the mean monthly rate of return for T-Bills between an expansive Fed monetary policy and a restrictive Fed monetary policy.

For the second model, β_1 is the difference in the mean monthly rate of return for Equity REIT between an expansive Fed monetary policy and a restrictive Fed monetary policy.

c.   The least squares prediction equation for the equity REIT index is:

$\hat{y} = 0.01863 - 0.01582x$.

When the Federal Reserve's monetary policy is restrictive, $x = 1$. The predicted mean monthly rate of return for the equity REIT index is

$\hat{y} = 0.01863 - 0.01582(1) = .00281$

When the Federal Reserve's monetary policy is expansive, $x = 0$. The predicted mean monthly rate of return for the equity REIT index is

$\hat{y} = 0.01863 - 0.01582(0) = .01863$.

11.75   a.   Let $x = \begin{cases} 1 \text{ if Lotion/cream} \\ 0 \text{ otherwise} \end{cases}$

The model is $E(y) = \beta_0 + \beta_1 x$.

b.   From MINITAB, the output is:

Regression Analysis: Cost/Use versus Type

```
The regression equation is
Cost/Use = 0.778 + 0.109 Type

Predictor         Coef      SE Coef          T          P
Constant        0.7775       0.2975       2.61      0.023
Type            0.1092       0.4545       0.24      0.814

S = 0.8415      R-Sq = 0.5%      R-Sq(adj) = 0.0%

Analysis of Variance

Source            DF           SS          MS          F          P
Regression         1       0.0409      0.0409       0.06      0.814
Residual Error    12       8.4973      0.7081
Total             13       8.5381
```

The fitted model is: $\hat{y} = 0.7775 + .1092x$

c.   To determine whether repellent type is a useful predictor of cost-per-use, we test:

$H_0 : \beta_1 = 0$

d.   The alternative hypothesis is

$H_a : \beta_1 \neq 0$

The test statistic is $t = 0.24$ and the p-value is $p = 0.814$.

Since the p-value is greater than α ($p = .814 > .10$), H_0 is not rejected. There is insufficient evidence to indicate that repellent type is a useful predictor of cost-per-use at $\alpha = .10$.

e.   The dummy variable will be defined the same way and the model will look the same (just the dependent variable will be different).

From MINITAB, the output is:

Regression Analysis: MaxProt versus Type

```
The regression equation is
MaxProt = 7.56 - 1.65 Type

Predictor         Coef      SE Coef          T          P
Constant         7.563        2.339       3.23      0.007
Type            -1.646        3.574      -0.46      0.653

S = 6.617       R-Sq = 1.7%      R-Sq(adj) = 0.0%

Analysis of Variance

Source            DF           SS          MS          F          P
Regression         1         9.29        9.29       0.21      0.653
Residual Error    12       525.43       43.79
Total             13       534.71
```

The fitted model is: $\hat{y} = 7.56 - 1.65x$

To determine whether repellent type is a useful predictor of cost-per-use, we test:

H_0: $\beta_1 = 0$
H_a: $\beta_1 \neq 0$

The test statistic is $t = -0.46$ and the *p*-value is $p = 0.653$.

Since the *p*-value is greater than α ($p = .653 > .10$), H_0 is not rejected. There is insufficient evidence to indicate that repellent type is a useful predictor of maximum number of hours of protection at $\alpha = .10$.

11.77   a.   Let $x_1 = \begin{cases} 1 & \text{if Group V} \\ 0 & \text{otherwise} \end{cases}$ Let $x_2 = \begin{cases} 1 & \text{if Group S} \\ 0 & \text{otherwise} \end{cases}$

The model would be: $E(y) = \beta_0 + \beta_1 x_1 + \beta_2 x_2$

b.   Using MINITAB, the results are:

Regression Analysis: Recall versus x1, x2

```
The regression equation is
Recall = 3.17 - 1.08 x1 - 1.45 x2


Predictor      Coef   SE Coef       T       P
Constant     3.1667    0.1670   18.96   0.000
x1          -1.0833    0.2362   -4.59   0.000
x2          -1.4537    0.2362   -6.15   0.000


S = 1.73596   R-Sq = 11.3%   R-Sq(adj) = 10.7%


Analysis of Variance

Source           DF        SS        MS       F       P
Regression        2   123.265    61.633   20.45   0.000
Residual Error  321   967.352     3.014
Total           323  1090.617


Source  DF    Seq SS
x1       1     9.150
x2       1   114.116
```

The least squares prediction equation is: $\hat{y} = 3.1667 - 1.0833x_1 - 1.4537x_2$.

c. To determine if the overall model is useful, we test:

H_0: $\beta_1 = \beta_2 = 0$
H_a: At least one $\beta_i \neq 0$

The test statistic is $F = 20.45$ and the *p*-value is $p = 0.000$. Since the *p*-value is less than $\alpha = .01$, H_0 is rejected. There is sufficient evidence to indicate the model is useful in predicting brand recall at $\alpha = .01$.

From the Chapter 8 SIA, the test statistic was $F = 20.45$ and the *p*-value was $p = 0.000$. These are identical to those above. The model is useful in predicting recall. This is the same as the conclusion that there is a difference in mean recall among the 3 groups.

d. With the dummy variable coding in part **a**, β_0 is the mean recall for group N. Thus, the estimated mean recall for Group N is 3.1667 or 3.17. β_1 is the difference in mean recall between Group V and Group N. Thus, the mean recall for Group V is $\beta_0 + \beta_1$ and is estimated to be $3.1667 - 1.0833 = 2.0834$ or 2.08. β_2 is the difference in mean recall between Group S and Group N. Thus, the mean recall for Group S is $\beta_0 + \beta_2$ and is estimated to be $3.1667 - 1.4537 = 1.7130$ or 1.71.

11.79   a. The complete second-order model is $E(y) = \beta_0 + \beta_1 x_1 + \beta_2 x_1^2$

b. The new model is $E(y) = \beta_0 + \beta_1 x_1 + \beta_2 x_1^2 + \beta_3 x_2 + \beta_4 x_3$

where $x_2 = \begin{cases} 1 \text{ if level 2} \\ 0 \text{ otherwise} \end{cases}$ $x_3 = \begin{cases} 1 \text{ if level 3} \\ 0 \text{ otherwise} \end{cases}$

c. The model with the interaction terms is:

$E(y) = \beta_0 + \beta_1 x_1 + \beta_2 x_1^2 + \beta_3 x_2 + \beta_4 x_3 + \beta_5 x_1 x_2 + \beta_6 x_1 x_3 + \beta_7 x_1^2 x_2 + \beta_8 x_1^2 x_3$

d. The response curves will have the same shape if none of the interaction terms are present or if $\beta_5 = \beta_6 = \beta_7 = \beta_8 = 0$.

e. The response curves will be parallel lines if the interaction terms as well as the second-order terms are absent or if $\beta_2 = \beta_5 = \beta_6 = \beta_7 = \beta_8 = 0$.

f. The response curves will be identical if no terms involving the qualitative variable are present or $\beta_3 = \beta_4 = \beta_5 = \beta_6 = \beta_7 = \beta_8 = 0$.

11.81 a. For $x_2 = 0$ and $x_3 = 0$, $\hat{y} = 48.8 - 3.4x_1 + .07x_1^2$

For $x_2 = 1$ and $x_3 = 0$, $\hat{y} = 48.8 - 3.4x_1 + .07x_1^2 - 2.4(1) + 3.7x_1(1) - .02x_1^2(1)$
$$= 46.4 + 0.3x_1 + .05x_1^2$$

For $x_2 = 0$ and $x_3 = 1$, $\hat{y} = 48.8 - 3.4x_1 + .07x_1^2 - 7.5(1) + 2.7x_1(1) - .04x_1^2(1)$
$$= 41.3 - 0.7x_1 + 0.03x_1^2$$

b. The plots of the lines are:

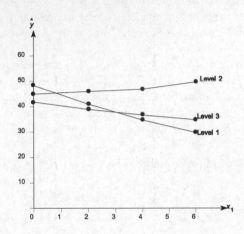

11.83 a. To determine if the model is adequate, we test:

H_o: $\beta_1 = \beta_2 = \beta_3 = \ldots \beta_{12} = 0$
H_a: At least 1 $\beta_i \neq 0$

The test statistic is $F = 26.9$.
Using Tables VII, VIII, IX, and X, Appendix B, with $v_1 = k = 12$ and $v_2 = n - (k + 1) = 148 - (12 + 1)$
$= 135$, the p-value associated with $F = 26.9$ is less than .001. Since the p-value is so small, H_0 is rejected. There is sufficient evidence to indicate the model is adequate.

$R^2 = .705$. 70.5% of the total variation of the natural logarithm of card prices is explained by the model with the 12 variables in the model.

Adj-$R^2 = .681$. 68.1% of the total variation of the natural logarithm of card prices is explained by the model with the 12 variables in the model, adjusting for the sample size and the number of variables in the model.

Since these R^2 values are fairly large, it indicates that the model is pretty good.

b. To determine if race contributes to the price, we test:

H_0: $\beta_1 = 0$
H_a: $\beta_1 \neq 0$

The test statistic is $t = -1.014$ and the p-value is $p = .312$. Since the p-value is so large, H_0 is not rejected. There is insufficient evidence to indicate race has an impact on the value of professional football player's rookie cards for any reasonable value of α, holding the other variables constant.

b. To determine if card vintage contributes to the price, we test:

$H_0: \beta_3 = 0$
$H_a: \beta_3 \neq 0$

The test statistic is $t = -10.92$ and the p-value is $p = .000$. Since the p-value is so small, H_0 is rejected. There is sufficient evidence to indicate card vintage has an impact on the value of professional football player's rookie cards for any reasonable value of α, holding the other variables constant.

d. The first order model is: $E(y) = \beta_0 + \beta_1 x_3 + \beta_2 x_5 + \beta_3 x_6 + \beta_4 x_7 + \beta_5 x_8 + \beta_6 x_9 + \beta_7 x_{10} + \beta_8 x_{11} + \beta_9 x_{12} + \beta_{10} x_5 x_3 + \beta_{11} x_6 x_3 + \beta_{12} x_7 x_3 + \beta_{13} x_8 x_3 + \beta_{14} x_9 x_3 + \beta_{15} x_{10} x_3 + \beta_{16} x_{11} x_3 + \beta_{17} x_{12} x_3$

11.85 a. For obese smokers, $x_2 = 0$. The equation of the hypothesized line relating mean REE to time after smoking for obese smokers is:

$E(y) = \beta_0 + \beta_1 x_1 + \beta_2(0) + \beta_3 x_1(0) = \beta_0 + \beta_1 x_1$

The slope of the line is β_1.

b. For normal weight smokers, $x_2 = 1$. The equation of the hypothesized line relating mean REE to time after smoking for normal smokers is:

$E(y) = \beta_0 + \beta_1 x_1 + \beta_2(1) + \beta_3 x_1(1) = (\beta_0 + \beta_2) + (\beta_1 + \beta_3) x_1$

The slope of the line is $\beta_1 + \beta_3$.

c. The reported p-value is .044. Since the p-value is small, there is evidence to indicate that interaction between time and weight is present for $\alpha > .044$.

For $\alpha = .01$, there is no evidence to indicate that interaction between time and weight is present.

11.87 a. Let $x_1 = \begin{cases} 1 & \text{if Channel catfish} \\ 0 & \text{otherwise} \end{cases}$ $x_2 = \begin{cases} 1 & \text{if Largemouth bass} \\ 0 & \text{otherwise} \end{cases}$

b. Let $x_3 = $ weight. The model would be: $E(y) = \beta_0 + \beta_1 x_1 + \beta_2 x_2 + \beta_3 x_3$

c. The model would be: $E(y) = \beta_0 + \beta_1 x_1 + \beta_2 x_2 + \beta_3 x_3 + \beta_4 x_1 x_3 + \beta_4 x_2 x_3$

d.   From MINITAB, the output is:

Regression Analysis: DDT versus x1, x2, Weight

```
The regression equation is
DDT = 3.1 + 26.5 x1 - 4.1 x2 + 0.0037 Weight

Predictor          Coef        SE Coef            T          P
Constant           3.13          38.89         0.08      0.936
x1                26.51          21.52         1.23      0.220
x2                -4.09          37.91        -0.11      0.914
Weight          0.00371        0.02598         0.14      0.887

S = 98.57        R-Sq = 1.7%       R-Sq(adj) = 0.0%

Analysis of Variance

Source              DF            SS           MS          F         P
Regression           3         23652         7884       0.81     0.490
Residual Error     140       1360351         9717
Total              143       1384003

Source         DF      Seq SS
x1              1       23041
x2              1         414
Weight          1         198
```

The least squares prediction equation is: $\hat{y} = 3.1 + 26.5x_1 - 4.1x_2 + 0.0037x_3$

e. $\hat{\beta}_3 = 0.0037$.   For each additional gram of weight, the mean level of DDT is expected to increase by 0.0037 units, holding species constant.

f.   From MINITAB, the output is:

Regression Analysis: DDT versus x1, x2, Weight, x1Weight, x2Weight

```
The regression equation is
DDT = 3.5 + 25.6 x1 - 3.5 x2 + 0.0034 Weight + 0.0008 x1Weight
          - 0.0013 x2Weight

Predictor          Coef        SE Coef            T          P
Constant           3.50          54.69         0.06      0.949
x1                25.59          67.52         0.38      0.705
x2                -3.47          84.70        -0.04      0.967
Weight          0.00344        0.03843         0.09      0.929
x1Weight        0.00082        0.05459         0.02      0.988
x2Weight       -0.00129        0.09987        -0.01      0.990

S = 99.29        R-Sq = 1.7%       R-Sq(adj) = 0.0%

Analysis of Variance

Source              DF            SS           MS          F         P
Regression           5         23657         4731       0.48     0.791
Residual Error     138       1360346         9858
Total              143       1384003

Source         DF      Seq SS
x1              1       23041
x2              1         414
Weight          1         198
x1Weight        1           4
x2Weight        1           2
```

The least squares prediction equation is:

$$\hat{y} = 3.5 + 25.6x_1 - 3.5x_2 + 0.0034x_3 + 0.0008x_1x_3 - .0013x_2x_3$$

g.　For Channel catfish, $x_1 = 1$ and $x_2 = 0$. The least squares line is

$$\hat{y} = 3.5 + 25.6(1) + 0.0034x_3 + 0.0008(1)x_3 = 29.1 + .0042x_3$$

The estimated slope is .0042.

11.89　a.　Let x_1 = sales volume

$$x_2 = \begin{cases} 1 \text{ if NW} \\ 0 \text{ if not} \end{cases} \qquad x_3 = \begin{cases} 1 \text{ if S} \\ 0 \text{ if not} \end{cases}$$

$$x_4 = \begin{cases} 1 \text{ if W} \\ 0 \text{ if not} \end{cases}$$

The complete second order model for the sales price of a single-family home is:

$$E(y) = \beta_0 + \beta_1 x_1 + \beta_2 x_1^2 + \beta_3 x_2 + \beta_4 x_3 + \beta_5 x_4 + \beta_6 x_1 x_2 + \beta_7 x_1 x_3 + \beta_8 x_1 x_4$$
$$+ \beta_9 x_1^2 x_2 + \beta_{10} x_1^2 x_3 + \beta_{11} x_1^2 x_4$$

b.　For the West, $x_2 = 0$, $x_3 = 0$, and $x_4 = 1$. The equation would be:

$$E(y) = \beta_0 + \beta_1 x_1 + \beta_2 x_1^2 + \beta_3(0) + \beta_4(0) + \beta_5(0) + \beta_6 x_1(0) + \beta_7 x_1(0)$$
$$+ \beta_8 x_1(0) + \beta_9 x_1^2(0) + \beta_{10} x_1^2(0) + \beta_{11} x_1^2(0)$$
$$= \beta_0 + \beta_1 x_1 + \beta_2 x_1^2 + \beta_5 + \beta_8 x_1 + \beta_{11} x_1^2$$
$$= \beta_0 + \beta_5 + \beta_1 x_1 + \beta_8 x_1 + \beta_2 x_1^2 + \beta_{11} x_1^2$$
$$= (\beta_0 + \beta_5) + (\beta_1 + \beta_8)x_1 + (\beta_2 + \beta_{11})x_1^2$$

c.　For the Northwest, $x_2 = 1$, $x_3 = 0$, and $x_4 = 0$. The equation would be:

$$E(y) = \beta_0 + \beta_1 x_1 + \beta_2 x_1^2 + \beta_3(1) + \beta_4(0) + \beta_5(0) + \beta_6 x_1(1) + \beta_7 x_1(0)$$
$$+ \beta_8 x_1(0) + \beta_9 x_1^2(1) + \beta_{10} x_1^2(0) + \beta_{11} x_1^2(0)$$

$$= \beta_0 + \beta_1 x_1 + \beta_2 x_1^2 + \beta_3 + \beta_6 x_1 + \beta_9 x_1^2$$

$$= \beta_0 + \beta_3 + \beta_1 x_1 + \beta_6 x_1 + \beta_2 x_1^2 + \beta_9 x_1^2$$
$$= (\beta_0 + \beta_3) + (\beta_1 + \beta_6)x_1 + (\beta_2 + \beta_9)x_1^2$$

d.　The parameters β_3, β_4, and β_5 allow for the y-intercepts of the 4 regions to be different. The parameters β_6, β_7, and β_8 allow for the peaks of the curves to be a different value of sales volume (x_1) for the four regions. The parameters β_9, β_{10}, and β_{11} allow for the shapes of the curves to be different for the four regions. Thus, all the parameters from β_3 through β_{11} allow for differences in mean sales prices among the four regions.

e.   Using MINITAB, the printout is:

Regression Analysis: Price versus X1, X1SQ, ...

The regression equation is
Price = 1904740 - 70.4 X1 + 0.000721 X1SQ + 159661 X2 + 5291908 X3 + 3663319 X4
        + 22.2 X1X2 - 23.9 X1X3 - 37 X1X4 - 0.000421 X1SQX2 - 0.000404 X1SQX3
        - 0.000181 X1SQX4

Predictor	Coef	SE Coef	T	P
Constant	1904740	1984278	0.96	0.351
X1	-70.44	72.09	-0.98	0.343
X1SQ	0.0007211	0.0006515	1.11	0.285
X2	159661	2069265	0.08	0.939
X3	5291908	4812586	1.10	0.288
X4	3663319	4478880	0.82	0.425
X1X2	22.25	73.74	0.30	0.767
X1X3	-23.86	92.09	-0.26	0.799
X1X4	-37.2	103.0	-0.36	0.723
X1SQX2	-0.0004210	0.0006589	-0.64	0.532
X1SQX3	-0.0004044	0.0006777	-0.60	0.559
X1SQX4	-0.0001810	0.0007333	-0.25	0.808

S = 24365.8   R-Sq = 85.0%   R-Sq(adj) = 74.6%

Analysis of Variance

Source	DF	SS	MS	F	P
Regression	11	53633628997	4875784454	8.21	0.000
Residual Error	16	9499097458	593693591		
Total	27	63132726455			

Source	DF	Seq SS
X1	1	3591326
X1SQ	1	64275360
X2	1	11338642654
X3	1	10081000583
X4	1	241539024
X1X2	1	18258475317
X1X3	1	5579187440
X1X4	1	7566169810
X1SQX2	1	138146367
X1SQX3	1	326425228
X1SQX4	1	36175888

Unusual Observations

Obs	X1	Price	Fit	SE Fit	Residual	St Resid
2	61025	235900	291659	18746	-55759	-3.58R
5	60324	345300	279697	15712	65603	3.52R
7	61025	240855	241084	24360	-229	-0.42 X

R denotes an observation with a large standardized residual.
X denotes an observation whose X value gives it large influence.

To determine if the model is useful for predicting sales price, we test:

H_0: $\beta_1 = \beta_2 = \ldots = \beta_{11} = 0$
H_a: At least one of the coefficients is nonzero

The test statistic is $F = \dfrac{MS(Model)}{MSE} = 8.21$

The p-value is $p = .000$. Since the p-value is less than $\alpha = .01$ ($p = .000 < .01$), H_0 is rejected. There is sufficient evidence to indicate the model is useful in predicting sales price at $\alpha = .01$.

11.91 The models in parts **a** and **b** are nested:

The complete model is $E(y) = \beta_0 + \beta_1 x_1 + \beta_2 x_2$
The reduced model is $E(y) = \beta_0 + \beta_1 x_1$

The models in parts **a** and **d** are nested.

The complete model is $E(y) = \beta_0 + \beta_1 x_1 + \beta_2 x_2 + \beta_3 x_1 x_2$
The reduced model is $E(y) = \beta_0 + \beta_1 x_1 + \beta_2 x_2$

The models in parts **a** and **e** are nested.

The complete model is $E(y) = \beta_0 + \beta_1 x_1 + \beta_2 x_2 + \beta_3 x_1 x_2 + \beta_4 x_1^2 + \beta_5 x_2^2$
The reduced model is $E(y) = \beta_0 + \beta_1 x_1 + \beta_2 x_2$

The models in parts **b** and **c** are nested.

The complete model is $E(y) = \beta_0 + \beta_1 x_1 + \beta_2 x_1^2$
The reduced model is $E(y) = \beta_0 + \beta_1 x_1$

The models in parts **b** and **d** are nested.

The complete model is $E(y) = \beta_0 + \beta_1 x_1 + \beta_2 x_2 + \beta_3 x_1 x_2$
The reduced model is $E(y) = \beta_0 + \beta_1 x_1$

The models in parts **b** and **e** are nested.

The complete model is $E(y) = \beta_0 + \beta_1 x_1 + \beta_2 x_2 + \beta_3 x_1 x_2 + \beta_4 x_1^2 + \beta_5 x_2^2$
The reduced model is $E(y) = \beta_0 + \beta_1 x_1$

The models in parts **c** and **e** are nested.

The complete model is $E(y) = \beta_0 + \beta_1 x_1 + \beta_2 x_2 + \beta_3 x_1 x_2 + \beta_4 x_1^2 + \beta_5 x_2^2$
The reduced model is $E(y) = \beta_0 + \beta_1 x_1 + \beta_2 x_1^2$

The models in parts **d** and **e** are nested.

The complete model is $E(y) = \beta_0 + \beta_1 x_1 + \beta_2 x_2 + \beta_3 x_1 x_2 + \beta_4 x_1^2 + \beta_5 x_2^2$
The reduced model is $E(y) = \beta_0 + \beta_1 x_1 + \beta_2 x_2 + \beta_3 x_1 x_2$

11.93 a. Including β_0, there are five β parameters in the complete model and three in the reduced model.

b. The hypotheses are:

H_0: $\beta_3 = \beta_4 = 0$
H_a: At least one $\beta_i \neq 0$, $i = 3, 4$

c.   The test statistic is $F = \dfrac{(\text{SSE}_R - \text{SSE}_C)/(k-g)}{\text{SSE}_C /[n-(k+1)]}$

$$= \frac{(160.44 - 152.66)/(4-2)}{152.66/[20-(4+1)]} = \frac{3.89}{10.1773} = .38$$

The rejection region requires $\alpha = .05$ in the upper tail of the F distribution with numerator df $= k - g$ $= 4 - 2 = 2$ and denominator df $= n - (k+1) = 20 - (4+1) = 15$. From Table VIII, Appendix B, $F_{.05} = 3.68$. The rejection region is $F > 3.68$.

Since the observed value of the test statistic does not fall in the rejection region ($F = .38 \not> 3.68$), H_0 is not rejected. There is insufficient evidence to indicate the complete model is better than the reduced model at $\alpha = .05$.

11.95   a.   To determine whether the quadratic terms in the model are statistically useful for predicting relative optimism, we test:

H_0: $\beta_4 = \beta_5 = 0$
H_a: At least 1 $\beta_i \neq 0$

b.   The complete model is $E(y) = \beta_0 + \beta_1 x_1 + \beta_2 x_2 + \beta_3 x_1 x_2 + \beta_4 x_2^2 + \beta_5 x_1 x_2^2$ and the reduced model is $E(y) = \beta_0 + \beta_1 x_1 + \beta_2 x_2 + \beta_3 x_1 x_2$.

b.   To determine whether the interaction terms in the model are statistically useful for predicting relative optimism, we test:

H_0: $\beta_3 = \beta_5 = 0$
H_a: At least 1$\beta_i \neq 0$

d.   The complete model is $E(y) = \beta_0 + \beta_1 x_1 + \beta_2 x_2 + \beta_3 x_1 x_2 + \beta_4 x_2^2 + \beta_5 x_1 x_2^2$ and the reduced model is $E(y) = \beta_0 + \beta_1 x_1 + \beta_2 x_2 + \beta_4 x_2^2$.

To determine whether the dummy variable terms in the model are statistically useful for predicting relative optimism, we test:

e. H_0: $\beta_1 = \beta_3 = \beta_5 = 0$
H_a: At least 1 $\beta_i \neq 0$

f.   The complete model is $E(y) = \beta_0 + \beta_1 x_1 + \beta_2 x_2 + \beta_3 x_1 x_2 + \beta_4 x_2^2 + \beta_5 x_1 x_2^2$ and the reduced model is $E(y) = \beta_0 + \beta_2 x_2 + \beta_4 x_2^2$.

11.97   a.   Let $x_1 = $ cycle speed and $x_2 = $ cycle pressure ratio. A complete second order model is:

$$E(y) = \beta_0 + \beta_1 x_1 + \beta_2 x_2 + \beta_3 x_1^2 + \beta_4 x_2^2 + \beta_5 x_1 x_2$$

b.   To determine whether the curvature terms in the complete 2nd –order model are useful for predicting heat rate, we test:

H_o: $\beta_3 = \beta_4 = 0$
H_a: At least one of the parameters β_3 , β_4 differs from 0

c.   The complete model is: $E(y) = \beta_0 + \beta_1 x_1 + \beta_2 x_2 + \beta_3 x_1^2 + \beta_4 x_2^2 + \beta_5 x_1 x_2$

The reduced model is: $E(y) = \beta_0 + \beta_1 x_1 + \beta_2 x_2 + \beta_5 x_1 x_2$

d. From the printout, $SSE_R = 25{,}310{,}639$, $SSE_C = 19{,}370{,}350$, and $MSE_C = 317{,}547$.

e. The test statistic is:

$$F = \frac{(SSE_R - SSE_C)/(k-g)}{SSE_C/[n-(k+1)]} = \frac{(25{,}310{,}639 - 19{,}370{,}350)/(5-3)}{19{,}370{,}350/[67-(5+1)]} = 9.35$$

f. The rejection region requires $\alpha = .10$ in the upper tail of the F-distribution with $v_1 = k - g = 5 - 3 = 2$ and $v_2 = n - (k+1) = 67 - (5+1) = 61$. From Table VII, Appendix B, $F_{.10} = 2.39$. The rejection region is $F > 2.39$.

g. Since the observed value of the test statistic falls in the rejection region ($F = 9.35 > 2.39$), H_0 is rejected. There is sufficient evidence to indicate at least one of the curvature terms in the complete 2nd–order model are useful for predicting heat rate at $\alpha = .10$.

11.99 a. The hypothesized equation for $E(y)$ is:

$$E(y) = \beta_0 + \beta_1 x_1 + \beta_2 x_2 + \beta_3 x_3 + \beta_4 x_4 + \beta_5 x_5 + \beta_6 x_6 + \beta_7 x_7 + \beta_8 x_8 + \beta_9 x_9 + \beta_{10} x_{10}$$

b. To determine if the initial model is sufficient, we test:

H_0: $\beta_3 = \beta_4 = \ldots = \beta_{10} = 0$
H_a: At least one $\beta_i \neq 0$ $i = 3, 4, \ldots, 10$

c. Since the F was significant, we reject H_0 at $\alpha = .05$. There is sufficient evidence to indicate that at least one of the additional variables (student ethnicity, socio-economic status, school performance, number of math courses taken in high school and overall GPA in the math courses) contributes to the prediction of the SAT-math score.

d. $R_{adj}^2 = .79$. 79% of the sample variability of SAT-math scores is explained by the model containing the 10 independent variables, adjusted for the sample size and the number of variables.

e. For confidence coefficient .95, $\alpha = .05$ and $\alpha/2 = .05/2 = .025$. From Table V, Appendix B, with df $= n - (k+1) = 3{,}492 - (10+1) = 3{,}481$, $t_{.025} = 1.96$. The confidence interval is:

$$\hat{\beta}_2 \pm t_{\alpha/2} s_{\hat{\beta}_2} \Rightarrow 14 \pm 1.96(3) \Rightarrow 14 \pm 5.88 \Rightarrow (8.12, \ 19.88)$$

We are 95% confident that the mean SAT-Math score for those who were coached was anywhere from 8.12 to 19.88 points higher than the mean for those who were not coached, holding all other variables constant.

f. Yes. The value of $\hat{\beta}_2$ decreased from 19 to 14 when the additional variables were added to the model. Thus, the increase from coaching is not as great.

g. Te new model including all the interaction terms is:

$$E(y) = \beta_0 + \beta_1 x_1 + \beta_2 x_2 + \beta_3 x_3 + \beta_4 x_4 + \beta_5 x_5 + \beta_6 x_6 + \beta_7 x_7 + \beta_8 x_8 + \beta_9 x_9 + \beta_{10} x_{10}$$
$$+ \beta_{11} x_1 x_2 + \beta_{12} x_3 x_2 + \beta_{13} x_4 x_2 + \beta_{14} x_5 x_2 + \beta_{15} x_6 x_2 + \beta_{16} x_7 x_2 + \beta_{17} x_8 x_2$$
$$+ \beta_{18} x_9 x_2 + \beta_{19} x_{10} x_2$$

h. To determine if the model with the interaction terms is better in predicting SAT-Math scores, we test:

H_0: $\beta_{11} = \beta_{12} = \ldots = \beta_{19} = 0$
H_a: At least one $\beta_i \neq 0$ $i = 11, 12, \ldots, 19$

We would fit the complete model above. We would then compare it to the fitted model from part a (Reduced model). The test statistic would be:

$$F = \frac{(SSE_R - SSE_C)/(k-g)}{SSE_C /[n-(k+1)]}$$

11.101 a. The model would be:

$E(y) = \beta_0 + \beta_1 x_1 + \beta_2 x_2 + \beta_3 x_3$

b. The model including the interaction terms is:

$E(y) = \beta_0 + \beta_1 x_1 + \beta_2 x_2 + \beta_3 x_3 + \beta_4 x_1 x_2 + \beta_5 x_1 x_3$

c. For AL, $x_2 = x_3 = 0$. The model would be:

$E(y) = \beta_0 + \beta_1 x_1 + \beta_2(0) + \beta_3(0) + \beta_4 x_1(0) + \beta_5 x_1(0) = \beta_0 + \beta_1 x_1$

The slope of the line is β_1.

For TDS-3A, $x_2 = 1$ and $x_3 = 0$. The model would be:

$E(y) = \beta_0 + \beta_1 x_1 + \beta_2(1) + \beta_3(0) + \beta_4 x_1(1) + \beta_5 x_1(0) = (\beta_0 + \beta_2) + (\beta_1 + \beta_4)x_1$

The slope of the line is $\beta_1 + \beta_4$.

For FE, $x_2 = 0$ and $x_3 = 1$. The model would be:

$E(y) = \beta_0 + \beta_1 x_1 + \beta_2(0) + \beta_3(1) + \beta_4 x_1(0) + \beta_5 x_1(1) = (\beta_0 + \beta_3) + (\beta_1 + \beta_5)x_1$

The slope of the line is $\beta_1 + \beta_5$.

d. To test for the presence of temperature-waste type interaction, we would fit the complete model listed in part **b** and the reduced model found in part **a**. The hypotheses would be:

H_0: $\beta_4 = \beta_5 = 0$
H_a: At least one $\beta_i \neq 0$, for $i = 4, 5$

The test statistic would be $F = \dfrac{(SSE_R - SSE_C)/(k-g)}{SSE_C /[n-(k+1)]}$ where $k = 5$, $q = 3$, SSE_R is the SSE for the reduced model, and SSE_C is the SSE for the complete model.

11.103 a. Using MINITAB, the output from fitting a complete second-order model is:

```
* NOTE *        X1 is highly correlated with other  predictor variables
* NOTE *        X2 is highly correlated with other  predictor variables
* NOTE *        X1X2 is highly correlated with other  predictor variables

The regression equation is
Y = 172788 - 10739 X1 - 499 X2 - 20.2 X1X2 + 198 X1SQ + 14.7 X2SQ

Predictor        Coef       Stdev      t-ratio        p
Constant        172788       97785       1.77      0.084
X1              -10739        2789      -3.85      0.000
X2                -499        1444      -0.35      0.731
X1X2             -20.20       21.36     -0.95      0.350
X1SQ             197.57       22.60      8.74      0.000
X2SQ             14.678       8.819      1.66      0.103


s = 13132       R-sq = 95.9%    R-sq(adj) = 95.5%

Analysis of Variance

SOURCE        DF            SS            MS          F          p
Regression     5 1.70956E+11 34191134720     198.27      0.000
Error         42  7242915328    172450368
Total         47 1.78199E+11

SOURCE        DF        SEQ SS
X1             1 1.56067E+11
X2             1     13214024
X1X2           1   1686339840
X1SQ           1  12711371776
X2SQ           1    477704384

Unusual Observations
Obs.       X1           Y     Fit Stdev.Fit  Residual   St.Resid
  14      62.9      203288  235455     6002    -32167     -2.75R
  22      45.4       27105   58567     3603    -31462     -2.49R
  34      28.2       28722   15156    11311     13566      2.03RX
  43      64.3      230329  248054     8790    -17725     -1.82 X
  47      63.9      212309  240469     4904    -28160     -2.31R

R denotes an obs. with a large st. resid.
X denotes an obs. whose X value gives it large influence.
```

b. To test the hypothesis H_0: $\beta_4 = \beta_5 = 0$, we must fit the reduced model

$$E(y) = \beta_0 + \beta_1 x_1 + \beta_2 x_2 + \beta_3 x_1 x_2$$

Using MINITAB, the output from fitting the reduced model is:

```
* NOTE *     X1X2 is highly correlated with other  predictor variables
```

```
The regression equation is
Y = - 476768 + 11458 X1 + 3404 X2 - 64.4 X1X2


Predictor       Coef       Stdev      t-ratio        p
Constant     -476768      100852       -4.73     0.000
X1             11458        1874        6.11     0.000
X2              3404        1814        1.88     0.067
X1X2           -64.35      33.77       -1.91     0.063


s = 21549       R-sq = 88.5%      R-sq(adj) = 87.8%

Analysis of Variance

SOURCE       DF          SS           MS          F        p
Regression    3 1.57767E+11 52588867584      113.25    0.000
Error        44 20431990784    464363424
Total        47 1.78199E+11


SOURCE       DF       SEQ SS
X1            1 1.56067E+11
X2            1     13214024
X1X2          1   1686339840


Unusual Observations
Obs.      X1          Y      Fit Stdev.Fit  Residual   St.Resid
  34     28.2      28722   -59713     11922     88435     4.93RX
  38     66.5     290411   250350      9553     40061     2.07R
  43     64.3     230329   202899     11574     27430     1.51 X


R denotes an obs. with a large st. resid.
X denotes an obs. whose X value gives it large influence.
```

The test is:

H_0: $\beta_4 = \beta_5 = 0$
H_a: At least one $\beta_i \neq 0$, for $i = 4, 5$

The test statistic is $F = \dfrac{(\text{SSE}_R - \text{SSE}_C)/(k - g)}{\text{SSE}_C\,/[n - (k+1)]}$

$$= \frac{(20,431,990,784 - 7,242,915,328)/(5-3)}{7,242,915,328/[48-(5+1)]} = 38.24$$

The rejection region requires $\alpha = .05$ in the upper tail of the F-distribution with $\nu_1 = k - g = 5 - 3 = 2$ and $\nu_2 = n - (k + 1) = 48 - (5 + 1) = 42$. From Table VIII, Appendix B, $F_{.05} \approx 3.23$. The rejection region is $F > 3.23$.

Since the observed value of the test statistic falls in the rejection region ($F = 38.24 > 3.23$), H_0 is rejected. There is sufficient evidence to indicate that at least one of the quadratic terms contributes to the prediction of monthly collision claims at $\alpha = .05$.

c. From part **b**, we know at least one of the quadratic terms is significant. From part **a**, it appears that none of the terms involving x_2 may be significant.

Thus, we will fit the model with just x_1 and x_1^2. The MINITAB output is:

```
The regression equation is
Y = 185160 - 11580 X1 + 196 X1SQ


Predictor       Coef        Stdev     t-ratio        p
Constant      185160        54791        3.38    0.002
X1            -11580         2182       -5.31    0.000
X1SQ          195.54        21.64        9.04    0.000


s = 13219       R-sq = 95.6%      R-sq(adj) = 95.4%

Analysis of Variance

SOURCE         DF           SS           MS          F        p
Regression      2  1.70335E+11  85167357952     487.36    0.000
Error          45   7863868416    174752624
Total          47  1.78199E+11


SOURCE         DF      SEQ SS
X1              1  1.56067E+11
X1SQ            1  14267676672


Unusual Observations
Obs.      X1          Y       Fit Stdev.Fit   Residual    St.Resid
 10     35.8      28957     21200      5825       7757       0.65 X
 14     62.9     203288    230397      4044     -27109      -2.15R
 22     45.4      27105     62456      2856     -35351      -2.74R
 34     28.2      28722     14099     11344      14623       2.15RX
 38     66.5     290411    279798      6189      10613       0.91 X
 47     63.9     212309    243611      4570     -31302      -2.52R


R denotes an obs. with a large st. resid.
X denotes an obs. whose X value gives it large influence.
```

To see if any of the terms involving x_2 are significant, we test:

H_0: $\beta_2 = \beta_3 = \beta_5 = 0$
H_a: At least one $\beta_i \neq 0$, for $i = 2, 3, 5$

The test statistic is $F = \dfrac{(\text{SSE}_R - \text{SSE}_C)/(k-g)}{\text{SSE}_C/[n-(k+1)]}$

$$= \frac{(7,863,868,416 - 7,242,915,328)/(5-2)}{7,242,915,328/[48-(5+1)]} = 1.20$$

The rejection region requires $\alpha = .05$ in the upper tail of the F-distribution with $v_1 = k - g = 5 - 2 = 3$ and $v_2 = n - (k+1) = 48 - (5+1) = 42$. From Table VIII, Appendix B, $F_{.05} \approx 2.84$. The rejection region is $F > 2.84$

Since the observed value of the test statistic does not fall in the rejection region ($F = 1.20 \not> 2.84$), H_0 is not rejected. There is insufficient evidence to indicate that any of the terms involving x_2 contribute to the model at $\alpha = .05$.

Thus, it appears that the best model is $E(y) = \beta_0 + \beta_1 x_1 + \beta_2 x_1^2$. The model does not support the analyst's claim. In the model above, the estimate for β_2 is positive. This would indicate that the higher claims are for both the young and the old. Also, there is no evidence to support the claim that there are more claims when the temperature goes down.

11.105 a.   In Step 1, all one-variable models are fit to the data. These models are of the form:

$$E(y) = \beta_0 + \beta_1 x_i$$

Since there are 7 independent variables, 7 models are fit. (Note: There are actually only 6 independent variables. One of the qualitative variables has three levels and thus two dummy variables. Some statistical packages will allow one to bunch these two variables together so that they are either both in or both out. In this answer, we are assuming that each x_i stands by itself.

       b.   In Step 2, all two-varirable models are fit to the data, where the variable selected in Step 1, say x_1, is one of the variables. These models are of the form:

$$E(y) = \beta_0 + \beta_1 x_1 + \beta_2 x_i$$

Since there are 6 independent variables remaining, 6 models are fit.

       c.   In Step 3, all three-variable models are fit to the data, where the variables selected in Step 2, say x_1 and x_2, are two of the variables. These models are of the form:

$$E(y) = \beta_0 + \beta_1 x_1 + \beta_2 x_2 + \beta_3 x_i$$

Since there are 5 independent variables remaining, 5 models are fit.

       d.   The procedure stops adding independent variables when none of the remaining variables, when added to the model, have a *p*-value less than some predetermined value. This predetermined value is usually $\alpha = .05$.

       e.   Two major drawbacks to using the final stepwise model as the "best" model are:

          (1)   An extremely large number of single β parameter *t*-tests have been conducted. Thus, the probability is very high that one or more errors have been made in including or excluding variables.

          (2)   Often the variables selected to be included in a stepwise regression do not include the high-order terms. Consequently, we may have initially omitted several important terms from the model.

11.107 a.   In step 1, all 1 variable models are fit. Thus, there are a total of 11 models fit.

       b.   In step 2, all two-variable models are fit, where 1 of the variables is the best one selected in step 1. Thus, a total of 10 two-variable models are fit.

       c.   In the 11th step, only one model is fit – the model containing all the independent variables.

d.   The model would be:

$$E(y) = \beta_0 + \beta_1 x_{11} + \beta_2 x_4 + \beta_3 x_2 + \beta_4 x_7 + \beta_5 x_{10} + \beta_6 x_1 + \beta_7 x_9 + \beta_8 x_3$$

e.   67.7% of the total sample variability of overall satisfaction is explained by the model containing the independent variables safety on bus, seat availability, dependability, travel time, convenience of route, safety at bus stops, hours of service, and frequency of service.

f.   Using stepwise regression does not guarantee that the best model will be found. There may be better combinations of the independent variables that are never found, because of the order in which the independent variables are entered into the model. In addition, there are no squared or interaction terms included. There is a high probability of making at least one Type 1 error.

11.109 Yes. x_2 and x_4 are highly correlated (.93), as well as x_4 and x_5 (.86). When highly correlated independent variables are present in a regression model, the results can be confusing. The researcher may want to include only one of the variables.

11.111 a.   Since the absolute value of the correlation coefficient is .983, this would imply there is a very high potential for multicollinearity.

b.   Since the absolute value of the correlation coefficient is .074, this would imply there is a very low potential for multicollinearity.

c.   Since the absolute value of the correlation coefficient is .722, this would imply there is a moderate potential for multicollinearity.

d.   Since the absolute value of the correlation coefficient is .528, this would imply there is a moderate potential for multicollinearity.

11.113 It is possible that company role of estimator and previous accuracy could be correlated with each other. This indicates multicollinearity may be present

11.115 a.   The normal probability plot should be used to check for normal errors. The points in this plot are fairly close to the straight line, so the assumption of normality appears to be satisfied.

b.   The graph of the residuals versus the fitted or predicted values should be used to check for unequal variances. The spread of the residuals appears to be fairly constant in this graph. It appears that the assumption of equal variances is satisfied.

11.117   Using MINITAB, the residual plots are:

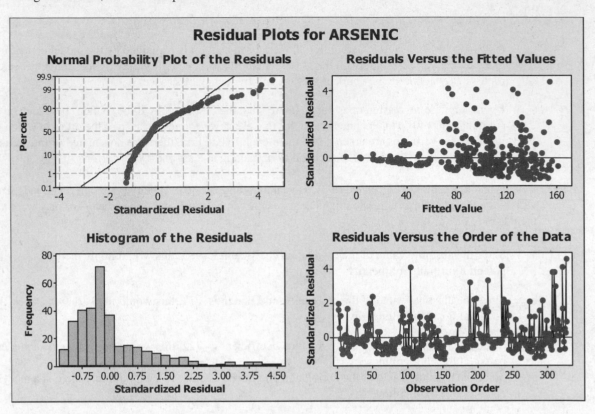

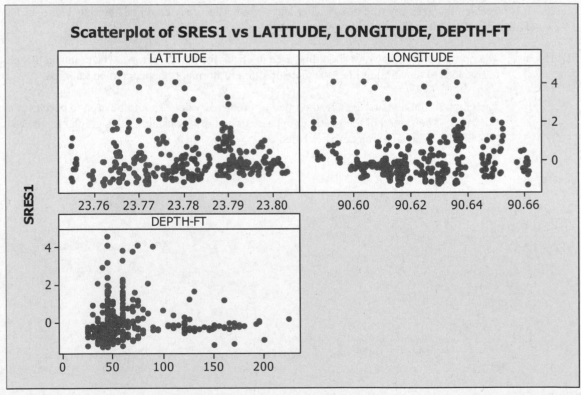

a. From the histogram of the standardized residuals, it appears that the mean of the residuals is close to 0. Thus, the assumption that the mean error is 0 appears to be met.

b. From the plot of the standardized residuals versus the fitted values, it appears that the spread of the residuals increases as the fitted values increase. Thus, it appears that the assumption of constant variance is violated.

c. From the plots of the standardized residuals versus the fitted values, it appears that there are some outliers. There are several observations with standardized residuals of 4 or more.

d. From the normal probability plot, the data do not form a straight line. Thus, it appears that the assumption of normal error terms is violated.

c. Using MINITAB, the correlations among the independent variables are:

Correlations: LATITUDE, LONGITUDE, DEPTH-FT

```
            LATITUDE   LONGITUDE
LONGITUDE     0.311
              0.000

DEPTH-FT      0.151      -0.328
              0.006       0.000


Cell Contents: Pearson correlation
               P-Value
```

None of the pairwise correlations are large in absolute value, so there is no evidence of multicollinearity. In addition, the global test indicates that at least one of the independent variables is significant and each of the independent variables is statistically significant. This also indicates that multicollinearity does not exist.

11.119 a. Using MINITAB, the results are:

Regression Analysis: Time versus Temp

```
The regression equation is
Time = 30856 - 192 Temp


Predictor      Coef   SE Coef       T      P
Constant      30856      2713   11.37  0.000
Temp        -191.57     18.49  -10.36  0.000


S = 1099.17   R-Sq = 84.3%   R-Sq(adj) = 83.5%


Analysis of Variance

Source         DF          SS         MS        F      P
Regression      1   129663987  129663987   107.32  0.000
Residual Error 20    24163399    1208170
Total          21   153827386
```

The fitted regression line is $\hat{y} = 30{,}856 - 191.57 temp$

b.   For temperature = 149, $\hat{y} = 30,856 - 191.57(150) = 2,312.07$. There are 2 observations with a temperature of 149. The residuals for the microchips manufactured at a temperature of 149° C are $r = y - \hat{y} = 1,100 - 2,312.07 = -1,212.07$ and $r = y - \hat{y} = 1,150 - 2,312.07 = -1,162.07$.

c.   Using MINITAB, the plot of the residuals versus temperature is:

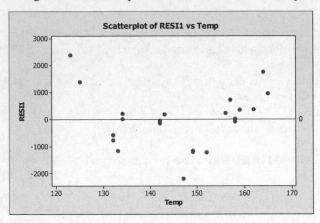

There appears to be a U-shaped trend to the data.

d.   Yes. Because there appears to be a U-shaped trend to the data, this indicates that there is a curvilinear relationship between temperature and time.

11.121   In multiple regression, as in simple regression, the confidence interval for the mean value of *y* is narrower than the prediction interval of a particular value of *y*.

11.123   The model-building step is the key to the success or failure of a regression analysis. If the model is a good model, we will have a good predictive model for the dependent variable *y*. If the model is not a good model, the predictive ability will not be of much use.

11.125   a.   The least squares equation is $\hat{y} = 90.1 - 1.836x_1 + .285x_2$

b. $R^2 = .916$. About 91.6% of the sample variability in the *y*'s is explained by the model $E(y) = \beta_0 + \beta_1 x_1 + \beta_2 x_2$

c.   To determine if the model is useful for predicting *y*, we test:

H_0: $\beta_1 = \beta_2 = 0$
H_a: At least one $\beta_i \neq 0$, $i = 1, 2$

The test statistic is $F = \dfrac{\text{MSR}}{\text{MSE}} = \dfrac{7400}{114} = 64.91$

The rejection region requires $\alpha = .05$ in the upper tail of the *F* distribution with $v_1 = k = 2$ and $v_2 = n - (k + 1) = 15 - (2 + 1) = 12$. From Table VIII, Appendix B, $F_{.05} = 3.89$. The rejection region is $F > 3.89$.

Since the observed value of the test statistic falls in the rejection region ($F = 64.91 > 3.89$), H_0 is rejected. There is sufficient evidence to indicate the model is useful for predicting *y* at $\alpha = .05$.

d. H_0: $\beta_1 = 0$
H_a: $\beta_1 \neq 0$

The test statistic is $t = \dfrac{\hat{\beta}_1}{s_{\hat{\beta}_1}} = \dfrac{-1.836}{.367} = -5.01$

The rejection region requires $\alpha/2 = .05/2 = .025$ in each tail of the t distribution with df $= n - (k + 1)$ $= 15 - (2 + 1) = 12$. From Table V, Appendix B, $t_{.025} = 2.179$. The rejection region is $t < -2.179$ or $t > 2.179$.

Since the observed value of the test statistic falls in the rejection region ($t = -5.01 < -2.179$), H_0 is rejected. There is sufficient evidence to indicate β_1 is not 0 at $\alpha = .05$.

e. The standard deviation is $\sqrt{\text{MSE}} = \sqrt{114} = 10.68$. We would expect about 95% of the observations to fall within $2(10.68) = 21.36$ units of the fitted regression line.

11.127 $E(y) = \beta_0 + \beta_1 x_1 + \beta_2 x_2 + \beta_3 x_3$

where $x_1 = \begin{cases} 1, \text{ if level 2} \\ 0, \text{ otherwise} \end{cases}$ $x_2 = \begin{cases} 1, \text{ if level 3} \\ 0, \text{ otherwise} \end{cases}$ $x_3 = \begin{cases} 1, \text{ if level 4} \\ 0, \text{ otherwise} \end{cases}$

11.129   The stepwise regression method is used to try to find the best model to describe a process. It is a screening procedure that tries to select a small subset of independent variables from a large set of independent variables that will adequately predict the dependent variable. This method is useful in that it can eliminate some unimportant independent variables from consideration.

11.130   a. $E(y) = \beta_0 + \beta_1 x_1 + \beta_2 x_2$

      b. $E(y) = \beta_0 + \beta_1 x_1 + \beta_2 x_1^2 + \beta_3 x_2 + \beta_4 x_2^2 + \beta_5 x_1 x_2$

11.131   Even though SSE $= 0$, we cannot estimate σ^2 because there are no degrees of freedom corresponding to error. With three data points, there are only two degrees of freedom available. The degrees of freedom corresponding to the model is $k = 2$ and the degrees of freedom corresponding to error is $n - (k + 1) = 3 - (2 + 1) = 0$. Without an estimate for σ^2, no inferences can be made.

11.133   a.   A confidence interval for the difference of two population means, $(\mu_1 - \mu_2)$, could be used. Since both sample sizes are over 30, the large sample confidence interval is used (with independent samples).

      b.   Let $x = \begin{cases} 1 \text{ if public college} \\ 0 \text{ otherwise} \end{cases}$

         The model is $E(y) = \beta_0 + \beta_1 x$

      c. β_1 is the difference between the two population means. A point estimate for β_1 is $\hat{\beta}_1$. A confidence interval for β_1 could be used to estimate the difference in the two population means.

11.135 a. The type of juice extractor is qualitative.
            The size of the orange is quantitative.

       b. The model is $E(y) = \beta_0 + \beta_1 x_1 + \beta_2 x_2$

           where x_1 = diameter of orange

           $$x_2 = \begin{cases} 1 \text{ if Brand B} \\ 0 \text{ if not} \end{cases}$$

       c. To allow the lines to differ, the interaction term is added:

           $$E(y) = \beta_0 + \beta_1 x_1 + \beta_2 x_2 + \beta_3 x_1 x_2$$

       d. For part **b**:

           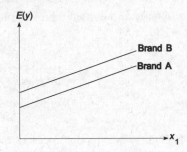

           For part **c**:

           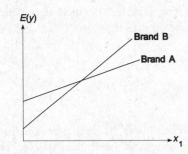

       e. To determine whether the model in part **c** provides more information for predicting yield than does
           the model in part **b**, we test:

           H_0: $\beta_3 = 0$
           H_a: $\beta_3 \neq 0$

       f. The test statistic would be $F = \dfrac{(\text{SSE}_R - \text{SSE}_C)/(k - g)}{\text{SSE}_C /[n - (k + 1)]}$

           To compute SSE_R: The model in part **b** is fit and SSE_R is the sum of squares for error.

           To compute SSE_C: The model in part **c** is fit and SSE_C is the sum of squares for error.

           $k - g$ = number of parameters in H_0 which is 1
           $n - (k + 1)$ = degrees of freedom for error in the complete model

11.137 Variables that are highly correlated with each other are x_4 and x_5 (r = -.84). When highly correlated independent variables are present in a regression model, the results can be confusing. Possible problems include:

    1.   Global test indicates at least one independent variable is useful in the prediction of *y*, but none of the individual tests for the independent variables is significant.

    2.   The signs of the estimated beta coefficients are opposite from what is expected.

11.139 a. $R^2 = .712$. 71.2% of the total sample variation in the fees charged by auditors is explained by the model containing 7 independent variables.

    b.   To determine if the model is adequate, we test:

H_0: $\beta_1 = \beta_2 = \beta_3 = \beta_4 = \beta_5 = \beta_6 = \beta_7 = 0$
H_a: At least one $\beta_i \neq 0$, $i = 1, 2, 3, ..., 7$

The test statistic is $F = 111.1$ (from table).

Since no α was given, we will use $\alpha = .05$. The rejection region requires $\alpha = .05$ in the upper tail of the *F*-distribution with $v_1 = k = 7$ and $v_2 = n - (k + 1) = 268 - (7 + 1) = 260$. From Table VIII, Appendix B, $F_{.05} \approx 2.01$. The rejection region is $F > 2.01$.

Since the observed value of the test statistic falls in the rejection region ($F = 111.1 > 2.01$), H_0 is rejected. There is sufficient evidence to indicate that the model is adequate for predicting the audit fees at $\alpha = .05$.

    c.   If new auditors charge less than incumbent auditors, then β_1 is negative. By definition, $x_1 = 1$ if new auditor and 0 if incumbent. Therefore, we will be adding to the mean only for new auditors. If new auditors charge less, we have to add a negative number.

11.141 The correlation coefficient between Importance and Replace is .2682. This correlation coefficient is fairly small and would not indicate a problem with multicollinearity between Importance and Replace. The correlation coefficient between Importance and Support is .6991. This correlation coefficient is fairly large and would indicate a potential problem with multicollinearity between Importance and Support. Probably only one of these variables should be included in the regression model. The correlation coefficient between Replace and Support is −.0531. This correlation coefficient is very small and would not indicate a problem with multicollinearity between Replace and Support. Thus, the model could probably include Replace and one of the variables Support or Importance.

11.143 a.   Let $x_2 = \begin{cases} 1 \text{ if intervention group} \\ 0 \text{ if otherwise} \end{cases}$

The first-order model would be:

$$E(y) = \beta_0 + \beta_1 x_1 + \beta_2 x_2$$

b. For the control group, $x_2 = 0$. The first-order model is:

$$E(y) = \beta_0 + \beta_1 x_1 + \beta_2(0) = \beta_0 + \beta_1 x_1$$

For the intervention group, $x_2 = 1$. The first-order model is:

$$E(y) = \beta_0 + \beta_1 x_1 + \beta_2(1) = \beta_0 + \beta_1 x_1 + \beta_2 = (\beta_0 + \beta_2) + \beta_1 x_1$$

In both models, the slope of the line is β_1.

c. If pretest score and group interact, the first-order model would be:

$$E(y) = \beta_0 + \beta_1 x_1 + \beta_2 x_2 + \beta_3 x_1 x_2$$

d. For the control group, $x_2 = 0$. The first-order model including the interaction is:

$$E(y) = \beta_0 + \beta_1 x_1 + \beta_2(0) + \beta_3 x_1(0) = \beta_0 + \beta_1 x_1$$

For the intervention group, $x_2 = 1$. The first-order model including the interaction is:

$$E(y) = \beta_0 + \beta_1 x_1 + \beta_2(1) + \beta_3 x_1(1) = \beta_0 + \beta_1 x_1 + \beta_2 + \beta_3 x_1$$
$$= (\beta_0 + \beta_2) + (\beta_1 + \beta_3) x_1$$

The slope of the model for the control group is β_1. The slope of the model for the intervention group is $\beta_1 + \beta_3$.

11.145 a. Not necessarily. If Nickel was highly correlated to several other variables, then it might be better to keep Nickel and drop some of the other highly correlated variables.

b. Using stepwise regression is a good start for selecting the best set of predictor variables. However, one should use caution when looking at the model selected using stepwise regression. Sometimes important variables are not selected to be entered into the model. Also, many *t*-tests have been run, thus inflating the Type I and Type II error rates. One must also consider using higher order terms in the model and interaction terms.

c. No, further exploration should be used. One should consider using higher order terms for the variables (i.e. squared terms) and also interaction terms.

11.147 a. Using MINITAB, the scattergram is:

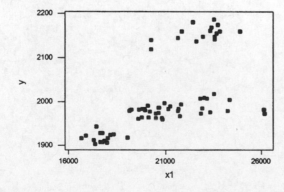

b. Let $x_2 = \begin{cases} 1 \text{ if } 1-35\text{W} \\ 0 \text{ if not} \end{cases}$

The complete second-order model would be

$$E(y) = \beta_0 + \beta_1 x_1 + \beta_2 x_1^2 + \beta_3 x_2 + \beta_4 x_1 x_2 + \beta_5 x_1^2 x_2$$

c. Using MINITAB, the printout is:

Regression Analysis

```
   The regression equation is
y = 776 + 0.104 x1 -0.000002 x1sq + 232 x2 - 0.0091 x1x2
        +0.000000 x1sqx2

Predictor        Coef       StDev         T        P
Constant        776.4       144.5      5.37    0.000
x1            0.10418     0.01388      7.50    0.000
x1sq      -0.00000223  0.00000033     -6.73    0.000
x2              232        1094        0.21    0.833
x1x2        -0.00914     0.09829      -0.09    0.926
x1sqx2     0.00000027  0.00000220      0.12    0.903


S = 15.58      R-Sq = 97.2%      R-Sq(adj) = 97.0%

Analysis of Variance

Source            DF          SS          MS         F        P
Regression         5      555741      111148    457.73    0.000
Residual Error    66       16027         243
Total             71      571767


Source       DF      Seq SS
x1            1      254676
x1sq          1       21495
x2            1      279383
x1x2          1         183
x1sqx2        1           4

Unusual Observations
Obs      x1        y       Fit  StDev Fit  Residual  St Resid
 27   19062  1917.64  1953.27       2.51    -35.63     -2.32R
 48   26148  1982.02  1978.23       9.10      3.79      0.30 X
 53   26166  1972.92  1978.01       9.15     -5.09     -0.40 X
 55   20250  2120.00  2130.56      10.57    -10.56     -0.92 X
 56   20251  2140.00  2130.57      10.57      9.43      0.82 X
 63   24885  2160.02  2161.81      12.67     -1.79     -0.20 X

R denotes an observation with a large standardized residual
X denotes an observation whose X value gives it large influence.
```

The fitted model is
$$\hat{y} = 776 + .104x_1 - .000002x_1^2 + 232x_2 - .0091x_1x_2 + .00000027x_1^2x_2 .$$

To determine if the curvilinear relationship is different at the two locations, we test:

H_0: $\beta_3 = \beta_4 = \beta_5 = 0$
H_0: At least one of the coefficients is nonzero

In order to test this hypothesis, we must fit the reduced model

$$E(y) = \beta_0 + \beta_1x_1 + \beta_2x_1^2$$

Using MINITAB, the printout from fitting the reduced model is:

Regression Analysis

```
The regression equation is
y = 197 + 0.149 x1 -0.000003 x1sq
```

Predictor	Coef	StDev	T	P
Constant	197.5	578.9	0.34	0.734
x1	0.14921	0.05551	2.69	0.009
x1sq	-0.00000295	0.00000132	-2.24	0.028

```
S = 65.45      R-Sq = 48.3%      R-Sq(adj) = 46.8%
```

Analysis of Variance

Source	DF	SS	MS	F	P
Regression	2	276171	138085	32.23	0.000
Residual Error	69	295597	4284		
Total	71	571767			

Source	DF	Seq SS
x1	1	254676
x1sq	1	21495

Unusual Observations

Obs	x1	y	Fit	StDev Fit	Residual	St Resid
30	16691	1916.13	1865.11	23.39	51.02	0.83 X
48	26148	1982.02	2079.68	33.08	-97.66	-1.73 X
53	26166	1972.92	2079.59	33.31	-106.67	-1.89 X
56	20251	2140.00	2007.88	10.43	132.12	2.04R

```
R denotes an observation with a large standardized residual
X denotes an observation whose X value gives it large influence.
```

The fitted regression line is $\hat{y} = 197 + .149x_1 - .000003x_1^2$

To determine if the curvilinear relationship is different at the two locations, we test:

H_0: $\beta_3 = \beta_4 = \beta_5 = 0$
H_a: At least one of the coefficients is nonzero

The test statistic is $F = \dfrac{(SSE_R - SSE_C)/(k-g)}{SSE_C /[n-(k+1)]} = \dfrac{(295,597 - 16,027)/(5-2)}{16,027 /[72-(5+1)]}$

$= 383.76$

Since no α was given we will use $\alpha = .05$. The rejection region requires $\alpha = .05$ in the upper tail of the F-distribution with $v_1 = (k-g) = (5-2) = 3$ and $v_2 = n - (k+1) = 72 - (5+1) = 66$. From Table VIII, Appendix B, $F_{.05} \approx 2.76$. The rejection region is $F > 2.76$.

Since the observed value of the test statistic falls in the rejection region ($F = 383.76 > 2.76$), H_0 is rejected. There is sufficient evidence to indicate the curvilinear relationship is different at the two locations at $\alpha = .05$.

d.   Using MINITAB, the plot of the residual versus x_1 is:

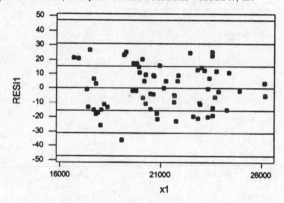

From this plot, we notice that there is only one point more than 2 standard deviations from the mean and no points that are more than 3 standard deviations from the mean. Thus, there do not appear to be any outliers. There is no curve to the residuals, so we have the appropriate model.

A stem-and-leaf display of the residuals is:

Character Stem-and-Leaf Display

```
Stem-and-leaf of RESI1     N  = 72
Leaf Unit = 1.0

    1    -3 5
    1    -3
    2    -2 5
    5    -2 210
   13    -1 99877755
   23    -1 4443221100
   29    -0 996655
  (10)   -0 4432111000
   33     0 03344
   28     0 5678899
   21     1 11222244
   13     1 577
   10     2 0012334
    3     2 556
```

The stem-and-leaf display looks fairly mound-shaped, so it appears that the assumption of normality is valid.

A plot of the residuals versus the fitted values is:

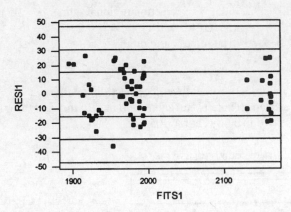

From this plot, there is no cone-shape. Thus, it appears that the assumption of constant variance is valid.

11.149   a.   The model is:

$$E(y) = \beta_0 + \beta_1 x_1 + \beta_2 x_2 + \beta_3 x_3$$

where y = market share

$$x_1 = \begin{cases} 1 \text{ if VH} \\ 0 \text{ otherwise} \end{cases} \quad x_2 = \begin{cases} 1 \text{ if H} \\ 0 \text{ otherwise} \end{cases} \quad x_3 = \begin{cases} 1 \text{ if M} \\ 0 \text{ otherwise} \end{cases}$$

We assume that the error terms (ε_i) or y's are normally distributed at each exposure level, with a common variance. Also, we assume the ε_i's have a mean of 0 and are independent.

     b.   No interaction terms were included because we have only one independent variable, exposure level. Even though we have 3 x_i's in the model, they are dummy variables and correspond to different levels of the one independent variable.

c. Using MINITAB, the output is:

Regression Analysis: y versus x1, x2, x3

```
The regression equation is
y = 10.2 + 0.500 x1 + 2.02 x2 + 0.683 x3

Predictor          Coef     SE Coef          T        P
Constant        10.2333      0.1084      94.41    0.000
x1               0.5000      0.1533       3.26    0.004
x2               2.0167      0.1533      13.16    0.000
x3               0.6833      0.1533       4.46    0.000

S = 0.2655      R-Sq = 90.4%      R-Sq(adj) = 89.0%


Analysis of Variance

Source             DF          SS         MS        F        P
Regression          3     13.3433     4.4478    63.09    0.000
Residual Error     20      1.4100     0.0705
Total              23     14.7533

Source         DF      Seq SS
x1              1      0.7200
x2              1     11.2225
x3              1      1.4008
```

The fitted model is $\hat{y} = 10.2 + .5x_1 + 2.02x_2 + .683x_3$

$$x_1 = \begin{cases} 1 \text{ if VH} \\ 0 \text{ otherwise} \end{cases}$$

$$x_2 = \begin{cases} 1 \text{ if H} \\ 0 \text{ otherwise} \end{cases}$$

$$x_3 = \begin{cases} 1 \text{ if M} \\ 0 \text{ otherwise} \end{cases}$$

d. To determine if the firm's expected market share differs for different levels of advertising exposure, we test:

H_0: $\beta_1 = \beta_2 = \beta_3 = 0$
H_a: At least one $\beta_i \neq 0$, $i = 1, 2, 3$

The test statistic is $F = 63.09$.

The rejection region requires $\alpha = .05$ in the upper tail of the F-distribution with $v_1 = k = 3$ and $v_2 = n - (k + 1) = 24 - (3 + 1) = 20$. From Table VIII, Appendix B, $F_{.05} = 3.10$. The rejection region is $F > 3.10$.

Since the observed value of the test statistic falls in the rejection region ($F = 63.09 > 3.10$), H_0 is rejected. There is sufficient evidence to indicate the firm's expected market share differs for different levels of advertising exposure at $\alpha = .05$.

11.151 a. $\hat{\beta}_0 = -105$ has no meaning because $x_3 = 0$ is not in the observable range. $\hat{\beta}_0$ is simply the y-intercept.

$\hat{\beta}_1 = 25$. The estimated difference in mean attendance between weekends and weekdays is 25, temperature and weather constant.

$\hat{\beta}_2 = 100$. The estimated difference in mean attendance between sunny and overcast days is 100, type of day (weekend or weekday) and temperature constant.

$\hat{\beta}_3 = 10$. The estimated change in mean attendance for each additional degree of temperature is 10, type of day (weekend or weekday) and weather (sunny or overcast) held constant.

b.   To determine if the model is useful for predicting daily attendance, we test:

H_0: $\beta_1 = \beta_2 = \beta_3 = 0$
H_a: At least one $\beta_i \neq 0$, $i = 1, 2, 3$

The test statistic is $F = \dfrac{R^2 / k}{(1 - R^2) / [n - (k+1)]} = \dfrac{.65 / 3}{(1 - .65) / [30 - (3+1)]} = 16.10$

The rejection region requires $\alpha = .05$ in the upper tail of the F distribution with numerator df $= k = 3$ and denominator df $= n - (k + 1) = 30 - (3 + 1) = 26$. From Table VIII, Appendix B, $F_{.05} \approx 2.98$. The rejection region is $F > 2.98$.

Since the observed value of the test statistic falls in the rejection region ($F = 16.10 > 2.98$), H_0 is rejected. There is sufficient evidence to indicate the model is useful for predicting daily attendance at $\alpha = .05$.

c.   To determine if mean attendance increases on weekends, we test:

H_0: $\beta_1 = 0$
H_a: $\beta_1 > 0$

The test statistic is $t = \dfrac{\hat{\beta}_1}{s_{\hat{\beta}_1}} = \dfrac{25 - 0}{10} = 2.5$

The rejection region requires $\alpha = .10$ in the upper tail of the t distribution with df $= n - (k + 1) = 30 - (3 + 1) = 26$. From Table V, Appendix B, $t_{.10} = 1.315$. The rejection region is $t > 1.315$.

Since the observed value of the test statistic falls in the rejection region ($t = 2.5 > 1.315$), H_0 is rejected. There is sufficient evidence to indicate the mean attendance increases on weekends at $\alpha = .10$.

d.   Sunny $\Rightarrow x_2 = 1$, Weekday $\Rightarrow x_1 = 0$, Temperature 95° $\Rightarrow x_3 = 95°$
$= -105 + 25(0) + 100(1) + 10(95) = 945$

e.   We are 90% confident that the actual attendance for sunny weekdays with a temperature of 95° is between 645 and 1245.

11.153 a. $E(y) = \beta_0 + \beta_1 x_1 + \beta_2 x_6 + \beta_3 x_7$

where $x_6 = \begin{cases} 1 \text{ if condition is good} \\ 0 \text{ otherwise} \end{cases}$

$x_7 = \begin{cases} 1 \text{ if condition is fair} \\ 0 \text{ otherwise} \end{cases}$

b.   The model specified in part **a** seems appropriate. The points for E, F, and G cluster around three parallel lines.

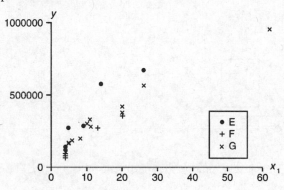

c.   Using MINITAB, the output is

```
The regression equation is
y = 188875 + 15617 x1 - 103046 x6 - 152487 x7

Predictor        Coef        StDev          T          P
Constant        188875       28588        6.61      0.000
x1               15617        1066       14.66      0.000
x6             -103046       31784       -3.24      0.004
x7             -152487       39157       -3.89      0.001
S = 64624      R-Sq = 91.8%    R-Sq(adj) = 90.7%

Analysis of Variance

Source          DF            SS            MS          F          P

Regression       3      9.86170E+11   3.28723E+11    78.71     0.000
Residual Error  21      87700442851    4176211564
Total           24      1.07387E+12


Source      DF         SeqSS
x1           1     9.15776E+11
x6           1        7061463149
x7           1       63332198206

Unusual Observations
Obs    x1        y        Fit      StDev Fit     Residual     St Resid
 10   62.0    950000   1054078      53911        -104078      -2.92RX
 23   14.0    573200    407512      26670         165688       2.81R

R denotes an observation with a large standardized residual
X denotes an observation whose X value gives it large influence.
```

The fitted model is $\hat{y} = 188{,}875 + 15{,}617x_1 - 103{,}046x_6 - 152{,}487x_7$

For excellent condition, $\hat{y} = 188{,}875 + 15{,}617x_1$
For good condition, $\hat{y} = 85{,}829 + 15{,}617x_1$
For fair condition, $\hat{y} = 36{,}388 + 15{,}617x_1$

d.

e.   We must first fit a reduced model with just x_1, number of apartments. Using MINITAB, the output is:

```
The regression equation is
y = 101786 + 15525 x1

Predictor        Coef        StDev            T          P
Constant       101786        23291         4.37      0.000
x1              15525         1345        11.54      0.000

S = 82908        R-Sq = 85.3%     R-Sq(adj) = 84.6%

Analysis of Variance

Source          DF           SS              MS          F          P
Regression       1    9.15776E+11     9.15776E+11    133.23     0.000
Residual Error  23    1.58094E+11      6873656705
Total           24    1.07387E+12

Unusual Observations
Obs     x1          y          Fit     StDev Fit      Residual     St Resid
  4   26.0     676200       505433        24930        170757        2.16R
 10   62.0     950000      1064353        69058       -114353       -2.49RX
 23   14.0     573200       319140        16765        254060        3.13R

R denotes an observation with a large standardized residual
X denotes an observation whose X value gives it large influence.
```

The fitted model is $\hat{y} = 101{,}786 + 15{,}525x_1$.

To determine if the relationship between sale price and number of units differs depending on the physical condition of the apartments, we test:

H_0: $\beta_2 = \beta_3 = 0$
H_a: At least one $\beta_i \neq 0$, $i = 2, 3$

The test statistic is:

$$F = \frac{(\text{SSE}_R - \text{SSE}_C)/(k - g)}{\text{SSE}_C / [n - (k + 1)]} = \frac{(1.58094 \times 10^{11} - 87,700,442,851)/2}{4,176,211,564} = 8.43$$

The rejection region requires $\alpha = .05$ in the upper tail of the F distribution with $v_1 = k - g = 3 - 1 = 2$ and $v_2 = n - (k + 1) = 25 - (3 + 1) = 21$. From Table VIII, Appendix B, $F_{.05} = 3.47$. The rejection region is $F > 3.47$.

Since the observed value of the test statistic falls in the rejection region ($F = 8.43 > 3.47$), H_0 is rejected. There is evidence to indicate that the relationship between sale price and number of units differs depending on the physical condition of the apartments at $\alpha = .05$.

f. We will look for high pairwise correlations.

	x1	x2	x3	x4	x5	x6
x2	-0.014					
x3	0.800	-0.188				
x4	0.224	-0.363	0.166			
x5	0.878	0.027	0.673	0.089		
x6	0.175	-0.447	0.271	0.112	0.020	
x7	-0.128	0.392	-0.118	0.050	-0.238	-0.564

When highly correlated independent variables are present in a regression model, the results are confusing. The researchers may only want to include one of the variables. This may be the case for the variables: x_1 and x_3, x_1 and x_5, x_3 and x_5

g. Use the following plots to check the assumptions on $\in$.

residuals vs x_1
residuals vs x_2
residuals vs x_3
residuals vs x_4
residuals vs x_5
resisduals vs predicted values
frequency distribution of the standardized residuals.

From the plots of the residuals, there do not appear to be any outliers - no standardized residuals are larger than 2.38 in magnitude. In all the plots of the residuals vs x_i, there is no trend that would indicate non-constant variance (no funnel shape). In addition, there is no U or upside-down U shape that would indicate that any of the variables should be squared. In the histogram of the residuals, the plot is fairly mound-shaped, which would indicate the residuals are approximately normally distributed. All of the assumptions appear to be met.

Residuals Versus x_1
(response is y)

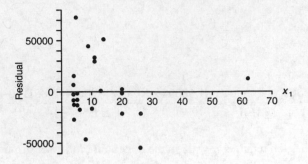

Residuals Versus x_2
(response is y)

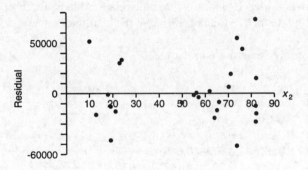

Residuals Versus x_3
(response is y)

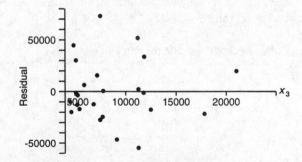

Residuals Versus x_4
(response is y)

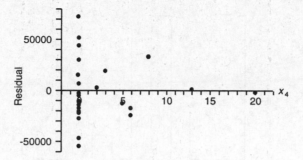

Residuals Versus x_5
(response is y)

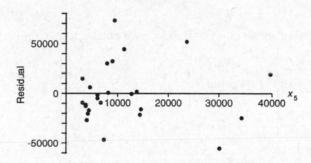

Residuals Versus the Predicted Valucs
(response is y)

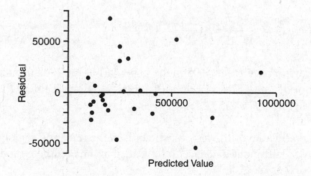

Histogram of the Residuals
(response is *y*)

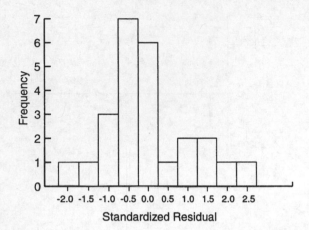

11.155 a.   To determine whether the complete model contributes information for the prediction of *y*, we test:

H_0: $\beta_1 = \beta_2 = \beta_3 = \beta_4 = \beta_5 = 0$
H_a: At least one of the β's is not 0, $i = 1, 2, 3, 4, 5$

b. $\text{MSR} = \dfrac{\text{SS(Model)}}{k} = \dfrac{4,911.56}{5} = 982.31$

$\text{MSE} = \dfrac{\text{SSE}}{n-(k+1)} = \dfrac{1,830.44}{40-(5+1)} = 53.84$

The test statistic is $F = \dfrac{\text{MSR}}{\text{MSE}} = \dfrac{982.31}{53.84} = 18.24$

The rejection region requires $\alpha = .05$ in the upper tail of the F distribution with numerator df $= k = 5$ and denominator df $= n - (k + 1) = 40 - (5 + 1) = 34$. From Table VIII, Appendix B, $F_{.05} \approx 2.53$. The rejection region is $F > 2.53$.

Since the observed value of the test statistic falls in the rejection region ($F = 18.24 > 2.53$), H_0 is rejected. There is sufficient evidence to indicate that the complete model contributes information for the prediction of *y* at $\alpha = .05$.

c.   To determine whether a second-order model contributes more information than a first-order model for the prediction of *y*, we test:

H_0: $\beta_3 = \beta_4 = \beta_5 = 0$
H_a: At least one $\beta_i \neq 0$, $i = 3, 4, 5$

d.   The test statistic is $F = \dfrac{(SSE_R - SSE_C)/(k-g)}{SSE_C/[n-(k+1)]} = \dfrac{(3197.16 - 1830.44)/(5-2)}{1830.44/(40-(5+1))}$

$$= \frac{455.5733}{53.8365} = 8.46$$

The rejection region requires $\alpha = .05$ in the upper tail of the F distribution with numerator df $= k - g$ $= 3$ and denominator df $= n - (k + 1) = 40 - (5 + 1) = 34$. From Table VIII, Appendix B, $F_{.05} \approx 2.92$. The rejection region is $F > 2.92$.

Since the observed value of the test statistic falls in the rejection region ($F = 8.46 > 2.92$), H_0 is rejected. There is sufficient evidence to indicate the second-order model contributes more information than a first-order model for the prediction of y at $\alpha = .05$.

e.   The second-order model, based on the test result in part **d**.

11.157   First, we will fit the simple linear regression model: $E(y) = \beta_o + \beta_1 x_1 + \beta_2 x_2$

Using MINITAB, the results are:

Regression Analysis: y versus x1, x2

```
The regression equation is
y = - 1.57 + 0.0257 x1 + 0.0336 x2

Predictor        Coef      SE Coef          T         P
Constant      -1.5705       0.4937      -3.18     0.003
x1           0.025732     0.004024       6.40     0.000
x2           0.033615     0.004928       6.82     0.000

S = 0.4023      R-Sq = 68.1%      R-Sq(adj) = 66.4%

Analysis of Variance

Source           DF           SS          MS         F         P
Regression        2      12.7859      6.3930     39.51     0.000
Residual Error   37       5.9876      0.1618
Total            39      18.7735

Source      DF      Seq SS
x1           1      5.2549
x2           1      7.5311

Unusual Observations
Obs      x1           y         Fit      SE Fit     Residual     St Resid
  4     100      1.5400      2.6498      0.1699      -1.1098       -3.04R
 32      39      1.2200      2.1558      0.1483      -0.9358       -2.50R

R denotes an observation with a large standardized residual
```

To determine if the model is useful in the prediction of y (GPA), we test:

H_0: $\beta_1 = \beta_2 = 0$
H_a: At least one $\beta_i \neq 0$, $i = 1, 2$

The test statistic is $F = 39.51$ and the p-value is $p = 0.000$. Since the p-value is so small, H_0 is rejected for any reasonable value of α. There is sufficient evidence to indicate at least one of the variables Verbal score or Mathematics score is useful in predicting GPA.

To determine if Verbal score is useful in predicting GPA, controlling for Mathematics score, we test:

H_0: $\beta_1 = 0$
H_a: $\beta_1 \neq 0$

The test statistic is $t = 6.40$ and the *p*-value is $p = 0.000$. Since the p-value is so small, H_0 is rejected for any reasonable value of α. There is sufficient evidence to indicate Verbal score is useful in predicting GPA, controlling for Mathematics score.

To determine if Mathematics score is useful in predicting GPA, controlling for Verbal score, we test:

H_0: $\beta_2 = 0$
H_a: $\beta_2 \neq 0$

The test statistic is $t = 6.82$ and the *p*-value is $p = 0.000$. Since the *p*-value is so small, H_0 is rejected for any reasonable value of α. There is sufficient evidence to indicate Mathematics score is useful in predicting GPA, controlling for Verbal score.

Thus, both terms in the model are significant. The *R*-squared value is $R^2 = .681$.
This indicates that 68.1% of the sample variance of the GPA's is explained by the model.

Now, we need to check the residuals. From MINITAB, the plots are:

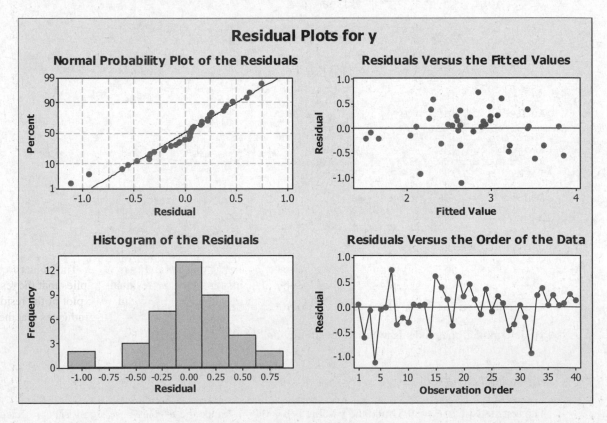

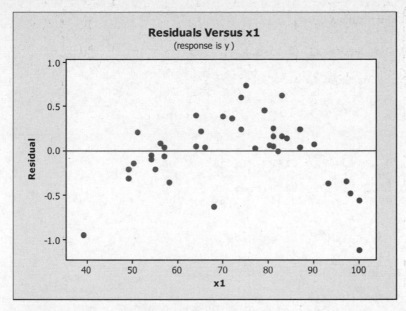

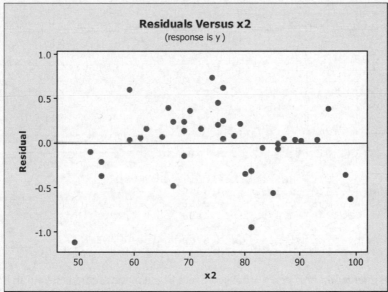

From the normal probability plot, it appears that the assumption of normality is valid. The points are very close to a straight line except for the first 2 points. The histogram of the residuals implies that the residuals are slightly skewed to the left. I would still consider the assumption to be valid. The plot of the residuals versus y-hat indicates a random spread of the residuals between the two bands. This indicates that the assumption of equal variances is probably valid. The plot of the residuals versus x_1 indicates that the relationship between GPA and Verbal score may not be linear, but quadratic because the points form a somewhat upside down U shape. The plot of the residuals versus x_2 indicates that the relationship between GPA and Mathematics score may or may not be quadratic.

Since the plots indicate a possible 2nd order model and the R^2 value is not real large, we will fit a complete 2nd order model:

$$E(y) = \beta_o + \beta_1 x_1 + \beta_2 x_2 + \beta_3 x_1^2 + \beta_4 x_2^2 + \beta_5 x_1 x_2$$

Using MINITAB, the results are:

Regression Analysis: y versus x1, x2, x1sq, x2sq, x1x2

```
The regression equation is
y = - 9.92 + 0.167 x1 + 0.138 x2 - 0.00111 x1sq - 0.000843 x2sq + 0.000241 x1x2


Predictor        Coef    SE Coef       T      P
Constant       -9.917      1.354   -7.32  0.000
x1            0.16681    0.02124    7.85  0.000
x2            0.13760    0.02673    5.15  0.000
x1sq       -0.0011082  0.0001173   -9.45  0.000
x2sq       -0.0008433  0.0001594   -5.29  0.000
x1x2        0.0002411  0.0001440    1.67  0.103


S = 0.187142   R-Sq = 93.7%   R-Sq(adj) = 92.7%


Analysis of Variance

Source          DF       SS       MS       F      P
Regression       5  17.5827   3.5165  100.41  0.000
Residual Error  34   1.1908   0.0350
Total           39  18.7735


Source  DF   Seq SS
x1       1   5.2549
x2       1   7.5311
x1sq     1   3.6434
x2sq     1   1.0552
x1x2     1   0.0982


Unusual Observations

Obs   x1      y     Fit  SE Fit  Residual  St Resid
  2   68  2.8900  3.2820  0.1002   -0.3920    -2.48R
  4  100  1.5400  1.5806  0.1404   -0.0406    -0.33 X
 34   70  3.8200  3.3940  0.0753    0.4260     2.49R

R denotes an observation with a large standardized residual.
X denotes an observation whose X value gives it large influence.
```

To determine if the interaction between Verbal score and Mathematics score is useful in the prediction of y (GPA), we test:

H_0: $\beta_5 = 0$
H_a: $\beta_5 \neq 0$

The test statistic is $t = 1.67$ and the p-value is $p = 0.103$. Since the p-value is not small, H_0 is not rejected for any value of $\alpha < .10$. There is insufficient evidence to indicate the interaction between Verbal score and Mathematics score is useful in predicting GPA.

Now, we will fit a model without the interaction term, but including the squared terms:

$$E(y) = \beta_o + \beta_1 x_1 + \beta_2 x_2 + \beta_3 x_1^2 + \beta_4 x_2^2$$

Using MINITAB, the results are:

Regression Analysis: y versus x1, x2, x1sq, x2sq

```
The regression equation is
y = - 11.5 + 0.189 x1 + 0.159 x2 - 0.00114 x1sq - 0.000871 x2sq


Predictor          Coef     SE Coef         T       P
Constant        -11.458       1.019    -11.24   0.000
x1              0.18887     0.01709     11.05   0.000
x2              0.15874     0.02417      6.57   0.000
x1sq         -0.0011412   0.0001186     -9.62   0.000
x2sq         -0.0008705   0.0001626     -5.35   0.000


S = 0.191905   R-Sq = 93.1%   R-Sq(adj) = 92.3%


Analysis of Variance

Source            DF        SS        MS        F       P
Regression         4   17.4845    4.3711   118.69   0.000
Residual Error    35    1.2890    0.0368
Total             39   18.7735


Source   DF   Seq SS
x1        1   5.2549
x2        1   7.5311
x1sq      1   3.6434
x2sq      1   1.0552


Unusual Observations

Obs    x1       y      Fit   SE Fit   Residual   St Resid
  2    68   2.8900   3.2921   0.1025    -0.4021     -2.48R
  4   100   1.5400   1.7059   0.1219    -0.1659     -1.12 X
 32    39   1.2200   1.3190   0.1240    -0.0990     -0.68 X
 34    70   3.8200   3.3954   0.0772     0.4246      2.42R

R denotes an observation with a large standardized residual.
X denotes an observation whose X value gives it large influence.
```

To determine if the relationship between Verbal score and GPA is quadratic, controlling for Mathematics score, we test:

H_0: $\beta_3 = 0$
H_a: $\beta_3 \neq 0$

The test statistic is $t = -9.62$ and the p-value is $p = 0.000$. Since the p-value is so small, H_0 is rejected for any reasonable value of α. There is sufficient evidence to indicate the relationship between Verbal score and GPA is quadratic, controlling for Mathematics score.

To determine if the relationship between Verbal score and GPA is quadratic, controlling for Mathematics score, we test:

H_0: $\beta_4 = 0$
H_a: $\beta_4 \neq 0$

The test statistic is $t = -5.35$ and the *p*-value is $p = 0.000$. Since the p-value is so small, H_0 is rejected for any reasonable value of α. There is sufficient evidence to indicate the relationship between Mathematics score and GPA is quadratic, controlling for Verbal score.

Thus, both quadratic terms in the model are significant. The R-squared value is $R^2 = .913$. This indicates that 91.3% of the sample variance of the GPA's is explained by the model.

Now, we need to check the residuals. From MINITAB, the plots are:

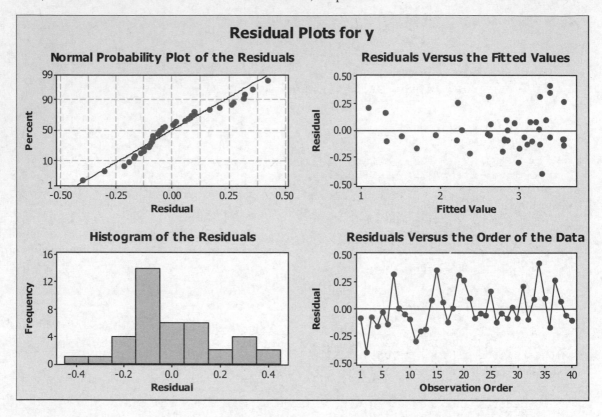

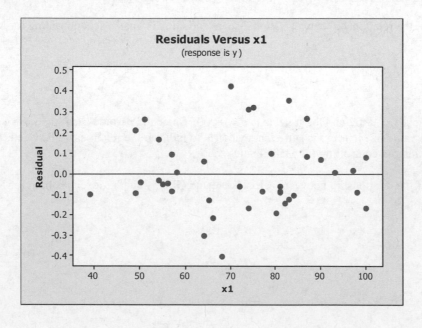

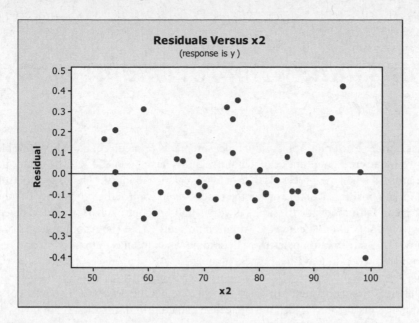

From the normal probability plot, it appears that the assumption of normality is valid. The points are very close to a straight line. The histogram of the residuals also implies that the residuals are approximately normal. The plot of the residuals versus y-hat indicates a random spread of the residuals between the two bands. This indicates that the assumption of equal variances is probably valid. The plot of the residuals versus x_1 indicates a random spread of the residuals between the two bands. This indicates that the order of x_1 (2nd) is appropriate. The plot of the residuals versus x_2 indicates a random spread of the residuals between the two bands. This indicates that the order of x_2 (2nd) is appropriate.

The model appears to be pretty good. All terms in the model are significant, the residual analysis indicates the assumptions are met and the R-squared value is fairly close to 1. The fitted model is

$$\hat{y} = -11.5 + 0.189x_1 + 0.159x_2 - 0.0114x_1^2 - 0.000871x_2^2.$$

Chapter 12
Methods for Quality Improvement: Statistical Process Control

12.1   A control chart is a time series plot of individual measurements or means of a quality variable to which a centerline and two other horizontal lines called control limits have been added. The center line represents the mean of the process when the process is in a state of statistical control. The upper control limit and the lower control limit are positioned so that when the process is in control the probability of an individual measurement or mean falling outside the limits is very small. A control chart is used to determine if a process is in control (only common causes of variation present) or not (both common and special causes of variation present). This information helps us to determine when to take action to find and remove special causes of variation and when to leave the process alone.

12.3   When a control chart is first constructed, it is not known whether the process is in control or not. If the process is found not to be in control, then the centerline and control limits should not be used to monitor the process in the future.

12.5   Even if all the points of an $\bar{x}$-chart fall within the control limits, the process may be out of control. Nonrandom patterns may exist among the plotted points that are within the control limits, but are very unlikely if the process is in control. Examples include six points in a row steadily increasing or decreasing and 14 points in a row alternating up and down.

12.7   Rule 1:   One point beyond Zone A: No points are beyond Zone A.

Rule 2:   Nine points in a row in Zone C or beyond: No sequence of nine points are in Zone C (on one side of the centerline) or beyond.

Rule 3:   Six points in a row steadily increasing or decreasing: No sequence of six points steadily increase or decrease.

Rule 4:   Fourteen points in a row alternating up and down: This pattern does not exist.

Rule 5:   Two out of three points in Zone A or beyond: There are no groups of three consecutive points that have two or more in Zone A or beyond.

Rule 6:   Four out of five points in a row in Zone B or beyond: Points 18 through 21 are all in Zone B or beyond. This indicates the process is out of control.

Thus, rule 6 indicates this process is out of control.

12.9   Using Table XI, Appendix B:

a.   With $n = 3$, $A_2 = 1.023$

b.   With $n = 10$, $A_2 = 0.308$

c.   With $n = 22$, $A_2 = 0.167$

12.11   a.   For each sample, we compute $\bar{x}_1 = \dfrac{\sum x}{n}$ and R = range = largest measurement - smallest measurement. The results are listed in the table:

Sample No.	$\bar{x}_1$	R	Sample No.	$\bar{x}_2$	R
1	20.225	1.8	11	21.225	3.2
2	19.750	2.8	12	20.475	0.9
3	20.425	3.8	13	19.650	2.6
4	19.725	2.5	14	19.075	4.0
5	20.550	3.7	15	19.400	2.2
6	19.900	5.0	16	20.700	4.3
7	21.325	5.5	17	19.850	3.6
8	19.625	3.5	18	20.200	2.5
9	19.350	2.5	19	20.425	2.2
10	20.550	4.1	20	19.900	5.5

b. $\bar{\bar{x}} = \dfrac{\bar{x}_1 + \bar{x}_2 + \cdots \bar{x}_{20}}{k} = \dfrac{402.325}{20} = 20.11625$

      $\bar{R} = \dfrac{R_1 + R_2 + \cdots R_{20}}{k} = \dfrac{66.2}{20} = 3.31$

c.   *Centerline* $= \bar{\bar{x}} = 20.116$

      From Table XI, Appendix B, with $n = 4$, $A_2 = .729$.

      Upper control limit $= \bar{\bar{x}} + A_2\bar{R} = 20.116 + .729(3.31) = 22.529$

      Lower control limit $= \bar{\bar{x}} - A_2\bar{R} = 20.116 - .729(3.31) = 17.703$

d.   *Upper* A-B *boundary* $= \bar{\bar{x}} + \dfrac{2}{3}(A_2\bar{R}) = 20.116 + \dfrac{2}{3}(.729)(3.31) = 21.725$

      Lower A-B *boundary* $= \bar{\bar{x}} - \dfrac{2}{3}(A_2\bar{R}) = 20.116 - \dfrac{2}{3}(.729)(3.31) = 18.507$

      Upper B-C *boundary* $= \bar{\bar{x}} + \dfrac{1}{3}(A_2\bar{R}) = 20.116 + \dfrac{1}{3}(.729)(3.31) = 20.920$

      Lower B-C *boundary* $= \bar{\bar{x}} - \dfrac{1}{3}(A_2\bar{R}) = 20.116 - \dfrac{1}{3}(.729)(3.31) = 19.312$

e.   The $\bar{x}$-chart is:

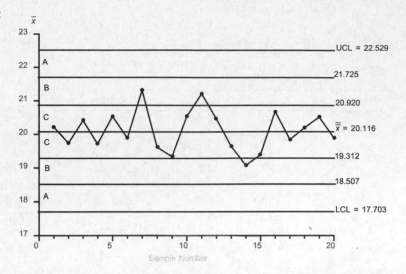

Rule 1:   One point beyond Zone A: No points are beyond Zone A.

Rule 2:   Nine points in a row in Zone C or beyond: No sequence of nine points are in Zone C (on one side of the centerline) or beyond.

Rule 3:   Six points in a row steadily increasing or decreasing: No sequence of six points steadily increase or decrease.

Rule 4:   Fourteen points in a row alternating up and down: This pattern does not exist.

Rule 5:   Two out of three points in Zone A or beyond: There are no groups of three consecutive points that have two or more in Zone A or beyond.

Rule 6:   Four out of five points in a row in Zone B or beyond: No sequence of five points has four or more in Zone B or beyond.

The process appears to be in control.

12.13   a.   From Table XI, Appendix B, with $n = 4$, $A_2 = .729$.

$$\bar{\bar{x}} = .6733 \quad and \quad \bar{R} = .335$$

Upper control limit $= \bar{\bar{x}} + A_2\bar{R} = .6733 + .729(.335) = .9175$

Lower control limit $= \bar{\bar{x}} - A_2\bar{R} = .6733 - .729(.335) = .4291$

Upper A $-$ B *boundary* $= \bar{\bar{x}} + \dfrac{2}{3}\left(A_2\bar{R}\right) = .6733 + \dfrac{2}{3}(.729)(.335) = .8361$

Lower A $-$ B *boundary* $= \bar{\bar{x}} - \dfrac{2}{3}\left(A_2\bar{R}\right) = .6733 - \dfrac{2}{3}(.729)(.335) = .5105$

Upper B $-$ C *boundary* $= \bar{\bar{x}} + \dfrac{1}{3}\left(A_2\bar{R}\right) = .6733 + \dfrac{1}{3}(.729)(.335) = .7547$

Lower A $-$ B *boundary* $= \bar{\bar{x}} - \dfrac{1}{3}\left(A_2\bar{R}\right) = .6733 - \dfrac{1}{3}(.729)(.335) = .5919$

b. Rule 1: One point beyond Zone A: No points are beyond Zone A.

Rule 2: Nine points in a row in Zone C or beyond: There are nine points (Points 9 through 17) in a row in Zone C (on one side of the centerline) or beyond. This indicates that the process is out of control.

Rule 3: Six points in a row steadily increasing or decreasing: No sequence of six points steadily increase or decrease.

Rule 4: Fourteen points in a row alternating up and down: This pattern does not exist.

Rule 5: Two out of three points in Zone A or beyond: There are no groups of three consecutive points that have two or more in Zone A or beyond.

Rule 6: Four out of five points in a row in Zone B or beyond: No sequence of five points has four or more in Zone B or beyond.

Rule 2 indicates the process in out of control.

b. These control limits should not be used to monitor future output because the process is out of control. One or more special causes of variation arc affecting the process mean. These should be identified and eliminated in order to bring the process into control.

12.15 a. From the problem, we are given LCL = 12.3 and UCL = 13.8. We are given the sample means for the 30 observations, but not the Ranges. Thus, we will have to compute $\bar{R}$ from the UCL and UCL. We can also compute $\bar{\bar{x}}$ from the UCL and LCL. From Table XI, Appendix B, with $n = 6$, $A_2 = .483$.

$$\bar{\bar{x}} = \frac{UCL + LCL}{2} = \frac{13.8 + 12.3}{2} = 13.05$$

$$UCL = \bar{\bar{x}} + A_2\bar{R} \Rightarrow \bar{R} = \frac{UCL - \bar{\bar{x}}}{A_2} = \frac{13.8 - 13.05}{.483} = 1.55$$

Upper A-B boundary $\quad \bar{\bar{x}} + \frac{2}{3}A_2\bar{R} = 13.05 + \frac{2}{3}(.483)(1.55) = 13.55$

Lower A-B boundary $\quad \bar{\bar{x}} - \frac{2}{3}A_2\bar{R} = 13.05 - \frac{2}{3}(.483)(1.55) = 12.55$

Upper B-C boundary $\quad \bar{\bar{x}} + \frac{1}{3}A_2\bar{R} = 13.05 + \frac{1}{3}(.483)(1.55) = 13.30$

Lower B-C boundary $\quad \bar{\bar{x}} - \frac{1}{3}A_2\bar{R} = 13.05 - \frac{1}{3}(.483)(1.55) = 12.80$

The $\bar{x}$-chart is:

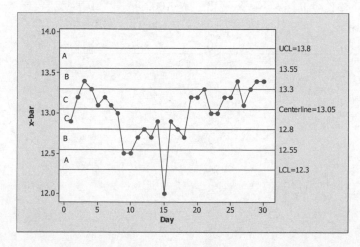

b.   To determine if the process is in or out of control, we check the six rules:
     Rule 1:   One point beyond Zone A: There is one point beyond Zone A.
     Rule 2:   Nine points in a row in Zone C or beyond: Points 8 though 18 are all in the lower
               Zone C or below
     Rule 3:   Six points in a row steadily increasing or decreasing: This pattern does not exist.
     Rule 4:   Fourteen points in a row alternating up and down: This pattern does not exist.
     Rule 5:   Two out of three points in Zone A or beyond: This pattern does not exist.
     Rule 6:   Four out of five points in a row in Zone B or beyond: Points 9 through 16 satisfy this rule.
     This process appears to be out of control. Rules 1, 2, and 6 indicate that the process is out of control.

c.   Nine of these ten observations fall below the lower control limit. This would be extremely unusual if
     there was no under-reporting. We would conclude that there is under-reporting for the emissions
     data for this 10-day period.

12.17   a.   The sample means and ranges are:

Sample	x-bar	Range	Sample	x-bar	Range
1	99.743	0.12	21	99.713	0.65
2	99.447	1.53	22	100.05	0.69
3	100.04	0.29	23	100.283	1.24
4	100.353	1.68	24	99.91	0.75
5	99.287	0.38	25	100.51	1.62
6	99.507	0.79	26	99.723	0.79
7	99.707	0.28	27	99.327	0.23
8	99.717	0.83	28	100.597	0.37
9	100.537	1.26	29	100.18	1.77
10	100.097	0.39	30	99.94	0.47
11	99.633	0.92	31	100.653	0.77
12	100.883	1.05	32	99.473	0.65
13	100.843	1.01	33	99.877	0.99
14	100.507	0.5	34	100.503	0.39
15	100.543	0.24	35	100.053	0.76
16	100.503	1.19	36	99.783	1.23
17	100.087	1.14	37	100.367	1.69
18	99.383	0.2	38	100.503	0.7
19	100.457	0.86	39	100.27	0.69
20	100.863	0.97	40	99.377	0.18

$$\overline{\overline{x}} = \frac{\overline{x}_1 + \overline{x}_2 + \ldots + \overline{x}_{40}}{k} = \frac{4{,}003.229}{40} = 100.081$$

$$\overline{R} = \frac{R_1 + R_2 + \ldots + R_{40}}{40} = \frac{32.26}{40} = .8065$$

$Centerline = \overline{\overline{x}} = 100.081$

From Table XI, Appendix B, with n = 3, $A_2 = 1.023$.

Upper control limit	$\bar{\bar{x}} + A_2\bar{R} = 100.081 + 1.023(.8065) = 100.906$
Lower control limit	$\bar{\bar{x}} - A_2\bar{R} = 100.081 - 1.023(.8065) = 99.256$

Upper A-B *boundary* $\quad \bar{\bar{x}} + \dfrac{2}{3}A_2\bar{R} = 100.081 + \dfrac{2}{3}(1.023)(.8065) = 100.631$

Lower A-B *boundary* $\quad \bar{\bar{x}} - \dfrac{2}{3}A_2\bar{R} = 100.081 - \dfrac{2}{3}(1.023)(.8065) = 99.531$

Upper B-C *boundary* $\quad \bar{\bar{x}} + \dfrac{1}{3}A_2\bar{R} = 100.081 + \dfrac{1}{3}(1.023)(.8065) = 100.356$

Lower B-C *boundary* $\quad \bar{\bar{x}} - \dfrac{1}{3}A_2\bar{R} = 100.081 - \dfrac{1}{3}(1.023)(.8065) = 99.806$

The $\bar{x}$-chart is:

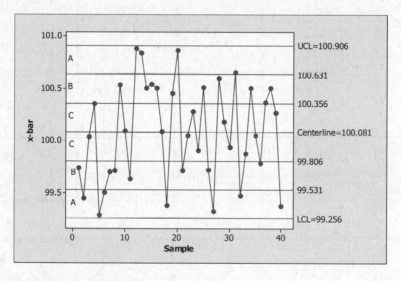

Using Rule 1, there are no points beyond Zone A. Therefore, the process appears to be in control.

b.   The sample means and ranges for the rounded data are:

Sample	x-bar	Range	Sample	x-bar	Range
1	100.000	0	21	99.667	1
2	99.333	1	22	100.000	0
3	100.000	0	23	100.333	1
4	100.333	2	24	100.000	0
5	99.000	0	25	100.667	1
6	99.667	1	26	99.667	1
7	100.000	0	27	99.000	0
8	99.667	1	28	100.333	1
9	100.667	1	29	100.000	2
10	100.000	0	30	100.000	0
11	99.667	1	31	100.667	1
12	101.333	1	32	99.667	1
13	101.333	1	33	99.667	1
14	100.333	1	34	100.333	1
15	100.667	1	35	100.000	0
16	100.667	1	36	99.667	1
17	100.333	1	37	100.333	1
18	99.000	0	38	100.333	1
19	100.667	1	39	100.333	1
20	101.333	1	40	99.000	0

$$\bar{\bar{x}} = \frac{\bar{x}_1 + \bar{x}_2 + ... + \bar{x}_{40}}{k} = \frac{4{,}003.667}{40} = 100.092$$

$$\bar{R} = \frac{R_1 + R_2 + ... + R_{40}}{40} = \frac{30}{40} = .75$$

$Centerline = \bar{\bar{x}} = 100.092$

From Table XI, Appendix B, with n = 3, A_2 = 1.023.

Upper control limit $\bar{\bar{x}} + A_2\bar{R} = 100.092 + 1.023(.75) = 100.859$

Lower control limit $\bar{\bar{x}} - A_2\bar{R} = 100.092 - 1.023(.75) = 99.325$

Upper A-B *boundary* $\bar{\bar{x}} + \frac{2}{3}A_2\bar{R} = 100.092 + \frac{2}{3}(1.023)(.75) = 100.604$

Lower A-B *boundary* $\bar{\bar{x}} - \frac{2}{3}A_2\bar{R} = 100.092 - \frac{2}{3}(1.023)(.75) = 99.581$

Upper B-C *boundary* $\bar{\bar{x}} + \frac{1}{3}A_2\bar{R} = 100.092 + \frac{1}{3}(1.023)(.75) = 100.348$

Lower B-C *boundary* $\bar{\bar{x}} - \frac{1}{3}A_2\bar{R} = 100.02 - \frac{1}{3}(1.023)(.75) = 99.836$

The $\bar{x}$-chart is:

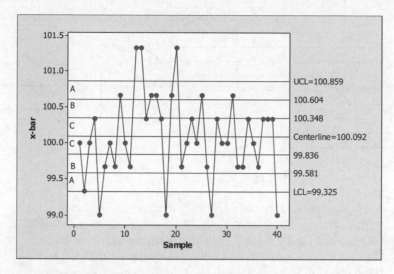

Using Rule 1, there are seven points beyond Zone A. This process appears to be out of control. When the data are rounded, the process is obviously out of control.

12.19　a.　$\bar{\bar{x}} = \dfrac{\bar{x}_1 + \bar{x}_2 + \cdots + \bar{x}_{20}}{k} = \dfrac{1,052.933333}{20} = 52.6467$

$\bar{R} = \dfrac{R_1 + R_2 + \cdots + R_{20}}{k} = \dfrac{15.1}{20} = .755$

Centerline $= \bar{\bar{x}} = 52.6467$

From Table XI, Appendix B, with $n = 3$, $A_2 = 1.023$

Upper control limit $= \bar{\bar{x}} + A_2\bar{R} = 52.6467 + 1.023(.755) = 53.419$

Lower control limit $= \bar{\bar{x}} - A_2\bar{R} = 52.6467 - 1.023(.755) = 51.874$

Upper A – B *boundary* $= \bar{\bar{x}} + \dfrac{2}{3}(A_2\bar{R}) = 52.6467 + \dfrac{2}{3}(1.023)(.755) = 53.162$

Lower A – B *boundary* $= \bar{\bar{x}} - \dfrac{2}{3}(A_2\bar{R}) = 52.6467 - \dfrac{2}{3}(1.023)(.755) = 52.132$

Upper B – C *boundary* $= \bar{\bar{x}} + \dfrac{1}{3}(A_2\bar{R}) = 52.6467 + \dfrac{1}{3}(1.023)(.755) = 52.904$

Lower B – C *boundary* $= \bar{\bar{x}} - \dfrac{1}{3}(A_2\bar{R}) = 52.6467 - \dfrac{1}{3}(1.023)(.755) = 52.389$

The $\bar{x}$-chart is:

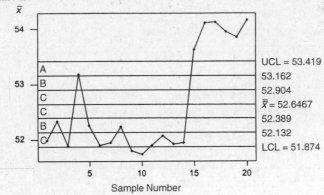

b.   To determine if the process is in or out of control, we check the six rules:

Rule 1:   One point beyond Zone A: Eight points are beyond Zone A.

Rule 2:   Nine points in a row in Zone C or beyond: Data points 5 through 14 (10 points) are in Zone C (on one side of the centerline) or beyond.

Rule 3:   Six points in a row steadily increasing or decreasing: No sequence of six points steadily increase or decrease.

Rule 4:   Fourteen points in a row alternating up and down: This pattern does not exist.

Rule 5:   Two out of three points in Zone A or beyond: There are several sets of three consecutive points that have two points in Zone A or beyond.

Rule 6:   Four out of five points in a row in Zone B or beyond: There are several sets of five points where four or more are in Zone B or beyond.

Special causes of variation appear to be present. The process appears to be out of control. Rules 1, 2, 5, and 6 indicate the process is out of control.

c.   Processes that are out of control exhibit variation that is the result of both common causes and special causes of variation. Common causes affect all output of the process. Special causes typically affect only local areas or operations within a process.

d.   Since the process is out of control, the control limits and centerline should not be used to monitor future output.

12.21   The control limits of the *R*-chart are a function of and reflect the variation in the process. If the variation were unstable (i.e., out of control), the control limits would not be constant. Under these circumstances, the fixed control limits of the $\bar{x}$-chart would have little meaning. We use the *R*-chart to determine whether the variation of the process is stable. If it is, the $\bar{x}$-chart is meaningful. Thus, we interpret the *R*-chart prior to the $\bar{x}$-chart.

12.23   a.   From Exercise 12.10, $\bar{R} = \dfrac{R_1 + R_2 + \cdots + R_{25}}{k} = \dfrac{198.7}{25} = 7.948$

Centerline = $\bar{R}$ = 7.948

From Table XI, Appendix B, with $n = 5$, $D_4 = 2.114$ and $D_3 = 0$.

Upper control limit = $\bar{R}D_4$ = 7.948(2.114) = 16.802

Since $D_3 = 0$, the lower control limit is negative and is not included on the chart.

b.   From Table XI, Appendix B, with $n = 5$, $d_2 = 2.326$, and $d_3 = .864$.

$$Upper\ \text{A–B}\ boundary = \bar{R} + 2d_3\,\frac{\bar{R}}{d_2} = 7.948 + 2(.864)\frac{7.948}{2.326} = 13.853$$

$$Lower\ \text{A–B}\ boundary = \bar{R} - 2d_3\,\frac{\bar{R}}{d_2} = 7.948 - 2(.864)\frac{7.948}{2.326} = 2.043$$

$$Upper\ \text{B–C}\ boundary = \bar{R} + d_3\,\frac{\bar{R}}{d_2} = 7.948 + (.864)\frac{7.948}{2.326} = 10.900$$

$$Lower\ \text{B–C}\ boundary = \bar{R} - d_3\,\frac{\bar{R}}{d_2} = 7.948 - (.864)\frac{7.948}{2.326} = 4.996$$

c.   The *R*-chart is:

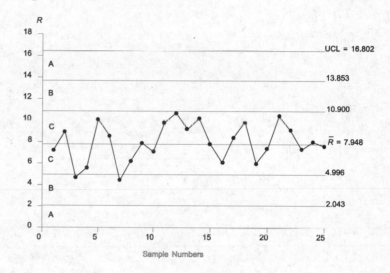

To determine if the process is in or out of control, we check the four rules:

Rule 1:   One point beyond Zone A: No points are beyond Zone A.

Rule 2:   Nine points in a row in Zone C or beyond: No sequence of nine points are in Zone C (on one side of the centerline) or beyond.

Rule 3:   Six points in a row steadily increasing or decreasing: No sequence of six points steadily increase or decrease.

Rule 4:   Fourteen points in a row alternating up and down: This pattern does not exist.

The process appears to be in control.

12.25   First, we construct an *R*-chart.

$$\bar{R} = \frac{R_1 + R_2 + \cdots + R_{20}}{k} = \frac{80.6}{20} = 4.03$$

Centerline = $\bar{R}$ = 4.03

From Table XI, Appendix B, with $n = 7$, $D_4 = 1.924$ and $D_3 = .076$.

Upper control limit = $\bar{R}D_4$ = 4.03(1.924) = 7.754
Lower control limit = $\bar{R}D_3$ = 4.03(0.076) = 0.306

From Table XI, Appendix B, with $n = 7$, $d_2 = 2.704$ and $d_3 = .833$.

$$\textit{Upper A–B boundary} = \overline{R} + 2d_3\,\frac{\overline{R}}{d_2} = 4.03 + 2(.833)\frac{4.03}{2.704} = 6.513$$

$$\textit{Lower A–B boundary} = \overline{R} - 2d_3\,\frac{\overline{R}}{d_2} = 4.03 - 2(.833)\frac{4.03}{2.704} = 1.547$$

$$\textit{Upper B–C boundary} = \overline{R} + d_3\,\frac{\overline{R}}{d_2} = 4.03 + (.833)\frac{4.03}{2.704} = 5.271$$

$$\textit{Lower B–C boundary} = \overline{R} - d_3\,\frac{\overline{R}}{d_2} = 4.03 - (.833)\frac{4.03}{2.704} = 2.789$$

The R-chart is:

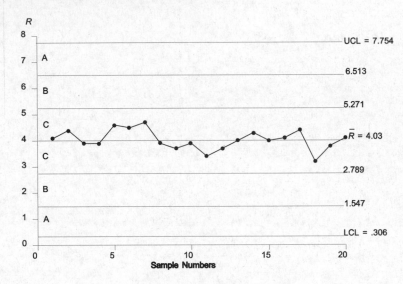

To determine if the process is in or out of control, we check the four rules:

Rule 1:   One point beyond Zone A: No points are beyond Zone A.

Rule 2:   Nine points in a row in Zone C or beyond: No sequence of nine points are in Zone C (on one side of the centerline) or beyond.

Rule 3:   Six points in a row steadily increasing or decreasing: No sequence of six points steadily increase or decrease.

Rule 4:   Fourteen points in a row alternating up and down: This pattern does not exist.

The process appears to be in control. Since the process variation is in control, it is appropriate to construct the $\overline{x}$ -chart.

To construct an $\overline{x}$ -chart, we first calculate the following:

$$\overline{\overline{x}} = \frac{\overline{x}_1 + \overline{x}_2 + \cdots + \overline{x}_{20}}{k} = \frac{434.56}{20} = 21.728$$

$$\overline{R} = \frac{R_1 + R_2 + \cdots R_{20}}{k} = \frac{80.6}{20} = 4.03$$

$$\textit{Centerline} = \overline{\overline{x}} = 21.728$$

From Table XI, Appendix B, with $n = 7$, $A_2 = .419$.

Upper control limit $= \bar{\bar{x}} + A_2\bar{R} = 21.728 + .419(4.03) = 23.417$

Lower control limit $= \bar{\bar{x}} - A_2\bar{R} = 21.728 - .419(4.03) = 20.039$

Upper A-B *boundary* $= \bar{\bar{x}} + \dfrac{2}{3}(A_2\bar{R}) = 21.728 + \dfrac{2}{3}(.419)(4.03) = 22.854$

Lower A-B *boundary* $= \bar{\bar{x}} - \dfrac{2}{3}(A_2\bar{R}) = 21.728 - \dfrac{2}{3}(.419)(4.03) = 20.602$

Upper B-C *boundary* $= \bar{\bar{x}} + \dfrac{1}{3}(A_2\bar{R}) = 21.728 + \dfrac{1}{3}(.419)(4.03) = 22.291$

Lower B-C *boundary* $= \bar{\bar{x}} - \dfrac{1}{3}(A_2\bar{R}) = 21.728 - \dfrac{1}{3}(.419)(4.03) = 21.165$

The $\bar{x}$-chart is:

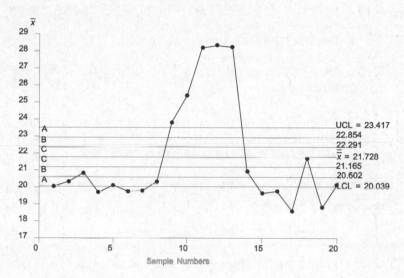

To determine if the process is in or out of control, we check the six rules:

Rule 1: One point beyond Zone A: There are 12 points beyond Zone A. This indicates the process is out of control.

Rule 2: Nine points in a row in Zone C or beyond: No sequence of nine points are in Zone C (on one side of the centerline) or beyond.

Rule 3: Six points in a row steadily increasing or decreasing: Points 6 through 12 steadily increase. This indicates the process is out of control.

Rule 4: Fourteen points in a row alternating up and down: This pattern does not exist.

Rule 5: Two out of three points in Zone A or beyond: There are several groups of three consecutive points that have two or more in Zone A or beyond. This indicates the process is out of control.

Rule 6: Four out of five points in a row in Zone B or beyond: Several sequences of five points have four or more in Zone B or beyond. This indicates the process is out of control.

Rules 1, 3, 5, and 6 indicate that the process is out of control.

12.27 a. From Table XI, Appendix B, with $n = 4$, $D_3 = 0$, and $D_4 = 2.282$.

$\overline{R} = .335$

Upper control limit $= \overline{R} D_4 = .335(2.282) = .7645$

Since $D_3 = 0$, the lower control limit is negative and is not included on the chart.

b. To determine if the process is in control, we check the four rules.

Rule 1: One point beyond Zone A: No points are beyond Zone A.
Rule 2: Nine points in a row in Zone C or beyond: There are not nine points are in a row in Zone C (on one side of the centerline) or beyond.
Rule 3: Six points in a row steadily increasing or decreasing: No sequence of six points steadily increase or decrease.
Rule 4: Fourteen points in a row alternating up and down: This pattern does not exist.

It appears that the process is in control.

c. Yes. This process appears to be in control. Therefore, these control limits could be used to monitor future output.

d. Of the 30 R values plotted, there are only 8 different values. Most of the R values take on one of three values. This indicates that the data must be discrete (take on a countable number of values), or that the path widths are multiples of each other.

12.29 a. $\overline{R} = \dfrac{R_1 + R_2 + \ldots + R_{16}}{16} = \dfrac{.3800}{16} = .0238$

Centerline $= \overline{R} = .0238$

From Table XI, Appendix B, with $n = 2$, $D_4 = 3.267$ and $D_3 = 0$.

Upper control limit $= \overline{R} D_4 = .0238(3.267) = .0778$

Since $D_3 = 0$, the lower control limit is negative and not included.

From Table XI, Appendix B, with $n = 2$, $d_2 = 1.128$ and $d_3 = .853$.

Upper A-B *boundary* $= \overline{R} + 2 d_3 \dfrac{\overline{R}}{d_2} = .0238 + 2(.853)\dfrac{.0238}{1.128} = .0598$

Lower A-B *boundary* $= \overline{R} - 2 d_3 \dfrac{\overline{R}}{d_2} = .0238 - 2(.853)\dfrac{.0238}{1.128} = -.0122$ or 0 (cannot be negative)

Upper B-C *boundary* $= \overline{R} + d_3 \dfrac{\overline{R}}{d_2} = .0238 + (.853)\dfrac{.0238}{1.128} = .0418$

Lower B-C *boundary* $= \overline{R} - d_3 \dfrac{\overline{R}}{d_2} = .0238 - (.853)\dfrac{.0238}{1.128} = .0058$

The R-chart is:

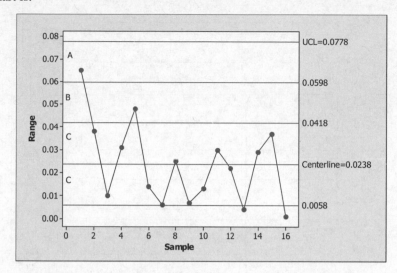

To determine if the process is in or out of control, we check the four rules:

Rule 1:   One point beyond Zone A: No points are beyond Zone A.
Rule 2:   Nine points in a row in Zone C or beyond: This pattern doe not exist.
Rule 3:   Six points in a row steadily increasing or decreasing: This pattern doe not exist.
Rule 4:   Fourteen points in a row alternating up and down: This pattern doe not exist.

The process appears to be in control.

b. $\bar{\bar{x}} = \dfrac{\bar{x}_1 + \bar{x}_2 + ... + \bar{x}_{16}}{k} = \dfrac{3.5430}{16} = .2214$

Centerline $= \bar{\bar{x}} = .2214$

From Table XI, Appendix B, with n = 2, $A_2 = 1.880$.

Upper control limit $\bar{\bar{x}} + A_2 \bar{R} = .2214 + 1.880(.0238) = .2661$

Lower control limit $\bar{\bar{x}} - A_2 \bar{R} = .2214 - 1.880(.0238) = .1767$

Upper A-B *boundary* $\bar{\bar{x}} + \dfrac{2}{3} A_2 \bar{R} = .2214 + \dfrac{2}{3}(1.880)(.0238) = .2512$

Lower A-B *boundary* $\bar{\bar{x}} - \dfrac{2}{3} A_2 \bar{R} = .2214 + \dfrac{2}{3}(1.880)(.0238) = .1916$

Upper B-C *boundary* $\bar{\bar{x}} + \dfrac{1}{3} A_2 \bar{R} = .2214 + \dfrac{1}{3}(1.880)(.0238) = .2363$

Lower B-C *boundary* $\bar{\bar{x}} - \dfrac{1}{3} A_2 \bar{R} = .2214 - \dfrac{1}{3}(1.880)(.0238) = .2065$

The $\overline{x}$-chart is:

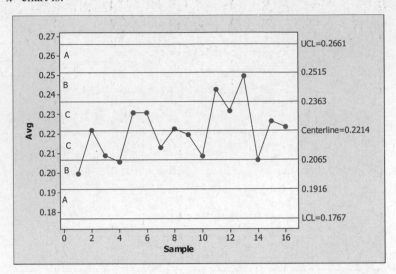

To determine if the process is in or out of control, we check the six rules:

Rule 1:   One point beyond Zone A: There are no points beyond Zone A.
Rule 2:   Nine points in a row in Zone C or beyond: This pattern does not exist.
Rule 3:   Six points in a row steadily increasing or decreasing: This pattern does not exist.
Rule 4:   Fourteen points in a row alternating up and down: This pattern does not exist.
Rule 5:   Two out of three points in Zone A or beyond: This pattern does not exist.
Rule 6:   Four out of five points in a row in Zone B or beyond: This pattern does not exist.

This process appears to be in control.

c.   Based on the R-chart and the $\overline{x}$-chart, the process appears to be in control. An estimate of the true average thickness of the expensive layer would be $\overline{\overline{x}} = .2214$.

12.31   a. $\overline{R} = \dfrac{R_1 + R_2 + \cdots + R_{16}}{k} = \dfrac{.4 + 1.4 + \cdots + 2.6}{16} = \dfrac{44.1}{16} = 2.756$

Centerline $= \overline{R} = 2.756$

From Table XI, Appendix B, with $n = 5$, $D_4 = 2.114$ and $D_3 = 0$.

Upper control limit $= \overline{R}D_4 = 2.756(2.114) = 5.826$

Since $D_3 = 0$, the lower control limit is negative and is not included on the chart.

From Table XI, Appendix B, with $n = 5$, $d_2 = 2.326$ and $d_3 = 0.864$.

Upper A – B *boundary* $= \overline{R} + 2d_3 \dfrac{\overline{R}}{d_2} = 2.756 + 2(.864)\dfrac{2.756}{2.326} = 4.803$

Lower A – B *boundary* $= \overline{R} - 2d_3 \dfrac{\overline{R}}{d_2} = 2.756 - 2(.864)\dfrac{2.756}{2.326} = .709$

Upper B – C *boundary* $= \overline{R} + d_3 \dfrac{\overline{R}}{d_2} = 2.756 + (.864)\dfrac{2.756}{2.326} = 3.780$

Lower B – C *boundary* $= \overline{R} - d_3 \dfrac{\overline{R}}{d_2} = 2.756 - (.864)\dfrac{2.756}{2.326} = 1.732$

The *R*-chart is:

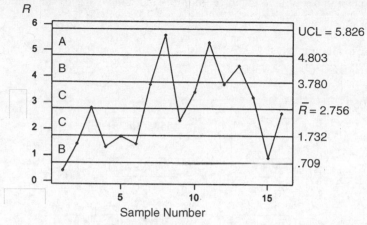

b.   The *R*-chart is designed to monitor the process variation.

c.   To determine if the process is in or out of control, we check the four rules:

Rule 1:   One point beyond Zone A: No points are beyond Zone A.
Rule 2:   Nine points in a row in Zone C or beyond: No sequence of nine points are in Zone C (on one side of the centerline) or beyond.
Rule 3:   Six points in a row steadily increasing or decreasing: No sequence of six points steadily increases or decreases.
Rule 4:   Fourteen points in a row alternating up and down: This pattern does not exist.

The process appears to be in control. None of the out-of-control signals are present. There is no indication that special causes of variation present.

12.33   The *p*-chart is designed to monitor the proportion of defective units produced by a process.

12.35   The sample size is determined as follows:

$$n > \frac{9(1-p_0)}{p_0} = \frac{9(1-.08)}{.08} = 103.5 \approx 104$$

12.37   a.   We must first calculate . To do this, it is necessary to find the total number of defectives in all the samples. To find the number of defectives per sample, we multiple the proportion by the sample size, 150. The number of defectives per sample are shown in the table:

Sample No.	*p*	No. Defectives	Sample No.	*p*	No. Defectives
1	.03	4.5	11	.07	10.5
2	.05	7.5	12	.04	6.0
3	.10	15.0	13	.06	9.0
4	.02	3.0	14	.05	7.5
5	.08	12.0	15	.07	10.5
6	.09	13.5	16	.06	9.0
7	.08	12.0	17	.07	10.5
8	.05	7.5	18	.02	3.0
9	.07	10.5	19	.05	7.5
10	.06	9.0	20	.03	4.5

Note: There cannot be a fraction of a defective. The proportions presented in the exercise have been rounded off. I have used the fractions to minimize the roundoff error.

To get the total number of defectives, sum the number of defectives for all 20 samples. The sum is 172.5. To get the total number of units sampled, multiply the sample size by the number of samples: $150(20) = 3000$.

$$\bar{p} = \frac{\text{Total defective in all samples}}{\text{Total units sampled}} = \frac{172.5}{3000} = .0575$$

$Centerline = \bar{p} = .0575$

$$Upper\ control\ limit = \bar{p} + 3\sqrt{\frac{\bar{p}(1-\bar{p})}{n}} = .0575 + 3\sqrt{\frac{.0575(.9425)}{150}} = .1145$$

$$Lower\ control\ limit = \bar{p} - 3\sqrt{\frac{\bar{p}(1-\bar{p})}{n}} = .0575 - 3\sqrt{\frac{.0575(.9425)}{150}} = .0005$$

b. $$Upper\ \text{A–B}\ boundary = \bar{p} + 2\sqrt{\frac{\bar{p}(1-\bar{p})}{n}} = .0575 + 2\sqrt{\frac{.0575(.9425)}{150}} = .0955$$

$$Lower\ \text{A-B}\ boundary = \bar{p} - 2\sqrt{\frac{\bar{p}(1-\bar{p})}{n}} = .0575 - 2\sqrt{\frac{.0575(.9425)}{150}} = .0195$$

$$Upper\ \text{B-C}\ boundary = \bar{p} + \sqrt{\frac{\bar{p}(1-\bar{p})}{n}} = .0575 + \sqrt{\frac{.0575(.9425)}{150}} = .0765$$

$$Lower\ \text{B-C}\ boundary = \bar{p} - \sqrt{\frac{\bar{p}(1-\bar{p})}{n}} = .0575 - \sqrt{\frac{.0575(.9425)}{150}} = .0385$$

c. The *p*-chart is:

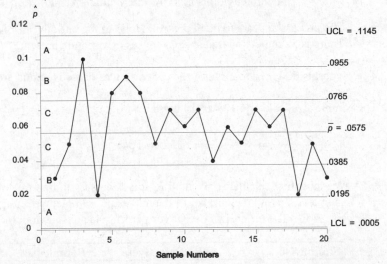

d. To determine if the process is in or out of control, we check the four rules:

Rule 1:   One point beyond Zone A: No points are beyond Zone A.
Rule 2:   Nine points in a row in Zone C or beyond: No sequence of nine points are in Zone C (on one side of the centerline) or beyond.
Rule 3:   Six points in a row steadily increasing or decreasing: No sequence of six points steadily increase or decrease.
Rule 4:   Fourteen points in a row alternating up and down: Points 7 through 20 alternate up and down. This indicates the process is out of control.

Rule 4 indicates that the process is out of control.

e. Since the process is out of control, the centerline and control limits should not be used to monitor future process output. The centerline and control limits are intended to represent the behavior of the process when it is under control.

12.39 a. To compute the proportion of defectives in each sample, divide the number of defectives by the number in the sample, 100:

$$\hat{p} = \frac{\text{No. of defectives}}{\text{No. in sample}}$$

The sample proportions are listed in the table:

Sample No.	$\hat{p}$	Sample No.	$\hat{p}$
1	.02	16	.02
2	.04	17	.03
3	.10	18	.07
4	.04	19	.03
5	.01	20	.02
6	.01	21	.03
7	.13	22	.07
8	.09	23	.04
9	.11	24	.03
10	.00	25	.02
11	.03	26	.02
12	.04	27	.00
13	.02	28	.01
14	.02	29	.03
15	.08	30	.04

To get the total number of defectives, sum the number of defectives for all 30 samples. The sum is 120. To get the total number of units sampled, multiply the sample size by the number of samples: $100(30) = 3000$.

$$\overline{p} = \frac{\text{Total defective in all samples}}{\text{Total units sampled}} = \frac{120}{3000} = .04$$

The centerline is $\overline{p} = .04$

$$\text{Upper control limit} = \overline{p} + 3\sqrt{\frac{\overline{p}(1-\overline{p})}{n}} = .04 + 3\sqrt{\frac{.04(1-.04)}{100}} = .099$$

$$\text{Lower control limit} = \overline{p} - 3\sqrt{\frac{\overline{p}(1-\overline{p})}{n}} = .04 - 3\sqrt{\frac{.04(1-.04)}{100}} = -.019 \text{ or } 0 \text{ (cannot be negative)}$$

$$\text{Upper A–B boundary} = \overline{p} + 2\sqrt{\frac{\overline{p}(1-\overline{p})}{n}} = .04 + 2\sqrt{\frac{.04(1-.04)}{100}} = .079$$

$$\text{Lower A–B boundary} = \overline{p} - 2\sqrt{\frac{\overline{p}(1-\overline{p})}{n}} = .04 - 2\sqrt{\frac{.04(1-.04)}{100}} = .001$$

$$\text{Upper B–C boundary} = \overline{p} + \sqrt{\frac{\overline{p}(1-\overline{p})}{n}} = .04 + \sqrt{\frac{.04(1-.04)}{100}} = .060$$

$$\text{Lower B–C boundary} = \sqrt{\frac{\overline{p}(1-p)}{n}} = .04 - \sqrt{\frac{.04(1-.04)}{100}} = .020$$

The *p*-chart is:

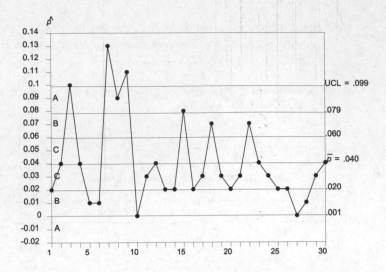

b. To determine if the process is in or out of control, we check the four rules for the *p*-chart.

    Rule 1:   One point beyond Zone A: There are 3 points beyond Zone A—points 2, 7, and 9.

    Rule 2:   Nine points in a row in Zone C or beyond: No sequence of nine points are in Zone C (on one side of the centerline) or beyond.

    Rule 3:   Six points in a row steadily increasing or decreasing: This pattern is not present.

    Rule 4:   Fourteen points in a row alternating up and down: This pattern does not exist.

The process does not appear to be in control. Rule 1 indicates that the process is out of control.

c. No. Since the process is not in control, then these control limits are meaningless.

12.41   a. To compute the proportion of leaky pumps in each sample, divide the number of leaky pumps by the number in the sample, 500:

$$\hat{p} = \frac{\text{No. leaky pumps}}{\text{No. in sample}}$$

The sample proportions are listed in the table:

Week	$\hat{p}$
1	0.72
2	.056
3	.048
4	.052
5	.040
6	.112
7	.052
8	.056
9	.062
10	.052
11	.068
12	.052
13	.064

To get the total number of leaky pumps, sum the number of leaky pumps for all 13 samples. The sum is 393. To get the total number of pumps sampled, multiply the sample size by the number of samples: 500(13) = 6,500.

$$\bar{p} = \frac{\text{Total leaky pumps in all samples}}{\text{Total pumps sampled}} = \frac{393}{6500} = .060$$

The *Centerline* is $\bar{p} = .060$

$$Upper\ control\ limit = \bar{p} + 3\sqrt{\frac{\bar{p}(1-\bar{p})}{n}} = .060 + 3\sqrt{\frac{.06(1-.06)}{500}} = .060 + .032 = .092$$

$$Lower\ control\ limit = \bar{p} - 3\sqrt{\frac{\bar{p}(1-\bar{p})}{n}} = .060 - 3\sqrt{\frac{.06(1-.06)}{500}} = .060 - .032 = .028$$

$$Upper\ \text{A-B}\ boundary = \bar{p} + 2\sqrt{\frac{\bar{p}(1-\bar{p})}{n}} = .060 + 2\sqrt{\frac{.06(1-.06)}{500}} = .060 + .021 = .081$$

$$Lower\ \text{A-B}\ boundary = \bar{p} - 2\sqrt{\frac{\bar{p}(1-\bar{p})}{n}} = .060 - 2\sqrt{\frac{.06(1-.06)}{500}} = .060 - .021 = .039$$

$$Upper\ \text{B-C}\ boundary = \bar{p} + \sqrt{\frac{\bar{p}(1-\bar{p})}{n}} = .060 + \sqrt{\frac{.06(1-.06)}{500}} = .060 + .011 = .071$$

$$Lower\ \text{B-C}\ boundary = \bar{p} - \sqrt{\frac{\bar{p}(1-\bar{p})}{n}} = .060 - \sqrt{\frac{.06(1-.06)}{500}} = .060 - .011 = .049$$

The p-chart is:

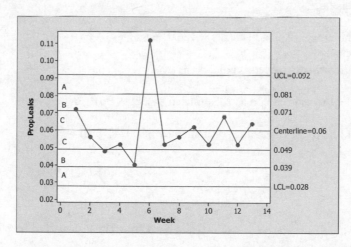

To determine if the process is in or out of control, we check the four rules:

Rule 1:   One point beyond Zone A: One point lies beyond Zone A.
Rule 2:   Nine points in a row in Zone C or beyond: This pattern doe not exist.
Rule 3:   Six points in a row steadily increasing or decreasing: This pattern doe not exist.
Rule 4:   Fourteen points in a row alternating up and down: This pattern doe not exist.

The process appears to be out of control because Rule 1 is not followed. One observation is beyond Zone A. It appears that the process is not stable.

12.43   A capability analysis is a methodology used to help determine when common cause variation is unacceptably high. If a process is not in statistical control, then both common causes and special causes of variation exist. It would not be possible to determine if the common cause variation is too high because it could not be separated from special cause variation.

12.45   One way to assess the capability of a process is to construct a frequency distribution or stem-and-leaf display for a large sample of individual measurements from the process. Then, the specification limits and the target value for the output variable are added to the graph. This is called a capability analysis diagram. A second way to assess the capability of a process is to quantify capability. The most direct way to quantify capability is to count the number of items that fall outside the specification limits in the capability analysis diagram and report the percentage of such items in the sample. Also, one can construct a capability index. This is the ratio of the difference in the specification spread and the difference in the process spread. This measure is called C_P. If C_P is less than 1, then the process is not capable.

12.47   a. $C_P = 1.00$. For this value, the specification spread is equal to the process spread. This indicates that the process is capable. Approximately 2.7 units per 1,000 will be unacceptable.

          b. $C_P = 1.33$. For this value, the specification spread is greater than the process spread. This indicates that the process is capable. Approximately 63 units per 1,000,000 will be unacceptable.

          c. $C_P = 0.50$. For this value, the specification spread is less than the process spread. This indicates that the process is not capable.

          d. $C_P = 2.00$. For this value, the specification spread is greater than the process spread. This indicates that the process is capable. Approximately 2 units per billion will be unacceptable.

12.49   The process spread is 6σ.

          a.   For $\sigma = 21$, the process spread is $6(21) = 126$

          b.   For $\sigma = 5.2$, the process spread is $6(5.2) = 31.2$

          c.   For $s = 110.06$, the process spread is estimated by $6(110.06) = 660.36$

          d.   For $s = .0024$, the process spread is estimated by $6(.0024) = .0144$

12.51   We know that $C_P = \dfrac{USL - LSL}{6\sigma}$

Thus, if $C_P = 2$, then $2 = \dfrac{USL - LSL}{6\sigma} \Rightarrow 12\sigma = USL - LSL$. The process mean is halfway between the USL and the LSL. Since the specification spread covers 12σ, then the USL must be $12\sigma/2 = 6\sigma$ from the process mean.

12.53   a.   A capability analysis diagram is:

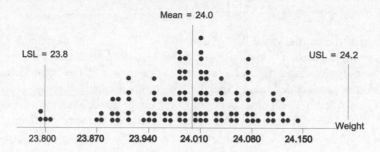

   b.   From the sample, $\bar{x} = 23.997$ and $s = .077$.

$$C_P = \frac{\text{USL - LSL}}{6\sigma} \approx \frac{24.2 - 23.8}{6(.077)} = \frac{.4}{.462} = .866$$

   Since the C_P value is less than 1, the process is not capable.

12.55   a.   The capability analysis diagram is:

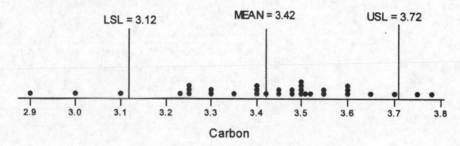

   b.   Two observations are above the upper specification limit and three observations are below the lower specification limit. Thus, the proportion of measurements that fall outside the specifications is 5 / 33 = .152.

   c.   From the sample, $\bar{x} = 3.43$ and $s = 0.1982$.

$$C_p = \frac{\text{USL} - \text{LSL}}{6\sigma} = \frac{3.72 - 3.12}{6(.1982)} = \frac{.6}{1.1892} = .505$$

   Since the C_p value is less than 1, the process is not capable.

12.57   The quality of a good or service is indicated by the extent to which it satisfies the needs and preferences of its users. Its eight dimensions are: performance, features, reliability, conformance, durability, serviceability, aesthetics, and other perceptions that influence judgments of quality.

12.59   A system is a collection or arrangement of interacting components that has an on-going purpose or mission. A system receives inputs from its environment, transforms those inputs to outputs, and delivers those outputs to its environment.

12.61   Yes. Even though the output may all fall within the specification limits, the process may still be out of control.

12.63   Solution will vary. See page 488 for Guided Solutions.

12.65   If a process is in control and remains in control, its future will be like its past. It is predictable in that its output will stay within certain limits. If a process is out of control, there is no way of knowing what the future pattern of output from the process may look like.

12.67   Control limits are a function of the natural variability of the process. The position of the limits is a function of the size of the process standard deviation. Specification limits are boundary points that define the acceptable values for an output variable of a particular product or service. They are determined by customers, management, and/or product designers. Specification limits may be either two-sided, with upper and lower limits, or one-sided with either an upper or lower limit. Specification limits are not dependent on the process in any way. The process may not be able to meet the specification limits even when it is under statistical control.

12.69   The C_P statistic is used to assess capability if the process is stable (in control) and if the process is centered on the target value.

12.71   a.   The centerline is:

$$\bar{x} = \frac{\sum x}{n} = \frac{96}{15} = 6.4$$

The time series plot is:

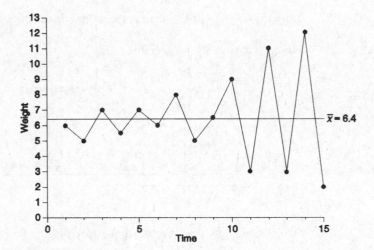

        b.   The type of variation best described by the pattern in this plot is increasing variance. The spread of the measurements increases with the passing of time.

12.73   To determine if the process is in or out of control, we check the six rules:

        Rule 1:   One point beyond Zone A: No points are beyond Zone A.
        Rule 2:   Nine points in a row in Zone C or beyond: Points 8 through 16 are in Zone C (on one side of the centerline) or beyond. This indicates the process is out of control.
        Rule 3:   Six points in a row steadily increasing or decreasing: No sequence of six points steadily increase or decrease.
        Rule 4:   Fourteen points in a row alternating up and down: This pattern does not exist.
        Rule 5:   Two out of three points in Zone A or beyond: No group of three consecutive points have two or more in Zone A or beyond.
        Rule 6:   Four out of five points in a row in Zone B or beyond: No sequence of five points has four or more in Zone B or beyond.

        Rule 2 indicates that the process is out of control. A special cause of variation appears to be present.

12.75   a.   To compute the range, subtract the larger score minus the smaller score. The ranges for the samples are listed in the table:

Sample No.	R	$\bar{x}$	Sample No.	R	$\bar{x}$
1	4	343.0	11	5	357.5
2	3	329.5	12	10	330.0
3	12	349.0	13	2	349.0
4	1	351.5	14	1	336.5
5	12	354.0	15	16	337.0
6	6	339.0	16	7	354.5
7	3	329.5	17	1	352.5
8	0	344.0	18	6	337.0
9	25	346.5	19	6	338.0
10	15	353.5	20	13	351.5

The centerline is $\bar{R} = \dfrac{\sum R}{k} = \dfrac{148}{20} = 7.4$

From Table XI, Appendix B, with $n = 2$, $D_3 = 0$, and $D_4 = 3.267$.

Upper control limit $= \bar{R}D_4 = 7.4(3.267) = 24.1758$

Since $D_3 = 0$, the lower control limit is negative and is not included on the chart.
From Table XI, Appendix B, with $n = 2$, $d_2 = 1.128$, and $d_3 = .853$.

Upper A–B boundary $= \bar{R} + 2d_3 \dfrac{\bar{R}}{d_2} = 7.4 + 2(.853) \dfrac{(7.4)}{1.128} = 18.5918$

Lower A–B boundary $= \bar{R} - 2d_3 \dfrac{\bar{R}}{d_2} = 7.4 - 2(.853) \dfrac{(7.4)}{1.128} = -3.7918$ or 0

(cannot have a negative value)

Upper B–C boundary $= \bar{R} + d_3 \dfrac{\bar{R}}{d_2} = 7.4 + (.853) \dfrac{(7.4)}{1.128} = 12.9959$

Lower B–C boundary $= \bar{R} - d_3 \dfrac{\bar{R}}{d_2} = 7.4 - (.853) \dfrac{(7.4)}{1.128} = 1.8041$

The *R*-chart is:

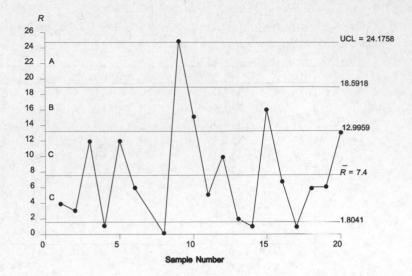

To determine if the process is in control, we check the four rules.

Rule 1:   One point beyond Zone A: Point 9 is beyond Zone A. This indicates the process is out of control.

Rule 2:   Nine points in a row in Zone C or beyond: There are not nine points in a row in Zone C (on one side of the centerline) or beyond.

Rule 3:   Six points in a row steadily increasing or decreasing: No sequence of six points steadily increase or decrease.

Rule 4:   Fourteen points in a row alternating up and down: This pattern does not exist.

Rule 1 indicates that the process is out of control. We should not use this to construct the $\bar{x}$ -chart.

b.   We will construct the $\bar{x}$ -chart even though the *R*-chart indicates the variation is out of control. First, compute the mean for each sample by adding the 2 observations and dividing by 2. These values are in the table in part **a.**

The centerline is $\bar{\bar{x}} = \dfrac{\sum \bar{x}}{k} = \dfrac{6883}{20} = 344.15$

From Table XII, Appendix B, with $n = 2$, $A_2 = 1.880$.

$\bar{\bar{x}} = 344.15$ and $\bar{R} = 7.4$

Upper control limit $= \bar{\bar{x}} + A_2 = 344.15 + 1.88(7.4) = 358.062$

Lower control limit $= \bar{\bar{x}} - A_2 = 344.15 - 1.88(7.4) = 330.238$

Upper A–B *boundary* $= \bar{\bar{x}} + \dfrac{2}{3}(A_2 \bar{R}) = 344.15 + \dfrac{2}{3}(1.88)(7.4) = 353.425$

Lower A–B *boundary* $= \bar{\bar{x}} - \dfrac{2}{3}(A_2 \bar{R}) = 344.15 - \dfrac{2}{3}(1.88)(7.4) = 334.875$

Upper B–C *boundary* $= \bar{\bar{x}} + \dfrac{1}{3}(A_2 \bar{R}) = 344.15 + \dfrac{1}{3}(1.88)(7.4) = 348.787$

Lower B–C *boundary* $= \bar{\bar{x}} - \dfrac{1}{3}(A_2 \bar{R}) = 344.15 - \dfrac{1}{3}(1.88)(7.4) = 339.513$

The $\bar{x}$-chart is:

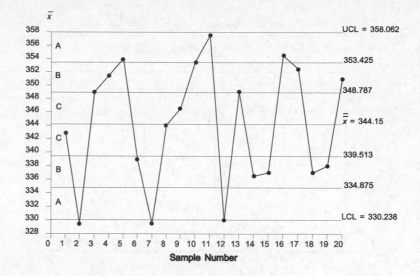

To determine if the process is in control, we check the six rules.

Rule 1:   One point beyond Zone A: Points 2 and 7 are beyond Zone A. This indicates the process is out of control.

Rule 2:   Nine points in a row in Zone C or beyond: There are nine points (Points 9 through 17) in a row in Zone C (on one side of the centerline) or beyond. This indicates that the process is out of control.

Rule 3:   Six points in a row steadily increasing or decreasing: No sequence of six points steadily increase or decrease.

Rule 4:   Fourteen points in a row alternating up and down: This pattern does not exist.

Rule 5:   Two out of three points in Zone A or beyond: Points 10 and 11 are in Zone 3 or beyond. This indicates that the process is out of control.

Rule 6:   Four out of five points in a row in Zone B or beyond: No sequence of five points has four or more in Zone B or beyond.

Rules 1 and 5 indicate the process is out of control. The $\bar{x}$-chart should not be used to monitor the process.

c.   These control limits should not be used to monitor future output because both processes are out of control. One or more special causes of variation are affecting the process variation and process mean. These should be identified and eliminated in order to bring the processes into control.

d.   Of the 40 patients sampled, 10 received care that did not conform to the hospital's requirement. The proportion is 10/40 = .25.

12.77   a.   For each sample, we compute $\bar{x} = \dfrac{\sum x}{n}$ and $R = $ range = largest measurement - smallest

measurement. The results are listed in the table:

Sample No.	$\bar{x}$	R	Sample No.	$\bar{x}$	R
1	4.36	7.1	11	3.32	4.8
2	5.10	7.7	12	4.02	4.8
3	4.52	5.0	13	5.24	7.8
4	3.42	5.8	14	3.58	3.9
5	2.62	6.2	15	3.48	5.5
6	3.94	3.9	16	5.00	3.0
7	2.34	5.3	17	3.68	6.2
8	3.26	3.2	18	2.68	3.9
9	4.06	8.0	19	3.66	4.4
10	4.96	7.1	20	4.10	5.5

$$\bar{\bar{x}} = \frac{\bar{x}_1 + \bar{x}_2 + \cdots + \bar{x}_{20}}{k} = \frac{77.24}{20} = 3.867$$

$$\bar{R} = \frac{R_1 + R_2 + \cdots + R_{20}}{k} = \frac{109.1}{20} = 5.455$$

First, we construct an R-chart.

Centerline $= \bar{R} = 5.455$

From Table XI, Appendix B, with $n = 5$, $D_4 = 2.114$, and $D_3 = 0$.

Upper control limit $= \bar{R}D_4 = 5.455(2.114) = 11.532$

Since $D_3 = 0$, the lower control limit is negative and is not included on the chart.

Upper A–B *boundary* $= \bar{R} + 2d_3 \dfrac{\bar{R}}{d_2} = 5.455 + 2(.864)\dfrac{(5.455)}{2.326} = 9.508$

Lower A–B *boundary* $= \bar{R} - 2d_3 \dfrac{\bar{R}}{d_2} = 5.455 - 2(.864)\dfrac{(5.455)}{2.326} = 1.402$

Upper B–C *boundary* $= \bar{R} + d_3 \dfrac{\bar{R}}{d_2} = 5.455 + (.864)\dfrac{(5.455)}{2.326} = 7.481$

Lower B–C *boundary* $= \bar{R} - d_3 \dfrac{\bar{R}}{d_2} = 5.455 - (.864)\dfrac{(5.455)}{2.326} = 3.429$

The *R*-chart is:

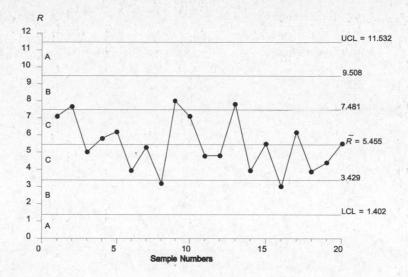

b.   To determine if the process is in or out of control, we check the four rules:

Rule 1:   One point beyond Zone A: No points are beyond Zone A.
Rule 2:   Nine points in a row in Zone C or beyond: No sequence of nine points are in Zone C (on one side of the centerline) or beyond.
Rule 3:   Six points in a row steadily increasing or decreasing: No sequence of six points steadily increase or decrease.
Rule 4:   Fourteen points in a row alternating up and down: This pattern does not exist.

The process appears to be in control. Since the process variation is in control, it is appropriate to construct the $\bar{x}$-chart.

c.   In order for the $\bar{x}$-chart to be valid, the process variation must be in control. The *R*-chart checks to see if the process variation is in control. For more details, see the answer to Exercise 12.21.

d.   To construct an $\bar{x}$-chart, we first calculate the following:

$$\bar{\bar{x}} = \frac{\bar{x}_1 + \bar{x}_2 + \cdots + \bar{x}_{20}}{k} = \frac{77.24}{20} = 3.867$$

$$\bar{R} = \frac{R_1 + R_2 + \cdots + R_{20}}{k} = \frac{109.1}{20} = 5.455$$

$Centerline = \bar{\bar{x}} = 3.867$

From Table XI, Appendix B, with $n = 5$, $A_2 = .577$.

$Upper\ control\ limit = \bar{\bar{x}} + A_2\bar{R} = 3.867 + .577(5.455) = 7.015$

$Lower\ control\ limit = \bar{\bar{x}} - A_2\bar{R} = 3.867 - .577(5.455) = .719$

$Upper\ A\text{--}B\ boundary = \bar{\bar{x}} + \frac{2}{3}(A_2\bar{R}) = 3.867 + \frac{2}{3}(.577)(5.455) = 5.965$

$Lower\ A\text{--}B\ boundary = \bar{\bar{x}} - \frac{2}{3}(A_2\bar{R}) = 3.867 - \frac{2}{3}(.577)(5.455) = 1.769$

$$Upper \text{ B–C } boundary = \overline{\overline{x}} + \frac{1}{3}(A_2\overline{R}) = 3.867 + \frac{1}{3}(.577)(5.455) = 4.916$$

$$Lower \text{ B–C } boundary = \overline{\overline{x}} - \frac{1}{3}(A_2\overline{R}) = 3.867 - \frac{1}{3}(.577)(5.455) = 2.818$$

The $\overline{x}$-chart is:

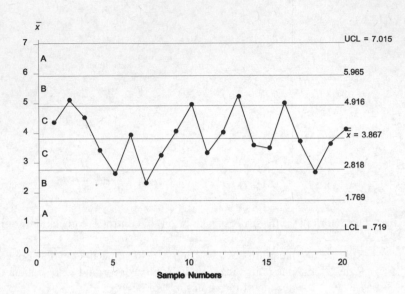

e.   To determine if the process is in or out of control, we check the six rules:

Rule 1:   One point beyond Zone A: No points are beyond Zone A.

Rule 2:   Nine points in a row in Zone C or beyond: No sequence of nine points are in Zone C (on one side of the centerline) or beyond.

Rule 3:   Six points in a row steadily increasing or decreasing: No sequence of six points steadily increases or decreases.

Rule 4:   Fourteen points in a row alternating up and down: This pattern does not exist.

Rule 5:   Two out of three points in Zone A or beyond: There are no groups of three consecutive points that have two or more in Zone A or beyond.

Rule 6:   Four out of five points in a row in Zone B or beyond: No sequence of five points has four or more in Zone B or beyond.

The process appears to be in control.

f.   Since both the *R*-chart and the $\overline{x}$-chart are in control, these control limits should be used to monitor future process output.

12.79   a.   The sample size is determined by the following:

$$n > \frac{9(1 - p_0)}{p_0} = \frac{9(1 - .06)}{.06} = 141$$

The minimum sample size is 141. Since the sample size of 150 was used, it is large enough.

b. To compute the proportion of defectives in each sample, divide the number of defectives by the number in the sample, 150:

$$\hat{p} = \frac{\text{No. of defectives}}{\text{No. in sample}}$$

The sample proportions are listed in the table:

Sample No.	$\hat{p}$	Sample No.	$\hat{p}$
1	.060	11	.047
2	.073	12	.040
3	.080	13	.080
4	.053	14	.067
5	.067	15	.073
6	.040	16	.047
7	.087	17	.040
8	.060	18	.080
9	.073	19	.093
10	.033	20	.067

To get the total number of defectives, sum the number of defectives for all 20 samples. The sum is 189. To get the total number of units sampled, multiply the sample size by the number of samples: 150(20) = 3000.

$$\bar{p} = \frac{\text{Total defectives in all samples}}{\text{Total units sampled}} = \frac{189}{3000} = .063$$

Centerline $= \bar{p} = .063$

Upper control limit $= \bar{p} + 3\sqrt{\dfrac{\bar{p}(1-\bar{p})}{n}} = .063 + 3\sqrt{\dfrac{.063(.937)}{150}} = .123$

Lower control limit $= \bar{p} - 3\sqrt{\dfrac{\bar{p}(1-\bar{p})}{n}} = .063 - 3\sqrt{\dfrac{.063(.937)}{150}} = .003$

Upper A-B *boundary* $= \bar{p} + 2\sqrt{\dfrac{\bar{p}(1-\bar{p})}{n}} = .063 + 2\sqrt{\dfrac{.063(.937)}{150}} = .103$

Lower A-B *boundary* $= \bar{p} - 2\sqrt{\dfrac{\bar{p}(1-\bar{p})}{n}} = .063 - 2\sqrt{\dfrac{.063(.937)}{150}} = .023$

Upper B-C *boundary* $= \bar{p} + \sqrt{\dfrac{\bar{p}(1-\bar{p})}{n}} = .063 + \sqrt{\dfrac{.063(.937)}{150}} = .083$

Lower B-C *boundary* $= \bar{p} - \sqrt{\dfrac{\bar{p}(1-\bar{p})}{n}} = .063 - \sqrt{\dfrac{.063(.937)}{150}} = .043$

The *p*-chart is:

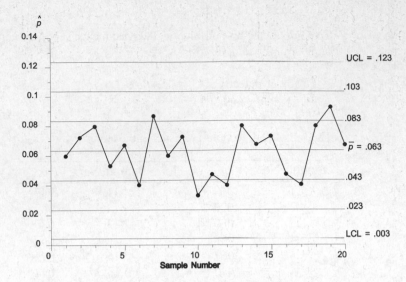

c.   To determine if the process is in or out of control, we check the four rules.

Rule 1:   One point beyond Zone A: No points are beyond Zone A.

Rule 2:   Nine points in a row in Zone C or beyond: No sequence of nine points are in Zone C (on one side of the centerline) or beyond.

Rule 3:   Six points in a row steadily increasing or decreasing: No sequence of six points steadily increase or decrease.

Rule 4:   Fourteen points in a row alternating up and down: Points 2 through 16 alternate up and down. This indicates the process is out of control.

Rule 4 indicates the process is out of control. Special causes of variation appear to be present.

e.   Since the process is out of control, the control limits should not be used to monitor future process output. It would not be appropriate to evaluate whether the process is in control using control limits determined during a period when the process was out of control.

12.81 First, we must compute the range for each sample. The range $= R =$ largest measurement $-$ smallest measurement. The results are listed in the table:

Sample No.	R	Sample No.	R	Sample No.	R
1	2.0	25	4.6	49	4.0
2	2.1	26	3.0	50	4.9
3	1.8	27	3.4	51	3.8
4	1.6	28	2.3	52	4.6
5	3.1	29	2.2	53	7.1
6	3.1	30	3.3	54	4.6
7	4.2	31	3.6	55	2.2
8	3.6	32	4.2	56	3.6
9	4.6	33	2.4	57	2.6
10	2.6	34	4.5	58	2.0
11	3.5	35	5.6	59	1.5
12	5.3	36	4.9	60	6.0
13	5.5	37	10.2	61	5.7
14	5.6	38	5.5	62	5.6
15	4.6	39	4.7	63	2.3
16	3.0	40	4.7	64	2.3
17	4.6	41	3.6	65	2.6
18	4.5	42	3.0	66	3.8
19	4.8	43	2.2	67	2.8
20	5.4	44	3.3	68	2.2
21	5.5	45	3.2	69	4.2
22	3.8	46	0.8	70	2.6
23	3.6	47	4.2	71	1.0
24	2.5	48	5.6	72	1.9

$$\bar{\bar{x}} = \frac{\bar{x}_1 + \bar{x}_2 + \cdots + \bar{x}_{72}}{k} = \frac{3537.3}{72} = 49.129$$

$$\bar{R} = \frac{R_1 + R_1 + \cdots + R_{72}}{k} = \frac{268.8}{72} = 3.733$$

Centerline $= \bar{\bar{x}} = 49.13$

From Table XI, Appendix B, with $n = 6$, $A_2 = .483$.

Upper control limit $= \bar{\bar{x}} + A_2\bar{R} = 49.129 + .483(3.733) = 50.932$

Lower control limit $= \bar{\bar{x}} + A_2\bar{R} = 49.129 - .483(3.733) = 47.326$

Upper A–B boundary $= \bar{\bar{x}} + \frac{2}{3}(A_2\bar{R}) = 49.129 + \frac{2}{3}(.483)(3.733) = 50.331$

Lower A–B boundary $= \bar{\bar{x}} + \frac{2}{3}(A_2\bar{R}) = 49.129 - \frac{2}{3}(.483)(3.733) = 47.927$

Upper B–C boundary $= \bar{\bar{x}} + \frac{1}{3}(A_2\bar{R}) = 49.129 + \frac{1}{3}(.483)(3.733) = 49.730$

Lower B–C boundary $= \bar{\bar{x}} - \frac{1}{3}(A_2\bar{R}) = 49.129 - \frac{1}{3}(.483)(3.733) = 48.528$

The $\bar{x}$-chart is:

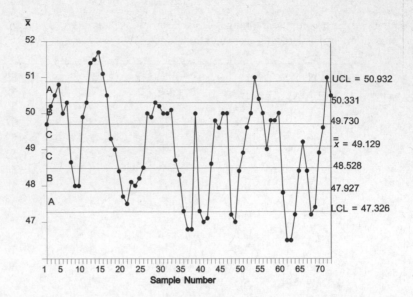

To determine if the process is in or out of control, we check the six rules:

Rule 1:   One point beyond Zone A: There are a total of 17 points beyond Zone A.

Rule 2:   Nine points in a row in Zone C or beyond: No sequence of nine points are in Zone C (on one side of the centerline) or beyond.

Rule 3:   Six points in a row steadily increasing or decreasing: There is one sequence of seven points that are steadily increasing—Points 15 through 21.

Rule 4:   Fourteen points in a row alternating up and down: This pattern does not exist.

Rule 5:   Two out of three points in Zone A or beyond: There are four groups of at least three points in Zone A or beyond—Points 12–16, Points 35–37, Points 39–41, and Points 60–63.

Rule 6:   Four out of five points in a row in Zone B or beyond: There are four groups of points that satisfy this rule—Points 10–16, Points 19–24, Points 26–32, and Points 60–64.

The process appears to be out of control. Rules 1, 3, 5, and 6 indicate that the process is out of control.

No. The problem does not give the times of the shifts. However, suppose we let the first shift be from 6:00 A.M. to 2:00 P.M., the second shift be from 2:00 P.M. to 10:00 P.M., and the third shift be from 10:00 P.M. to 6:00 A.M. If this is the case, the major problems are during the second shift.

Chapter 13
Time Series: Descriptive Analyses, Models, and Forecasting

13.1   To calculate a simple index number, first obtain the prices or quantities over a time period and select a base year. For each time period, the index number is the number at that time period divided by the value at the base period multiplied by 100.

13.3   A Laspeyres index uses the purchase quantity at the base period as the weights for all other time periods. A Paasche index uses the purchase quantity at each time period as the weight for that time period. The weights at the specified time period are also used with the base period to find the index.

13.5   a.   To find Laspeyres index, we use the quantities for the base period as the weights. We multiply the quantity for quarter 1 times the prices for quarters 1 and 4 for each product (A, B, or C). We then sum the products for both time periods. Finally, we divide the sum for quarter 4 by the sum for quarter 1. The sum of the products for quarter 1 is $100(3.25) + 20(1.75) + 50(8.00) = 325 + 35 + 400 = 760$. The sum of the products for quarter 4 is $100(4.25) + 20(1.00) + 50(10.50) = 425 + 20 + 525 = 970$. Laspeyres index is $(970 / 760) \times 100 = 127.63$.

        b.   To find Paasche index, we use the quantities for all time periods as weights. We multiple the quantity for each quarter and each product by the corresponding price. We then sum these products for the base period quarter 2 and the quarter for which we want to compute Paasche's index (quarter 4). The sum for quarter 2 is $200(3.50) + 25(1.25) + 35(9.35) = 700 + 31.25 + 327.25 = 1058.5$. The sum of the products for quarter 4 is $300(4.25) + 100(1.00) + 20(10.50) = 1275 + 100 + 210 = 1585$. Paasche's index is $(1585 / 1058.5) \times 100 = 149.74$.

13.7   a.   To compute the simple index, divide each U.S. Beer Production value by the 1980 value, 188, and then multiply by 100.

Year	Simple Index		Year	Simple Index	
1980	$(188/188) \times 100 =$	100.00	1994	$(202/188) \times 100 =$	107.45
1981	$(194/188) \times 100 =$	103.19	1995	$(199/188) \times 100 =$	105.85
1982	$(194/188) \times 100 =$	103.19	1996	$(201/188) \times 100 =$	106.91
1983	$(195/188) \times 100 =$	103.72	1997	$(199/188) \times 100 =$	105.85
1984	$(193/188) \times 100 =$	102.66	1998	$(198/188) \times 100 =$	105.32
1985	$(193/188) \times 100 =$	102.66	1999	$(198/188) \times 100 =$	105.32
1986	$(195/188) \times 100 =$	103.72	2000	$(199/188) \times 100 =$	105.85
1987	$(195/188) \times 100 =$	103.72	2001	$(199/188) \times 100 =$	105.85
1988	$(198/188) \times 100 =$	105.32	2002	$(200/188) \times 100 =$	106.38
1989	$(200/188) \times 100 =$	106.38	2003	$(195/188) \times 100 =$	103.72
1990	$(204/188) \times 100 =$	108.51	2004	$(198/188) \times 100 =$	105.32
1991	$(203/188) \times 100 =$	107.98	2005	$(197/188) \times 100 =$	104.79
1992	$(202/188) \times 100 =$	107.45	2006	$(198/188) \times 100 =$	105.32
1993	$(203/188) \times 100 =$	107.98	2007	$(199/188) \times 100 =$	105.85

The index value for 2007 is 105.85. Thus, the beer production in 2007 increased by $105.85 - 100 = 5.85\%$ over the beer production in the base year of 1980.

b.   This is a quantity index because the numbers collected were the number of barrels produced rather than the price.

c.   To compute the simple index, divide each U.S. Beer Production value by the 1990 value, 204, and then multiply by 100.

Year	Simple Index		Year	Simple Index	
1980	$(188/204) \times 100 =$	92.16	1994	$(202/204) \times 100 =$	99.02
1981	$(194/204) \times 100 =$	95.10	1995	$(199/204) \times 100 =$	97.55
1982	$(194/204) \times 100 =$	95.10	1996	$(201/204) \times 100 =$	98.53
1983	$(195/204) \times 100 =$	95.59	1997	$(199/204) \times 100 =$	97.55
1984	$(193/204) \times 100 =$	94.61	1998	$(198/204) \times 100 =$	97.06
1985	$(193/204) \times 100 =$	94.61	1999	$(198/204) \times 100 =$	97.06
1986	$(195/204) \times 100 =$	95.59	2000	$(199/204) \times 100 =$	97.55
1987	$(195/204) \times 100 =$	95.59	2001	$(199/204) \times 100 =$	97.55
1988	$(198/204) \times 100 =$	97.06	2002	$(200/204) \times 100 =$	98.04
1989	$(200/204) \times 100 =$	98.04	2003	$(195/204) \times 100 =$	95.59
1990	$(204/204) \times 100 =$	100.00	2004	$(198/204) \times 100 =$	97.06
1991	$(203/204) \times 100 =$	99.51	2005	$(197/204) \times 100 =$	96.57
1992	$(202/204) \times 100 =$	99.02	2006	$(198/204) \times 100 =$	97.06
1993	$(203/204) \times 100 =$	99.51	2007	$(199/204) \times 100 =$	97.55

The plots of the two simple indices are:

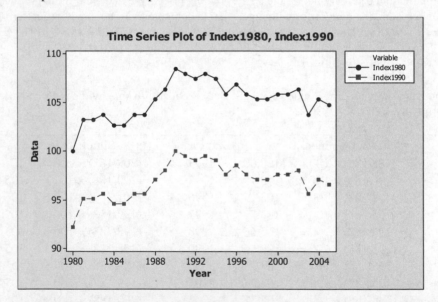

The two plots have the same shape, just at different levels. For both, there is a fairly steep increase in the indices from 1987 to 1990. After 1990, there is a steady decrease in the indices.

13.9   a.   To compute the simple index, divide each natural gas price by the 1980 value, 3.68, and then multiply by 100.

Year	Simple Index	
1980	(3.68/3.68) x 100 =	100.00
1990	(5.80/3.68) x 100 =	157.61
1991	(5.82/3.68) x 100 =	158.15
1992	(5.89/3.68) x 100 =	160.05
1993	(6.16/3.68) x 100 =	167.39
1994	(6.41/3.68) x 100 =	174.18
1995	(6.06/3.68) x 100 =	164.67
1996	(6.34/3.68) x 100 =	172.28
1997	(6.94/3.68) x 100 =	188.59
1998	(6.82/3.68) x 100 =	185.33
1999	(6.69/3.68) x 100 =	181.79
2000	(7.76/3.68) x 100 =	210.87
2001	(9.63/3.68) x 100 =	261.68
2002	(7.89/3.68) x 100 =	214.40
2003	(9.63/3.68) x 100 =	261.68
2004	(10.75/3.68) x 100 =	292.12
2005	(12.70/3.68) x 100 =	345.11
2006	(13.75/3.68) x 100 =	373.64
2007	(13.01/3.68) x 100 =	353.53

The plot of the index is:

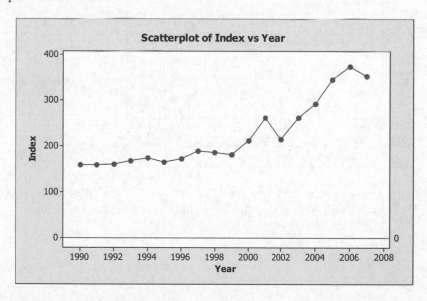

b.   From 1980 to 1990 there was an increase in the price of natural gas. From 1990 to 2000, there was again a slight increase in the price of natural gas. From 2000 to 2007, the price was very volatile, with sharp increases from 2000 to 2001, a sharp decrease from 2001 to 2002, sharp increases from 2002 to 2006, and sharp decreases from 2006 to 2007.

c.   The index constructed is a price index since it is based on the price of natural gas.

13.11   a.   To compute the simple composite index, first sum the three values (durables, nondurables, and services) for every time period. Then, divide each sum by the sum in 1970, 646.5, and then multiply by 100. The simple composite index for 1970 is:

Year	Sum	Simple Composite Index-1970	Simple Composite Index-1980
1960	332.5	51.43	19.02
1965	444.6	68.77	25.43
1970	646.5	100.00	36.98
1975	1,024.8	158.52	58.62
1980	1,748.1	270.39	100.00
1985	2,667.4	412.59	152.59
1990	3,761.2	581.78	215.16
1995	4,969.0	768.60	284.26
2000	6,739.30	1,042.43	385.53
2005	8,694.10	1,344.80	497.35

   b.   To update the 1970 index to the 1980 index, divide the 1970 index values by the 1970 index value for 1980, 270.39, and then multiply by 100. The 1980 simple composite index is also listed in the table in part **a**.

   c.   The graph of the two indices is:

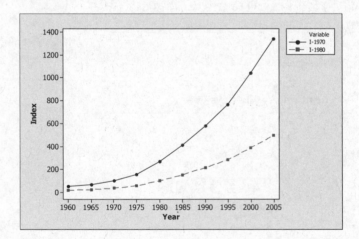

Changing the base year from 1970 to 1980 flattens out the graph. Also, the spread of the values for the 1980 index is much smaller than the spread of the values in the 1970 index.

13.13   a.   To compute the simple index for the average hourly earnings for manufacturing workers, divide the hourly earnings for each year by the hourly earnings for the base year, 4.83, and multiply by 100. To compute the simple index for the average hourly earnings for transportation and public utilities workers, divide the hourly earnings for each year by the hourly earnings for the base year, 5.88, and multiply by 100. The two indices are:

Year	Manufacturing Index	Transportation/Utilities Index
1975	100.00	100.00
1980	150.52	150.85
1985	197.52	193.88
1990	224.22	220.58
1995	256.11	242.01
2000	297.72	275.85

   b.   The two plots are:

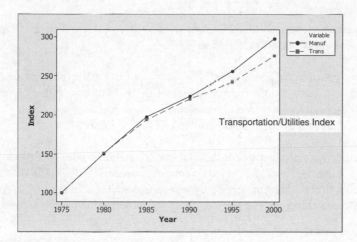

The simple earnings indices are very similar. From 1975 to 2000, the hourly earnings have increased 175.85% for the transportation and public utilities workers and 197.72% for the manufacturing workers.

   c.   To compute the simple composite index for the hourly earnings, sum the earnings for the three industries for each time period. Then divide the sum at each year by the sum at the base year, 15.43, and multiply by 100. To compute the simple composite index for weekly hours, sum the weekly hours for the three industries for each time period. Then divide the sum at each year by the sum at the base year, 117.8, and multiply by 100. The two composite indices are:

Year	Earnings	Hours	Earnings Index	Hours Index
1975	15.43	117.80	100.00	100.00
1980	23.09	117.70	149.64	99.92
1985	30.09	118.40	195.01	100.51
1990	34.59	117.80	224.17	100.00
1995	39.03	119.40	252.95	101.36
2000	45.80	119.70	296.82	101.61

d.   The plots of the two composite indices are:

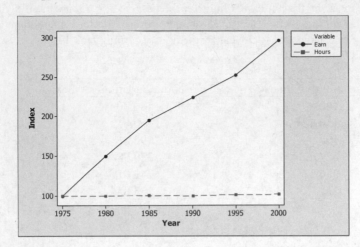

The composite earnings index increased 196.82% from 1975 to 2000. However, the composite weekly hours has increased only 1.61% from 1975 to 2000.

13.15   The smaller the value of w, the smoother the series. With $w = .2$, the current value receives a weight of .2 while the previous exponentially smoothed value receives a weight of .8. With $w = .8$, the current value receives a weight of .8 while the previous exponentially smoothed value receives a weight of .2. The smaller the value of w, the less chance the series can be affected by large jumps.

13.17   a.   The exponentially smoothed beer production for the first period is equal to the beer production for that period. For the rest of the time periods, the exponentially smoothed beer production is found by multiplying the beer production of that time period by $w = .2$ and adding to that $(1 - .2)$ times the exponentially smoothed value above it. The exponentially smoothed value for the second period is $.2(194) + (1 - .2)(188) = 189.2$.

The rest of the values are shown in the following table.

Year	Beer Production	Exponentially Smoothed Production w = .2	Exponentially Smoothed Production w = .8
1980	188	188.0	188.0
1981	194	189.2	192.8
1982	194	190.2	193.8
1983	195	191.1	194.8
1984	193	191.5	193.4
1985	193	191.8	193.1
1986	195	192.4	194.6
1987	195	193.0	194.9
1988	198	194.0	197.4
1989	200	195.2	199.5
1990	204	196.9	203.1
1991	203	198.1	203.0
1992	202	198.9	202.2
1993	203	199.7	202.8
1994	202	200.2	202.2
1995	199	200.0	199.6
1996	201	200.2	200.7
1997	199	199.9	199.3
1998	198	199.5	198.3
1999	198	199.2	198.1
2000	199	199.2	198.8
2001	199	199.1	199.0
2002	200	199.3	199.8
2003	195	198.5	196.0
2004	198	198.4	197.6
2005	197	198.1	197.1
2006	198	198.1	197.8
2007	199	198.3	198.8

b.   The exponentially smoothed beer production for the first period is equal to the beer production for that period. For the rest of the time periods, the exponentially smoothed beer production is found by multiplying .8 times the beer production of that time period and adding to that $(1 - .8)$ times the value of the exponentially smoothed beer production figure of the previous time period. The exponentially smoothed beer production for the second time period is $.8(194) + (1 - .8)(188) = 192.8$. The rest of the values are shown in the table in part **a**.

c.   The plot of the two series is:

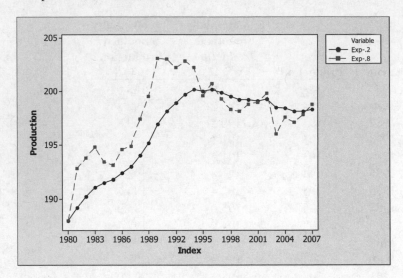

The exponentially smoothed series with $w = .2$ is smoother than the series with $w = .8$. Thus, the series with $w = .2$ best portrays the long-term trend.

13.19   a.   The exponentially smoothed gold price for the first period is equal to the gold price for that period. For the rest of the time periods, the exponentially smoothed gold price is found by multiplying the price for the time period by $w = .8$ and adding to that $(1 − .8)$ times the exponentially smoothed value from the previous time period. The exponentially smoothed value for the second time period is $.8(362) + (1 − .8)(384) = 366.40$. The rest of the values are shown below.

Year	Price	$w=.8$ Exponentially Smoothed Price
1990	384	384.00
1991	362	366.40
1992	344	348.48
1993	360	357.70
1994	384	378.74
1995	384	382.95
1996	388	386.99
1997	331	342.20
1998	294	303.64
1999	279	283.93
2000	279	279.99
2001	271	272.80
2002	310	302.56
2003	363	350.91
2004	410	398.18
2005	445	435.64
2006	603	569.53
2007	695	669.91
2008	872	831.58

b. The plot of the two series is:

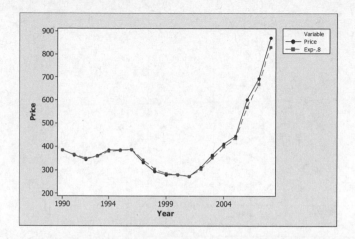

The exponentially smooth series with $w = .8$ is almost the same as the original series.

13.21 a. The exponentially smoothed imports for the first period is equal to the imports that period. For the rest of the time periods, the exponentially smoothed imports is found by multiplying $w = .1$ times the imports for that time period and adding to that $(1 − .1)$ times the value of the exponentially smoothed imports figure of the previous time period. The exponentially smoothed imports for the second time period is $.1(1,233) + (1 − .1)(1,283) = 1,278.0$. The rest of the values are shown in the table.

The same procedure is followed for $w = .9$. The exponentially smoothed imports/exports for the second time period is $.9(1,233) + (1 − .9)(1,283) = 1,238$. The rest of the values are shown in the table.

Year	t	Imports	Exponentially Smoothed Series $w = .1$	Exponentially Smoothed Series $w = .9$
1990	1	1,283	1,283.0	1,283.0
1991	2	1,233	1,278.0	1,238.0
1992	3	1,247	1,274.9	1,246.1
1993	4	1,339	1,281.3	1,329.7
1994	5	1,307	1,283.9	1,309.3
1995	6	1,219	1,277.4	1,228.0
1996	7	1,258	1,275.5	1,255.0
1997	8	1,378	1,285.7	1,365.7
1998	9	1,522	1,309.3	1,506.4
1999	10	1,543	1,332.7	1,539.3
2000	11	1,659	1,365.3	1,647.0
2001	12	1,770	1,405.8	1,757.7
2002	13	1,490	1,414.2	1,516.8
2003	14	1,671	1,439.9	1,655.6
2004	15	1,948	1,490.7	1,918.8
2005	16	1738	1,515.4	1,756.1
2006	17	1745	1,538.4	1,746.1
2007	18	1969	1,581.5	1,946.7

b.   The plot of the three series is:

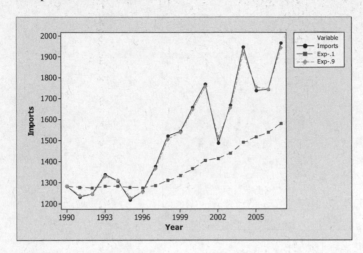

The exponentially smoothed series with $w = .9$ looks more like the original series. The closer w is to 1 the closer the exponentially smoothed curve looks like the original.

13.23   If w is small (near 0), one will obtain a smooth, slowly changing series of forecasts. If w is large (near 1), one will obtain more rapidly changing forecasts that depend mostly on the current values of the series.

13.25   a.   We first compute the exponentially smoothed values $E_1, E_2, \ldots, E_t$ for years 1980 – 2004.

$E_1 = Y_1 = 188$

For $w = .3$, $E_2 = wY_2 + (1 - w)E_1 = .3(194) + (1 - .3)(188) = 189.80$
$E_3 = wY_3 + (1 - w)E_2 = .3(194) + (1 - .3)(189.80) = 191.06$

The rest of the values appear in the table.

For $w = .7$, $E_2 = wY_2 + (1 - w)E_1 = .7(194) + (1 - .7)(188) = 192.20$
$_3 = wY_3 + (1 - w)E_2 = .7(194) + (1 - .7)(192.20) = 193.46$

The rest of the values appear in the table.

Year	Beer Production	$w = .3$ Exponentially Smoothed Value	$w = .7$ Exponentially Smoothed Value
1980	188	188.00	188.00
1981	194	189.80	192.20
1982	194	191.06	193.46
1983	195	192.24	194.54
1984	193	192.47	193.46
1985	193	192.63	193.14
1986	195	193.34	194.44
1987	195	193.84	194.83
1988	198	195.09	197.05
1989	200	196.56	199.11
1990	204	198.79	202.53
1991	203	200.05	202.86
1992	202	200.64	202.26
1993	203	201.35	202.78
1994	202	201.54	202.23
1995	199	200.78	199.97
1996	201	200.85	200.69
1997	199	200.29	199.51
1998	198	199.60	198.45
1999	198	199.12	198.14
2000	199	199.09	198.74
2001	199	199.06	198.92
2002	200	199.34	199.68
2003	195	198.04	196.40
2004	198	198.03	197.52
2005	197		
2006	198		
2007	199		

To forecast using exponentially smoothed values, we use the following:

For $w = .3$:
$$F_{2005} = F_{t+1} = E_t = 198.03$$
$$F_{2006} = F_{t+2} = F_{t+1} = 198.03$$
$$F_{2007} = F_{t+3} = F_{t+1} = 198.03$$

For $w = .7$:
$$F_{2005} = F_{t+1} = E_t = 197.52$$
$$F_{2006} = F_{t+2} = F_{t+1} = 197.52$$
$$F_{2007} = F_{t+3} = F_{t+1} = 197.52$$

b. We first compute the Holt-Winters values for the years 1980-2004.

With $w = .7$ and $v = .3$,

$E_2 = Y_2 = 194$
$E_3 = wY_3 + (1 - w)(E_2 + T_2) = .7(194) + (1 - .7)(194 + 6) = 195.8.$

$T_2 = Y_2 - Y_1 = 194 - 188 = 6$
$T_3 = v(E_3 - E_2) + (1 - v)T_2 = .3(195.8 - 194) + (1 - .3)6 = 4.74$

The rest of the E_t's and T_t's appear in the table that follows.

With $w = .3$ and $v = .7$,

$E_2 = Y_2 = 194$
$E_3 = wY_3 + (1 - w)(E_2 + T_2) = .3(194) + (1 - .3)(194 + 6) = 198.2.$

$T_2 = Y_2 - Y_1 = 194 - 188 = 6$
$T_3 = v(E_3 - E_2) + (1 - v)T_2 = .7(198.2 - 194) + (1 - .7)6 = 4.74$

The rest of the E_t's and T_t's appear in the table that follows.

Year	Beer	E_t $w = .7$ $v = .3$	T_t $w = .7$ $v = .3$	E_t $w = .3$ $v = .7$	T_t $w = .3$ $v = .7$
1980	188				
1981	194	194	6.00	194.00	6.00
1982	194	195.80	4.74	198.20	4.74
1983	195	196.66	3.58	200.56	3.07
1984	193	195.17	2.06	200.44	0.84
1985	193	194.27	1.17	198.80	-0.90
1986	195	195.13	1.08	197.03	-1.51
1987	195	195.36	0.82	195.36	-1.62
1988	198	197.46	1.20	195.02	-0.72
1989	200	199.60	1.49	196.01	0.47
1990	204	203.13	2.10	198.74	2.05
1991	203	203.67	1.63	201.45	2.52
1992	202	202.99	0.94	203.38	2.10
1993	203	203.28	0.74	204.74	1.58
1994	202	202.61	0.32	205.02	0.67
1995	199	200.18	-0.51	203.69	-0.73
1996	201	200.60	-0.23	202.37	-1.14
1997	199	199.41	-0.52	200.56	-1.61
1998	198	198.27	-0.70	198.66	-1.81
1999	198	197.87	-0.61	197.20	-1.57
2000	199	198.48	-0.25	196.64	-0.86
2001	199	198.77	-0.08	196.75	-0.18
2002	200	199.61	0.19	197.59	0.54
2003	195	196.44	-0.82	197.19	-0.12
2004	198	197.29	-0.32	197.35	0.08
2005	197				
2006	198				
2007	199				

To forecast using the Holt-Winters Model:

For $w = .7$ and $v = .3$,

$F_{2005} = F_{t+1} = E_t + T_t = 197.29 - .32 = 196.97$
$F_{2006} = F_{t+2} = E_t + 2T_t = 197.29 - 2(.32) = 196.65$
$F_{2007} = F_{t+3} = E_t + 3T_t = 197.29 - 3(.32) = 196.33$

For $w = .3$ and $v = .7$,

$F_{2005} = F_{t+1} = E_t + T_t = 197.35 + .08 = 197.43$
$F_{2006} = F_{t+2} = E_t + 2T_t = 197.35 + 2(.08) = 197.51$
$F_{2007} = F_{t+3} = E_t + 3T_t = 197.35 + 3(.08) = 197.59$

13.27   a.   Using MINITAB, the time series plot is:

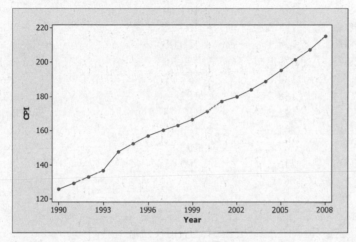

There appears to be an increasing trend in CPI over time.

b.   To compute the exponentially smoothed values, we follow these steps:

$E_1 = Y_1 = 125.8$

$E_2 = wY_2 + (1 - w)E_1 = .4(129.1) + (1 - .4)(125.8) = 127.12$
$E_3 = wY_3 + (1 - w)E_2 = .4(132.8) + (1 - .4)(127.12) = 129.39$

The rest of the values are computed in a similar manner and are listed in the table:

Year	CPI	Exponentially Smoothed Value $w=.4$
1990	125.8	125.80
1991	129.1	127.12
1992	132.8	129.39
1993	136.8	132.36
1994	147.8	138.53
1995	152.4	144.08
1996	156.9	149.21
1997	160.5	153.72
1998	163.0	157.43
1999	166.6	161.10
2000	171.5	165.26
2001	177.1	170.00
2002	179.9	173.96
2003	184.0	177.97
2004	188.9	182.34
2005	195.3	187.53
2006	201.6	193.16
2007	207.3	198.81
2008	215.3	205.41

Using MINITAB, the plot is:

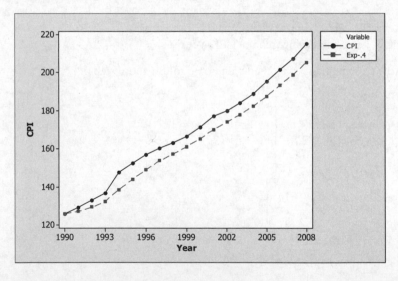

To forecast using exponentially smoothed values, we use the following:

$$F_{2009} = F_{t+1} = E_t = 205.41$$

c.   We first compute the Holt-Winters values for the years 1990-2005.

With $w = .4$ and $v = .5$,

$E_2 = Y_2 = 129.1$
$E_3 = wY_3 + (1 - w)(E_2 + T_2) = .4(132.8) + (1 - .4)(129.1 + 3.3) = 132.56.$

$T_2 = Y_2 - Y_1 = 129.1 - 125.8 = 3.3$
$T_3 = v(E_3 - E_2) + (1 - v)T_2 = .5(132.56 - 129.1) + (1 - .5)(3.3) = 3.38$

The rest of the E_t's and T_t's appear in the table that follows.

Year	CPI	E_t $w = .4$ $v = .5$	T_t $w = .4$ $v = .5$
1990	125.8		
1991	129.1	129.10	3.30
1992	132.8	132.56	3.38
1993	136.8	136.28	3.55
1994	147.8	143.02	5.14
1995	152.4	149.86	5.99
1996	156.9	156.27	6.20
1997	160.5	161.68	5.81
1998	163.0	165.69	4.91
1999	166.6	169.00	4.11
2000	171.5	172.47	3.79
2001	177.1	176.59	3.96
2002	179.9	180.29	3.83
2003	184.0	184.07	3.80
2004	188.9	188.28	4.01
2005	195.3	193.50	4.61
2006	201.6	199.50	5.31
2007	207.3	205.81	5.81
2008	215.3	213.09	6.54

To forecast using the Holt-Winters Model:

For $w = .4$ and $v = .5$,

$F_{2009} = F_{t+1} = E_t + T_t = 213.09 + 6.54 = 219.63$

13.29   a.   To compute the exponentially smoothed values, we follow these steps:

$E_t = Y_1 = 1,160.3$

For $w = .7$,

$E_2 = wY_2 + (1 - w)E_1 = .7(1,224.4) + (1 - .7)(1,160.3) = 1,205.2$
$E_3 = wY_3 + (1 - w)E_2 = .7(1,040.7) + (1 - .7)(1,205.2) = 1,090.2$

The rest of the values are computed in a similar manner and are listed in the table:

Year	Quarter	S&P 500	Exponentially Smoothed $w = .7$	Exponentially Smoothed $w = .3$
2001	1	1,160.3	1,160.3	1,160.3
	2	1,224.4	1,205.2	1,179.5
	3	1,040.9	1,090.2	1,137.9
	4	1,148.1	1,130.7	1,141.0
2002	1	1,147.4	1,142.4	1,142.9
	2	989.8	1,035.6	1,097.0
	3	815.3	881.4	1,012.5
	4	879.8	880.3	972.7
2003	1	848.2	857.8	935.3
	2	974.5	939.5	947.1
	3	996.0	979.0	961.8
	4	1,111.9	1,072.0	1,006.8
2004	1	1,126.2	1,110.0	1,042.6
	2	1,140.8	1,131.5	1,072.1
	3	1,114.6	1,119.7	1,084.8
	4	1,211.9	1,184.2	1,123.0
2005	1	1,180.6	1,181.7	1,140.2
	2	1,191.3	1,188.4	1,155.6
	3	1,228.8	1,216.7	1,177.5
	4	1,248.3	1,238.8	1,198.8
2006	1	1,294.9	1,278.1	1,227.6
	2	1,270.2	1,272.6	1,240.4
	3	1,335.8	1,316.8	1,269.0
	4	1,418.3	1,387.9	1,313.8
2007	1	1,420.9	1,411.0	1,345.9
	2	1,503.3	1,475.6	1,393.1
	3	1,526.7	1,511.4	1,433.2
	4	1,468.4	1,481.3	1,443.8
2008	1	1,322.7		
	2	1,280.0		
	3	1,164.7		
	4	903.3		

The forecasts using the exponentially smoothed values with $w = .7$ are:

$$F_{2008,1} = F_{t+1} = E_t = 1,481.3$$
$$F_{2008,2} = F_{t+2} = F_{t+1} = 1,481.3$$
$$F_{2008,3} = F_{t+3} = F_{t+1} = 1,481.3$$
$$F_{2008,4} = F_{t+4} = F_{t+1} = 1,481.3$$

b.   To compute the exponentially smoothed values, we follow these steps:

$E_t = Y_1 = 1,160.3$

For $w = .3$,

$E_2 = wY_2 + (1 - w)E_1 = .3(1,224.4) + (1 - .3)(1,160.3) = 1,779.5$
$E_3 = wY_3 + (1 - w)E_2 = .3(1,040.9) + (1 - .3)(1,179.5) = 1,137.9$

The rest of the values are computed in a similar manner and are listed in the table above.

The forecasts using the exponentially smoothed values with $w = .3$ are:

$F_{2008,1} = F_{t+1} = E_t = 1,443.8$
$F_{2008,2} = F_{t+2} = F_{t+1} = 1,443.8$
$F_{2008,3} = F_{t+3} = F_{t+1} = 1,443.8$
$F_{2008,4} = F_{t+4} = F_{t+1} = 1,443.8$

13.31   a.   We first compute the exponentially smoothed values $E_1, E_2, \ldots, E_t$ for 2001 through 2008.

$E_1 = Y_1 = 265.5$

For $w = .5$,

$E_2 = wY_2 + (1 - w)E_1 = .5(261.9) + (1 - .5)(265.5) = 263.70$
$E_3 = wY_3 + (1 - w)E_2 = .5(263.0) + (1 - .5)(263.7) = 263.35$

The rest of the values are found in the table:

Year	Month	Gold Price	Exponentially Smoothed $w=.5$	Holt-Winters Et $w=.5$	Tt $v=.5$
2001	Jan	265.5	265.50		
	Feb	261.9	263.70	261.90	-3.60
	Mar	263.0	263.35	260.65	-2.43
	Apr	260.5	261.93	259.36	-1.86
	May	272.4	267.16	264.95	1.87
	Jun	270.2	268.68	268.51	2.71
	Jul	267.5	268.09	269.36	1.78
	Aug	272.4	270.25	271.77	2.10
	Sep	283.4	276.82	278.63	4.48
	Oct	283.1	279.96	283.11	4.48
	Nov	276.2	278.08	281.89	1.63
	Dec	275.9	276.99	279.71	-0.28

2002	Jan	281.7	279.35	280.57	0.29
	Feb	295.5	287.42	288.18	3.95
	Mar	294.0	290.71	293.07	4.42
	Apr	302.7	296.71	300.09	5.72
	May	314.5	305.60	310.16	7.89
	Jun	321.2	313.40	319.63	8.68
	Jul	313.3	313.35	320.80	4.93
	Aug	310.3	311.83	318.02	1.07
	Sep	319.2	315.51	319.14	1.10
	Oct	316.6	316.06	318.42	0.19
	Nov	319.2	317.63	318.91	0.34
	Dec	333.4	325.51	326.32	3.88
2003	Jan	356.9	341.21	343.55	10.55
	Feb	359.0	350.10	356.55	11.78
	Mar	340.6	345.35	354.46	4.85
	Apr	328.2	336.78	343.75	-2.93
	May	355.7	346.24	348.26	0.79
	Jun	356.5	351.37	352.77	2.65
	Jul	351.0	351.18	353.21	1.54
	Aug	359.8	355.49	357.28	2.81
	Sep	378.9	367.20	369.49	7.51
	Oct	378.9	373.05	377.95	7.98
	Nov	389.9	381.47	387.92	8.98
	Dec	407.6	394.54	402.25	11.65
2004	Jan	414.0	404.27	413.95	11.68
	Feb	405.3	404.78	415.46	6.60
	Mar	406.7	405.74	414.38	2.76
	Apr	403.0	404.37	410.07	-0.78
	May	383.4	393.89	396.34	-7.25
	Jun	392.0	392.94	390.55	-6.52
	Jul	398.1	395.52	391.06	-3.00
	Aug	400.5	398.01	394.28	0.11
	Sep	405.3	401.66	399.84	2.83
	Oct	420.5	411.08	411.59	7.29
	Nov	439.4	425.24	429.14	12.42
	Dec	441.7	433.47	441.63	12.46
2005	Jan	424.2	428.83	439.14	4.98
	Feb	423.4	426.12	433.76	-0.20
	Mar	434.2	430.16	433.88	-0.04
	Apr	428.9	429.53	431.37	-1.28
	May	421.9	425.71	426.00	-3.32
	Jun	430.7	428.21	426.69	-1.32
	Jul	424.5	426.35	424.93	-1.54
	Aug	437.9	432.13	430.65	2.09
	Sep	456.0	444.06	444.37	7.91
	Oct	469.9	456.98	461.09	12.31
	Nov	476.7	466.84	475.05	13.14
	Dec	509.8	488.32	498.99	18.54

2006	Jan	549.9	519.11	533.72	26.63
	Feb	555.0	537.06	557.67	25.29
	Mar	557.1	547.08	570.03	18.83
	Apr	610.6	578.84	599.73	24.26
	May	676.5	627.67	650.25	37.39
	Jun	596.2	611.93	641.92	14.53
	Jul	633.8	622.87	645.12	8.87
	Aug	632.6	627.73	643.30	3.52
	Sep	598.2	612.97	622.51	-8.63
	Oct	585.8	599.38	599.84	-15.65
	Nov	627.8	613.59	605.99	-4.75
	Dec	629.8	621.70	615.52	2.39
2007	Jan	631.2	626.45	624.56	5.71
	Feb	664.7	645.57	647.48	14.32
	Mar	654.9	650.24	658.35	12.59
	Apr	679.4	664.82	675.17	14.71
	May	666.9	665.86	678.39	8.96
	Jun	655.5	660.68	671.43	1.00
	Jul	665.3	662.99	668.86	-0.78
	Aug	665.4	664.19	666.74	-1.45
	Sep	712.7	688.45	688.99	10.40
	Oct	754.6	721.52	727.00	24.20
	Nov	806.3	763.91	778.75	37.98
	Dec	803.2	783.56	809.96	34.60
2008	Jan	889.6	836.58	867.08	45.86
	Feb	922.3	879.44	917.62	48.20
	Mar	968.4	923.92	967.11	48.84
	Apr	909.7	916.81	962.83	22.28
	May	888.7	902.75	936.90	-1.82
	Jun	889.5	896.13	912.29	-13.22
	Jul	939.8	917.96	919.44	-3.04
	Aug	839.0	878.48	877.70	-22.39
	Sep	829.9	854.19	842.61	-28.74
	Oct	806.6	830.40	810.23	-30.56
	Nov	760.9	795.65	770.29	-35.25
	Dec	816.1	805.87	775.57	-14.99

To forecast the monthly prices for 2008 using the data through December 2007:

$$F_{t+1} = E_t \qquad F_{t+I} = F_{t+i} = E_t \text{ for } i = 2, 3, \dots$$
$$F_{t+1} = E_{\text{Dec},2007} = 783.56$$

Year	Month	Forecast
2008	Jan	783.56
	Feb	783.56
	Mar	783.56
	Apr	783.56
	May	783.56
	Jun	783.56
	Jul	783.56
	Aug	783.56
	Sep	783.56
	Oct	783.56
	Nov	783.56
	Dec	783.56

b. To compute the one-step-ahead forecasts for 2008, we use $F_{t+1} = E_t$, where E_t is recomputed each time period (month). The forecasts are obtained from the table in part **a**.

Year	Month	Forecast
2008	Jan	783.56
	Feb	836.58
	Mar	879.44
	Apr	923.92
	May	916.81
	Jun	902.75
	Jul	896.13
	Aug	917.96
	Sep	878.48
	Oct	854.19
	Nov	830.40
	Dec	795.65

c. First, we compute the Holt-Winters values for the years 2001-2008.

With $w = .5$ and $v = .5$,

$$E_2 = Y_2 = 261.9$$
$$E_3 = wY_3 + (1 - w)(E_2 + T_2) = .5(263.0) + (1 - .5)(261.9 - 3.6) = 260.65.$$

$$T_2 = Y_2 - Y_1 = 261.9 - 265.5 = -3.6$$
$$T_3 = v(E_3 - E_2) + (1 - v)T_2 = .5(260.65 - 261.9) + (1 - .5)(-3.6) = -2.43$$

The rest of the E_t's and T_i's appear in the table in part a.

To forecast the monthly prices for 2008 using the data through December 2007:

$$F_{t+1} = E_t + T_t = 809.96 + 34.60 = 844.56$$
$$F_{t+2} = E_t + 2T_t = 809.96 + 2(34.60) = 879.16$$
$$F_{t+n} = E_t + nT_t$$

The rest of the forecasts appear in the table:

Year	Month	Forecast
2008	Jan	844.56
	Feb	879.16
	Mar	913.76
	Apr	948.36
	May	982.96
	Jun	1,017.56
	Jul	1,052.16
	Aug	1,086.76
	Sep	1,121.36
	Oct	1,155.96
	Nov	1,190.56
	Dec	1,225.16

To compute the one-step-ahead forecasts for 2008, we use $F_{t+1} = E_t + T_t$ where E_t and T_t are recomputed each time period. The forecasts are obtained from the table in part **a**.

$$F_{\text{Jan},2008} = E_{\text{Dec, 2007}} + T_{\text{Dec, 2007}} = 809.96 + 34.60 = 844.56$$
$$F_{\text{Feb},2008} = E_{\text{Jan, 2008}} + T_{\text{Jan, 2008}} = 867.08 + 45.86 = 912.94$$

The rest of the values appear in the table:

Year	Month	Forecast
2008	Jan	844.56
	Feb	912.94
	Mar	965.81
	Apr	1015.95
	May	985.11
	Jun	935.08
	Jul	899.07
	Aug	916.40
	Sep	855.32
	Oct	813.87
	Nov	779.68
	Dec	735.04

13.33   a.   From Exercise 13.25b, the Holt-Winters forecasts for 2005-2007 using $w = .3$ and $v = .7$ are:
$$F_{2005} = 196.97$$
$$F_{2006} = 196.65$$
$$F_{2007} = 196.33$$

The errors are the differences between the actual values and the predicted values. Thus, the errors are:

$$Y_{2005} - F_{2005} = 197 - 196.97 = 0.03$$
$$Y_{2006} - F_{2006} = 198 - 196.65 = 1.35$$
$$Y_{2007} - F_{2007} = 199 - 196.33 = 2.67$$

b.   From Exercise 13.25b, the Holt-Winters forecasts for 2005-2007 using $w = .7$ and $v = .3$ are:
$$F_{2005} = 197.43$$
$$F_{2006} = 197.51$$
$$F_{2007} = 197.59$$

The errors are:
$$Y_{2005} - F_{2005} = 197 - 197.43 = -0.43$$
$$Y_{2006} - F_{2006} = 198 - 197.51 = 0.49$$
$$Y_{2007} - F_{2007} = 199 - 197.59 = 1.41$$

c.   For the Holt-Winters forecasts with $w = .3$ and $v = .7$,

$$\text{MAD} = \frac{\sum_{i=1}^{m} |Y_t - F_t|}{m} = \frac{|197 - 196.97| + |198 - 196.65| + |199 - 196.33|}{3} = \frac{4.05}{3} = 1.35$$

$$\text{MAPE} = \left[\frac{\sum_{i=1}^{m} \left| \frac{(Y_t - F_t)}{Y_t} \right|}{m} \right] 100$$

$$= \left[\frac{\left| \frac{197 - 196.97}{197} \right| + \left| \frac{198 - 196.65}{198} \right| + \left| \frac{199 - 196.33}{199} \right|}{3} \right] 100 = \left[\frac{.02039}{3} \right] 100 = 0.68$$

$$\text{RMSE} = \sqrt{\frac{\sum_{i=1}^{m} (Y_t - F_t)^2}{m}} = \sqrt{\frac{(197 - 196.97)^2 + (198 - 196.65)^2 + (199 - 196.33)^2}{3}}$$

$$= \sqrt{\frac{8.9523}{3}} = 1.73$$

d. For the Holt-Winters forecasts with $w = .7$ and $v = .3$,

$$\text{MAD} = \frac{\sum_{i=1}^{m}|Y_t - F_t|}{m} = \frac{|197 - 197.43| + |198 - 197.51| + |199 - 197.59|}{3} = \frac{2.33}{3} = .78$$

$$\text{MAPE} = \left[\frac{\sum_{i=1}^{m}\left|\frac{(Y_t - F_t)}{Y_t}\right|}{m}\right]100$$

$$= \left[\frac{\left|\frac{197 - 197.43}{197}\right| + \left|\frac{198 - 197.51}{198}\right| + \left|\frac{199 - 197.59}{199}\right|}{3}\right]100 = \left[\frac{.011743}{3}\right]100 = .39$$

$$\text{RMSE} = \sqrt{\frac{\sum_{i=1}^{m}(Y_t - F_t)^2}{m}} = \sqrt{\frac{(197 - 197.43)^2 + (198 - 197.51)^2 + (199 - 197.59)^2}{3}}$$

$$= \sqrt{\frac{2.4131}{3}} = .90$$

13.35 a. From Exercise 13.30, the forecasts for the 4 quarters of 2008 using the Holt-Winters forecasts with $w = .3$ and $v = .5$ are:

$F_{2008,1} = 1,574.90$
$F_{2008,2} = 1,610.72$
$F_{2008,3} = 1,646.64$
$F_{2008,4} = 1,682.51$

$$\text{MAD} = \frac{\sum_{i=1}^{m}|Y_t - F_t|}{m}$$

$$= \frac{|1322.7 - 1574.90| + |1280.0 - 1610.72| + |1164.7 - 1646.64| + |903.3 - 1682.51|}{4}$$

$$= \frac{1844.12}{4} = 461.0$$

$$\text{MAPE} = \left[\frac{\sum_{i=1}^{m} \left| \frac{(Y_t - F_t)}{Y_t} \right|}{m} \right] 100$$

$$= \left[\frac{\left| \frac{1322.7 - 1574.90}{1322.7} \right| + \left| \frac{1280.02 - 1610.77}{1280.0} \right| + \left| \frac{1164.7 - 1646.64}{1164.7} \right| + \left| \frac{903.3 - 1682.51}{903.3} \right|}{4} \right] 100$$

$$= \left[\frac{1.7255}{4} \right] 100 = 43.1$$

$$\text{RMSE} = \sqrt{\frac{\sum_{i=1}^{m} (Y_t - F_t)^2}{m}}$$

$$= \sqrt{\frac{(1322.7 - 1574.90)^2 + (1280.0 - 1610.77)^2 + (1164.7 - 1646.64)^2 + (903.3 - 1682.51)^2}{4}}$$

$$= \sqrt{\frac{1,012,448.021}{4}} = 503.1$$

b. From Exercise 13.30, the forecasts for the 4 quarters of 2008 using the Holt-Winters forecasts with $w = .7$ and $v = .5$ are:

$$F_{2008,1} = 1,508.61$$
$$F_{2008,2} = 1,515.92$$
$$F_{2008,3} = 1,523.23$$
$$F_{2008,4} = 1,530.54$$

$$\text{MAD} = \frac{\sum_{i=1}^{m} |Y_t - F_t|}{m}$$

$$= \frac{|1322.7 - 1508.61| + |1280.0 - 1515.92| + |1164.7 - 1523.23| + |903.3 - 1530.54|}{4}$$

$$= \frac{1407.6}{4} = 351.9$$

$$\text{MAPE} = \left[\frac{\sum\limits_{i=1}^{m} \left| \frac{(Y_t - F_t)}{Y_t} \right|}{m} \right] 100$$

$$= \left[\frac{\left| \frac{1322.7 - 1508.61}{1322.7} \right| + \left| \frac{1280.0 - 1515.92}{1280.0} \right| + \left| \frac{1164.7 - 1523.23}{1164.7} \right| + \left| \frac{903.3 - 1530.54}{903.3} \right|}{4} \right] 100$$

$$= \left[\frac{1.327084}{4} \right] 100 = 33.2$$

$$\text{RMSE} = \sqrt{\frac{\sum\limits_{i=1}^{m} (Y_t - F_t)^2}{m}}$$

$$= \sqrt{\frac{(1322.7 - 1508.61)^2 + (1280.0 - 1515.92)^2 + (1164.7 - 1523.23)^2 + (903.3 - 1530.54)^2}{4}}$$

$$= \sqrt{\frac{612,194.6}{4}} = 391.2$$

c. For all three measures of error, the Holt-Winters series with $w = .7$ and $v = .5$ is smaller than the Holt-Winters series with $w = .3$ and $v = .5$. Thus, the more accurate series would be the Holt-Winters series with $w = .7$ and $v = .5$.

13.37 a. To compute the exponentially smoothed values, we follow these steps:

$E_1 = Y_1 = 61,267$
$E_2 = wY_2 + (1 - w)E_1 = .8(61,605) + (1 - .8)(60,267) = 61,337.4$
$E_3 = wY_3 + (1 - w)E_2 = .8(62,686) + (1 - .8)(61,337.4) = 62,416.3$

The rest of the values are computed in a similar manner and are listed in the table:

Year	Enroll	Exponentially Smoothed $w = .8$	E_t $w = .8$ $v = .7$	T_t $w = .8$ $v = .7$
1990	60,267	60,267.0		
1991	61,605	61,337.4	61,605.0	1338.0
1992	62,686	62,416.3	62,737.4	1194.1
1993	63,241	63,076.1	63,379.1	807.4
1994	63,986	63,804.0	64,026.1	695.1
1995	64,764	64,572.0	64,755.4	719.1
1996	65,743	65,508.8	65,689.3	869.4
1997	66,470	66,277.8	66,487.7	819.7
1998	66,983	66,842.0	67,047.9	638.0
1999	67,667	67,502.0	67,670.8	627.4
2000	68,146	68,017.2	68,176.4	542.2
2001	69,936	69,552.2	69,692.5	1223.9
2002	71,215	70,882.4	71,155.3	1391.1
2003	71,442	71,330.1	71,662.9	772.6
2004	71,688	71,616.4	71,837.5	354.0
2005	72,075	71,983.3	72,098.3	288.8
2006	73,318			
2007	73,685			
2008	74,079			

The forecasts for 2006-2008 using the exponential smoothing series with w = .8 are:

$F_{2006} = F_{t+1} = E_t = 71,983.3$
$F_{2007} = F_{t+2} = F_{t+1} = 71,983.3$
$F_{2008} = F_{t+3} = F_{t+1} = 71,983.3$

b. To compute the Holt-Winters values with $w = .8$ and $v = .7$:
$E_2 = Y_2 = 61,605$
$E_3 = wY_3 + (1 - w)(E_2 + T_2) = .8(62,686) + (1 - .8)(61,605 + 1,338) = 62,737.4$

$T_2 = Y_2 - Y_1 = 61,605 - 60,267 = 1,338$
$T_3 = v(E_3 - E_2) + (1 - v)T_2 = .7(62,737.4 - 61,605) + (1 - .7)(1,338) = 1,194.1$

The rest of the E_t's and T_t's appear in the table in part a,

The forecasts for 2006-2008 using the Holt-Winters series with w = .8 and v = .7 are:
$F_{2006} = F_{t+1} = E_t + T_t = 72,098.3 + 288.8 = 72,387.1$
$F_{2007} = F_{t+2} = E_t + 2T_t = 72,098.3 + 2(288.8) = 72,675.9$
$F_{2008} = F_{t+3} = E_t + 3T_t = 72,098.3 + 3(288.8) = 72,964.7$

b. For the exponential smoothing forecasts with $w = .8$:

$$\text{MAD} = \frac{\sum\limits_{i=1}^{m}|Y_t - F_t|}{m}$$

$$= \frac{|73,318 - 71,983.3| + |73,685 - 71,983.3| + |74,079 - 71,983.3|}{3} = \frac{5,132.1}{3} = 1,710.7$$

$$\text{MAPE} = \left[\frac{\sum\limits_{i=1}^{m}\left|\dfrac{(Y_t - F_t)}{Y_t}\right|}{m}\right]100$$

$$= \left[\frac{\left|\dfrac{73,318 - 71,983.3}{73,318}\right| + \left|\dfrac{73,685 - 71,983.3}{73,685}\right| + \left|\dfrac{74,079 - 71,983.3}{74,079}\right|}{3}\right]100$$

$$= \left[\frac{.06959}{3}\right]100 = 2.32$$

$$\text{RMSE} = \sqrt{\frac{\sum\limits_{i=1}^{m}(Y_t - F_t)^2}{m}}$$

$$= \sqrt{\frac{(73,318 - 71,983.3)^2 + (73,685 - 71,983.3)^2 + (74,079 - 71,983.3)^2}{3}}$$

$$= \sqrt{\frac{9,069,165.47}{3}} = 1,738.36$$

For the Holt-Winters forecasts with $w = .8$ and $v = .7$:

$$\text{MAD} = \frac{\sum\limits_{i=1}^{m}|Y_t - F_t|}{m}$$

$$= \frac{|73,318 - 72,387.1| + |73,685 - 72,675.9| + |74,079 - 72,964.7|}{3} = \frac{3,054.3}{3} = 1,018.1$$

$$\text{MAPE} = \left[\frac{\sum\limits_{i=1}^{m}\left|\dfrac{(Y_t - F_t)}{Y_t}\right|}{m}\right]100$$

$$= \left[\frac{\left|\dfrac{73,318 - 72,387.1}{73,318}\right| + \left|\dfrac{73,685 - 72,675.9}{73,685}\right| + \left|\dfrac{74,079 - 72,964.7}{74,079}\right|}{3}\right]100$$

$$= \left[\frac{.041434}{3}\right]100 = 1.38$$

$$RMSE = \sqrt{\frac{\sum_{i=1}^{m}(Y_t - F_t)^2}{m}}$$

$$= \sqrt{\frac{(73,318 - 72,387.1)^2 + (73,685 - 72,675.9)^2 + (74,079 - 72,964.7)^2}{3}}$$

$$= \sqrt{\frac{3,126,522.1}{3}} = 1,020.9$$

For all three measures of forecast errors, the Holt-Winters forecasts have smaller errors than the exponential smoothing forecasts. Thus, the Holt-Winters forecasts are better.

13.39   a.   Let $x_1 = \begin{cases} 1 \text{ if quarter 1} \\ 0 \text{ otherwise} \end{cases}$ $x_2 = \begin{cases} 1 \text{ if quarter 2} \\ 0 \text{ otherwise} \end{cases}$ $x_3 = \begin{cases} 1 \text{ if quarter 3} \\ 0 \text{ otherwise} \end{cases}$

$t = \text{time} = 1, 2, \dots, 40$

The model is $E(Y_t) = \beta_0 + \beta_1 t + \beta_2 x_1 + \beta_3 x_2 + \beta_4 x_3$

b.   Using MINITAB, the output is:

Regression Analysis: Y versus T, X1, X2, X3

```
The regression equation is
Y = 11.5 + 0.510 T - 3.95 X1 - 2.09 X2 - 4.52 X3

Predictor        Coef       SE Coef          T         P
Constant       11.4933       0.2420       47.49     0.000
T             0.509848      0.007607      67.02     0.000
X1             -3.9505       0.2483      -15.91     0.000
X2             -2.0903       0.2477       -8.44     0.000
X3             -4.5202       0.2473      -18.28     0.000

S = 0.5528      R-Sq = 99.3%      R-Sq(adj) = 99.2%

Analysis of Variance

Source            DF          SS          MS          F         P
Regression         4      1558.79      389.70    1275.44     0.000
Residual Error    35        10.69        0.31
Total             39      1569.48

Source          DF      Seq SS
T                1     1433.96
X1               1       22.56
X2               1        0.21
X3               1      102.06
```

The fitted model is $\hat{Y}_t = 11.4933 + .5098t - 3.9505x_1 - 2.0903x_2 - 4.5202x_3$.

To determine if the model is adequate, we test:

H_0: $\beta_1 = \beta_2 = \beta_3 = \beta_4 = 0$
H_a: At least one $\beta_i \neq 0$, $i = 1, 2, 3, 4$

The test statistic is $F = 1275.44$.

The rejection region requires $\alpha = .05$ in the upper tail of the F-distribution with numerator df $= k = 4$ and denominator df $= n - (k + 1) = 40 - (4 + 1) = 35$. From Table VIII, Appendix B, $F_{.05} \approx 2.69$. The rejection region is $F > 2.69$.

Since the observed value of the test statistic falls in the rejection region ($F = 1275.44 > 2.69$), H_0 is rejected. There is sufficient evidence to indicate the model is useful at $\alpha = .05$.

c. From MINITAB, the predicted values and prediction intervals are:

Predicted Values for New Observations

```
New Obs      Fit      SE Fit        95.0% CI              95.0% PI
1        28.4467     0.2420   ( 27.9554, 28.9379)   ( 27.2217, 29.6716)
```

Values of Predictors for New Observations

```
New Obs        T        X1        X2        X3
1           41.0      1.00  0.000000  0.000000
```

Predicted Values for New Observations

```
New Obs      Fit      SE Fit        95.0% CI              95.0% PI
1        30.8167     0.2420   ( 30.3254, 31.3079)   ( 29.5917, 32.0416)
```

Values of Predictors for New Observations

```
New Obs        T        X1        X2        X3
1           42.0  0.000000      1.00  0.000000
```

Predicted Values for New Observations

```
New Obs      Fit      SE Fit        95.0% CI              95.0% PI
1        28.8967     0.2420   ( 28.4054, 29.3879)   ( 27.6717, 30.1216)
```

Values of Predictors for New Observations

```
New Obs        T        X1        X2        X3
1           43.0  0.000000  0.000000      1.00
```

Predicted Values for New Observations

```
New Obs      Fit      SE Fit        95.0% CI              95.0% PI
1        33.9267     0.2420   ( 33.4354, 34.4179)   ( 32.7017, 35.1516)
```

Values of Predictors for New Observations

```
New Obs        T        X1        X2        X3
1           44.0  0.000000  0.000000  0.000000
```

From the above output, the predicted values and 95% prediction intervals are:

For year $= 11$, quarter $= 1$, $\hat{y} = 28.4467$ and the 95% PI is (27.22, 29.67)
For year $= 11$, quarter $= 2$, $\hat{y} = 30.8167$ and the 95% PI is (29.59, 32.04)
For year $= 11$, quarter $= 3$, $\hat{y} = 28.8967$ and the 95% PI is (27.67, 30.12)
For year $= 11$, quarter $= 4$, $\hat{y} = 33.9267$ and the 95% PI is (32.70, 35.15)

13.41   a.   Using MINITAB, the results are:

Regression Analysis: Interest versus t

```
The regression equation is
Interest = 11.4 - 0.278 t


Predictor      Coef   SE Coef       T       P
Constant    11.4004    0.3708   30.75   0.000
t          -0.27826   0.02886   -9.64   0.000


S = 0.918188   R-Sq = 81.6%   R-Sq(adj) = 80.7%


Analysis of Variance

Source           DF       SS      MS      F       P
Regression        1   78.358  78.358  92.94   0.000
Residual Error   21   17.704   0.843
Total            22   96.063


Predicted Values for New Observations

New
Obs   Fit  SE Fit      95% CI           95% PI
  1  4.444   0.447  (3.514, 5.374)  (2.320, 6.568)


Values of Predictors for New Observations

New
Obs    t
  1  25.0
```

The fitted model is: $\hat{Y}_t = 11.4004 - .27826t$

b.   For 2010, $t = 25$. The forecast for the average interest rate in 2010 is
$\hat{Y}_{25} = 11.4004 - .27826(25) = 4.44$

From the printout, the 95% prediction interval is (2.32, 6.57).

13.43   a.   Using MINITAB, the results are:

Regression Analysis: Policies versus t

```
The regression equation is
Policies = 394 - 1.14 t


Predictor      Coef   SE Coef       T       P
Constant    393.877     4.168   94.51   0.000
t            -1.1447    0.2601   -4.40   0.000


S = 10.5283   R-Sq = 43.6%   R-Sq(adj) = 41.4%


Analysis of Variance

Source          DF       SS      MS       F       P
Regression       1   2146.3  2146.3   19.36   0.000
Residual Error  25   2771.1   110.8
Total           26   4917.4
```

Predicted Values for New Observations

```
New
Obs    Fit  SE Fit        95% CI             95% PI
 1  361.83    4.17  (353.24, 370.41)  (338.51, 385.15)
```

Values of Predictors for New Observations

```
New
Obs     t
 1   28.0
```

Predicted Values for New Observations

```
New
Obs    Fit  SE Fit        95% CI             95% PI
 1  360.68    4.40  (351.63, 369.74)  (337.18, 384.18)
```

Values of Predictors for New Observations

```
New
Obs     t
 1   29.0
```

Defining $t = 1$ for year 1980, the fitted model is:
$$\hat{Y}_t = 393.877 - 1.447t$$

b.   From the printout, the forecasted values for 2004 and 2005 ($t = 35$ and $t = 36$) are:

2007: 361.83
2008: 360.68

c.   From the printout, the 95% prediction intervals for 2004 and 2005 are:

2007: (338.51, 385.15)
2008: (337.18, 384.18)

13.45   Autocorrelation is the correlation between time series residuals at different points in time.

13.47   a.   For $\alpha = .05$, the rejection region is $d < d_{L,\alpha} = d_{L,.05} = 1.10$. The value of $d_{L,.05}$ is found in Table XII, Appendix B, with $k = 2$, $n = 20$, and $\alpha = .05$. Also, $d_{U,.05} = 1.54$.

Since the test statistic falls between $d_{L,.05}$ and $d_{U,.05}$ $(1.10 \leq 1.10 \leq 1.54)$, no decision can be made.

b.   For $\alpha = .01$, the rejection region is $d < d_{L,\alpha} = d_{L,.01} = .86$. The value of $d_{L,.01}$ is found in Table XIII, Appendix B, with $k = 2$, $n = 20$, and $\alpha = .01$. Also, $d_{U,.01} = 1.27$.

Since the test statistic falls between $d_{L,.01}$ and $d_{U,.01}$ $(.86 \leq 1.10 \leq 1.27)$, no decision can be made.

c.   For $\alpha = .05$, the rejection region is $d < d_{L,\alpha} = d_{L,.05} = 1.44$. The value of $d_{L,.05}$ is found in Table XII, Appendix B, with $k = 5$, $n = 65$, and $\alpha = .05$.

Since the test statistic falls in the rejection region $(d = .95 < 1.44)$, H_0 is rejected.

d.   For $\alpha = .01$, the rejection region is $d < d_{L,\alpha} = d_{L,.01} = 1.15$. The value of $d_{L,.01}$ is found in Table XIII, Appendix B, with $k = 1$, $n = 31$, and $\alpha = .01$. Also, $d_{U,.01} = 1.27$.

Since the test statistic does not fall in the rejection region $(d = 1.35 \not< 1.15)$, and the test statistic is above $d_{U,.01}$ $(d = 1.35 > 1.27)$ H_0 is not rejected.

13.49   a.   For Bank 1, $R^2 = .914$. 91.4% of the sample variation of the deposit shares of Bank 1 is explained by the model containing expenditures on promotion-related activities, expenditures on service-related activities, and expenditures on distribution-related activities.

For Bank 2, $R^2 = .721$. 72.1% of the sample variation of the deposit shares of Bank 2 is explained by the model containing expenditures on promotion-related activities, expenditures on service-related activities, and expenditures on distribution-related activities.

For Bank 3, $R^2 = .926$. 92.6% of the sample variation of the deposit shares of Bank 3 is explained by the model containing expenditures on promotion-related activities, expenditures on service-related activities, and expenditures on distribution-related activities.

For Bank 4, $R^2 = .827$. 82.7% of the sample variation of the deposit shares of Bank 4 is explained by the model containing expenditures on promotion-related activities, expenditures on service-related activities, and expenditures on distribution-related activities.

For Bank 5, $R^2 = .270$. 27.0% of the sample variation of the deposit shares of Bank 5 is explained by the model containing expenditures on promotion-related activities, expenditures on service-related activities, and expenditures on distribution-related activities.

For Bank 6, $R^2 = .616$. 61.6% of the sample variation of the deposit shares of Bank 6 is explained by the model containing expenditures on promotion-related activities, expenditures on service-related activities, and expenditures on distribution-related activities.

For Bank 7, $R^2 = .962$. 96.2% of the sample variation of the deposit shares of Bank 7 is explained by the model containing expenditures on promotion-related activities, expenditures on service-related activities, and expenditures on distribution-related activities.

For Bank 8, $R^2 = .495$. 49.5% of the sample variation of the deposit shares of Bank 8 is explained by the model containing expenditures on promotion-related activities, expenditures on service-related activities, and expenditures on distribution-related activities.

For Bank 9, $R^2 = .500$. 50.0% of the sample variation of the deposit shares of Bank 9 is explained by the model containing expenditures on promotion-related activities, expenditures on service-related activities, and expenditures on distribution-related activities.

b.   For all banks, to determine if the model is adequate, we test:

H_0: $\beta_1 = \beta_2 = \beta_3 = 0$
H_a: At least 1 $\beta_i \neq 0$ $i = 1, 2, 3$

For Bank 1, the *p*-value is $p = .000$. Since the *p*-value is less than $\alpha = .01$, H_0 is rejected. There is sufficient evidence to indicate the model is adequate at $\alpha = .01$.

For Bank 2, the *p*-value is $p = .004$. Since the *p*-value is less than $\alpha = .01$, H_0 is rejected. There is sufficient evidence to indicate the model is adequate at $\alpha = .01$.

For Bank 3, the *p*-value is $p = .000$. Since the *p*-value is less than $\alpha = .01$, H_0 is rejected. There is sufficient evidence to indicate the model is adequate at $\alpha = .01$.

For Bank 4, the *p*-value is $p = .000$. Since the *p*-value is less than $\alpha = .01$, H_0 is rejected. There is sufficient evidence to indicate the model is adequate at $\alpha = .01$.

For Bank 5, the *p*-value is $p = .155$. Since the *p*-value is not less than $\alpha = .01$, H_0 is not rejected. There is insufficient evidence to indicate the model is adequate at $\alpha = .01$.

For Bank 6, the *p*-value is $p = .012$. Since the *p*-value is not less than $\alpha = .01$, H_0 is not rejected. There is insufficient evidence to indicate the model is adequate at $\alpha = .01$.

For Bank 7, the *p*-value is $p = .000$. Since the *p*-value is less than $\alpha = .01$, H_0 is rejected. There is sufficient evidence to indicate the model is adequate at $\alpha = .01$.

For Bank 8, the *p*-value is $p = .014$. Since the *p*-value is not less than $\alpha = .01$, H_0 is not rejected. There is insufficient evidence to indicate the model is adequate at $\alpha = .01$.

For Bank 9, the *p*-value is $p = .011$. Since the p-value is not less than $\alpha = .01$, H_0 is not rejected. There is insufficient evidence to indicate the model is adequate at $\alpha = .01$.

c.   To determine if positive autocorrelation is present, we test:

H_0: No positive first-order autocorrelation
H_a: Positive first-order autocorrelation of residuals

The test statistics is *d*.
For $\alpha = .01$, the rejection region is $d < d_{L, \alpha} = d_{L, .01} = .77$. The value $d_{L, .01}$ is found in Table XIII, Appendix B, with $k = 3$, $n = 20$, and $\alpha = .01$. Also, $d_{U, .01} = 1.41$.

For Bank 1, $d = 1.3$. Since the observed value of the test statistic does not fall in the rejection region ($d = 1.3 \not< .77$) and is not greater thn $d_{U, .01}$ ($d = 1.3 \not> 1.41$), no decision can be made at $\alpha = .01$.

For Bank 2, $d = 3.4$. Since the observed value of the test statistic does not fall in the rejection region ($d = 3.4 \not< .77$) and is greater than $d_{U, .01}$ ($d = 3.4 > 1.41$), H_0 is not rejected. There is insufficient evidence to indicate the time series residuals are positively autocorrelated at $\alpha = .01$.

For Bank 3, $d = 2.7$. Since the observed value of the test statistic does not fall in the rejection region ($d = 2.7 \not< .77$) and is greater than $d_{U, .01}$ ($d = 2.7 > 1.41$), H_0 is not rejected. There is insufficient evidence to indicate the time series residuals are positively autocorrelated at $\alpha = .01$.

For Bank 4, $d = 1.9$. Since the observed value of the test statistic does not fall in the rejection region ($d = 1.9 \not< .77$) and is greater than $d_{U, .01}$ ($d = 1.9 > 1.41$), H_0 is not rejected. There is insufficient evidence to indicate the time series residuals are positively autocorrelated at $\alpha = .01$.

For Bank 5, $d = .85$. Since the observed value of the test statistic does not fall in the rejection region ($d = .85 \not< .77$) and is not greater thn $d_{U, .01}$ ($d = 1.3 \not> 1.41$), no decision can be made at $\alpha = .01$.

For Bank 6, $d = 1.8$. Since the observed value of the test statistic does not fall in the rejection region ($d = 1.8 \not< .77$) and is greater than $d_{U, .01}$ ($d = 1.8 > 1.41$), H_0 is not rejected. There is insufficient evidence to indicate the time series residuals are positively autocorrelated at $\alpha = .01$.

For Bank 7, $d = 2.5$. Since the observed value of the test statistic does not fall in the rejection region ($d = 2.5 \not< .77$) and is greater than $d_{U, .01}$ ($d = 2.5 > 1.41$), H_0 is not rejected. There is insufficient evidence to indicate the time series residuals are positively autocorrelated at $\alpha = .01$.

For Bank 8, $d = 2.3$. Since the observed value of the test statistic does not fall in the rejection region ($d = 2.3 \not< .77$) and is greater than $d_{U, .01}$ ($d = 2.3 > 1.41$), H_0 is not rejected. There is insufficient evidence to indicate the time series residuals are positively autocorrelated at $\alpha = .01$.

For Bank 9, $d = 1.1$. Since the observed value of the test statistic does not fall in the rejection region ($d = 1.1 \not< .77$) and is not greater thn $d_{U, .01}$ ($d = 1.1 \not> 1.41$), no decision can be made at $\alpha = .01$.

13.51   a.   Using MINITAB, the plot of the residuals against t is:

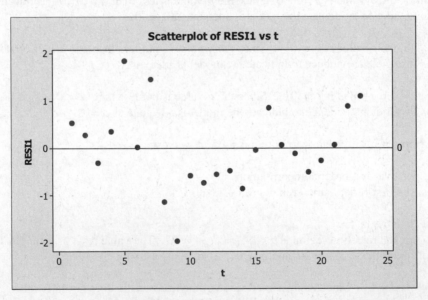

Since there appear to be groups of consecutive positive and groups of consecutive negative residuals, the data appear to be autocorrelated.

b.   Using MINITAB, the output is:

Regression Analysis: Interest versus t

```
The regression equation is
Interest = 11.6 - 0.273 t


Predictor        Coef   SE Coef       T       P
Constant      11.5915    0.3815   30.38   0.000
t            -0.27331   0.02783   -9.82   0.000


S = 0.885218   R-Sq = 82.1%   R-Sq(adj) = 81.3%


Analysis of Variance

Source           DF       SS       MS       F       P
Regression        1   75.595   75.595   96.47   0.000
Residual Error   21   16.456    0.784
Total            22   92.051


Durbin-Watson statistic = 1.28788
```

To determine if positive autocorrelation is present, we test:

H_0: No first-order autocorrelation
H_a: Positive first-order autocorrelation of residuals

The test statistics is $d = 1.28788$.

For $\alpha = .05$, the rejection region is $d < d_{L,\alpha} = d_{L,.05} = 1.26$. The value $d_{L,.05}$ is found in Table XII, Appendix B, with $k = 1$, $n = 23$, and $\alpha = .05$.

Since the observed value of the test statistic does not fall in the rejection region ($d = 1.28788 \not< 1.26$), H_0 is not rejected. There is insufficient evidence to indicate the time series residuals are positively autocorrelated at $\alpha = .05$.

c.   Since the error terms appear to be independent, the validity of the test for model adequacy appears to be OK.

13.53 a.   To determine if the overall model contributes information for the prediction of future spot exchange rates for the British pound, we test:

H_0: $\beta_1 = 0$
H_a: $\beta_1 = 0$

The test statistic is

$$F = \frac{R^2 / k}{(1 - R^2)/[n - (k + 1)]} = \frac{.957/1}{(1 - .957)/[81 - (1 + 1)]} = 1758.21$$

The rejection region requires $\alpha = .05$ in the upper tail of the F distribution with $v_1 = k = 1$ and $v_2 = n - (1 + 1) = 81 - (1 + 1) = 79$. From Table IX, Appendix B, $F_{.05} \approx 3.96$. The rejection region is $F > 3.96$.

Since the observed value of the test statistic falls in the rejection region ($F = 1758.21 > 3.96$), H_0 is rejected. There is sufficient evidence to indicate the overall model contributes information for the prediction of future spot exchange rates for the British pound at $\alpha = .05$.

b.   The value of s is .025. Almost all of the observations will fall within $\pm 2s$ or $\pm 2(.025)$ or $\pm .05$ of their least squares predicted values.

$R^2 = .957$. 95.7% of the sample variation in the future spot exchange rates for the British pound values are explained by the model containing the forward exchange rate.

c.   To determine if positive autocorrelation is present, we test:

H_0: No first-order autocorrelation
H_a: Positive first-order autocorrelation of residuals

The test statistics is $d = 0.962$

For $\alpha = .05$, the rejection region is $d < d_{L, \alpha} = d_{L, .05} = 1.61$. The value $d_{L, .05}$ is found in Table XII, Appendix B, with $k = 1$, $n = 81$, and $\alpha = .05$.

Since the observed value of the test statistic falls in the rejection region ($d = 0.962 < 1.61$, H_0 is rejected. There is sufficient evidence to indicate the time series residuals are positively autocorrelated at $\alpha = .05$.

d.   No. Since the error terms do not appear to be independent, the validity of the test for model adequacy is in question.

13.55   a.   The simple composite index is found by summing the three worker quantities, dividing by 325.3, the sum for the base period, 2000, and multiplying by 100. The values appear in the table.

Year	Fully Permanent	Fully Not Permanent	Event Disability	Total Quantity	Index
2000	140.9	44.9	139.5	325.3	100.0
2001	142.9	45.2	141.7	329.8	101.4
2002	144.9	45.3	143.5	333.7	102.6
2003	147.0	45.0	144.9	336.9	103.6
2004	149.0	44.8	146.2	340.0	104.5
2005	151.1	44.7	147.7	343.5	105.6
2006	153.3	45.1	150.1	348.5	107.1
2007	155.4	45.6	152.3	353.3	108.6
2008	157.4	46.0	154.5	357.9	110.0

b.   This is a quantity index because it is based on the numbers of workers rather than prices.

c.   The index value for 2008 is 110.0. This means that the total number of insured workers in 2008 is $110.0 - 100 = 10\%$ higher in 2008 than in 2000.

13.57 a.   Using MINITAB, the output is:

Regression Analysis: Daily Visits versus t

```
The regression equation is
Daily Visits = 38.2 + 7.32 t

Predictor        Coef      SE Coef          T        P
Constant       38.171        4.420       8.64    0.000
t               7.3192       0.7123      10.27    0.000

S = 6.470       R-Sq = 93.0%     R-Sq(adj) = 92.1%

Analysis of Variance

Source           DF          SS          MS        F        P
Regression        1      4419.5      4419.5   105.57    0.000
Residual Error    8       334.9        41.9
Total             9      4754.4
```

Predicted Values for New Observations

```
New Obs     Fit      SE Fit        95.0% CI            95.0% PI
1         118.68       4.42   ( 108.49, 128.87)  ( 100.61, 136.75)
```

Values of Predictors for New Observations

```
New Obs        t
1           11.0
```

Predicted Values for New Observations

```
New Obs     Fit      SE Fit        95.0% CI            95.0% PI
1         126.00       5.06   ( 114.33, 137.67)  ( 107.06, 144.94)
```

Values of Predictors for New Observations

```
New Obs        t
1           12.0
```

Predicted Values for New Observations

```
New Obs     Fit      SE Fit        95.0% CI            95.0% PI
1         133.32       5.72   ( 120.13, 146.51)  ( 113.40, 153.24)
```

Values of Predictors for New Observations

```
New Obs        t
1           13.0
```

The fitted regression line is: $\hat{Y}_t = 38.171 + 7.319t$

The forecasts for the next 3 years are:

$$\hat{Y}_{11} = 38.171 + 7.319(11) = 118.68$$

$$\hat{Y}_{12} = 38.171 + 7.319(12) = 126.00$$

$$\hat{Y}_{13} = 38.171 + 7.319(13) = 133.32$$

b.   From the printout, the 95% prediction intervals for the 3 years are:

Year 11: (100.61, 136.75)
Year 12: (107.06, 144.94)
Year 13: (113.40, 153.24)

c.   There are basically two problems with using simple linear regression for predicting time series data. First, we must predict values of the time series for values of time outside the observed range. We observe data for time periods 1, 2, …, t and use the regression model to predict values of the time series for $t + 1$, $t + 2$, … . The second problem is that simple linear regression does not allow for any cyclical effects such as seasonal trends.

d.   We could use an exponentially smoothed series to forecast patient visits or we could use a Holt-Winters series to forecast patient visits.

13.59   a.   To compute the Holt-Winters series, we use:

$E_2 = Y_2 = 11.33$ $\qquad\qquad$ $T_2 = Y_2 - Y_1 = 11.33 - 11.85 = -.52$
$E_3 = wY_3 + (1 - w)(E_2 + T_2)$ $\qquad$ $T_3 = v(E_3 - E_2) + (1 - v)T_2$
$\quad = .3(10.46) + (1 - .3)(11.33 - .52)$ $\qquad = .7(10.71 - 11.33) + (1 - .7)(-.52)$
$\quad = 10.71$ $\qquad\qquad\qquad\qquad\qquad = -.59$

The rest of the values appear in the table:

		Holt-Winters	
		$w = .3$	$v = .7$
Year	Interest	Et	Tt
1985	11.85		
1986	11.33	11.33	-0.52
1987	10.46	10.71	-0.59
1988	10.86	10.34	-0.44
1989	12.07	10.55	0.02
1990	9.97	10.39	-0.11
1991	11.14	10.54	0.07
1992	8.27	9.91	-0.42
1993	7.17	8.80	-0.91
1994	8.28	8.01	-0.82
1995	7.86	7.39	-0.68
1996	7.76	7.02	-0.46
1997	7.57	6.86	-0.25
1998	6.92	6.71	-0.18
1999	7.46	6.80	0.01
2000	8.08	7.20	0.28
2001	7.01	7.33	0.18
2002	6.56	7.23	-0.02
2003	5.89	6.81	-0.30
2004	5.86	6.32	-0.43
2005	5.93	5.90	-0.43
2006	6.47	5.77	-0.22
2007	6.40	5.81	-0.04

The forecasts for 2008-2010 using the Holt-Winters series with $w = .3$ and $v = .7$ are:

$F_{2008} = F_{t+1} = E_t + T_t = 5.81 + (-.04) = 5.77$
$F_{2009} = F_{t+2} = E_t + 2T_t = 5.81 + 2(-.04) = 5.73$
$F_{2010} = F_{t+3} = E_t + 3T_t = 5.81 + 3(-.04) = 5.69$

From Exercise 13.41, the forecasts for 2008-2010 are:

2008: $\hat{Y}_{23} = 11.4004 - .29826(23) = 5.00$

2009: $\hat{Y}_{24} = 11.4004 - .29826(24) = 4.72$

2010: $\hat{Y}_{25} = 11.4004 - .29826(25) = 4.44$

The forecasts from the Holt-Winters series are larger than those of the regression forecasts.

13.61   a.   Using MINITAB, the printout from fitting the model $E(Y_t) = \beta_0 + \beta_1 t$ is:

Regression Analysis: Price versus t

```
The regression equation is
Price = 42.6 + 0.379 t


Predictor    Coef   SE Coef      T      P
Constant   42.629     5.200   8.20  0.000
t          0.3788    0.4561   0.83  0.418


S = 10.8893   R-Sq = 3.9%   R-Sq(adj) = 0.0%


Analysis of Variance

Source          DF       SS     MS      F      P
Regression       1     81.8   81.8   0.69  0.418
Residual Error  17   2015.8  118.6
Total           18   2097.6

Durbin-Watson statistic = 1.73871
```

Predicted Values for New Observations

```
New
Obs    Fit   SE Fit        95% CI            95% PI
  1  50.20     5.20   (39.23, 61.18)   (24.74, 75.66)


Values of Predictors for New Observations

New
Obs     t
  1  20.0
```

Predicted Values for New Observations

```
New
Obs    Fit   SE Fit        95% CI            95% PI
  1  50.58     5.60   (38.76, 62.41)   (24.74, 76.42)


Values of Predictors for New Observations

New
Obs     t
  1  21.0
```

The fitted model is $\hat{Y}_t = 42.629 - .3788t$.

b.   The plot of the data is:

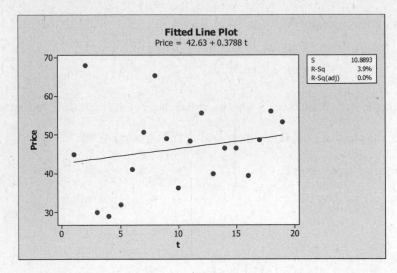

c.   From the printout in part a,

$$F_{2009} = 50.2$$
$$F_{2010} = 50.6$$

d.   Also from the printout in part a, the 95% prediction intervals are:

2009: (24.7, 75.7)   We are 95% confident that the actual closing price for
                       2009 will be between 24.7 and 75.7.

2010: (24.7, 76.4)   We are 95% confident that the actual closing price for
                       2010 will be between 24.7 and 76.4.

e.   To determine if autocorrelation is present, we test:

       H_0: Autocorrelation is not present
       H_a: Autocorrelation is present

The test statistic is $d = 1.739$.

Since α is not given, we will use $\alpha = .10$. The rejection region is $d < d_{L,\alpha/2} = d_{L,.05} = 1.18$ or $4 - d < d_{L,.05} = 1.18$, where $d_{L,.05}$ is from Table XII, Appendix B, for $k = 1$, $n = 19$, and $\alpha = .10$.

Since the observed value of the test statistic does not fall in the rejection region ($d = 1.739 \not< 1.18$), H_0 is not rejected. There is insufficient evidence to indicate that autocorrelation is present at $\alpha = .10$.

13.63   To compute the Holt-Winters values for the years 2001-2005:

With $w = .5$ and $v = .5$,

$E_2 = Y_2 = 11,610$
$E_3 = wY_3 + (1 - w)(E_2 + T_2) = .5(11,779) + (1 - .5)(11,610 + 204) = 11,796.50.$

$T_2 = Y_2 - Y_1 = 11,610 - 11,406 = 204$
$T_3 = v(E_3 - E_2) + (1 - v)T_2 = .5(11,796.50 - 11,610) + (1 - .5)(204) = 195.25$

The rest of the values appear in the table:

| | | | Holt-Winters | |
| | | | $w = .5$ | $v = .5$ |
Year	Quarter	GDP	E_t	T_t
2004	1	11,406		
	2	11,610	11,610.00	204.00
	3	11,779	11,796.50	195.25
	4	11,949	11,970.38	184.56
2005	1	12,155	12,154.97	184.58
	2	12,298	12,318.77	174.19
	3	12,538	12,515.48	185.45
	4	12,696	12,698.47	184.22
2006	1	12,960	12,921.34	203.55
	2	13,134	13,129.44	205.82
	3	13,250	13,292.63	184.51
	4	13,370	13,423.57	157.72
2007	1	13,511	13,546.15	140.15
	2	13,738	13,712.15	153.07
	3	13,951	13,908.11	174.52
	4	14,031	14,056.82	161.61
2008	1	14,151	14,184.71	144.75
	2	14,295	14,312.23	136.14
	3	14,413	14,430.69	127.29
	4	14,200	14,378.99	37.80

The forecasts for the four quarters of 2009 are:

$F_{2009,1} = F_{t+1} = E_t + T_t = 14,798.99 + 37.80 = 14,836.8$
$F_{2009,2} = F_{t+2} = E_t + 2T_t = 14,798.99 + 2(37.80) = 14,874.6$
$F_{2009,3} = F_{t+3} = E_t + 3T_t = 14,798.99 + 3(37.80) = 14,912.4$
$F_{2009,4} = F_{t+4} = E_t + 4T_t = 14,798.99 + 4(37.80) = 14,950.2$

13.65   Solution will vary. See page 488 for Guided Solutions.

13.67   a.   Real income $1990 = \dfrac{\$50,000}{125.8} \times 100 = \$39,745.63$

Real income $2008 = \dfrac{\$95,000}{215.3} \times 100 = \$44,124.48$

The real income for 2008 was greater than that for 1990. Since the real income in 2008 is greater than that in 1990, you would be able to buy more in 2008 than in 1990.

b.   Let x = monetary income in 2008.

Then $\dfrac{x}{215.3} = \dfrac{\$20,000}{125.8}$

Solving for x, we get $x = \$34,228.93$.

Chapter 14
Nonparametric Statistics

14.1   The sign test is preferred to the t-test when the population from which the sample is selected is not normal.

14.3   a. $P(x \geq 7) = 1 - P(x \leq 6) = 1 - .965 = .035$

      b. $P(x \geq 5) = 1 - P(x \leq 4) = 1 - .637 = .363$

      c. $P(x \geq 8) = 1 - P(x \leq 7) = 1 - .996 = .004$

      d. $P(x \geq 10) = 1 - P(x \leq 9) = 1 - .849 = .151$
         $\mu = np = 15(.5) = 7.5$ and $\sigma = \sqrt{npq} = \sqrt{15(.5)(.5)} = 1.9365$

$$P(x \geq 10) \approx P\left(z \geq \frac{(10-.5)-7.5}{1.9365} \right) = P(z \geq 1.03) = .5 - .3485 = .1515 \text{ (Using Table IV, Appendix B)}$$

      e. $P(x \geq 15) = 1 - P(x \leq 14) = 1 - .788 = .212$
         $\mu = np - 25(.5) = 12.5$ and $\sigma = \sqrt{npq} = \sqrt{25(.5)(.5)} = 2.5$

$$P(x \geq 15) \approx P\left(z \geq \frac{(15-.5)-12.5}{2.5} \right) = P(z \geq .80) = .5 - .2881 = .2119 \text{ (Using Table IV, Appendix B)}$$

14.5   To determine if the median is greater than 75, we test:

    H_0: $\eta = 75$
    H_a: $\eta > 75$

The test statistic is S = number of measurements greater than 75 = 17.

The p-value = $P(x \geq 17)$ where x is a binomial random variable with $n = 25$ and $p = .5$. From Table II,

    p-value = $P(x \geq 17) = 1 - P(x \leq 16) = 1 - .946 = .054$

Since the p-value = .054 < α = .10, H_0 is rejected. There is sufficient evidence to indicate the median is greater than 75 at α = .10.

We must assume the sample was randomly selected from a continuous probability distribution.

Note: Since $n \geq 10$, we could use the large-sample approximation.

14.7   a.   To determine if the median income of graduates of the MBA program was more than $125,000 in 2008, we test:

    H_0: $\eta = 125,000$
    H_a: $\eta > 125,000$

b.   The test statistic is $S = \{$Number of observations greater than $125{,}000\} = 9$.

The p-value $= P(x \geq 9)$ where x is a binomial random variable with $n = 15$ and $p = .5$. From Table II,

p-value $= P(x \geq 9) = 1 - P(x \leq 8) = 1 \ .696 = .304$.

Since the p-value $= .304 > \alpha = .05$, H_0 is not rejected. There is insufficient evidence to indicate the median income of graduates of the MBA program was more than \$125,000 in 2008 at $\alpha = .05$.

c.   We must assume only that the sample is selected randomly from a continuous probability distribution.

14.9   a.   To determine whether half of all banks with recent acquisitions charge more than \$200 billion, we test:
H_0: $\eta = 200$ billion
H_a: $\eta > 200$ billion

b.   The test statistic is $S = \{$Number of observations greater than 200 billion$\} = 4$.
The p-value $= P(x \geq 4)$ where x is a binomial random variable with $n = 5$ and $p = .5$. From Table II. Appendix B,
$\qquad p$-value $= P(x \geq 4) = 1 - P(x \leq 3) = 1 - .812 = .188$

c.   Since the p-value $= .188 > \alpha = .10$, H_0 is not rejected. There is insufficient evidence to indicate half of all banks with recent acquisitions charge more than \$200 billion at $\alpha = .10$.

d.   For the above test to be valid, we need a random sample. Since this sample represents the banks with the highest amounts charged in 2007, it is not a random sample. However, if we could not reject H_0 with this sample, we would not be able to reject H_o with a random sample.

14.11   a.   In order for the inference to be valid, we must assume that the population we are sampling from is normal. From the sample data, it appears that the data are not from a normal distribution, but rather from a distribution that is skewed to the right.

b.   To determine if the median 5-year revenue growth rate is less than 5,000%, we test:

$\qquad H_0$: $\eta = 5{,}000$
$\qquad H_a$: $\eta < 5{,}000$

c.   The test statistic is $S = \{$Number of observations less than $5{,}000\} = 10$.

The p-value $= P(x \geq 10)$ where x is a binomial random variable with $n = 12$ and $p = .5$.

$$p - \text{value} = P(x \geq 10) = P(x = 10) + P(x = 11) + P(x = 12)$$

$$= \binom{12}{10}.5^{10}(.5)^{12-10} + \binom{12}{11}.5^{11}(.5)^{12-11} + \binom{12}{12}.5^{12}(.5)^{12-12}$$

$$= \frac{12!}{10!2!}.5^{10}(.5)^2 + \frac{12!}{11!1!}.5^{11}(.5)^1 + \frac{12!}{12!0!}.5^{12}(.5)^0$$

$$= .0161 + .0029 + .0002 = .0192$$

Since the p-value $= .0192 < \alpha = .05$, H_0 is rejected. There is sufficient evidence to indicate the median 5-year revenue growth is less than 5,000% at $\alpha = .05$.

14.13   To determine if the median productivity z-score of all such Ph.D. programs differs from 0, we test:

H_0: $\eta = 0$
H_a: $\eta \neq 0$

$S_1 = \{\text{Number of observations} < 0\} = 8$
$S_2 = \{\text{Number of observations} > 0\} = 2$

The test statistic is S = larger of S_1 and $S_2 = 8$.

The p-value $= 2P(x \geq 8)$ where x is a binomial random variable with $n = 10$ and $p = .5$. Using Table II, Appendix B,

p-value $= 2P(x \geq 8) = 2(1 - P(x \leq 7)) = 2(1 - .945) = 2(.055) = .110$.

Since the p-value $= .110 > \alpha = .05$, H_0 is not rejected. There is insufficient evidence to indicate the median productivity z-score of all such Ph.D. programs differs from 0 at $\alpha = .05$.

14.15   To determine if the distribution of A is shifted to the left of distribution B, we test:

H_0: The two sampled populations have identical distributions
H_a: The probability distribution for population A is shifted to the left of population B.

The test statistic is $z = \dfrac{T_1 - \dfrac{n_1(n_1 + n_2 + 1)}{2}}{\sqrt{\dfrac{n_1 n_2 (n_1 + n_2 + 1)}{12}}} = \dfrac{173 - \dfrac{15(15 + 15 + 1)}{2}}{\sqrt{\dfrac{15(15)(15 + 15 + 1)}{12}}} = -2.47$

The rejection region requires $\alpha = .05$ in the lower tail of the z-distribution. From Table IV, $z_{.05} = 1.645$. The rejection region is $z < -1.645$.

Since the observed value of the test statistic falls in the rejection region ($z = -2.47 < -1.645$), H_0 is rejected. There is sufficient evidence to indicate the distribution of A is shifted to the left of distribution B.

14.17

Sample from Population 1	Rank	Sample from Population 2	Rank
15	13	5	2.5
10	8.5	12	10.5
12	10.5	9	6.5
16	14	9	6.5
13	12	8	4.5
8	4.5	4	1
		5	2.5
		10	8.5
$T_1 = 62.5$		$T_2 = 42.5$	

a. H_0: The two sampled populations have identical probability distributions
        H_a: The probability distribution for population 1 is shifted to the left or to the right of that for 2

The test statistic is $T_1 = 62.5$ since sample A has the smallest number of measurements.

The null hypothesis will be rejected if $T_1 \leq T_L$ or $T_1 \geq T_U$ where T_L and T_U correspond to $\alpha = .05$ (two-tailed), $n_1 = 6$ and $n_2 = 8$. From Table XIV, Appendix B, $T_L = 29$ and $T_U = 61$. Reject H_0 if $T_1 \leq 29$ or $T_1 \geq 61$.

Since $T_1 = 62.5 \geq 61$, we reject H_0 and conclude there is sufficient evidence to indicate population 1 is shifted to the left or right of population 2 at $\alpha = .05$.

b. H_0: The two sampled populations have identical probability distributions
H_a: The probability distribution for population 1 is shifted to the right of population 2

The test statistic remains $T_1 = 62.5$.

The null hypothesis will be rejected if $T_1 \geq T_U$ where T_U corresponds to $\alpha = .05$ (one-tailed), $n_1 = 6$ and $n_2 = 8$. From Table XIV, Appendix B, $T_U = 58$.

Reject H_0 if $T_1 \geq 58$.

Since $T_1 = 62.5 \geq 58$, we reject H_0 and conclude there is sufficient evidence to indicate population 1 is shifted to the right of population 2 at $\alpha = .05$.

14.19   a.   The ranks of the data are:

Old Design	Rank	New Design	Rank
210	9	216	16.5
212	13.5	217	18.5
211	11	162	4
211	11	137	1
190	7	219	20
213	15	216	16.5
212	13.5	179	6
211	11	153	3
164	5	152	2
209	8	217	18.5
	$T_1=104$		$T_2=106$

b.   The sum of the ranks are $T_1 = 104$.

c.   The sum of the ranks are $T_2 = 106$.

d.   Since $n_1 = n_2 = 10$, either T_1 or T_2 can be used. We will pick $T_1 = 104$.

e.   To determine if the distributions of bursting strengths differ for the two designs, we test:

H_0: The two sampled populations have identical probability distributions
H_a: The probability distribution of the new design is located to the right or left of that for the old design.

The test statistic is $T_1 = 104$.

The null hypothesis will be rejected if $T_1 \leq T_L$ or $T_1 \geq T_U$ where T_L and T_U correspond to $\alpha = .05$ (two-tailed) and $n_1 = n_2 = 10$. From Table XIV, Appendix B, $T_L = 79$ and $T_U = 131$.

Reject H_0 if $T_1 \leq 79$ or $T_1 \geq 131$.

Since $T_1 = 104 \not\leq 79$ and $T_1 = 104 \not\geq 131$, H_0 is not rejected. There is insufficient evidence to indicate the distributions of bursting strengths differ for the two designs at $\alpha = .05$.

14.21   a.   Since the data are not normal, we will use the Wilcoxon Rank Sum test. There is some concern with this test as there are many ties in the data. One of the assumptions for the Wilcoxon Rank Sum test is that the data are continuous, with relatively few ties.

b.   To determine if the scores of those in the CMC group tend to be lower than the scores of those in the FTF group, we test:

H_0: The two sampled populations have identical probability distributions
H_a: The probability distribution of the FTF is located to the right of that for the CMC group.

c.   Since $n_1 = n_2 = 24$, the large sample test statistic must be used. The rejection region requires $\alpha = .10$ in the lower tail of the z distribution. From Table IV, Appendix B, $z_{.10} = 1.28$. The rejection region is $z < -1.28$.

d.   Some preliminary calculations are:

CMC	Rank	FTF	Rank
4	34.5	5	47
3	13.5	4	34.5
3	13.5	4	34.5
4	34.5	4	34.5
3	13.5	3	13.5
3	13.5	3	13.5
3	13.5	3	13.5
3	13.5	4	34.5
4	34.5	3	13.5
4	34.5	3	13.5
3	13.5	3	13.5
4	34.5	3	13.5
3	13.5	4	34.5
3	13.5	4	34.5
2	2	4	34.5
4	34.5	4	34.5
2	2	4	34.5
4	34.5	3	13.5
5	47	3	13.5
4	34.5	3	13.5
4	34.5	4	34.5
4	34.5	4	34.5
5	47	2	2
3	13.5	4	34.5
	$T_1 = 578$		$T_2 = 598$

The test statistic is

$$z = \frac{T_1 - \dfrac{n_1(n_1 + n_2 + 1)}{2}}{\sqrt{\dfrac{n_1 n_2 (n_1 + n_2 + 1)}{12}}} = \frac{578 - \dfrac{24(24 + 24 + 1)}{2}}{\sqrt{\dfrac{24(24)(24 + 24 + 1)}{12}}} = \frac{-10}{48.4974} = -.21$$

Since the observed value of the test statistic does not fall in the rejection region ($z = -.206 \not< -1.28$), H_0 is not rejected. There is insufficient evidence to indicate the scores of those in the CMC group tend to be lower than the scores of those in the FTF group at $\alpha = .10$.

14.23   a.   To determine if the distribution of the recalls for those receiving audiovisual presentation differs from that of the recalls of those receiving only the visual presentation, we test:

H_0: The two sampled distributions are identical
H_a: The distribution of recalls for those receiving audiovisual presentation is shifted to the right or left of that for those receiving only visual presentation

b.   First, we rank all of the data:

Audiovisual Group				Video Only Group			
Recall	Rank	Recall	Rank	Recall	Rank	Recall	Rank
0	1.5	1	5	6	34.5	6	34.5
4	24	2	12	3	19	2	12
6	34.5	6	34.5	6	34.5	3	19
6	34.5	1	5	2	12	1	5
1	5	3	19	2	12	3	19
2	12	0	1.5	4	24	2	12
2	12	2	12	7	40	5	28
6	34.5	5	28	6	34.5	2	12
6	34.5	4	24	1	5	4	24
4	24	5	28	3	19	6	34.5
	$T_1 = 385.5$				$T_2 = 434.5$		

The test statistic is $z = \dfrac{T_1 - \dfrac{n_1(n_1 + n_2 + 1)}{2}}{\sqrt{\dfrac{n_1 n_2 (n_1 + n_2 + 1)}{12}}} = \dfrac{385.5 - \dfrac{20(20 + 20 + 1)}{2}}{\sqrt{\dfrac{20(20)(20 + 20 + 1)}{12}}} = -.66$

c.   The rejection region requires $\alpha/2 = .10/2 = .05$ in each tail of the z-distribution. From Table IV, Appendix B, $z_{.05} = 1.645$. The rejection region is $z < -1.645$ and $z > 1.645$.

d.   Since the observed value of the test statistic does not fall in the rejection region ($z = -.66 \not< -1.645$), H_0 is not rejected. There is insufficient evidence to indicate the distribution of the recalls for those receiving audiovisual presentation differs from that of the recalls of those receiving only the visual presentation at $\alpha = .10$. This supports the researchers' theory.

14.25   a.   Using MINITAB, the histrograms of the data are:

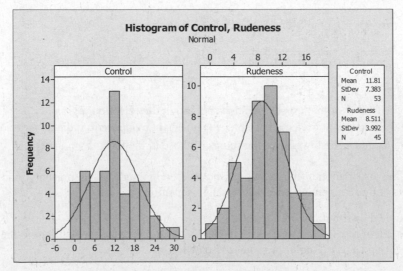

As you can see from the above graphs, the distribution for the control group is skewed to the right while the distribution for the Rudeness group is fairly normal.

b. We first rank the data:

Control Group				Rudeness Condition			
Score	Rank	Score	Rank	Score	Rank	Score	Rank
1	5.5	9	42	4	17	7	30.5
24	96	12	66.5	11	58.5	11	58.5
5	22	18	85.5	18	85.5	4	17
16	81.5	5	22	11	58.5	13	73
21	93.5	21	93.5	9	42	5	22
7	30.5	30	98	6	25.5	4	17
20	91	15	78	5	22	7	30.5
1	5.5	4	17	11	58.5	8	36
9	42	2	9	9	42	3	12.5
20	91	12	66.5	12	66.5	8	36
19	88	11	58.5	7	30.5	15	78
10	50	10	50	5	22	9	42
23	95	13	73	7	30.5	16	81.5
16	81.5	11	58.5	3	12.5	10	50
0	2	3	12.5	11	58.5	0	2
4	17	6	25.5	1	5.5	7	30.5
9	42	10	50	9	42	15	78
13	73	13	73	11	58.5	13	73
17	84	16	81.5	10	50	9	42
13	73	12	66.5	7	30.5	2	9
0	2	28	97	8	36	13	73
2	9	19	88	9	42	10	50
12	66.5	12	66.5	10	50		
11	58.5	20	91				
7	30.5	3	12.5				
1	5.5	11	58.5				
19	88						

$$T_1 = 2{,}964.5 \qquad\qquad T_2 = 1{,}886.5$$

To determine if the distribution of the rudeness condition is shifted to the left of that for the control group, we test:

H_0: The distributions of the two sampled populations are identical
H_a: The distribution of the rudeness group scores is shifted to the left of that for the control group

The test statistic is $z = \dfrac{T_1 - \dfrac{n_1(n_1+n_2+1)}{2}}{\sqrt{\dfrac{n_1 n_2 (n_1+n_2+1)}{12}}} = \dfrac{2964.5 - \dfrac{53(53+45+1)}{2}}{\sqrt{\dfrac{53(45)(53+45+1)}{12}}} = 2.43$

The rejection region requires $\alpha = .01$ in the upper tail of the z-distribution. From Table IV, Appendix B, $z_{.01} = 2.33$. The rejection region is $z > 2.33$.

Since the observed value of the test statistic falls in the rejection region ($z = 2.43 > 2.33$), H_0 is rejected. There is sufficient evidence to indicate the distribution of the rudeness condition scores is shifted to the left of that for the control group at $\alpha = .01$.

c. Since the sample sizes for both groups were over 30, the Central Limit Theorem applies. Thus, the parametric 2-sample test in Exercise 7.19 is appropriate.

14.27   a. Using MINITAB, histograms of the two data sets are:

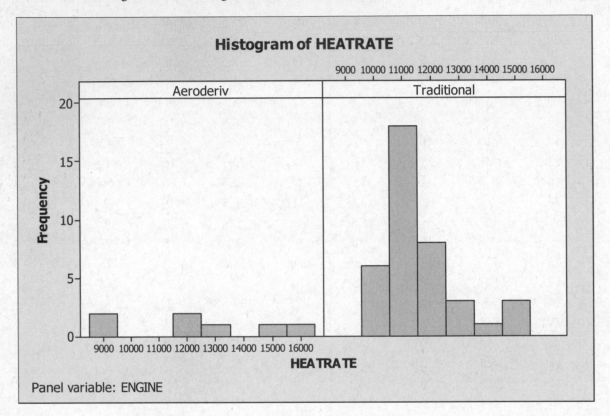

From the histograms, the data for each group do not look like they are mound-shaped. The variance of the aeroderivative engines is greater than that of the traditional engines. Thus, the assumptions of normal distributions and equal variances necessary for the t-test are probably not met.

b. The p-value = .3431. Since this p-value is not small, H_0 is not rejected. There is no evidence to indicate that the heat rate distribution of the traditional turbine engines is shifted to the right or left of that for the aeroderivative turbine engines.

14.29 a. The hypotheses are:

H_0: The two sampled populations have identical probability distributions
H_a: The probability distributions for population A is shifted to the right of that for population B

b. Some preliminary calculations are:

Treatment A	B	Difference A - B	Rank of Absolute Difference
54	45	9	5
60	45	15	10
98	87	11	7
43	31	12	9
82	71	11	7
77	75	2	2.5
74	63	11	7
29	30	−1	1
63	59	4	4
80	82	−2	2.5
			$T_- = 3.5$

The test statistic is $T_- = 3.5$

The rejection region is $T_- \leq 8$, from Table XV, Appendix B, with $n = 10$ and $\alpha = .025$.

Since the observed value of the test statistic falls in the rejection region ($T_- = 3.5 \leq 8$), H_0 is rejected. There is sufficient evidence to indicate the responses for A tend to be larger than those for B at $\alpha = .025$.

14.31 a. H_0: The two sampled populations have identical probability distributions
H_a: The probability distribution for population 1 is located to the right of that for population 2

b. The test statistic is:

$$z = \frac{T_+ - \dfrac{n(n+1)}{4}}{\sqrt{\dfrac{n(n+1)(2n+1)}{24}}} = \frac{354 - \dfrac{30(30+1)}{4}}{\sqrt{\dfrac{30(30+1)(60+1)}{24}}} = \frac{121.5}{48.6184} = 2.50$$

The rejection region requires $\alpha = .05$ in the upper tail of the z-distribution. From Table IV, Appendix B, $z = 1.645$. The rejection region is $z > 1.645$.

Since the observed value of the test statistic falls in the rejection region ($z = 2.499 > 1.645$), H_0 is rejected. There is sufficient evidence to indicate population 1 is located to the right of that for population 2 at $\alpha = .05$.

c. The p-value = $P(z \geq 2.499) = .5 - .4938 = .0062$ (using Table IV, Appendix B).

d. The necessary assumptions are:

1. The sample of differences is randomly selected from the population of differences.
2. The probability distribution from which the sample of paired differences is drawn is continuous.

14.33   a.   The differences between the scores for first and the third sessions are probably not normally distributed. Thus, a paired t-test probably will not be appropriate. The nonparametric Wilcoxan signed ranks test will be more appropriate.

b.   To determine if the relational intimacy scores for the CMC group will tend to be higher at the third meeting than at the first meeting, we test:

H_0: The two sampled populations have identical probability distributions.
H_a: The probability distribution at the third session for the CMC group is shifted to the right of that at the first session.

c.   Since no α was given, we will use $\alpha = .05$. The rejection region is $T_- \leq T_o$ where T_o corresponds to $\alpha = .05$ (one-tailed) and $n = 24$. From Table XV, Appendix B, $T_o = 92$. The rejection region is $T_- \leq 92$.

d.   To determine if the relational intimacy scores for the FTF group will be different at the third meeting than at the first meeting, we test:

H_0: The two sampled populations have identical probability distributions.
H_a: The probability distribution at the third session for the FTF group is shifted to the right or left of that at the first session.

e.   Since no α was given, we will use $\alpha = .05$. The rejection region is $T \leq T_o$ where T_o corresponds to $\alpha = .05$ (two-tailed) and $n = 24$. T is the smaller of T_- and T_+. From Table XV, Appendix B, $T_o = 81$. The rejection region is $T_- \leq 81$.

14.35   To determine if the photo-red enforcement program is effective in reducing red-light-running crash incidents at intersections, we test:

H_0: The two sampled populations have identical probability distributions
H_a: The probability distribution after the camera installation is shifted to the left of that before the camera installation

From the printout, the test statistic is $T = 79$ and the p-value is $p = .011$. Since the p-value is so small, H_0 is rejected. There is sufficient evidence to indicate the photo-red enforcement program is effective in reducing red-light-running crash incidents at intersections for any value of α greater than .011.

14.37

Operator	Before Policy	After Policy	Difference	Rank of Absolute Difference
1	10	5	5	5.5
2	3	0	3	4
3	16	7	9	8
4	11	4	7	7
5	8	6	2	2.5
6	2	4	−2	2.5
7	1	2	−1	1
8	14	3	11	9
9	5	5	0	(eliminated)
10	6	1	5	5.5

Negative rank sum $T_- = 3.5$
Positive rank sum $T_+ = 41.5$

To determine if the distributions of the number of complaints differs for the two time periods, we test:

H_0: The distributions of the number of complaints for the two years are the same
H_a: The distribution of the number of complaints after the policy change is shifted to the right or left of the distribution before the policy change.

The test statistic is $T_- = 3.5$.

Since no α is given we will use $\alpha = .05$. The null hypothesis will be rejected if $T_- \leq T_0$ where T_0 corresponds to $\alpha = .05$ (two-tailed) and $n = 9$. From Table XV, Appendix B, $T_0 = 6$.

Reject H_0 if $T_- \leq 6$.

Since the observed value of the test statistic falls in the rejection region ($T_- = 3.5 \leq 6$), H_0 is rejected. There is sufficient evidence to indicate the distributions of the complaints are different for the two years at $\alpha = .05$.

14.39   a.   Some preliminary calculations are:

Circuit	Standard Method	Huffman-coding Method	Difference S-H	Rank of Absolute Differences
1	0.80	0.78	0.02	2
2	0.80	0.80	0.00	(eliminated)
3	0.83	0.86	-0.03	3
4	0.53	0.53	0.00	(eliminated)
5	0.50	0.51	-0.01	1
6	0.96	0.68	0.28	8
7	0.99	0.82	0.17	5
8	0.98	0.72	0.26	7
9	0.81	0.45	0.36	9
10	0.95	0.79	0.16	4
11	0.99	0.77	0.22	6
				$T_- = 4$

To determine if the Huffman-coding method yields a smaller mean compression ratio, we test:

   H_0: The two sampled populations have identical probability distributions.
   H_a: The probability distribution of the Standard Method is shifted to the right of that for the Huffman-coding Method.

The test statistic is $T_- = 4$.

The rejection region is $T_- \leq 8$, from Table XV, Appendix B, with $n = 9$ and $\alpha = .05$ (one-tailed).

Since the observed value of the test statistic falls in the rejection region ($T_- = 4 \leq 8$), H_0 is rejected. There is sufficient evidence to indicate the Huffman-coding method yields a smaller mean compression ratio at $\alpha = .05$

   b.   In Exercise 7.33, we concluded that the Huffman-coding method yields a smaller mean compression ratio than the standard method which is the same as the conclusion above.

14.41   The χ^2 distribution provides an appropriate characterization of the sampling distribution of H if the p sample sizes exceed 5.

14.43   a.   A completely randomized design was used.

   b.   The hypotheses are:

   H_0: The three probability distributions are identical
   H_a: At least two of the three probability distributions differ in location

   c.   The rejection region requires $\alpha = .01$ in the upper tail of the χ^2 distribution with df $= p - 1 = 3 - 1 = 2$. From Table VI, Appendix B, $\chi^2_{.01} = 9.21034$. The rejection region is $H > 9.21034$.

   d.   Some preliminary calculations are:

I		II		III	
Observation	**Rank**	**Observation**	**Rank**	**Observation**	**Rank**
66	13	19	2	75	14.5
23	3	31	6	96	19
55	10	16	1	102	21
88	18	29	4	75	14.5
58	11	30	5	98	20
62	12	33	7	78	16
79	17	40	8		
49	9				
	$R_A = 93$		$R_B = 33$		$R_C = 105$

The test statistic is:

$$H = \frac{12}{n(n+1)} \sum \frac{R_j^2}{n_j} - 3(n+1)$$

$$= \frac{12}{21(21+1)} \left[\frac{93^2}{8} + \frac{33^2}{7} + \frac{105^2}{6} \right] - 3(21+1) = 79.85 - 66 = 13.85$$

Since the observed value of the test statistic falls in the rejection region ($H = 13.85 > 9.21034$), H_0 is rejected. There is sufficient evidence to indicate at least two of the three probability distributions differ in location at $\alpha = .01$.

14.45   a.   To determine if the distributions of recalls differ among the three groups, we test:

   H_0: The three probability distributions are identical
   H_a: At least two of the three probability distributions differ in location

   b.   The test statistic is $H = 36.04$ and the p-value is $p = 0.000$.

   c.   Since the p-value is less than α ($p = 0.000 < \alpha = .01$), H_0 is rejected. There is sufficient evidence to indicate that at least two of the distributions of recalls differ in location at $\alpha = .01$.

14.47 a. To determine if the distributions of office rental growth rates differ among the four market cycle phases, we test:

H_0: The four probability distributions are identical
H_a: At least two of the growth rate distributions differ

b. The ranks of the measurements are:

Phase I	Rank	Phase II	Rank	Phase III	Rank	Phase IV	Rank
2.7	9	10.5	20	6.1	14	−1.0	4.5
−1.0	4.5	11.5	23	1.2	7	6.2	15.5
1.1	6	9.4	19	11.4	22	−10.8	1
3.4	10	12.2	24	4.4	13	2.0	8
4.2	12	8.6	18	6.2	15.5	−1.1	3
3.5	11	10.9	21	7.6	17	−2.3	2
$R_1 = 52.5$		$R_2 = 125$		$R_3 = 88.5$		$R_4 = 34$	

c. The rank sums appear in the table above. The test statistic is:

$$H = \frac{12}{n(n+1)} \sum \frac{R_j^2}{n_j} - 3(n+1) = \frac{12}{24(24+1)} \left(\frac{52.5^2}{6} + \frac{125^2}{6} + \frac{88.5^2}{6} + \frac{34^2}{6} \right) - 3(24+1)$$

$$= 16.23$$

d. The rejection region requires $\alpha = .05$ in the upper tail of the χ^2 distribution with $df = p - 1 = 4 - 1 = 3$. From Table VI, Appendix B, $\chi^2_{.05} = 7.81473$. The rejection region is $H > 7.81473$.

e. Since the observed value of the test statistic falls in the rejection region ($H = 16.23 > 7.81473$), H_0 is rejected. There is sufficient evidence to indicate the distributions of office rental growth rates differ among the four market cycle phases at $\alpha = .05$.

14.49 a. The F-test would be appropriate if:

1. All p populations sampled from are normal.
2. The variances of the p populations are equal.
3. The p samples are independent.

b. The variances for the three populations are probably not the same and the populations are probably not normal.

c. To determine whether the salary distributions differ among the three cities, we test:

H_0: The three probability distributions are identical
H_a: At least two of the three probability distributions differ in location

Some preliminary calculations are:

1 Atlanta	Rank	2 Los Angeles	Rank	3 Washington,D.C.	Rank
39,600	1	47,400	4	43,000	2
89,900	19	140,000	21	81,900	16
66,700	11	68,000	12	53,000	6
43,900	3	48,700	5	77,600	14
82,200	17	74,400	13	78,200	15
88,600	18	102,000	20	56,800	8
64,800	10	54,500	7	60,000	9
	$R_1 = 79$		$R_2 = 82$		$R_3 = 70$

The test statistic is $H = \dfrac{12}{n(n+1)} \sum \dfrac{R_j^2}{n_j} - 3(n+1)$

$$= \dfrac{12}{21(22)} \left(\dfrac{79^2}{7} + \dfrac{82^2}{7} + \dfrac{70^2}{7} \right) - 3(22) = 66.2894 - 66 = .29$$

The rejection region requires $\alpha = .05$ in the upper tail of the χ^2 distribution with df $= p - 1 = 3 - 1 = 2$. From Table VI, Appendix B, $\chi^2_{.05} = 5.99147$. The rejection region is $H > 5.99147$.

Since the observed value of the test statistic does not fall in the rejection region ($H = .2894 \not> 5.99147$), H_0 is not rejected. There is insufficient evidence to indicate the salary distributions differ among the three cities at $\alpha = .05$.

We must assume we have independent random samples, sample sizes greater than or equal to 5 from each population, and that all populations are continuous.

14.51   Some preliminary calculations:

Change	Rank	Change	Rank	Change	Rank	Change	Rank	Change	Rank	Change	Rank
	Honey Dosage				DM Dosage				No Dosage		
12	88	12	88	4	12	6	24.5	5	18.5	5	18.5
11	78.5	8	47	6	24.5	8	47	8	47	11	78.5
15	102	12	88	9	59	12	88	6	24.5	9	59
11	78.5	9	59	4	12	12	88	1	3	5	18.5
10	70.5	11	78.5	7	35	4	12	0	1	6	24.5
13	96.5	15	102	7	35	12	88	8	47	8	47
10	70.5	10	70.5	7	35	13	96.5	12	88	8	47
4	12	15	102	9	59	7	35	8	47	6	24.5
15	102	9	59	12	88	10	70.5	7	35	7	35
16	105	13	96.5	10	70.5	13	96.5	7	35	10	70.5
9	59	8	47	11	78.5	9	59	1	3	9	59
14	99	12	88	6	24.5	4	12	6	24.5	4	12
10	70.5	10	70.5	3	6	4	12	7	35	8	47
6	24.5	8	47	4	12	10	70.5	7	35	7	35
10	70.5	9	59	9	59	15	102	12	88	3	6
8	47	5	18.5	12	88	9	59	7	35	1	3
11	78.5	12	88	7	35			9	59	4	12
12	88							7	35	3	6
								9	59		
		$R_1 = 2549$				$R_2 = 1693.5$				$R_3 = 1322.5$	

To determine if the distributions of improvement scores for the three groups differ in location, we test:

H_0: The three probability distributions are identical
H_a: At least two of the three improvement distributions differ in location

The test statistic is

$$H = \frac{12}{n(n+1)} \sum \frac{R_j^2}{n_j} - 3(n+1)$$

$$= \frac{12}{105(105+1)} \left[\frac{2549^2}{35} + \frac{1693.5^2}{33} + \frac{1322.5^2}{37} \right] - 3(105+1) = 26.82$$

The rejection region requires $\alpha = .01$ in the upper tail of the χ^2 distribution with degrees of freedom = $p - 1 = 3 - 1 = 2$. From Table VI, Appendix B, $\chi^2_{.01} = 9.21034$. The rejection region is $H > 9.21034$.

Since the observed value of the test statistic falls in the rejection region ($H = 26.82 > 9.21034$), H_0 is rejected. There is sufficient evidence to indicate the distributions of improvement scores for the three groups differ in location at $\alpha = .01$.

14.53   a.   The hypotheses are:

H_0:   The probability distributions for three treatments are identical
H_a: At least two of the probability distributions differ in location

b.   The rejection region requires $\alpha = .10$ in the upper tail of the χ^2 distribution with df = $p - 1 = 3 - 1 = 2$. From Table VI, Appendix B, $\chi^2_{.10} = 4.60517$. The rejection region is $F_r > 4.60517$.

c. Some preliminary calculations are:

Error! Bookmark not defined.Block	A	Rank	B	Rank	C	Rank
1	9	1	11	2	18	3
2	13	2	13	2	13	2
3	11	1	12	2.5	12	2.5
4	10	1	15	2	16	3
5	9	2	8	1	10	3
6	14	2	12	1	16	3
7	10	1	12	2	15	3
		$R_A = 10$		$R_B = 12.5$		$R_C = 19.5$

The test statistic is $F_r = \dfrac{12}{bp(p+1)} \sum R_j^2 - 3b(p+1)$

$$= \dfrac{12}{7(3)(4)}\left[10^2 + 12.5^2 + 19.5^2\right] - 3(7)(4) = 90.9286 - 84 = 6.93$$

Since the observed value of the test statistic falls in the rejection region ($F_r = 6.93 > 4.60517$), H_0 is rejected. There is sufficient evidence to indicate the effectiveness of the three different treatments differ at $\alpha = .10$.

14.55 a. From the printout, the rank sums are 23 (before), 32 (after 2 months), and 35 (after 2 days).

b. $F_r = \dfrac{12}{bp(p+1)} \sum R_j^2 - 3b(p+1) = \dfrac{12}{15(3)(3+1)}\left[23^2 + 32^2 + 35^2\right] - 3(15)(3+1) = 185.2 - 180 = 5.2$

c. From the printout, the test statistic is $F_r = 5.20$ and the p-value is $p = .074$.

d. To determine if the distributions of the competence levels differ in location among the 3 time periods, we test:

H_0: The probability distributions of the three sampled populations are the same
H_a: At least two of the distributions of the competence levels differ in location

The test statistic is $F_r = 5.20$ and the p-value is $p = .074$. Since the p-value is not small, we would not reject H_0 for any values of $\alpha < .074$. There is insufficient evidence to indicate the distributions of the competence levels differ in location among the 3 time periods for $\alpha < .074$.

If we use $\alpha = .10$, then we would reject H_0.

14.57   a.   To determine if the distributions of rotary oil rigs differ among the three states, we test:

H_0: The probability distributions of the rotary oil rigs for the 3 states are the same
H_a: At least two of the probability distributions of rotary oil rigs differ in location

b.   The ranked data are:

Month/Year	California	Utah	Alaska
Nov. 2000	3	2	1
Oct. 2001	3	2	1
Nov. 2001	3	2	1
	$R_1 = 9$	$R_2 = 6$	$R_3 = 3$

c.   The test statistic is

$$F_r = \frac{12}{bp(p+1)} \sum R_j^2 - 3b(p+1) = \frac{12}{3(3)(3+1)}\left(9^2 + 6^2 + 3^2\right) - 3(3)(3+1) = 6$$

d.   The rejection region requires $\alpha = .05$ in the upper tail of the χ^2 distribution with df = $p - 1 = 3 - 1 = 2$. From Table VI, Appendix B, $\chi^2_{.05} = 5.99147$. The rejection region is $F_r > 5.99147$.

e.   Since the observed value of the test statistic falls in the rejection region ($F_r = 6 > 5.99147$), H_0 is rejected. There is sufficient evidence to indicate the distributions of rotary oil rigs differ among the three states at $\alpha = .05$.

14.59   Some preliminary calculations are:

Student	Rank Live Plant	Rank Plant Photo	Rank No Plant
1	1	2	3
2	2	3	1
3	3	2	1
4	1	2	3
5	2	3	1
6	3	2	1
7	2	1	3
8	1	3	2
9	2	1	3
10	2	1	3
	$R_1 = 19$	$R_2 = 20$	$R_3 = 21$

To determine if the students' finger temperatures depend on the experimental conditions, we test:

H_0: The probability distributions of finger temperatures are the same for the three conditions
H_a: At least two probability distributions of finger temperatures differ in location

The test statistic is $F_r = \dfrac{12}{bp(p+1)} \sum R_j^2 - 3b(p+1)$

$$= \frac{12}{10(3)(3+1)}(19^2 + 20^2 + 21^2) - 3(10)(3+1) = 0.2$$

Since no α was given, we will use $\alpha = .05$. The rejection region requires $\alpha = .05$ in the upper tail of the χ^2 distribution with df $= p - 1 = 3 - 1 = 2$. From Table VI, Appendix B, $\chi^2_{.05} = 5.99147$. The rejection region is $F_r > 5.99147$.

Since the observed value of the test statistic does not fall in the rejection region ($F_r = 0.2 \not> 5.99147$), H_0 is not rejected. There is insufficient evidence to indicate that the students' finger temperatures depend on the experimental conditions at $\alpha = .05$.

Because the value of the test statistic is so small, H_0 would not be rejected for any reasonable value of α.

14.61   Some preliminary calculations are:

Metal	I	Rank	II	Rank	III	Rank
1	4.6	2	4.2	1	4.9	3
2	7.2	3	6.4	1	7.0	2
3	3.4	1.5	3.5	3	3.4	1.5
4	6.2	3	5.3	1	5.9	2
5	8.4	3	6.8	1	7.8	2
6	5.6	2	4.8	1	5.7	3
7	3.7	1.5	3.7	1.5	4.1	3
8	6.1	1	6.2	2	6.4	3
9	4.9	3	4.1	1	4.2	2
10	5.2	3	5.0	1	5.1	2
		$R_1 = 23$		$R_2 = 13.5$		$R_3 = 23.5$

To determine if there is a difference in the probability distributions of the amounts of corrosion among the three types of sealers, we test:

H_0:   The probability distributions of corrosion amounts are identical for the three types of sealers
H_a: At least two of the probability distributions differ in location

The test statistic is $F_r = \dfrac{12}{bp(p+1)} \sum R_j^2 - 3b(p+1)$

$$= \frac{12}{10(3)(3+1)} [23^2 + 13.5^2 + 23.5^2] - 3(10)(3 + 1) = 126.35 - 120 = 6.35$$

The rejection region requires $\alpha = .05$ in the upper tail of the χ^2 distribution with df $= p - 1$ $= 3 - 1 = 2$. From Table VI, Appendix B, $\chi^2_{.05} = 5.99147$. The rejection region is $F_r > 5.99147$.

Since the observed value of the test statistic falls in the rejection region ($F_r = 6.35 > 5.99147$), reject H_0. There is sufficient evidence to indicate a difference in the probability distributions among the three types of sealers at $\alpha = .05$.

14.63 a. For $n = 22$, $P(r_s > .508) = .01$

b. For $n = 28$, $P(r_s > .448) = .01$

c. For $n = 10$, $P(r_s \leq .648) = 1 - .025 = .975$

d. For $n = 8$, $P(r_s < -.738$ or $r_s > .738) = 2(.025) = .05$

14.65 Since there are no ties, we will use the shortcut formula.

a. Some preliminary calculations are:

x Rank (u_i)	y Rank (v_i)	$d_i = u_i - v_i$	d_i^2
3	2	1	1
5	4	1	1
2	5	−3	9
1	1	0	0
4	3	1	1
			Total = 12

$$r_s = 1 - \frac{6\sum d_i^2}{n(n^2 - 1)} = 1 - \frac{6(12)}{5(5^2 - 1)} = 1 - .6 = .4$$

b.

x Rank (u_i)	y Rank (v_i)	$d_i = u_i - v_i$	d_i^2
2	3	−1	1
3	4	−1	1
4	2	2	4
5	1	4	16
1	5	−4	16
			Total = 38

$$r_s = 1 - \frac{6\sum d_i^2}{n(n^2 - 1)} = 1 - \frac{6(38)}{5(5^2 - 1)} = 1 - 1.9 = -.9$$

c.

x Rank (u_i)	y Rank (v_i)	$d_i = u_i - v_i$	d_i^2
1	2	−1	1
4	1	3	9
2	3	−1	1
3	4	−1	1
			Total = 12

$$r_s = 1 - \frac{6\sum d_i^2}{n(n^2 - 1)} = 1 - \frac{6(12)}{4(4^2 - 1)} = 1 - 1.2 = -.2$$

d.

x Rank (u_i)	y Rank (v_i)	$d_i = u_i - v_i$	d_i^2
2	1	1	1
5	3	2	4
4	5	-1	1
3	2	1	1
1	4	-3	9
			Total = 16

$$r_s = 1 - \frac{6\sum d_i^2}{n(n^2 - 1)} = 1 - \frac{6(16)}{5(5^2 - 1)} = 1 - .8 = .2$$

14.67 a. The ranks of the 2 values appear in the table:

Brick	Apparent Porosity	Rank, u	Pore Diameter	Rank, v	Difference d_i	d_i^2
A	18.8	5	12.0	5	0	0
B	18.3	4	9.7	3	1	1
C	16.3	2	7.3	2	0	0
D	6.9	1	5.3	1	0	0
E	17.1	3	10.9	4	-1	1
F	20.4	6	16.8	6	0	0
						$\sum d_i^2 = 2$

b. $$r_s = 1 - \frac{6\sum d_i^2}{n(n^2 - 1)} = 1 - \frac{6(2)}{6(6^2 - 1)} = 1 - .0571 = .9429$$

c. To determine if apparent porosity and mean pore diameter are positively correlated, we test:

H_0: $\rho_s = 0$
H_a: $\rho_s > 0$

The test statistic is $r_s = .9429$.

Reject H_o if $r_s > r_{s,\alpha}$ where $\alpha = .01$ and $n = 6$. From Table XVI, Appendix B, $r_{s,.01} = .943$.
Reject H_o if $r_s > .943$.

Since the observed value of the test statistic does not fall in the rejection region ($r_s = .9429 \ngtr .943$), H_0 is not rejected. There is insufficient evidence to indicate the apparent porosity and mean pore diameter are positively correlated at $\alpha = .01$.

14.69 a. **Navigability**: $r_s = .179$. Since this value is close to 0, there is a very weak positive correlation between the ranks of organizational internet use and the ranks of navigability.

Transactions: $r_s = .334$. Since this value is relatively close to 0, there is a weak positive correlation between the ranks of organizational internet use and the ranks of transactions.

Locatability: $r_s = .590$. Since this value is about half way between 0 and 1, there is a moderate positive correlation between the ranks of organizational internet use and the ranks of locatability.

Information Richness: $r_s = -.115$. Since this value is close to 0, there is a very weak negative correlation between the ranks of organizational internet use and the ranks of information richness.

Number of files: $r_s = .114$. Since this value is close to 0, there is a very weak positive correlation between the ranks of organizational internet use and the ranks of number of files.

b. For each indicator, we will test:

H_o: $\rho_s = 0$
H_a: $\rho_s \neq 0$

Navigability: p-value = .148. Since the p-value is greater than $\alpha = .10$, H_0 is not rejected. There is insufficient evidence to indicate a positive correlation between organizational internet use and navigability.

Transactions: p-value = .023. Since the p-value is less than $\alpha = .10$, H_0 is rejected. There is sufficient evidence to indicate a positive correlation between organizational internet use and transactions.

Locatability: p-value = .000. Since the p-value is less than $\alpha = .10$, H_0 is rejected. There is sufficient evidence to indicate a positive correlation between organizational internet use and locatability.

Information Richness: p-value = .252. Since the p-value is greater than $\alpha = .10$, H_0 is not rejected. There is insufficient evidence to indicate a positive correlation between organizational internet use and information richness.

Number of files: p-value = .255. Since the p-value is greater than $\alpha = .10$, H_0 is not rejected. There is insufficient evidence to indicate a positive correlation between organizational internet use and number of files.

14.71 Some preliminary calculations are:

Punish	Rank, u	Payoff	Rank, v	u^2	v^2	uv
0	1	0.50	13	1	169	13
1	2	0.20	9	4	81	18
2	3	0.30	11.5	9	132.25	34.5
3	4	0.25	10	16	100	40
4	5	0.00	6	25	36	30
5	6	0.30	11.5	36	132.25	69
6	7	0.10	7	49	49	49
8	8	-0.20	3.5	64	12.25	28
10	9	0.15	8	81	64	72
12	10	-0.30	1	100	1	10
14	11	-0.10	5	121	25	55
16	12	-0.20	3.5	144	12.25	42
17	13	-0.25	2	169	4	26
	$\sum u = 91$		$\sum v = 91$	$\sum u^2 = 819$	$\sum v^2 = 818$	$\sum uv = 486.5$

$$SS_{uv} = \sum uv - \frac{\left(\sum u\right)\left(\sum v\right)}{n} = 486.5 - \frac{91(91)}{13} = -150.5$$

$$SS_{uu} = \sum u^2 - \frac{\left(\sum u\right)^2}{n} = 819 - \frac{91^2}{13} = 182$$

$$SS_{vv} = \sum v^2 - \frac{\left(\sum v\right)^2}{n} = 818 - \frac{91^2}{13} = 181$$

$$r_s = \frac{SS_{uv}}{\sqrt{SS_{uu}SS_{vv}}} = \frac{-150.5}{\sqrt{182(181)}} = -.829$$

To determine if "punishers tend to have lower payoffs", we test:

H_0: $\rho_s = 0$
H_a: $\rho_s < 0$

The test statistic is $r_s = -.829$

Since no α was given, we will use $\alpha = .05$.

Reject H_0 if $r_s < r_{s,\alpha}$ where $\alpha = .05$ and $n = 13$.

Reject H_0 if $r_s < -.475$ (from Table XVI, Appendix B)

Since the observed value of the test statistic falls in the rejection region ($r = -.829 < .475$), H_0 is rejected. There is sufficient evidence to indicate "punishers tend to have lower payoffs" at $\alpha = .05$.

14.73 **Method I and Method II**: $r_s = .189$. Since this value is close to 0, there is a very weak positive rank correlation between the ranks of Method I and the ranks of Method II.

Method I and Method III: $r_s = .592$. Since this value is about half way between 0 and 1, there is a moderate positive rank correlation between the ranks of Method I and the ranks of Method III.

Method I and Method IV: $r_s = .340$. Since this value is fairly close to 0, there is a weak positive rank correlation between the ranks of Method I and the ranks of Method IV.

Method II and Method III: $r_s = .205$. Since this value is close to 0, there is a very weak positive rank correlation between the ranks of Method II and the ranks of Method III.

Method II and Method IV: $r_s = .324$. Since this value is fairly close to 0, there is a weak positive rank correlation between the ranks of Method II and the ranks of Method IV.

Method III and Method IV: $r_s = .314$. Since this value is fairly close to 0, there is a weak positive rank correlation between the ranks of Method III and the ranks of Method IV.

14.75 Some preliminary calculations are:

Company	2007 Rank	Rank, u	2008 Rank	Rank, v	u^2	v^2	uv
1	2	1	1	1	1	1	1
2	3	2	5	4	4	16	8
3	18	10	8	6	100	36	60
4	10	5.5	9	7	30.25	49	38.5
5	12	7	13	9	49	81	63
6	44	14	14	10	196	100	140
7	8	3	16	11	9	121	33
8	38	13	24	14	169	196	182
9	10	5.5	11	8	30.25	64	44
10	46	15	35	15	225	225	225
11	9	4	18	12	16	144	48
12	16	9	3	2	81	4	18
13	15	8	19	13	64	169	104
14	27	12	4	3	144	9	36
15	23	11	7	5	121	25	55

$$\sum u = 120 \qquad \sum v = 120 \qquad \sum u^2 = 1239.5 \qquad \sum v^2 = 1240 \qquad \sum uv = 1055.5$$

$$SS_{uv} = \sum uv - \frac{\left(\sum u\right)\left(\sum v\right)}{n} = 1055.5 - \frac{120(120)}{15} = 95.5$$

$$SS_{uu} = \sum u^2 - \frac{\left(\sum u\right)^2}{n} = 1239.5 - \frac{120^2}{15} = 279.5$$

$$SS_{vv} = \sum v^2 - \frac{\left(\sum v\right)^2}{n} = 1240 - \frac{120^2}{15} = 280$$

$$r_s = \frac{SS_{uv}}{\sqrt{SS_{uu}SS_{vv}}} = \frac{95.5}{\sqrt{279.5(280)}} = .341$$

To determine if the 2007 and 2000 reputation ranks are positively correlated, we test:

$H_0: \rho_s = 0$
$H_a: \rho_s > 0$

The test statistic is $r_s = .341$.

Reject H_0 if $r_s > r_{s,\alpha}$ where $\alpha = .05$ and $n = 15$.

Reject H_0 if $r_s > .441$ (From Table XVI, Appendix B)

Since the observed value of the test statistic does not fall in the rejection region ($r_s = .341 \not> .441$), H_0 is not rejected. There is insufficient evidence to indicate that the 2007 and 2000 reputation ranks are positively correlated at $\alpha = .05$.

14.77 a. Some preliminary calculations are:

Pair	X	Rank u_i	Y	Rank v_i	u_i^2	v_i^2	$u_i v_i$
1	19	5	12	5	25	25	25
2	27	7	19	8	49	64	56
3	15	2	7	1	4	1	2
4	35	9	25	9	81	81	81
5	13	1	11	4	1	16	4
6	29	8	10	2.5	64	6.25	20
7	16	3.5	16	6	12.25	36	21
8	22	6	10	2.5	36	6.25	15
9	16	3.5	18	7	12.25	49	24.5

$$\sum u_i = 45 \qquad \sum v_i = 45 \qquad \sum u_i^2 = 284.5 \qquad \sum v_i^2 = 284.5 \qquad \sum u_i v_i = 248.5$$

$$SS_{uv} = \sum u_i v_i - \frac{\sum u_i v_i}{n} = 248.5 - \frac{45(45)}{9} = 23.5$$

$$SS_{uu} = \sum u_i^2 - \frac{\left(\sum u_i\right)^2}{n} = 284.5 - \frac{45^2}{9} = 59.5$$

$$SS_{vv} = \sum v_i^2 - \frac{\left(\sum v_i\right)^2}{n} = 284.5 - \frac{45^2}{9} = 59.5$$

To determine if the Spearman rank correlation differs from 0, we test:

H_0: $\rho_s = 0$
H_a: $\rho_s \neq 0$

The test statistic is $r_s = \dfrac{SS_{uv}}{\sqrt{SS_{uv}SS_{vv}}} = \dfrac{23.5}{\sqrt{59.5(59.5)}} = .40$

Reject H_0 if $r_s < -r_{s,\alpha/2}$ or if $r_s > r_{s,\alpha/2}$ where $\alpha/2 = .025$ and $n = 9$:

Reject H_0 if $r_s < -.683$ or if $r_s > .683$ (from Table XVI, Appendix B)

Since the observed value of the test statistic does not fall in the rejection region ($r_s = .40 \not> .683$), H_0 is not rejected. There is insufficient evidence to indicate that Spearman's rank correlation between x and y is significantly different from 0 at $\alpha = .05$.

b. Use the Wilcoxon signed rank test. Some preliminary calculations are:

Pair	X	Y	Difference	Rank of Absolute Difference
1	19	12	7	3
2	27	19	8	4.5
3	15	7	8	4.5
4	35	25	10	6
5	13	11	2	1.5
6	29	10	19	8
7	16	16	0	(eliminated)
8	22	10	12	7
9	16	18	-2	1.5
				$T_- = 1.5$

To determine if the probability distribution of x is shifted to the right of that for y, we test:

H_0: The probability distributions are identical for the two variables
H_a: The probability distribution of x is shifted to the right of the probability distribution of y

The test statistic is $T = T_- = 1.5$.
Reject H_0 if $T \leq T_0$ where T_0 is based on $\alpha = .05$ and $n = 8$ (one-tailed):

Reject H_0 if $T \leq 6$ (from Table XV, Appendix B).

Since the observed value of the test statistic falls in the rejection region ($T = 1.5 \leq 6$), reject H_0 at $\alpha = .05$. There is sufficient evidence to conclude that the probability distribution of x is shifted to the right of that for y.

14.79 Some preliminary calculations are:

Block	1	Rank	2	Rank	3	Rank	4	Rank	5	Rank
1	75	4	65	1	74	3	80	5	69	2
2	77	3	69	1	78	4	80	5	72	2
3	70	4	63	1.5	69	3	75	5	63	1.5
4	80	3.5	69	1	80	3.5	86	5	77	2
		$R_1 = 14.5$		$R_2 = 4.5$		$R_3 = 13.5$		$R_4 = 20$		$R_5 = 7.5$

To determine whether at least two of the treatment probability distributions differ in location, use Friedman F_r test.

H_0: The five treatments have identical probability distributions
H_a: At least two of the populations have probability distributions that differ in location

The test statistic is $F_r = \dfrac{12}{bp(p+1)} \sum R_j^2 - 3b(p+1)$

$$= \frac{12}{4(5)(6)}[(14.5)^2 + (4.5)^2 + (13.5)^2 + (20)^2 + (7.5)^2] - 3(4)(6) = 14.9$$

The rejection region requires $\alpha = .05$ in the upper tail of the χ^2 distribution with df $= p - 1 = 5 - 1 = 4$. From Table VI, Appendix B, $\chi^2_{.05} = 9.48773$. The rejection region is $F_r > 9.48773$.

Since the observed value of the test statistic falls in the rejection region ($F_r = 14.9 > 9.48773$), H_0 is rejected. There is sufficient evidence to indicate that at least two of the treatment means differ in location at $\alpha = .05$.

14.81   a. $$H = \frac{12}{n(n+1)} \sum \frac{R_j^2}{n_j} - 3(n+1)$$

$$= \frac{12}{217(217+1)} \left[\frac{1804^2}{11} + \frac{6398^2}{49} + \frac{7328^2}{62} + \frac{4075^2}{39} + \frac{2660^2}{35} + \frac{1388^2}{21} \right] - 3(217+1)$$

$$= 35.23$$

   b.   The rejection region requires $\alpha = .01$ in the upper tail of the χ^2 distribution with df $= p - 1 = 6 - 1 = 5$. From Table VI, Appendix B, $\chi^2_{.01} = 15.0863$. The rejection region is $H > 15.0863$.

   c.   To determine if the biting rates for the six wind speed conditions differ, we test:

   H_0:   The probability distributions of the number of bites are the same for the six wind speed conditions
   H_a: At least two of the six probability distributions differ in location

   Since the observed value of the test statistic falls in the rejection region ($H = 35.23 > 15.0863$), H_0 is rejected. There is sufficient evidence to indicate that the biting rates for the six wind speed conditions differ at $\alpha = .01$.

   d.   The p-value is $p < .01$. Since the p-value is less than $\alpha = .01$, H_0 is rejected. This supports the inference in part **c**.

14.83   a.   To calculate the median, we first arrange the data in order from the smallest to the largest:

   22, 28, 32, 33, 39, 41, 43, 43, 45, 47, 50, 54, 54, 59, 62

   Since n is odd, the median is the middle number, which is 43.

   b.   To determine if the median age of the terminated workers exceeds the entire company's median age, we test:

   H_0: $\eta = 37$
   H_a: $\eta > 37$

   c.   The test statistic is $S =$ number of measurements greater than $37 = 11$.

   The p-value $= P(x \geq 11)$ where x is a binomial random variable with $n = 15$ and $p = .5$. From Table II, Appendix B,

   p-value $= P(x \geq 11) = 1 - P(x \leq 10) = 1 - .941 = .059$.

   Since no α value was given, we will use $\alpha = .05$. Since the p-value $= .059 > \alpha = .05$, H_0 is not rejected. There is insufficient evidence to indicate that the median age of the terminated workers exceeds the entire company's median age at $\alpha = .05$.

(Note: If $\alpha = .10$ was used, the conclusion would be to reject H_0.)

Using MINITAB, the results are:

Sign Test for Median: Age

```
Sign test of median = 37.00 versus  >  37.00

               N  Below  Equal  Above      P   Median
Age           15      4      0     11  0.0592    45.00
```

From the printout, the *p*-value is .0592. Again, using $\alpha = .05$, we would not reject H_0.

    d.   Since the conclusion using $\alpha = .10$ is to reject H_0 and conclude that there is sufficient evidence to indicate that the median age of the terminated workers exceeds the entire company's median age, we would advise the company to reevaluate its planned RIF. With the proposed sample, there is evidence that the company is discriminating with respect to age.

14.85   a.   Since only 70 of the 80 customers responded to the question, only the 70 will be included.

           To determine if the median amount spent on hamburgers at lunch at McDonald's is less than $2.25, we test:

$$H_0: \eta = 2.25$$
$$H_a: \eta < 2.25$$

           S = number of measurements less than 2.25 = 20.

           The test statistic is $z = \dfrac{(S - .5) - .5n}{.5\sqrt{n}} = \dfrac{(20 - .5) - .5(70)}{.5\sqrt{70}} = -3.71$

           No α was given in the exercise. We will use $\alpha = .05$. The rejection region requires $\alpha = .05$ in the lower tail of the z-distribution. From Table IV, Appendix B, $z_{.05} = 1.645$. The rejection region is $z > 1.645$.

           Since the observed value of the test statistic does not fall in the rejection region ($z = -3.71 \not> 1.645$), H_0 is not rejected. There is insufficient evidence to indicate that the median amount spent on hamburgers at lunch at McDonald's is less than $2.25 at $\alpha = .05$.

    b.   No. The survey was done in Boston only. The eating habits of those living in Boston are probably not representative of all Americans.

    c.   We must assume that the sample is randomly selected from a continuous probability distribution.

14.87   a.   From the printout, the rank sums are: $R_1 = 27.0$, $R_2 = 32.5$, $R_3 = 29.0$, and $R_4 = 31.5$.

    b. $F_r = \dfrac{12}{bp(p+1)} \sum R_j^2 - 3b(p+1) = \dfrac{12}{12(4)(4+1)}(27^2 + 32.5^2 + 29^2 + 31.5^2) - 3(12)(4+1) = .925$

    c.   From the printout, $F_r = S = .93$ and the p-value is p = .819.

    d.   To determine if the atlas theme ranking distributions of the four groups differ, we test:

H_0: The probability distributions of the atlas theme rankings are the same for the four groups
H_a: The probability distributions of the atlas theme rankings differ in location

The test statistic is $F_r = .925$ and the *p*-value is $p = .819$. Since the p-value is so large, there is no evidence to reject H_0 for any reasonable value of α. There is insufficient evidence to indicate that the atlas theme ranking distributions of the four groups differ.

14.89   The appropriate test for paired samples is the Wilcoxon signed rank test. Some preliminary calculations are:

Subject	Aspirin	Drug	Difference	Rank of Absolute Difference
1	15	7	8	6
2	20	14	6	3.5
3	12	13	−1	1
4	20	11	9	7
5	17	10	7	5
6	14	16	−2	2
7	17	11	6	3.5
				$T_- = 3.0$
				$T_+ = 25.0$

To determine if the probability distribution of the times required to obtain relief with aspirin is shifted to the right of the probability distribution of the times required to obtain relief with the drug, we test:

H_0:   The probability distributions of length of time required for pain relief are identical for aspirin and the new drug
H_a: The probability distribution of the length of time required for pain relief with aspirin is shifted to the right of that for the new drug

The test statistic is $T_- = 3$.

Reject H_0 if $T_- \leq T_0$ where $\alpha = .05$ (one-tailed) and $n = 7$:

Reject H_0 if $T_- \leq 4$ (from Table XV, Appendix B).

Since $T_- = 3 \leq 4$, reject H_0. There is sufficient evidence to indicate the probability distribution of time required to obtain relief with aspirin is shifted to the right of that for the new drug at $\alpha = .05$.

14.91 a. We first rank all the data:

Firms with Successful MIS (1)				Firms with Unsuccessful MIS (2)			
Score	Rank	Score	Rank	Score	Rank	Score	Rank
52	5	90	25.5	60	10.5	65	12.5
70	15	75	17	50	4	55	7
40	1.5	80	19	55	7	70	15
80	19	95	29.5	70	15	90	25.5
82	21	90	25.5	41	3	85	22
65	12.5	86	23	40	1.5	80	19
59	9	95	29.5	55	7	90	25.5
60	10.5	93	28				
	$T_1 = 290.5$				$T_2 = 174.5$		

To determine whether the distribution of quality scores for the successfully implemented systems differs from that for the unsuccessfully implemented systems, we test:

H_0: The two sampled distributions are identical
H_a: The probability distribution for the successful MIS is shifted to the right or left of that for the unsuccessful MIS

The test statistic is $z = \dfrac{T_1 - \dfrac{n_1(n_1 + n_2 + 1)}{2}}{\sqrt{\dfrac{n_1 n_2(n_1 + n_2 + 1)}{12}}} = \dfrac{290.5 - \dfrac{16(16 + 14 + 1)}{2}}{\sqrt{\dfrac{16(14)(16 + 14 + 1)}{12}}} = 1.77$

The rejection region requires $\alpha/2 = .05/2 = .025$ in each tail of the z-distribution. From Table IV, Appendix B, $z_{.025} = 1.96$. The rejection region is $z < -1.96$ or $z > 1.96$.

Since the observed value of the test statistic does not fall in the rejection region $(z = 1.77 \not> 1.96)$, H_0 is not rejected. There is insufficient evidence to indicate the distribution of quality scores for the successfully implemented systems differs from that for the unsuccessfully implemented systems at $\alpha = .05$.

b. We could use the two-sample t-test if:

1. Both populations are normal.
2. The variances of the two populations are the same.

14.93   Some preliminary calculations are:

Before		After	
Observation	Rank	Observation	Rank
10	19	4	5.5
5	8.5	3	3.5
3	3.5	8	16.5
6	12	5	8.5
7	14.5	6	12
11	20	4	5.5
8	16.5	2	2
9	18	5	8.5
6	12	7	14.5
5	8.5	1	1
$T_{\text{Before}} = 132.5$		$T_{\text{After}} = 77.5$	

To determine if the situation has improved under the new policy, we test:

H_0:   The two sampled population probability distributions are identical
H_a: The probability distribution associated with after the policy was instituted is shifted to the l
         left of that before
The test statistic is $T_{\text{Before}} = 132.5$.

The rejection region is $T_{\text{Before}} \geq 127$ from Table XIV, Appendix B, with $n_A = n_B = 10$ and $\alpha = .05$.

Since the observed value of the test statistic falls in the rejection region ($T_{\text{Before}} = 132.5 \geq 127$), H_0 is rejected. There is sufficient evidence to indicate the situation has improved under the new policy at $\alpha = .05$.

14.95   Since the data are already ranked, it is clear that:

$R_1 = 19.0$ $R_2 = 21.5$ $R_3 = 27.5$ $R_4 = 32.0$

To determine if the probability distributions of ratings differ for at least two of the items, we test:

H_0: The probability distributions of responses are identical for the four aspects
H_a: At least two of the probability distributions differ in location

The test statistic is $F_r = \dfrac{12}{bp(p+1)} \sum R_j^2 - 3b(p+1)$

$$= \dfrac{12}{10(4)(4+1)}[19.0^2 + 21.5^2 + 27.5^2 + 32.0^2] - 3(10)(4+1)$$

$$= 156.21 - 150 = 6.21$$

The rejection region requires $\alpha = .05$ in the upper tail of the χ^2 distribution with df $= p - 1 = 4 - 1 = 3$. From Table VI, Appendix B, $\chi_{.05}^2 = 7.81473$. The rejection region is $F_r > 7.81473$.

Since the observed value of the test statistic does not fall in the rejection region ($F_r = 6.21 \not> 7.81473$), do not reject H_0. There is insufficient evidence to conclude that at least two of the items negotiated differ at $\alpha = .05$.

14.97 a. To determine if the median TCDD level in the fat tissue of Vietnam vets exceeds 3 ppt, we test:

H_0: $\eta = 3$
H_a: $\eta > 3$

The test statistic is S = {Number of observations greater 3} = 14.

The p-value = $P(x \geq 14)$ where x is a binomial random variable with $n = 20$ and $p = .5$. From Table II, Appendix B, p-value = $P(x \geq 14) = 1 - P(x \leq 13) = 1 - .942 = .058$

Since the p-value = .058 > α = .05, H_0 is not rejected. There is insufficient evidence to indicate the median TCDD level in the fat tissue of Vietnam vets exceeds 3 ppt at α = .05.

b. To determine if the median TCDD level in the plasma of Vietnam vets exceeds 3 ppt, we test:

H_0: $\eta = 3$
H_a: $\eta > 3$

The test statistic is S = {Number of observations greater 3} = 12.

The p-value = $P(x \geq 12)$ where x is a binomial random variable with $n = 20$ and $p = .5$. From Table II, Appendix B, p-value = $P(x \geq 12) = 1 - P(x \leq 11) = 1 - .748 = .252$

Since the p-value = .252 > α = .05, H_0 is not rejected. There is insufficient evidence to indicate the median TCDD level in the plasma of Vietnam vets exceeds 3 ppt at α = .05.

c. Some preliminary calculations are:

Vet	Fat	Plasma	Difference	Rank
1	4.9	2.5	2.4	11.5
2	6.9	3.5	3.4	16
3	10.0	6.8	3.2	15
4	4.4	4.7	-0.3	4
5	4.6	4.6	0.0	(eliminated)
6	1.1	1.8	-0.7	8
7	2.3	2.5	-0.2	2.5
8	5.9	3.1	2.8	14
9	7.0	3.1	3.9	17
10	5.5	3.0	2.5	13
11	7.0	6.9	0.1	1
12	1.4	1.6	-0.2	2.5
13	11.0	20.0	-9.0	19
14	2.5	4.1	-1.6	9
15	4.4	2.1	2.3	10
16	4.2	1.8	2.4	11.5
17	41.0	36.0	5.0	18
18	2.9	3.3	-0.4	5
19	7.7	7.2	0.5	6.5
20	2.5	2.0	0.5	6.5

$T_- = 50$
$T_+ = 140$

To determine if the distribution of TCDD levels in fat is shifted above or below that of the distribution of TCDD levels in plasma, we test:

H_0: The probability distributions for the two populations are identical
H_a: The probability distribution of TCDD levels in fat is shifted above or below that of the distribution of TCDD levels in plasma

The test statistic is $T =$ smaller of T_- or $T_+ = 50$.

Reject H_0 if $T \le T_o$ where T_o is based on $\alpha = .05$ and $n = 19$ (two-tailed).

Reject H_0 if $T \le 46$ (from Table XV, Appendix B)

Since the observed value of the test statistic does not fall in the rejection region ($T = 50 \nleq 46$), H_0 is not rejected. There is insufficient evidence to indicate the distribution of TCDD levels in fat is shifted above or below that of the distribution of TCDD levels in plasma at $\alpha = .05$.

d.   Some preliminary calculations are:

Vet	Fat	u	Plasma	v	u^2	v^2	uv
1	4.9	11	2.5	6.5	121	42.25	71.5
2	6.9	14	3.5	12	196	144	168
3	10.0	18	6.8	16	324	256	288
4	4.4	8.5	4.7	15	72.25	225	127.5
5	4.6	10	4.6	14	100	196	140
6	1.1	1	1.8	2.5	1	6.25	2.5
7	2.3	3	2.5	6.5	9	42.25	19.5
8	5.9	13	3.1	9.5	169	90.25	123.5
9	7.0	15.5	3.1	9.5	240.25	90.25	147.25
10	5.5	12	3.0	8	144	64	96
11	7.0	15.5	6.9	17	240.25	289	263.5
12	1.4	2	1.6	1	4	1	2
13	11.0	19	20.0	19	361	361	361
14	2.5	4.5	4.1	13	20.25	169	58.5
15	4.4	8.5	2.1	5	72.25	25	42.5
16	4.2	7	1.8	2.5	49	6.25	17.5
17	41.0	20	36.0	20	400	400	400
18	2.9	6	3.3	11	36	121	66
19	7.7	17	7.2	18	289	324	306
20	2.5	4.5	2.0	4	20.25	16	18
		$\sum u = 210$		$\sum v = 210$	$\sum u^2 = 2869$	$\sum v^2 = 2869$	$\sum uv = 2719$

$$SS_{uv} = \sum uv - \frac{\left(\sum u\right)\left(\sum v\right)}{n} = 2719 - \frac{210(210)}{20} = 514$$

$$SS_{uu} = \sum u^2 - \frac{\left(\sum u\right)^2}{n} = 2869 - \frac{210^2}{20} = 664$$

$$SS_{vv} = \sum v^2 - \frac{\left(\sum v\right)^2}{n} = 2869 - \frac{210^2}{20} = 664$$

$$r_s = \frac{SS_{uv}}{\sqrt{SS_{uu}SS_{vv}}} = \frac{514}{\sqrt{664(664)}} = .774$$

To determine if there is a positive association between the two TCDD measures, we test:

H_0: $\rho_s = 0$
H_a: $\rho_s > 0$

The test statistic is $r_s = .774$

Reject H_o if $r_s > r_{s,\alpha}$ where $\alpha = .05$ and n = 20.

Reject H_o if $r_s > .377$ (from Table XVI, Appendix B)

Since the observed value of the test statistic falls in the rejection region ($r = .774 > .377$), H_0 is rejected. There is sufficient evidence to indicate there is a positive association between the two TCDD measures at $\alpha = .05$.

14.99 Using MINITAB, the results of the Wilcoxon Rank Sum Test (Mann-Whitney Test) for each of the Variables are:

Mann-Whitney Test and CI: CREATIVE-S, CREATIVE-NS

```
              N   Median
CREATIVE-S   47   5.0000
CREATIVE-NS  67   4.0000


Point estimate for ETA1-ETA2 is 1.0000
95.0 Percent CI for ETA1-ETA2 is (0.9999,1.0000)
W = 3734.5
Test of ETA1 = ETA2 vs ETA1 not = ETA2 is significant at 0.0000
The test is significant at 0.0000 (adjusted for ties)
```

Mann-Whitney Test and CI: INFO-S, INFO-NS

```
          N   Median
INFO-S   47   5.000
INFO-NS  67   5.000


Point estimate for ETA1-ETA2 is 0.000
95.0 Percent CI for ETA1-ETA2 is (-0.000,1.000)
W = 2888.5
Test of ETA1 = ETA2 vs ETA1 not = ETA2 is significant at 0.2856
The test is significant at 0.2743 (adjusted for ties)
```

Mann-Whitney Test and CI: DECPERS-S, DECPERS-NS

```
            N   Median
DECPERS-S   47   3.000
DECPERS-NS  67   2.000


Point estimate for ETA1-ETA2 is -0.000
95.0 Percent CI for ETA1-ETA2 is (-0.000,1.000)
W = 2963.5
Test of ETA1 = ETA2 vs ETA1 not = ETA2 is significant at 0.1337
The test is significant at 0.1228 (adjusted for ties)
```

Mann-Whitney Test and CI: SKILLS-S, SKILLS-NS

```
           N   Median
SKILLS-S   47   6.0000
SKILLS-NS  67   5.0000


Point estimate for ETA1-ETA2 is 1.0000
95.0 Percent CI for ETA1-ETA2 is (0.9999,1.9999)
W = 3498.5
Test of ETA1 = ETA2 vs ETA1 not = ETA2 is significant at 0.0000
The test is significant at 0.0000 (adjusted for ties)
```

Mann-Whitney Test and CI: TASKID-S, TASKID-NS

```
           N   Median
TASKID-S   47   5.000
TASKID-NS  67   4.000


Point estimate for ETA1-ETA2 is 1.000
95.0 Percent CI for ETA1-ETA2 is (-0.000,1.000)
W = 3028.0
Test of ETA1 = ETA2 vs ETA1 not = ETA2 is significant at 0.0614
The test is significant at 0.0566 (adjusted for ties)
```

Mann-Whitney Test and CI: AGE-S, AGE-NS

```
         N   Median
AGE-S    47   47.000
AGE-NS   67   45.000


Point estimate for ETA1-ETA2 is 1.000
95.0 Percent CI for ETA1-ETA2 is (-1.000,4.001)
W = 2891.5
Test of ETA1 = ETA2 vs ETA1 not = ETA2 is significant at 0.2779
The test is significant at 0.2771 (adjusted for ties)
```

Mann-Whitney Test and CI: EDYRS-S, EDYRS-NS

```
          N   Median
EDYRS-S   47   13.000
EDYRS-NS  67   13.000


Point estimate for ETA1-ETA2 is -0.000
95.0 Percent CI for ETA1-ETA2 is (0.000,-0.000)
W = 2664.0
Test of ETA1 = ETA2 vs ETA1 not = ETA2 is significant at 0.8268
The test is significant at 0.8191 (adjusted for ties)
```

A summary of the tests above and the *t*-tests from Chapter 7 are listed in the table:

Variable	Wilcoxon Test Statistic, T_2	p-value	t	p-value
CREATIVE	3734.5	0.000	8.847	0.000
INFO	2888.5	0.274	1.503	0.136
DECPERS	2963.5	0.123	1.506	0.135
SKILLS	3498.5	0.000	4.766	0.000
TASKID	3028.0	0.057	1.738	0.087
AGE	2891.5	0.277	0.742	0.460
EDYRS	2664.0	0.819	-0.623	0.534

The *p*-values for the Wilcoxon Rank Sum Tests and the *t*-tests are similar and the decisions are the same.

Since the sample sizes are large ($n = 47$ and $n = 67$), the Central Limit Theorem applies. Thus, the *t*-tests (or *z*-tests) are valid. One assumption for the Wilcoxon Rank Sum test is that the distributions are continuous. Obviously, this is not true. There are many ties in the data, so the Wilcoxon Rank Sum tests may not be valid.

Guided Solutions to Exercises with Solutions that Vary

4.157   The answers to this will vary. After selecting 100 samples of size n = 2 from the bag with coins marked 0, 2, 4, and 6 with replacement, the values of $\bar{x}$ for the 100 samples are:

x_1	x_2	$\bar{x}$	x_1	x_2	$\bar{x}$	x_1	x_2	$\bar{x}$	x_1	x_2	$\bar{x}$
2	2	2	2	6	4	6	2	4	6	0	3
2	4	3	4	0	2	6	0	3	2	4	3
0	2	1	2	4	3	2	4	3	2	4	3
6	0	3	6	4	5	0	0	0	2	2	2
4	4	4	2	4	3	2	4	3	6	2	4
4	2	3	4	6	5	0	4	2	2	6	4
2	2	2	0	4	2	4	6	5	4	6	5
2	4	3	4	2	3	2	4	3	6	0	3
2	0	1	0	2	1	2	6	4	6	4	5
2	2	2	2	4	3	4	6	5	6	0	3
0	0	0	6	4	5	2	4	3	4	4	4
4	0	2	4	6	5	2	4	3	2	6	4
6	4	5	2	4	3	2	0	1	0	0	0
2	0	1	4	2	3	4	4	4	4	6	5
4	4	4	0	2	1	0	4	2	4	2	3
4	2	3	6	2	4	0	4	2	4	0	2
4	4	4	0	2	1	4	2	3	2	6	4
4	6	5	6	2	4	2	4	3	2	2	2
2	6	4	4	2	3	2	4	3	6	6	6
2	4	3	0	2	1	4	4	4	2	6	4
6	4	5	4	4	4	2	4	3	4	4	4
4	2	3	2	2	2	4	6	5	6	2	4
6	6	6	0	2	1	4	0	2	2	6	4
0	0	0	0	0	0	6	4	5	4	2	3
6	6	6	4	4	4	4	4	4	2	2	2

Using MINITAB, a histogram of the values of $\bar{x}$ is:

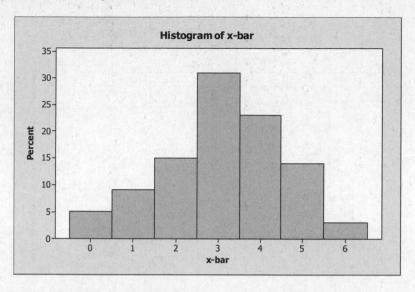

Although it is not exactly the same as the graph in Exercise 4.156 e, is it very similar.

4.161 a-b. The answers to this will vary. The results of the first 10 generated samples of size 15 with the computed means and medians are:

Sample																Mean	Median
1	198	155	188	170	200	178	178	168	158	197	176	156	168	193	176	177.27	176
2	164	158	161	199	170	161	179	167	184	161	193	154	178	171	179	171.93	170
3	191	186	156	196	194	157	188	180	171	152	177	191	170	193	160	177.47	180
4	169	183	198	163	154	176	199	192	186	198	179	178	188	159	170	179.47	179
5	192	181	159	163	173	161	177	190	164	165	167	179	158	164	157	170.00	165
6	172	159	164	163	176	194	183	157	163	174	191	190	185	172	152	173.00	172
7	190	162	159	176	173	187	191	171	193	167	180	180	175	159	189	176.80	176
8	168	178	160	172	166	171	160	173	176	184	172	172	171	155	191	171.27	172
9	196	165	183	166	179	176	173	196	162	185	194	195	191	171	158	179.33	179
10	190	182	162	190	184	200	175	167	159	195	190	150	188	183	189	180.27	184

Using MINITAB, histograms of the means and medians are:

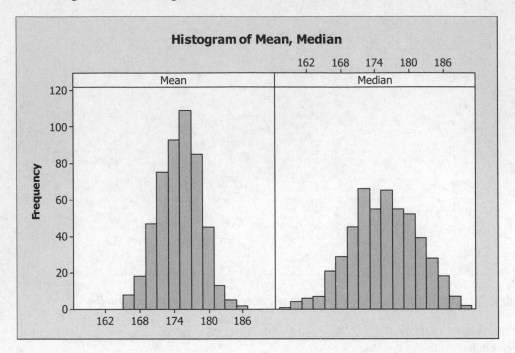

The histogram of the medians is more spread out than the histogram of the means. The values of the mean tend to cluster around μ to a greater extent than do the values of the median.

5.113   a.   Answers will vary. Using MINITAB, a random sample of 100 was selected from the numbers 1 through 5000. The numbers selected are listed below with those ending in 0 highlighted.

3718	1987	1163	3466	70
4062	1329	2251	2511	17
2226	2905	3307	2146	4743
3261	1706	540	4068	3288
2624	718	87	4592	1231
3708	4152	1591	2055	2218
616	2781	301	505	4991
1888	2298	592	2023	2370
3957	3046	2293	4259	2297
4155	203	1074	1042	4573
1614	4180	180	3408	2270
4988	2	518	3030	3874
581	2225	4025	2138	813
2052	1302	464	1221	3763
3816	1647	724	2698	1629
2639	3153	626	2714	2909
3331	737	1727	2615	3815
2178	3509	2430	1057	1278
2752	3112	4910	3874	966
4191	317	4887	2149	689

b.   From the sample, there were 9 numbers ending in 0, so there were 9 invoices in error.

$$\hat{p} = \frac{x}{n} = \frac{9}{100} = .09$$

For confidence coefficient .90, $\alpha = .10$ and $\alpha/2 = .10/2 = .05$. From Table IV, Appendix B, $z_{.05} = 1.645$. The 90% confidence interval for the proportion of invoices in error is:

$$\hat{p} \pm z_{.05} \sqrt{\frac{\hat{p}\hat{q}}{n}} \Rightarrow .09 \pm 1.645 \sqrt{\frac{.09(.91)}{100}} \Rightarrow .09 \pm .047 \Rightarrow (.043, .137)$$

c.   Yes, the confidence interval that was constructed in part b does contain the true proportion of .10.

12.63   Answers may vary. One possible cause-and-effect diagram to help explain why $\bar{x} \neq \mu$ is:

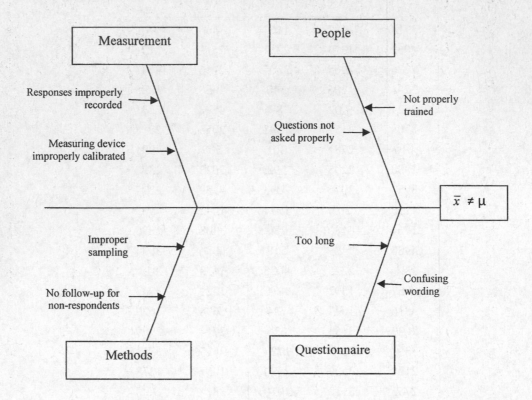

13.65   At press time, the 2009 quarterly GDP values were not available. Suppose the quarterly values were:

Year	Quarter	GDP
2009	I	13998
	II	13973
	III	14356
	IV	14417

Using the above values, the 3 criteria are computed for each of the 3 different forecast models.

From Exercise 13.63 and 13.64, the forecasts for the 4 quarters of 2009 are:

Year	Quarter	Holt-Winters	Simple Linear Regression	Seasonal Model
2009	I	14,836.8	14,780.5	14,799.7
	II	14,874.6	14,843.2	14,978.1
	III	14,912.4	15,105.9	15,149.3
	IV	14,950.2	15,268.7	15,212.2

For the Holt-Winters forecasts, the errors are:

$$MAD = \frac{\sum\limits_{i=1}^{m} |Y_t - F_t|}{m}$$

$$= \frac{|13998-14836.8| + |13973-14874.6| + |14356-14912.4| + |14417-14950.2|}{4} = \frac{2830}{4} = 707.5$$

$$MAPE = \left[\frac{\sum\limits_{i=1}^{m} \frac{|(Y_t - F_t)|}{Y_t}}{m} \right] 100$$

$$= \left[\frac{\left|\frac{13998-14836.8}{13998}\right| + \left|\frac{13973-14874.6}{13973}\right| + \left|\frac{14356-14912.4}{14356}\right| + \left|\frac{14417-14950.2}{14417}\right|}{3} \right] 100$$

$$= \left[\frac{.20019}{4} \right] 100 = 5.005$$

$$RMSE = \sqrt{\frac{\sum\limits_{i=1}^{m} (Y_t - F_t)^2}{m}}$$

$$= \sqrt{\frac{(13998-14836.8)^2 + (13973-14874.6)^2 + (14356-14912.4)^2 + (14417-14950.2)^2}{4}}$$

$$= \sqrt{\frac{2110351.2}{4}} = 726.35$$

For the Simple Linear regression forecasts, the errors are:

$$MAD = \frac{\sum\limits_{i=1}^{m} |Y_t - F_t|}{m}$$

$$= \frac{|13998-14780.5| + |13973-14843.2| + |14356-15105.9| + |14417-15268.7|}{4}$$

$$= \frac{3254.3}{4} = 813.6$$

$$\text{MAPE} = \left[\frac{\displaystyle\sum_{i=1}^{m} \left| \frac{(Y_t - F_t)}{Y_t} \right|}{m} \right] 100$$

$$= \left[\frac{\left| \frac{13998 - 14780.5}{13998} \right| + \left| \frac{13973 - 14843.2}{13973} \right| + \left| \frac{14356 - 15105.9}{14356} \right| + \left| \frac{14417 - 15268.7}{14417} \right|}{3} \right] 100$$

$$= \left[\frac{.22949}{4} \right] 100 = 5.737$$

$$\text{RMSE} = \sqrt{\frac{\displaystyle\sum_{i=1}^{m} (Y_t - F_t)^2}{m}}$$

$$= \sqrt{\frac{(13998 - 14780.5)^2 + (13973 - 14843.2)^2 + (14356 - 15105.9)^2 + (14417 - 15268.7)^2}{4}}$$

$$= \sqrt{\frac{2657297.2}{4}} = 815.06$$

For the Seasonal Model forecasts, the errors are:

$$\text{MAD} = \frac{\displaystyle\sum_{i=1}^{m} |Y_t - F_t|}{m}$$

$$= \frac{|13998 - 14799.7| + |13973 - 14978.1| + |14356 - 15149.3| + |14417 - 15212.2|}{4} = \frac{3395.3}{4} = 848.8$$

$$\text{MAPE} = \left[\frac{\displaystyle\sum_{i=1}^{m} \left| \frac{(Y_t - F_t)}{Y_t} \right|}{m} \right] 100$$

$$= \left[\frac{\left| \frac{13998 - 14799.7}{13998} \right| + \left| \frac{13973 - 14978.1}{13973} \right| + \left| \frac{14356 - 15149.3}{14356} \right| + \left| \frac{14417 - 15212.2}{14417} \right|}{3} \right] 100$$

$$= \left[\frac{.23962}{4} \right] 100 = 5.991$$

$$RMSE = \sqrt{\frac{\sum_{i=1}^{m}(Y_t - F_t)^2}{m}}$$

$$= \sqrt{\frac{(13998-14799.7)^2 + (13973-14978.1)^2 + (14356-15149.3)^2 + (14417-15212.2)^2}{4}}$$

$$= \sqrt{\frac{2914616.8}{4}} = 853.61$$

The Holt-Winters model performs the best for all three criteria. The MAD, MAPE, and RMSE values for the Holt-Winter forecasts are the smallest.